International Environmental Law and Policy Series

The Environmental Policy
of the
European Communities

Second Edition

International Environmental Law and Policy Series

The Environmental Policy of the European Communities

Second Edition

Stanley P. Johnson
*Former Member of the European Parliament and Vice-Chairman,
European Parliament Committee on Environment, Public Health and
Consumer Protection*

Guy Corcelle
*Directorate General for Environment, Civil Protection and Nuclear
Safety, Commission of the European Communities*

KLUWER LAW
INTERNATIONAL
LONDON – THE HAGUE – BOSTON

Published by Kluwer Law International
Sterling House
66 Wilton Road
London SW1V 1DE
United Kingdom

Kluwer Law International incorporates
the publishing programmes of
Graham & Trotman Ltd,
Kluwer Law & Taxation Publishers
and Martinus Nijhoff Publishers.

Sold and distributed in the USA and Canada
by Kluwer Law International
675 Massachusetts Ave
Cambridge, MA 02139
USA

In all other countries, sold and distributed
by Kluwer Law International
P.O. Box 322
3300 AD Dordrecht
The Netherlands

© S.P. Johnson and G. Corcelle, 1995
First edition published 1989
Second edition published 1995

Reprinted 1997

ISBN: 90-411-0826-9
Series ISBN: 1-85333-275-5

**British Library Cataloguing in Publication Data and Library of Congress
Cataloguing-in-Publication Data is available**

Typeset in 10/11 Times by EXPO Holdings, Malaysia
Printed and bound in Great Britain by Athenæum Press Ltd, Gateshead, Tyne & Wear

Contents

Part One The Basic Sectors of Community Environment Policy

Chapter 7 Noise   **280**

Chapter 8 Flora and Fauna   **298**

Part Two Specific Aspects of Community Environment Policy

Chapter 9 Preventive Action   339

Chapter 13 The Integration of Environmental Protection in the Other Community Policies

The International Environmental Law and Policy Series

Series General Editor
Stanley P. Johnson

Advisory Editor
Günther Handl

Other titles in the series

Transferring Hazardous Technologies and Substances, G. Handl, R.E. Lutz
(ISBN 0-86010-704-3)
Understanding US and European Environmental Law: A Practitioner's Guide,
T.T. Smith, P. Kromarek
(ISBN 1-85333-305-0)
*Air Pollution Control in the European Community: Implementation of the EC
Directives in the Twelve Member States*, G. Bennett (ed.)
(ISBN 1-85333-567-3)
International Responsibility for Environmental Harm, F. Francioni and
T. Scovazzi (eds.)
(ISBN 1-85333-579-7)
Environmental Protection and International Law, W. Lang, H. Neuhold,
K. Zemanek (eds.)
(ISBN 1-85333-611-4)
International Law and Global Climate Change, R. Churchill, D. Freestone (eds.)
(ISBN 1-85333-629-7)
International Legal Problems of the Environmental Protection of the Baltic Sea,
M. Fitzmaurice
(ISBN 0-7923-1402-6)
Basic Documents of International Environmental Law, H. Hohmann (ed.)
(ISBN 1-85333-628-9)
The Antarctic Environment and International Law, J. Verhoeven, P. Sands,
M. Bruce (eds.)
(ISBN 1-85333-630-0)
*Environmental Pollution Control: An Introduction to Principles and Practice of
Administration*, J. McLoughlin, E.G. Bellinger
(ISBN 1-85333-577-0)
*The Earth Summit: The United Nations Conference on Environment and
Development (UNCED)*, S.P. Johnson
(ISBN 1-85333-784-6)

Amazonia and Siberia: Legal Aspects of the Preservation of the Environment and Development in the Last Open Spaces, M. Bothe, T. Kurzidem, C. Schmidt (eds.)
(ISBN 1-85333-903-2)
Pollution Insurance: International Survey of Coverages and Exclusions,
W. Pfennigstorf (ed.)
(ISBN 1-85333-941-5)
Civil Liability for Transfrontier Pollution, G. Betlem
(ISBN 1-85333-951-2)
Transboundary Movements and Disposal of Hazardous Wastes in International Law, B. Kwiatkowska, A. H. A. Soons
(ISBN 0-7923-1667-3)
The Legal Regime for Transboundary Water Pollution: Between Discretion and Constraint, A. Nollkaemper
(ISBN 0-7923-2476-5)
The Environment after Rio: International Law and Economics, L. Campiglio,
L. Pineschi, D. Siniscalco, T. Treves (eds.)
(ISBN 1-85333-949-0)
Overcoming National Barriers to International Waste Trade, E. Louka
(ISBN 0-7923-2850-7)
Precautionary Legal Duties and Principles in Modern International Environmental Law, H. Hohmann
(ISBN 1-85333-077-0)
Negotiating International Regimes: Lessons Learned from the UN Conference on Environment and Development, B. Spector, G. Sjöstedt, I. Zartman (eds.)
(ISBN 1-85966-077-0)
Conserving Europe's Natural Heritage: Towards a European Ecological Network,
G. Bennett (ed.)
(ISBN 1-85966-090-8)
US Environmental Liability Risks, J. T. O'Reilly
(ISBN 1-85966-093-2)
Environmental Liability and Privatization in Central and Eastern Europe,
G. Goldenmann *et al* (eds.)
(ISBN 1-85966-094-0)
German Environmental Law, G. Winter (ed.)
(ISBN 0-7923-3055-2)
The Peaceful Management of Transboundary Resources, G. H. Blake *et al* (eds.)
(ISBN 1-85966-173-4)
Pollution from Offshore Installations, M. Gavouneli
(ISBN 1-85966-186-6)
Sustainable Development and International Law, W. Lang
(ISBN 1-85966-179-3)

European Environmental law, J. Salter (Looseleaf Service)
(Basic Work ISBN 1-85966-050-9)

(Please order by ISBN or title)

Preface

Launched in 1972 by the Heads of State and Government, Community Environment Policy has made significant progress in recent years. It has also benefited from considerable political and public support.

Much nevertheless remains to be done. The environment continues to deteriorate in many areas of the Community – pollution affects natural resources as a whole, be they streams, rivers, or the atmosphere – recycling of waste still presents numerous problems and the improvement of urban areas is a matter of priority.

Natural resources, the foundation and limit of our economic and social development, still seem to be misused. We should favour a new form of development by increasing our control over the industrial process, and by encouraging farmers both to use methods of cultivation which are compatible with the needs of nature protection, and to accept new responsibilities in contributing to the conservation of the Community's rural heritage.

Given the non-renewable character of certain natural resources and given the considerable rate of demographic growth on a world-wide level, it is essential that we follow the path of promoting an active environmental policy.

The protection of the environment is vital for the long term if satisfactory economic growth and optimal conditions of life for each individual are to be guaranteed.

The Single European Act has recently acknowledged the Community's competence in developing a European environment policy, the main elements of which appear in the Fourth Environmental Action Programme for the period 1987–1992. This policy is an essential counterpart to the creation of a European Internal Market where the speeding up of commercial transactions will undoubtedly result in risks from which the environment must be protected.

This book illustrates the growing dimension of the Community's activities and underlines the little-known contribution which it is making to "environmental" progress in Europe and throughout the world. Its authors have succeeded in giving a clear presentation of every aspect of the problems and outlining the solutions which sooner or later should become a reality. This book certainly merits wide circulation.

Jacques Delors
President of the Commission
of the European Community

Author's Note

In 1979 Graham & Trotman published my book *The Pollution Control Policy of the European Communities*. The second edition of this work, expanded and brought up to date, appeared in 1983. In 1987, Guy Corcelle and I jointly produced a book in French, using the same format but incorporating much new material, entitled: *L'autre Europe verte: la politique communautaire de l'environnement*. This was published in the "Collection Europe" series put out by Fernand Nathan, Paris; Editions Labor, Brussels, and RLT, Luxembourg.

Our colleague, Alison Davies, to whom both Guy Corcelle and I are immeasurably grateful, produced an English version of *L'autre Europe verte* early in 1988. Since then, we have been able to expand and update the material still further. *The Environmental Policy of the European Communities*, as the work is now entitled, covers developments up to the end of 1988. Since the new Commission took office on 6 January 1989, this seemed to be an appropriate moment to draw the line. There have, however, been numerous significant developments in the Community's environmental policy since the beginning of the year. At the Environmental Council held on 8 and 9 June 1989, for example, standards for exhaust emission from small cars were finally adopted in a far more stringent form than originally proposed by the Commission (see Chapter 4) and on 12 July 1989, the Commission proposed the creation of a European Environment Agency, open to third countries, e.g. those of the European Free Trade Area. The central task of the Agency would be to provide the Community and Member States with objective scientific data necessary for the formulation and implementation of environmental policy. At the time of writing, it seems probable that the Council will adopt the Commission's proposal for a European Environment Agency in the relatively near future. But that is something for a future edition of this book.

As I indicated in the Preface to the first Edition of *The Pollution Control Policy of the European Communities*, the approach taken in this book is, on the whole, documentary rather than analytical. It is an attempt to assemble a collection of texts – some well known, some less known – into a coherent whole. The facts which are cited, the motives and methods which are described and the details which are given of a particular proposal or project, are those officially approved and published by the various Community institutions. There is nothing secret or confidential here. No inside material has been used.

Stanley Johnson
Brussels, 18 July 1989

Author's Note: Second Edition

This new edition of *The Environmental Policy of the European Communities* carries the story forward from December 1988 to January 1995, the month which saw the end of the Delors Commission.

From the environmental point of view they were six extremely busy years. In the European Commission Carlo Ripa di Meana, a former Italian Member of the European Parliament, ran the environment portfolio with a substantially raised profile, a flair for publicity and fine political judgement. Mr Ripa di Meana returned to Italy before the end of his mandate to become Minister for the Environment and was succeeded by the Greek Commissioner, Mr Yannis Paleokrassas. In January 1995, a Danish Commissioner, Mrs Ritt Bjerregaard, took over.

For most of the period, DG XI — the Commission's Directorate-General for Environmental Protection and Nuclear Safety — enjoyed the dedicated leadership of Laurens Jan Brinkhorst, a former Dutch State Secretary for Foreign Affairs. In June 1994 Mr Brinkhorst was elected a Member of the European Parliament. He was succeeded by a fellow Dutchman, Marius Enthoven, former Director General of the Environment Ministry at the Hague.

Over these six years the Commission was able to count as before on the active support of the European Parliament, and in particular on that of the Committee on Environment, Public Health and Consumer Protection under the leadership of the German MEP, Mrs Beate Weber, and the UK MEP, Ken Collins. The latter had already served as Chairman of the Environment Committee during the 1979–1984 period when this co-author acted as Vice-Chairman.

The Commission also found an increasing number of allies in the Council. The entry into force of the Single European Act with its environment chapter and, latterly, of the Maastricht Treaty which expanded and reinforced the treaty's environmental provisions certainly gave a new impetus to the Community's environmental policy during the period under review. With the arrival of Austria, Finland and Sweden, the "greening of the Council" seems likely to continue.

This volume concentrates on the legislative texts relating to the environment rather than on the application of other Community instruments, such as incentive measures and the financing of projects, which are playing an increasingly important part in environmental policy. Even with this self-imposed limitation on the scope of the study, we have had to expand the work by over 150 pages. The descriptions given are inevitably summary but, as before, we have tried to include relevant tabular material, particularly where quantitative norms are being established with legal force, and we have almost always given Official Journal references so that the full document can be consulted if necessary.

Guy Corcelle and I are grateful to Alison Davies and to Robin Ratchford for their help in updating the book. The errors — of omission or commission — remain ours.

Stanley Johnson
London, 18 April, 1995

Structure and methodology of the book

1. This book consists of 17 chapters, which mainly fall into two large sections. Part One brings together the traditional headings of any environmental policy, be it at national, Community or international level. It is made up of six chapters, dealing mainly with the fight against pollution and nuisances, and divided into the following areas:

- water;
- air;
- waste;
- chemicals;
- noise;
- flora and fauna.

Part Two deals with the aspects of Community environment policy which are more directly linked to the specific activities of the European Communities, such as the environment and research, the environment and its economic implications for the functioning of the Common Market, the environment and Community law, etc. Part Two consists of the following eight chapters:

- preventive action;
- economic aspects of pollution control;
- research;
- international conventions;
- integration of environmental protection in other Community policies;
- environment and development aid;
- nuclear safety;
- implementation of the directives.

2. These two main sections of the book are preceded by an introductory section and by a summary of the Environmental Action Programmes. The introduction contains a political and legal analysis of the basic principles of Community Environment Policy. Any judgment on the value of this policy which this analysis might imply reflects the opinion of the authors. Because of this, the introduction differs from the rest of the book which is basically a "work of reference" and which generally restricts itself to a brief description of the main provisions of the regulations made at Community level. The introductory part also includes a chapter on the Environmental Action Programmes of the European Communities which have been adopted since 1973. These programmes, each running for a period of five years, in some ways represent a "charter of reference" for Community Policy as a whole. They describe the principles, objectives and nature of the different actions to be implemented within the framework of this policy.

3. Most of the chapters in Part One of the book are preceded by a short introduction drawing attention to the salient points of the actions described in the chapter in question. Similarly, they are concluded with a brief description of actions envisaged for the future. For practical reasons, the method used for the description of the different regulations follows the institutional system of the Community, namely the fundamental "partnership" of Commission/Council. The description of each action, therefore, first includes a brief indication of the content of the "proposal of the Commission", together with the date when this proposal was presented to the Council of Ministers. Secondly the description specifies the date on which the Council adopted the legal act in question, which is generally a "directive", and indicates in a footnote in which Official Journal it is to be found. It then gives a summary of the main provisions of the directive. In the case of major directives or ones which might be of direct interest to the public (e.g. "drinking water" or "bathing water" directives) the book also reproduces in tabular form certain technical annexes which form part of the directives in question.

Where the Council has not approved the Commission's proposal, the book restricts itself to a general description of the provisions suggested by the Commission. Two situations might occur here. The first is when the proposal, presented relatively recently by the Commission, is still being considered by the Council, the average period for consideration being around two years. The second is when it has not been possible for the proposal to receive the approval of the Council because of differences of opinion between Member States. These differences mean that it is not possible to arrive at the unanimity which until recently has been required in order for decisions to be taken on Community environment policy. In the latter case the main reasons for the deadlock are mentioned.

4. The pre-eminence given to the "Commission/Council" partnership can be explained by the need to limit the size of the book to a reasonable number of pages. The institutional structure of the Community does, in fact, generally allow for the intervention of two additional bodies, namely the European Parliament and the Economic and Social Committee, each of which should give an opinion on the proposals presented by the Commission. This opinion is, nevertheless, usually of a purely consultative nature and the final decision rests with the Council of Ministers which brings together all of the Member States. This somewhat categorical statement has, however, to be qualified in the light of experience resulting from the application of the cooperation procedure between Council and Parliament introduced in the Single European Act and from the incorporation of an environment chapter in the amended treaty. In cases where the European Parliament has played a particularly active role, for example by setting up a committee of enquiry into dangerous wastes, or by proposing a fund for the environment, this will be mentioned.

5. Finally, it should be noted that this book was completed at the end of 1994, and that consequently only the official proposals submitted by the Commission to the Council prior to that date are taken into consideration.

Chapter 1

Introduction

I. ORIGIN AND EVOLUTION OF COMMUNITY ENVIRONMENT POLICY

1. Environment policy does not appear in the 1957 Treaty of Rome

From the political and legal points of view, Community Environment Policy differs fundamentally from other Community policies, such as agricultural, commercial or transport policies, in that no mention of it is made in the treaty establishing the European Economic Community, namely the Treaty of Rome of March 1957. This omission is explained by the fact that in the years during which the Treaty of Rome was being drawn up the idea of environment policy or of "environmental protection", as it is understood today, was not a major preoccupation of public policy. Only two articles in the Treaty can be seen as offering some kind of link with an environment policy. First, there is Article 2 of the Treaty which expresses in a very general way a preoccupation with the quality of life, in as much as it refers to a "harmonious" development of economic activities and to a "balanced" expansion. The second article of the EEC Treaty which refers to the idea of environmental protection is Article 36. Again, the reference is somewhat negative in that, unlike the basic principle of the Common Market which aims at freedom of exchange, Article 36 allows for the continuation or introduction of the banning or restriction of trade for reasons of public health and the protection of animals and plants.

2. The birth of Community Environment Policy: the 1972 Paris Summit

It was not until 15 years after the signing of the Treaty of Rome, at the summit of the Community Heads of State and Government held in Paris in 1972, that Community environment policy eventually came into being. The Heads of State and Government felt that economic expansion should equally result in an improvement in the quality of life, and that to this end particular attention should be given to environmental protection. Aware too of the need to bring the European Economic Community closer to the citizens, the Heads of State and Government proposed that the institutions of the Community establish an Environmental Action

Programme in the course of 1973, as well as other programmes in the areas of social and regional policy and consumer protection.

3.   Uncertain and modest beginnings

The beginnings of Community Environment Policy coincided with the economic and oil crises of 1973–1974, thus making it more difficult to impose restrictions and new burdens on enterprises and the economy in general. Furthermore, it should be remembered that historically speaking the protection of the environment developed as a reaction to the excesses of the period of extremely rapid industrialization during the 1960s. Given these conditions one could legitimately wonder if the ecological thrust, typified to an extreme degree in the ideas launched by the "Club of Rome" which advocated reduced economic expansion and a more qualitative management approach ("zero growth"), might be likely to disappear with the end of economic growth which came in the years 1973–1975. However, despite numerous obstacles of a political, legal, economic and even administrative nature, and, doubtless, through the tenacity and power of initiative of the Commission, the Community was finally able, during the 1970s, progressively to set up and put into action a genuinely substantial environment policy.

4.   An undeniable success

More than 20 years after its birth, Community Environment Policy can be seen to be not only a major Community policy, but also an undeniable success, despite certain gaps and weaknesses. This success is all the more evident if one compares it to other Community policies, be it transport policy, referred to in the Treaty of Rome itself, or consumer policy, which was also established in 1972 at the same time as environment policy. This success of Community Environment Policy is confirmed by the adoption of over 400 legislative acts relating to all aspects of the environment, as well as by a growing interest in this policy within all the Community institutions – in particular the European Parliament and also the European Council, which brings together the Community Heads of State and Government. This success was confirmed with the introduction into the "Single European Act", of an important chapter on environmental protection and with the further emphasis given to the environment in the Treaty on European Union (the Maastricht Treaty) as indicated in Chapter 17.

Different factors explain the success of Community Environment Policy. The first of these is undoubtedly the dynamism of the European Commission, which has taken its responsibilities as the initiator of policy extremely seriously and which has brought the Council to examine, not always with unmitigated enthusiasm, a considerable number of proposals. The second is the ever-growing interest of the public, in some Member States in particular, in matters concerning the protection of the natural environment, which has in turn stimulated the interest and support of the European Parliament. Finally, and possibly most importantly, a series of spectacular catastrophes which have occurred over recent years has provided concrete proof of the reality and importance of problems of environmental protection. One need only think of "environmental" headlines such as: the *Amoco Cadiz*; Seveso; acid rain; Bhopal; Chernobyl; pollution of the Rhine, etc.

II. THE CONSTITUENT ELEMENTS OF COMMUNITY ENVIRONMENT POLICY

1. The political framework

The general political framework surrounding Community Environment Policy consists basically of five action programmes, the main characteristics of which are explained in the following chapter. Another important political element is the relatively recent tendency of the European Council of Heads of State and Government, which is the highest political authority of the Community, to pay particular attention to the environmental situation within the Community. This first became evident in 1978 when the European Council decided on a specific Community action on sea pollution, but also more recently in 1983 and 1985. In 1983 the Stuttgart European Council underlined the urgent need to speed up and reinforce the action carried out at all levels in the fight against environmental pollution. It put particular emphasis on the serious danger threatening European forest areas, and decided that environmental protection policy should be treated as a priority within the Community. In March 1985 at its Brussels session the European Council judged that environmental protection policy should become a fundamental part of economic, industrial, agricultural, and social policies set up by the Community and its Member States. It asked that the years to come be marked by significant progress in Community action for environmental protection in Europe and the rest of the world.

The year 1987 was declared by the Council as European Year of the Environment and saw the adoption of the Community's 4th Environmental Action Programme. It was also the year in which the report of the World Commission on Environment and Development, the so-called Brundtland Commission, was published, setting the stage for the United Nations Conference on Environment and Development (UNCED) to be held in June 1992.

In general, the European Community, supported by the EFTA countries, can be said to have taken a reasonably progressive stance at the 1992 Earth Summit in Rio de Janeiro. Aiming to promote greater environmental protection whilst understanding concerns of developing countries, the Community sought to help bring about compromises between the very different positions held by countries such as India and Malaysia on the one hand, and the United States on the other. Nevertheless, many observers felt that the Community did not take advantage of the opportunity to take a serious lead in influencing global environmental policies which was posed by the somewhat reluctant stance adopted by the United States.

The signature, ratification and entry into force of the Treaty on European Union were events of major political importance for the Community's environmental policy as for other dimensions of the Community's activities. The treaty, which was signed by all Member States on 7 February 1992 and entered into force on 1 November 1993, introduced into the treaties in Article 2 the principal objective of promoting sustainable growth respecting the environment. The activities of the Union it created include specifically that of an environment policy which it states must aim at a high level of protection. Furthermore, environmental protection considerations must be integrated into the drawing up of and implementation of other Community policies (Article 130r.2). Article 3b gives special value to the subsidiarity principle, which states that decisions ought to be taken as closely as possible to the citizens (Article A). An important and interesting development is the concept in Article 130r.1 that Community environment policy contributes to the promotion of measures at international level to combat regional or global environmental problems.

2. The legal framework

The most frequently used legal instrument with regard to environment policy is the "directive", as defined in Article 189 of the EEC Treaty. Since the beginning of Community Environment Policy, that is since 1973–1975 and until the coming into force of the Single European Act in 1987, the legal basis used in almost all of the directives is that of Articles 100 and 235 of the EEC Treaty, these two articles sometimes being combined. Article 100 is the basic article relating to the bringing together of the laws of the Member States which have a direct effect on the functioning of the Common Market; this article consequently provides a link between environmental and economic policies. Article 235 indicates that the treaty establishing the Community has not provided a basis for the actions proposed and that it is therefore a matter of creating a new policy, for which purpose Article 235 may be used. The fundamental characteristic is nevertheless that in both cases, be it Article 100 or 235, decision-making requires the unanimity of the members of the Council, and not a qualified or simple majority. This legal requirement has had a number of consequences which have profoundly influenced Community Environment Policy. Indeed, the need to have unanimity first and foremost implies at best a permanent effort to find a compromise in order to reach an agreement. At worst, and this occurs fairly frequently, it leads to an agreement based on the lowest common denominator, if not a total impasse. Because of this, those Member States which feel the Community provisions to be insufficient have in turn often insisted that environmental directives be "minimal" directives, that is to say that they give Member States a legal right, if they so wish, to take more severe environmental protection measures in their own countries than those fixed by the Community directives. These then represent no more than a sort of bottom level which all Member States must respect, but do not specify any common ceiling or upper limit. This lack of total harmonization in the "environment" directives, unlike most of those dealing with the elimination of technical obstacles and the internal market, can cause considerable difficulties on the international level as well as for businesses when the subjects in question have important economic and industrial implications.

As for the future, if it is true that for the first time the Single Act devoted a specific chapter to the environment, the method of decision to be used was nevertheless that of unanimity, excepting the case of proposals which contributed equally to the realization of the internal market, when the decision could be taken on the basis of a qualified majority. Under the Maastricht Treaty the field of majority voting in respect of environmental measures was further extended.

3. Legislative and regulatory action

The bulk of the activities carried out by the Community in the area of environment has been of a legislative or regulatory nature. From 1973–1975 until the end of

1988 more than 100 texts had been adopted, which was no mean feat, especially given the lack of a "legal basis" in the treaty establishing the Common Market. These 100 legislative measures, either regulatory or administrative, mostly concern the fight against pollution and nuisances, and consequently the curative aspects involved, often described as the "command and control" approach. However, some of the measures adopted deal with the improvement of the environment and the surroundings, as well as the protection of natural resources. The measures in this last category, the majority of which were adopted towards the end of the 1980s, aimed at a more *preventive* approach to environment policy. Despite the reticence expressed by certain Member States over this category of measures, it is this approach which has received the greater emphasis in recent years.

The first category of measures, the command and control category, mainly covers regulations in the area of water pollution, air pollution, waste management, control of chemicals and noise reduction. The second category, consisting of the "preventive" or "incentive" measures, covers a more varied area. It brings together several types of preventive actions, be it the directive establishing the principle of prior evaluation of the effect on the environment which would result from major development projects ("environmental impact assessment") or the directive on the industrial risks of major accidents. Since 1984 it has also provided for measures of financial aid in the area of development of clean technologies and the conservation of certain biotopes. Despite the extremely limited financial allowances made for these measures, it is clear that the so-called ACE regulation, which set up a sort of mini-fund in favour of the protection of the environment, marked an important turning point in Community Environment Policy and paved the way for the further measures which have been adopted more recently, notably the so-called LIFE programme.

Another sector to be included in this second category of action concerns the protection of flora and fauna, particularly the most endangered species. Finally, there are a certain number of more specific actions which range from the creation of a European foundation for research and information regarding living and working conditions, to the production of ecological maps and an information system of the state of natural resources in the Community, or else to the taking of specific measures concerning environmental problems in the Mediterranean regions (soil erosion; forest fires; insufficient water resources) and the creation of a European environmental agency.

4.   Other actions: research and information

Parallel with the legislative action, the Community has undertaken a vast programme of research and development within the area of the environment. This programme, which has expanded considerably since 1973, is carried out either directly by the Commission itself in its research centre at Ispra in Italy, or indirectly in laboratories in Member States through contracts with the Community. It should be stressed that a large part of this programme is devoted to the safety of nuclear installations and nuclear waste management. Another area of activity within Community policy concerns information and awareness raising of environmental matters amongst the population at large. In this respect pilot projects have been started in different schools in the Member States and regular contacts have been established with environmental associations brought together at Community level in a "European Environment Bureau". Initially, this information action was carried out on an extremely modest scale. However, it became increasingly clear that there was a need to expand this activity considerably in the future, particularly in order to draw the population's attention to the importance of environmental questions and so to create favourable conditions for the application of and respect for Community legislation already adopted. This is why the European Council decided to launch a major information and awareness campaign in 1987–1988 in the form of a European Year of the Environment. One of the main aims of this "Year" was to show that economic development and environmental protection, far from being incompatible, are complementary, and that the protection of the environment can result in job creation. Significantly, a number of the pilot projects and actions launched then continue to operate at Community level with a considerable degree of success.

5.   Structure and means

On the organizational level, the Commission has within its services a directorate-general responsible for "environment and nuclear safety" (Directorate-General number XI). Originally known as the Environment and Consumer Protection Service numbering some 20 permanent officials at the time of its creation in 1973, DG XI now has a permanent staff of some 150 officials who are in turn assisted by around 150 temporary officials or consultants.

To assist it in the drawing up of its proposals, the Commission has established a number of consultative committees made up of experts from Member States and responsible for giving consultative advice to the Commission (Consultative Committee on waste management; Ecotoxicology Committee; Consultative Committee on marine pollution, etc.)

On the financial level, the Commission currently has an annual environment budget of around 100 million Ecus (1 Ecu is equivalent to approximately 75p). Though the Commission's environment budget has grown substantially in recent years (during the 1980s annual expenditure on the environment, including research, was around 20–30 million Ecus), today's figure nonetheless represents an extremely small, if not negligible, part of the Community budget.

Apart from the funds coming from the mini-funds intended for "environmental" actions for the Community (ACE and LIFE, etc.), the bulk of the environment funds is used to pay for scientific studies carried out prior to the drawing up of directive proposals, and for grants made to different environmental protection associations.

On the institutional level, it should be noted that the Council of Environment Ministers meets regularly two or three times a year. The European Parliament has also set up a special committee on environment questions, public health and consumer protection. So has the Economic and Social Committee of the European Communities, which brings together representatives of employers, workers and "diverse activities", covering, for example, family or consumer organizations, as well as professional or scientific associations. It is as much the role of the Parliament as of the Economic and Social Committee to give the Council its views on proposals drawn up by the Commission. In most cases the Council can in fact only give rulings on proposals presented to it by the Commission after having consulted the Parliament and the Economic and Social Committee. The Council is not, however, obliged to follow the advice of these two institutions. However, it should be stressed that the Single Act allowed for a procedure of "cooperation" or concili-ation between Parliament, Council and Commission in areas where the decisions are taken on the basis of a qualified majority: internal market; social policy; research. This new procedure undoubtedly increased the powers of the Parliament in a general sense by providing for the more active involvement of that institution in the Community's legislative process. Though the cooperation procedures envis-aged under the Single Act were not applicable to the environment sector, where decisions had to be taken unanimously, except in so far as the measures were pro-posed on the basis of Article 100A or 130S, paragraph 2, the extension of majority voting under the Maastricht Treaty to certain aspects of the environment has had the effect of confirming the increasing importance of the Parliament in this field.

6. The international dimension of Community Environment Policy

It is clear that by its very nature pollution recognizes no borders, and that the envir-onment is a field of action which enjoys a large degree of international cooperation. Moreover, since the 1973 1st Action Programme the Community has given an important place to the international dimension of Community Environment Policy. This international action is to be seen first and foremost in an active participation in numerous international conventions to which the Community has become a legal contracting party. These conventions mainly concern water pollution, but also to a lesser extent air pollution and the protection of flora and fauna. They are either of a worldwide dimension as with the 1985 Vienna Convention on the protection of the ozone layer, or the 1973 Washington Convention on the protection of the threat-ened flora and fauna, or of a regional dimension, bringing together several countries in the same geographical area (Mediterranean; Atlantic; the North Sea, etc.). In this respect it should be stressed that some of these conventions have played a consider-able political role, the protection of the environment having constituted a common objective and a uniting factor between countries or political systems which are often opposed in many other areas. So the Geneva Convention of 1979 on trans-boundary atmospheric pollution made it possible to create an exemplary field of cooperation between Eastern and Western European countries and even between the USA and the Soviet Union. Equally the joint signing of this convention by the Community and the Community countries indirectly represented the first political and diplomatic recognition of the Community by the Soviet Union and by the Eastern European countries as a whole.

Another notable convention from the political point of view is the 1975 Convention of Barcelona on the protection of the Mediterranean which made it possible to establish the only common framework in which both Israel and the Arab countries, including Libya, cooperate. Apart from participating in numerous inter-national conventions, the Community has established regular relations with certain third countries, such as the United States, Canada, Switzerland, Sweden and Austria, with a view to exchanging information on environmental matters. There is a special declaration on environmental cooperation between EC and EFTA coun-tries known as the 1987 Nordwijk Declaration. The Community also participates in a number of international organizations dealing with environmental questions, such as the United Nations Environmental Programme (UNEP), the United Nations Economic Commission for Europe in Geneva (UN-ECE) or the Organization for

Economic Cooperation and Development in Paris (OECD). Finally, the Community has passed several agreements on scientific and technical cooperation in environmental research with third countries in Western Europe (COST), as well as agreements on technical cooperation which have "environmental" aspects with certain developing countries, such as Egypt, Jordan or China.

Both the preparations for, as well as the follow-up to, the 1992 Earth Summit have served to focus the Community's attention on international environmental questions, particularly those relating to climate change, biodiversity and the protection of forests issues which were high up on the agenda of the Rio Conference.

III.   ASSESSMENT AND PERSPECTIVES

1.   The position of Member States with regard to Community Environment Policy

The nine countries making up the EC when Community Environment Policy came into being in 1973–1975 can, generally speaking, be divided into three categories. The first, which covers the "ecological" countries and the most advanced when it comes to environmental protection, includes the Federal Republic of Germany, the Netherlands and Denmark. As far as Germany is concerned, the awakening of particular interest in the environment coincided with the arrival of the "greens" on the German political scene and the awareness of the phenomenon of acid rain. As for Denmark, it finds itself in a special situation inasmuch as this country appears to be profoundly split between its interests in the environment and its general reticence with regard to the Community. Generally speaking, these countries have an increasing tendency to consider that Community Environment Policy does not go far enough and represents a slowing influence in comparison with the stricter environmental protection measures which they would wish to introduce in their countries.

The second category, which covers the countries which could be classed as "neutral", includes France, Luxembourg, Italy and Belgium. These countries generally accept the proposals of the Commission without any particular enthusiasm, but without causing any particular difficulties either.

The third category, made up of the United Kingdom and Ireland, has frequently shown a certain reticence with regard to over-restrictive and over-harmonized Community solutions in environmental matters. One of the best-known cases which illustrates this more restrictive approach concerns the conflict between "emission norms" and "quality objectives" which ranged the United Kingdom against all the other Member States on the subject of water pollution policy.

As for the position of the three Member States, Greece, Spain and Portugal, which joined the Community in 1981 (Greece) and 1986 (Spain and Portugal) respectively, all three not surprisingly experienced, and in some cases continue to experience, certain difficulties in respecting and applying the whole of Community legislation, as is illustrated for example by the dispensations granted to Portugal regarding certain directives (drinking water directive; bathing water directive, etc.). Over the years these countries have tried to turn Community Environment Policy towards a less normalizing or legislative approach, wanting to direct it towards more specific actions and interventions on the ground, for example in the area of soil quality, erosion, forest fires, insufficient water resources, or coastal protection, all of these being matters where the Southern countries have a particular concern and appear to hope that Community resources, sometimes in the form of inter–regional transfers through the Community's structural funds, will help meet the often substantial costs.

2.   The assessment: an undeniable success, despite certain weaknesses

Compared with other Community policies on the one hand, and bearing in mind certain handicaps such as economic crises, the principle of unanimity, and the dif- fering interests of Member States on the other, Community Environment Policy can be seen to represent an undeniable success. Moreover, this policy, the import- ance of which was originally rather neglected by some, has become over the years a major Community policy, and is fully recognized as such, as has been stressed by several sessions of the European Council. It is equally clear, however, that this success has also been accompanied by some weaknesses. Numerous adopted direct- ives are not applied by Member States, as is shown by several cases brought before the Court of Justice in Luxembourg. What is more, a number of directives are the result of successive political compromises, which often explains a certain incoher- ence in the texts and provisions retained. Finally, it is clear that legislation, although very important, could never be enough on its own to prevent certain types of pollution or accidents. To that extent the development of other means of action, particularly those involving the application of economic and financial instruments, must be a vital complement to the original command and control approach.

3.   The prospects for Community Environment Policy

The first prospect in view for environment policy will concern a broadening of its field of activities. Indeed, while continuing the efforts against pollution and nuisances, notably through a more global, so-called "multi–media" approach, this policy will no doubt take on new aspects aiming at a more preventive and general conception of environmental protection. For example, actions will be undertaken in favour of better management of natural resources, and better protection of sensitive regions such as coastal zones or urban centres; more care will be taken in national and regional developments and in the spread of economic activities. In addition, the entry of Spain and Portugal has encouraged the Community to conceive actions aimed at increasing natural resources which are often insufficient in Southern Europe, for example, the development of water resources, or afforestation in order to prevent soil erosion. This orientation is likely to be maintained. Finally, the Community should also make better known the considerable successes of its en- vironment policy by improving its information and awareness activities at all levels of the population.

The second prospect in view will be the increased integration of Community Environment Policy with the other sectoral policies of the Community. This idea, the importance of which has already been stressed within the context of the 1983 3rd Action Programme, was expanded during the 4th Action Programme by the launching over the years 1987–1992 of a certain number of new actions, such as the

ENVIREG Programme, the aim of which was to favour regional development on the basis of investments for environmental purposes. It was also expected that environmental protection would be increasingly taken into account in the two big Community policies, which are the Common Agricultural Policy and the Development Aid Policy.

The Community's 5th Environmental Action Programme already reflects the emphasis being placed on both the broadening of environmental instruments and the integration of environment into other sectors. Entitled "Towards Sustainability" and reflecting many of the preoccupations of the Brundtland Commission's report, the 5th Action Programme was approved by the Council in March 1992 in the run-up to the UNCED Conference. In line with the subsidiarity principle (see Chapter 17), the 5th Action Programme commits the Community to a departure from the "top-down" approach to a broader-based, "bottom-up" strategy in which industry, business, citizens and consumers all have a role to play. The basis of the programme is to break existing trends of behaviour and consumption and replace them with a more sustainable pattern of development and production. Environmental policy is intended to be integrated into all other policy areas and decision-making structures. To this end, the programme calls for the use not only of legislative instruments, but also of market-based instruments, horizontal and supporting measures, and financial support mechanisms. More specifically, it targets five priority sectors: industry, energy, transport, agriculture and tourism.

Finally, the third prospect in view for Community Environment Policy over the coming years will concern the application and implementation of the "environment" chapter in the Maastricht Treaty which builds on and expands the environmental provisions contained in the Single European Act. The challenge for the Community, and more especially the Commission, will be to ensure that they select the best part of the new elements contained in these texts, while avoiding any hidden pitfalls. Only practical implementation will allow the true value and merits of the new treaty to be fully appreciated.

4.   Enlargement

Between 1989 and 1992 four EFTA countries – Austria, Sweden, Finland and Norway – applied to join the EC, the ECSC and Euratom. Negotiations began with the first three on 1 February 1993 and with Norway on 5 April 1993 with the view to the countries acceding by 1 January 1995.

As predicted, the issue of environmental standards was one of the more difficult issues during the negotiations. All four applicant states have environmental rules in certain areas which give a higher level of protection than that afforded in the Community, and even some legislation for which there are no corresponding statutes in the Community. Environmental awareness is high in all four states and their governments were keen to ensure that accession to the Union would not result in, or be seen to result in, a reduction in the high environmental standards which prevail in those states.

In a few areas, the Community has stricter environmental legislation than that of the applicants but much of the *acquis communautaire* in the area of environment was already adopted by the applicant states in the context of the European Economic Area (EEA) Agreement.

In its opinions on Finland's and Austria's applications for membership, the Commission noted that Finnish legislation concerning nuclear safety and radiation protection would need to be changed, while in Austria's case there could be some legal or technical difficulties arising from the more progressive nature of EU legislation.[1]

During the negotiations, however, Austria requested permanent or temporary derogations for a number of areas including the use, marketing, labelling and classification of dangerous substances; substances that deplete the ozone layer; dangerous waste; and lead in petrol. In the case of dangerous substances, Austrian legislation is stricter than that of the Community: the Austrian list of classified substances corresponding to Directive 67/548 contains 1500 substances that do not feature in Annex I of the directive.

Difficulties were also encountered in the product-related area where concern for high environmental standards had to be reconciled with the requirements of free circulation. In the case of Sweden, this issue applied notably to CFCs and the classification of dangerous substances, the waste directives, approved pesticides and rules on exhaust emissions. In other areas, such as biotechnology and major industrial hazards, Sweden would have to develop further its framework legislation in order to bring it into line with the rest of the Community.

Norway has a higher level of environmental protection than the Community in similar areas to Austria and Sweden. In addition, the decision in 1993 of Norway to resume whaling also posed a problem as the Community and its Member States no longer continue this practice. The application of the directive banning the import or marketing of certain seal products was also contentious.

In the area of environment, Finland identified only Directive 75/716 on the sulphur content of certain fuels as being a problem, since the Finns want to maintain stricter rules on the sulphur content of diesel oils, to keep the right to use light fuel oils with a sulphur content of less than 0.1%, and to continue to use economic regulators to promote the use of fuel oils with a low sulphur content. Accordingly, Finland requested special arrangements until Community rules are in line with hers.

The accession of Sweden, Finland and Norway would add a sixth biogeographical region – Boreal – to the Union in addition to the existing regions: Alpine, Atlantic, Continental, Macronesian and Mediterranean. Consequently, the annexes to the Habitats Directive would have to be adapted to take account of habitat types and species not found elsewhere in the Union.

The Commission noted in its opinion on the prospective enlargement that the sound and long-term environmental policies of the applicant states would "not only add to the quality of environmental standards, but would also promote a comprehensive approach aiming at an overall integration of environmental considerations in all relevant policy areas".

In 1994, negotiations were successfully concluded between the Community and the four applicant countries. It was anticipated that the four countries would become members of the European Union (as the Community became known following the entry into force of the Maastricht Treaty) on 1 January 1995. In the event, Norway voted to stay out – for the second time in 20 years – in a referendum held at the end of November 1994.

[1] Bulletin of the European Community, Supplements 4/92 and 5/92.

Chapter 2

The Environmental Action Programmes of the European Community (1973–1977–1983–1987–1993)

I. INTRODUCTION

All of the actions envisaged by the Community in the area of the environment have been defined and described in several "action programmes", each of which represents the basic reference framework for Community Environment Policy. These programmes, which generally cover a period of four to five years, follow the procedure of other measures which are approved by the Council after being proposed by the Commission. The instrument used for the adoption of these programmes is usually a Council "resolution", which shows the political will of the Member States to apply the measures contained in the programme, but which does not imply any legal obligation to do so. For this reason, certain actions which were clearly provided for in the 1st Action Programme of 1973 and which related to particular branches of industry, such as the paper pulp sector, have never been realized due to a lack of agreement between the Member States in the Council. What is more, except in the case of the 1st Action Programme where the Council approved not only the general orientation but also the specific actions, the Council has generally been careful in the drawing up of the texts of the "resolutions" on the different programmes to approve only the general directions or guidelines, and not the detailed programmes as such.

Since 1973, which marks the beginning of Community Environment Policy, five action programmes have been approved by the Council:

- the first programme, adopted on 22 November 1973,[1] covered the years 1973–1976; it defined for the first time the basic principles and objectives of Community Environment Policy and specifically described the actions to be carried out in the different sectors of the environment;
- the second programme, adopted on 17 May 1977,[2] covered the years 1977–1981; this programme simply followed on from the first and specified the general

[1] OJ No C 112 of 20/12/73.
[2] OJ No C 139 of 13/6/77.

12

actions provided for within the framework of the first programme of 1973 and which were still fully valid;

- the third programme, adopted on 17 February 1983,[3] covered the period 1982–1986; this established for the first time the priorities for action and introduced a certain number of new concepts such as the integration of the "environmental" dimension into other policies, or the need for a preventive approach to environment policy;
- the fourth programme, adopted on 19 October 1987,[4] covered the period 1987–1992 and contained several innovations both as to format and content;
- the fifth programme, adopted on 27 March 1992,[5] covers the period 1992–1997.

In addition to the summary presented in this chapter, details of the fifth programme are also given in subsequent chapters under the heading "future action".

II.   THE 1973 1ST ACTION PROGRAMME (1973–1976)

In its introduction, the 1st Programme mentions that among the other objectives set out in the preamble to the 1957 Treaty of Rome establishing the European Economic Community, the signatories affirmed as goals "the constant improvement of the living and working conditions of their peoples" and "the harmonious development of their economies".

In addition, in Article 2 of the treaty the following are included in the statement of the task assigned to the Community: to promote throughout the Community "a harmonious development of economic activities", and "continuous" and "balanced" expansion. When they met in Paris in October 1972, the Heads of State and Government of the Member States (consisting of the "original" six, namely: Belgium, the Netherlands, France, West Germany, Italy, and Luxembourg, plus the three "adherent states", Denmark, Ireland and the United Kingdom) also declared that "economic expansion should result in an improvement in the quality of life as well as in standards of living and that particular attention should be given to intangible values and to protecting the environment". Thus emphasizing the importance of a Community Environment Policy the Heads of State and Government invited the Community institutions to establish, before 31 July 1973, a programme of action accompanied by a precise timetable.

In response to this invitation in March 1973, the Commission sent a proposal to the Council for a 1st Environmental Action Programme. After consulting the European Parliament, the Economic and Social Committee, and the professional and trade union organizations, the Council adopted this programme on 22 November 1973[6] in the form of a "Declaration of the Council of the European Communities, and of the representatives of the Governments of the Member States meeting in the Council". The Council retained this mixed form of declaration because it felt that actions provided for in the programme should be carried out either at Community level, or at national level by Member States, depending on the action in question, thereby providing an early example, in fact if not in name, of

---

[3] OJ No C 46 of 17/2/83.
[4] OJ No C 328 of 7/12/87.
[5] OJ No C 138 of 17/5/93.
[6] OJ No C 1122 of 20/12/73.

the importance it attached to the application of what would later come to be called the "subsidiarity" principle to the field of environment. In this declaration the Council approved the objectives and principles of a Community Environment Policy, as well as the general actions to be undertaken at Community level. It also committed itself in principle to deciding on the Commission's proposals within a period of nine months from the date of their despatch.

1.   The objectives of Community Environment Policy

The aim of a Community Environment Policy, as defined in the 1st Action Programme, is to improve the quality of life, and the surroundings and living conditions. To this end it should:

- prevent, reduce and as far as possible eliminate pollution and nuisances;
- ensure sound management of and avoid any exploitation of resources or of nature which causes significant damage to the ecological balance;
- guide development in accordance with quality requirements, especially by improving working conditions and the settings of life;
- ensure that more account is taken of environmental aspects in town planning and land use;
- seek common solutions to environment problems with countries outside the Community, particularly in international organizations.

2.   The principles of Community Environment Policy

The general principles of Community Environment Policy are also defined by the 1st Action Programme and are as follows:

1. The best environment policy consists in preventing the creation of pollution and nuisance at source, rather than subsequently trying to counteract their effects. To this end, technical progress must be conceived and devised so as to take into account the concern for protection of the environment and for the improvement of the quality of life at the lowest cost to the Community. This environment policy can and must be compatible with economic and social development.

2. Effects on the environment should be taken into account at the earliest possible stage in all the technical planning and decision-making processes.

3. Any exploitation of natural resources or of nature which causes significant damage to the ecological balance must be avoided. The natural environment has only limited resources; it can only absorb pollution and neutralize its harmful effects to a limited extent. It represents an asset which can be used, but not abused.

4. The standard of scientific and technological knowledge in the Community should be improved with a view to taking effective action to conserve and improve the environment and to combat pollution and nuisances. Research in this field should therefore be encouraged.

5. The cost of preventing and eliminating nuisances must in principle be borne by the polluter. However, there may be certain exceptions and special arrangements, in particular for transitional periods, provided that they cause no significant distortion to international trade and investment.

6. In accordance with the Declaration on the Environment of the United Nations Conference on the Human Environment which took place in Stockholm in 1972, care should be taken to ensure that activities carried out in one state do not cause any degradation of the environment in another state.

7. The Community and its Member States must take into account in their environment policy the interests of developing countries, and must in particular examine any repercussions of the measures contemplated under that policy on the economic development of such countries and on trade with them.

8. The effectiveness of effort aimed at promoting a global environmental policy will be increased by a clearly defined long-term concept of a European environmental policy. In this respect, the Community and the Member States must make their voices heard in the international organizations dealing with aspects of the environment and must make an original contribution in these organizations, with the authority which a common point of view confers on them.

9. The protection of the environment being a matter for all, public opinion should be made aware of its importance. The success of an environment policy presupposes that all categories of the population and all the social forces of the Community help to protect and improve the environment. This means that at all levels continuous and detailed educational activity should take place.

10. In each different category of pollution, it is necessary to establish the level of action (local, regional, national, Community, international) that befits the type of pollution, and the geographical zone to be protected.

11. On the basis of a common long-term concept, national programmes in these fields of the environment should be coordinated, and national policies should be harmonized within the Community. Such coordination and harmonization should be achieved without, however, hampering potential or actual progress at the national level. However, the latter should be carried out in such a way as not to jeopardize the satisfactory operation of the Common Market.

3.   General description of the actions to be undertaken under the 1st Action Programme

The protection of the natural environment and the improvement of living conditions requires the implementation of a body of actions which should be undertaken as much within the framework of Community Environment Policy as that of the other sectoral policies – agricultural; regional; industrial; energy; research, etc. The 1st Action Programme provides for the following three categories of action:

(a)   Action to reduce and prevent pollution and nuisances

In order to arrive at an objective evaluation of pollution and to perfect common methods of reference, the Commission will undertake the following tasks:

● The establishment of scientific criteria for the degree of harm caused by the principal forms of air and water pollution and for noise. This action will go hand in hand with the standardization or alignment of the methods and instruments used in measuring these pollutants and nuisances. In the laying-down of criteria, priority will be given to the following pollutants: organic halogen compounds, sulphur compounds and particles in suspension, nitrogen oxides, carbon monoxide, mercury, phenols and hydrocarbons.

- The definition, on the basis of a common methodology, of parameters in connection with the laying-down of quality objectives.
- The promotion of exchanges of technical information between the regional and national pollution surveillance and monitoring networks.
- The adoption of a common method of estimating the cost of anti-pollution measures allowing for the application of the principle of making the polluter pay, without prejudice to the rules of the Common Market.
- The standardization or harmonization of the methods and techniques for sampling, analysis and measurement of pollutants. Priority will be given in this respect to oils and natural gases having carcinogenic effects, photochemical oxidants, asbestos and vanadium.
- The establishing of quality objectives determining the various requirements an environment must meet, bearing in mind its allotted purpose.
- The determination of emission standards concerned mainly with water pollutants.
- The harmonization of the specifications of polluting products. This harmonization, which is already being implemented in the elimination of technical barriers to trade, will be accompanied by studies on the noxious effects of pollutants contained in such products, and on the possibilities, if necessary, of their replacement by non-polluting or less polluting substitute products. Priority will be given to vehicles, noisy products and other fuels and combustibles, cleaning and washing products.
- The establishment of a common research programme, and a European documentation system for the dissemination of information on environmental protection, particularly with regard to anti-pollution technologies and the effects of pollution on human health and the natural environment.
- Studies in individual industries on pollution caused by industrial activities and energy production, relating to the principal polluting industrial activities, will be carried out. In the first place work will be undertaken on paper and pulp, iron and steel and titanium dioxide manufacturing.
- With regard to the problems raised by toxic or persistent waste, such as waste oils for example, possible means of action will be examined, such as harmonization of regulations, promotion of the development of new techniques, or the possible establishment of a system for pooling information.
- The serious problems posed by the pollution of certain zones of common interest (marine pollution, pollution of the Rhine Basin and certain frontier zones) will be the subject of special measures taking into account the geographical characteristics of such zones. As far as marine pollution is concerned, Community action will consist in particular of coordinating and harmonizing the rules for implementing international conventions, and of implementing projects to combat land-based marine pollution. With regard to the protection of the environment in frontier zones, Member States will be recommended to establish consultation procedures for the conclusion of agreements on the protection of the environment in such zones.

(b)   Action to improve the quality of the environment

In order to improve the quality of the environment in general, the 1st Action Programme provides for a certain number of actions being undertaken in the following areas:

- safeguarding the natural environment, for example, in the areas of mountain farming and farming in certain poorer areas;
- study of the problems raised by the growing scarcity of water resources and of the exploitation of natural resources;
- study of the environmental problems connected with urban development and the geographical distribution of human activities;
- improvement of the working environment and, linked to this, the creation of a European Foundation for the Improvement of Working and Living Conditions;
- promotion of activities to strengthen environmental awareness among the population, in order to encourage them to accept their own responsibility towards environmental protection.

(c) Action in international organizations

The Community will enter into active cooperation in the area of the environment with international bodies, particularly the OECD, the Council of Europe and the United Nations Organization. This cooperation will facilitate the carrying out of common activities by the Member States within these bodies without prejudicing any action by the Community itself, within the framework of its own competencies.

III. THE 1977 2ND ACTION PROGRAMME (1977–1981)

On 17 May 1977 the Council adopted a Resolution, establishing the 2nd Environmental Action Programme of the European Communities for the years 1977–1981.[7] This programme basically represented a continuation and expansion of the actions undertaken within the framework of the 1st Programme of 1973. It reaffirmed in full the general principles and objectives of the 1973 programme. As far as the description and the timetable of the actions to be undertaken is concerned, it gave a certain priority to anti-pollution measures in the areas of water and air. It also provided for wider and more specific measures in the area of noise pollution. Finally, it reinforced the preventive nature of Community Environment Policy and gave particular attention to the rational protection and management of space, the surrounding environment and natural resources.

IV. THE 1983 3RD ACTION PROGRAMME (1982–1986)

The 3rd Environmental Action Programme for the years 1982–1986 was adopted by a Resolution of the Council on 7 February 1983.[8] This Resolution, as with preceding instruments, was of a mixed character, associating both the Council and the governments of Member States. The 3rd Programme, without bringing into question the principles and objectives of the preceding two, introduced particularly important new elements, which were indications of the evolution of Community

[7] OJ No C 139 of 13/6/77.
[8] OJ No C 46 of 17/2/83.

Environment Policy. These new elements mainly concerned the following four aspects:

- The first concerned the desire, expressed by Commission and Council alike, to integrate environment policy into the other sectoral policies of the Community; in this respect the Resolution equally emphasized the economic and social aspects of environment policy, particularly the fact that this policy could contribute to the lessening of current economic problems such as unemployment.
- The second aspect clearly underlined the need to reinforce the preventive character of environment policy, particularly within the framework of a global strategy aiming at the most economic use possible of natural resources; great importance was attached in this respect to the procedure for evaluating environmental effect (impact assessment).
- The third aspect lay in the fact that for the first time a certain number of priority areas were established by the Council. These priorities were the following:
  - integration of the environmental dimension into other Community policies;
  - environmental impact assessment procedure;
  - reduction of pollution and nuisance if possible at source, in the context of an approach to prevent the transfer of pollution from one part of the environment to another, in the following three areas: atmospheric pollution (especially by NOx, heavy metals and SO_2); freshwater and marine pollution; pollution of the soil;
  - environmental protection in the Mediterranean region;
  - noise pollution and particularly noise pollution caused by transport;
  - transfrontier pollution;
  - dangerous chemical substances and preparations;
  - waste, and in particular toxic and dangerous waste, including transfrontier transport of such waste;
  - encouraging the development of clean technologies, e.g. by improving the exchange of information between Member States;
  - protection of areas of importance to the Community which are particularly sensitive environmentally;
  - cooperation with developing countries on environmental matters.
- The fourth aspect concerned the listing of a certain number of considerations which the Commission should use as a basis for the drawing up of its proposals. These considerations concerned, for example, the need to avoid any unnecessary overlaps, and the obligation to evaluate, where possible, the costs and benefits of the actions planned. It was also stated that the Commission must take into account the different economic and ecological conditions and the different structures existing in the Community.

While the first three aspects could be considered as a significant step forward in Community Environment Policy, the latter would however seem to have a tendency to place the Commission's proposals into a more restrictive framework.

V. THE 4TH ACTION PROGRAMME (1987–1992)

The 4th Action Programme began in 1987 and ended in 1992 – the year which saw the more or less complete realization of the "internal market" of the

Community, and thus the abolition of a large number of obstacles to trade and free movement. From the point of view of format and content, this programme moved away somewhat from the preceding programmes. As regards format, the Commission chose a new structure, highlighting the different conceptual approaches in the area of pollution control and prevention; multi-media approach; substance-directed approach; pollution source-directed approach, etc. As far as content is concerned, the 4th Programme developed a number of new ideas and principles. One of the main ideas of the programme concerned, for example, the need to establish environmental standards which are sufficiently strict, which had hardly been the case in the past. Indeed, such standards not only largely conformed with the desires of the public, but had also become an economic necessity for Community industry, both within the internal market of the Community, and outside it. A second idea of the 4th Action Programme concerned the need to give greater importance to the control and practical implementation of Community directives in the area of the environment. A third direction aimed to achieve the progressive implementation of a true environmental education and information policy, to accompany and increase the efficacy of the legislative approach followed until now.

The 4th Programme developed and specified principles which had already appeared in the 1983 3rd Action Programme, notably the need to integrate environmental protection into the other Community policies (employment; agriculture; transport; development, etc.), or the need to intensify the global or integrated fight against pollution, in order to avoid the transfer of pollution from one area of the environment to another (air; water; soil). Finally, the 4th Programme provided for a number of initiatives in new areas, in particular in the sectors of biotechnology and the management of natural resources with regard to soil protection on the one hand, and the protection of urban, coastal and mountain zones on the other. As far as marine coastal areas are concerned, on 14 November 1986, the Commission sent the Council an initial communication on the integrated improvement of coastal zones and its place in Community Environment Policy.

As noted above (see p. 13), the 4th Environmental Action Programme was adopted by the Council on 19 October 1987. The Resolution of the Council followed the pattern established by earlier Council Resolutions, e.g. that under which the 3rd Environmental Action Programme was adopted (see p. 17), in that it was of a mixed character, associating both the Council and the governments of Member States. As with earlier "programme" Resolutions, the Council Resolution of 19 October 1987 laid down certain priorities which, in the Council's view, ought to guide the work of the Community in the environmental field over the period of the 4th Programme. The main themes stressed in the Resolution were:

- pollution prevention;
- improvement in management of resources;
- international activities;
- development of appropriate instruments.

The full text of the Council Resolution is set out in Annex 1.

VI.   THE 5TH ACTION PROGRAMME (1993–2000)

The draft 5th Action Programme was presented to the Council in 1992 under the form of a proposal entitled "Towards Sustainability". The choice of title underlined the stress which the programme placed on the principle of sustainable development. For the first time, the aim is not simply environmental protection, but also properly managed growth without detriment to the environment and the natural resources and the achievement of balance between economic and social improvement and respect for the needs of the environment. The programme is broadly based on the principle of subsidiarity and the concept of shared responsibility.

In its introduction, the programme notes that attaining a balance between human activity and the development and protection of the environment calls for a sharing of responsibilities which is both equitable and clearly defined by reference to consumption of and behaviour towards the environment and natural resources. On this basis, environmental factors must be integrated into the formulation and carrying out of other policies, public policy decisions, the production process, and individual behaviour. The programme uses the word "sustainable" to refer to "continued economic and social development without detriment to the environment and natural resources on the quality of which continued human activity and further development depend" (p. 3, para. 5). The programme sets out three practical requirements for the achievement of sustainable development: optimize reuse and recycling, thus avoiding wastage and helping prevent depletion of finite natural resources; rationalization of production and consumption of energy; and the alteration of consumption and behaviour patterns. The fundamental aim of the programme is to break current trends.

The programme addresses itself to a range of issues which it describes not as problems but as symptoms of mismanagement and abuse. The environmental problems faced by the Community are the consumption and behaviour patterns which are the cause of environmental degradation. In line with the principle of subsidiarity, the programme concentrates on those issues which have a Community-wide dimension, be it because they are cross-boundary, of shared resource or cohesion implications, or as a result of the single market: climate change; acidification and air pollution; depletion of natural resources and biodiversity; depletion and pollution of water resources; deterioration of the urban environment; deterioration of coastal zones; waste.

Accordingly, the programme gives priority to six areas for Community action with the aim of achieving real improvements or changes during its operational lifetime:

- sustainable management of natural resources, namely water, soil, natural areas and coastal zones;
- integrated pollution control and prevention of waste;
- reduction in the consumption of non-renewable energy;
- improved management of mobility, such as more environmentally rational and efficient location policies and modes of transport;
- coherent packages of measures to attain gains in urban environmental quality;
- improvement of public health and safety, in particular industrial risk assessment and management, nuclear safety and radiation protection.

In addition, the programme highlights five target sectors for special attention for which it sees policy conducted at Community level as being the most efficient: industry, energy, transport, agriculture and tourism.

As regards industry, the programme refers to a realization in the business world that not only is industry a major part of environmental problems, but that it must also be part of the solution. Accordingly, the programme calls for a new approach with greater dialogue and self-regulation.

In the area of energy, apart from boosting efficiency, the programme sets the objective of moving towards less carbon-intensive energy, especially renewable energies.

In response to the even greater pressure being imposed on the environment by transport with the completion of the internal market and the economic development of Central and Eastern Europe, the programme proposes a strategy of "sustainable mobility". This is to cover the development of public transport and the improvement of its competitive position; the continued technical improvement of vehicles and fuels; the encouragement of more environmentally rational use of the private car (including driving rules and habits); and the incorporation of the real costs of infrastructure and environment in investment policies, decisions and user costs.

As regards agriculture, the programme sets out to build on the Commission's proposals for the reform of the CAP and for the development of the Community's forests with the aim of fostering balanced and dynamic rural development. In response to the overexploitation and degradation by farming practices of soil, water and air, the programme calls for a more sustainable balance to be established between agriculture, other types of rural development and environmental considerations.

The fifth target area, tourism, notes the programme, is predicted to grow rapidly in Europe during the 1990s, with most of the increase occurring in the Mediterranean region. In line with the subsidiarity principle, however, the programme sees that the main effort to reconcile tourism and the protection of natural and cultural assets must be by Member States, regional and local authorities and the tourism industry itself.

In contrast to previous environmental action programmes, the 5th Programme proposes using not only legislative measures but a variety of other instruments in order to bring about what it describes as fundamental changes in trends and practices and to involve all parts of society. Perhaps the most important of the other instruments are those based on the market. These aim to internalize environmental costs by economic and fiscal incentives and disincentives thus helping ensure that environmentally friendly goods and services are not at a disadvantage compared to wasteful or polluting competitors. Such measures also encourage the responsible use of natural resources by both producers and consumers. In addition, the programme calls for greater use of horizontal supporting instruments such as scientific research and technological development. The programme refers to the Community's existing financial support mechanisms for the environment, namely LIFE and the Structural Funds, in particular ENVIREG, as well as to the new Cohesion Funds, but contains no provision for the setting up of new budget lines in this area.

Another departure from previous action programmes is the espousal of a bottom-up strategy involving all social and economic partners rather than a top-down, legislation-based approach. To this end, the Commission proposed to establish

three *ad hoc* dialogue groups: a General Consultative Forum (comprising representatives of consumers, unions, professional organizations, NGOs, and business); an
Implementation Network (made up of representatives of relevant national authorities and of the Commission involved in the practical implementation of
Community measures); and an Environmental Policy Review Group (comprising
representatives of the Commission and the Member States at Director-General level)
aimed at developing mutual understanding on environment policy and measures.

Within this broader approach, the programme points out that "Towards
Sustainability" is not just for the Commission or environmentalists, but for all citizens and consumers, as well as all levels of the political and economic spectrums.

Just as the challenge of the 1980s was the completion of the internal market, the
5th Action Programme sees the reconciliation of environment and development as
one of the main challenges of the 1990s. The programme is targeted towards the
year 2000 but will be reviewed in 1995 in light of improvements in data, results of
research and reviews of other Community policies.

The publication of the Commission's proposal for a 5th Environmental Action
Programme was accompanied by a new report on the "State of the Environment".[9]
This points to a slow but continuing deterioration of the general state of the
Community's environment, in spite of the hundreds of measures adopted as a result
of the preceding four programmes. Sectors of particular concern include climate
change, acidification, air pollution, depletion of natural resources and biodiversity,
depletion and pollution of water resources, deterioration of the urban and coastal
environment, and waste.

The full text of the Council Resolution is set out in Annex 2.

VII.   THE ROLE OF THE EUROPEAN COUNCIL IN ENVIRONMENTAL POLICY

The Community's environment policy and programmes have been a subject of
growing importance at the regular meetings of the Community's Heads of State or
Government known as the European Council. Thus, the meeting of the European
Council held in Stuttgart, under the German Presidency in June 1983 adopted the
following statement:

> The European Council underlines the urgent necessity of accelerating and reinforcing
> action at national, Community and international level aimed at combating the pollution
> of the environment. It underlines in particular the acute danger threatening the
> European forest areas, which calls for immediate action.
>
> The European Council welcomes in this connection the memorandum from the
> Federal German Government and the Commission Communication which illustrates the
> urgency of the question and the necessity to take coordinated and effective initiatives
> both within the Community and internationally, particularly within the ECE, if an irre-
> versible situation is to be avoided. It calls on the Environment Council to pursue its
> work on the different specific dossiers relevant to this problem and examine relevant
> initiatives proposed by the Commission, with a view to rapid significant progress.
>
> The European Council also welcomed the Conclusions of the Environment Council
> on the special case of lead in petrol. It emphasized the importance of reducing the

---

[9] COM (92) 23 final of 27/3/92.

amount of lead in the environment and called for progress which may lead to the use of leadless petrol.

The Conclusions of the Stuttgart Summit gave an impetus to the Community's environmental work, particularly in air pollution.

Similarly, the European Council held in Brussels in March 1985 adopted some language on environmental policy which would later be incorporated in substance in the Single European Act. The European Council of March 1985 "affirmed its determination to give environmental protection policy the dimension of an essential component of the economic, industrial, agricultural and social policies implemented by the Community and by its Member States". Article 130R, paragraph 2 of the Single European Act (see p. 489) lays down that "environmental protection requirements shall be a component of the Community's other policies".

The March 1985 Summit also decided to designate 1987 as "European Year of the Environment".

The relevant text from the Conclusions of the Presidency following the European Council of March 1985 read as follows:

> The European Council considers that a Community environmental protection policy must be based on the following considerations:
>
> (i) Having acknowledged that this policy can contribute to improved economic growth and job creation, it affirms its determination to give this policy the dimension of an essential component of the economic, industrial, agricultural and social policies implemented by the Community and by its Member States.
>
> (ii) It acknowledges the need for the Member States to take coherent action in the Community framework to protect the air, the sea and the soil, where isolated action is unlikely to prove effective and may even be harmful.
>
> It requests the Council to expedite its proceedings and to make every effort, together with the Commission, to ensure that the years to come are marked by significant progress in Community action for the protection of the environment in Europe and throughout the world.

The European Council returned to environmental questions at its meeting in Hanover on 27 and 28 June 1988, again under the German Presidency, expressing "its concern about the danger to the environment in general and in particular that caused by the pollution of air and water". Since the Single European Act had already entered into force, the Hanover Summit went on to state that "the concept that environmental considerations must be integrated into all areas of economic policy-making is in conformity with the environmental objectives of the Single European Act".

At the Rhodes meeting of 2 and 3 December 1988, and on the initiative of the Greek Presidency, the European Council adopted a Declaration on the Environment in the following terms:

> 1. Today's world is confronted by environmental problems of increasing magnitude. In the interests of sustained growth and a better quality of life, it is urgent to find solutions to such global issues as the depletion of the ozone layer, the rise in the temperature of the earth's atmosphere ("the greenhouse" effect), threats to the natural environment, the problem of water resources, soil erosion, safe management of toxic chemicals and waste, air pollution, particularly "acid rain", and problems of urban areas. Effective action will in many cases require better scientific research and understanding.

2. The goals of environmental protection laid down for the Community have recently been defined by the Single European Act. Some progress has been made in reducing pollution and in ensuring prudent management of natural resources. But these actions by themselves are not enough. Within the Community, it is essential to increase efforts to protect the environment directly and also to ensure that such protection becomes an integral component of other policies. Sustainable development must be one of the overriding objectives of all Community policies.

3. The expected achievement of the Single Market by 1992 and the accompanying economic growth offers both a challenge and an opportunity. Europe's industrial future and international competitiveness will depend in part on applying the high level of environmental protection foreseen in the Treaty. Special attention needs to be devoted to the seas and coastal regions of the Member States, which are of outstanding importance from the economic and ecological stand-point, particularly the Mediterranean region, the North Sea and the Irish Sea. The Community should redouble its efforts to protect these vital resources.

4. In the wider international context, the Community and the Member States are determined to play a leading role in the action needed to protect the world's environment and will continue to strive for an effective international response, particularly to such global problems as depletion of the ozone layer, the greenhouse effect and the ever-growing threats to the natural environment, thus contributing to a better quality of life for all the peoples of the world.

Eighteen months later at its meeting in Dublin in June 1990, the Council issued a declaration entitled "The Environmental Imperative". This declaration recognized that "the very life support system of the planet is at risk" and that the Community "has a special responsibility to protect and enhance the natural environment not just of the Community itself but of the world of which it is a part".

The Council stated the Community had a responsibility to play a leading role in concerted and effective action on a global level and to work with other industrialized regions to help developing countries overcome their particular problems. The declaration also noted that the impetus to growth that would arise from the completion of the single market in 1992 must be accompanied by a greater effort to ensure that such growth was sustainable and environmentally sound, especially in the areas of transport, energy and infrastructure. Whilst confirming that the regulatory approach would remain the "cornerstone" of Community environmental policy, the declaration announced that the "command and control" approach should be supplemented by economic and fiscal measures to enable environmental considerations to be integrated fully into other policy areas.

The Heads of State and Government announced that the Community and its Member States had an "enormous" capacity to provide leadership in tackling global environmental problems and called for the Community to use its "moral, economic and political authority" as a motor for international action. In a wide-ranging declaration, the Community's leaders expressed their concern about the depletion of the ozone layer, the destruction of tropical rainforests, and the particular problems faced by Central and Eastern Europe. Accordingly, the leaders called upon the Commission to draw up concrete proposals relating to carbon dioxide emissions, recognized that the question of tropical deforestation could only be effectively tackled in the context of North–South relationships generally, and underlined the need to expand the PHARE programme (see p. 468).

The positive note of the declaration seemed to indicate that the Community was ready to adopt a much more active role as regards environmental policy, both within and beyond the Community. As preparations continued for the 1992 United Nations Conference on the Environment and Development, it seemed as if the Community might take the leading role in environmental policy, particularly as the United States administration did not appear to be giving much priority to environmental issues. As the UNCED drew nearer, however, it became clear that the Council was not prepared to go as far in providing the leadership it had proclaimed in Dublin as some had hoped or expected. In the end, declarations of intent were scaled down to comply with political necessities.

A particularly crucial summit meeting from the perspective of the European Community's environmental policy was the European Council held in December 1992 in Edinburgh. The Summit's conclusions included a re-emphasis of the basic tenet that the European Union rests "on the principle of subsidiarity ... which contributes to the respect for the identities of Member States and safeguards their powers". The Commission undertook to review existing and proposed legislation and to report to the December 1993 meeting of the European Council. In the area of the environment, the Commission announced that it intended to simplify, consolidate and update existing texts, particularly those on air and water to take account of developments in knowledge and technical progress.

Part One

The Basic Sectors of Community Environment Policy

Chapter 3

Water

I. INTRODUCTION

1. Water pollution policy is the oldest and the most complete sector of Community Environment Policy. This actually reflects the historical situation in most Member States, where problems of water pollution have also been dominant both internally and externally. Indeed one of the first cases of litigation between France and Belgium, newly created in 1830, is said to have concerned a particularly polluted river.

This part of Community Environment Policy represents the oldest sector in that the first major proposals were presented by the Commission and adopted by the Council from 1973 to 1975. By way of comparison, the first significant measure in the area of air pollution, and one which can be seen in many ways as the first element of a true Community air pollution policy, namely, the directive fixing air quality standards for sulphur dioxide, was only adopted by the Council in 1980. It should also be noted that the impetus for the adoption of that directive was more external than internal, namely the signing in 1979, within the framework of the United Nations, of the Convention on Long-Range Transboundary Air Pollution. But besides being the oldest, Community water pollution policy is also the most complete, in that some 70 or so directives or decisions have been adopted, covering both freshwater and seawater pollution.

This policy largely operates on a two-pronged approach, the first being of a general nature, which consists in fighting against the discharge of dangerous substances into the aquatic environment of the Community, the other of a more specific nature which aims to define certain water quality standards according to the proposed use: water to be used for the production of drinking water; bathing water; water for shellfish, etc.

The policy refers both to a system of "quality objectives", based on the desired quality of the receiving environment, and to a system of "emission standards" which are considered to be more restrictive, and which fix the maximum permissible quantities of pollutants to be discharged into the aquatic environment.

2. Since the first discussions held in 1974–1976 within the Council, Community policy on water pollution has known some difficult moments which have almost led to its being seriously called into question. The difficulties which have caused delays in the setting up of this policy have mainly been over the conflict between emission standards and quality objectives with regard to pollution caused by dangerous substances, and to a lesser extent over the problems of competence in the area of marine pollution.

The main difficulty, which was both a philosophical and economic one, concerned the need to establish whether Community policy on dangerous substances discharged into the aquatic environment, namely those coming mainly from industry, should be based, as the Commission proposed, on the fixing of emission standards, that is maximum Community limits which must not be exceeded, or on the fixing of quality objectives for the water in question.

The Commission's proposal (see p. 74) was supported by eight Member States, while the United Kingdom alone argued for the system of quality objectives. Finally a compromise was reached within the Council which allowed for the adoption in 1976 of the framework directive on the pollution of the aquatic environment of the Community. This compromise, known as the "parallel approach", while giving a certain priority as far as principles and presentation are concerned to the emission standards system, also allows for a quality objectives approach, even if the latter is considered rather the exception than the rule. The conflict between emission standards and quality objectives was reawakened in 1980–1982 when the first proposals for the implementing directives of the 1976 framework directive were examined, and when the system applicable for new industrial establishments had to be established. Again an intermediate solution was found within the Council in 1982–1983 with the adoption of the "alkaline mercury" and "cadmium" directives. Nevertheless, the problem of the system to be applied to newly built industrial establishments largely explains the delay in the adoption of the different implementing directives drawn up in accordance with the framework directive of 1976.

The second difficulty, which is of less importance, but which should nevertheless be mentioned in that it also slightly delayed the implementation of Community measures, concerns marine pollution. Problems linked to the distribution of competences between the Community and its Member States did indeed arise within the Council when it came to examine the first measures submitted by the Commission in 1977 regarding marine pollution, in particular those involving the Community's participation in certain international conventions.

However, the political and psychological impact provoked by the accident of the oil tanker, the *Amoco-Cadiz*, off the Brittany coast, made it possible, due in particular to the interest taken in the affair by the European Council in Copenhagen in 1978, to unfreeze the situation and to adopt an action programme in the area of marine pollution by hydrocarbons.

3. Despite the difficulties encountered, the record of Community water pollution policy can be considered as very satisfactory, both quantitatively and qualitatively speaking. The work accomplished is substantial, in spite of certain weaknesses, if not a failure in specific high-pollutant industrial sectors such as the paper pulp sector, for which the Commission's proposal of 1975 was never adopted by the Council, or the titanium dioxide industry where it proved very difficult to adopt a truly harmonious anti-pollution regulation.

Nevertheless, the achievement is very largely positive, compared not only with other sectors of Community Environment Policy, but also with existing regulations in non-Community countries. The difficulties encountered by the newer Member States (Spain and Portugal) in applying the current Community regulations is evidence of the importance and quality of Community water pollution policy since

1975. This policy was further completed and enlarged between 1987 and 1992 within the framework of the 4th Environmental Action Programme.

II. QUALITY OBJECTIVES

The 1973 1st Action Programme on the Environment stressed the need to establish quality objectives at Community level. "Quality objectives" were defined by the Council as "a set of requirements which must be fulfilled at a given time, now or in the future, by a given environment or particular part thereof". Quality objectives were to be established for the following uses of water: drinking, swimming, farming, pisciculture, industry, recreation, and aquatic life in general.

To date, more than 30 directives establishing quality objectives for different uses of water have been adopted by the Council. These directives can be seen as environmental management directives and allow a certain freedom to Member States having to apply them. In most cases it is up to the Member States themselves to specify the areas in which the quality objectives must be respected. For the most part these quality objectives are in any case made up of "guide values" (G) which Member States must try to respect. The most constricting element of these directives concerns a number of mandatory values (I) which Member States are obliged to respect and which generally correspond to public health requirements.

1. Quality of surface water intended for the abstraction of drinking water

(a)   The first Council directive of 1975

The Commission's first proposal for a directive on quality objectives was sent to the Council on 21 January 1974 and concerned the quality of surface water intended for the abstraction of drinking water in the Member States. Drinking water supplies are most frequently abstracted from groundwater or surface water such as lakes, water courses or artificial reservoirs. Generally speaking, purification is necessary, particularly in the case of watercourses which are often polluted by effluents of various origins. This is why the proposal included a detailed definition of the pollution levels which were not to be exceeded if health requirements were to be fulfilled. It also laid down standard methods of treatment for transforming surface water of various qualities into drinking water.

The Council adopted the directive on surface water quality objectives on 16 June 1975.[1] Although health requirements were a primary motivation for this directive, the international and ecological aspects were also taken into consideration. In fact the directive goes beyond public health requirements, in that it represents a means of achieving improvements in the quality of surface waters in general whenever they are used for the abstraction of drinking water. What is more, because the directive applies equally to water crossing the borders of Member States, it must also be seen as an instrument for dealing with certain problems of cross-border pollution.

---

[1]   OJ No L 194 of 15/7/75.

The directive requires Member States to take the necessary measures to ensure that their surface water intended for the abstraction of drinking water conforms to the values laid down (see Table 3.1). These values correspond to about 50 parameters selected as pollution indicators and fall into two categories. The first covers "mandatory values" (I) which Member States must respect under all circumstances (except under exceptional circumstances such as floods or natural disasters, for example). The second covers "guide values" (G), which are stricter and which should serve as guidelines for Member States to endeavour to respect. Member States must respect the values both for their own national surface waters and for those crossing their borders. Only three categories of surface water can, under normal circumstances, be used for the abstraction of drinking water. These three categories (A1 – A2 – A3) correspond to different treatment methods which allow for the transformation of surface water into drinking water. The Member States must draw up a plan of action, including a timetable, for the improvement of their surface waters, particularly those falling into category A3. Considerable improvements had to be achieved over the 10-year period from 1975 onwards within the framework of the national action plans which would be examined by the Commission.

(b)   The complementary directive of 1979 specifying measuring methods

On 25 July 1978 the Commission submitted a proposal for a directive to the Council which specified the reference methods of measurement, as well as the minimum annual frequency for the sampling and analysis of surface waters intended for the abstraction of drinking water in the Member States. The Council adopted this directive on 9 October 1979.[2]

2.   Quality of bathing water

(a)   Council directive of 8 December 1975

On 7 February 1975 the Commission sent the Council a second proposal for a directive dealing with quality objectives, this time for bathing water. In drawing up this proposal the Commission took into account the health problems which can be caused through polluted bathing water, especially when it is polluted by sewage water. This question was not only one of national concern, but also of Community concern, in that polluted bathing water, be it seas or rivers, frequently had international implications, particularly from the point of view of tourism. But the Commission's aim was not only to satisfy public health requirements with this directive; it also aimed to include other criteria such as amenity, aesthetic attractiveness, and the improvement of the quality of the environment in general.

The Council adopted this directive on 8 December 1975.[3] In the context of the directive, "bathing water" covers all fresh water or sea water in which "bathing is either explicitly authorized by the Member States, or is not prohibited and is traditionally practised by a large number of bathers". Water in swimming-pools and spas is not covered by the directive. The aim of the directive is to guarantee a

---

[2] OJ L 271 of 29/10/79.
[3] OJ L 31 of 5/2/76.

Table 3.1: Council Directive of 16 June 1975
Quality requirements for surface water intended for the abstraction of drinking water

	Parameter		A1 G	A1 I	A2 G	A2 I	A3 G	A3 I
1	pH		6.5 to 8.5		5.5 to 9		5.5 to 9	
2	Coloration (after simple filtration)	mg/l Pt scale	10	20 (0)	50	100 (0)	50	200 (0)
3	Total suspended solids	mg/l SS						
4	Temperature	°C	22	25 (0)	22	25 (0)	22	25 (0)
5	Conductivity	s/cm^{-1} at 20°C	1000		1000		1000	
6	Odour	(dilution factor at 25°C)	3		10		20	
7*	Nitrates	mg/l NO$_1$	25	50 (0)		50 (0)		50 (0)
8^1	Fluorides	mg/l F	0.7 to 1	1.5	0.7 to 1.7		0.7 to 1.7	
9	Total extractable organic chlorine	mg/l Cl						
10*	Dissolved iron	mg/l Fe	0.1	0.3	1	2	1	
11*	Manganese	mg/l Mn	0.05		0.1		1	
12	Copper	mg/l Cu	0.02	0.05 (0)	0.05			
13	Zinc	mg/l Zn	0.5	3	1	5	1	5
14	Boron	mg/l B	1		1			
15	Beryllium	mg/l Be						
16	Cobalt	mg/l Co						
17	Nickle	mg/l Ni						
18	Vanadium	mg/l V						
19	Arsenic	mg/l As	0.01	0.05		0.05	0.05	0.1
20	Cadmium	mg/l Cd	0.001	0.005	0.001	0.005	0.001	0.005
21	Total chromium	mg/l Cr		0.05		0.05		0.05
22	Lead	mg/l Pb		0.05		0.05		0.05
23	Selenium	mg/l Se		0.01		0.01		0.01
24	Mercury	mg/l Hg	0.005	0.001	0.005	0.001	0.0005	0.001

Table 3.1 continued

	Parameter		A1 G	A1 I	A2 G	A2 I	A3 G	A3 I
25	Barium	mg/l Ba		0.1		1		1
26	Cyanide	mg/l Cn		0.05		0.05		0.05
27	Sulphates	mg/l SO_4	150	250	150	250 (0)	150	250 (0)
28	Chlorides	mg/l Cl	200		200		200	
29	Surfactants (reacting with methyl blue)	mg/l (laurylsulphate)	0.2		0.2		0.5	
30*2	Phosphates	mg/l P_2O_5	0.4		0.7		0.7	
31	Phenols (Phenol index) paranitraniline 4 aminoantipyrine	mg/l C_6H_5OH		0.001	0.001	0.005	0.01	0.1
32	Dissolved or emulsified hydrocarbons (after extraction by petroleum ether)	mg/l		0.05		0.2	0.5	1
33	Polycyclic aromatic hydrocarbons	mg/l		0.0002		*0.0002		0.001
34	Total pesticides (parathion, BHC, dieldrin)	mg/l		0.001		0.0025		0.005
35*	Chemical oxygen demand (COD)	mg/l O_2					30	
36*	Dissolved oxygen saturation rate		>70		>50		>30	
37*	Biochemical oxygen demand (BOD) (at 20°C without nitrification)	mg/l O	<3		<5		>7	

Table 3.1 continued

	Parameter		A1 G	A1 I	A2 G	A2 I	A3 G	A3 I
38	Nitrogen by Kjeldahl method (except NO_1)	mg/l N	1		2		3	
39	Ammonia	mg/l NH_4	0.05		1	1.5	2	3(0)
40	Substances extractable with chloroform	mg/l SEC	0.1		0.2		0.5	
41	Total organic carbon	mg/l C						
42	Residual organic carbon after flocculation and membrane filtration (5) (TOC)	mg/l C						
43	Total coliforms 37 C	/100 ml	50		5000	5000	5000	
44	Faecal coliforms	/100 ml	20		2000		2000	
45	Faecal streptococci	/100 ml	20		1000		1000	
46	Salmonella		Not present in 1000 ml		Not present in 1000 ml			

I = mandatory; G = guide; O = exceptional climatic or geographical conditions; * = see Article 8 (d)

[1] The values given are upper limits set in relation to the mean annual temperature (high and low)
[2] This parameter has been included to satisfy the ecological requirements of certain types of environment.

minimum quality of bathing water by laying down a number of values corresponding to various microbiological and physico-chemical parameters. Other parameters regarded as pollution indicators, such as pesticides or heavy metals, can also be considered by Member States (see Table 3.2). The directive establishes two categories of values for these parameters; one category covers the mandatory values (I) which Member States are obliged to respect; the second covers the guide values (G) which Member States must endeavour to achieve and respect.

The Member States were given a period of 10 years following notification of the directive, that is 1975, in which to ensure that the quality of their bathing water conforms with the mandatory limit values (I) laid down by the directive. However, in exceptional circumstances, Member States could be granted derogations, provided that they notify the Commission of the justifications. These were to be included in water management plans for the area in question. For transborder bathing waters, i.e. ones which are situated close to borders, the directive stipulates that quality objectives must be determined jointly by the bordering Member States and that the Commission can participate in this. The directive also establishes a detailed sampling procedure, particularly with regard to minimum frequency of the sampling, and indicates the methods of analysis to be used.

The Member States must send the Commission a regular report on their bathing waters and their most significant characteristics. With the consent of the Member States concerned, the Commission will publish the information obtained. It should be noted that the detailed information they provide on the cleanliness and quality of the different beaches of the Community has made these reports the object of growing interest to public opinion and consumer associations.

(b)   Commission proposal for a revised directive on the quality of bathing water

On 16 February 1994, the Commission proposed a revised directive on the quality of bathing water, the purposes of which are to:

● maintain the protection of the environment and public health, taking advantage of technical progress and focusing on the most significant parameters;
● simplify the operation of the directive by removing redundant parameters and making certain definitions more explicit;
● ensure that Member States take action on deteriorating water quality and identify new bathing waters, while allowing time for water to be brought up to the standards required by the directive.

3.   Water for freshwater fish

On 2 August 1976 the Commission submitted a proposal for a directive to the Council on the quality requirements for water capable of supporting freshwater fish. The Commission had noted that degradation in the quality of water due to the discharge of pollutants has adverse effects on certain species of fish. These effects are seen either in the form of a reduction in the number of fish, or even in the disappearance of some species. The quality objectives contained in this directive aim to allow fish belonging to indigenous species or whose presence is considered desirable for water management, to live in favourable conditions. When laying down parameters and numerical values for determining water quality, the Commission

**Table 3.2: Council Directive of 8 December 1975
Quality requirements for bathing water**

Parameters		G	I	Minimum sampling frequency	Method of analysis and inspection
MICROBIOLOGICAL					
1	Total coliforms	500	10000	Fort-nightly (1)	Fermentation in multiple tubes subculturing of the positive tubes on a confirmation medium.
2	Faecal coliforms	100	2000	Fort-nightly (1)	Count according to MPN (most probable number) or membrane filtration and culture on an appropriate medium such as Tergitol lactose agar, endo agar. 0.4% Teepol broth, subculturing and identification of the suspect colonies.

In the case of 1 and 2, the incubation temperature is variable according to whether total or faecal coliforms are being investigated. |
| 3 | Faecal streptococci | 100 | – | (2) | Litsky method. Count according to MPN (most probable number) or filtration on membrane. Culture on an appropriate membrane. |
| 4 | Salmonella | – | 0 | (2) | Concentration by membrane filtration. Inoculation on a standard membrane. Enrichment – subculturing on isolating – agar identification. |

Note: /100 ml for parameters 1, 2, 3; /1 litre for parameter 4.

Table 3.2 continued

	Parameters		G	I	Minimum sampling frequency	Method of analysis and inspection
5	Entero viruses	Pfu/10 litres	—	0	(2)	Concentrating by filtration, flocculation or centrifuging and confirmation.
	PHYSICO-CHEMICAL:					
6	pH		—	6 to 9 (0)	(2)	Electrometry with calibration at pH 7 and 9.
7	Colour		—	No abnormal change in colour (0)	Fort-nightly (1) (2)	Visual inspection or photometry with standards on the Pt. Co scale.
8	Mineral oils	mg/litre	— / —	— / No film visible on the surface of the water and no odour	Fort-nightly (1)	Visual and olfactory inspection or extraction using an adequate volume and weighing the dry residue.
9	Surface-active substances reacting with methylene blue	mg/litre (lauryl-sulfate)	<0.3 / —	— / No lasting foam	(2) / Fort-nightly (1) (2)	Visual inspection or absorption spectrophotometry with methylene blue.
10	Phenols (phenol indices)	mg/litre C_6H_5OH	<0.3 / — / ≤0.005	— / No specific odour / ≤0.05	Fort-nightly (1) (2)	Verification of the absence of specific odour due to phenol or absorption spectrophotometry 4-aminoantipyrine (4 AAP) method.
11	Transparency	m	2	1 (0)	Fort-nightly (1)	Secchi's disc.

Table 3.2 continued

	Parameters		G	I	Minimum sampling frequency	Method of analysis and inspection
12	Dissolved oxygen	% saturation O_2	80 to 190	—	(2)	Winkler's method or electrometric method (oxygen meter).
13	Tarry residues and floating materials such as wood, plastic articles, bottles, containers of glass, plastic, rubber or any other substance. Waste or splinters.		Absence		Fortnightly (1)	Visual inspection
14	Ammonia	mg/litre NH_4			(3)	Absorption spectrophotometry. Nessler's method, or indophenol blue method.
15	Nitrogen Kjeldahl	mg/litre N			(3)	Kjeldahl method
16	Pesticides (parathion, HCH, dieldrin)	mg/litre mg/litre			(2)	Extraction with appropriate solvents and chromatographic determination.
17	Heavy metals such as – arsenic – cadmium – chrom VI – lead – mercury	mg/litre As Cd CrVI Pb Hg			(2)	Atomic absorption possible preceded by extraction

Table 3.2 continued

Parameters	G	I	Minimum sampling frequency	Method of analysis and inspection
18 Cyanides	mg/litre CN		(2)	Absorption spectrophotometry using a specific reagent
19 Nitrates and phosphates	mg/litre NI_1 PO_4		(2)	Absorption spectrophotometry using a specific reagent.

G guide; I mandatory; (0) Provision exists for exceeding the limits in the event of exceptional geographical or meteorological conditions;
(1) When a sampling taken in previous years produced results which are appreciably better than those in this Annex and when no new factor likely to lower the quality of the water has appeared, the competent authorities may reduce the sampling frequency by a factor of 2;
(2) Concentration to be checked by the competent authorities when an inspection in the bathing area shows that the substance may be present or that the quality of the water has deteriorated; (3) These parameters must be checked by the competent authorities when there is a tendency towards the eutrophication of the water.

paid particular attention to the effects of each parameter not only on the survival of the fish at the different stages of their life-cycle, but also on their growth and reproduction, as well as on other components of the aquatic ecosystem which might provide them with shelter and food.

The Council adopted this directive on 18 July 1978.[4] Under it, Member States must themselves designate the waters to which the directive applies, and must either respect the mandatory values (I) or attempt to reach the guide values (G), corresponding to the different parameters given in the directive (see Table 3.3). For each parameter the directive specifies the method of analysis and the minimum frequency of sampling to be carried out by the Member States. The Member States must also establish programmes with a view to reducing pollution and so to ensuring that within a period of five years the waters they have designated conform with the values and sampling procedures laid down in the directive.

Five years after the designation of the areas in question, the Member States had to send a detailed report to the Commission on water for freshwater fish and its main characteristics.

4. Water for shellfish

On 3 November 1976 the Commission submitted to the Council a proposal for a directive on the quality requirements for water favourable to shellfish growth. In fixing the parameters and numerical values which characterize the quality of the water, the Commission took due account, as with the previous directive on the quality of pisciculture waters, not only of the survival of the shellfish populations at the different stages of their life-cycle, but also of the effects on growth, reproduction and other characteristics of the aquatic ecosystem. The proposal did not deal directly with health aspects in relation to human consumption of shellfish, but only with the changes in flavour of the shellfish meat brought about by certain substances.

The Council adopted the directive on 30 October 1979.[5] The structure of the directive is identical to that of the directive of 18 July 1978 on the quality of pisciculture waters. Member States must designate coastal or brackish waters needing protection or improvement in order to support shellfish life and growth and so to contribute to the quality of shellfish products intended for human consumption. With this aim Member States must see that the designated waters respect the mandatory values (I) and attempt to reach the guide values (G) corresponding to the different parameters determined by the directive (see Table 3.4). The parameters include the method of analysis and minimum frequency of sampling and measuring to which Member States must conform. Within six years after designation Member States must also establish programmes with a view to reducing pollution and ensuring that designated waters conform to the specified values. The Commission was to publish regular reports on the state of the waters designated by the Member States as being water for shellfish.

---

[4] OJ No L 222 of 14/8/78.
[5] OJ No L 281 of 10/11/79.

Table 3.3: Council Directive of 18 July 1978
Quality of fresh waters needing protection or improvement in order to support fish life

Parameter	Salmonid waters		Cyprinid waters	
	G	I	G	I
1 Temperature °C	1° – Temperature measured downstream of a point of thermal discharge (at the end of the mixing zone) must not exceed the unaffected temperature by more than:			
		1.5°C		3°C
	Derogations limited in geographical scope may be decided by Member States in particular conditions if the competent authority can prove that there are no harmful consequences for the balanced development of the fish population.			
	2° – Thermal discharge must not cause the temperature downstream of the point of thermal discharge (at the edge of the mixing zone) to exceed the following:			
		21.5 (0)		28 (0)
		10 (0)		10 (0)
	The 10° temperature limit applies only to breeding periods of species which need cold water for reproduction and only to waters which may contain such species.			
	Temperature limits may, however, be exceeded for 2% of the time.			
2 Dissolved oxygen mg/l O₂	50% ≥ 9	50% ≥ 9	50% ≥ 8	50% ≥ 7
	100% ≥ 7		100% ≥ 5	
		When the oxygen concentration falls below 6 mg/l, Member States shall implement the provisions of Article 7(3). The competent authority must prove that this situation will have no harmful consequences for the balanced development of the fish population.		When the oxygen concentration falls below 4 mg/l, Member States shall implement the provisions of Article 7(3). The competent authority must prove that this situation will have no harmful consequences for the balanced development of the fish population.
3 pH		6–9 (0)		6–9 (0)
		x)		x)
	x) Artificial pH variations with respect to the unaffected values shall not exceed +0.5 of a pH unit within the limits falling between 6.0 and 9.0 provided that these variations do not increase the harmfulness of other substances present in water.			
4 Suspended solids mg/l	≤25 (0)		≤25 (0)	

Note: Temperature parameter values — $1.5°C$ and $3°C$; $21.5 (0)$, $28 (0)$; $10 (0)$, $10 (0)$. Dissolved oxygen values as in table. O_2 in mg/l.

Table 3.3 continued

Methods of analysis or inspection	Minimum sampling and measuring frequency	OBSERVATIONS
Thermometry	Weekly, both upstream and downstream of the point of thermal discharge	Over-sudden variations in temperature shall be avoided
– Winkler's method or – specific electrodes (electro-chemical method)	Monthly, minimum one sample representative of low oxygen conditions of the day of sampling. However, where major daily variations are suspected, a minimum of two samples in one day shall be taken	
Electrometry calibration by means of two solutions with known pH values, preferably on either side of, and close to, the pH being measured	Monthly	
Filtration through a 0.45 μm filtering membrane, or centrifugation (5 minutes minimum, average acceleration of 2800–3200g) drying at 105°C and weighing	The values shown are average concentration and do not apply to suspended solids with harmful chemical properties. Floods are liable to cause particularly high concentration.	

Table 3.3 continued

Parameter	Salmonid waters		Cyprinid waters	
	G	I	G	I
5 BOD$_5$ mg/l O$_2$	≤3		≤6	
6 Total phosphorus mg/l P				
7 Nitrites mg/l NO$_2$	≤0.01		≤0.03	
8 Phenolic compounds mg/l C$_6$H$_5$OH	(*)		(*)	

(*) Phenolic compounds must not be present in such concentrations that they adversely affect fish flavour

| 9 Petroleum hydro- carbons | (*) | | (*) | |

(*) Petroleum products must not be present in water in such quantities that they:
form a visible film on the surface of the water or form coatings on the beds of watercourses and lakes,
– impart a detectable 'hydrocarbon' taste to fish,
– produce harmful effects in fish

Table 3.3 continued

Methods of analysis or inspection	Minimum sampling and measuring frequency	OBSERVATIONS
Determination of O_2 by the Winkler method before and after 5-day incubation in complete darkness at $20°\pm1°C$ (nitrification should not be inhibited)		
Molecular absorption spectrophotometry		In the case of lakes of average depth between 18 and 300 metres the following formula could be applied $$L \leqslant 10\frac{\overline{Z}}{Tw}(1+\sqrt{Tw})$$ L = loading expressed in mg/l per square metre lake in one year $\overline{Z}$ = mean depth of lake in metres Tw = theoretical renewal time of lake water in years. In other cases limit values of 0.2 mg/l for salmonid and of 0.4 mg/l for cyprinid water, expressed as PO_4, may be regarded as indicative in order to reduce eutrophication
Molecular absorption spectrophotometry		
By taste		An examination by taste shall be made only where the presence of Phenolic compounds is presumed
Visual By taste	Monthly	A visual examination shall be made regularly once a month, with an examination by taste only where the presence of hydrocarbon is presumed

Table 3.3 continued

Parameter	Salmonid waters		Cyprinid waters	
	G	I	G	I
10 Non-ionized ammonia mg/l NH$_3$	≤0.005	≤0.025	≤0.005	≤0.025
	In order to diminish the risk of toxicity due to non-ionized ammonia, of oxygen consumption due to nitrification and eutrophication, the concentrations of total ammonium should not exceed the following:			
11 Total ammonium mg/l NH$_4$	≤0.04	≤1 (*)	≤0.2	≤1 (*)
	(*) In particular geographical or climatic conditions and particularly in cases of low water temperature and of reduced nitrification or where the competent authority can prove that there are no harmful consequences for the balanced development of the fish population, Member States may fix values high than 1 mg/l.			
12 Total residual chlorine mg/l HOCl		≤0.005		≤0.005
13 Total zinc mg/l Zn		≤0.3		≤1.0
14 Dissolved copper mg/l Cu	≤0.04		≤0.04	

Table 3.3 continued

Methods of analysis or inspection	Minimum sampling and measuring frequency	OBSERVATIONS
Molecular absorption spectrophotometry using indophenol blue or Nessler's method associated with pH and temperature determination	Monthly	
DPD-method (diethyl-p-phenylene-diamene)	Monthly	The I-values correspond to pH = 6. Higher concentrations of total chlorine can be accepted if the pH is higher
Atomic absorption spectrometry	Monthly	The I-values correspond to a water hardness of 100 mg/l $CaCO_3$. For hardness levels between 10 and 500 mg/l corresponding limit values can be found in Annex II
Atomic absorption spectrometry		The G-values correspond to a water hardness of 100 mg/l $CaCO_3$. For hardness levels between 10 and 500 mg/l corresponding limit values can be found in Annex II

General observations:
   It should be noted that the parametric values listed in this Annex assume that the other parameters, whether mentioned in this Annex or not, are favourable. This implies, in particular, that the concentrations of other harmful substances are very low.
   Where two or more harmful substances are present in mixture, joint effects (additive, synergic or antagonistic effects) may be significant.
   G   guide
   I   mandatory
   (0) Derogations are possible in accordance with Article II.

**Table 3.4: Council Directive of 30 October 1979
Quality of shellfish waters**

	Parameters	G	I	Reference methods of analysis	Minimum sampling and measuring frequency
1	pH pH unit		7–9	Electrometry Measured *in situ* at the time of sampling	Quarterly
2	Temperature °C	A discharge affecting shellfish waters must not cause the temperature of the waters to exceed by more than 2°C the temperature of waters not so affected		Thermometry Measured *in situ* at the time of sampling	Quarterly
3	Coloration (after filtration) mg Pt/l		A discharge affecting shellfish waters must not cause the colour of the waters after filtration to deviate by more than 10 mg Pt/l from the colour of waters not so affected	Filter through a 0.45 µm membrane Photometric method, using the platinum/cobalt scale	Quarterly
4	Suspended solids mg/l		A discharge affecting shellfish waters must not cause the suspended solid content of the waters to exceed by more than 30% the content of waters not so affected	Filtration through a 0.45 µm membrane, drying at 105°C and weighing Centrifuging (for at least five minutes, with mean acceleration 2,800 to 3,200 g), drying at 105°C and weighing	Quarterly

Table 3.4 continued

	Parameters	G	I	Reference methods of analysis	Minimum sampling and measuring frequency
5	Salinity%	12 to 38%	≤40% Discharge affecting shellfish waters must not cause their salinity to exceed by more than 10% the salinity of waters not so affected	Conductimetry	Monthly
6	Dissolved oxygen saturation %	≥80%	≥70% (average value) Should an individual measurement indicate a value lower than 70%, measurements shall be repeated An individual measurement may not indicate a value of less than 60% unless there are no harmful consequences for the development of shellfish colonies	Winkler's method Electrochemical method	Monthly, with a minimum of one sample representative of low oxygen conditions on the day of sampling. However, where major daily variations are suspected, a minimum of two samples in one day shall be taken
7	Petroleum hydrocarbons		Hydrocarbons must not be present in the shellfish water in such quantities as to: produce a visible film on the surface of the water and/or a deposit on the shellfish, have harmful effects on the shellfish	Visual examination	Quarterly

Table 3.4 continued

	Parameters	G	I	Reference methods of analysis	Minimum sampling and measuring frequency
8	Organohalogenated substances	The concentration of each substance in shell-fish flesh must be so lim-ited that it contributes, in accordance with Article I, to the high quality of shellfish products	The concentration of each substance in the shellfish water or in shellfish flesh must not reach or exceed a level which has harmful effects on the shellfish and larvae	Gas chromatography after extraction with suitable solvents and purification	Half-yearly
9	*Metals* Silver Ag Arsenic As Cadmium Cd Chromium Cr Copper Cu Mercury Hg Nickel Ni Lead Pb Zinc Zn mg/l	The concentration of each substance in shellfish flesh must be so limited that it contributes in accordance with Article I, to the high quality of shellfish products	The concentration of each substance in the shellfish water or in the shellfish flesh must not exceed a level which gives rise to harmful effects on the shellfish and their larvae The synergic effects of these metals must be taken into consideration	Spectrometry or atomic absorption preceded, where appropriate, by concentration and/or extraction	Half-yearly

Table 3.4 continued

Parameters	G	I	Reference methods of analysis	Minimum sampling and measuring frequency
10 Faecal coliforms/ 100 ml	≤300 in the shellfish flesh and intervalvular liquid ([1])		Method of dilution with fermentation in liquid substrates in at least three tubes in three dilutions. Subculturing of the positive tubes on a confirmation medium. Count according to MPN (most probable number). Incubation temperature 44°C ± 0.5°C	Quarterly
11 Substances of affecting the taste of the shellfish		Concentration lower than that liable to impair the taste of the shellfish	Examination of the shellfish by tasting where the presence of one of these substances is presumed	
12 Saxitoxin (produced by dinoflagellates)				

Abbreviations: G = guide, I = mandatory

([1]) However, pending the adoption of a Directive on the protection of consumers of shellfish products, it is essential that this value be observed in waters in which live shellfish directly edible by man.

5.   First proposal for a directive on water quality objectives for chromium

Because of the Member States' delay with regard to the "grey list" substances (see below p. 75), the Commission submitted to the Council on 7 January 1986 a proposal for a directive on water quality objectives for chromium.[6] The presentation of this directive represented an important and new initiative on the part of the Commission in the area of management of the aquatic environment as defined by the 1976 framework directive.

It was in fact the first time that the Commission had intervened by means of a proposal for a directive, i.e. by a legally binding act, for a substance which simply appears on the "grey list" of the 1976 framework directive, namely, in this case, chromium.

Until then the Commission had limited itself to acting only in the area of the most dangerous and most toxic substances on the "black list" of the 1976 directive. To this end from 1978 onwards it put forward several proposals for directives, most of which have been adopted by the Council (see pp. 79ff). However, for substances on the grey list considered to be of a lesser priority because less toxic, the 1976 framework directive only stipulates that Member States must put together programmes at national level to reduce water pollution caused by these substances. These national programmes must in particular, in line with Article 7 of the 1976 directive, include a system of prior authorization for all discharges into water. The authorizations must be based on and calculated according to the *quality objectives* set for the waters in question.

Since 1982 the Commission had asked Member States to inform it of their national programmes for the reduction of pollution by chromium. It became apparent that these programmes were for the most part incomplete and imprecise as far as the quality objectives set and timetable envisaged were concerned, and so did not meet in a coherent and harmonious way the requirements of Article 7 of the 1976 directive.

In order to remedy this unsatisfactory situation, the Commission judged it necessary to draw up a proposal for a directive, aimed both at improving the harmonization of the national programmes for chromium, and at speeding up their implementation. This proposal basically aimed to fix at Community level water quality objectives for chromium. Chromium, a substance judged to be a priority on the grey list, is present in several industrial sectors: surface treatment (40%); pigments (25%); tanneries and textiles (20%).

The proposal gave three quality objectives (for fresh water capable of supporting fish life; sea water; sediments and shellfish), from which the Member State selects one or more which it considers to be most appropriate for the zone in question.

It should be noted that the Commission determined these quality objectives while taking into consideration those already fixed for chromium in the directives already in force, in line with Article 7, paragraph 3 of the 1976 directive.

The proposal required that the quality objectives be respected by Member States by 1991 at the latest within the framework of the respective national programmes for the reduction of water pollution by chromium.

---

[6] OJ No C 351 of 31/12/85.

The Council has not yet adopted this new form of directive, which was to be followed by several others dealing with other priority substances on the grey list, such as zinc, nickel, lead or arsenic. In the case of arsenic, it should be noted that the Commission sent a Communication to the Council on 8 June 1983 indicating that arsenic would remain on List II, or the "grey list", of the framework directive, despite certain carcinogenic tendencies.

6.   Proposal for a Council directive on the ecological quality of water

On 15 July 1994, the Commission put forward a proposal for a Council directive on the ecological quality of water.[7] The proposal followed the conclusions of the Community Water Policy Ministerial Seminar held in Frankfurt on 27 and 28 June 1988 (see p. 121) as well as the Council Resolution on the 5th Environmental Action Programme[8] and the Commission's commitment following the European Council in Edinburgh in December 1992 to simplify, and increase the consistency of, Community surface water legislation.

The Commission pointed out that according to "The State of the Environment in the European Community",[9] 25% of the rivers and canals in the Community have water which is not suitable for the production of drinking water. The environmental objective to be reached is to maintain water quality of Community waters where it is already good and ultimately achieve good ecological water quality elsewhere. A body of water is considered to be of good ecological quality when the self-purification of the water body is maintained, the diversity of naturally occurring species is preserved and the structure and quality of the sediments are able to sustain the naturally occurring biological community of the ecosystem.

The proposed directive requires that for each water or for groups of waters Member States set an operational quality target for good ecological quality as defined in Article 2 of the proposal and that they draw up integrated proposals with the ultimate aim of meeting these targets.

Table 3.5 gives the specifications for good ecological water quality as these appear in Annex II of the proposed directive.

III.   QUALITY STANDARDS

The 1973 Action Programme defined "environmental quality standards" as standards "which, with legally binding force, prescribe the levels of pollution or nuisance not to be exceeded in a given environment or part thereof". Where the maximum levels of pollution apply to a product rather than a specific environment, "product standards" are used, which are thus a variation on the general quality standard.

Given these definitions, the mandatory values (I) contained in the four "quality objective" directives described in the previous section can be combined with the "quality standards", in that Member States are obliged to respect these values.

---

[7] COM (93) 680 final of 15/6/94.

[8] OJ No C 351 of 31/12/85.

[9] COM (92) 23 final of 27/3/92.

Table 3. 5: Proposal for a Council Directive on the ecological quality of water

ANNEX II

GOOD ECOLOGICAL WATER QUALITY – SPECIFICATIONS

Member States shall, based on the precautionary principle, fix the operational targets to be reached in accordance with this Directive within the framework of representative elements from the following list which are relevant to the individual waters concerned:

1   Dissolved oxygen should allow survival and reproduction of indigenous animals

2   Concentrations of toxic or other harmful substances in water, sediment and biota should not go beyond levels which have been demonstrated to pose no threat to aquatic species and should not prevent the normal uses of the water body.

3   There should be no evidence of elevated levels of disease in animal life, including fish, and in plant life due to anthropogenic influence.

4   The diversity of invertebrate communities (planktonic and bottom-dwelling) should resemble that of similar water bodies with insignificant anthropogenic disturbance. Key species/taxa normally associated with the undisturbed condition of the ecosystem should be present.

5   The diversity of aquatic plant communities should resemble that of similar water bodies with insignificant anthropogenic disturbance.

     Key species/taxa normally associated with the undisturbed condition of the ecosystem should be present. There should be no evidence of excessive macrophytic or algal growth due to elevated nutrient levels of anthropogenic origin.

6   The diversity of the fish population should resemble that of similar water bodies with insignificant anthropogenic disturbance.

     Key species/taxa normally associated with the undisturbed condition of the ecosystem should be present. There should be no significant artificial hindrance to the passage of migratory fish.

7   Higher vertebrate life (amphibians, birds, and mammals) should reflect that of similar water bodies with insignificant anthropogenic disturbance. Key species/taxa normally associated with the undisturbed condition of the ecosystem should be present.

8   Sediment structure and quality should allow the occurrence of biological communities typical of the region.

9   The status of riparian and coastal zones should, in non-urban areas, reflect either the absence of any significant influence by human activity, or care for the preservation of the biological community and for the aesthetics of the site.

However, the basic characteristic of these directives is that it is entirely up to the Member States to choose the area in which to apply the quality objectives which do include mandatory values, but which also, and more importantly, include guide values.

Only one directive in the area of water can be considered to be basically a "quality standards" or even "products standards" directive, and that is the directive defining the quality of water intended for human consumption. This directive actually applies to all the Member States, and all the parameters defining the quality of water involve mandatory standards in the form of maximum admissible concentrations (MAC), even if these also include guide values (G).

The 1980 directive on the quality of drinking water

On 22 July 1975 the Commission sent the Council a proposal for a directive on the quality of water for human consumption, more commonly termed "drinking water". The proposal aimed to fix the guide values and mandatory values for different parameters for water quality. The mandatory values could consist either of maximum admissible concentrations, or alternatively of minimum required concentrations, determined with a view to protecting public health with relation to the toxicity and noxiousness of the different substances in question.

The Council adopted this directive on 15 July 1980.[10] The directive applies to all water intended for human consumption, from whatever origin. These waters, which may or may not have undergone prior treatment, are either intended for direct human consumption (drinking water), or for food production (e.g. ice-creams). The directive does not however apply to medicinal waters or natural mineral waters. These are in fact covered at Community level by a specific directive which was also adopted on 15 July 1980.

Under the "drinking water" directive the Member States must fix the values to be applied to water for human consumption for each of the parameters indicated in the directive, in accordance with the guide values and mandatory values given. (See Table 3.6.) The directive also establishes how often and by what means monitoring should be carried out and, by way of reference, gives a method of analysis for each parameter.

IV.   THE CONTROL OF THE DISCHARGE OF DANGEROUS SUBSTANCES

The 1973 Action Programme indicated that a detailed examination would be carried out of the different possible methods, such as establishing discharge or emission standards, in order to achieve and respect the quality objectives fixed with regard to water pollution. The programme stated that priority would be given to the regulation of discharges of toxic, persistent and bioaccumulative substances into fresh water.

10 OJ No L 129 of 30/8/80.

Table 3.6: Council Directive of 15 July 1980
Quality of water for human consumption

LIST OF PARAMETERS

A. ORGANOLEPTIC PARAMETERS

	Parameters	Expression of the results (¹)	Guide level (GL)	Maximum admissible concentration (MAC)	Comments
1	Colour	mg/l Pt/Co scale	1	20	
2	Turbidity	mg/l SiO_2 Jackson units	1 0.4	10 4	Replaced in certain circumstances by a transparency test, with a Secchi disc reading in meters: GL: 6 m MAC: 2 m
3	Odour	Dilution number	0	2 at 12°C 3 at 25°C	To be related to the taste tests.
4	Taste	Dilution number	0	2 at 12°C 3 at 25°C	To be related to the odour tests.

(¹) If, on the basis of Directive 71/354/EEC as last amended, a Member State uses in its national legislation, adopted in accordance with this Directive, units of measurement other than these indicated in this Annex, the values thus indicated must have the same degree of precision.

Table 3.6 continued

B. PHYSICO-CHEMICAL PARAMETERS

(in relation to the water's natural structure)

Parameters	Expression of the results	Guide level (GL)	Maximum admissible concentration (MAC)	Comments
5 Temperature	°C	12	25	
6 Hydrogen ion concentration	pH unit	$6.5 \leqslant pH \leqslant 8.5$		The water should not be aggressive. The pH values do not apply to water in closed containers. Maximum admissible value: 9.5.
7 Conductivity	$\mu S\ cm^{-1}$ at 20°C	400		Corresponding to the mineralization of the water. Corresponding relativity values in ohms/cm: 2,500.
8 Chlorides	Cl mg/l	25		Approximate concentration above which effects might occur: 200 mg/l.
9 Sulphates	SO_4 mg/l	25	250	
10 Silica	SiO_2 mg/l			See Article 8.
11 Calcium	Ca mg/l	100		
12 Magnesium	Mg mg/l	30	50	

Table 3.6 continued

	Parameters	Expression of the results	Guide level (GL)	Maximum admissible concentration (MAC)	Comments
13	Sodium	Na mg/l	20	175 (as from 1984 and with a percentile of 90) 150 (as from 1987 and with a percentile of 80) (these percentiles should be calculated over a reference period of three years)	The values of this parameter take account of the recommendations of a WHO working party (The Hague, May 1978) on the progressive reduction of the current total daily salt intake to 6 g. As from 1 January 1984 the Commission will submit to the Council reports on trends in the total daily intake of salt per population. In these reports the Commission will examine to what extent the 120 mg/l MAC suggested by the WHO working party is necessary to achieve a satisfactory total salt intake level, and, if appropriate, will suggest a new salt MAC value to the Council and a deadline for compliance with that value. Before 1 January 1984 the Commission will submit to the Council a report on whether the reference period of three years for calculating these percentiles is scientifically well founded.
14	Potassium	K mg/l	10	12	
15	Aluminium	Al mg/l	0.05	0.2	

Table 3.6 continued

Parameters	Expression of the results	Guide level (GL)	Maximum admissible concentration (MAC)	Comments
16 Total hardness				
17 Dry residues	mg/l after drying at 180°C		1,500	
18 Dissolved oxygen	% O_2 saturation			Saturation value >75% except for underground water.
19 Free carbon dioxide	CO_2 mg/l			The water should not be aggressive.

Table 3.6 continued

C. PARAMETERS CONCERNING SUBSTANCES UNDESIRABLE IN EXCESSIVE AMOUNTS (¹)

	Parameters	Expression of the results (¹)	Guide level (GL)	Maximum admissible concentration (MAC)	Comments
20	Nitrates	NO_3 mg/l	25	50	
21	Nitrites	NO_2 mg/l		0.1	
22	Ammonium	NH_4 mg/l	0.05	0.5	
23	Kjeldahl Nitrogen (excluding N in NO_2 and NO_3)	N mg/l		1	
24	(K Mn O_4) Oxidizability	O_2 mg/l	2	5	Measured when heated in acid medium.
25	Total organic carbon (TOC)	C mg/l			The reason for any increase in the usual concentration must be investigated.
26	Hydrogen sulphide	S μg/l		undetectable organoleptically	
27	Substances extractable in chloroform	mg/l dry residue	0.1		

(¹) Certain of these substances may even be toxic when present in very substantial quantities.

Table 3.6 continued

	Parameters	Expression of the results	Guide level (GL)	Maximum admissible concentration (MAC)	Comments
28	Dissolved or emulsified hydrocarbons (after extraction by petroleum ether); Mineral oils	$\mu g/l$		10	
29	Phenols (phenol index)	C_6H_5OH $\mu g/l$		0.5	Excluding natural phenols which do not react to chlorine.
30	Boron	B $\mu g/l$	1,000		
31	Surfactants (reacting with methylene blue)	$\mu g/l$ (lauryl sulphate)		200	
32	Other organochlorine compounds not covered by parameter No 55	$\mu g/l$	1		Haloform concentrations must be as low as possible.
33	Iron	Fe $\mu g/l$	50	200	
34	Manganese	Mn $\mu g/l$	20	50	

Table 3.6 continued

Parameters	Expression of the results	Guide level (GL)	Maximum admissible concentration (MAC)	Comments
35 Copper	Cu μg/l	100 At outlets of pumping and/or treatment works and their substations 3,000 After the water has been standing for 12 hours in the piping and at the point where the water is made available to the consumer		Above 3,000 μg/l astringent taste discoloration + corrosion may occur.
36 Zinc	Zn μg/l	100 At outlets of pumping and/or treatment works and their substations 5,000 After the water has been standing for 12 hours in the piping and at the point where the water is made available to the consumer		Above 5,000 μg/l astringent taste, opalescence and sand-like deposits may occur.

Table 3.6 continued

Parameters	Expression of the results	Guide level (GL)	Maximum admissible concentration (MAC)	Comments
37 Phosphorus	P₂O₅ μg/l	400	5,000	
38 Fluoride	F μg/l 8–12°C 25–30°C		1,500 700.	MAC varies according to average temperature in geographical area concerned.
39 Cobalt	Co μg/l			
40 Suspended solids		None		
41 Residual Chlorine	CL μg/l			See Article 8.
42 Barium	Ba μg/l	100		
43 Silver	Ag μg/l		10	If, exceptionally, silver is used non-systematically to process the water, a MAC value of 80 μg/l may be authorized.

Table 3.6 continued

D. PARAMETERS CONCERNING TOXIC SUBSTANCES

	Parameters	Expression of the results	Guide level (GL)	Maximum admissible concentration (MAC)	Comments
44	Arsenic	As µg/l		50	
45	Beryllium	Be µg/l			
46	Cadmium	Cd µg/l		5	
47	Cyanides	CN µg/l		50	
48	Chromium	Cr µg/l		50	
49	Mercury	Hg µg/l		1	
50	Nickel	Ni µg/l		50	
51	Lead	Pb µg/l		50 (in running water)	Where lead pipes are present, the lead content should not exceed 50 µg/l in a sample taken after flushing. If the sample is taken either directly or after flushing and the lead content either frequently or to an appreciable extent exceeds 100 µg/l, suitable measures must be taken to reduce the exposure to lead on the part of the consumer.
52	Antimony	Sb µg/l		10	
53	Selenium	Se µg/l		10	
54	Vanadium	V µg/l			

Table 3.6 continued

	Parameters	Expression of the results	Guide level (GL)	Maximum admissible concentration (MAC)	Comments
55	Pesticides and related products substances considered separately	μg/l		0.1	'Pesticides and related products' means: insecticides: persistent organochlorine compounds organophosphorous compounds carbamates
	total			0.5	herbicides fungicides PCBs and PCTs
56	Polycyclic aromatic hydrocarbons	μg/l		0.2	reference substances: fluoranthene/benzo 3.4 fluoranthene/benzo 11.12 fluoranthene/benzo 3.4 pyrene/benzo 1.12 perylene/indeno (1, 2, 3–cd) pyrene

Table 3.6 continued

E. MICROBIOLOGICAL PARAMETERS

| | Results: volume of the sample (in ml) | Guide level (GL) | Maximum admissible concentration (MAC) | |
			Membrane filter method	Multiple tube method (MPN)
57 Total coliforms (^{1})	100	—	0	MPN < 1
58 Faecal coliforms	100	—	0	MPN < 1
59 Faecal streptococci	100	—	0	MPN < 1
60 Sulphite-reducing Clostridia	20	—	—	MPN ≦ 1

Water intended for human consumption should not contain pathogenic organisms.
It is necessary to supplement the microbiological analysis of water intended for human consumption, the samples should be examined not only for the bacteria referred to in Table E but also for pathogens including:
salmonella,
pathogenic staphylococci,
faecal bacteriophages,
entero-viruses;
nor should such water contain:
parasites
algas,
other organisms such as animalcules.

(^{1}) Provided a sufficient number of samples is examined (95% consistent results).

Table 3.6 continued

Parameters	Results: size of sample (in ml)	Guide level (GL)	Maximum admissible concentration (MAC)	Comments
61 Total bacteria counts for water supplied for human consumption	37°C 1 22°C 1	10(^{1})(^{2}) 100(^{1})(^{2})	— —	On their own responsibility and where parameters 57, 58, 59 and 60 are complied with, and where the pathogen organisms given above are absent, Member States may process water for their internal use the total bacteria count of which exceeds the MAC values laid down for parameter 62. MAC values should be measured within 12 hours of being put into closed containers with the sample water being kept at a constant temperature during that 12-hour period.
62 Total bacteria counts for water in closed containers	37°C 1 22°C 1	5 20	20 100	

(^{1}) For disinfected water the corresponding values should be considerably lower at the point where it leaves the processing plant.
(^{2}) If, during successive sampling, any of these values is consistently exceeded a check should be carried out.

Table 3.6 continued

F. MINIMUM REQUIRED CONCENTRATION FOR SOFTENED WATER INTENDED FOR HUMAN CONSUMPTION

	Parameters	Expression of the results	Minimum required concentration (softened water)	Comments
1	Total hardness	m/l Ca	60	Calcium or equivalent cations.
2	Hydrogen ion concentration	pH	–	The water should not be aggressive.
3	Alkalinity	mg/l HCO_3	30	
4	Dissolved oxygen			

NB: The provisions for hardness, hydrogen ion concentration, dissolved oxygen and calcium also apply to desalinated water. If, owing to its excessive natural hardness, the water is softened in accordance with Table F before being supplied for consumption, its sodium content may, in exceptional cases, be higher than the values given in the 'Maximum admissible concentration' column. However, an effort must be made to keep the sodium content at as low a level as possible and the essential requirements for the protection of public health may not be disregarded.

TABLE OF CORRESPONDENCE BETWEEN THE VARIOUS UNITS OF WATER HARDNESS MEASUREMENT

	French degree	English degree	German degree	Milligrams of Ca	Millimoles of Ca
French degree	1	0.70	0.56	4.008	0.1
English degree	1.43	1	0.80	5.73	0.143
German degree	1.79	1.125	1	7.17	0.179
Milligrams of Ca	0.25	0.175	0.140	1	0.025
Millimoles of Ca	10	7	5.6	40.08	1

Table 3.6 continued

PATTERNS AND FREQUENCY OF STANDARD ANALYSES

A. TABLE OF STANDARD PATTERN ANALYSES

(Parameters to be considered in monitoring)

Standard analyses / Parameters to be considered	Minimum monitoring (C1)	Current monitoring (C2)	Periodic monitoring (C3)	Occasional monitoring in special situations or in case of accidents (C4)
A ORGANOLEPTIC PARAMETERS	– odour (^{1}) – taste (^{1})	– odour – taste – turbidity (appearance)		The competent national authorities of the Member States will determine the parameters (^{5}) according to circumstances, taking account of all factors which might have an adverse affect on the quality of drinking water supplied to consumers.
B PHYSICO-CHEMICAL PARAMETERS	– conductivity or other physico-chemical parameter – residual chlorine (^{3})	– temperature (^{2}) – conductivity or other physico-chemical parameter – pH – residual chlorine (^{3})	Current monitoring analyses + other parameters as in footnote 4	
C UNDESIRABLE PARAMETERS		– nitrates – nitrites – ammonia		
D TOXIC PARAMETERS				
E MICRO-BIOLOGICAL PARAMETERS	– total coliforms or total counts of 22° and 37° – faecal coliforms	– total coliforms – faecal coliforms – total counts of 22° and 37°		

Note: An initial analysis, to be carried out before a source is exploited, should be added. The parameters to be considered would be the current monitoring analyses plus *inter alia* various toxic or undesirable substances presumed present. The list would be drawn up by the competent national authorities.

(^{1}) Qualitative assessment.
(^{2}) Except for water supplied in containers.
(^{3}) Or other disinfectants and only in the case of treatment.
(^{4}) These parameters will be determined by the competent national authority, taking account of all factors which might affect the quality of drinking water supplied to users and which could enable the ionic balance of the constituents to be assessed.
(^{5}) The competent national authority may use parameters other than those mentioned in Annex I to this Directive.

Table 3.6 continued

B. *Table of minimum frequency of standard analyses* (³)

Volume of water produced or distributed in m³/day	Population concerned (assuming 200 l/day per person)	Analysis C 1 Number of samples per year	Analysis C 2 Number of samples per year	Analysis C 3 Number of samples per year	Analysis C 4
100	500	(¹)	(¹)	(¹)	Frequency to be determined by the competent national authorities as the situation requires
1000	5000	(¹)	(¹)	(¹)	
2000	10 000	12	3	1	
10 000	50 000	60	6	1	
20 000	100 000	120	12	2	
30 000	150 000	180	18	3	
60 000	300 000	360 (²)	36	6	
100 000	500 000	360 (²)	60	10	
200 000	1 000 000	360 (²)	120 (²)	20 (²)	
1 000 000	5 000 000	360 (²)	120 (²)	20 (²)	

(¹) Frequency left to the discretion of the competent national authorities. However, water intended for the food-manufacturing industries must be monitored at least once a year.

(²) The competent health authorities should endeavour to increase this frequency as far as their resources allow.

(³) (a) In the case of water which must be disinfected, microbiological analysis should be twice as frequent.
    (b) Where analyses are very frequent, it is advisable to take samples at the most regular intervals possible.
    (c) Where the values of the results obtained from samples taken during the preceding years are constant and significantly better than the limits laid down in Annex 1, and where no factor likely to cause a deterioration in the quality of the water has been discovered, the minimum frequencies of the analyses referred to above may be reduced:
    – for surface waters, by a factor of 2 with the exception of the frequencies laid down for microbiological analyses;
    – for ground waters, by a factor of 4, but without prejudice to the provisions of point (a) above.

Table 3.6 continued

REFERENCE METHODS OF ANALYSIS

A. *Organoleptic parameters*

1	Colour	Photometric method calibrated on the Pt/co scale.
2	Turbidity	Silica method – Formazine test – Secchi's method.
3	Odour	Successive dilutions, tested at 12°C or 25°C.
4	Taste	Successive dilutions, tested at 12°C or 25°C.

B. *Physico-chemical parameters*

5	Temperature	Thermometry.
6	Hydrogen ion concentration	Electrometry.
7	Conductivity	Electrometry.
8	Chlorides	Titrimetry – Mohr's method.
9	Sulphates	Gravimetry – complexometry – spectrophotometry.
10	Silica	Absorption spectrophotometry.
11	Calcium	Atomic absorption – complexometry.
12	Magnesium	Atomic absorption.
13	Sodium	Atomic absorption.
14	Potassium	Atomic absorption.
15	Aluminium	Atomic absorption – absorption spectrophotometry.
16	Total hardness	Complexometry.
17	Dry residue	Dessication at 180 °C and weighing.
18	Dissolved oxygen	Winkler's method – Specific electrode method.
19	Free carbon dioxide	Acidimetry.

C. *Parameters concerning undesirable substances*

20	Nitrates	Absorption spectrophotometry – Specific electrode method.
21	Nitrites	Absorption spectrophotometry.
22	Ammonium	Absorption spectrophotometry.
23	Kjeldahl Nitrogen	Oxidation with Titrimetry or Absorption spectrophotometry.
24	Oxidizability	Boiling for 10 minutes with $KMnO_4$ in acid medium.
25	Total organic carbon (TOC)	–
26	Hydrogen sulphide	Absorption spectrophotometry.
27	Substances extractable in chloroform	Liquid/liquid extraction using purified chloroform at neutral pH, weighing the residue.
28	Hydrocarbons (dissolved or in emulsion); Mineral oils	Infra-red absorption spectrophotometry.

Table 3.6 continued

29	Phenols (phenol index)	Absorption spectrophotometry, paranitroaniline method and 4-aminoantipyrine method.
30	Boron	Atomic absorption – Absorption spectrophotometry.
31	Surfactants (reacting with methylene blue)	Absorption spectrophotometry with methylene blue.
32	Other organo-chlorine compounds	Gas-phase or liquid-phase chromotagraphy after extraction by appropriate solvents and purification – Identification of the constituents of mixtures if necessary. Quantitative determination.
33	Iron	Atomic absorption – Absorption spectrophotometry.
34	Manganese	Atomic absorption – Absorption spectrophotometry.
35	Copper	Atomic absorption – Absorption spectrophotometry.
36	Zinc	Atomic absorption – Absorption spectrophotometry.
37	Phosphorus	Absorption spectrophotometry.
38	Fluoride	Absorption spectrophotometry – Specific electrode method.
39	Cobalt	–
40	Suspended solids	Method of filtration on to μ 0.45 porous membrane or centrifuging (for at least 15 minutes with an average acceleration of 2 800 to 3 200 g) dried at 105°C and weighed.
41	Residual chlorine	Titrimetry–Absorption spectrophotometry.
42	Barium	Atomic absorption.

D. *Parameters concerning toxic substances*

43	Silver	Atomic absorption.
44	Arsenic	Absorption spectrophotometry – Atomic absorption.
45	Beryllium	–
46	Cadmium	Atomic absorption.
47	Cyanides	Absorption spectrophotometry.
48	Chromium	Atomic absorption – Absorption spectrophotometry.
49	Mercury	Atomic absorption.
50	Nickel	Atomic absorption.
51	Lead	Atomic absorption.
52	Antimony	Absorption spectrophotometry.
53	Selenium	Atomic absorption.
54	Vanadium	–
55	Pesticides and related products	See method 32.
56	Polycyclic aromatic hydrocarbons	Measurement of intensity of fluorescence ultraviolet after extraction using hexane – gas-phase chromatography or measurement in ultraviolet after thin layer chromatography – Comparative measurements against a mixture of six standard substances of the same concentration ([1]).

Table 3.6 continued

E. *MICROBIOLOGICAL PARAMETERS*

	Fermentation in multiple tubes. Subculturing of the positive tubes on a confirmation medium. Count according to MPN (most probable number)
	or
57 (^{2}) Total coliforms	Membrane filtration and culture on an appropriate medium
58 (^{2}) Faecal coliforms	such as Tergitol lactose agar, endo, agar, 0.4% Teepol broth, subculturing and identification of the suspect colonies – Incubation temperature for total coliforms: 37°C Incubation temperature for faecal coliforms: 44°C

59 (^{2}) Faecal streptococci   Sodium azide method (Litsky). Count according to MPN –

Membrane filtration and culture on an appropriate medium.

60 (^{2}) Sulphite-   A spore count, after heating the sample to 80°C by:

      reducing   – seeding in a medium with glucose, sulphite and iron,
      Clostridia   counting the black-halo colonies;

– membrane filtration, deposition of the inverted filter on a medium with glucose, sulphite and iron covered with agar, count of black colonies;

– distribution in tubes of differential reinforced clostridial medium (DRCM), subculturing of the black tubes in a medium of litmus-treated milk, count according to MPN.

61/62 (^{2}) Total counts   Inoculation by placing in nutritive agar.

ADDITIONAL TESTS

Salmonella   Concentration by membrane filtration. Inoculation on a pre-enriched medium. Enrichment, subculturing on isolating agar. Identification.

Pathogenic
staphylococci   Membrane filtration and culture on a specific medium (e.g. Chapman's hypersaline medium). Test for pathogenic characteristics.

Faecal bacteriophages   Guelin's process.

Enteroviruses   Concentration by filtration, flocculation or centrifuging, and identification.

Protozoa   Concentration by filtration on a membrane, microscopic examination, test for pathogenicity.

Animalcules
(worms – larvae)   Concentration by filtration on a membrane. Microscopic examination. Test for pathogenicity.

F. *MINIMUM REQUIRED CONCENTRATION*

Alkalinity   Acidimetry with Methyl orange

(^{1}) Standard substances to be considered: fluoranthene/benzo-3,4, fluoranthene/benzo-11,12, fluoranthene/benzo- 3,4, pyrene/benzo- 1,12, perylene and indeno (1,2,3-cd)pyrene.

(^{2}) Comments: The incubation period is generally 24 or 48 hours except for total counts, when it is 48 or 72 hours.

1.   The 1976 framework directive on the discharge of dangerous substances into the aquatic environment

On 21 October 1974 the Commission presented a proposal for a directive to the Council which aimed to reduce pollution caused by certain dangerous substances discharged into the aquatic environment of the Community. The Commission noted that three draft conventions on water pollution were currently being drawn up (the Paris Convention on marine pollution from land-based sources; the Strasbourg Convention on the protection of international watercourses against pollution; and the Convention on the protection of the Rhine against chemical pollution), which could have led to disparities in the legal requirements in different Member States. The aim of the proposal was therefore both to ensure a coherent approach by Member States to draft conventions, and to move in the direction indicated by the 1973 Community Action Programme with regard to water pollution.

The proposal was submitted to the Council of Environment Ministers on 16 October 1975. Despite lengthy discussions, the Council was not able to reach an agreement. The main problem was that the UK, which advocated an approach based on a system of "quality objectives" for the ambient environment, refused to accept a system which aimed to regulate pollution caused by the more dangerous substances, that is those on the "black list", by means of Community "emission standards". The latter approach, which corresponded to the Commission's proposal, was supported by all the other Member States. Following this first inconclusive debate, the Council asked the Commission to submit a proposal allowing for a compromise between the emission standards approach advocated by the majority of Member States and the quality objectives argument defended by the UK.

In its compromise, the Commission proposed that the Council fix both quality objectives and emission standards, with the understanding that emission standards would not be applicable in cases where Member States could prove to the Commission that the quality objectives were reached and maintained. Emission standards should however be applied in cases where quality objectives could not be established and respected. An agreement in principle was finally reached at Council level on 8 December 1975. This agreement echoed the main points of the Commission's compromise proposal. At this session, Belgium, Denmark, the Federal Republic of Germany, France, Ireland, Italy, Luxembourg and the Netherlands reaffirmed their opinion that measures taken against water pollution caused by the discharge of "black list" substances will only be effective if Community limit values are applied which national emission standards must not exceed. These countries indicated that they would therefore apply such a system based on Community emission standards.

For its part, the Commission stated that it would propose the reduction and elimination by phases of pollution caused by dangerous substances. With this in mind it would first examine the different substances on the black list in the light of the results of examinations carried out by experts and using the "best technical means available". As far as the latter are concerned, the Commission also stated that it would take into account the economic viability of these means.

The Council finally adopted the directive on pollution caused by certain dangerous substances discharged into the aquatic environment of the Community on 4 May 1976.[11] This framework directive is particularly important, given that it

---

[11] OJ No L 129 of 18/5/76.

determines the basic principles of the fight against aquatic pollution in the Community, and that it was to be followed by a number of implementing directives.

The directive covers the whole of the aquatic environment of the Community, that is the inland surface waters, internal coastal waters and territorial seas. The directive groups the dangerous substances into two categories. The first, called the "black list" or "List I", includes the substances considered to be the most dangerous due to their toxicity, persistence or bioaccumulation in the aquatic environment. The second category, called the "grey list" or "List II", covers other substances which are considered to have a less harmful effect on the aquatic environment. (See Table 3.7.)

The general aim of the directive is both to "eliminate" water pollution caused by substances on the black list, and also to "reduce" pollution caused by substances on the grey list.

With regard to substances on the black list, the directive establishes the basic principle according to which any discharge of a black list substance must be authorized beforehand by the relevant authority in the Member State concerned. This authorization, which can only be granted for a limited period, must as a general rule lay down an emission standard to be respected. This emission standard will establish the maximum concentration and the maximum quantity of substance permissible in a discharge. The Council will subsequently lay down Community emission standards, or "limit values", for each substance on the black list, which must be respected by the different sectors of industry discharging polluting effluents into water. In establishing these emission standards the Council will take into account not only the toxicity, persistence, and bioaccumulation of each substance, but also the best technical means available to eliminate or reduce the pollution caused by that substance.

But following the compromise of 8 December 1975, the directive states that parallel to the emission standards the Council should also establish "quality objectives" for substances on the black list. This double system has been called the "parallel approach". Once the Council has fixed emission standards on the one hand, and quality objectives on the other for a particular "black substance", which of the two systems should Member States apply? Here the directive indicates clearly that as a general rule the emission standards should be applied, except where a Member State can prove to the Commission, on the basis of an agreed monitoring procedure, that the quality objectives are being met and continuously maintained throughout the geographic area affected by the discharge. The Commission must report to the Council on all cases where recourse to the quality objective method has been accepted.

As far as substances on the "grey list" are concerned, the directive states that in order to "reduce" pollution caused by these substances, Member States must establish programmes which cover the fixing of quality objectives within a certain period. In addition, the directive indicates that any discharge of a grey list substance must also receive prior authorization from the competent authority in the Member State. These national programmes must be communicated to the Commission which must carry out a comparative study of the programmes in cooperation with the Member States, in order to ensure harmonized and rapid progress towards a reduction in pollution.

Table 3.7: Council Directive of 4 May 1976
Pollution caused by certain dangerous substances discharged into the acquatic environment

List 1 of families and groups of substances

List 1 contains certain individual substances which belong to the following families and groups of substances, selected mainly on the basis of their toxicity, persistence and bioaccumulation, with the exception of those which are biologically harmless or which are rapidly converted into substances which are biologically harmless:

1. organohalogen compounds and substances which may form such compounds in the aquatic environment;
2. organophosphorous compounds;
3. organotin compounds;
4. substances in respect of which it has been proved that they posses carcinogenic properties in or via the aquatic environment;
5. mercury and its compounds;
6. cadmium and its compounds;
7. persistent mineral oils and hydrocarbons of petroleum origin; and for the purposes of implementing Articles 2, 8, 9 and 14 of this Directive;
8. persistent synthetic substances which may float, remain in suspension or sink and which may interfere with any use of the waters.

List II of families and groups of substances

List II contains:
    substances belonging to the families and groups of substances in List I for which the limit values referred to in Article 6 of the Directive have not been determined;
    certain individual substances and categories of substances belonging to the families and groups of substances listed below;
and which have a deleterious effect on the aquatic environment, which can, however, be confined to a given area and which depend on the characteristics and location of the water into which they are discharged.

Families and groups of substances referred to in the second indent

1. The following metalloids and metals and their compounds:

1. zinc	6. selenium	11. tin	16. vanadium
2. copper	7. arsenic	12. barium	17. cobalt
3. nickel	8. antimony	13. beryllium	18. thalium
4. chromium	9. molybdenum	14. boron	19. tellurium
5. lead	10. titanium	15. uranium	20. silver

2. Biocides and their derivatives not appearing in List I.
3. Substances which have a deleterious effect on the taste and/or smell of the products for human consumption derived from the aquatic environment, and compounds liable to give rise to such substances in water.
4. Toxic or persistent organic compounds of silicon, and substances which may give rise to such compounds in water, excluding those which are biologically harmless or are rapidly converted in water into harmless substances.
5. Inorganic compounds of phosphorus and elemental phosphorus.
6. Non-persistent mineral oils and hydrocarbons of petroleum origin.
7. Cyanides, fluorides.
8. Substances which have an adverse effect on the oxygen balance, particularly: ammonia nitrites.

[1] Where certain substances in List II are carcinogenic, they are included in category 4 of this list.

Statement on Article 8
With regard to the discharge of waste water into the open sea by means of pipelines, Member States undertake to lay down requirements which shall be not less stringent than those imposed by this Directive.

2.   The 1979 directive on the protection of groundwater against pollution caused by dangerous substances

On 24 January 1978 the Commission submitted a proposal for a directive to the Council concerning the protection of groundwater against pollution caused by certain dangerous substances.

The proposal defined a number of measures intended to prevent, reduce or eliminate pollution of groundwater caused by the discharge of dangerous substances. The structure of the proposal largely followed that of the directive of 4 May 1976 with regard both to the division of the dangerous substances into two distinct lists ("black list" and "grey list"), and to the general provisions concerning monitoring. One of the basic principles of the proposal concerned the Member States' obligation to grant prior authorization for any direct or indirect discharge of dangerous substances into groundwater.

The Council adopted the directive on the protection of groundwater against pollution by dangerous substances on 17 December 1979.[12] The directive aims to prevent pollution caused by certain dangerous substances appearing on the "black" and "grey" lists. The substances which appear on these lists are not identical to those in the basic directive of 4 May 1976. (See Table 3.8.) The directive defines groundwater as all water below the surface of the ground in the saturation zone and in direct contact with the ground or subsoil. It does not cover discharges of domestic effluents from isolated dwellings, discharges of matter containing radioactive substances, or discharges which in the opinion of the competent authority are not of a sufficient quantity and concentration to cause any risk to the quality of the receiving groundwater.

Where "black list" substances are concerned, Member States must prevent any introduction of such substances into groundwater. This objective must be achieved by prohibiting "direct" discharges, that is those introduced into the groundwater without percolation through the ground or subsoil, and by subjecting all "indirect" discharges (i.e. those which percolate the ground or subsoil) to a prior investigation.

In the case of "grey list" substances, Member States must subject to prior investigation all direct or indirect discharge of such substances into groundwater. This investigation must include a study of the hydrogeological conditions of the area concerned and of the possible purifying power of the soil and subsoil. Following the investigation authorization may or may not be given by the Member States. This authorization must specify in particular the place and method of discharge, the maximum permissible quantity of the substance concerned, the precautions to be taken and the monitoring measures to be applied.

Any authorization given must be reviewed every four years, and must appear on a regularly updated inventory. At its request Member States must provide the Commission with information on the results of prior investigations, and of checks carried out, as well as detailed information on authorizations granted.

[12] OJ No L 20 of 26/1/80.

Table 3.8: Council Directive of 17 December 1979
Protection of groundwater against pollution by certain dangerous substances

List I of families and groups of substances

List I contains the individual substances which belong to the families and groups of substances enumerated below, with the exception of those which are considered inappropriate to List I on the basis of a low risk of toxicity, persistence and bioaccumulation.

Such substances which, with regard to toxicity, persistence and bioaccumulation, are appropriate to List II are to be classed in List II.

1. Organohalogen compounds and substances which may form such compounds in the aquatic environment
2. Organophosphorous compounds
3. Organotin compounds
4. Substances which posses carcinogenic, mutagenic or teratogenic properties in or via the aquatic environment ([1])
5. Mercury and its compounds
6. Cadmium and its compounds
7. Mineral oils and hydrocarbons
8. Cyanides

List II of families and groups of substances

List II contains the individual substances and the categories and the categories of substances belonging to the families and groups of substances listed below which would have a harmful effect on groundwater.
1. The following metalloids and metals and their compounds:

1. Zinc	6. Selenium	11. Tin	16. Vanadium
2. Copper	7. Arsenic	12. Barium	17. Cobalt
3. Nickel	8. Antimony	13. Beryllium	18. Thalium
4. Chrome	9. Molybdenum	14. Boron	19. Tellurium
5. Lead	10. Titanium	15. Uranium	20. Silver

2. Biocides and their derivatives not appearing in List I.
3. Substances which have a deleterious effect on the taste and/or odour of groundwater, and compounds liable to cause the formation of such substances in such water and to render it unfit for human consumption.
4. Toxic or persistent organic compounds of silicon, and substances which may cause the formation of such compounds in water, excluding those which are biologically harmless or are rapidly converted in water into harmless substances.
5. Inorganic compounds of phosphorus and elemental phosphorus.
6. Fluorides.
7. Ammonia and nitrites.

([1]) Where certain substances in List II are carcinogenic, mutagenic or teratogenic, they are included in category 4 of this list.

3.   The 1983 Council Resolution on the implementation of the 1976 framework directive on "black list" substances[13]

On 22 June 1982 the Commission sent a Communication to the Council on dangerous substances which might be included on the "black list", or List I, of the 1976 framework directive. In this Communication the Commission informed the Council of the work and priorities envisaged for the implementation of the requirements concerning the discharge of particularly dangerous substances appearing on the black list into the aquatic environment of the Community. Since the black list does not generally mention substances individually, but only the family or group of substances, the Commission had to select, from these families or groups, the different substances which were to be studied and which could possibly be the subject of directive proposals. To do this the Commission first selected 21 substances considered to be priorities on the basis of their toxicity, persistence and bioaccumulation.

As a second step the Commission carried out studies with a view to establishing not only the priorities, but also a complete list of substances which might appear on the black list of the 1976 framework directive. These studies led to the identification of 1500 substances. Another study, taking into account both the quantities produced in the Community and the risks to the aquatic environment and human health, made it possible to reduce the number of substances from 1500 to 108. Once the priority substances established at the first stage were added, this came to a total of 129 substances which might be used in the future.

On 7 February 1983, and in the light of the Commission's Communication of 22 June 1982, the Council adopted a Resolution on water pollution.[14] This established the direction and priorities which the Council intended to follow in combating water pollution caused by the discharge into the aquatic environment of the Community of dangerous substances appearing on the black list of the 1976 directive. In this Resolution the Council, having noted the Commission's Communication of 1982, indicated that the list of 129 substances which appears in the Commission's Communication (see Table 3.9) should form the basis for the continuation of work on the implementation of the 1976 directive. It also stated that Member States should communicate to the Commission as soon as possible, and within three years at the latest, all readily available information on these 129 substances, concerning in particular:

● production, use and discharge by industrial sectors;
● concentration in surface water, sediments and living organisms;
● measures already taken or planned with a view to remedying the situation, and the effects of these measures on the quantity of discharges.

4.   Directives on the implementation of the framework directive of 1976 on "black list" substances

(a)   Discharge of aldrin, dieldrin and endrin

On 16 May 1979 the Commission presented the first implementing directive proposals on black list substances. The first of these directives fixed "emission

---

[13] The concepts of "black list" or List 1 are identical.
[14] OJ No C 46 of 17/2/83.

standards" and the second concerned "quality objectives" for the particularly toxic pesticides, aldrin, dieldrin and endrin. The production of these pesticides was very low in the Community, and 95% of their discharge into water came from the textile industry, particularly from the production of wool products.

No agreement was reached within the Council on these proposals. The Commission indicated that in future it would propose a simplified procedure for such substances, given that discharge of these pesticides only concerned a limited number of Member States. This new simplified proposal corresponded with the implementing provisions of the directive of 12 June 1986, and was submitted to the Council on 20 October 1986.[15]

The directive was agreed in principle by the Council at its meeting of 21–22 May 1987, and finally approved, after the opinions of the European Parliament and the Economic and Social Committee had been received, on 16 June 1988. A quality objective of 5 nanograms per litre for endrin and isodrin and 10 ng/litre for aldrin and dieldrin had to be achieved by January 1994 but an interim objective of 30 ng/litre for all four "drins" would apply in January 1989. Member States were to take the measures necessary to comply with this directive by 1 January 1989, as far as the above substances are concerned.

The limit values for emission standards as well as the quality objectives for the "drins" are set out in the Table 3.10.

(b)   Mercury discharges by the chlor-alkali electrolysis industry

On 26 June 1979 the Commission submitted to the Council two specific proposals for directives concerning respectively "emission standards" and "quality objectives" to be applied to mercury discharges by the chlor-alkali electrolysis industry. The aim of these two directives was to reduce and eliminate pollution caused by such discharges. These proposals were the object of long and difficult negotiations within the Council, particularly on the question of the system to apply to new industrial establishments.

The Council finally reached an agreement on the basis of a single directive which was adopted on 22 March 1982.[16] The directive fixed "limit values" to which authorizations given by Member States had to conform, except where a Member State decided to use the quality objectives system following the conditions set out in the base directive of 1976. In this case the Member State in question must respect the quality objective requirements as well as the methods of monitoring fixed by the directive (see Table 3.10). As far as new plants are concerned, the directive specified that Member States cannot grant authorizations unless they include references to the standards corresponding to the "best technical means available" for preventing mercury discharges. In addition, the directive states that whatever the method chosen (emission standard or quality objective), in cases where for technical reasons the intended measures do not correspond to the best technical means available, and prior to the granting of any authorization, the Member State must justify its reasons to the Commission. In an interpretative declaration published in the Official Journal, the Council and the Commission considered that the use of the "best technical means available" makes it possible to

15 OJ No C 309 of 3/12/86.
16 OJ No L 291 of 24/10/83.

Table 3.9: List of substances which could belong to List 1 of Council Directive 76/464 EEC

1	***	309-00-2	Aldrin
2		95-85-2	2-Amino-4-chlorophenol
3		120-12-7	Anthracene
4	**	7440-38-2	Arsenic and its mineral compounds
5		2642-71-9	Azinphos-ethyl
6		86-50-0	Azinphos-methyl
7	**	71-43-2	Benzene
8	**	92-87-5	Benzidine
9		100-44-7	Benzyl chloride (Alpha-chlorotoluene)
10		98-87-3	Benzylidene chloride (Alpha, alpha-dichlorotoluene)
11		92-52-4	Biphenyl
12	***	7440-43-9	Cadmium and its compounds
13	**	56-23-5	Carbon tetrachloride
14		302-17-0	Chloral hydrate
15	***	57-74-9	Chlordane
16		79-11-8	Chloroacetic acid
18		108-42-9	3-Chloroaniline
19		106-47-8	4-Chloroaniline
20	*	108-90-7	Chlorobenzene
21		97-00-7	1-Chloro-2, 4-dinitrobenzene
22		107-07-3	2-Chloroethanol
23	**	67-66-3	Chloroform
24		59-50-7	4-Chloro-3-methylphenol
25		90-13-1	1-Chloronaphthalene
26			Chloronaphthalenes (technical mixture)
27		89-63-4	4-Chloro-2-nitroaniline
28		89-21-4	1-Chloro-2-nitrobenzene
29		88-73-3	1-Chloro-3-nitrobenzene
30		121-73-3	1-Chloro-4-nitrobenzene
31		89-59-8	4-Chloro-2-nitrotoluene
32			Chloronitrotoluenes (other than 4-Chloro-2-nitrotoluene)
33		95-57-8	2-Chlorophenol
34		108-43-0	3-Chlorophenol
35		106-48-9	4-Chlorophenol
36		126-99-8	Chloroprene (2-Chlorobuta-1,3-diene)
37		107-05-1	3-Chloropropene (Allyl chloride)
38		95-49-8	2-Chlorotoluene
39		108-41-8	3-Chlorotoluene
40		106-43-4	4-Chlorotoluene
41			2-Chloro-p-toluidine
42			Chlorotoluidines (other than 2-Chloro-p-toluidine)
43		56-72-4	Coumaphos
44		108-77-0	Cyanuric chloride (2,4,6-Trichloro-1,3,5-triazine)
45		94-75-7	2,4-D (including 2,4-D-salts and 2,4-D-esters)
46	**	50-29-3	DDT (including metabolites DDD and DDE)
47		298-03-3	Demeton (including Dementon-o, Demeton-s, Demeton-s-methyl and Demeton-s-methylsulphone)
48	*	106-93-4	1,2-Dibromoethane

Table 3.9 continued

49			Dibutyltin dichloride
50			Dibutyltin oxide
51			Dibutyltin salts (other than Dibutyltin dichloride and Dibutyltin oxide)
52			Dichloroanilines
53		95-50-1	1,2-Dichlorobenzene
54		541-73-1	1,3-Dichlorobenzene
55		106-46-7	1,4-Dichlorobenzene
56			Dichlorobenzidines
57		108-60-1	Dichlorodiisopropyl ether
58	*	75-34-3	1,1-Dichloroethane
59	*	107-06-2	1,2-Dichloroethane
60	*	75-35-4	1,1-Dichloroethylene (Vinylidene chloride)
61	*	540-59-0	1,2-Dichloroethylene
62	*	75-09-2	Dichloromethane
63			Dichloronitrobenzenes
64		120-83-2	2,4-Dichlorophenol
65	*	78-87-5	1,2-Dichloropropane
66		96-23-1	1,3-Dichloropropan-2-ol
67		542-75-6	1,3-Dichloropropene
68		78-88-6	2,3-Dichloropropene
69		120-36-5	Dichlorprop
70		62-73-7	Dichlorvos
71	***	60-57-1	Dieldrin
72		109-89-7	Diethylamine
73		60-51-5	Dimethoate
74		124-40-3	Dimethylamine
75		298-04-4	Disulfoton
76	**	115-29-7	Endosulfan
77	***	72-20-8	Endrin
78		106-89-8	Epichlorohydrin
79		100-41-4	Ethylbenzene
80		122-14-5	Fenitrothion
81		55-38-9	Fenthion
82	***	76-44-8	Heptachlor (including Heptachlorepoxide)
83	**	118-74-1	Hexachlorobenzene
84	**	87-68-3	Hexachlorobutadiene
85	**	608-73-1 58-89-9	Hexachlorocyclohexane (including all isomers and Lindane)
86		67-72-1	Hexachloroethane
87		98-83-9	Isopropylbenzene
88		330-55-2	Linuron
89	*	121-75-5	Malathion
90		94-74-6	MCPA
91		93-65-2	Mecoprop
92	***	7439-97-6	Mercury and its compounds
93		10265-92-6	Methamidophos
94		7786-34-7	Mevinphos
95		1746-81-2	Monolinuron

Table 3.9 continued

96		91-20-3	Naphthalene
97		113-02-6	Omethoate
98		301-12-2	Oxydemeton-methyl
99	**		PAH (with special reference to: 3,4-Benzopyrene and 3,4-Benzofluoranthene)
100		56-38-2 298-00-0	Parathion (including Parathion-methyl)
101	**		PCB (including PCT)
102	**	87-86-5	Pentachlorophenol
103		14816-18-3	Phoxim
104		709-98-8	Propanil
105		1698-60-8	Pyrazon
106		122-34-9	Simazine
107		93-76-5	2,4,5-T (including 2,4,5-T salts and 2,4,5-T esters)
108			Tetrabutyltin
109		95-94-3	1,2,4,5-Tetrachlorobenzene
110	*	79-34-5	1,1,2,2-Tetrachloroethane
111	*	127-18-4	Tetrachloroethylene
112		108-88-3	Toluene
113		24017-47-8	Triazophos
114		126-73-8	Tributyl phosphate
115			Tributyltin oxide
116		52-68-6	Trichlorfon
117	*		Trichlorobenzene (technical mixture)
118		120-82-1	1,2,4-Trichlorobenzene
119	*	71-55-6	1,1,1-Trichloroethane
120	*	79-00-5	1,1,2-Trichloroethane
121	*	79-01-6	Trichloroethylene
122	**	95-95-4 88-06-2	Trichlorophenols
123		76-13-1	1,1,2-Trichlorotrifluoroethane
124		1582-09-8	Trifluralin
125		900-95-8	Triphenyltin acetate (Fentin acetate)
126			Triphenyltin chloride (Fentin chloride)
127		76-87-9	Triphenyltin hydroxide (Fentin hydoxide)
128		75-01-4	Vinyl chloride (Chloroethylene)
129			Xylenes (technical mixture of isomers)

*** Substances which are the subject of a proposal or a communication to the Council.
** Substances which have been or are being studied.
*   Substances to be studied next.
309-00-2 CAS number (Chemical Abstract Service)

Table 3.10: Council Directive of 16 June 1988 amending Annex II to Directive 86/280/EEC on limit values and quality objectives for discharges of certain dangerous substances included in List I of the Annex to Directive 76/464/EEC

Heading A (1, 71, 77, 130): Limit values for emission standards ([1])

| Type of industrial plant ([2]) | Type of average value | Limit value expressed as | | To be complied with as from |
		Weight	Concentration in effluent µg/l of water discharged ([3])	
Production of aldrin and/or dieldrin and/or endrin including formulation of these substances on the same site	Monthly	3 g per tonne of total production capacity (g/tonne)	2	1.1.1989
	Daily	15 g per tonne of total production capacity (g/tonne) ([4])	10 ([4])	1.1.1989

([1]) The limit values indicated in this heading shall apply to the total discharge of aldrin, dieldrin and endrin.
     If the effluent resulting from the production or use of aldrin, dieldrin and/or endrin (including formulation of these substances) also contains isodrin, the limit values laid down above shall apply to the total discharges of aldrin, dieldrin, endrin and isodrin.
([2]) Among the industrial plants referred to under heading A, point 3, of Annex I, reference is made in particular to plants formulating aldrin and/or dieldrin and/or endrin away from the production site.
([3]) This figures take account of the total amount of water passing through the plant.
([4]) If possible, daily values should not exceed twice the monthly value.

Heading B (1, 71, 77, 130): Quality objectives

| Environment | Substance | Quality objectives ng/l to be complied with as from | |
		1.1.1989	1.1.1994
Inland surface waters	Aldrin	30 for the four substances in total with a maximum of 5 for endrin	10
Estuary waters	Dieldrin		10
Internal coastal waters other than estuary waters	Endrin		5
Territorial waters	Isodrin		5

Standstill: The concentration(s) of aldrin and/or dieldrin and/or endrin and/or isodrin in sediments and/or molluscs and/or shellfish and/or fish must not increase significantly with time.

limit discharges of mercury from new industrial plants to less than 0.5 grammes of recycled brine per tonne of the production capacity of installed chloride.

(c)   Cadmium discharges

On 17 February 1981 the Commission submitted a proposal for a directive to the Council on limit values and quality objectives for cadmium discharges into the aquatic environment of the Community. This proposal aimed to reduce and if possible eliminate pollution caused by effluents containing cadmium which is a toxic, persistent, and bioaccumulating substance. The proposal mainly concerned the prime metal industries (extraction and refinement of lead and zinc) and secondary metal industries (manufacture of stabilizers and batteries).

The Council adopted this directive on 26 September 1983.[17] Following the framework directive of 4 May 1976, it applies to interior surface waters, territorial and interior coastal waters, and concerns all industrial establishments where the treatment of cadmium or any other substance containing cadmium is carried out.

The directive fixes both limit values including time periods and monitoring procedures, and also quality objectives. (See Table 3.11.) A two-stage system of limit values exists for discharges into the aquatic environment. According to the 1976 framework directive, a Member State can only grant an industrial plant authorization to discharge substances if the effluents in question conform to the limit values specified by the directive.

Member States having recourse to the derogation provided for by Article 6, paragraph 3 of the framework directive must respect the quality objectives specified by the directive.

The directive also contains specific provisions for new industrial plants. It stipulates that as a general rule Member States can only issue authorizations for discharges into the aquatic environment on condition that the new plants apply the standards corresponding to the "best technical means available" when this is necessary for the elimination of pollution or for the prevention of distortion of competition.

Where discharges affect several Member States, the directive states that the Member States concerned must collaborate with a view to harmonizing monitoring procedures. The directive also defines reference measurement methods to be used in order to determine the cadmium content of the waters, sediments and living organisms, and lays down a monitoring procedure for quality objectives.

Every five years the Commission will draw up a comparative analysis of the implementation of the directive by Member States.

(d)   Mercury discharges by sectors other than the chlor-alkali electrolysis industry

On 22 December 1982 the Commission submitted a proposal for a directive to the Council on limit values and quality objectives for discharges of mercury other than by the chlor-alkali electrolysis industry. This proposal concerned six industries, in particular chemical industries using mercurial catalysts, industries manufacturing mercury batteries, and the non-ferrous metal industries. The Council adopted this directive on 8 March 1984.[18] This text constitutes the third implementing directive of the 1976 framework directive on pollution caused by the discharge of dangerous substances into the waters of the Community.

[17] OJ No L 291 of 24/10/83.
[18] OJ No L 47 of 17/3/84.

Table 3.11: Council Directive of 26 September 1983
Limit values and quality objectives for cadmium discharges

Limit values, time limits fixed for compliance with these values and monitoring procedures to be applied to discharges

1. Limit values and time limits

Industrial sector [1]	Unit of measurement	Limit values which must be complied with as from	
		1.1.1986	1.1.1989 [2]
1. Zinc mining, lead and zinc refining, cadmium metal and non-ferrous metal industry	Milligrams of cadmium per litre of discharge	0.3 [3]	0.2 [3]
2. Manufacture of cadmium compounds	Milligrams of cadmium per litre of discharge	0.5 [3]	0.2 [3]
	Grams of cadmium discharged per kilogram of cadmium handled	0.5 [4]	[5]
3. Manufacture of pigments	Milligrams of cadmium per litre of discharge	0.5 [3]	0.2 [3]
	Grams of cadmium discharged per kilogram of cadmium handled	0.3 [4]	[5]
4. Manufacture of stabilizers	Milligrams of cadmium per litre of discharge	0.5 [3]	0.2 [3]
	Grams of cadmium discharged per kilogram of cadmium handled	0.5 [4]	[5]
5. Manufacture of primary and secondary batteries	Milligrams of cadmium per litre of discharge	0.5 [3]	0.2 [3]
	Grams of cadmium discharged per kilogram of cadmium handled	1,5 [4]	[5]
6. Electroplating [6]	Milligrams of cadmium per litre of discharge	0.5 [3]	0.2 [3]
	Grams of cadmium discharged per kilogram of cadmium handled 0.3 [4]		[5]
7. Manufacture of phosphoric acid and/or phosphatic fertilizer from phosphatic rock [7]		—	—

Table 3.11 continued

(1) Limit values for industrial sectors not mentioned in this table will, if necessary, be fixed by the Council at a later stage. In the meantime the Member States will fix emission standards for cadmium discharges autonomously in accordance with Directive 76/464/EEC. Such standards must take into account the best technical means available and must not be less stringent than the most nearly comparable limit value in this Annex.

(2) On the basis of experience gained in implementing this Directive, the Commission will, pursuant to Article 5 (3), submit in due course to the Council proposals for fixing more restrictive limit values with a view to their coming into force by 1992.

(3) Monthly flow-weighted average concentration of total cadmium.

(4) Monthly average.

(5) It is impossible for the moment to fix limit values expressed as load. If need be, these values will be fixed by the Council in accordance with Article 5 (3) of this Directive. If the Council does not fix any limit values, the values expressed as load given in column '1.1.1986' will be kept.

(6) Member States may suspend application of the limit values until 1 January 1989 in the case of plants which discharge less than 10 kg of cadmium a year and in which the total volume of the electroplating tanks is less than 1.5 m³, if technical or administrative considerations make such a step absolutely necessary.

(7) At present there are no economically feasible technical methods for systematically extracting cadmium from discharges arising from the production of phosphoric acid and/or phosphatic fertilizers from phosphatic rock. No limit values have therefore been fixed for such discharges. The absence of such limit values does not release the Member States from their obligation under Directive 76/464/EEC to fix emission standards for these discharges.

2. Limit values expressed as concentrations which in principle must not be exceeded are given in the above table for the industrial sectors in sections 2, 3, 4, 5 and 6. In no instance may limit values expressed as maximum concentrations be greater than those expressed as maximum quantities divided by water requirements per kilogram of cadmium handled. However, because the concentration of cadmium in effluents depends on the volume of water involved, which differs for different processes and plants, the limit values, expressed in terms of the quantity of cadmium discharged in relation to the quantity of cadmium handled, given in the above table must be complied with in all cases.

3. The daily average limit values are twice the corresponding monthly average limit values given in the above table.

4. A monitoring procedure must be instituted to check whether the discharges comply with the emission standards which have been fixed in accordance with the limit values laid down in this Annex.

This procedure must provide for the taking and analysis of samples and for measurement of the flow of the discharge and the quantity of cadmium handled.

Should the quantity of cadmium handled be impossible to determine, the monitoring procedure may be based on the quantity of cadmium that may be used in the light of the production capacity on which the authorization was based.

5. A sample representative of the discharge over a period of 24 hours will be taken. The quantity of cadmium discharged over a month must be calculated on the basis of the daily quantities of cadmium discharged.

However, a simplified monitoring procedure may be instituted in the case of industrial plants which do not discharge more than 10 kg of cadmium per annum. In the case of industrial electroplating plants, a simplified monitoring procedure may only be instituted if the total volume of the electroplating tanks is less than 1.5 m³.

This directive completes the existing Community regulation on mercury discharges, the Council having already adopted in 1982 a first directive on mercury discharges from the chlor-alkali electrolysis industry.

The provisions of the directive are based on those of the "cadmium" directive. This is why it fixes two series of limit values, progressively stricter, to be applied from 1 July 1986 and 1 July 1989 respectively (see Table 3.12).

It also covers the quality objectives to be respected by Member States who have recourse to the derogation mentioned in Article 6, paragraph 3 of the 1976 framework directive.

(e) Discharge of hexachlorocyclohexane (HCH)

On 19 July 1983, the Commission submitted a proposal for a directive to the Council on limit values and quality objectives for the discharge of hexachlorocyclohexane, and of lindane in particular. This substance, which due to its toxicity also appears on the "black list" of the 1976 directive, is mainly linked to the production of agricultural pesticides. Unlike the "mercury" and "cadmium" directives, this proposal concerns substances whose production is declining, and only applies to a limited number of industrial plants.

The Council adopted the directive fixing the limit values and quality objectives for HCH on 9 October 1984.[19] The structure chosen by the Council is identical to that of the 1983 "cadmium" directive with regard to the general field of application as well as the specific requirements for new industrial plants or for cross-border discharges affecting the waters of several Member States.

The directive fixes two series of increasingly severe limit values to be respected from 1986 and 1988 onwards. It also defines several quality objectives expressed as a total concentration of HCH for different categories of water: interior surface waters, sea water used for the production of drinking water, etc.

(f) Discharges of carbon tetrachloride, DDT and pentachlorophenol, and "codifying" of the application provisions of the framework directive of 1976

On 28 January 1985 the Commission submitted to the Council a new proposal for a directive concerning limit values and quality objectives for four new substances appearing on the "black list" of the 1976 framework directive, as it was defined and specified by the Council Resolution of 7 February 1983.

The Council adopted the directive on 12 June 1986.[20] This directive first fixes the limit values, quality objectives and measuring methods of the following three substances: carbon tetrachloride, DDT and pentachlorophenol. The Council did not in fact retain chloroform, which was the fourth substance proposed by the Commission, since it felt that this did not sufficiently fulfil the criteria regarding the noxiousness of black list substances.

The second characteristic of this directive which should be stressed concerns the "codifying" in one text of the general implementation provisions of the framework directive of 4 May 1976 on the protection of the aquatic environment of the Community. This meant that in future there would be no need to have recourse to a repetitive and awkward legislative procedure, as had previously been the case with

[19] OJ No L 274 of 17/10/84.
[20] OJ No L 181 of 4/7/86.

Table 3.12: Council Directive of 8 March 1984 Limit Values and quality objectives for mercury discharges by sectors other than the chlor-alkali electrolysis industry

Limit values, time limits by which they must be complied with, and the procedure for monitoring discharges

1. The limit values and the time limits for the industrial sectors concerned are set out together in the table below:

Industrial sector ([1])	Limit value which must be complied with as from:		Unit of measurement
	1 July 1986	1 July 1989	
1. Chemical industries using mercury catalysts: (a) in the production of vinyl chloride	0.1	0.05	mg/l effluent
	0.2	0.1	g/t vinyl chloride production capacity
(b) in other processes	0.1 10	0.05 5	mg/l effluent g/kg mercury processed
2. Manufacture of mercury catalysts used in the production of vinyl chloride	0.1	0.05	mg/l effluent
	1.4	0.7	g/kg mercury processed
3. Manufacture of organic and non-organic mercury compounds (except for products referred to in point 2)	0.1	0.05	mg/l effluent
	0.1	0.05	g/kg mercury processed
4. Manufacture of primary batteries containing mercury	0.1	0.05	mg/l effluent
	0.05	0.03	g/kg mercury processed
5. Non-ferrous metal industry ([2]) 5.1 Mercury recovery plants	0.1	0.05	mg/l effluent
5.2 Extraction and refining of non-ferrous metals	0.1	0.05	mg/l effluent
6. Plants for the treatment of toxic wastes containing mercury	0.1	0.05	mg/l effluent

([1]) Limit values for industrial sectors other than the chlor-alkali electrolysis industry which are not mentioned in this table, such as the paper and steel industries or coal-fired power stations, will, if necessary, be fixed by the Council at a later stage. In the meantime, the Member States will fix emission standards for mercury discharges autonomously in accordance with Directive 76/464/EEC. Such standards must take into account the best technical means available and must not be less stringent than the most nearly comparable limit value in this Annex.

([2]) On the basis of experience gained in the implementation of this Directive the Commission will, pursuant to Article 6 (3), submit to the Council proposals for more stringent limit values to be introduced 10 years after the notification of this Directive.

Table 3.12 continued

The limit values given in the table correspond to a monthly average concentration or to a maximum monthly load.

The amounts of mercury discharged are expressed as a function of the amount of mercury used or handled by the industrial plant over the same period or as a function of the installed vinyl chloride production capacity.

2. Limit values expressed as concentrations which in principle must not be exceeded are given in the above table for the industrial sectors 1 to 4. In no instance may limit values expressed as maximum concentrations be greater than those expressed as maximum quantities divided by water requirements per kilogram of mercury handled or per tonne of installed vinyl chloride production capacity.

   However, because the concentration of mercury in effluents depends on the volume of water involved, which differs for different processes and plants, the limit values, expressed in terms of the quantity of mercury discharged in relation to the quantity of mercury handled or to the installed vinyl chloride production capacity, given in the above table, must be complied with in all cases.

3. The daily average limit values are twice the corresponding monthly average limit values given in the table.

4. A monitoring procedure must be instituted to check whether the discharges comply with the emission standards which have been fixed in accordance with the limit values laid down in this Annex.

   This procedure must provide for the taking and analysis of samples and for measurement of the flow of the discharge and, where appropriate, the quantity of mercury handled.

   Should the quantity of mercury handled be impossible to determine, the monitoring procedure may be based on the quantity of mercury that may be used in the light of the production capacity on which the authorization was based.

5. A sample representative of the discharge over a period of 24 hours will be taken. The quantity of mercury discharged over a month must be calculated on the basis of the daily quantities of mercury discharged.

   However, a simplified monitoring procedure may be instituted in the case of industrial plants which do not discharge more than 7.5 kilograms of mercury per annum.

implementation directives on mercury, cadmium or hexachlorocyclohexane (HCH). This simplification should also make it possible to speed up the work on 129 substances on the black list in line with the directions established in the Council Resolution of 7 February 1983.

The third characteristic of this directive is that on the one hand it sets out the methods of application of the principles contained in the framework directive of 4 May 1976 when the legal codification is exercised, and on the other it sets out complementary provisions on certain specific points. These concern, for example, diffused or indirect discharge of "grey list" substances by industries which do not constitute the main source of pollution. For these types of discharge coming from numerous and diffuse sources, Member States must establish specific pollution reduction and elimination programmes. Another new provision concerns the general obligation of Member States to monitor the aquatic environment affected by discharges from industrial plants.

Table 3.13: Council Decision of 12 December 1977 Establishing a common procedure for the exchange of information on the quality of surface fresh water in the Community

PARAMETERS IN RESPECT OF WHICH INFORMATION IS TO BE
EXCHANGED

(Modes of expression and significant figures for the parametric data)

	Parameter	Mode of expression	Significant figures	
			Before the decimal comma	After the decimal comma
physical	Rate of flow (¹) (at the time of sampling)	m³/sec	x x x x	x x
	Temperature	°C	x x	x
	pH	pH	x x	x
	Conductivity at 20°C	μS cm⁻¹	(<100) x x (≥ 100) x x x	
chemical	Chlorides	Cl mg/l	(<100) x x (≥ 100) x x x	
	Nitrates	NO₃ mg/l	x x x	x x
	Ammonia	NH₄ mg/l	x x x	x x
	Dissolved oxygen	O₂ mg/l	x x	x
	BOD₅	O₂ mg/l	x x x	x
	COD	O₂ mg/l	x x x	x
	Total phosphorus	P mg/l	x x	x x
	Surfactants reacting to methylene blue	Sodium lauryl sulphate eq. mg/l	x x	x x
	Total cadmium	Cd mg/l	x	x x x x
	Mercury	Hg mg/l	x	x x x x
micro-biological	Faecal coliforms	/ 100 ml	x x x x x x	
	Total coliforms (²)	/ 100 ml	x x x x x x	
	Faecal streptococci (²)	/ 100 ml	x x x x x x	
	Salmonella (²)	/ 1 l	x	
biological	biological quality (²) (³)			

(¹) The date of sampling must be given.
(²) The data relating to this parameter shall be exchanged when it is measured.
(³) The frequency of sampling of this parameter and the mode of expression of results shall be decided on by Member States.

(g)   Heptachloride and chlordan discharges

On 3 October 1981 the Council noted a Commission Communication which expressed the view that it was not necessary to draw up specific proposals for controlling the discharge of heptachloride and chlordan into the aquatic environment. These two substances were not actually produced in the Community, nor were they used to any great extent.

(h)   Hexachlorobenzene, hexachlorobutadine, chloroform

On 16 June 1988, the Council adopted a directive amending Annex II to Directive 86/280/EEC on limit values and quality objectives for discharges of certain dangerous substances included in List I of the Annex to Directive 76/464/EEC for the above substances.

The limit values for emission standards, and the quality objectives, for the substances in question are set out in Table 3.14. Member States had to take the measures necessary to comply with this directive by 1 January 1990, as far as the above substances are concerned.

5.   Pollution reduction programmes for the "grey list" substances of the 1976 framework directive

Since 1978 the Commission has organized meetings with Member States in order to compare the national pollution reduction programmes for substances on the "grey list" or List II of the 1976 directive. The Commission noted that few Member States had submitted their pollution reduction programmes, so preventing the Commission from going on to the comparative study intended to ensure a uniform implementation of these programmes, as mentioned in Article 7 of the 1976 framework directive.

V.   INDUSTRIAL SECTORS

The 1973 Action Programme also considered that the protection of the environment demanded that particular attention be paid to industrial activities in which the manufacturing processes entail the introduction of pollution or nuisances into the environment.

1.   Paper pulp industry

(a)   Technical report of the Commission

In 1975 the Commission submitted to the Council a technical report on the pollution of water by pulp manufacturing industry in the Member States. This report showed that pulp mill effluents contained considerable quantities of suspended solids which could severely deplete the oxygen content of the receiving water course, discolour the water and cause foaming. The extent of such pollution depended on the type of pulp-producing process used, the volume and type of discharge, and the environmental characteristics of the receiving medium.

Table 3.14: Council Directive of 16 June 1988 amending Annex II to Directive 86/280/EEC on limit values and quality objectives for discharges of certain dangerous substances included in List I of the Annex to Directive 76/464/EEC

V. SPECIFIC PROVISIONS RELATING TO HEXACHLOROBENZENE (HCB) (NO 83)

CAS-118-74-1

Heading A (83): Limit values for emission standards

Standstill: There must be no significant direct or indirect increase over time in pollution arising from discharges of HCB and affecting concentrations in sediments and/or molluscs and/or shellfish and/or fish.

Type of industrial plant (^{1}) (^{2}) (^{3})	Type of average value	Limit values expressed as		To be complied with as from
		weight	*concentration*	
1. HCB production and processing	monthly	10 g HCB/tonne of HCB production capacity	1 mg/l of HCB	1.1.1990
	daily	20 g HCB/tonne of HCB production capacity	2 mg/l of HCB	
2. Production of perchloro-ethylene (PER) and carbon tetrachloride (CCl$_4$) by perchlorination	monthly	1.5 g HCB/tonne of PER + CCl$_4$ total production capacity	1.5 mg/l of HCB	1.1.1990
	daily	3 g HCB/tonne of PER + CCl$_4$ total production capacity	3 mg/l of HCB	
3. Production of trichloroethylene and/or perchloroethylene by any other process (^{4})	monthly	—	—	—
	daily	—	—	—

(^{1}) A simplified monitoring procedure may be introduced if annual discharges do not exceed 1 kg a year.

(^{2}) Among the industrial plants referred to in Annex I, heading A, point 3, reference is made in particular to industrial plants producing quintozene and tecnazene, industrial plants producing chlorine by chlor-alkali electrolysis with graphite electrodes, industrial rubber processing plants, plants manufacturing pyrotechnic products and plants producing vinylchloride.

(^{3}) On the basis of experience gained in implementing the Directive, and taking into account the fact that the use of best technical means already makes it possible to apply in some cases much more stringent values than those indicated above, the Council shall decide, on the basis of proposals from the Commission, upon more stringent limit values, such decision to be taken by 1 January 1995.

(^{4}) It is not possible at present to adopt limit values for this sector. The Council shall adopt such limit values at a later stage, acting on a proposal from the Commission. In the meantime, Member States will apply national emission standards in accordance with Annex I, heading A, point 3.

Table 3.14 continued

Heading B (83): Quality objectives ([1])

Standstill: The concentration of HCB in sediments and/or molluscs and/or shellfish and/or fish must not increase significantly with time.

([1]) The Commission shall keep under review the possibility of setting more stringent quality objectives, taking into account measured concentrations of HCB in sediments and/or molluscs and/or shellfish and/or fish, and will report to the Council, by 1 January 1995, for decision as to whether any changes should be made to the Directive.

Environment	Quality objective	Unit of measurement	To be complied with as from
Inland surface waters Estuary waters Internal coastal waters other than estuary waters Territorial waters	0.03	μg/l	1.1.1990

Heading C (83): Reference method of measurement

1. The reference method of measurement to be used for determining the presence of HCB in effluents and waters in gas chromatography with electron-capture detection after extraction by means of an appropriate solvent.

   The limit of determination ([1]) for HCB shall be within the range 1 to 10 ng/l for waters and 0.5 to 1 μg/l for effluents depending on the number of extraneous substances present in the sample.

2. The reference method to be used for determining HCB in sediments and organisms is gas chromatography with electron-capture detection after appropriate preparation of the sample. The limit of determination ([1]) shall be within the range 1 to 10 μg/kg of dry matter.

3. The accuracy and precision of the method must be ± 50% at a concentration which represents twice the value of the limit of determination ([1]).

([1]) The "limit of determination" × g of a given substance is the smallest quantity, quantitatively determinable in a sample on the basis of a given working method, which can still be distinguished from zero.

VI. SPECIFIC PROVISIONS RELATING TO HEXACHLOROBUTADINE (HCBD) (NO 84)

CAS-87-68-3

Heading A (84): Limit values for emission standards

Standstill: There must be no significant direct or indirect increase over time in pollution arising from discharges of HCBD and affecting concentrations in sediments and/or molluscs and/or shellfish and/or fish.

Table 3.14 continued

| Type of industrial plant (¹) (²) (³) | Type of average value | Limit values expressed as | | To be complied with as from |
		weight	concentration	
1. Production of perchloroethylene (PER) and carbon tetrachloride (CCl₄) by perchlorination	monthly	1.5 g HCBD/tonne of total production capacity of PER + CCl₄	1.5 mg/l of HCBD	
	daily	3 g HCBD/tonne of total production capacity of PER + CCl₄	3 mg/l of HCBD	1.1.1990
2. Production of trichloroethylene and/or perchloroethylene by any other process (⁴)	monthly	—	—	—
	daily	—	—	—

(¹) A simplified monitoring procedure may be introduced if annual discharges do not exceed 1 kg a year.

(²) Among the industrial plants referred to in Annex I, heading A, point 3, reference is made in particular to industrial plants using HCBD for technical purposes.

(³) On the basis of experience gained in implementing this Directive, and taking into account the fact that the use of best technical means already makes it possible to apply in some cases much more stringent values than those indicated above, the Council shall decide, on the basis of proposals from the Commission, upon more stringent limit values, such decision to be taken by 1 January 1995.

(⁴) It is not possible at present to adopt limit values for this sector. The Council shall adopt such limit values at a later stage, acting on a proposal from the Commission. In the meantime, Member States will apply national emission standards in accordance with Annex I, heading A, point 3.

Heading B (84): Quality objectives (¹)

Standstill: The concentration of HCBD in sediments and/or molluscs and/or shellfish and/or fish must not increase significantly with time.

(¹) The Commission shall keep under review the possibility of setting more stringent quality objectives, taking into account measured concentrations of HCBD in sediments and/or molluscs and/or shellfish and/or fish, and will report to the Council, by 1 January 1995, for decision as to whether any changes should be made to the Directive.

Environment	Quality objective	Unit of measurement	To be complied with as from
Inland surface waters Estuary waters Internal coastal waters other than estuary waters Territorial waters	0.1	µg/l	1.1.1990

Table 3.14 continued

Heading C (84): Reference method of measurement

1. The reference method of measurement to be used for determining HCBD in effluents and waters is gas chromatograpy with electron-capture detection after extraction by means of an appropriate solvent.
   The limit of determination ([1]) for HCBD shall be within the range 1 to 10 ng/l for waters and 0.5 to 1 μg/l for effluents, depending on the number of extraneous substances present in the sample.

2. The reference method to be used for determining HCBD in sediments and organisms is gas chromatography with electron-capture detection after appropriate preparation of the sample. The limit of determination ([1]) shall be within the range 1 to 10 μg/kg of dry matter.

3. The accuracy and precision of the method just be ± 50 % at a concentration which represents twice the value of the limit of determination ([1]).

([1]) The "limit of determination" x g of a given substance is the smallest quantity, quantitatively determinable in a sample on the basis of a given working method, which can still be distinguished from zero.

VII. SPECIFIC PROVISIONS RELATING TO CHLOROFORM (CHCl$_3$) (NO 23) ([1])

CAS-67-66-3

Heading A (23): Limit values for emission standards

Type of industrial plant ([2]) ([3])	Limit value (monthly averages) expressed as ([4]) ([5])		To be complied with as from
	weight	concentration	
1. Production of chloromethanes from methanol or from a combination of methanol and methane ([6])	10 g CHCl$_3$/tonne of total production capacity of chloromethanes	1 mg/l	1.1.1990
2. Production of chloromethanes by chlorination of methane	7.5 g CHCl$_3$/tonne of total production capacity of chloromethanes	1 mg/l	1.1.1990
3. Production of chlorofluorocarbon (CFC) ([7])	—	—	—

([1]) In the case of chloroform, Article 3 of Directive 76/464/EEC shall apply to discharges from industrial processes which may in themselves contribute significantly to the level of chloroform in the aquenous effluent; in particular it shall apply to those mentioned under heading A of this Annex. Article 5 of this Directive applies if sources other than those listed in this Annex are identified.

([2]) Among the industrial plants referred to under heading A, point 3 of Annex I, special reference is made, in the case of chloroform, to plants manufacturing monomer vinyl chloride using dichlorethane pyrolysis, those producing bleached pulp and other plants using CHCl$_3$, as a solvent and plants in which cooling waters or other effluents are chlorinated. The Council shall adopt limit values for these sectors at a later stage, acting on proposals from the Commission.

([3]) A simplified monitoring procedure may be introduced if annual discharges do not exceed 30 kg a year.

([4]) Daily average limit values are equal to twice the monthly average values.

Table 3.14 continued

(^{5}) In view of the volatility of chloroform and in order to ensure compliance with Article 3 (6), where a process involving agitation in the open air of effluent containing chloroform is used, the Member States shall require compliance with the limit values upstream of the plant concerned; they shall ensure that all water likely to be polluted is taken fully into account.

(^{6}) I.e. by hydrochlorination of methanol, then chlorination of methyl chloride.

(^{7}) It is not possible at present to adopt limit values for this sector. The Council shall adopt such limit values at a later date, acting on a proposal from the Commission. In the meantime, Member States will apply national emission standards in accordance with Annex I, heading A, point 3.

Heading B (23): Quality objectives (^{1})

(^{1}) Without prejudice to Article 6 (3) of Directive 76/464/EEC, where there is no evidence of any problem in meeting and continuously maintaining the quality objective set out above, a simplified monitoring procedure may be introduced.

Environment	Quality objectives	Unit of measurement	To be complied with as from
Inland surface waters Estuary waters Internal coastal waters other than estuary waters Territorial waters	12	µg/l	1.1.1990

Heading C (23): Reference method of measurement

1. The reference method of measurement to be used for determining the presence of chloroform in effluents and the aquatic environment is gas chromatography.

    A sensitive detector must be used when concentration levels are below 0.5 mg/l and in this case the determination limit (^{1}) is 0.1 µg/l. For concentration levels higher than 0.5 mg/l a determination limit of 0.1 mg/l is acceptable.

2. The accuracy and precision of the method must be ± 50 % at a concentration which represents twice the value of the determination limit.

(^{1}) The "determination limit" × g of a given substance is the smallest quantity, quantitatively determinable in a sample on the basis of a given working method, which can still be distinguished from zero.

Article 2

Member States shall take the measures necessary to comply with this Directive by 1 January 1989 with regard to aldrin, dieldrin, endrin and isodrin, and by 1 January 1990 with regard to the other substances. They shall forthwith inform the Commission thereof.

Member States shall communicate to the Commission, the provisions of national law which they adopt in the field governed by this Directive.

Article 3

This Directive is addressed to the Member States.

Done at Luxembourg, 16 June 1988.

For the Council
The President
K. TÖPFER

(b)   The Commission's proposal for a directive of 1975

In addition to the technical report, the Commission also presented to the Council on 20 January 1975 a proposal for a directive on the reduction of water pollution by paper pulp mills in the Member States.[21] The aim of this proposal was to fix emission standards at Community level for the paper pulp industry, to be applied according to the manufacturing method used. However, a certain measure of flexibility was provided for in the application of the proposed standards, in order to take into account the assimilative capacity of the receiving waters, as well as the desired quality of water and the local, social and economic conditions.

The Council has examined this proposal on several occasions but has been unable to reach an agreement due to opposition on principle and for reasons of protection of the interests of national industries. The proposal was withdrawn in August 1993.[22]

2.   Titanium dioxide industry

(a)   Technical report of the Commission

The 1973 Action Programme also mentioned the titanium dioxide industry among those industrial sectors to be studied as a matter of priority.

In 1975 the Commission presented a technical report to the Council on pollution caused by the titanium dioxide industry. The report noted that the vast majority of factories manufacturing titanium dioxide dumped their waste at sea or in estuaries, relying on the "buffer effect" of the sea to neutralize the acid part of the waste, and on the capacity of the oxygen present to convert the ferrous sulphate into ferric sulphate, the other waste of heavy metals sinking naturally to the seabed.

Monitoring of the pollution of the discharge areas showed that industrial discharge of titanium dioxide was potentially or actually harmful. These adverse effects on the marine environment are mainly due to acidity, the presence of ferrous sulphate and other heavy metals. These effects can take the following forms, depending on the method and place of dumping:

- reduced oxygenation and pH of the water and increased concentration of iron and heavy metals;
- temporary shortage of zooplankton biomass;
- change in the colour, transparency and turbidity of the water, and temporary reduction of photosynthesis and of phytoplankton, particularly in the case of surface dumping;
- covering of the seabed by iron oxides where dumping is carried out in estuaries and shallow water.

In conclusion, the report suggested that the industries concerned should, within a reasonable period of time, store on land the insoluble matter and make certain reductions in the total pollution.

---

[21] OJ No C 99 of 2/5/75.
[22] OJ No C 228/4 of 24/8/93.

(b)   1978 first framework directive on waste from the titanium dioxide industry

In the light of its technical report the Commission submitted to the Council on 18 July 1975 a proposal for a directive on waste from the titanium dioxide industry.

The proposal had three main aspects: the principle of prior authorization for discharges; the ecological receiving environment; measures to be taken to reduce and prevent pollution.

After long and difficult discussions, the Council finally adopted this first directive on waste from the titanium dioxide industry on 20 February 1978.[23] It retained the two principles on prior authorization for any discharge of waste and on the ecological control of the affected zone. However, it was not able to accept the Commission's proposals on a progressive reduction of waste from the titanium dioxide industry. It did, nevertheless, insist that Member States draw up national programmes for the progressive reduction of pollution caused by waste coming from existing industrial plants. These programmes, which had to be implemented by 1 January 1982, at the latest, were to fix general objectives for the reduction of pollution by liquid, solid and gaseous wastes, to be reached by 1 July 1987. They were also to include intermediary objectives and contain information on the state of the environment concerned, on the measures of pollution reduction and on the methods of treating wastes caused by the manufacturing processes.

The national programmes had to be submitted to the Commission by 1 July 1980 so that it might within a period of six months of receipt of all national programmes, submit suitable proposals to the Council for the harmonization of these programmes with regard to the reduction of pollution and the improvement of the conditions of competition in the titanium dioxide industry.

The directive requires that national programmes cover all existing industrial plants and indicate the measures to be taken in each plant. However, if in special circumstances a Member State considers that in the case of a specific industrial plant no additional measures are necessary to satisfy the requirements of the directive, that Member State must justify this conclusion to the Commission within six months of notification of the directive. After having conducted any independent verification that may be necessary, the Commission may give its agreement to the Member State. The Commission's agreement must be given within six months. If the Commission does not give its agreement to a Member State, specific additional measures concerning the plant in question must be included in the national programme of the Member State concerned.

(c)   1982 second directive on the monitoring of discharges from the titanium dioxide industry

On 30 December 1980 the Commission submitted a proposal to the Council for a directive dealing with methods of monitoring and control of the areas affected by the discharges of the titanium dioxide industry, in line with the provisions of Article 7, paragraph 3 of the directive of 20 February 1978 on discharges from the titanium dioxide industry. The Council adopted this directive on 3 December 1982.[24] The directive defines the system for the surveillance and monitoring of the effects of the discharge, dumping, storage on, tipping on or injection into the

---

[23] OJ No L 54 of 25/2/78.
[24] OJ No L 378 of 31/12/82.

ground of waste from the titanium dioxide industry on the environment, from the physical, chemical, biological and ecological points of view. With this aim, the directive fixes a body of control parameters for each method of waste elimination (in sea water, fresh water, or storage and dumping on land). These parameters are either obligatory or optional, and contain both the minimum frequency of sampling and a reference method of measurement. The directive also covers control of atmospheric pollution due to discharges into the air.

In line with Article 14 of the directive of 20 February 1978, Member States must include in the general report to the Commission precise data on monitoring and surveillance. With the permission of the Member States, the Commission will publish a summary of the information received.

(d)   Council directive of 21 June 1989 on procedures for harmonizing the programmes for the reduction and eventual elimination of pollution caused by waste from the titanium dioxide industry

On 18 April 1983 the Commission submitted a new proposal to the Council which aimed to harmonize the programmes for the reduction of pollution caused by the titanium dioxide industry.[25] This proposal arose directly from the framework directive of 20 February 1978, and more particularly from Article 9 of that directive. In 1978 the Council was unable to overcome the differences between Member States on the Commission's proposals for a progressive elimination of waste from existing industrial plants and had reported this problem previously. It had restricted itself to requiring Member States to set up national programmes for the reduction of pollution caused by the titanium dioxide industry (see p. 99). These programmes were to be sent to the Commission so that it could present proposals during 1981 with a view to harmonizing them. Because of the delay in receiving the national programmes, the Commission was unable to submit such proposals until 1983, two years later than planned. Having examined the programmes sent by the Member States, the Commission realized that the harmonizing objective of the 1978 directive was all the more essential since the programmes differed greatly from one another, both on the technical level and on the level of anti-pollution investment made. In addition, they did not fulfil one of the conditions of competition in the sector of titanium dioxide production.

The proposal for a directive included both the prohibiting of the most polluting discharges, e.g. "copperas" (ferrous sulphate), and also Community limit values for discharges of liquid acid. The structures of the proposal rested on two major distinctions:

● first, the different processes of production of titanium dioxide: the sulphate process, which is by far the most polluting, and the chlorine process, less polluting, but also less used in Europe;
● secondly, the receiving environment of the discharge, i.e. sea water (estuaries, coastal waters or sea waters) and surface fresh water.

The limit values proposed were spread out in time, and there were two stages of reduction so that industries would be able to adapt and make towards the necessary investments.

[25] OJ No C 138 of 26/5/83.

The proposal also covered the possibility of derogations in case of technical difficulties.

Despite numerous discussions at both technical and political levels, the Council was not able to reach early agreement on this directive. Certain progress was, however, realized at the meetings of the Environment Council held in Luxembourg on 16–17 and 28–29 June 1988, when the Council approved guidelines on procedures for harmonizing the programmes for the reduction of pollution caused by waste from the titanium dioxide industry.

The guidelines were drawn up to serve as a basis for further discussion within the Council bodies on the proposal for a directive submitted by the Commission and took account of the outcome of the discussions held to date. It was accepted that all dumping should end by 31 December 1989. Discharges of solid wastes, strong acid and treatment wastes from the sulphate process, as well as solid waste and strong acid wastes from the chloride process would be banned from all waters by 31 December 1989. However, the possibility of exceptions were envisaged which might extend the period for the "final prohibition" up until 1992 at the latest. If a Member State was going to avail itself of the possibility of extending the date, it would have to inform the Commission within three months of the notification of the directive and present a programme for effective reduction of both dumping and discharge. It was accepted that all discharges of weak acid wastes from the sulphate process into all waters would be substantially reduced by 1 July 1993, by limit values to be established, and that discharges of weak acid wastes and treatment wastes from the chloride process into all waters would be substantially reduced by 31 December 1989, by further limit values to be established. It was also agreed that Member States might alternatively apply quality objectives to be fixed in such a way that they are equivalent to the limit values in terms of the protection of the environment and competition. Emissions into the air would also be limited.

The Council meetings of 16–17 and 28–29 June 1988 did not reach agreement on the legal basis for the directive. The Commission's position was that Article 100A was the correct legal base, the proposal having as its objective not only the protection of the environment, but also the need to avoid distortions of competition, one of the basic objectives of the internal market. The Council disagreed and changed the legal basis to Article 130S, dealing specifically with the environment.[26]

Subsequently, the European Parliament, with the support of the Commission, took the Council to court over the legal base used for this directive. As a result, the Court agreed that the European Parliament's complaint was valid. The Court struck down the directive, accepting the Commission's argument for basing its proposal on Article 100A.[27]

3.   Future work concerning specific industrial sectors

Taking into account the differences of opinion existing between Member States and the difficulties encountered within the Council in adoption of the sectoral proposals for directives, the Commission indicated in 1980 that generally speaking it would no longer submit proposals aimed directly at specific industrial sectors.

[26] OJ No L 201 of 14/7/89.
[27] Case 300/89 *Commission* v. *Council* (1991).

However, in the 4th Environment Action Programme, the following passage occurred:

> The "source-oriented" approach as defined in Chapter 5 of the First Environment Action Programme (actions specific to certain industrial sectors and to energy production) has not made much progress at least at Community level even though 15 key industrial sectors were identified in that programme and numerous studies were undertaken. In fact, proposals were made for only two industrial sectors – titanium dioxide (where a multi-media approach was adopted) and pulp-and-paper (where the emphasis was on discharges to water). The pulp-and-paper proposal remains unadopted, and even unconsidered, by the Council, whilst the history of the titanium dioxide proposal has not been encouraging. Nevertheless a source-oriented approach (aimed at individual industries or target groups of industries, and covering all discharges to air, land, or water and including the generation of solid as well as liquid or gaseous wastes) is appropriate in certain circumstances and is one of the alternative approaches available that may be worth considering again.[28]

VI.   CONTROL OF WATER POLLUTION

Under the heading "Exchange of information between surveillance and monitoring networks", the 1973 Action Programme specified the aims and content of Community action in the control of water pollution as being:

- to organize and develop technical exchanges between the regional and national pollution surveillance and monitoring networks;
- to improve the efficiency, accuracy and comparative value of the provisions already in force;
- to set up a system of information exchange on data collected by the networks.

1.   Decision of 1977 establishing a system of information exchange on water quality

On 1 April 1976 the Commission submitted a proposal to the Council for a decision to establish a uniform procedure for the exchange of information on the quality of surface fresh water in the Community. The proposal laid down criteria for the selection of measuring stations which should form part of the Community network and sets out a list of parameters on which information should be exchanged. These parameters must allow for the physical, chemical and microbiological properties of the waters. Those for radioactivity were excluded as they are to be measured according to the basic standards established by the Euratom Treaty (see p. 471). In order for a meaningful comparison to be made between the data at Community level, the information transmitted by the central bodies of the Member States should not only include numerical data on the parameters, but also a description of the measuring methods used and of the sampling procedures (depth and location). The Council adopted this decision on 12 December 1977.[29] According to this, each Member State must select a certain number of measuring stations, respecting the following criteria:

---

[28] See paras 3.4.1 and 3.4.2 of the 4th Environment Action Programme, OJ C 328 of 7/12/87.
[29] OJ No L 334 of 24/12/77.

- the stations must be situated at points which are representative of the conditions of the surrounding aquatic environment and must not be under direct or immediate influence from a source of pollution;
- they must be able to measure periodically all the parameters considered (see Table 3.12);
- they must be situated not more than 100 km apart on the principal rivers, excluding tributaries;
- they must be upstream of confluences and not below the tidal limit.

Each Member State must also name a central body which will transmit the information gathered to the Commission. This information must be submitted annually (based on the calendar year). On the basis of the information received, the Commission was to prepare a synthesis report which is sent to Member States. There are 18 parameters which must be measured and which form the subject of the information exchange and these are divided into three categories: physical, chemical and microbiological. It should be noted that by one of its own decisions taken on 24 July 1984 the Commission amended the list of measuring stations participating in the information exchange, following requests from France, Ireland, the Netherlands and the United Kingdom.[30]

2.   1986 decision modifying and extending the 1977 information system

On 19 November 1985 the Commission put a proposal to the Council which modified the 1977 decision on information exchange on the quality of fresh water in the Community. In the light of experience gained since 1977, the proposal aimed to update, complete and improve the current information system.

The Council accepted this modifying decision on 24 November 1986.[31] The main new provision is the addition of an annex which sets out the reference measurement methods to be used by the Member States for the different water quality parameters to be measured. Laboratories using methods other than these should start cross-testing and inter-calibrating the different methods so that the results obtained are comparable. Samples should always be taken from the same places and the procedures used should always be identical. Other measures in the decision which are intended to complete and improve the efficiency of the information system concerned:

- the setting up of a monthly sampling and analysis of the parameters; this could however be carried out less frequently in certain strictly defined conditions, especially when the water quality does not show any significant variations;
- the addition of a new parameter for the biological quality of the water.

Finally, the decision proposed simplifying the methods of drawing up the synthesis report which the Commission should prepare on the basis of information received from Member States. This will only be produced every three years, and not annually. In particular it should bring out the long-term trends which have become apparent in the water quality.

[30] OJ No L 237 of 5/9/84.
[31] OJ No L 335 of 28/11/86.

It should be noted that when the Council adopted this decision it asked the Commission to come up with a simplification and regrouping of all the information and reports on the directives on the aquatic environment of the Community (e.g. directives on water quality).

3.   Council directive of 12 December 1991 concerning the protection of waters against pollution caused by nitrates from agricultural sources

The increasing level of nitrates in Community surface, coastal and groundwaters causes two basic problems as far as the environment is concerned: the risk of degradation of drinking water, and the eutrophication of coastal and interior waters. In recent years, the Baltic Sea, North Sea and Adriatic have been particularly affected in spring and summer by the appearance of algae as a result of eutrophication. These algae can cause severe damage to biotopes, especially fisheries, and can affect the touristic value of the areas concerned.

The two main sources of nitrate pollution are agriculture and discharges of waste water. As far as agriculture is concerned, this stems from certain types of land use and the excessive use of chemical fertilizers.

Directive 80/778/EEC fixes at 50 mg/litre the maximum concentration in nitrates of distributed drinking water. If the nitrate content is above this, the water must be treated or mixed with clean water in order to bring it back below the permitted level. The Commission recognized that these measures proved to be extremely onerous and did not attack the origin of the problem. Also, it was often very difficult to deal with small quantities of water. The adoption by some Member States of legislation on intensive agriculture highlighted the need to move quickly towards common action, not only with a view to protecting the environment, but also in order to avoid distortions in competition.

The new Council directive of 12 December 1991[32] aimed to define the framework which must be respected by the Member States when they draw up individually or in collaboration with other Member States programmes devoted to this problem. In the first place, the Member States must identify within two years the zones likely to be subject to nitrate pollution. This identification is based on criteria defined in Annex I of the directive. Within four years (or longer in special circumstances) Member States must take specific measures, including those necessary to ensure that the quantity of animal manure spread on land by an individual farmer does not exceed the limits outlined in Annex II of the directive in relation to the number of animals; and must establish rules concerning the periods during which the spreading of animal manure is prohibited; conditions for spreading manure on sloping, flooded or frozen land; and measures governing the size and construction of containers for manure. The waste waters of towns with a population of more than 5000 which are discharged directly or indirectly into zones designated as vulnerable must be treated to ensure that their total nitrate content does not exceed 10 mg per litre.

In their reports on the implementation of the directive, Member States must indicate the respective levels of nitrates contained in the chemical fertilizers and the

---

[32] OJ L 375 of 31/12/91.

Table 3.15: Council Directive of 12 December 1991 concerning the protection of waters against pollution caused by nitrates from agricultural sources

ANNEX I

CRITERIA FOR IDENTIFYING WATERS REFERRED TO IN ARTICLE 3 (1)

A. Waters referred to in Article 3 (1) shall be identified making use, *inter alia*, of the following criteria:

1. whether surface fresh waters, in particular those used or intended for the abstraction of drinking water, contain or could contain if action pursuant to Article 5 is not taken, more than the concentration of nitrates laid down in accordance with Directive 75/440/EEC;

2. whether ground waters contain more than 50 mg/l nitrates or could contain more than 50 mg/l nitrates if action pursuant to Article 5 is not taken;

3. whether natural freshwater lakes, other freshwater bodies, estuaries, coastal waters and marine waters are found to be eutrophic or in the near future may become eutrophic if action pursuant to Article 5 is not taken.

B. In applying this criteria, Member States shall also take account of:

1. the physical and environmental characteristics of the waters and land;

2. the current understanding of the behaviour of nitrogen compounds in the environment (water and soil);

3. the current understanding of the impact of the action taken pursuant to Article 5.

ANNEX II

CODE(S) OF GOOD AGRICULTURAL PRACTICE

A. A code or codes of good agricultural practice with the objective of reducing pollution by nitrates and taking account of conditions in the different regions of the Community should certain provisions covering the following items, in so far as they are relevant:

1. periods when the land application of fertilizer is inappropriate;

2. the land application of fertilizer to steeply sloping ground;

3. the land application of fertilizer to water-saturated, flooded, frozen or snow-covered ground;

4. the conditions for land application of fertilizer near watercourses;

5. the capacity and construction of storage vessels for livestock manures, including measures to prevent water pollution by run-off and seepage into the groundwater and surface water of liquids containing livestock manures and effluents from stored plant materials such as silage;

6. procedures for the land application, including rate and uniformity of spreading, of both chemical fertilizer and livestock manure, that will maintain nutrient losses to water at an acceptable level.

Table 3.15 continued

B. Member States may also include in their code(s) of good agricultural practices the following items:

   7. land use management, including the use of crop rotation systems and the proportion of the land area devoted to permanent crops relative to annual tillage crops;

   8. the maintenance of a minimum quantity of vegetation cover during (rainy) periods that will take up the nitrogen from the soil that could otherwise cause nitrate pollution of water;

   9. the establishment of fertilizer plans on a farm-by-farm basis and the keeping of records on fertilizer use;

  10. the prevention of water pollution from run-off and the downward water movement beyond the reach of crop roots in irrigation systems.

ANNEX III

MEASURES TO BE INCLUDED IN ACTION PROGRAMMES AS REFERRED TO IN ARTICLE 5 (4) (a)

1. The measures shall include rules relating to:

   1. periods when the land application of certain types of fertilizer is prohibited;

   2. the capacity of storage vessels for livestock manure; this capacity must exceed that required for storage throughout the longest period during which land application in the vulnerable zone is prohibited, except where it can be demonstrated to the competent authority that any quantity of manure in excess of the actual storage capacity will be disposed of in a manner which will not cause harm to the environment;

   3. limitation of the land application of fertilizers, consistent with good agricultural practice and taking into account the characteristics of the vulnerable zone concerned, in particular:

   (a) soil conditions, soil type and slope;

   (b) climatic conditions, rainfall and irrigation;

   (c) land use and agricultural practices, including crop rotation systems;

   and to be based on a balance between:

   (i) the foreseeable nitrogen requirements of the crops,

     and

   (ii) the nitrogen supply to the crops from the soil and from fertilization corresponding to:

     – the amount of nitrogen present in the soil at the moment when the crop starts to use it to a significant degree (outstanding amounts at the end of winter),

     – the supply of nitrogen through the net mineralization of the reserves of organic nitrogen in the soil,

     – additions of nitrogen compounds from livestock manure,

     – additions of nitrogen compounds from chemical and other fertilizers.

Table 3.15 continued

2. These measures will ensure that, for each farm or livestock unit, the amount of livestock manure applied to the land each year, including by the animals themselves, shall not exceed a specified amount per hectare.

The specified amount per hectare be the amount of manure containing 170 kg N. However:

(a) for the first four-year action programme Member States may allow an amount of manure containing up to 210 kg N;

(b) during and after the first four-year action programme, Member States may fix different amounts from those referred to above. These amounts must be fixed so as not to prejudice the achievement of the objectives specified in Article 1 and must be justified on the basis of objectives criteria, for example:

   – long growing seasons,

   – crops with high nitrogen uptake,

   – high net precipitation in the vulnerable zone,

   – soils with exceptionally high denitrification capacity.

   If a Member State allows a different amount under subparagraph (b), it shall inform the Commission which will examine the justification in accordance with the procedure laid down in Article 9.

3. Member States may calculate the amounts referred to in paragraph 2 on the basis of animal numbers.

4. Member States shall inform the Commission of the manner in which they are applying the provisions of paragraph 2. In the light of the information received, the Commission may, if it considers necessary, make appropriate proposals to the Council in accordance with Article 11.

ANNEX IV

REFERENCE METHODS OF MEASUREMENT

Chemical fertilizer

Nitrogen compounds shall be measured using the method described in Commission Directive 77/535/EEC of 22 June 1977 on the approximation of the laws of the Member States relating to methods of sampling and analysis for fertilizers ([1]), as amended by Directive 89/519/EEC ([2]).

Fresh waters, coastal waters and marine waters

Nitrate concentration shall be measured in accordance with Article 4a (3) of Council Decision 77/795/EEC of 12 December 1977 establishing a common procedure for the exchange of information on the quality of surface fresh water in the Community ([3]), as amended by Decision 86/574/EEC ([4]).

---

[1] OJ No L 213, 22. 8. 1977, p. 1.
[2] OJ No L 265, 12. 9. 1989, p. 30.
[3] OJ No L 334, 24. 12. 1977, p. 29.
[4] OJ No L 335, 28. 11. 1986, p. 44.

Table 3.15 continued

ANNEX V

INFORMATION TO BE CONTAINED IN REPORTS TO IN ARTICLE 10

1. A statement of the preventive action taken pursuant to Article 4.

2. A map showing the following:

    (a) waters identified in accordance with Article 3 (1) and Annex I indicating for each water which of the criteria in Annex I was used for the purpose of identification;

    (b) the location of the designed vulnerable zones, distinguishing between existing zones and zones designated since the previous report.

3. A summary of the monitoring results obtained pursuant to Article 6, including a statement of the considerations which led to the designation of each vulnerable zone and to any revision of or addition to designations of vulnerable zones.

4. A summary of the action programmes drawn up pursuant to Article 5 and, in particular:

    (a) the measures required by Article 5 (4) (a) and (b);

    (b) the information required by Annex III (4);

    (c) any additional measures or reinforced actions taken pursuant to Article 5 (5);

    (d) a summary of the results of the monitoring programmes implemented pursuant to Article 5 (6);

    (e) the assumptions made by the Member States about the likely timescale within which the waters identified in accordance with Article 3 (1) are expected to respond to the measure in the action programme, along with an indication of the level of uncertainty incorporated in these assumptions.

manure spread each year in vulnerable zones, the total area of these zones, as well as the number of animals per hectare. These measures include the definition at Commmunity level of maximum amounts of manure, the fixing at national level of maximum amounts of chemical fertilizers, the types of land use and a limit on the nitrate content of municipal waste waters. It is explicitly recognized that not all waters are at risk from nitrate pollution.

4. Council directive of 21 May 1991 concerning urban waste water treatment

The directive[33] sets up a comprehensive system for controlling the quality of urban waste water treatment and discharge from most areas that are populated. It includes industrial waste water discharged from 11 types of industry, all in the food process-

---

[33] OJ L 135 of 30/5/91.

ing sector (such as brewers and producers of alcoholic drinks, soft drinks, milk processing, fruit and vegetable products, potato processing, and the meat industry), into waste water collection systems and treatment plants. As of 31 December 1993, such discharges have required a permit issued by the Member State and which must satisfy the requirements of Annex I (C) (see Table 3.16).

Urban areas of different sizes are given a series of deadlines, between 31 December 1995 and 31 December 2005, by which time they must provide collection systems and, as a minimum, secondary, biological treatment for urban waste water (defined as domestic waste water) which may be mixed with run-off rain water or industrial waste water.

Annex I (B) of the directive lists five general requirements that urban waste water treatment plants must meet. It also provides parameters for biochemical oxygen demand, chemical oxygen demand and for total suspended solids, as well as for total nitrogen and phosphorous content to be applied in sensitive areas subject to eutrophication. Plants constructed to comply with the directive have to be built and operated to ensure adequate performance under all normal climatic conditions.

Under the terms of the directive, Member States had by 31 December 1993 to have identified sensitive areas, such as surface waters used as a source of drinking water which could exceed the nitrate concentration specified in the 1975 directive on surface water for drinking (75/440/EEC), areas subject to eutrophication, and areas where further treatment is required to meet other conditions stipulated in other directives. This classification must be reviewed every four years. Where a Member State applies sensitive area discharge standards throughout its territory, there is no requirement to identify specific areas.

Where a Member State can provide sufficient evidence that discharges to a less sensitive area will not result in environmental degradation, under certain circumstances such discharges need only be subject to primary biological or chemical treatment. Exemptions to discharge requirements to less sensitive waters from urban areas of more than 150,000 inhabitants may be obtained via a committee procedure, which can also be used to amend permit requirements for Annex I (B), (C), and (D) and to adapt monitoring guidelines.

The Member States, through their relevant authorities, are required to set up monitoring programmes and publish reports every two years. Each Member State was obliged to set up an implementing programme by 31 December 1993 and communicate it to the Commission by 30 June 1994, followed by biennial updates.

VII. SEA POLLUTION

The 1973 Action Programme recognizes that, of all forms of pollution, marine pollution is undoubtedly one of the most dangerous due to the effects it has on the fundamental biological and ecological balances governing life on our planet, the level of pollution already reached, the diversity of pollution sources and the difficulty of ensuring that any measures adopted are complied with. Indeed the sea represents an essential source of proteins and plays a vital role in maintaining the natural ecological balance by supplying a large proportion of the oxygen upon which life depends. The sea and coastal areas are also of great importance for recreation and leisure.

The Community is affected by sea pollution both because of the role played by the sea in the preservation and development of species, and because of the importance

Table 3.16: Council Directive of 21 May 1991 concerning urban waste water treatment

ANNEX I

REQUIREMENTS FOR URBAN WASTE WATER

A. *Collecting systems* (¹)

Collecting systems shall take into account waste water treatment requirements.

The design, construction and maintenance of collecting systems shall be undertaken in accordance with the best technical knowledge not entailing excessive costs, notably regarding:

– volume and characteristics of urban waste water,

– prevention of leaks,

– limitation of pollution of receiving waters due to storm water overflows.

B. *Discharge from urban waste water treatment plants to receiving waters* (¹)

1. Waste water treatment plants shall be designed or modified so that representative samples of the incoming waste water and of treated effluent can be obtained before discharge to receiving waters.

2. Discharges from urban waste water treatment plants subject to treatment in accordance with Articles 4 and 5 shall meet the requirements shown in Table 1.

3. Discharges from urban waste water treatment plants to those sensitive areas which are subject to eutrophication as identified in Annex II.A (a) shall in addition meet the requirements shown in Table 2 of this Annex.

4. More stringent requirements than those shown in Table 1 and/or Table 2 shall be applied where required to ensure that the receiving waters satisfy any other relevent Directives.

5. The points of discharge of urban waste water shall be chosen, as far as possible, so as to minimize the effects on receiving waters.

C. *Industrial waste water*

Industrial waste water entering collecting systems and urban waste water treatment plants shall be subject to such pre-treatment as is required in order to:

– protect the health of staff working in collecting systems and treatment plants,

– ensure that collecting systems, waste water treatment plants and associated equipment are not damaged,

– ensure that the operation of the waste water treatment plant and the treatment of sludge are not impeded,

---

(¹) Given that it is not possible in practice to construct collecting systems and treatment plants in a way such that all waste water can be treated during situations such as unusually heavy rainfall, Member States shall decide on measures to limit pollution from storm water overflows. Such measures could be based on dilution rates or capacity in relation to dry weather flow, or could specify a certain acceptable number of overflows per year.

Table 3.16 continued

  – ensure that discharges from the treatment plants do not adversely affect the environment, or prevent receiving water from complying with other Community Directives,

  – ensure that sludge can be disposed of safely in an environmentally acceptable manner.

D. *Reference methods for monitoring and evaluation of results*

1. Member States shall ensure that a monitoring method is applied which corresponds at least with the level of requirements described below.

   Alternative methods to those mentioned in paragraphs 2, 3 and 4 may be used provided that it can be demonstrated that equivalent results are obtained.

   Member States shall provide the Commission with all relevant information concerning the applied method. If the Commission considers that the conditions set out in paragraphs 2, 3 and 4 are not met, it will submit an appropriate proposal to the Council.

2. Flow-proportional or time-based 24-hour samples shall be collected at the same well-defined point in the outlet and if necessary in the inlet of the treatment plant in order to monitor compliance with the requirements for discharged waste water laid down in this Directive.

   Good international laboratory practices aiming at minimizing the degradation of samples between collection and analysis shall be applied.

3. The minimum annual number of samples shall be determined according to the size of the treatment plant and be collected at regular intervals during the year:

   – 2000 to 9 999 p.e.:   12 samples during the first year.

                             four samples in subsequent years,
                             if it can be shown that the water
                             during the first year complies
                             with the provisions of the
                             Directive; if one sample of the
                             four fails, 12 samples must be
                             taken in the year that follows.

   – 10 000 to 49 999 p.e.: 12 samples.

   – 50 000 p.e. or over: 24 samples.

4. The treated waste water shall be assumed to conform to the relevant parameters if, for each relevant parameter considered individually, samples of the water show that it complies with the relevant parametric value in the following way:

   (a) for the parameters specified in Table 1 and Article 2 (7), a maximum number of samples which are allowed to fail the requirements, expressed in concentrations and/or percentage reductions in Table 1 and Article 2 (7), is specified in Table 3;

   (b) for the parameters of Table 1 expressed in concentrations, the failing samples taken under normal operating conditions must not deviate from the parametric values by more than 100%. For the parametric values in concentration relating to total suspended solids deviations of up to 150% may be accepted;

   (c) for those parameters specified in Table 2 the annual mean of the samples for each parameter shall conform to the relevant parametric values.

5. Extreme values for the water quality in question shall not be taken into consideration when they are the result of unusual situations such as those due to heavy rain.

Table 3.16 continued

Table 1: Requirements for discharges from urban waste water treatment plants subject to Articles 4 and 5 of the Directive. The values for concentration or for the percentage of reduction shall apply.

Parameters	Concentration	Minimum percentage of reduction ([1])	Reference method of measurement
Biochemical oxygen demand (BOD5 at 20°C) without nitrification ([2])	25 mg/l O_2	70–90 40 under Article 4 (2)	Homogenized, unfiltered, undecanted sample. Determination of dissolved oxygen before and after five-day incubation at 20°C ± 1°C, in complete darkness. Addition of a nitrification inhibitor
Chemical oxygen demand (COD)	125 mg/l O_2	75	Homogenized, infiltered, undecanted sample Potassium dichromate
Total suspended solids	35 mg/l ([3]) 35 under Article 4 (2) (more than 10 000 p.e.) 60 under Article 4 (2) (2 000– 10 000 p.e.)	90 ([3]) 90 under Article 4 (2) (more than 10 000 p.e.) 70 under Article (2 000– 10 000 p.e.)	– Filtering of a representative sample through a 0.45 μm filter membrane. Drying at 105°C and weighing – Centrifuging of a representative sample (for at least five mins with mean acceleration of 2,800 to 3,200 g), drying at 105°C and weighing

([1])   Reduction in relation to the load of the influent.

([2])   The parameter can be replaced by another parameter: total organic carbon (TOC) or total oxygen demand (TOD) if a relationship can be established between BOD5 and the substitute parameter.

([3])   This requirement is optional.

Analyses concerning discharges from lagooning shall be carried out on filtered samples; however, the concentration of total suspended solids in unfiltered water samples shall not exceed 150 mg/l.

Table 2: Requirements for discharges from urban waste water treatment plants to sensitive areas which are subject to eutrophication as identified in Annex II.A (a). One or both parameters may be applied depending on the local situation. The values for concentration or for the percentage of reduction shall apply.

Parameters	Concentration	Minimum percentage of reduction ([1])	Reference method of measurement
Total phosphorus	2 mg/l P (10 000–100 000 p.e.) 1 mg/l P (more than 100 000 p.e.)	80	Molecular absorption spectrophotometry
Total nitrogen ([2])	15 mg/l N (10 000–100 000 p.e.) 10 mg/l N (more than 100 000 p.e.) ([3])	70–80	Molecular absorption spectrophotometry

Table 3.16 continued

(^{1}) Reduction in relation to the load of the influent.
(^{2}) Total nitrogen means: the sum of total Kjeldahl-nitrogen (organic N + NH$_3$), nitrate (NO$_3$)-nitrogen and nitrite (NO$_2$)-nitrogen.
(^{3}) Alternatively, the daily average must not exceed 20 mg/l N. This requirement refers to a water temperature of 12°C or more during the operation of the biological reactor of the waste water treatment plant. As a substitute for the condition concerning the temperature, it is possible to apply a limited time of operation, which takes into account the regional climatic conditions. This alternative applies if it can be shown that paragraph 1 of Annex I.D is fulfilled.

Table 3

Series of samples taken in any year	*Maximum permitted number of samples which fail to conform*
4–7	1
8–16	2
17–28	3
29–40	4
41–53	5
54–67	6
68–81	7
82–95	8
96–110	9
111–125	10
126–140	11
141–155	12
156–171	13
172–187	14
188–203	15
204–219	16
220–235	17
236–251	18
252–268	19
269–284	20
285–300	21
301–317	22
318–334	23
335–350	24
351–365	25

ANNEX II

CRITERIA FOR IDENTIFICATION OF SENSITIVE AND LESS SENSITIVE AREAS

A. *Sensitive areas*

A water body must be identified as a sensitive area if it falls into one of the following groups:

(a) natural freshwater lakes, other freshwater bodies, estuaries and coastal waters which are found to be eutrophic or which in the near future may become eutrophic if protective action is not taken.

The following elements may be taken into account when considering which nutrient should be reduced by further treatment:

Table 3.16 continued

(i) lakes and streams reaching lakes/reservoirs/closed bays which are found to have a poor water exchange, whereby accumulation may take place. In these areas, the removal of phosphorus should be included unless it can be demonstrated that the removal will have no effect on the level of eutrophication. Where discharges from large agglomerations are made, the removal of nitrogen may also be considered;

(ii) estuaries, bays and other coastal waters which are found to have a poor water exchange, or which receive large quantities of nutrients. Discharges from small agglomerations are usually of minor importance in those areas, but for large agglomerations, the removal of phosphorus and/or nitrogen should be included unless it can be demonstrated that the removal will have no effect on the level of eutrophication;

(b) surface fresh waters intended for the abstraction of drinking water which could contain more than the concentration of nitrate laid down under the relevant provisions of Council Directive 75/440/EEC of 16 June 1975 concerning the quality required of surface water intended for the abstraction of drinking water in the Member States ([1]) if action is not taken;

(c) areas where further treatment than that prescribed in Article 4 of this Directive is necessary to fulfil Council Directives.

B. Less sensitive areas

A marine water body or area can be identified as a less sensitive area if the discharge of waste water does not adversely affect the environment as a result of morphology, hydrology or specific hydraulic conditions which exist in that area.

When identifying less sensitive areas, Member States shall take into account the risk that the discharged load may be transferred to adjacent areas where it can be cause detrimental environmental effects. Member states shall recognize the presence of sensitive areas outside their national jurisdiction.

The following elements shall be taken into consideration when identifying less sensitive areas:

open bays, estuaries and other coastal waters with a good water exchange and not subject to eutrophication or oxygen depletion or which are considered unlikely to become eutrophic or to develop oxygen depletion due to the discharge of urban waste water.

ANNEX III

INDUSTRIAL SECTORS

1. Milk-processing
2. Manufacture of fruit and vegetable products
3. Manufacture and bottling of soft drinks
4. Potato-processing
5. Meat industry
6. Breweries
7. Production of alcohol and alcoholic beverages
8. Manufacture of animal feed from plant products
9. Manufacture of gelatine and of glue from hides, skin and bones
10. Malt-houses
11. Fish-processing industry

of sea navigation and transport for economic development. The 1973 Action Programme specified four main sources of marine pollution:

- discharge of effluent from land;
- deliberate dumping of waste at sea;
- exploitation of marine and submarine resources, especially exploitation of the seabed;
- sea transport and navigation.

1. Land-based sea pollution

The measures for reducing telluric or land-based sea pollution, that is, effluents discharged directly from the land into the sea, have already been examined in the context of the framework directive of 1976 on pollution caused by the discharge of certain dangerous substances into the aquatic environment of the Community. Reference should also be made to the chapter on international conventions (see p. 403ff) which describes the Community's role in different conventions, such as the Paris Convention for the Prevention of Marine Pollution arising from Land-Based Sources in the North-East Atlantic; the Barcelona Convention for the Protection of the Mediterranean Sea, etc.

2. Dumping of wastes at sea

(a) International conventions

As far as the deliberate dumping of wastes at sea is concerned, there are two major international agreements which are designed to protect the marine environment from this form of pollution, namely:

- The Convention for the Prevention of Marine Pollution by Dumping from Ships and Aircraft, concerning the areas of the north-east Atlantic, the North Sea and their dependent seas, which was signed at Oslo on 15 February 1972 and came into force on 7 April 1974 (Oslo Convention). On 19 December 1978 the Council authorized the Commission to enter into negotiations regarding the participation of the Community in the Oslo Convention.
- The Convention on the Dumping of Wastes at Sea, concerning all the seas in the world, which was signed in London on 13 November 1972 and came into force on 31 August 1975 (London Convention).

(b) The Commission's first proposal for a directive on the dumping of wastes at sea of 1976

On 12 January 1976 the Commission presented the Council with a proposal on the dumping of wastes at sea. This proposal aimed to define the field of application of common rules for the deliberate dumping of waste into the sea in order to prevent and reduce marine pollution as far as possible. Despite several years of discussions, the Council was not able to reach an agreement on this directive proposal.

(c)   The Commission's new proposal for a directive on the dumping of wastes at sea of 1985

On 13 August 1985 the Commission presented a new proposal to the Council which concerned the dumping of wastes at sea[34] and which replaced the 1976 proposal.

The proposal aimed to introduce throughout the Community harmonized common rules which were already the object of various international conventions, or worldwide agreement (London Convention; Marpol Convention), or regional agreements (Barcelona Convention; Bonn Agreement; Oslo Convention). As these conventions had themselves developed considerably, it was necessary to bring the 1976 proposal up to date.

Although all of these international conventions generally had the same objective, i.e. the prevention of the pollution of the sea by the discharge of dangerous substances, their provisions were sometimes different, particularly with regard to the lists of discharges considered as dangerous. This proposal stressed the basic importance of the seas surrounding the Community. One of the main difficulties consisted in trying to impose rules which are applicable to the North Sea or the Mediterranean and vice versa. The importance of the proposal, in the Commission's view, was due to its wide field of application even though radioactive discharges and substances were not included. Since the seas had become an important dumping ground for the discharge of wastes, such discharges should be regulated, restricted, and even prohibited in order to reduce sea pollution, which was becoming an increasingly important economic factor.

The proposal's field of application covered all deliberate discharges of wastes into the sea, as well as the incineration and combustion at sea of wastes or substances. The temporary depositing of wastes on the seabed was also covered. The types of discharge considered were those carried out from ships but also by aircraft or any other means, including platforms. The proposal applied to the marine waters coming under the jurisdiction of the Member States.

The main provisions of the proposal foresaw either a banning of the discharge of the most toxic substances, or a monitoring procedure, the strictness of which would depend on the nature of the substances in question.

The dumping or incineration of the most dangerous substances mentioned in the "black list" was to be forbidden. The dumping of less toxic substances which appear on the "grey list" was to be subject to the prior granting by the relevant authorities of a specific permit.

As far as all other substances are concerned, that is those that do not appear on either the "black" or "grey" list, the discharge of such substances at sea was to be subject to the prior granting of a general permit. This would be granted in the light of the fulfilment of criteria applying to the type of waste concerned, the area in which the discharge was to take place, and the effect on the marine environment. Special consideration would be given to the possible effects on leisure and bathing areas, as well as on waters used for pisciculture and shellfish.

As far as the incineration of wastes at sea is concerned, the proposal stipulated, where there is not a total ban in the case of certain substances, that such incineration can only be authorized if there is no alternative method of treatment or disposal on land. In addition, the Member States must establish, from 1990 onwards, a date after which incineration at sea will be prohibited.

34 OJ No C 245 of 26/9/85.

In spite of the reformulation in 1985 of the original 1976 proposal, the Council's reaction was lukewarm. Delegations questioned the need for Community legislation in an area where, it could be argued, international conventions were already sufficient. Besides raising the issue of "unnecessary duplication" some delegations were also reluctant to see any extension of the Community's competence in maritime matters. In the end, the Commission's proposal was a casualty of the wide-ranging debate over the application of the "subsidiarity" principle which took place in connection with the ratification of the Maastricht Treaty; together with several other proposals in the environmental field, it was officially withdrawn by the Commission in the summer of 1993.[35]

3.   Marine resources exploitation and sea transport

(a)   The Commission's first Communication of 1977 on hydrocarbon pollution

On 9 June 1977 the Commission sent to the Council a Communication and a draft Resolution on the prevention, control and reduction of pollution caused by accidental discharges of hydrocarbons into the sea.

This Communication was drawn up by the Commission following the accident which took place on 22 April 1977 on the drilling rig Bravo-Ekofisk which was situated in an area of the North Sea under the control of the Norwegian authorities. This accident occurred when a safety valve was being attached to the top of a drilling pipe, and resulted in the escape of 20,000 tonnes of oil, the blow-out not being halted until 30 April 1977.

According to the Commission, the Ekofisk accident underlined the need for a more effective policy to fight marine pollution. With this in mind, the Community should have powers and means allowing it to take effective action in such situations, so expressing the solidarity of the Member States among themselves and towards (non-Member) third countries hit by a disaster of this type. In particular the Commission recommended the creation of a data bank at Community level recording the means available for taking action in the event of accidental discharges of hydrocarbons. It also proposed the drawing up of a research programme concerning the technologies for collecting and dispersing hydrocarbons, what happens to hydrocarbons in the sea, and their effects on marine flora and fauna.

The meeting of the Council of Environment Ministers held in June 1977 was not able to examine the Communication and the draft Resolution. However, most of the ideas and proposals contained in the two texts were included some months later in the framework of the action programme presented by the Commission to the Council following the accident of the *Amoco-Cadiz* (see below).

(b)   The Amoco-Cadiz *disaster of 1978*

The ecological, social and economic consequences of the *Amoco-Cadiz* disaster had made the general public acutely aware of the absence of effective measures against marine pollution caused by oil tankers. At the meeting of the Council on 4 April 1978, the French External Affairs minister appealed to the Community to implement a number of practical measures in this area. At its meeting in Copenhagen on 7–8 April 1978 the European Council decided that the Community

35 See OJ No C 228/4 of 24/8/93.

should make the prevention and combating of marine pollution, particularly by hydrocarbons, a major objective. It invited the Council, acting on proposals of the Commission, and the Member States to take appropriate measures within the Community and to adopt common attitudes in the competent international bodies concerning in particular:

- the swift implementation of existing international rules, in particular those regarding minimum standards for the operation of ships;
- the prevention of accidents through coordinated action by the Member States with regard to a satisfactory functioning of the system of compulsory shipping lanes, and more effective control over vessels which do not meet the standards;
- research into and implementation of effective measures to combat pollution.

In response to the decisions of the European Council of Copenhagen, the Commission sent to the Council on 27 April 1978 a second Communication containing a number of proposals on sea pollution caused by the transport of hydrocarbons.

(c) Adoption by the Council in 1978 of an action programme concerning hydrocarbons at sea following the Amoco-Cadiz accident

On 26 June 1978 the Council adopted a Resolution setting up an action programme on the control and reduction of pollution caused by oil spills at sea.[36] This programme requires the Commission to undertake a series of studies in order to establish areas where additional measures are needed to control and reduce this type of pollution. These studies would allow the Commission to present appropriate proposals to the Council in the following six areas:

- (i) computer processing of the existing data, or data still to be collected, on ways of dealing with marine pollution by oil with a view to the immediate use of this data in the event of accidental pollution;
- (ii) the availability of data on tankers likely to pollute the seas surrounding the Community or the coasts of Member States, as well as the artificial structures placed under the jurisdiction of Member States;
- (iii) the adoption of measures allowing for the strengthening of cooperation and effectiveness of emergency teams which have been or which are to be set up by Member States;
- (iv) the possible participation of the Community in the development of clean-up vessels to which might be fitted equipment needed for the effective treatment of oil spills;
- (v) the amendments which may have to be made to the rules of law regarding insurance against the risks of accidental pollution from oil spills;
- (vi) the drawing up of a research programme into the chemical and mechanical means of combating pollution due to oil discharged at sea, and into its effects on marine flora and fauna.

(d) The Commission's decision of 1980 to create a consultative committee on marine pollution caused by hydrocarbons

On 25 June 1980 the Commission decided to set up a consultative committee, made up of government experts, which should advise the Commission on any

[36] OJ No C 162 of 8/7/78.

question connected with marine pollution by hydrocarbons and other dangerous substances.

(e)   Decision of 1981 to create a Community information system on marine pollution caused by hydrocarbons

In the light of the results of the studies undertaken within the framework of the *Amoco-Cadiz* action programme, the Commission sent to the Council on 2 July 1980 a first proposal for a decision on the setting up of a Community information system for the control and reduction of pollution caused by hydrocarbons discharged at sea. The Council adopted this decision on 3 December 1981, but did not include the Commission's suggestion which aimed to create a general computerized inventory on oil tankers. The information system concerns three categories of information, and includes:

● an inventory of the means for combating such pollution;
● a list of national and joint contingency plans, including a brief description of their content and an indication of the relevant authority;
● a compendium of hydrocarbon properties and their behaviours and of methods of treatment of mixtures of water – hydrocarbon solid matter recovered from the seas along the coasts.

The Commission is responsible for implementing the system on the basis of information from Member States. The Commission will make available to all Member States a copy of the information contained in the system. The Commission will produce a regular report on the functioning of the information system and on its use by Member States. The first of these reports was published by the Commission in 1985.

(f)   1986 decision extending the Community information systems of 1981 to include chemical substances other than hydrocarbons

On 2 April 1983 the Commission presented the Council with a proposal modifying the decision of 3 December 1981 on the establishment of a Community information system on the control and reduction of pollution caused by the discharge of hydrocarbons into the sea.

This modification aimed to extend the field of application of the information system, by including dangerous substances other than hydrocarbons. The widening of the substances covered corresponds with the preoccupations caused by a recent and important development in the transport of dangerous chemicals by sea, and the consequent increase in the risk of accidents where such transport is concerned.

As an example, there was the accident which occurred in 1984 to the French cargo ship the *Mont-Louis*, which was carrying uranium hexafluoride and which ran aground off the Belgian coast.

The Council adopted this modification on 6 March 1986.[37] For practical reasons the decision repeats the contents of the earlier Council decision of 1981 which dealt only with hydrocarbons. Where other chemical substances are concerned, the decision basically allows for the drawing up of an inventory of methods of

---

[37] OJ No L 77 of 22/2/86.

intervention in case of an accidental discharge of these substances into the sea. This inventory will include data on the specialized personnel and material means available, including the location and time needed to implement these means. The Commission will be responsible for producing this inventory based on the information provided by the Member States. The Commission will provide a copy of the inventory for each Member State so that the information gathered, which will be regularly updated, will be immediately available in case of emergency anywhere in the Community.

In addition to the inventory dealing with the means available, the decision also calls for the progressive drawing up by the Commission of a collection of information on the different properties and reaction of dangerous substances following an accident at sea.

At its meeting of 3 December 1987, the Environment Council arrived at a considerable measure of agreement on a draft decision intended to extend to inland waters the scope of Decision 86/85. This proposal constituted a first reaction by the Commission to the accidental pollution of the Rhine which occurred near Basle in November 1986. The decision was formally adopted by the Council on 16 June 1988.[38]

(g)   1983 Commission proposal for a directive on the establishment of emergency intervention plans to combat the accidental discharge at sea of hydrocarbons and other dangerous substances

On 27 September 1983, the Commission presented the Council with a proposal on the setting up of emergency intervention plans to combat the accidental discharge of hydrocarbons at sea.[39] In 1984 the Commission proposed to extend the field of application to cover other dangerous substances.[40] This proposal comes into the action programme on the control and reduction of pollution caused by the discharge of hydrocarbons at sea, adopted by the Council on 26 June 1978 (see p. 118). It also completed the decisions of 1981 and 1986 in setting up a Community information system for the control and reduction of pollution caused by the discharge at sea of hydrocarbons and other dangerous substances. The proposal would make it compulsory for Member States to establish emergency intervention plans to combat sea pollution, these plans nevertheless remaining under the exclusive responsibility of the Member States. It specifies the minimum content of the emergency plans, for example, with regard to inventories of risk areas and equipment. The proposal also organizes the cooperation of Member States in case of emergency. With this aim, it establishes an exchange of information on the accidents and on the presence of slicks of hydrocarbons or other substances, and also the drawing up by Member States of joint intervention plans for common areas of sea. Finally it specifies that Member States must test national or joint intervention plans by carrying out regular simulation exercises.

The Council has not yet adopted this directive which appears to cause problems for some Member States with regard to the Community's competence in the areas covered by the proposal.

---

[38] OJ No L 158/32–33 of 25/6/88.
[39] OJ No C 7273 of 12/10/83.
[40] OJ No C 7215 of 16/8/84.

VIII. FUTURE ACTION

1. The 4th Environment Action Programme

During the 4th Action Programme it was envisaged that the Commission would continue the actions already started in the following areas: pollution by dangerous substances, marine pollution and the control and improvement of water quality.

In the area of pollution caused by dangerous substances discharged into the aquatic environment, the Commission would re-examine the advantages and limitations of the so-called "parallel" approach (emission standards and quality objectives), particularly with a view to paying more attention to point or diffuse sources of pollution. Pending the results of this examination, the Commission would accelerate the establishment of values for the 129 substances appearing on the "black list" of the base directive of 1976 (see p. 74). This speeding up would be assisted by the adoption in 1986 of the general application directive (see p. 88).

The Commission would also draw up proposals in the light of experience gained at national level where "grey list" substances are concerned, particularly with regard to lead, copper, nickel and zinc.

In the area of sea pollution, the Commission would give priority to dangerous substances other than oil. It would also see that the different international conventions were applied more effectively, and that there was a better integration of environmental requirements in the policies of maritime transport. Demonstration pilot projects for marine protection against oil pollution and other dangerous substances would be implemented, and the training of those responsible for combating marine pollution would be developed.

As far as the control of pollution and the general improvement of water quality was concerned, the Commission would present new proposals on the control of livestock effluents (see p. 427) and the use of fertilizers and pesticides in agriculture. It also intended to propose the fixing of minimum standards to apply in the long term in all Community waters, as well as the establishing of quality objectives for industrial and agricultural uses of water. Finally, particular attention would be paid to water supply and management, especially in arid regions and islands. The 4th Environmental Action Programme noted that problems are indeed increasingly common in Mediterranean regions, notably in Greece, Spain and Portugal. Actions would be undertaken by the Community in this respect within the framework of the environmental Mediterranean Action Plan (MEDSPA) (see p. 343).

2. The Frankfurt Seminar of June 1988

On 27–28 June 1988, EEC Environment Ministers, the European Commission and high-level officials from the Member States attended a special Ministerial Conference in Frankfurt. The participants agreed, within the context of the Single Act, to expand and intensify Community policy and legislation on the protection and management of Community water resources.

Without prejudice to existing directives, there was support for legislation providing in general for a high ecological standard. At the same time, participants recognized that such a standard could not be made mandatory everywhere in the short term. Key elements would be, *inter alia*, maintenance of the capacity for self-purification, preservation of the diversity of naturally occurring species and the protection of the quality of sediments. With regard to the three main sources of water pollution (industrial, municipal and agricultural), there was broad support for addressing dangerous substances simultaneously and in a complementary way, by the quality objective and emission standard approaches.

The point was also made that, ultimately, the aim should be the elimination of certain dangerous substances from waste water. Until this goal is achieved, emission norms for these substances should be defined on the basis of best available technology (understood to mean the best available technology not entailing excessive costs (BATNEEC)).

Most delegations urged that, in order to speed up the progress, the identification of substances to be included in the "black list" should be decided by unanimity and that the values to be subsequently applied should be decided by qualified majority followed by Article 130S.

The Commission was urged to propose action on a number of substances in parallel, to group similar substances in families and to address specific sectors.

3.   The 5th Environment Action Programme

The 5th Environment Action Programme ("Towards Sustainability – A European Community Programme of Policy and Action in Relation to the Environment and Sustainable Development"), whose "general approach and strategy" was approved by the Council at the meeting of the Environment Council on 15–16 December 1992, indicated that Community policies must aim at:

- prevention of pollution of fresh and marine surface waters and groundwater, with particular emphasis on prevention at source;
- restoration of natural ground and surface waters to an ecologically sound condition, thus ensuring (*inter alia*) a suitable source for extraction of drinking water;
- ensuring that water demand and water supply are brought into equilibrium on the basis of more rational use and management of water resources.

Table 3.17 indicates the overall objectives on water quantity and water quality to be realized in the long term, the targets to be reached in the year 2000 and the actions needed in the short term. They are in line with the programme of action outlined in the The Hague Declaration on the future Community Groundwater Policy as agreed at the EC Ministerial Meeting on 26 and 27 November 1991.[41]

---

[41] As confirmed by Council Resolution on 12/12/91.

Table 3.17: The fifth environment action programme: water quantity and water quality

	Objectives	EC Targets up to 2000	Actions	Time-frame	Actors
Quantitative Aspects Groundwater & Surface fresh water	– Sustainable use of freshwater resources: demand for water should be in balance with its availability	– Prevent permanent overdraft – Integration of resource conservation and sustainable use criteria into other policies, including, in particular, agriculture and land use planning, but also industry (development, location and production procedures) – Marked reduction of pollution of both groundwater and fresh surface water	– Collection and updating of data on groundwater – Monitoring and control measures on groundwater – Integrated water management and protection, including legislation – Measures to protect and rehabilitate aquifers – Measures to promote more effective water use – Economic and fiscal measures	1992/3 by 1995 mid 1993 id id ongoing	MS + LAs id EC + MS + LAs MS MS + EC + sectors + LAs MS + LAs + EC
Qualitative Aspects Groundwater	– To maintain the quality of uncontaminated groundwater – To prevent further contamination of contaminated groundwater – To restore contaminated groundwater to a quality required for drinking water production purposes	– Groundwater: to prevent all pollution from point sources and to reduce pollution from diffuse sources according to best environmental practices and best available technology	– Groundwater and surface fresh water: – strict implementation of the existing directives on urban waste water and nitrate pollution to reduce the input of nutrients to the soil, water and sediments. With regard to fresh water: examination of the need for a directive on phosphate reduction. – Elaboration of further specific emission standards encouraging	continuous 1995 1992 ⇒	MS + LAs EC EC + MS + Industry +

Table 3.17 continued

Objectives	EC Targets up to 2000	Actions	Time-frame	Actors
		the development of production processes and performance standards for products to prevent foreseeable negative effects on water (use of best available technology combined with target standards to be achieved later)		standardization bodies (e.g. CEN)
		– Influence standardization bodies by participation of water industry where concerned	id	id
		– Proposals for progressive replacement of harmful pesticides and progressive use limitations	1993	EC + MS
		– Economic and fiscal measures	ongoing	MS + LAs + EC
Surface water – Fresh water	To maintain a high standard of ecological quality with a biodiversity corresponding as much as possible to the unperturbed state of a given water	– Surface water: quality improvement towards a better ecological quality and safeguard of high quality where it exists		
		– Surface fresh water: proposal for a directive to be presented. Member States' programmes for all waters taking into account their specific situation; practical measures, partly financed through national environment protection funds	1992	EC + MS
– Marine water	Reduction of discharges of all substances, which due to their toxic persistence	– Marine water: objectives and actions similar to the North Sea conference to		
		– Marine water: further to the measures to achieve a high ecological quality and to	1997	MS

Table 3.17 continued

Objectives	EC Targets up to 2000	Actions	Time-frame	Actors
or accumulating impact could negatively affect the environment, to levels which are not harmful to a high standard of ecological quality of all surface waters	other sensitive sea areas of the EC	reduce surface water pollution:		
		* Proposals on maritime transport preventing environmental damage from shipping activities (oil spills, loss of cargo, reduction of operational pollution) to be developed	1993 ⇒	EC + MS
		* Surveillance of geographic zones with appropriate monitoring techniques	ongoing	MS
		* Proposal for a directive on the reduction of operational and accidental pollution from small-tonnage boats	1993 ⇒	EC + MS
		* Economic and fiscal measures	ongoing	MS + EC

Chapter 4

Air

I. INTRODUCTION

1. Generally speaking, the development of Community policy concerning air pollution has very much lagged behind that of water pollution. A difference of approximately five years can be seen between the adoption of the first directive on water pollution and that establishing the first general quality standards for air, which was only approved by the Council in 1980.

Apart from the directives concerning quality objectives or standards, the comparative "delay" in Community air policy is equally clear when it comes to regulations on pollution emissions of industrial origin. So it is that while the framework directive regarding dangerous substances discharged by industry into the aquatic environment dates from 1976, its counterpart in the area of atmospheric pollution coming from industrial installations was only adopted at the end of 1984.

Since 1975 the Council has, nevertheless, adopted certain specific measures contributing to the fight against atmospheric pollution (for example, the 1975 directive on the sulphur content of gas oil). Even so, these measures, which were more related to product standards, were rather of a specific nature, and were directly linked to the objective of allowing free circulation of these products in the Common Market.

The delay apparent in the implementation of a Community policy against atmospheric pollution is largely explained by the oil crisis which struck the world, and Europe in particular, from 1974–1975 onwards. The continual increase in the price of oil, the risk of shortages, and the scarcity or overpricing of light high-quality oils with a low sulphur content made it all the more difficult to reach an agreement within the Council on the Commission's proposals. As an example of these difficulties one has only to look at a Commission proposal for a directive presented in 1975 which aimed to restrict the sulphur content of heavy fuel oils used in power stations. The Council was never able to adopt this proposal, and it eventually had to be officially withdrawn by the Commission.

A second reason for the delay in this important sector in environment policy has to do with the determined opposition shown at that time by certain large countries of the Community regarding the proposals of the Commission. Curiously enough these included Germany, which did not then feel that it could respect the standards established by the directives in certain of its highly industrialized regions (for example, the Ruhr). It is indeed true that such countries would have been forced to implement a large number of costly measures in order to meet the required standards.

It was only on 15 March 1980 that the first directive establishing atmospheric quality standards of a general nature for sulphur dioxide and suspended particulates was finally approved by the Council. The adoption of this first directive was very probably facilitated by the external pressure represented by the fact that in Geneva in 1979 almost all the countries in Western and Eastern Europe (including the USSR), plus the United States, Canada, and the Community itself, had signed a Convention on Long-Range Transboundary Air Pollution (see p. 412). This external event, and in particular the signing of this important convention by the Community, to some extent forced the Council to speed up its work and to arrive at an initial agreement.

2. From 1983–1984 onwards, a total change of direction took place with regard to policy on air pollution. This has now become an issue of major concern, and is a priority sector in Community Environment Policy. The new direction can of course be largely explained by the considerable damage caused to forests by acid rain in the northern countries of the Community, and in particular in Germany. Indeed before 1983–1984, the damage caused by acid rainfall due mainly to air pollution, had only affected the Scandinavian peninsula. It was not until the early 1980s that the phenomenon reached Germany, both ecologically and politically speaking. This country found itself obliged to take Draconian measures against air pollution and led the Community itself to adopt such measures. Even if most Community measures do not go as far as the German government might have wished, they do nevertheless have a much wider field of application, so increasing the effectiveness of the fight against atmospheric pollution, which by its very nature recognizes no borders. What is more, as far as standards to be applied to products are concerned (motor vehicles or fuels, for example), Community measures make it possible to avoid a split in the Common Market which would have many major consequences, at the very time when the Community wants to achieve a true interior market.

The renewal of interest by the Community in the air sector was particularly evident in June 1983 at the European Council session in Stuttgart which brought together the Heads of State and Government of the Member States, and which asked that immediate actions be taken with a view to fighting the serious dangers threatening European forests because of air pollution. In connection with this it should be noted that in 1983 the European Council, the orienting body and supreme decision-maker of the Community, followed the German initiative and looked for a second time at the theme of environmental protection. (The first time that it had applied itself to a question specifically linked to environmental protection was after the *Amoco-Cadiz* disaster in 1978 which led the Heads of State and Government, at France's request, to launch a Community programme in the area of marine pollution; see p. 118.)

Already a matter of serious concern to governments, in 1985 air pollution became equally an environmental theme which, for what was certainly the first time in Europe, directly affected and concerned a majority of Community citizens, particularly motorists. In 1985 the question of introducing a "clean car" was not only an issue of considerable economic importance, but also of direct personal concern to a large number of Community citizens. Indeed for the first time a link was established at the level of the ordinary citizen between the rather abstract theme of environmental protection and the daily use by Mr Average of an object dear to his heart, namely his car. The questions of the introduction of lead-free petrol and the drastic reduction of pollutants coming from motor vehicles have not only aroused a great interest, but have also resulted in a certain degree of environmental awareness in public opinion in many Community countries. The importance of new Community standards with regard to car pollution justifies the special place which they occupy in this book in the chapter on air pollution.

3. In conclusion, it can be said that as far as air pollution policy is concerned, the Community is beginning to make up for the "delay" suffered in comparison with the other areas of Community Environment Policy. This attempt to make up for lost time is illustrated in particular by the adoption in 1984 and 1985 of new directives establishing general quality standards for lead and nitrogen oxide in air. However, a fundamental test of the desire of Member States to make progress in the fight against atmospheric pollution was the agreement which the Council reached at its meeting of 28–29 June 1988 on the limitation of emissions of pollutants into the air coming from large combustion installations, i.e. coal, oil or gas-fired thermal power stations (see p. 156).

II. AIR QUALITY STANDARDS

1. Quality standards for sulphur dioxide

(a) Public health "criteria"[1]

The 1973 1st Action Programme dealt with the evaluation of risks to human health and the environment by pollution. Priority was given to so-called "first category" pollutants, which were chosen on the grounds both of their toxicity and of the current state of scientific knowledge of their significance in the health and ecological fields. As far as air pollution is concerned, sulphur dioxide and suspended particulate matter in the atmosphere were considered as "first category" pollutants, i.e. as requiring priority consideration.

On 19 February 1976 the Commission presented the Council with a draft resolution on the determination of "criteria" for sulphur dioxide and suspended particulate matter in urban atmospheres. In the Commission's view, these two pollutants were among those substances for which an objective evaluation of the scientific data available could be carried out with the certainty necessary for the development of "criteria" for the public health aspects.

(b) The establishment of air quality standards (1980)

On the basis of these criteria the Commission also put a proposal to the Council on 19 February 1976 for a directive concerning the setting of health protection standards for sulphur dioxide and suspended particulate matter in urban atmospheres.

The Council was not able to adopt this directive[2] until 15 July 1980, after more than four years of long and difficult discussions, and to a certain extent under the

---

[1] In the terminology of the 1973 Environmental Action Programme the term "criteria" is used to describe "the relationship between the exposure of the target to pollution or nuisance, and the risk and/or the magnitude of the adverse or undesirable effect resulting from the exposure in given circumstances".

[2] OJ No L 229 of 30/8/90.

external pressure provided by the signing by the Community in 1979 of the Geneva Convention on Long-Range Transboundary Air Pollution (see p. 412). The directive adopted by the Council does however have a wider field of application than that proposed by the Commission, since it is not restricted to urban atmospheres alone, but involves all of the territory of the Member States. The directive sets "limit values" and "guide values" for sulphur dioxide and suspended particulate matter in the atmosphere, together with the conditions for their application, with the aim of improving the protection of human health and the environment. Details of the limit and guide values are given in Table 4.1.

The "limit values" are defined as concentrations in sulphur dioxide (SO_2) and in suspended particulate matter which must not be exceeded through the territory of the Member State during set periods, with a view to the protection of human health in particular. The "guide values" are intended to serve as long-term precautions for health and the environment and as reference points for the establishment of specific schemes within zones determined by the Member States. The directive required Member States as of 1 April 1983 to take appropriate measures to respect the limit values set. It nevertheless makes provision for certain exceptions under strictly defined conditions. This is why Member States which could not respect the limit values in certain zones had to inform the Commission before 1 October 1982, sending details of plans for the progressive improvement of the quality of the environment in those zones. These plans had to include concrete measures enabling the limit values to be respected as soon as possible, and by 1 April 1983 at the latest.

The directive also provides for a procedure of prior consultation between Member States for the fixing of values to apply in border regions. The Commission may attend such consultations. In this respect the directive constitutes one of the first Community rulings to make such a provision for transboundary pollution.

Finally, while making provision for a reference method of sampling and analysis, the directive allows the Member States a certain freedom to choose other methods of measurement. However, in order to avoid any distortion or discrimination, the Commission was given the responsibility of checking the results of the measurements made by methods other than the reference method. The Commission's first synthesis report on the application of the directive was published in March 1985. It covered the period 1983–1985 and showed that numerous problems still exist. The Commission therefore planned to launch a common measurement programme with a view to arriving at a more harmonized application of the directive. The second Commission report was published at the end of 1986. A series of further annual reports followed.

(c)   The 1980 Council Resolution on transboundary pollution

At the same time as the Council adopted the directive on air quality standards for SO_2 and suspended particulates, it also approved a general Resolution according to which Member States will endeavour to limit, and as far as possible gradually reduce and prevent, transboundary air pollution by sulphur dioxide and suspended particulates.[3]

---

[3] OJ No C 222 of 30/8/80.

Table 4.1: Council Directive of 15 July 1980 Air quality limit values and guide values for sulphur dioxide and suspended particulates in the atmosphere

LIMIT VALUES FOR SULPHUR DIOXIDE AND SUSPENDED PARTICULATES

(As measured by the black-smoke method)

TABLE A

Limit values for sulphur dioxide expressed in $\mu g/m^3$ with the associated values for suspended particulates (as measured by the black-smoke method ([1])) expressed in $\mu g/m^3$

Reference period	Limit value for sulphur dioxide	Associated value for suspended particulates
Year	80 (median of daily mean values taken throughout the year)	> 40 (median of daily mean values taken throughout the year)
	120 (median of daily mean values taken throughout the year)	≤ 40 (median of daily mean values taken throughout the year)
Winter (1 October to 31 March)	130 (median of daily mean values taken throughout the winter)	> 60 (median of daily mean values taken throughout the winter)
	180 (median of daily mean values taken throughout the winter)	≤ 60 (median of daily mean values taken throughout the winter)
Year (made up of units of measuring periods of 24 hours)	250 ([2]) (98 percentile of all daily mean values taken throughout the year)	> 150 (98 percentile of all daily mean values taken throughout the year)
	350 ([2]) (98 percentile of all daily mean values taken throughout the year)	≤ 150 (98 percentile of all daily mean values taken throughout the year)

([1]) The results of the measurements of black smoke taken by the OECD method have been converted into gravimetric units as described by the OECD (see Annex III).

([2]) Member States must take all appropriate steps to ensure that this value is not exceeded for more than three consecutive days. Moreover, Member States must endeavour to prevent and to reduce any such instances in which this value has been exceeded.

Table 4.1 continued

TABLE B

Limit values for suspended particulates (as measured by the black-smoke method (^{1})) expressed in μg/m^3

Reference period	Limit value for suspended particulates
Year	80 (median of daily mean values taken throughout the year)
Winter (1 October to 31 March)	130 (median of daily mean values taken throughout the winter)
Year (made up of units of measuring periods of 24 hours)	250 (^{2}) (98 percentile of all daily mean values taken throughout the year)

(^{1}) The results of the measurements of black smoke taken by the OECD method have been converted into gravimetric units as described by the OECD (see Annex III).
(^{2}) Member States must take all appropriate steps to ensure that this value is not exceeded for more than three consecutive days. Moreover, Member States must endeavour to prevent and to reduce any such instances in which this value has been exceeded.

GUIDE VALUES FOR SULPHUR DIOXIDE AND SUSPENDED PARTICULATES

(as measured by the black-smoke method)

TABLE A

(Guide values for sulphur dioxide expressed in μg/m^3)

Reference period	Guide value for sulphur dioxide
Year	40 to 60 (arithmetic mean of daily mean values taken throughout the year)
24 hours	100 to 150 (daily mean value)

TABLE B

Guide values for suspended particulates (as measured by the black-smoke method (^{1})) expressed in μg/m^3

Reference period	Guide value for suspended particulates
Year	40 to 60 (arithmetic mean of daily mean values taken throughout the year)
24 hours	100 to 150 (daily mean value)

(^{1}) The results of the measurements of black smoke taken by the OECD method have been converted into gravimetric units as described by the OECD (see Annex III).

2.   Air quality standards for lead

(a)   Public health "criteria"

The 1973 Action Programme classified lead and its compounds as "first category" pollutants requiring priority consideration. The Commission sent a Communication to the Council on 16 April 1975 concerning the toxic effects of lead on man. Basing itself on the relationship established between "dose and effect", i.e. the quantity of lead absorbed on the one hand, and the effect determined on man on the other, the Commission drew up public health criteria intended to be used for the protection of individuals from lead. At the same time as the Communication, and in the light of the health criteria, the Commission also submitted two directive proposals to the Council on 16 April 1975. The first concerned the fixing of biological standards for lead in man, as well as the screening of the population for lead. The second fixed air quality standards for lead.

(b)   Screening of the population for lead (1977)

The first proposal for a directive was only partially accepted by the Council on 29 March 1977.[4] The Council refused to fix biological standards relating to the maximum concentrations of lead in the blood. It restricted the directive's field of application to a simple common procedure for biological screening in order to assess the exposure of the population to lead outside the working environment. The biological screening consisted of taking a measurement of the blood lead levels based on blood sampling carried out on volunteers from three categories: people from urban areas with more than 0.5 million inhabitants; people exposed to significant sources of lead pollution; critical groups. The sampling of the three categories of people was to be carried out during at least two campaigns, in 1979 and 1983, in each area investigated simultaneously. In assessing the results of the biological screening the Member States had to consider certain blood lead reference levels fixed by the directive. Where the results of the analyses indicated that the reference levels had been exceeded in one or more cases, Member States had to trace the exposure sources responsible for the level being exceeded and take appropriate measures. This investigation would concern anyone having a blood lead level over 35 microgrammes per 100 millilitres of blood.

During these sampling campaigns, more than 1800 volunteers were examined. These were made up of an equal number of men and women and a significant percentage of children. More than 50 laboratories in the Community took part in the programme of verifying the analyses and the screening campaign covered 168 geographical zones and separate groups of people.

The conclusions of this biological screening revealed that generally speaking the blood lead level measured was lower than might have been expected on the basis of earlier studies. However, the tests carried out in urban areas not including specific known sources of lead (sources of incidental emissions from industry or lead pipes) seemed to indicate that there was particular risk to the population, according to the reference values of the directive. Moreover, the analyses carried out in areas where the specific sources of lead were known and involving, in particular, critical groups of the population (e.g. children of lead workers, or children living near a factory

4   OJ No L 105 of 28/4/77.

working with lead) confirmed that there could be a health danger since the reference levels were exceeded in several cases.

(c)   Establishment of air quality standards for lead (1982)

The second proposal sent by the Commission to the Council on 16 April 1975 aimed to establish air quality standards for lead with the intention of protecting public health. These standards were determined according to the maximum concentrations of lead below which lead has no specific effects on the lungs. The Commission proposed two standards: one to be respected in residential urban zones and in zones exposed to sources of lead in the air other than from car traffic; the other, less stringent, to be respected, in zones exposed to car traffic.

On 3 December 1982, after seven years of consideration and discussion, the Council finally adopted a directive establishing a limit value for lead in the air.[5] Unlike the Commission proposal which made provision for two values, the directive retains only one limit value for lead in air. The aim of this limit value is specifically to help protect human beings against the effects of lead in the environment, and does not apply to occupational exposure in the work-place. The limit value set by the Council is 2 microgrammes of lead per cubic metre, expressed as an annual mean concentration, with the understanding that Member States may fix a more stringent value for their own territories. Member States had a period of five years after notification of the directive in which to respect the set value of 2 microgrammes.

The structure of the directive retained by the Council is largely based on that of the 1980 directive on sulphur dioxide, particularly with regard to the approach of progressive improvement of the air quality in certain zones of the territory of a Member State.

If a Member State considers that in certain zones it will not be able to respect the set limit value within the period allowed, it must inform the Commission. In this case, the Member State concerned will have to draw up plans for the progressive improvement of the quality of the air in the zones in question. These plans must contain concrete measures and procedures which make it possible for the concentrations of lead in the atmosphere to be brought down to the limit value of 2 microgrammes, as soon as possible, and at the latest within seven years of notification of the directive, i.e. December 1989.

The directive required Member States to install sampling stations at places where individuals may be exposed continually for a long period and where there is a danger of the limit value being exceeded. The directive also establishes the characteristics to be respected for the choice of sampling and analysis procedures. The Commission must publish a regular report on the application of the directive by the Member States.

3.   Air quality standards for nitrogen dioxide

(a)   The 1985 directive fixing air quality standards

Following the extensive work carried out on nitrogen oxides within the framework of the 1973 Action Programme, the Commission sent a proposal to the Council on

---

[5]   OJ No L 378 of 31/1/82.

13 September 1983 which aimed to fix air quality standards for nitrogen dioxide with a view to improving the health of man and contributing to the protection of the environment.

The Council adopted the directive on 7 March 1985.[6] This directive, the general structure of which is largely similar to that of the 1980 directive on sulphur dioxide (see p. 128) and that of the 1982 directive on lead (see p. 133), provided for the fixing of both limit values and guide values (see Table 4.2).

Table 4.2: Council Directive of 7 March 1988
Air quality standards for nitrogen dioxide

LIMIT VALUE FOR NITROGEN DIOXIDE

(The value limit shall be expressed in $\mu g/m^3$. The volume must be standardized at the following conditions of temperature and pressure: 293°K and 101.3 kPa)

Reference period (^{1})	Limit value for nitrogen dioxide
Year	200
	98th percentile calculated from the mean values per hour or per period of less than an hour recorded throughout the year (^{2})

(^{1}) The annual reference period begins on 1 January in any given calendar year and ends on 31 December.

(^{2}) To ensure that the validity of the calculation of the 98th percentile is recognized, 75% of the possible values must be available and, as far as possible, distributed uniformly throughout the year in question for that particular measurement site.
In cases where the values measured on certain sites are not available over a period exceeding 10 days, the calculated percentile must mention this fact.

The calculation of the 98th percentile on the basis of the values recorded throughout the year is to be carried out as follows: the 98th percentile must be calculated from the values actually measured. The measured values should be rounded off to the nearest $\mu g/m^3$. All the values are to be listed in increasing order for each site:

$$X_1 \leqslant X_2 \leqslant X_3 \leqslant \ldots \ldots \ldots \leqslant X_k \leqslant \ldots \ldots \ldots \leqslant X_{N-1} \leqslant X_N$$

The 98th percentile is the value of the component of rank k where k is calculated from the following formula:

$$k = (q \times N)$$

where q is equal to 0.98 for the 98th percentile and to 0.50 for the 50th percentile, N being the number of values actually measured. The value of (q x N) should be rounded off to the nearest whole number.

Where measuring equipment does not yet allow the production of discrete values but provides only classes of values higher than 1 $\mu g/m^3$, the Member State concerned may, for the calculation of the percentile, use an interpolation, provided that the interpolation formula is accepted by the Commission and that the classes of values are not higher than 10 $\mu g/m^3$. This temporary waiver is only valid for equipment currently installed for a time span not exceeding the life of the equipment and in any case limited to 10 years from the application of this Directive.

[6] OJ No L 87 of 27/3/85.

Table 4.2 continued

GUIDE VALUES FOR NITROGEN DIOXIDE

(The value limit shall be expressed in $\mu g/m^3$. The volume must be standardized at the following conditions of temperature and pressure: 293°K and 101, 3 kPa)

Reference period	Guide values for nitrogen dioxide
	50
Year	50th percentile calculated from the mean values per hour or per period of less than an hour recorded throughout the year
	135
	98th percentile calculated from the mean values per hour or per period of less than an hour recorded throughout the year

The formula given in footnote (^{2}) of Annex 1 must be used in calculating these percentiles, the value of q being 0.50 for the 50th percentile and 0.98 for the 98th percentile.

The guide values, more stringent than the limit value, are intended in particular to serve as reference points for the establishment of specific schemes within certain zones determined by the Member States. They are intended especially to contribute to long-term environmental protection. The directive does not apply to the occupational exposure of workers or to the interior of buildings. The imperative limit value, i.e. 200 microgrammes per cubic metre, was established in the light of the work of the World Health Organization and is specifically aimed at the protection of human beings from the effects of nitrogen dioxide in the air.

The Member States must respect the limit value set from 1 July 1987 onwards. However, when this limit value is likely to be exceeded in certain zones, the Member States concerned must inform the Commission and forward plans for the gradual improvement of the quality of the air in those zones. The plans had to contain measures and procedures aimed at respecting the limit values set as soon as possible, and by 1 January 1994 at the latest.

The directive authorizes Member States to set more stringent values than those of the directive if they so wish. This provision applies, for example, to zones where urban or industrial development has taken place, and for which a Member State considers it necessary to limit pollution by fixing a more stringent limit value than that of the directive. Similarly, a Member State can fix values which are lower than the guide values in zones afforded special environmental protection.

The directive also includes a standstill clause according to which the measures taken by Member States, pursuant to this directive, must not lead to a significant deterioration in the quality of the air in zones outside urban areas, where the level of pollution by nitrogen dioxide is low in relation to the limit value laid down.

In order to measure the concentrations of nitrogen dioxide in the environment, Member States must set up measuring stations, particularly in zones where the limit value is exceeded or is likely to be exceeded. In this respect, Member States must take into consideration zones predominantly affected by pollution from motor vehicles and which are situated in the vicinity of roads carrying heavy traffic, and also more extensive zones in which discharges from fixed sources also make a significant contribution to pollution by nitrogen dioxide.

Apart from the requirements concerning the installation of measuring stations, the directive also contains a reference method for the analysis of measures of concentrations of nitrogen dioxide. The Member States can however use another method of analysis, provided that they show the Commission that it is equivalent to the reference method.

Member States must inform the Commission of instances in which the limit value has been exceeded, giving the reasons and the measures they have taken to deal with them. Other information must be communicated to the Commission at its request, concerning, for example, the concentrations measured, or the values fixed in the zones afforded special protection. The directive also requires the Member States to make this information available to the public.

The directive also includes an article on cross-border pollution, according to which any Member State proposing to fix values for nitrogen dioxide in protected border regions must organize prior consultations with the other Member State concerned. Member States must also hold consultations in case of cross-border pollution when the limit values of the directive or the particular values of specific border regions have been exceeded or are likely to be exceeded following significant pollution originating from another Member State. In both cases the Commission must be informed and may attend the consultations.

Finally, the directive requires the Commission to publish a regular synthesis report on the application of the directive by the Member States.

(b)   Commission Communication on the fixing of long-term limit values for nitrogen dioxide (1985)

In adopting the "nitrogen dioxide" directive on 7 March 1985, the Council invited the Commission to present a report on the establishment of long-term limit values for nitrogen dioxide, taking into particular consideration the protection of the environment, and if necessary to submit a proposal on this. In a Communication addressed to the Council on 15 July 1985, the Commission considered that it was not appropriate to fix a long-term limit value for nitrogen dioxide specifically intended to protect land and aquatic ecosystems due to the insufficient scientific knowledge and lack of available studies on cost/benefits. The Commission also felt that it was not necessary at this stage to strengthen the long-term guide value fixed by the directive of 7 March 1985. However, the Commission indicated that it would intensify its research and monitoring activities for nitrogen dioxide, and that it would prepare proposals on the combating of photochemical atmospheric pollutants.

4.   Proposal for a Council directive on ambient air quality assessment and management[7]

On 4 July 1994 the Commission forwarded to the Council and Parliament the above proposal which addressed the need for a harmonized assessment and management of ambient air quality throughout the Community. It aims to define a strategy which

---

[7] COM (94) 109 final of 4/7/94.

limits or prevents harmful effects of air pollution on human health and the environment. It sets out the principles to be used to:

- fix objectives for ambient air quality in the European Community;
- assess the air quality in a uniform manner;
- make information on air pollution available to the public;
- maintain or improve ambient air quality.

Under Article 4, the Commission would be required to submit to the Council proposals for ambient air quality objectives not later than 31 December 1996 for sulphur dioxide (SO_2); nitrogen dioxide/oxides (NO_2/NOx); Black Smoke (BS); Suspended Particulate Matter (SPM) and lead. For ozone, the Commission would submit proposals for ambient air quality objectives in accordance with Article 8 of the Council Directive 92/72/EEC. For carbon monoxide (CO); cadmium (Cd); acid deposition; benzene (C_6H_6), poly-aromatic hydrocarbons (PAH), arsenic (As), fluoride and nickel (Ni) the Commission would submit proposals not later than 31 December 1999.

Once quality objectives are set, measurement would be mandatory in areas with agglomerations of more than 250,000 inhabitants with a population density of more than 1000 inhabitants per km^2 and in areas of poor and improving air quality. Steps would have to be taken by the Member States to ensure that the Community limit values are not exceeded according to the timetables set in the individual directives adopted under the provisions of Article 4.

III.   PRODUCT QUALITY STANDARDS

In the light of a Communication from the Commission of 3 April 1974 concerning problems of pollution due to the production of energy, the Council adopted on 3 March 1975[8] a general resolution on the relationship between energy and the environment, including nuclear energy. This resolution listed a certain number of principles and gave guidelines for possible actions. It also foresaw certain actions concerning in particular thermal discharges, and emissions of sulphur dioxide and nitrogen oxide. In the area of sulphur dioxide, the resolution announced initiatives aimed at reducing the sulphur content of gas oils and regulations on the use of heavy fuel oils.

1.   Sulphur content of gas oils

(a)   The 1975 directive fixing the sulphur content of gas oils

The consumption of gas oil having substantially increased in the Community, the Commission sent a directive proposal to the Council on 13 February 1974 concerning the approximation of the laws of the Member States relating to the sulphur content of certain liquid fuels such as gas oils.

---

[8] OJ No C 168 of 25/7/75.

The Council adopted this directive on 24 November 1975.[9] In order to arrive at a reduction in sulphur dioxide emissions caused by gas oil fuels, the directive defines two type of gas oil according to their sulphur content.

The directive, which does not concern gas oils used in power stations or by shipping, stipulated that from 1 October onwards only two qualities of gas oil could be allowed within the internal market of the Community:

- low sulphur gas oil, or type A, for which the sulphur content must not exceed 0.5% as of 1 October 1976, and then 0.3% as of 1 October 1980; this low sulphur gas oil was not subject to any restrictions on use in the Member States;
- type B gas oil was intended for use in zones either where atmospheric pollution by sulphur dioxide was sufficiently low, or where gas oil accounted for an insignificant proportion of atmospheric sulphur dioxide pollution. It was up to Member States to determine the zones in which the use of type B higher sulphur gas oil was permitted. The Member States must send the Commission the list of zones concerned and the criteria used for the choice of the zones.

This solution offered a certain degree of flexibility which was partly justified by the difficult energy situation being experienced at that time by the Community with its supply of crude oil.

(b)   The 1987 directive reducing the sulphur content of gas oils

On 28 July 1985 the Commission sent a proposal to the Council which modified the directive of 24 November 1975 on the sulphur content of gas oils.[10] In line with its general air pollution policy, the Commission proposed to reduce the limit values for the sulphur content of gas oil which were fixed by the directive of 1975, that is, before the damage caused by atmospheric pollution had reached a considerable level in certain regions of the Community. The gas oils in question included heating oil for domestic, commercial or industrial use, as well as diesel fuel. Although the use of gas oil represented a relatively small proportion of sulphur dioxide (SO_2) emissions as a whole, it could be the cause of important specific problems, e.g. in urban centres, particularly under unfavourable meteorological conditions.

The Council adopted the directive on 20 March 1987.[11] The directive makes provisions, first, for the reduction of the limit value for the sulphur content of all gas oils to 0.3% in all Member States, thereby doing away with the old distinction made by the 1975 directive between type A low sulphur gas oil used in all zones, and type B intended for use in zones where pollution is low (see above). Secondly, unlike the 1975 directive, the directive allows Member States wishing to do so to enforce the use of gas oil with a sulphur content below 0.3%, but not lower than 0.2%, in certain zones of their territories or throughout their territories, when there are serious environmental problems.

(c)   The 1993 directive introducing a single limit value

On 22 June 1991 the Commission submitted to the Council a proposal for a directive, proposing the creation of a single limit value for the sulphur content of gas oil.

---

[9] OJ No L 307 of 27/11/75.

[10] OJ No C 205 of 14/8/85.

[11] OJ No L 91 of 3/4/87.

The objective was to ensure ground-level atmospheric concentrations are kept within the limit values set by Directive 80/779 and to ensure compatibility with the reductions in emissions of gaseous and particulate pollutants from diesel engines set out in the Commission's 1990 proposals to amend Directive 88/77 on particulate emissions from diesel engines (see p. 149). Whilst noting that the total consumption of gas oil had remained constant since 1980, the Commission pointed out that though use of gas oils for domestic heating was expected to decline, their use as diesel fuel was forecast to continue increasing. Emissions from gas oils accounted for only 5% of total EC SO_2 emissions, which in the decade 1980–1990 fell by some 30%, but at ground level such emissions could have a greater impact on urban air. The draft directive proposed further reductions in the sulphur content of gas oils used for heating, in industry and in diesel engines, besides proposing limits for those gas oils used in fishing and coastal shipping. The proposal made a distinction between automotive diesel fuels and gas oils used for heating, industrial and marine purposes. It proposed to reduce the sulphur content of both categories in two stages:

Diesel fuels:

● from 1 October 1994 sulphur content should not exceed 0.20%
● from 1 October 1996 sulphur content should not exceed 0.05%

Other gas oils:
● from 1 October 1994 sulphur content should not exceed 0.20%
● from 1 October 1999 sulphur content should not exceed 0.10%

Member States would be required to ensure the availability and balanced distribution of 0.05% diesel fuel by 1 October 1995.

The proposal was adopted in March 1993 as Directive 93/12.[12]

2.   Sulphur content of heavy fuels

On 19 December 1975 the Commission sent the Council a proposal on the use of fuel oils with a view to reducing sulphur emissions.[13] This proposal aimed to define the conditions of use for fuel oils with a low sulphur content, i.e. not exceeding 2% from 1978, and 1% from 1983 onwards. It required Member States to create so-called special protection zones in regions where high levels of sulphur dioxide are measured. The proposal made provision for the permanent use of low sulphur fuel oil in the special protected zones and for its temporary use outside these zones in certain unfavourable conditions. This proposal resulted in objections from several Member States, and no progress was made during the examination of the proposal by the Council of Environment Ministers in 1977.

In 1981 the Commission announced that it was withdrawing the proposal. The large reduction in the consumption of heavy fuel oils since 1974 due to the increase in the price of oil had somewhat lessened the usefulness of the proposal. Indeed, the energy policy of the Community was tending to reduce the consumption of crude oil through more rational use of energy, and greater recourse to nuclear and

---

[12] OJ No L 74 of 27/3/93.
[13] OJ No C 54 of 8/3/76.

coal-fired energies. Subsequently, in an attempt to strengthen measures against acid rain, the Commission indicated that it was examining the possibility of drawing up a new proposal intended to reduce sulphur emissions by regulating the conditions of use of liquid fuels (heavy fuel oil) and solid fuels (coal) in installations not covered by the directive proposal on "large combustion plants" (see p. 156).

3.   Lead in petrol

On 5 December 1973 the Commission sent the Council a proposal on the approximation of the laws of the Member States concerning the composition of petrol.

Lead emissions from motor vehicles represented a significant proportion of the total quantity of lead released into the atmosphere, especially in large towns, and could thus be the cause of serious difficulties from the point of view of environmental protection and public health.

The disparity between the legal and administrative provisions of the Member States governing the lead content of petrol was also likely to create obstacles to the free movement of both fuel and motor vehicles within the Community.

The Council did not adopt this directive until 29 June 1978.[14] It stipulates that from 1 January 1981 onwards the maximum authorized lead content of "regular" or "premium" petrol put on the internal market of the Community should not exceed 0.40 grammes per litre. However, any Member State may require the petrol sold on its territory to have a lead content inferior to the general standard of 0.40 grammes per litre, provided that this is not lower than 0.15 grammes per litre. This provision was included in view of the situation in Germany where the lead content had already been reduced to 0.15 grammes per litre. In the other countries of the Community, however, the average level was well above 0.40 grammes per litre. The directive specified that Member States must take any appropriate measures to ensure that the reduction of the level of lead does not cause a significant increase in the quantity of other pollutants in the petrol, such as benzene, for example, or a deterioration in the quality of the petrol.

The 1978 directive was only meant to be a first stage in the move towards the approximation of the laws of the Member States in this area. This is why at the time of its adoption the Commission pointed out that it would take into account, in its future proposals on the lead content of petrol, the need not only to reduce still further emissions of lead into the atmosphere, but also to improve the workings of the internal market of the Community by reducing the differences between the lead content levels permitted in the different Member States.

Shortly after 1981, the date of the compulsory implementation of the 0.40 grammes per litre standard, pressure was therefore brought to bear in favour of the lowering of this content, and more generally in favour of lead-free petrol. The European Parliament adopted several resolutions asking the Commission to propose measures in order to introduce lead-free petrol into the Community, and to make the use of such petrol compulsory for new vehicles. All of the problems associated with the question of lead-free petrol are examined in the following section entitled "The Introduction of 'Clean' Vehicles into the Community".

[14] OJ No L 197 of 22/7/78.

IV. THE INTRODUCTION OF "CLEAN" VEHICLES INTO THE COMMUNITY

The concept of "clean" vehicles covers a group of measures taken or envisaged by the Community, in order not only to encourage the use of lead-free petrol, but also and especially to reduce the pollutants contained in motor vehicle exhaust gases. With this aim the Commission presented to the Council in 1984 two directive proposals concerning the introduction of lead-free petrol and the regulation of gaseous pollutants from motor vehicles up to 3.5 tonnes (including vans). At the request of the Council, the Commission also submitted a series of proposals in 1986 for directives covering both the roadworthiness tests for motor vehicles, and the regulation of particulate emissions from diesel cars and the exhaust fumes of lorries and buses.

A. 1984: the Commission's proposals on lead-free petrol and car exhaust fumes
On 6 June 1984 the Commission presented simultaneously to the Council two proposals[15] aimed at amending existing Community regulations on the lead content of petrol and on air pollution from car exhaust fumes.

These proposals were intended to respond to the directions of the Stuttgart European Council of June 1983 which stressed the urgent need to confront the danger threatening the European forest areas. Although there had been a Community regulation on motor vehicles' exhaust since the adoption in 1970 of a specific directive in this area,[16] a directive which had moreover been constantly improved and strengthened, it was clear that in the 1980s the legislation on car pollution was in many ways less stringent in the Community than in most other industrialized countries (USA, Japan). This is why the Commission suggested in 1984 the total elimination of lead from petrol, together with a reduction by nearly 70% compared with existing legislation, i.e. the 1983 Directive 351/EEC, of harmful emission of the following three pollutants: carbon monoxide; nitrogen oxide; and unburnt hydrocarbons.

The general aims on which the Commission based its proposals were:

- to establish the objectives to be achieved with the aim of protecting health and the environment, without actually specifying the technical means needed to respect those objectives;
- to maintain the unity of the Common Market in the two basic sectors of the car market and the oil (product) market, while respecting the rules of the treaty.

1. The 1985 directive on the lead content of petrol and the introduction of lead-free petrol

The Council adopted the directive on the lead content of petrol and the introduction of lead-free petrol, on 20 March 1985.[17]

This directive, which from the legal point of view abrogates the previous 1978 directive on the lead content of petrol (see p. 140), concerns both leaded and unleaded petrol.

---

[15] OJ No C 178 of 6/7/84.
[16] Directive 70/220/EEC (OJ No L 76 of 6/4/70).
[17] OJ No L 96 of 3/4/85.

As far as leaded petrol is concerned, the directive returns to the maximum permitted lead (compound) content level fixed by the 1978 directive, i.e. a lead content of between 0.40 and 0.15 grammes per litre of petrol. It also stipulates that Member States are to reduce the lead content of petrol to 0.15 grammes per litre as soon as they judge it appropriate. The directive sets out the general principle according to which the Member States must continue to guarantee the availability on their territory of leaded petrol; it also makes provisions for exemption conditions in cases of difficulties in supply of oil products.

As far as lead-free petrol is concerned, which represents the major new aspect of the directive, Member States must ensure the compulsory introduction and balanced distribution within their territories of this new type of petrol from 1 October 1989. The directive states that the introduction of lead-free petrol can be done on a voluntary basis prior to 1 October 1989. It also establishes the octane number for "premium" lead-free petrol, i.e. 95.0 "research octane" as the minimum number at the pump.

The directive also fixes as of 1 October 1989 the benzene content of leaded and unleaded petrol at 5% maximum by volume.

2.   The 1987 directive amending the 1985 directive on the lead content in petrol and the introduction of lead-free petrol

At its meeting of 19–20 March 1987, the Council considered favourably a German request that Member States should be able to prohibit the distribution of regular leaded petrol (while retaining the "super" grade). In so doing, the Council stipulated that this was not a first step towards prohibiting regular leaded petrol at Community level and could not be invoked as a precedent for justifying such a prohibition. On 21 July 1987, the Council formally adopted a directive amending Directive 85/210/EEC which provided that Member States may prohibit the marketing in their territory of leaded petrol having a motor octane number (MON) lower than 85 at the pump and a research octane number (RON) lower than 95 at the pump if such a measure were justified on grounds of the protection of human health and the environment and promoted the availability and balanced distribution of unleaded petrol within their territory.[18]

3.   The directive on polluting exhaust gases from petrol and diesel motor cars

(a)   The Commission proposal of June 1984

This proposal provided for a two-stage reduction in pollutants, the first to be achieved from 1989–1991, the second in 1995. At the first stage[19] the limit values should be respected by all categories of vehicle, regardless of their weight,[20] from

[18]   OJ No L 225/323 of 13/8/87.

[19]   The limits of the first stage corresponded to a reduction in emissions, compared to the Community legislation in force (Directive 83/351/EEC of June 1983), of the order of 30–40% for the three pollutants in question.

[20]   The 1983 Community legislation made provision for a differentiation between the limit values according to vehicle weight.

1 October 1989 onwards for all new car models, and from 1 October 1991 for all new cars, even if they are old models.

The second stage[21] provided for a reduction in polluting emissions, so making it possible to obtain values which were more or less equivalent to those in force in the United States and Japan, while taking account of the particular traffic conditions which existed in Europe.[22] The limit values of the second stage were to be respected as of 1 October 1995 for both new models and new cars.

(b)   Discussions within the Council during 1985

The measures taken in 1985 to make vehicles "cleaner" were examined at three sessions of the Council of Environment Ministers held respectively in March, June and November 1985. The Council's approach differed greatly from that contained in the initial proposal of the Commission. The Council's progress was gradual and marked by a certain cautiousness, due to the importance of what was at stake, and the many pressures being exerted on all sides.

March 1985: definition of vehicle categories and fixing of calendar for implementation

In March 1985 the Council defined a general framework, both for dividing vehicles into different categories depending on their cylinder capacity, and for establishing periods for implementation.

This differentiation between capacities made it easier from the technical point of view for industry, and from the financial point of view for motorists, to impose relatively strict standards, similar to those in force in the United States, whether for large cars (10% of the European market) or for small to medium-sized cars.

The periods decided on by the ministers in March 1985 for the introduction of the new standards were between three years (1988 at the earliest for large capacity) and eight years (1993 at the latest for small capacity engines), and vary depending on whether the vehicle is a new model or simply a new vehicle but an old model (see Table 4.3).

As far as the (actual) level of the standards is concerned, the Council merely indicated in March 1985 that these standards had to be fixed for 1 July 1985 and set out some general principles. These were the following:

- the European standards must be fixed according to each category of vehicle, so as to ensure that their effect on the environment is equivalent to that of the standards in force in the United States, taking into account the different conditions of use in Europe and the United States;
- the respect of these standards must be achieved at a reasonable cost and through different technical means.

---

[21] The limit values of the second stage corresponded to a reduction in emissions compared to Directive 83/351/EEC of the order of 70–80%.

[22] The traffic conditions in European differ from those in the United States, notably from the point of view of the average traffic speed, the average cylinder capacity and the average annual mileage, which made it difficult to compare European and American standards and necessitated the elaboration of a new European test cycle.

June 1985: establishing the emission standards for the different pollutants in exhaust fumes

For large cars (10% of the European market) the standards adopted corresponded to those in force in the United States. The need to respect such strict standards meant that manufacturers of this type of car would have to fit their vehicles with a three-way catalyst with electronic combustion control and compulsory use of lead-free petrol.

The standards which will have to be respected during the first stage (1990–1991) by small vehicles, that is, those of less than 1400 c.c., were not particularly restrictive and did not involve any major difficulties for the manufacturers, at least as far as the modern engines currently being produced are concerned.

But the main problem for the Council of June 1985 was medium-sized cars, which represented the largest part of the European car market, and which concerned the activities of most of the European manufacturers (in Italy, France, Belgium, Germany, the Netherlands and Spain).

The essential question was whether the standards to be fixed for medium-sized cars would require the use of a three-way catalyst or if they could be respected through less costly and more promising techniques in the relatively near future, such as the "lean burn" engine, including if necessary some kind of additional equipment (simple oxidization catalyst, for example). Despite considerable differences of opinion between Member States (Germany, the Netherlands and Denmark on the one hand, the United Kingdom supported to a great extent by France and Italy on the other), the Council finally managed to reach a compromise solution for medium-sized cars, by abolishing the specific value for nitrogen dioxide (NOx), this pollutant no longer being measured on its own, but together with hydrocarbons (HC). Such a solution allowed for a certain flexibility in the perfecting of the new engine technologies. What is more, while being relatively restrictive, the combined value used (NOx + HC) did not appear to require the use of a three-way catalyst.

All the Member States were able to support this compromise solution, with the exception of Denmark, which felt that the standards were not strict enough and would not bring about any real progress in environmental protection in that country.

The emission standards arrived at by the Council in June 1985 are summarized in Table 4.3.

November 1985: the remaining technical problems are resolved, but Denmark's opposition prevents adoption of the proposal

The Council, meeting in November 1985, settled a number of unresolved questions, of a mainly technical nature, but which were, nevertheless, very important from the industrial and trade points of view. These included for example:

- the relation between the new emission standards and the test cycle which vehicles undergo during the so-called "approval" of a vehicle;
- the fixing of more flexible standards for some specific vehicles (cars with automatic transmission; direct injection diesel cars; four-wheel drive vehicles);
- the possibility of Member States being able to make the use of lead-free petrol compulsory on their territory (establishment of a gradual timetable).

Table 4.3: "Luxembourg compromise" Emission standards to be respected by motor vehicles weighing up to 3.8 tonnes

Vehicle category	Date of introduction of new emission norms		European emission standards (in grams per test) for carbon monoxide, oxides of nitrogen and hydrocarbons
	new types of vehicles	new vehicles	
More than 2,000 cm³	1988	1989	CO25; HC–NOx6.5; NOx3.5
From 1,400 to 2,000 cm³	1991	1993	CO30; HC–NOx8
Less than 1,400 cm³	1990	1991	CO45; HC–NOx15 NOx6
	1992	1993	to be fixed in 1987

The body of problems linked to the general introduction into the Community of a less polluting car having found a solution, the directive reflecting the decisions taken since March 1985 should have been officially adopted by the Council in November 1985. However, as Denmark maintained its objections, the unanimity required by Article 100 of the EEC Treaty, the legal basis of the directive, could not be achieved, thereby preventing any legal force being given to the provisions so laboriously arrived at. But see under 5 below.

Economic impact

For the car industry, the new framework of regulations for anti-pollution standards undoubtedly represented an additional constraint. It should however be stressed that the solutions arrived at made it possible to avoid the fragmentation of the Common Market for cars, which would certainly have degenerated into different retaliatory or internal protection measures.

The possibility of such a breaking up of the large European markets for a product as economically important as the car, which also has a very special symbolic value, would have led to extremely serious distortions, at the very time when the Community was endeavouring to create a real "internal" market.

For the motorist it was probable that the new standards would come to mean an increase in the price of cars although it was difficult to estimate the likely amount. This would vary mainly according to the technology used: three-way catalyst, simple catalyst, etc. But whatever the category of car, it was probable that the additional cost that would be asked of the customer by the manufacturers would depend not only on the cost of the various pieces of anti-pollution equipment, but also on the more general conditions with which the car industry would be faced, in particular competition and tax conditions.

As far as tax was concerned, it should be noted that some Member States, namely Germany and the Netherlands, which wanted to encourage the trade and marketing of "clean" vehicles on their territories as quickly as possible, obtained from the Council the right to grant people purchasing such vehicles substantial tax incentives during the period preceding the coming into force of the Community standards.

The ecological impact

Compared with the previous regulation adopted by the Council in June 1983,[23] it is thought that from the environmental protection point of view, the new standards represented a global increase in severity of about 50%, which is considerable. This estimate was however subject to question, in that the figures applied to systems which were not totally comparable as far as vehicle categories and methods of measuring pollutants were concerned.

It was also clear that the gain for the protection of the environment would depend on the size and speed of turnover of the stock of new cars subject to the new regulation. Other parameters also had to be taken into consideration: the increase in the number of vehicles (for example); the increase or decrease in the annual mileage of each vehicle; driving conditions and the possible harmonization of stricter speed limits; the application of a roadworthiness test to check that anti-pollution standards are being respected; the fixing of standards for lorries, etc. In this context it should however be remembered that the polluting emissions due to mobile sources, which are mainly from motor vehicles, represented only about 25–30% of the total atmospheric pollution of the Community.

4.   Pollution by gases from cars with small cubic capacities

The "Luxembourg" compromise provided that emission standards for small cars would be fixed by the Council in 1987 on the basis of a Commission proposal. In the event, the Commission's proposal for a Council directive amending Directive 70/220/EEC to provide for European emission standards for cars below 1.4 litres was sent to the Council on 10 February 1988. The Commission proposed the reduction of permitted limit values for HC and NOx emissions by 58% and those for CO emissions by 48%. The resulting limit values are:

In the Commission's view, adoption of these values would mean that nearly all European car production, i.e. about 90%, would, from the early 1990s, be submitted to uniform air emission standards. This would allow industry to carry over into the small car category the technical solutions which it was at present developing for the medium category, i.e. the cost-efficient techniques which allow both for lower emissions and for little or even positive effects on fuel consumption. The increase in consumer prices which would result from these techniques – 4–5% – fitted in with the approach of equal incremental costs for improved emission characteristics of all car categories.

Table 4.4

	Carbon monoxide	Combined mass of hydrocarbons and nitrogen oxides
type-approval	30 grams/test	8 grams/test
production conformity	36 grams/test	10 grams/test

[23] Reg. 15/04 of the United Nations Economic Commission for Europe (ECE) was transposed into Directive 83/351/EEC applying to the European Economic Community.

In its memorandum the Commission pointed out that the proposal allowed industry to continue using existing engine components and did not force technology, i.e. ruling out the use of carburettors, leaving only recourse to injection systems.

As far as the dates of implementation were concerned, the Commission proposed to stick to the dates specified in the Luxembourg Agreement, i.e.:

- 1 October 1992 for new vehicle types, and
- 1 October 1993 for all new vehicles.

Without prejudice to the opinion of the European Parliament, the Council's discussions at its meetings on 16–17 and 28–29 June 1988, made it clear that the initial reaction of the majority was favourable to the standards proposed by the Commission. As reported by Europe Environment in its issue of 29 June 1988:

Eager to secure agreement on this issue and the draft directive on power plants, Germany finally parted ways with the Netherlands, Denmark and Greece in the early hours of the morning to align with eight other Member States including producing countries, France, UK, Italy and Spain on the Commission's original proposal ... Germany's support was made conditional on the following additional elements:
- the directive would include a clause committing the Council to consider a further reduction in emission limits by the end of 1991;
- the Commission would propose before 30 June 1989, a test cycle which represents driving conditions outside urban areas;
- the Commission would submit a report by 31 December 1990, on the effect of the overall clean car package and would make proposals for improving the limit values for the various categories of car, bearing in mind the request of some delegations for an NOx and HC limit of 5 grams per test;
- the Commission noted that nine Member States declared they would not introduce further fiscal incentives for less polluting cars ...

In the event, the then French Environment Minister, Brice Lalonde, informed his Community partners on 20 July that, on reflection, France could not go along with the agreement reached in Luxembourg because it did not offer car manufacturers sufficient market unity nor legislative certainty. As Europe Environment commented (28 July 1988): "France has now joined Greece, the Netherlands and Denmark to form a blocking majority of countries against the agreement which was tacked together under the German Presidency at the Environment Council Meeting on 28–29 June 1988. ..."

The impasse appeared to be resolved when, at its meeting of 24 November 1988, the Council reached a common position, confirming the agreement as to principle reached at the meeting on 28 and 29 June 1988; it incorporated the limit values and the dates which the Commission proposed for reducing emissions and the compromise arrangement for fiscal incentives.

The existing statutory requirements were to be cut by 58% for hydrocarbons and nitrogen oxide, and 48% for carbon monoxide, giving the following limit values:

- Carbon monoxide:
  = type approval: 30 grams/test
  = production conformity: 36 grams/test
- Combined emissions of hydrocarbons and nitrogen oxide:
  = type approval: 8 grams/test
  = production conformity: 10 grams/test.

These reductions were applicable with effect from 1992 to new models and with effect from 1993 to all new vehicles put on the road.

Under the cooperation procedure, the text of the directive still had to be communicated to the European Parliament and its opinion sought.

On 12 April 1989 the European Parliament rejected the "common position" by an overwhelming majority in favour of "US" standards. The Commissioner then responsible for the Environment, Carlo Ripa di Meana, indicated that the Commission would follow the opinion of the Parliament and amend its proposal accordingly. The Commission's "volte-face" was seen as a victory both for the growing environmental movement and for the European Parliament (at a time when MEPs were about to face their electorates!). At the Council meeting of 8 June 1989, US standards were finally adopted by a qualified majority. Values of 19 grams/test were agreed for carbon monoxide (22 grams/test for production conformity) and 5 grams/test for combined emissions of hydrocarbons and nitrogen oxide (5.8 grams/test for production conformity). Not later than the end of 1991, the Council undertook to examine on the basis of a Commission proposal a further reduction in emission levels for polluting gases.

5.   Final adoption of the "Luxembourg Compromise" as far as large and medium-sized cars are concerned

With the entry into force of the Single European Act, and the change in the legal basis of the Commission's proposal from Article 100 (unanimity) to 100A (majority voting), a new situation was created. The Danish President of the EEC's Council of Environment Ministers, Mr Christian Christensen, promoted a solution to the impasse whereby his own country was outvoted, the vote being taken on the basis of Article 100A. Mr Christensen described the meeting, which lasted barely four hours, as being "extremely constructive and efficient". The common position adopted by the Council on 21 July 1987 embodied the norms agreed by all Member States except Denmark at the Luxembourg Council in June 1985 (Table 4.3). Press comment following the meeting indicated that Denmark was in a minority of one. Europe Environment added in its 22 July 1987 edition: "fears that Denmark's plans to be outvoted on the issue of motor vehicle emission norms would be thwarted by the United Kingdom's insistence that the proposal's legal basis should be changed from Article 100A to Article 130 melted away when the delegation announced that it was withdrawing its reservations on the subject. The Danish delegation made quite clear its dissatisfaction with the proposed emission norms and warned its partners that it would be seeking a derogation under the terms of the Single European Act's new Article in due course."

The text of both directives was formally adopted by the Council on 3 December 1987.[24] However, this was not necessarily the end of the long saga since the Commission indicated in April 1989 that, in the light of developments on the question of emission norms for small cars, it would be coming forward with new proposals for the other categories of vehicles as well, notably medium-sized cars where there was a substantial discrepancy between European and US norms.

24 See OJ No L 36/1–61 of 9/2/88.

B. 1986: New series of Commission proposals concerning regulations on pollutants from lorries and diesel cars and on roadworthiness tests for motor vehicles
In 1985, during discussions on standards for cars, the Council also asked the Commission to submit proposals for regulations on:

- regular tests for motor vehicles;
- particulate emissions from diesel cars;
- gaseous pollutants from vehicles of over 3.5 tonnes (lorries and buses).

Responding to this request, the Commission sent three proposals to the Council during 1986.

1. Directive on roadworthiness tests for motor vehicles

On 2 May 1986 the Commission sent the Council a proposal amending the 1977 Directive 143/EEC on roadworthiness tests for motor vehicles and their trailers.[25]

The 1977 directive limited the periodic roadworthiness safety tests to buses and lorries of more than 3.5 tonnes, together with taxis and ambulances. The new proposal extended this test to all vehicles up to 3.5 tonnes (including vans), both for reasons of road safety, and for checking exhaust pollution. The proposal made provision for an initial roadworthiness test three years after the date of registration of the vehicle, followed by a second test two years later, i.e. five years after registration, and then an annual test, the aim being to keep emissions at a low level throughout the lifetime of a vehicle and to have withdrawn from service heavy polluting vehicles. The proposal also provided for the harmonization of the compulsory items to be tested. The Council finally approved the proposal in 1992 (Directive 92/55 of 22 June 1992).

2. Directive regulating particulate emissions from diesel engines

The proposal for the above directive, which was sent to the Council on 23 June 1986, aimed to limit all particulate emissions from diesel engines of cars (used for pleasure) and vans up to 3.5 tonnes.

Black smoke, that is, soot which only represented part – the most visible part – of all particulates emitted by diesel engines, was already covered by a directive adopted by the Council in 1972 (Directive 72/306/EEC).[26] The new proposal on air pollution was important because the number of diesel cars in the Community was forecast to double by the 1990s, and because no such regulation currently existed in Europe. (The USA has had particulate standards for diesel cars since 1982.) The Commission's proposal consisted of the following principal elements:

- the limit values proposed for particulates were 1.3 grammes/test for the "reception" of new types of car, regardless of their weight and cylinder capacity, and 1.7 grammes/test for new cars, at the time of product quality control;
- in order to avoid inflicting too many legal amendments on manufacturers, and in order to reduce to a minimum the administrative procedures for grouping together the different types of vehicles, the limit values suggested should be

---

[25] OJ No C 174 of 12/7/86.
[26] OJ No L 190 of 20/8/72.

applied to the same categories of cylinder capacity and by the same dates as those established in 1985 for gaseous pollutants from motor vehicles.

The Commission based its proposal on the current performance of the best available technology in the whole of the car industry of the Community. This technology being likely to make significant progress in the near future, the Commission's proposal should be considered as a first stage in the regulation of particulate emissions from diesel vehicles.

At the meeting of 3 December 1987, by qualified majority, the Environment Council reached a common position on the directive, to be transmitted to the European Parliament. As agreed, the directive (EEC 88/77)[27] provided for:

- *first stage*: (from 1.10.1989 for new types; from 1.10.1990 for all new vehicles) limit value of 1.1 g/test
- *second stage*: the Council considered that a second stage in the reduction of particulate emissions must be implemented as quickly as possible and that a level of 0.8 g/test should be achieved, taking into account the technical/economic possibilities which exist at that time.

The Council declared its intention to decide on the implementation of the second stage of the proposals before the end of 1989. The second stage in the reduction of particulate emissions was achieved by Directive 88/436.

3.   The 1988 directive on the emission of gaseous pollutants from diesel lorries and buses

The proposal for this directive, which was also submitted to the Council by the Commission on 23 June 1986,[28] aimed to complete the Community's anti-pollution standards applicable to diesel engine heavy vehicles of over 3.5 tonnes. Until then only emissions of black smoke had been covered by Community rules (under Directive 72/306/EEC), yet commercial vehicles represented a significant and growing proportion of the total road transport sector.

The Commission based its proposal on the 1982 draft prepared by the United Nations Economic Commission for Europe (known as R.49). Compared with this, the limit values proposed by the Commission were about 20% stricter for carbon monoxide and nitrogen oxide, and 30% stricter for hydrocarbons (CO: 11.2 g/kw; HC: 2.4 g/kw; NOx: 14.4 g/kw). Given the differences in the test procedures, these figures put European values at a level that was equivalent to that currently in force in the United States for the same vehicles. The limit values were to be respected from 1 January 1988 for new types of engine, and from 1 October 1990 for all new vehicles.

But, as with the preceding proposal on diesel car particulates, this proposal should be seen as a first stage only. The Commission intended to make a global proposal which would define an approach to the whole problem of diesel engine emissions, namely gaseous pollutants, black smoke and particulates, including if need be a new specification for diesel fuel. This global approach would include an analysis of the effects of pollutant emissions on public health and the environment, as well as a study of the technological possibilities of reducing these

[27] OJ No L 36 of 9/2/88.
[28] OJ No C 193 of 31/7/86.

Table 4.5: Emission standards for gaseous pollutants from
heavy vehicles

Mass of carbon monoxide (CO) grams per KWh	Mass of hydrocarbons (HC) grams per KWh	Mass of nitrogen oxides grams per KWh
11.2	2.4	14.4

The mass of the carbon monoxide, the mass of the hydrocarbons and the mass of the oxides of nitrogen obtained shall not exceed the amounts shown in the table.

emissions and of the economic and energy related impact of these possibilities (see p. 150 above).

The directive was finally adopted on 3 December 1987.[29] It specified that from 1 October 1990, the following standards would apply as far as the type-approval of diesel engines was concerned:

4.   Regulation on speed limits

In order to respond to the wishes expressed by the Council of Environment Ministers in 1985, the Commission initiated several studies into a Community regulation on speed limits. Before submitting a formal proposal on this question, which raised numerous political, psychological and industrial problems, the Commission sent the Council a Communication on the subject on 30 December 1986. Initial reactions in the Council were not encouraging.

C.   Further developments

1.   Directives 91/441 and 91/542; Directive 93/59

These directives set stringent standards for the control of exhaust pollutants from cars and heavy commercial vehicles, i.e. over three tonnes. For intermediate vehicles, transitional provisions in Directive 91/441 require emissions standards equal to the more lenient limits previously applicable to cars.[30]

On 23 December 1992 the Commission sent the Council a proposal for a directive amending Directive 70/220/EEC. The proposal set out new requirements for the control of gaseous and particulate emissions from large passenger cars, off-road vehicles and light-duty commercial vehicles, both diesel and petrol. The proposal sought to align the standards for intermediate vehicles to a level of equivalent technical severity as those established for cars and heavy commercial vehicles in Directives 91/441 and 91/542.

The main elements of the proposal included the establishment of the following uniform set of limit values:
- for cars below 2500 kg designed to carry six or more occupants (excluding off-road vehicles) and commercial vehicles below 1251 kg:
  - 2.72 g/km CO
  - 0.97 g/km HC + NOx
  - 0.14 g/km particulates (for diesels)

[29] OJ NO L 36 of 9/2/88.
[30] OJ No L 242 of 30/8/91 and OJ No L 295 of 25/10/91.

- for off-road vehicles below 1701 kg and commercial vehicles between 1251 kg and 1700 kg:
    - 5.17 g/km CO
    - 1.4 g/km HC + NOx
    - 0.19 g/km particulates for diesels
- for off-road vehicles and commercial vehicles between 1701 kg and 3500 kg:
    - 6.9 g/km CO
    - 1.7 g/km HC + NOx
    - 0.25 g/km particulates for diesels.

Mandatory introduction dates were set at 1 October 1993 for new-type approvals and 1 October 1994 for all new registrations. The proposal also called for a change to the test cycle to reduce the maximum speed from 120 km/h to 90 km/h for low-powered vehicles and for the application of the evaporative emission test and durability tests required by Directive 91/441 for cars to apply to the vehicles covered by the proposal.

The proposal was adopted as Council Directive 93/59.[31]

Table 4.6

		Directive 88/76			
				Implementation date	
Engine capacity (cm³)	*CO*	*HC+NO$_x$* *(g/test)*	*NO$_x$*	*New models*	*All new cars*
>2000	25	6.5	3.5	01.10.88	01.10.89
1400–2000	30	8	–	01.10.91	01.10.93
<1400 Stage 1	45	15	6	01.10.90	01.10.91

		Directive 89/458			
<1400 Stage II	19	5	–	31.7.92	31.12.92

Directive 91/441 *(All passenger cars)*				
CO	*HC/NO$_x$* *(g/km)*	*VOCs* *(g/test)*	*particulates(1)*	*CO at idling speed* *(% by volume)*
2.72	0.97	<2	0.14	3.5–4.5

Table 4.7: Emissions from commercial vehicles (Directive 91/542)

Implementation date	*CO*	*HC*	*NO$_x$ (g/Kwh)*	*Particulates*
New models				
1 July 1992	4.5	1.1	8.0	0.36
1 October 1995	4.0	1.1	7.0	0.15
New Registrations				
1 October 1993	4.9	1.23	9.0	0.4
1 October 1996	4.0	1.1	7.0	0.15

[31] OJ No L 186 of 27/8/93.

Table 4.8: Emission from light commercial vehicles (Directive 93/59)

Category (kg)	CO (g/km)	HC/NO$_x$ (g/km)	Particulates
I. <1250	2.72	0.97	0.14
II. 1250–1700	5.17	1.4	0.19
III. >1700	6.9	1.7	0.25

2. Council Directive 94/12/EC

Council Directive 94/12/EC further amends Directive 70/220/ on pollution from motor vehicles, marking another stage in the increasing stringency of emission standards (see Table 4.9).

Table 4.9: Directive 94/12/EC of the European Parliament and the Council of 23 March 1994 relating to measures to be taken against air pollution by emissions from motor vehicles and amending Directive 70/220/EEC

'Category of vehicle	Reference mass		Limit values		
		Mass of carbon monoxide L_1 (g/km)		Combined mass of hydrocarbons and oxides of nitrogen L_2 (g/km)		Mass of particulates L_3 (g/km)
	RM (kg)	Petrol	Diesel	Petrol	Diesel	Diesel
M (^{2})	all	2.2	1.0	0.5	0.7 (^{1})	0.08 (^{1})

(^{1}) For vehicles fitted with diesel engines of the direct-injection type the value L_2 is 0.9 g/km and the value L_3 is 0.10 g/km until 30 September 1999.
(^{2}) Except: – vehicles designed to carry more than six occupants including the driver,
               – vehicles whose maximum mass exceeds 2 500 kilograms.'

V. AIR POLLUTION FROM INDUSTRIAL PLANTS

1. Framework directive of 1984

On 15 April 1983 the Commission presented the Council with a proposal for a directive on the combating of atmospheric pollution from industrial plants. This is the first "framework" or general directive on the combating of air pollution. It therefore has links with the framework directive of 4 May 1976 on pollution caused by dangerous substances discharged into the aquatic environment of the Community (see p. 74). The proposal made provision for a body of measures and procedures which should facilitate the prevention and reduction of atmospheric pollution from industrial plants in the Community. In particular it established the basic principle of prior authorization for the operation of any new industrial plant. The Council adopted this directive on 28 June 1984.[32] The main provision of the directive was the requirement that as of 1 July 1987 Member States submit any new industrial plant belonging to certain specific industrial sectors to a system of prior authorization (with the understanding that any substantial alteration of an existing plant must be considered as a new plant). The authorization will only be granted if certain conditions are respected. An authorization may be issued only when the competent authority is satisfied that:

- all appropriate preventive measures against air pollution have been taken, including the application of the best available technology;
- the use of the plant will not cause significant air pollution;
- none of the emission or air quality limit values applicable will be exceeded.

However, the directive tempers the requirement for Member States to use the best available technology by adding that this should not entail "excessive costs".

The directive establishes the categories of industrial plants which require prior authorization (see Table 4.10).

As for the definition of atmospheric pollution, the directive does not exclude any harmful substance, but it mentions eight substances which are considered to be the most important (see Table 4.10).

The directive also makes specific provision for existing industrial plants, i.e. those which are working before 1 July 1987. It stipulates that the Member States must implement measures for the gradual adaptation of existing plants belonging to the same industrial sectors as those mentioned in Table 4.4 to the best available technology. This adaptation must be carried out taking into account the technical characteristics of the plant, the nature and volume of polluting emissions from it, and the desirability of not entailing excessive costs for the plant concerned, having regard to the economic situation of undertakings belonging to the category in question.

Apart from the basic provision on "prior authorization", the directive maintains the principle, contained in the Commission's proposal, of the fixing by the Council of Community "emission limit values", based on the best available technology not entailing excessive costs. Even if the force of this principle is somewhat weakened by the fact that in order to fix these emission limits the Council will have to be unanimous, and will act only when it appears strictly necessary, it is nevertheless true that in this provision the Council recognized the justification, in certain cases, of a Community limit value system. Until then, Community policy in the area of air pollution had in fact been restricted to the less demanding system, from the point of view of the Member States and economic agents, of the fixing of atmospheric "quality standards" (see SO_2 directive – lead and nitrogen dioxide – pp. 128 ff).

Among the other provisions of the directive is the compulsory exchange of information between the Member States on their experience in atmospheric pollution reduction and the procedures and technical equipment used. This exchange of information is all the more useful if the Member States are also required to follow the developments of the best available technologies and of the environmental situation.

---

[32] OJ No L 188 of 16/7/84.

Table 4.10: Council Directive of 28 June 1984 Combating air pollution from industrial plants

CATEGORIES OF PLANT([1])

(covered by Article 3)

1. *Energy industry*

1.1 Coke ovens

1.2 Oil refineries (excluding undertakings manufacturing only lubricants from crude oil)

1.3 Coal gasification and liquefaction plants

1.4 Thermal power stations (excluding nuclear power stations) and other combustion installations with a nominal heat output of more than 50 MW.

2. *Production and processing of metals*

2.1 Roasting and sintering plants with a capacity of more than 1 000 tonnes of metal ore per year

2.2 Integrated plants for the production of pig iron and crude steel

2.3 Ferrous metal foundries having melting installations with a total capacity of over 5 tonnes

2.4 Plants for the production and melting of non-ferrous metals having installations with a total capacity of over 1 tonne for heavy metals or 0.5 tonne for light metals.

3. *Manufacture of non-metallic mineral products*

3.1 Plants for the production of cement and rotary kiln lime production

3.2 Plants for the production and processing of asbestos and manufacture of asbestos-based products

3.3 Plants for the manufacture of glass fibre or mineral fibre

3.4 Plants for the production of glass (ordinary and special) with a capacity of more than 5 000 tonnes per year

3.5 Plants for the manufacturer of coarse ceramics notably refractory bricks, stoneware pipes, facing and floor bricks and roof tiles.

4. *Chemical industry*

4.1 Chemical plants for the production of olefins, derivatives of olefins, monomers and polymers

4.2 Chemical plants for the manufacture of other organic intermediate products

4.3 Plants for the manufacture of basic inorganic chemicals.

5. *Waste disposal*

5.1 Plants for the disposal of toxic and dangerous waste by incineration

5.2 Plants for the treatment by incineration of other solid and liquid waste.

Other industries
Plants for the manufacture of paper pulp by chemical methods with a production capacity of 25 000 tonnes or more per year.

([1]) The thresholds given in this Annex refer to production capacities.

Table 4.10 continued

LIST OF MOST IMPORTANT POLLUTING SUBSTANCES

(within the meaning of Article 4 (2))

1. Sulphur dioxide and other sulphur compounds
2. Oxides of nitrogen and other nitrogen compounds
3. Carbon monoxide
4. Organic compounds, in particular hydrocarbons (except methane)
5. Heavy metals and their compounds
6. Dust; asbestos (suspended particulates and fibres), glass and mineral fibres
7. Chlorine and its compounds
8. Fluorine and its compounds

In the light of these developments Member States will be able to adopt the conditions of authorization and impose new conditions on authorized plants.

Finally, the directive stipulates that Member States must make available to the public concerned the decisions taken by the competent authority regarding authorization requests for industrial plants. This information must also be sent to those Member States which might be interested by the authorization of an industrial plant likely to create cross-border pollution.

2.   The 1988 Directive 88/609 on the limitation of emissions of pollutants into the air from large combustion plants

On 19 December 1983 the Commission presented the Council with a proposal for a directive on the limitation of emissions of pollutants into the air from large combustion plants.[33]

This proposal represented the Commission's first response to the call by the European Council, meeting in Stuttgart in June 1983, concerning the need for immediate action to combat air pollution, and especially dangers threatening the forest zones of Northern Europe. (The two proposals concerning car pollution, namely the one on lead in petrol, and the one on vehicle exhaust, were not presented to the Council until six months later, in June 1984.)

The main characteristic of the proposal on large combustion plants is that it was the first time that the system of fixing Community limit values for discharges to the air, also known as air emission standards, was given concrete recognition.

Taking into account the different laws existing or about to be adopted in several Member States (Germany and the Netherlands) on the one hand, and the substantial cost of the anti-pollution investments in question on the other, the proposal also aimed to contribute to the harmonization of national provisions in this area.

As far as the importance of these anti-pollution investments was concerned, their cost could vary considerably from one economic sector to another; in some cases, for example in that of the old coal-fired power stations, it could come to 20% of the initial investment. Generally the cost of implementing the directive was estimated to be up to 10% of the production cost of the energy produced, which was far from negligible.

[33]   OJ No C 49 of 21/2/84.

The extra cost should however be compared with the benefits expected from the reduction in emissions, for example, from the point of view of corrosion of materials, damage caused to forests, losses of yield in agriculture, or negative influences on public health. While it was very difficult to put a figure on the benefits expected, it was quite possible that the real cost of damage caused would be higher than the cost of the proposed reductions in emissions.

The reduction proposal covered all large combustion plants (above 50 MW), both old and new, regardless of the type of fossil fuel used (oil; coal; gas; lignite). The term "large combustion plant" covers both electricity power stations with a thermal output (generally more than 300 MW) and industrial generators used for heat production.

New plants must respect the stated limit values or emission values for the three pollutants specified, namely sulphur dioxide (SO_2); dust, and nitrogen oxides (NOx).

In order to take account of technological developments under way, the emission standards for SO_2 and NOx are spread out in time and made gradually stricter. Two stages are envisaged: the first to be reached by 1985, the second by 1995. Generally the emission standards proposed take into account the best available technology, after its reliability from the industrial point of view has been proved, according to the fuel and type of plant in question.

Old plants will not be subject to emission standards or limit values as such, but their emissions will have to be reduced. To this end Member States must draw up reduction programmes which may differ as to the choice of means to be used but which must lead, by the end of 1995, to the same percentage of reduction of annual global emissions. The percentages of reduction proposed for all large combustion plants, i.e. both old and new, are, compared with the reference period of 1980, 60% for sulphur dioxide (SO_2), 40% for dust, and 40% for oxides of nitrogen (NOx).

Although the reduction percentages envisaged are fairly severe, this approach allows relative flexibility to the Member States in arriving at the global objectives established. Either they can apply a policy of systematic recourse to the emission limit values to be respected for old plants, or they can take selective measures, concentrating efforts only on certain particular plants. They can, for example, encourage the speedy replacement of old plants by new ones, make more use of low pollutant fuels, or use other forms of energy (e.g. nuclear energy).

The proposal also made provision for the possibility of the Commission granting exemptions to Member States, particularly in the following situations:

• where the structure of a Member State's energy production is based to a large extent on the use of indigenous solid fuel which contains sulphur to such an extent that the emission standards could only be complied with at a disproportionate cost;
• where the total annual emissions (in the reference period) in a Member State are lower than the levels in other Member States (in Ireland and Greece, for example).

Provision is also made for exemptions in cases of absolute necessity, for example a breakdown of purification facilities, or interruption in the supply of low-sulphur fuel.

After several years of discussions, agreement was finally reached in principle on the main aspects of the directive at the Environmental Council Meeting on 16–17 June 1988.

The aspects agreed on concerned in particular:

- reductions in overall emissions of SO_2 from existing plants in three stages: 1993, 1998 and 2003. The reductions were differentiated according to Member State to reflect the need for a balanced distribution of the effort required, taking account of the specific situation obtaining in each Member State.
- reductions in overall NOx emissions from existing plants in two stages. These reductions were determined using a similar approach to that adopted for SO_2 emissions;
- Community emission limit values for SO_2, NOx and dust for new plants, subject to: the adoption of specific provisions for certain types of fuel and plant, i.e. high sulphur fuel, lignite, peak-load installations and refineries;
- Spain being granted a derogation for solid fuel to allow for its specific energy situation.

As it can be seen from the tables, implementation of the directive should reduce overall emissions of SO_2 from existing plants with a production capacity of over 50 MW by 25%, 43% and 60% over 1980 levels in three phases – 1993, 1998 and 2003. However, the reductions to be achieved by each Member State differ markedly according to their economic, energy and environmental situation so that Belgium, France, Germany and the Netherlands are aiming at 40%, 60% and 70% cuts while the UK is aiming at 20%, 40% and 60% reductions and both Ireland and Portugal will be allowed to increase their 1980 emissions by a quarter before the year 2003. In total, implementation of the directive would mean a cut of more than six million tonnes a year in emissions of SO_2 from existing power plants and oil refineries by 1998 and the halving of emissions by the year 2003. NOx emissions for existing plants will be reduced by 20% and 36% over 1980 levels by first 1993 and then 1998.

The standards contained in the directive on new plants (commissioned after July 1987) will reduce emissions of SO_2 by more than 80% and of NOx by half (as compared with emissions of unmodified plants). It was agreed that Spain should receive a derogation permitting the authorization of new solid-fuel burning plants over 500 MW until the end of 1999. These installations would have to respect an SO_2 emission limit value of 800 g/Nm^3 and, in the case of installations burning indigenous solid fuels, at least a 60% rate of desulphurization. However, the total authorized capacity of such plants to which this derogation would apply, should not exceed:

- 2000 MWe in the case of plants burning indigenous solid fuels;
- 7500 MWe or 50% of all the new capacity of all plants burning solid fuels authorized before 31 December 1999, whichever is the lower;
- in the case of plants burning imported solid fuels, either 7500 MWe or 50% of all the new capacity of all plants burning solid fuels authorized before 31 December 1999, whichever is the lower.

Commissioner Stanley Clinton-Davis commented after agreement had been reached in principle at the 16–17 June 1988 meeting that "it signalled the solution to the Community's acid-rain problem".

The directive on the limitation of pollutants into the air from large combustion plants was formally adopted by the Council on 24 November 1988.[34]

34 OJ No L 336 of 7/12/88.

The table showing SO_2 overall emission ceilings for "existing" large combustion plants contains two headings:

- % reduction over LCI emissions 1980, and
- % reduction over *adjusted* LCI emissions 1980.

In certain cases, e.g. Belgium, Denmark, France, Luxembourg, UK, the percentage reductions to be achieved by the dates in question – 1993, 1998, 2003 – are the same. In other cases, however, there is a difference between the two columns.

For the purpose of calculating adjusted LCI emissions, plants added to Member States' capacity between 1980 and 1987 have been taken into account. The SO_2 emissions from these plants have been added on a hypothetical basis to the base year (1980) emissions. Hence the term "adjusted" LCI emissions 1980.

3.   The 1992 proposal for a directive amending Directive 88/609 on emissions from large combustion plants

On 18 December 1992 the Commission sent the Council a proposal to amend the 1988 directive on emissions from large combustion plants.[35] The proposed amendment sets a limit of 2000 mg/SO_2/cubic metre for plants with a thermal input of 50–100 MMWth. In its report to the Council, the Commission considered the availability of low sulphur content (LSC) coal which it defined as containing 1.5 g per kcal sulphur. Emissions from burning LSC coal could be limited to the 2000 mg/SO_2/cubic metre limit without extra measures being taken. As coal available on world markets was on the whole cheaper than that produced in the Community, the Commission concluded that there was enough LSC coal available at an acceptable price and that accordingly the lower limit was justified.

The Council adopted Common Position (EC) No 21/94 on the proposal. The only amendment made by the Council was to extend the time for compliance.[36]

VI.   CONTROL OF AIR POLLUTION

1.   The 1975 decision setting up a system for the exchange of information on sulphur compounds and suspended particulates

On 24 June 1975 the Council adopted a decision establishing a common procedure for the exchange of information between the surveillance and monitoring networks based on data relating to atmospheric pollution caused by sulphur compounds and suspended particulates.[37] The exchange of information relates to the results of measures taken by fixed stations sampling continuously. The data to be sent to the Commission on a monthly basis concern the average daily concentrations of sulphur dioxide and suspended particulates.

The basic objectives of the information exchange are to monitor the long-term development of air quality and to study the transfer of atmospheric pollution across

[35] OJ No C 17/12 of 22/1/93.
[36] OJ No C 213/11 of 3/8/94.
[37] OJ No L 194 of 25/7/75.

Table 4.11: Council Directive of 24 November 1988
Limitation of emissions of certain pollutants into the air from large combustion plants

CEILINGS AND REDUCTION TARGETS FOR EMISSIONS OF SO_2 FROM EXISTING PLANTS ([1]) ([2])

	0	1	2	3	4	5	6	7	8	9
	SO_2 emissions	Emission ceiling (ktonnes/year)			% reduction over 1980 emissions			% reduction over adjusted 1980 emissions		
Member State	by large combustion plants 1980	Phase 1	Phase 2	Phase 3	Phase 1	Phase 2	Phase 3	Phase 1	Phase 2	Phase 3
	ktonnes	1993	1998	2003	1993	1998	2003	1993	1998	2003
Belgium	530	318	212	159	− 40	− 60	− 70	− 40	− 60	− 70
Denmark	323	213	141	106	− 34	− 56	− 67	− 40	− 60	− 70
Germany	2 225	1 335	890	668	− 40	− 60	− 70	− 40	− 60	− 70
Greece	303	320	320	320	+ 6	+ 6	+ 6	− 45	− 45	− 45
Spain	2 290	2 290	1 730	1 440	0	− 24	− 37	− 21	− 40	− 50
France	1 910	1 146	764	573	− 40	− 60	− 70	− 40	− 60	− 70
Ireland	99	124	124	124	+ 25	+ 25	+ 25	− 29	− 29	− 29
Italy	2 450	1 800	1 500	900	− 27	− 39	− 63	− 40	− 50	− 70
Luxembourg	3	1,8	1,5	1,5	− 40	− 50	− 60	− 40	− 50	− 50
Netherlands	299	180	120	90	− 40	− 60	− 70	− 40	− 60	− 70
Portugal	115	232	270	206	+102	+135	+ 79	− 25	− 13	− 34
United Kingdom	3 883	3 106	2 330	1 553	− 20	− 40	− 60	− 20	− 40	− 60

([1]) Additional emissions may arise from capacity authorized on or after 1 July 1987.
([2]) Emissions coming from combustion plants authorized before 1 July 1987 but not yet in operation before that date and which have not been taken into account in establishing the emission ceilings fixed by this Annex shall either comply with the requirements established by this Directive for new plants or be accounted for in the overall emissions from existing plants that must not exceed the ceilings fixed in this Annex.

CEILINGS AND REDUCTION TARGETS FOR EMISSIONS OF NO_x FROM EXISTING PLANTS ([1]) ([2])

	0	1	2	3	4	5	6
Member State	NO_x emissions (as NO_2 by large combustion plants 1980 (ktonnes)	NO_x emission ceilings (ktonnes/year)		% reduction over 1980 emissions		% reduction over adjusted 1980 emissions	
		Phase 1	Phase 2	Phase 1	Phase 2	Phase 1	Phase 2
		1993 ([3])	1998	1993 ([3])	1998	1993 ([3])	1998
Belgium	110	88	66	− 20	− 40	− 20	− 40
Denmark	124	121	81	− 3	− 35	− 10	− 40
Germany	870	696	522	− 20	− 40	− 20	− 40
Greece	36	70	70	+ 94	+ 94	0	0
Spain	366	368	277	+ 1	− 24	− 20	− 40
France	400	320	240	− 20	− 40	− 20	− 40
Ireland	28	50	50	+ 79	+ 79	0	0
Italy	580	570	428	− 2	− 26	− 20	− 40
Luxembourg	3	2,4	1,8	− 20	− 40	− 20	− 40
Netherlands	122	98	73	− 20	− 40	− 20	− 40
Portugal	23	59	64	+ 157	+ 178	− 8	0
United Kingdom	1 016	864	711	− 15	− 30	− 15	− 30

([1]) Additional emissions may arise from capacity on or after 1 July 1987.
([2]) Emissions coming from combustion plants authorized before 1 July 1987 but not yet in operation before that date and which have not been taken into account in establishing the emission ceilings fixed by this Annex shall either comply with the requirements established by this Directive for new plants or be accounted for in the overall emissions from existing plants that must not exceed the ceilings fixed in this Annex.
([3]) Member States may for technical reasons delay for up to two years the phase 1 date for reduction in NO_x emissions by notifying the Commission within one month of the notification of this Directive.

Table 4.11 continued

EMISSION LIMIT VALUES FOR SO$_2$, FOR NEW PLANT[1]

Solid fuels

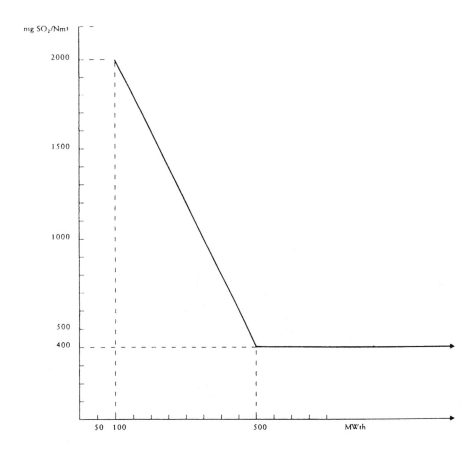

---

[1] In 1990, on the basis of a commission report on the availability of low-sulphur fuel and
a relevant Commission proposal, the Council will decide on emission limit values for
plants between 50 and 100 MWth.

Table 4.11 continued

EMISSION LIMIT VALUES FOR SO₂, FOR NEW PLANTS
Liquid fuels

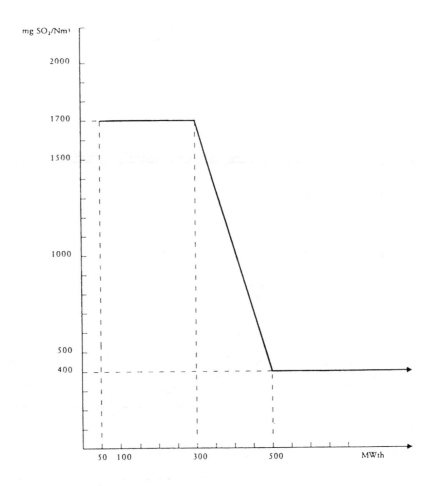

Table 4.11 continued

EMISSION LIMIT VALUES FOR SO₂ FOR NEW PLANTS

Gaseous fuels

Type of fuel	Limit values (mg/Nm³)
Gaseous fuels in general	35
Liquefied gas	5
Low calorific gases from gasification of refinery residues, coke oven gas, blast-furnace gas	800
Gas from gasification of coal	(¹)

(¹) The Council will fix the emission limit values applicable to such gas at a later stage on the basis of proposals from the Commission to be made in the light of further technical experience.

EMISSION LIMIT VALUES FOR NOₓ FOR NEW PLANTS

Type of fuel	Limit values (mg/Nm³)
Solid in general	650
Solid with less than 10 % volatile compounds	1 300
Liquid	450
Gaseous	350

EMISSION LIMIT VALUES FOR DUST FOR NEW PLANTS

Type of fuel	Thermal capacity (MW)	Emission limit values (mg/Nm³)
Solid	≥ 500 < 500	50 100
Liquid (¹)	all plants	50
Gaseous	all plants	5 as a rule 10 for blast-furnace gas 50 for gases produced by the steel industry which can be used elsewhere

(¹) A limit value of 100 mg/Nm³ may be applied to plants with a capacity of less than 500 MWth burning liquid fuel with an ash content of more than 0.06%.

Table 4.11 continued

RATES OF DESULPHURIZATION

(pursuant to Article 5 (2))

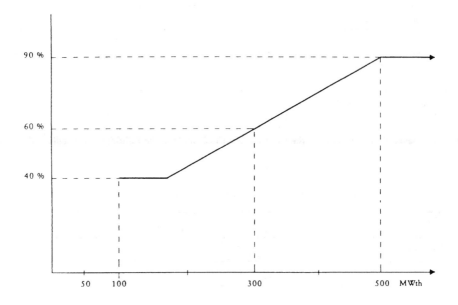

regional, national and Community borders. It also represents the Community's contribution to the United Nation's "global environmental monitoring system" (GEMS).

According to this decision, each Member State, after consultation with the Commission, must select the measuring stations established or planned on their territories, which will participate in the information exchange. Nearly 300 test stations have been selected for this in the Community. The choice of stations should depend mainly on geographic and demographic parameters (urban and rural areas; size of cities; residential or industrial areas) and on pollution levels (maximum – average – minimum). The network of stations will consist of four categories: high impact zones; rural situation; pilot towns; and comparative stations.

With regard to the comparability of measuring methods, the Commission will carry out studies with a view to harmonizing these methods. This will enable direct comparison to be made between the data received from the different measuring stations participating in the information system.

The work carried out by the Commission has also made it possible to define more clearly the structure of the network, to arrive at a uniform interpretation of the parameters set out in the decision, and so to assist Member States to use a common method to select the participating stations. The first general synthesis report on the implementation of this information system was produced by the Commission in 1979.

2.   The 1982 decision extending the 1975 information system to pollutants other than sulphur

On 26 July 1981 the Commission sent the Council a proposal for an amendment to the decision extending the information system of 24 June 1975 to cover pollutants other than sulphur compounds and suspended particulates. The Council adopted this amendment decision on 24 June 1982.[38] Formally speaking, this decision abrogated the preceding decision of 1975. In practice, however, it maintained the principal characteristics of the 1975 information system, while extending its field of application to cover pollutants other than SO_2 and particulates, namely heavy metals (e.g. lead or cadmium in the form of suspended particulates), nitrogen oxides, carbon monoxide and ozone.

The measuring stations already participating in the 1975 information exchange system were to be integrated into the new system, but other stations selected by the Member States would be added. These new stations would have to reflect as far as possible the different types of urbanization, topography and climatic conditions, as well as the different levels of pollution on the territory of the Member State in question. Priority should also be given to stations using several sampling and analysis techniques, in order to make it easier to compare them and assess their value.

On the basis of the information transmitted by the Member States, the Commission was to organize comparative programmes covering, for example, the equipment and methods used for sampling and analysis. The Commission was also to publish regular reports on this system for the reciprocal exchange of information on the measurement of atmospheric pollution in the Member States.

3.   1992 Directive 92/72 of 21 September 1992 on air pollution by ozone

On 2 July 1991 the Commission submitted a proposal to the Council for a directive on air pollution by ozone. The proposal set out to achieve a better understanding of the complex mechanisms of ground level ozone formation and the long-range transport of ozone and its precursors with the objective of providing information for future policy on ozone control. Ground level ozone is formed from oxides of nitrogen (NOx) and volatile organic compounds (VOCs) by a series of complicated reactions in the presence of sunlight, which causes it to be chiefly a summer pollutant. It is a component of photochemical smog, as well as a major transboundary air pollutant, and in high concentrations can damage human health, building materials and plant growth.

The directive as adopted by the Council in September 1992 has three main elements.[39] It requires the consistent monitoring throughout the Community of atmospheric concentrations of ground level ozone; the sharing of selected monitoring information between the Member States and the Commission; and the issue of precautionary health warnings to the public whenever ozone concentration exceeds given thresholds. The directive requires the Commission to submit proposals for

---

[38]   OJ No L 210 of 19/7/82.
[39]   OJ No L 297 of 13/10/92.

the control of air pollution five years after entry into force of the directive and after evaluation of the monitoring data collected by Member States.

VII.   THE CONTROL OF FLUOROCARBONS IN THE ENVIRONMENT

1.   The 1978 Council Resolution on a standstill in the production capacity of certain chlorofluorocarbons

With regard to the control of chlorofluorocarbons (CFCs), the Commission sent a proposal for a Recommendation to the Council on 29 August 1977 which advocated preventive measures in order to take account of the problems caused by the effects of emissions of chlorofluorocarbons on the ozone layer and by ultraviolet rays on health. The Council adopted this proposal on 30 May 1978 in the form of a Resolution.[40] The Resolution called on Member States:

- to present the research that they have carried out into the effects of chlorofluorocarbons on man and the environment, and to cooperate on a Community basis so that the research can be planned and the results made available;
- to take steps to encourage all the aerosol and plastic foam industries using chlorofluorocarbons F-11 and F-12 to intensify research into alternative products and to promote the development of alternative methods of application;
- to encourage the manufacturers and users of equipment containing chlorofluorocarbons F-11 and F-12 to eliminate the discharge of these compounds;
- to ensure that the industry situated within the Community does not increase its production capacity in respect of chlorofluorocarbons F-11 and F-12.

The Resolution also specified that the Commission would re-examine the effect of fluorocarbons on the environment during the second half of 1978, in the light of the information then available with a view to arriving at a Community policy on chlorofluorocarbons.

2.   The Council Decision of 1980 imposing a reduction in the use of chlorofluorocarbons in aerosols

At an international conference on chlorofluorocarbons held in Munich in 1978, the Member States of the Community and other participating countries agreed to achieve over the coming years a substantial reduction in emissions of chlorofluorocarbons. In line with the conclusions of the Munich conference, the Commission presented a proposal for a Decision to the Council on 16 March 1979 regarding fluorocarbons in the environment.

The Council adopted this Decision on 26 March 1980.[41] The Decision required Member States to ensure that industry situated in their territories should not increase its chlorofluorocarbon production capacity of F-11 and F-12 (standstill principle), and that it should achieve not later than 31 December 1981 a reduction of at least

---

[40] OJ No C 133 of 7/6/78.
[41] OJ No L 90 of 3/4/80.

30% compared with 1976 levels in the use of the fluorocarbons F-11 and F-12 in the filling of aerosol cans. The Decision also provided for a re-examination of the situation in the light of new scientific and economic data available. When adopting this Decision, the Council also undertook to take any new measures as might be deemed necessary in the light of this re-examination no later than 30 June 1981.

Following this provision, the Commission presented two Communications to the Council on 16 June 1980 and 26 May 1981 respectively, containing elements of information and evaluation on the carrying out of Community policy on the limiting of CFC emissions. The Council took note of these Communications and asked the Commission to prepare a proposal for a Decision on the measures of prevention and precaution to be taken by the Member States after 31 December 1981, the date for the implementation of the 30% reduction in the use of the chlorofluorocarbons F-11 and F-12 in aerosols.

3.   The Council Decision of 1982 renewing and consolidating the measures taken in 1980

In line with the conclusions of the Council of Environment Ministers on 11 June 1981, the Commission drew up a new proposal for a Decision which was sent to the Council on 7 October 1981. This proposal was intended to renew and consolidate the precautionary measures taken in 1980.

The Council approved this Decision on 15 November 1982.[42] The Decision confirmed and specified the measures taken by the Council on 26 March 1980. In this way it defined with greater precision the methods of application of the standstill principle for the production capacity of the chlorofluorocarbons F-11 and F-12, so as to avoid differing interpretations by the Member States.

Moreover, the Decision extended the field of application of precautionary measures, until then confined to the aerosol sector, to other sectors using chlorofluorocarbons such as synthetic foam, refrigeration and solvents; for these sectors the Decision required Member States to cooperate with the Commission with a view to reducing the loss of CFCs, and to perfect the best possible techniques for limiting their emission.

Finally, the Decision, like the previous ones on CFCs, contained a clause regarding scientific and economic re-examination.

4.   The Commission's Communications of 1983, 1985 and 1986 on the re-examination of the scientific and economic situation regarding chlorofluorocarbons

(a) In line with the Decision of 15 November 1982, the Commission presented a Communication to the Council on 31 May 1983 which assessed scientific knowledge and economic data with regard to CFCs. From the scientific point of view, the Commission, basing itself on the international work carried out within the framework of the United Nations' Environment Programme, stressed that the ozone layer might have been reduced by 3–5% due to the chlorofluorocarbons F-11 and F-12, while previous estimates had been of the order of 5–10%. From the economic

[42] OJ No L 329 of 25/11/82.

point of view, the Commission noted that the use of aerosols containing CFCs had been reduced by 1982 by an average throughout the Community of about 37% compared with 1976, which was well above the 30% reduction required by the Council Decision of 1980. Finally, the Commission indicated that in collaboration with the industries concerned, it had drawn up codes of good practice with a view to restricting to a minimum emissions of CFCs in the sectors of refrigeration, plastic foam and solvents.

(b) On 19 November 1985, the Commission presented the Council with a new Communication on chlorofluorocarbons. This did not bring in any new elements compared with 1983, the work launched in the framework of the Convention for the Protection of the Ozone Layer, signed in Vienna on 22 March 1985, not yet having resulted in any concrete measures.

(c) On 21 November 1986 the Commission sent the Council a third Communication concerning the re-examination of control measures for CFCs. The Communication summed up the economic tendencies with regard to the production and use of different CFCs and assessed the scientific and technical situation. This situation was examined before the recent recording of significant reductions in the ozone above the Antarctic. Moreover, the "greenhouse" effect caused by different gases might be the reason for a heating up of the globe and might cause climatic disturbances. The Commission therefore indicated that it would pay great attention to the development of the situation in the coming months, especially in the light of the results of the satellite observation programmes which would shortly be undertaken by the United States National Aeronautic and Space Administration (NASA) and the World Meteorological Organization (WMO). In the meantime, the Commission proposed that the Community control measures currently in force be maintained, these being measures which would be adapted within the framework of future negotiations on the drawing up of the "CFC" protocol of the 1985 Vienna Convention on the protection of the ozone layer (see p. 414). With this in view, the Council authorized the Commission on 24 November 1986 to participate in the negotiation of the protocol and established the directives relating to the Commission's mandate to negotiate.

The Community signed the Vienna Convention in March 1985 and the Montreal Protocol in September 1987. At its meeting on 16–17 June 1988, the Council reached substantive agreement on:

- a Decision concluding and implementing the Vienna Convention for the Protection of the Ozone Layer and the Montreal Protocol on Substances that Deplete the Ozone Layer, and
- a Regulation (3322/88) laying down common rules applicable to certain products which deplete the ozone layer.

To enable the Vienna Convention and the Montreal Protocol to enter into force on 1 January 1989, the Decision approved at the June 1988 meeting required Member States to take the necessary steps to ratify the convention by 1 October 1988, and the protocol by the end of the year. The regulation set down specific rules for restricting the production, sale and import of CFCs and halons, in order to apply the Montreal Protocol in the Community, and in particular the provisions for:

- a freeze on the production and consumption of CFCs and halons at 1986 levels, to take effect one year after the protocol entered into force on 1 January 1989;
- reduction to 80% of 1986 levels from 1 July 1993, and to 50% from 1 July 1988.

At the same meeting (June 1988) the Council reached agreement on a Resolution on the use of CFCs and halons in products. In this Resolution, the Council:

1. Stresses that in addition to the regulation implementing the Montreal Protocol in the Community urgent action should be taken in order to limit the use of CFCs and halons in products and equipment containing them or in processes using them, in particular by the measures mentioned below;
2. Underlines the need for the Community and the Member States to encourage further research into climate change and the ozone layer and, in consultation with industry, into alternative, environmentally sound products, equipment or processes;
3. Invites the Commission, in cooperation with the Member States, to initiate discussions on voluntary agreements at the Community level with all the industries concerned, wherever feasible to substitute CFCs and halons in products, such as aerosols, or in equipment or processes using them, or if such substitution is not feasible to reduce the use of these substances, so that the total amounts of these substances used will be reduced to the maximum possible extent. It further invites the Commission to report on progress made;
4. Invites the Commission, in cooperation with the Member States, to initiate discussions with the industries concerned with a view to concluding a voluntary agreement on a common Community label for CFC-free products.

Europe Environment commented (29 June 1988): "Although the Ministers' commitment to go further than is strictly necessary under the Protocol on chlorofluorocarbons (CFCs) and halons is a purely political one, officials felt that this may achieve more for the environment than a tightly-worded legal text."

By Council Decision 88/540/EC of 14 October 1988, the Community became a party to the Vienna Convention on the protection of the ozone layer and to the Montreal Protocol on substances which damage the ozone layer. The Montreal Protocol is applied in the Community through Regulation No 3322/88 of 14 October 1988 on certain chlorofluorocarbons and halons which destroy the ozone layer.

The Montreal Protocol was signed in September 1987. Since then, scientific evidence has shown that the measures contained in that regulation are inadequate in view of the continued deterioration of the ozone layer. This evidence is based in particular on studies concerning the hole in the ozone layer over the Antarctic, disturbances in the chemical exchanges in the Arctic region and reductions from 3 to 5.5% over a long period recorded in the Northern Hemisphere during the winter months from 1969 to 1988. The same study also shows that carbon tetrachloride and methyl chloroform also damage the ozone layer.

It was against this background that the Council decided on 2 March 1989 that it was necessary to introduce as soon as possible, at both Community and global levels, reductions in the production and use of CFCs of at least 85% compared to current levels, with a view to eliminating them totally by the end of the century.

At the "Save the Ozone Layer" Conference in London, the Commission called for a reduction of 85% by 1995 and total elimination well before the end of the century, in 1996 or 1997.

The Commission went on to produce a proposal for a modification to the Council Regulation EEC No 3322/88 introducing stricter controls of CFCs and halons aimed at eliminating them by 1997 and 1999 respectively. Controls were also introduced on carbon tetrachloride, methyl chloroform and other halogenic CFCs.

This regulation applies to the import, export, production and use of chlorofluorocarbons, other fully halogenated chlorofluorocarbons, halons, carbon tetrachloride, and 1,1,1 trichloroethane. It was proposed, in the light of scientific evidence which proved the existing controls over such substances to be inadequate given the rate of deterioration of the ozone layer, and in order to reflect the decision taken at the second meeting of the parties to the Montreal Protocol, to adopt additional measures for the protection of the ozone layer. The regulation introduces revised phase-out schedules for the substances in question.

5. The 1991 Regulation on substances that deplete the ozone layer

The Montreal Protocol set levels of production and consumption for certain ozone depleting substances – chlorofluorocarbons 11, 12, 113, 114 and 115 (used in refrigeration, aerosols, foam blowing and as solvents), and halons 1211, 1301 and 2402 (used in fire fighting). The provisions of the protocol were implemented within the Community by Regulation 3322/88. In the time since the 1987 protocol had been agreed though, scientific evidence had shown that the measures it contained did not go far enough to stop ozone depletion in the stratosphere. Accordingly, in May 1989, at the first meeting of the parties to the Montreal Protocol in Helsinki, the signatories undertook in a Declaration to phase out CFCs completely by 2000. At the second meeting of the parties held in London in June 1990, the protocol was formally revised to provide for the phasing out by 2000 of the consumption and production of CFCs and halons, with certain exemptions for essential use of halons. Other chemicals not covered by the original protocol were brought under control: carbon tetrachloride (used in paints, pesticides and pharmaceuticals) and 1,1,1 trichloroethane (a widely used solvent). These were also to be phased out by 2000, apart from 1,1,1 trichloroethane for which the phase-out date was set at 2005. A further group of chemicals – HCFCs – were identified as transitional substances. HCFCs cause much less damage to the ozone layer and are currently the only likely replacements in the short to medium term for some uses of CFCs. The only provision for HCFCs was the collection of production and trade data, although the parties to the protocol called in a Resolution for their responsible use.

Regulation 594/91[43] implements the terms of the revised protocol. Accordingly, it controls the production, consumption and import of all chlorofluorocarbons (CFCs), halons, 1,1,1 trichloroethane and carbon tetrachloride within the Community. But it imposes stricter controls on CFCs than the protocol, phasing out their production and consumption by 1 July 1997 instead of 1 January 2000, and of carbon tetrachloride by 1 January 1998 rather than 2000. Phase-out dates for halons and 1,1,1 trichloroethane remain the same as in the protocol, namely 1 January 2000 and 1 January 2005 respectively. In accordance with the revised protocol, the regulation set interim cuts in production and consumption at 85% by 1 July 1995 for CFCs, 50% by 1 January 1995 for halons, 85% by 1 January 1995 for carbon tetrachloride, and for 1,1,1 trichloroethane reductions of 30% by 1 January 1995 and 70% by 1 January 2000.

6. The 1992 proposal for a regulation to speed up the phasing out of substances that deplete the ozone layer

On 20 March 1992 the Commission sent the Council a proposal for a regulation amending Regulation 594/91. The proposal aimed to speed up the phasing out of

---

[43] OJ No L 67 of 14/3/91.

substances that deplete the ozone layer. Recent scientific evidence indicated that the stratospheric ozone layer is being depleted more rapidly than expected with significant losses being recorded over Northern Europe. This loss of ozone co-incides with a rise in ground level UV radiation. The Technical and Economic Assessment Panel of the Montreal Protocol concluded that progress made in developing alternative technologies would make it feasible to phase out ozone depleting substances sooner than the dates contained in the Montreal Protocol and in the existing EC Regulation 594/91. Accordingly, the Commission proposed to bring forward the dates for all substances to 1 January 1996. It also proposed bringing forward and increasing the interim cuts in production and consumption to 85% by 1 January 1994.

The regulation (3952/92) was adopted by the Council in December 1992.[44]

VIII.   A NEW TYPE OF DIRECTIVE: THE MULTI-MEDIA APPROACH

1.   The pollution of the environment by asbestos

On 6 December 1985, the Commission sent the Council a proposal for a directive on the prevention of environmental pollution by asbestos.[45] Although this proposal mainly concerned air pollution, hence its place in the "air" chapter, it also concerned the protection of other parts of the environment, such as soil and water. It therefore had a horizontal aspect which distinguished it from the other proposals drawn up by the Commission to date since the beginning of Community Environment Policy. This new "multi-media" approach has since been increasingly used, as was expressly provided for by the 4th Environmental Action Programme for 1987–1992.

After more than 10 years of Community Environment Policy, the Commission felt that environment problems should from now on be approached in a more global way, not only from the sectoral point of view (water, air, soil, etc.) but also from the point of view of the different polluting substances, so as to avoid any transfer of pollution from one sector to another. With this in view, the Commission's proposal concerned the prevention of asbestos pollution throughout the environment. It did not however concern the protection of workers exposed to asbestos in the workplace. The objective of the proposal was to prevent emissions of asbestos from different sources both from putting the health of the population directly at risk and from causing the gradual general contamination of the environment.

Asbestos is in fact a toxic substance which is already the object of several Community regulations regarding the protection of workers (1983 directive),[46] trade in certain asbestos products (1983 directive),[47] and the disposal of toxic and dangerous waste (1978 directive).[48] The proposal did not make provision for the general prohibiting of asbestos. This was due to the difficulties of finding reliable substitute products for the many uses of asbestos. In the case of the production of cement asbestos, the main problem was the aqueous effluent which contains

---

[44] OJ No L 405 of 31/12/92.
[45] OJ No C 349 of 31/12/85.
[46] OJ No L 263 of 24/9/83.
[47] OJ No L 262 of 27/9/76 and OJ No L 263 of 24/9/83
[48] OJ No L 84 of 31/3/78.

asbestos. The main provisions of the proposal concerned the fixing of limit values to be respected for the aqueous effluents and emissions into the air, and more general measures regarding the manufacture of products containing asbestos, the demolition of buildings containing asbestos, and the processing, transport and disposal of waste containing asbestos.

The proposal also required the Member States to use the best available technology not involving excessive costs, in order to ensure that the aqueous effluents emissions into the air and production of solid waste containing asbestos are reduced to a minimum and are recycled or processed in an appropriate way. It specified that the emissions into the air and aqueous effluents must be measured regularly using the sampling and analysis methods mentioned in the directive.

Finally, the proposal asked Member States to establish and follow codes of good practice, at national or Community levels, in order to prevent any pollution by asbestos during the demolition of buildings, the transport of asbestos waste, and the maintenance of tips containing asbestos. The Council adopted this directive on 19 March 1987.[49]

2.   Integrated pollution prevention and control (IPC)

For the Commission's proposals in this field, see p. 365.

IX.   THE "GREENHOUSE EFFECT"

The emergence of the "greenhouse effect" as a major international environmental problem has undoubtedly reshaped the Community's priorities in recent years as far as environment policy is concerned. On 16 November 1988 the Commission sent a Communication to the Council entitled "The Greenhouse Effect and the Community" (COM (88) 656 final) which set out a Commission work programme concerning the evaluation of policy options to deal with the greenhouse effect. The Communication was accompanied by a draft Council Resolution on the greenhouse effect and the Community. In its Communication, the Commission assessed the state of knowledge of the greenhouse issue in the following terms:

1. The composition of the earth's atmosphere is being significantly modified by human activities. Based on results of global climatic models, scientists agree that a doubling of the equivalent CO_2 atmospheric concentration will bring an increase of the average surface temperature in the range 1.5–4.5C. Such doubling is likely to happen within the first half of next century. According to climatic data the resulting change in average global climatic conditions will be beyond the range of climates that have existed during the historical past and during recent geological times.
2. The various impacts of such climatic change and their socio-economic consequences cannot be reliably assessed in detail at present. However the preliminary studies made on this subject show that the risks are alarmingly high and the likely direct and indirect consequences potentially disruptive.
3. Recent international events have introduced a sense of urgency in the worldwide debate on the issue. It has come out clearly that this is the time to work out viable strategies while accelerating research efforts.

49 OJ No L 85 of 28/3/87.

In the light of its assessment of the current state of knowledge, the Commission reached the following operational conclusions:

1. The Community should implement fully the Vienna Convention for the protection of the ozone layer and the Montreal Protocol on substances that deplete the ozone layer and it should participate actively in the renegotiation of such Protocol.
2. The Community should welcome initiation of discussions on the possibilities of an international agreement for the future protection of the atmosphere. It should be prepared to give an important contribution to the preparation and negotiation of such an agreement which might include the establishment of specific targets for limiting emissions of greenhouse gases as well as definition of emission reduction measures and programmes.
3. Therefore, the Commission will take the initiative to launch a substantial policy-options study programme to evaluate the feasibility, costs and likely results of possible measures to limit greenhouse gases emissions. The main areas of such programme should be:
   - identification and technical assessment of measures and technologies capable of reducing greenhouse gases emissions;
   - analysis of economic, industrial, energy, social and institutional implications and impacts of the above mentioned possible measures and technologies;
   - structuring and evaluating policy scenarios referring in particular to possible strategic targets for CO_2 emission ceilings;
   - establishing a decision analysis framework;
   - identifying and evaluating adaptive policies.
4. The Community and its Member States should take into account in their policy decisions (related to energy or other sectors relevant to the issue) the problem of potential climate changes linked to the greenhouse effect. Early consideration of such issue could avoid higher costs in future.
5. Moreover, the Commission will take action to reinforce and expand efforts in the field of energy savings, energy efficiency improvement, development of new energy sources, use of safe nuclear technology. The accelerated development and promotion of innovative commercial-scale technologies in these fields should be given high priority. There is no doubt that such action is justified because of both energy and environmental requirements, independent of uncertainties on some scientific aspects of the greenhouse issue. Of special importance would be the possibility to quantify energy efficiency improvements in terms of CO_2 reductions.
6. The Community should sustain vigorous research programmes on all the relevant aspects of the greenhouse issue and should provide new energy technologies having the potential to limit CO_2 emissions.

Among the possible actions, the Commission identified both preventive and adaptive actions. In the case of CO_2, it considered the energy sector in general and forestry and the tropical regions as the most relevant areas for intervention. Examples of energy measures which could contribute to curb CO_2 emissions were:

- increase energy efficiency (both on the supply and on the demand side);
- switch to less carbon intensive fuels;
- promote renewable energy sources and sustainable use of biomass;
- promote safe nuclear energy.

The promotion of innovative energy technologies to support such measures seemed to be of particular importance. In the long term new non-carbon based energy systems could give a significant contribution to curbing CO_2 emissions. Of course not all the above mentioned measures were equally effective. Moreover, a careful assessment of their economic viability was required.

Forestry policies should tend to reverse present deforestation trends especially in the equatorial regions. This would in particular require promoting substitutes for wood used massively as fuel in those regions and promoting sustainable agricultural practices so that agricultural expansion did not involve large-scale forest burning to clear land.

Possible actions to decrease emissions of greenhouse gases such as CH_4 and N_2O were less easy to identify given the uncertainties surrounding emissions of these substances. The following subjects could be explored:

- minimizing CH_4 losses in extraction, transport and use of natural gas;
- minimizing CH_4 losses from landfills;
- minimizing N_2O emission from fossil fuel burning;
- studying possible improvements in livestock management, rice cultivation and lagoon management, aiming at reducing CH_4 release;
- studying possible improved fertilizing management practices to reduce N_2O release from nitrogen fertilizer use.

In the case of CFCs, the nearly total elimination of CFCs emissions should be feasible by the year 2000 by constraining production and recapturing, recycling or destroying CFCs in existing products. Adaptation measures (i.e. those required in order to prevent or decrease damage due to climatic changes and associated impacts) might be required to deal with effects which, despite preventive actions, proved to be unavoidable. At this stage it was not possible to detail adaptation measures which could be required in the Community because of the lack of a reliable regional assessment of potential impacts. In general, adaptation to deal with sea-level rise could include sea wall/flood barriers, national flood insurance programmes, construction of reservoirs (to combat increased salinity), abandonment of developed regions in low-lying areas, other relocation of populations away from vulnerable sites, protection of coastal ecosystems, etc. More study was needed to identify possible adaptation measures in other sectors such as agriculture and forestry.

The Commission's Communication on the "greenhouse effect" and the draft Council Resolution was presented by Stanley Clinton-Davis, the Commissioner responsible for the Environment, to the Environment Council at its meeting on 24 November 1988. Since governments had only recently received the paper from the Commission, the Council limited itself to taking note of the Commissioner's statement, while leaving it to the incoming (Spanish) Presidency to progress the work further.

At its meeting in Dublin in June 1990, the European Council called for the adoption at the earliest possible opportunity of targets and strategies to limit emissions of greenhouse gases, in particular carbon dioxide. Later that year, at the meeting of the energy and environment ministers, the Council undertook to stabilize Community CO_2 emissions at 1990 levels by 2000. In the end, though, it was almost three years after its 1988 Communication before the Commission put forward proposals for a Community strategy for stabilizing carbon dioxide emissions at 1990 levels by 2000. In its Communication to the Council of 14 October 1991 (SEC (91) 1744 final of 14 October 1991), the Commission set out a four-pronged strategy:

- conventional measures and instruments, including research and development programmes, and technical measures to reduce CO_2 emissions;
- national programmes aimed at supplementing the other measures in the light of Member States' own economic, cultural, geographical or technical circumstances;

- measures to help Member States in areas where pollution poses the biggest problems for them either in terms of abatement or because of economic constraints;
- tax measures, including the possibility of a specific CO_2/energy tax.

At its meeting of 13 December 1991, the Council of Energy and Environment Ministers called on the Commission to table official proposals for concrete measures to implement the strategy, including proposals for the tax measures necessary at Community level.

1. SAVE programme (L 307/34)

On 29 October 1991 the Council adopted the SAVE programme (Specific Actions for Vigorous Energy Efficiency) – a five-year programme for energy efficiency running from 1 January 1991 to 31 December 1995. The SAVE programme is intended to comprise a set of legal and regulatory measures as well as a series of back-up measures part-financed by the Community and aimed at complementing the activities geared to energy efficiency in the Member States. The financial resource estimated as necessary for the programme's implementation amounted to Ecu 35 million. The programme focuses on three mutually complementary categories of action:

- technical measures – in particular setting Community level standards or specifications compatible with energy efficiency in the building, domestic appliances or transport sectors;
- financial measures – using financial instruments to provide additional incentives for investments concerning energy efficiency, especially third party financing;
- action relating to user behaviour – information and training to help change consumer habits and to increase the awareness of economic operators.

At the same as it adopted the SAVE programme the Commission also adopted a proposal concerning energy efficiency requirements for boilers. This proposal was adopted within the framework of the SAVE programme by the Council as Directive 92/42 of 21 May 1992 on efficiency requirements for new hot-water boilers fired with liquid or gaseous fuels. The directive sets efficiency requirements for boilers with an output of 4 kW – 400 kW.

On 20 May 1992, also within the framework of the SAVE programme, the Commission sent the Council a proposal for a directive to limit carbon dioxide emissions by improving energy efficiency, which set out seven types of measures, including thermal insulation of new buildings, energy audits of businesses, the billing of heating, air-conditioning and hot water costs on the basis of real consumption, and the regular inspection of boilers.

2. ALTENER programme

The Altener programme set out to increase the contribution made from renewable energy sources to total energy demand from 4% to 8% by 2005. It also aims to treble the production of electricity from renewable energy sources, as well as to ensure that biofuels account for 5% of fuel consumption by motor vehicles.

3.   1992 proposal for a directive introducing a tax on carbon dioxide emissions and energy

On 2 June 1992 the Commission sent the Council a proposal for a directive to intro-duce a tax on carbon dioxide emissions and on energy as part of the Community strategy to cut CO_2 emissions. The proposed tax would be one of the most import-ant elements of the strategy to reduce CO_2 emissions and would seek to encourage more economical use of energy and fossil fuels, as well as to provide an incentive for fuel switching from carbon-rich fuels, such as coal, to fuels with a lower carbon content, such as natural gas. The tax would be levied on all solid, viscous or gaseous fossil fuels, either in their crude state or in their final form with 50% levied on the carbon content of fuel and 50% on the calorific value of the energy source, whether fossil or not, but excluding renewables. Although the Commission realized that a tax solely on carbon would be more effective in reducing CO_2 emissions, it was felt that the advantage that a pure carbon tax would give to France, which is heavily dependent on nuclear energy, would be unacceptable to other Member States. In any case, a tax with an energy element as well would serve to encourage more rational and efficient use of all types of energy.

In accordance with guidelines laid down in the Communication of 14 October 1991, a basic rate, common to all Member States, would be set at Ecu 2.81 per tonne of carbon dioxide emitted by fossil fuels and at Ecu 0.21 per gigajoule for the energy component, a total tax of Ecu 17.75 per tonne of oil equivalent (toe), corre-sponding to US$3 per barrel at 1991 prices. However, electricity would be taxed at the rate of Ecu 2.1 per MW/h, with the exception of electricity generated by hydro-electric installations which would be taxed at the rate of Ecu 0.76 per MW/h.

The tax would increase by the equivalent of US$1 per barrel each consecutive year until it reached $10 per barrel equivalent, although the Council would be able to authorize one or more Member States temporarily to suspend application of the tax if particular circumstances relating to the economic situation arose. The Commission estimated the tax would raise the price of anthracite by some 58%, natural gas by 14% and petrol by 6% if the entire tax were passed on to the con-sumer. Member States could apply higher rates if they wished. Introduction of the tax would be conditional on the Community's main competitors, namely other OECD countries, imposing similar measures having an equivalent financial impact. Nevertheless, if this conditionality were not sufficient to safeguard the competi-tiveness of energy intensive industries, additional provisions would be allowed in the form of exemptions and graduated reductions in the tax.

The proposal states the tax must respect the principle of tax neutrality, i.e. that Member States must not use the tax as a means for raising more revenue and increasing the overall tax burden. If the tax were introduced, it would have to be offset in full by tax incentives or by reductions in taxes and other statutory contri-butions for both firms and individuals. As the Member States would be responsible for collecting and administering the tax, it is they who would have to decide on the arrangements for determining overall neutrality. The proposal suggests that meas-ures taken to this effect could include reductions in direct taxation or social security contributions, or reductions in indirect taxation. The proposal suggests that tax incentives, the effectiveness of which has been shown by the tax advantage given to unleaded petrol, could also be used. Examples are tax incentives for electrically powered vehicles or for other environmentally friendly modes of transport, or for forestry investment to promote the use of forests as CO_2 "sinks", or for the residential and tertiary sector which are responsible for 25% of CO_2 emissions.

The proposal for a tax on carbon dioxide emissions and energy was put forward as part of the Community's contribution to the effort by industrialized countries to reduce their CO_2 emissions and in line with the commitment undertaken by the Community to this end at the 1992 UNCED in Rio de Janeiro (see p. 465). It also represented a first attempt to move towards pollution taxes in line with the commitments in the Community's successive Environment Action Programmes which have increasingly stressed the need to use economic instruments for environmental policy in addition to traditional "command and control" measures.

The Ecofin Council meeting of 14 December 1992 considered the proposals to introduce an energy and CO_2 tax and concluded that the likely impact of the tax on energy consumption, economic activity and competitiveness should be analysed. The Council requested that the Economic Policy Committee should examine, *inter alia*, the question of the appropriate rate of tax and how it should be applied, the balance between the carbon and the energy elements, exemptions to offset negative effects on industrial competition, measures to ensure that the tax does not produce distortions between Member States or prejudice fiscal harmonization and whether Member States should be required to ensure tax neutrality.

On 28 January 1993, Mrs Scrivener, the Commissioner responsible for taxation matters, welcomed the declaration by the new Clinton administration in the USA that it was considering the introduction of an energy tax given the element of "conditionality" that had been introduced in the Commission's own proposal.

However, the Ecofin Council meeting on 7 June 1993 failed to agree in principle on proposals for an energy tax, national differences appearing to present insurmountable problems. Not least among such difficulties was the reluctance of Member States such as the United Kingdom to see an increase in the Community's powers over taxation and revenue-raising. Even though the product of a "carbon tax" according to the Commission's proposal was to be spent at the national level and was not to be seen as a way of increasing the Community's "own resources", the tax would have been mandated by the Community institutions and as such could be seen as a further encroachment on national sovereignty in what was probably the most sensitive area.

The Ecofin Council of 7 June 1993 nevertheless published "Conclusions of the Presidency" which "agreed that fiscal instruments will play an important role in developing the Community's overall strategy to limit carbon dioxide emissions and to improve energy efficiency", and noted that "a number of Member States have indicated that fiscal instruments will make a significant contribution to their planned reductions in CO_2 emissions and that a decision on such instruments at Community level should be reached as soon as possible".[50]

X.   FUTURE ACTION

In its programme "Towards Sustainability",[51] the Commission proposed new European Community themes and targets in the area of climate change,

---

[50] *European Environmental Law Review*, Vol 2, No 6, August/September 1993.

[51] COM (92) 23 final – Vol II, 27 March 1992.

Table 4.12: The fifth environment action programme: climate change

Objectives	EC Targets up to 2000	Actions	Time-frame	Sectors
CO_2	* stabilization on 1990 levels #) (progressive reductions at the horizon 2005 and 2010[(1)]	* Energy conservation measures e.g. – env. benign energy use – behavioural changes – economic and fiscal measures	continuous	Energy Transport Industry Public
		* Improvement of energy efficiency e.g. – R & D – infrastructural changes – change in transport modes – economic and fiscal measures	id	Energy Waste Transport Industry Consumer
		* Fuel substitution towards less or no CO_2 emitting sources (renewables, natural gas etc.) e.g. – R & D – infrastructural changes – economic and fiscal measures	id	Energy
Methane (CH_4) Nitrous oxide (N_2O)	* measures to be identified not later than 1994 and applied (possibly reduction targets)	* Inventory of data	before 1994	Energy Agriculture Waste

Table 4.12 continued

	Objectives	EC Targets up to 2000	Actions	Time-frame	Sectors
CFCs + carbon-tetrachloride + Halons + LII trichlorethane	no emissions of ozone layer depleting substances	* phase out before 1.1.1996 (except for some essential uses)			Industry
HCFCs etc		* limitation of use to maximum 5% of 1990 CFC use levels			

#) targets already set by the EC

N.B. The EC commits itself to help and support countries which seek for it, in their aim for stabilization and reduction measures in relation to greenhouse gases. The following measures could be used: debt trading, technology transfer, general trade arrangements, participation in global financial mechanisms.

(¹) Conclusions of the Joint Energy/Environment Council of 29 October 1990.

acidification and air quality. As far as climate change is concerned, Table 4.12 indicates overall objectives, targets for the year 2000, types of action required and the main sectors involved.

As far as acidification and air quality is concerned, "Towards Sustainability" signalled a new emphasis on the "critical load" approach, defined as "quantitative estimates of an exposure to one or more pollutants below which, according to present knowledge, significant harmful effects on specified elements of the environment do not occur". "Significant harmful effects are assumed to occur when critical values of chemical compounds in forest soils and freshwaters are exceeded."

Table 4.13 gives an indication of the overall EC targets and instruments which should be aimed for by the year 2000 on the way to a sustainable situation.

Table 4.14 indicates the measures needed to guarantee levels of air quality which are not detrimental to health and the environment.

Table 4.13: The fifth environment action programme: acidification

	Objective	EC Targets up to 2000	Actions + time-frame	Sectors/Actors
NOx 1)	no exceedance ever	* stabilization at EC level emissions in 1994 (1990 level) #) * 30% reduction in 2000	* actions listed in Table 7 on global scale also apply for NOx and SOx	Energy Transport Agriculture Industry
SOx 1)		* 35% at EC level reduction of emissions in 2000 (1985 level)	* proposals for products standards for coal, fuel oils and residuals before 1995	Tourism EC + MS + Energy and Industry
NH3 (ammonia)	of critical	* variable targets in accordance with problems identified in regions	* Inventory of NH3 emissions + trends before 1994; standards on new farm buildings before 1996	MS + LAs + EC EEA + AGRI
General VOCs	loads and	* 10% reduction of man-made emissions in 1996 * 30% reduction (1990 level) in 1999	* reductions in transport sector – idem in industry solvents and paints, and chemical industry	EC + MS + Industry
Dioxins	levels	* 90% reduction of dioxins emissions of identified sources by 2005 (1985 levels)	* Directive (revision) on standards for municipal waste incineration plants before 1994 * proposal for Directive on incineration of hazardous waste: 1992	EC + MS EC + MS
Heavy metals		* at least 70% reduction from all pathways of Cd, Hg and Pb emissions in 1995	* Integrated pollution control and revised BAT	EC + MS + LAs + Industry

#) Target already set by EC
1) In 1990 the Commission has presented a set of scenarios on energy demand and supply and their consequences for NOx, SO$_2$ and CO$_2$ emissions. On the basis of computer calculations with the RAINS model, regions listed under objectives 1 and 2 of the Structural Funds would still have room for considerable development from the point of view of acidification. However, where areas within these regions would reach or exceed the critical loads, further reduction over and above those provided for in the existing EC legislation will require to be introduced. In all other EC-regions the reduction targets as listed should apply without any exceptions requiring a substantial decrease in energy demand through higher efficiency and increased energy savings.

Table 4.14: The fifth environment action programme: air quality

Objectives	Targets up to 2000	Actions	Time-frame	Actors
* All people should be effectively protected against recognized health risks from Air Pollution	* implementation and enforcement of existing legislation on SO_2, NO_2, Lead, Particulates and Black Smoke	* identification of existing or potential problems * proposals for amendments of existing legislation	before 1995 id	*EC* + MS + EEA *EC* + MS
* Permitted concentration levels of air pollutants should take into account the protection of the environment	* WHO values become mandatory at EC level	* Air quality monitoring and control of concentration levels with regard to norms on all substances covered by legislation	not later than 1998	*MS + LAs* + EEA
* Extension of the list of regulated substances which cause pollution and danger to public health and the environment	For Ozone (O_3): * for health protection: current levels if not exceeding the mean value over 1-hour of 175 $\mu g/m^3$ and the mean value over 8-hour of 110 $\mu g/m^3$ * for protection of vegetation: a 200 $\mu g/m^3$ mean value over 1-hour and a 65 $\mu g/m^3$ mean over 24 hours should not be exceeded	* Directive	in 1992	*EC* + MS

AIR

183

Table 4.14 continued

Objectives	Targets up to 2000	Actions	Time-frame	Actors
	For Carbon monoxide (CO) and Cadmium (Cd): * knowledge of existing levels and setting of norms	* identification of potential or existing problems	before 1997	EC + MS + EEA
	* compliance with norms for concentrations			
	For other substances, such as heavy metals, organic compounds and deposition of Sulphur and Nitrogen: * knowledge of existing levels	* identification of potential or existing problems	before 1999	id
	* different targets according to different existing situations			

Chapter 5

Waste Management

I. INTRODUCTION

1. Community waste management policy started at about the same time as water pollution policy, in 1975. The Commission estimated that the Community was then generating over 2000 million tonnes of waste each year, which by virtue of its quantity or nature posed a whole series of problems for man and the environment. The quantity of waste was growing steadily. Most of it was disposed of to land though about 80% was potentially re-usable or recyclable for raw materials or energy. Moreover, the use of improved production processes in both industry and agriculture would make it possible to halt the growth of waste production. Given this situation, the Commission made it clear that it intended over the coming years to strengthen and expand its waste management policy.

Though contemporaneous with water pollution policy, the Community's waste management policy nevertheless has a number of particular characteristics which distinguish it from both water and air policy. Unlike water policy, waste management policy did not cause any particular difficulties within the Council during the discussion of the first proposals for the directives. On the contrary, the oil and energy crisis of 1973–1975 highlighted the importance of avoiding any waste of natural resources and led to renewed interest in recovering raw materials and energy through the re-use and recycling of wastes. These favourable circumstances allowed for the adoption in 1975 of a framework directive on waste, and of several specific directives, on waste oils or polychlorinated biphenyls for example. All of these regulations contain fairly detailed and restrictive provisions for the Member States to observe, to the extent that certain Member States have been unable to respect several of these texts within the prescribed period of time.

This favourable and promising start to waste management policy, on both the qualitative and quantitative levels, is all the more remarkable in that it contrasts with the relatively modest orientations of the 1973 1st Action Programme regarding waste management. Indeed, the 1973 programme considered that Community actions in the area of waste management should mainly concern the elimination of wastes which, because of their toxicity, their non-degradability and their bulk, required a solution extending beyond national borders.

The 1977 2nd Environmental Action Programme considerably extended the field of application of actions in the area of waste management policy. It established three guiding objectives in this respect which were confirmed by the 1983 3rd Action Programme. These three objectives concern:

- the prevention and reduction of quality non-recoverable waste;
- the recovery, recycling and re-use of waste for raw materials and energy;
- the proper management and harmless disposal of non-recoverable waste.

Thus, while the objectives and orientations in the area of waste management from 1977 onwards were becoming more precise and ambitious within the framework of the 2nd Action Programme, the rate at which the Council adopted new directives and legislative measures tended to slacken off between 1978 and 1984.

2. On several occasions during this period (1978–1984) the European Parliament criticized the inadequacy of Community actions in the area of waste management, as much with regard to the failure of Member States to respect the first directives adopted between 1975 and 1978, as to the inadequacy of new measures. These criticisms were accentuated by the coming to light of several incidents or scandals linked to toxic or dangerous wastes, the best known of which concerns the "Seveso" affair. On that occasion the European Parliament took the initiative of setting up, apparently for the first time, a committee of enquiry which took evidence from the main people responsible for waste management policy in the different Member States. The Seveso affair and the European Parliament committee of enquiry highlighted the fundamental importance of issues linked to the transport of toxic and dangerous wastes. Despite the external pressure brought about by this affair, it was almost two years before the Council adopted the proposal put forward by the Commission in January 1983 which was specifically intended to control the cross-border transfer of toxic and dangerous wastes.

3. Parallel with the legislative action, Community waste management policy has experienced a notable evolution since 1984 towards the development of a "clean technologies" programme. Thanks to the adoption in June 1984 of a regulation allowing for Community financial aid in certain specific sectors (Reg. 1872/84 known as the ACE regulation) (see p. 339), the Community has been able to increase its activities in the area of waste prevention. It expects to extend this programme, which is aimed at clean technologies, to cover new industrial sectors. Such a programme is closely linked with the efforts undertaken elsewhere by the Community to develop new technologies and to improve its competitiveness.

Finally it should be noted that radioactive waste and the discharge of waste into the sea have always occupied an important position within the Community waste management policy. As far as radioactive wastes are concerned, the Community became interested at a very early stage in the problems presented by the treatment and elimination of such wastes, particularly within the framework of the European Atomic Energy Community (Euratom). The main efforts undertaken by the Community in this sensitive area concern research actions.

As far as the discharge of waste into the sea is concerned, the Community has been prevented until now from adopting a specific regulation in this area because of the opposition of several Member States within the Council. However, in 1985 the Commission drew up a new proposal for a directive aiming to control the international discharge of waste into the sea. This proposal does not cover the discharge of radioactive waste (see p. 116).

II. WASTE IN GENERAL

1. The 1975 framework directive on waste

On 17 September 1974 the Commission sent a proposal to the Council on the disposal of waste. The Council approved this directive on 15 July 1975.[1] It is a framework directive containing general provisions on waste disposal. The idea of "waste disposal" is defined very broadly, in that:

- "waste" means any substance or object which the holder disposes of or is required to dispose of pursuant to the provisions of national law in force;
- "disposal" covers the collection, sorting, transport and treatment of waste as well as its storage and tipping above or under ground, together with the transformation operations necessary for its re-use, recovery or recycling.

The scope of the directive nevertheless excludes certain specific categories of waste, such as radioactive waste, waste resulting from mineral resources and the working of quarries, agricultural waste including animal carcasses, waste water, and gaseous effluents.

The directive first contains a general provision according to which Member States are required to take appropriate steps to encourage the prevention, recycling and reprocessing of waste, the extraction of raw materials and energy and any other process for the re-use of waste. It then requires Member States to take the necessary measures to ensure that waste is disposed of without endangering human health and without harming the environment, and in particular:

- without risk to water, air, soil, plants and animals;
- without causing a nuisance through noise and odours;
- without adversely affecting the countryside or places of specific interest.

To this end, Member States must designate the competent authorities to be responsible, in a given zone, for the planning, organization, authorization and supervision of waste disposal operations. These authorities must draw up plans relating in particular to the type and quantity of waste to be disposed of, the general technical requirements to be respected, and suitable disposal sites.

Member States are also required to take the necessary measures to ensure that any holder of waste has it handled by a private or public waste collector or by a disposal undertaking, or disposes of it himself without harming the environment. According to the directive, any installation or undertaking, treating, storing or tipping waste on behalf of third parties must obtain a permit from the competent authorities relating in particular to the type and quantity of waste to be treated, general technical requirements, and precautions to be taken. These installations or undertakings must be checked periodically by the competent authority.

Finally, the directive specifies that, in accordance with the "polluter pays" principle, the cost of disposing of waste, less any proceeds derived from treating the waste, shall be borne by the holder of the waste, and, where relevant, by the producer of the product from which the waste came. As far as information is concerned, the Member States must draw up a situation report every three years on

---

[1] OJ No L 194 of 25/7/75.

waste disposal in their respective countries and send it to the Commission. The Commission is also required to report every three years to the Council and to the European Parliament on the application of the directive.

On 5 August 1988, the Commission sent the Council a proposal for a Council directive amending Directive 75/442/EEC on waste. The proposal was adopted by the Council on 18 March 1991 as Directive 91/156. The directive provides for a new definition of waste as follows:

- "Waste" shall mean any substance or object in the categories set out in Annex I which the holder discards or intends or is required to discard.

The Commission is required to draw up a list of waste belonging to the categories listed in Annex I (see below).

Table 5.1: Council Directive of 18 March 1991 amending Directive 75/442/EEC on waste

'ANNEX I

CATEGORIES OF WASTE

Q1   Production or consumption residues not otherwise specified below

Q2   Off-specification products

Q3   Products whose date for appropriate use has expired

Q4   Materials spilled, lost or having undergone other mishap, including any materials, equipment, etc., contaminated as a result of the mishap

Q5   Materials contaminated or soiled as a result of planned actions (e.g. residues from cleaning operations, packing materials, containers, etc.)

Q6   Unusable parts (e.g. reject batteries, exhausted catalysts, etc.)

Q7   Substances which no longer perform satisfactorily (e.g. contaminated acids, contaminated solvents, exhausted tempering salts, etc.)

Q8   Residues of industrial processes (e.g. slags, still bottoms, etc.)

Q9   Residues from pollution abatement processes (e.g. scrubber sludges, baghouse dusts, spent filters, etc.)

Q10   Machining/finishing residues (e.g. lathe turnings, mill scales, etc.)

Q11   Residues from raw materials extraction and processing (e.g. mining residues, oil field slops, etc.)

Q12   Adulterated materials (e.g. oils contaminated with PCBs, etc.)

Q13   Any materials, substances or products whose use has been banned by law

Q14   Products for which the holder has no further use (e.g. agricultural, household, office, commercial and shop discards, etc.)

Q15   Contaminated materials, substances or products resulting from remedial action with respect to land

Q16   Any materials, substances or products which are not contained in the above categories.

The directive in Annexes II A and B (see Table 5.2) defines the disposal and recovery operations which are to be subject to a permit to be granted by the competent authority. In the case of disposal, the permit has to cover:

- the types and quantities of waste,
- the technical requirements,
- the security precautions to be taken,
- the disposal site, and
- the treatment method.

In accordance with Article 5, each Member State, in cooperation with other Member States where this is necessary or advisable, is to establish an integrated

Table 5.2: Council Directive of 18 March 1991 amending Directive 75/442/EEC on waste

ANNEX IIA

DISPOSAL OPERATIONS

NB: This Annex is intended to list disposal operations such as they occur in practice. In accordance with Article 4, waste must be disposed of without endangering human health and without the use of processes or methods likely to harm the environment.

D1   Tipping above or underground (e.g. landfill, etc.)

D2   Land treatment (e.g. biodegradation of liquid or sludge discards in soils, etc.)

D3   Deep injection (e.g. injection of pumpable discards into wells, salt domes or naturally occurring repositories, etc.)

D4   Surface impoundment (e.g. placement of liquid or sludge discards into pits, ponds or lagoons, etc.)

D5   Specially engineered landfill (e.g. placement into lined discrete cells which are capped and isolated from one another and the environment, etc.)

D6   Release of solid waste into a water body except seas/oceans

D7   Release into seas/oceans including seabed insertion

D8   Biological treatment not specified elsewhere in this Annex which results in final compounds or mixtures which are disposed of by means of any of the operations in this Annex

D9   Physico-chemical treatment not specified elsewhere in this Annex which results in final compounds or mixtures which are disposed of by means of any of the operations in this Annex (e.g. evaporation, drying, calcination, etc.)

D10 Incineration on land

D11 Incineration at sea

D12 Permanent storage (e.g. emplacement of containers in a mine, etc.)

D13 Blending or mixture prior to submission to any of the operations in this Annex

D14 Repackaging prior to submission to any of the operations in this Annex

D15 Storage pending any of the operations in this Annex, excluding temporary storage, pending collection, on the site where it is produced.

Table 5.2 continued

ANNEX IIB

OPERATIONS WHICH MAY LEAD TO RECOVERY

NB: This Annex is intended to list recovery operations as they are carried out in practice. In accordance with Article 4, waste must be recovered without endangering human health and without the use of processes or methods likely to harm the environment.

R1   Solvent reclamation/regeneration

R2   Recycling/reclamation of organic substances which are not used as solvents

R3   Recycling/reclamation of metals and metal compounds

R4   Recycling/reclamation of other inorganic materials

R5   Regeneration of acids or bases

R6   Recovery of components used for pollution abatement

R7   Recovery of components from catalysts

R8   Oil re-refining or other re-uses of oil

R9   Use principally as a fuel or other means to generate energy

R10 Spreading on land resulting in benefit to agriculture or ecological improvement, including composting and other biological transformation processes, except in the case of waste excluded under Article 2 (1) (b) (iii)

R11 Use of wastes obtained from any of the operations numbered R1 – R10

R12 Exchange of wastes for submission to any of the operations numbered R1 – R11

R13 Storage of materials intended for submission to any operation in this Annex, excluding temporary storage, pending collection, on the site where it is produced.'

and adequate network of disposal installations, taking account of the best available technology not involving excessive costs. The network must enable the Community as a whole to become self-sufficient in waste disposal and the Member States to move towards that aim individually, taking into account geographical circumstances or the need for specialized installations for certain types of waste.

The Commission Decision of 20 December 1993[2] established a list of waste belonging to the categories listed in Annex I of the directive, commonly referred to as the European Waste Catalogue (EWC). The EWC applies to all wastes irrespective of whether they are destined for disposal or for recovery operations. The EWC is a harmonized, non-exhaustive list of wastes which will be periodically reviewed and if necessary revised in accordance with the committee procedure.

The EWC index is shown in Table 5.3.

2.   The Consultative Committee on Waste Management

Through a decision taken on 21 April 1976, the Commission set up a Committee on Waste Management.[3] The task of this consultative committee is to supply the

[2] OJ No L 5 of 7/1/94.
[3] OJ No C 115 of 1/5/76.

Table 5.3: Commission Decision of 20 December 1993 establishing a list of wastes pursuant to Article 1(a) of Council Directive 75/442/EEC on waste

INDEX

01 00 00	Waste resulting from exploration, mining, dressing and further treatment of minerals and quarrying
02 00 00	Waste from agricultural, horticultural, hunting, fishing and aquaculture primary production, food preparation and processing
03 00 00	Wastes from wood processing and the production of paper, cardboard, pulp, panels and furniture
04 00 00	Wastes from the leather and textile industries
05 00 00	Wastes from petroleum refining, natural gas purification and pyrolytic treatment of coal
06 00 00	Wastes from inorganic chemical processes
07 00 00	Wastes from organic chemical processes
08 00 00	Wastes from manufacture, formulation, supply and use (MFSU) of coatings, (paints, varnishes and vitreous enamels), adhesives, sealants and printing inks
09 00 00	Wastes from the photographic industry
10 00 00	Inorganic wastes from thermal processes
11 00 00	Inorganic waste with metals from metal treatment and the coating of metals; non-ferrous hydrometallurgy
12 00 00	Wastes from shaping and surface treatment of metals and plastics
13 00 00	Oil wastes (except edible oils, 05 00 00 and 12 00 00)
14 00 00	Wastes from organic substances employed as solvents (except 07 00 00 and 08 00 00)
15 00 00	Packaging; absorbents, wiping cloths, filter materials and protective clothing not otherwise specified
16 00 00	Waste not otherwise specified in the catalogue
17 00 00	Construction and demolition waste (including road construction)
18 00 00	Wastes from human or animal health care and/or related research (excluding kitchen and restaurant wastes which do not arise from immediate health care)
19 00 00	Wastes from waste treatment facilities, off-site water treatment plants and the water industry
20 00 00	Municipal wastes and similar commercial, industrial and institutional wastes including separately collected fractions

Commission with opinions, either at the request of the Commission or on its own initiative, on all matters relating to:

● the formulation of a policy for waste management having regard to the need to ensure the best use of resources and the safe and effective disposal of waste;

- the different technical, economic, administrative and legal measures which could prevent the production of wastes or ensure their re-use, recycling or disposal;
- the implementation of directives on waste management and the formulation of fresh proposals for directives in this field.

The Committee is headed by a representative of the Commission and includes two representatives per Member State. It met for the first time in March 1977, and established the following priorities: toxic waste; waste paper; packaging; use of waste for fuel. The other fields singled out by the Committee concerned agricultural waste, textile wastes, and material resulting from demolition.

The Committee later approved action programmes in the packaging and waste paper sector, and defined the mandate of different working groups whose purpose was mainly to increase the energy possibilities offered by agricultural waste. More recently it has identified new directions to be taken in the area of transfrontier shipment of toxic and dangerous waste, has established criteria for the burning of used oils, and has decided to set up a data bank on waste.

III.   DANGEROUS WASTE

1.   Toxic and dangerous waste

(a)   The 1978 directive on toxic and dangerous waste

In accordance with the 1973 and 1977 Action Programmes which stress the need for Community actions to control the disposal of toxic and dangerous waste, the Commission presented a proposal to the Council on 22 July 1976 for a directive which is devoted specifically to toxic and dangerous waste. The content and structure of this directive largely follows that of the earlier framework directive of 15 July 1975 on waste in general.

The Council adopted the directive on toxic and dangerous waste on 20 March 1978, after two years of extensive discussions.[4]

The directive's field of application is basically defined by a precise list of dangerous substances which is annexed to the directive (see Table 5.3). The directive considers as "toxic and dangerous" any waste containing or contaminated by one or more of the substances listed in Table 5.3, in such quantities or concentrations as to constitute a risk to health or the environment. Some specific wastes are excluded from the directive's field of application, for example, radioactive waste; animal carcasses and agricultural waste of faecal origin; explosives; hospital waste; mining waste; household waste, etc. First of all, the directive instructs Member States to encourage as a matter of priority the prevention, recycling, and processing of toxic and dangerous waste, particularly with a view to extracting raw materials and energy from them.

It must be ensured that the disposal of such waste does not endanger human health, or harm the environment, that is, it is carried out without risk to water, air, soil, plants or animals; without causing a nuisance through noise or odours; and without adversely affecting the countryside or places of interest. To achieve these

[4] OJ No L 84 of 31/3/78.

Table 5.4: Council Directive of 20 March 1978
Toxic and Dangerous Waste

List of toxic or dangerous substances and materials

This list consists of certain toxic or dangerous substances and materials selected as requiring priority consideration

1   Arsenic: arsenic compounds
2   Mercury: mercury compounds
3   Cadmium: cadmium compounds
4   Thallium: thallium compounds
5   Beryllium: beryllium compounds
6   Chrome 6 compounds
7   Lead: lead compounds
8   Antimony: antimony compounds
9   Phenols: phenol compounds
10 Cyanides, organic and inorganic
11 Isocyanates
12 Organic-halogen compounds, excluding inert polymeric materials and other substances referred to in this list or covered by other Directives concerning the disposal of toxic or dangerous waste
13 Chlorinated solvents
14 Organic solvents
15 Biocides and phyto-pharmaceutical substances
16 Tarry materials from refining and tar residues from distilling
17 Pharmaceutical compounds
18 Peroxides, chlorates, perchlorates and azides
19 Ethers
20 Chemical laboratory materials, not identifiable and/or new, whose effects on the environment are not known
21 Asbestos (dust and fibres)
22 Selenium: selenium compounds
23 Tellurium: tellurium compounds
24 Aromatic polycyclic compounds (with carcinogenic effects)
25 Metal carbonyls
26 Soluble copper compounds
27 Acids and/or basic substances used in the surface treatment and finishing of metals

objectives, the directive prohibits in particular the abandonment and uncontrolled discharge of toxic and dangerous waste.

Member States must also designate or establish competent authorities to be responsible, in a given area, for the planning, organization and supervision of operations for the disposal of toxic and dangerous waste.

The installations, establishments or undertakings which carry out the "disposal" of toxic and dangerous waste in the broadest sense of the term, i.e. the storage, treatment and or deposit of these wastes, must obtain a permit from the competent authorities in the Member States. This permit should cover specific indications concerning the type and quality of waste; the technical requirements; the precautions to be taken; and the sites and methods of disposal.

Apart from the provision concerning authorization of undertakings, the directive also contains an obligation for undertakings which produce, hold or dispose of toxic and dangerous waste to keep a permanent record of the quantity and characteristics of the waste, together with the dates of receipt and disposal.

The directive also requires Member States to take the necessary measures to ensure that the toxic and dangerous waste is only handled by competent undertakings which have received authorization from the controlling authorities. It obliges any person holding toxic and dangerous waste to have it stored and treated by an authorized installation or undertaking.

Apart from the specific responsibilities regarding the designation, authorization and monitoring of individual "disposal" undertakings, the competent authorities must also establish general plans for the disposal of toxic and dangerous waste, which must be published and sent to the Commission. These plans cover the type and quantity of waste to be disposed of, the methods of disposal, the treatment centres and the disposal sites. The Commission arranges for comparisons of these plans in order to ensure that implementation of the directive is sufficiently coordinated.

(b)   The committee of enquiry set up in 1983 by the European Parliament into the treatment of toxic and dangerous substances

A few weeks after the Commission had sent in January 1983 a proposal for a directive intended to regulate the transfrontier shipment of toxic and dangerous waste (see p. 201), came the affair concerning the "disappearance" of the 41 "Seveso" barrels containing dioxin coming from Seveso. This "disappearance" was widely publicized in the press and on television, and agitated public opinion in Europe. Concerned by this affair, and by the lack of information available, the European Parliament, having voted on an initial resolution on 14 April 1983, decided on 21 June 1983 to set up a committee of enquiry into the "treatment of toxic and dangerous waste in the Community". Such a move is quite exceptional and should be underlined, since it constituted something of a "first" from the institutional point of view.

The "Seveso barrels" committee of enquiry, following the example of American parliamentary commissions, held a number of hearings. These made it possible to hear not only from the Community institutions (Commission, Council) and independent experts, but also from representatives of the Member States. Some Member States, such as Italy and France, were even represented at ministerial level, which was also an important event from the procedural point of view.

Although the parliamentary enquiry committee's mandate was relatively broad, the discussions mainly concentrated on the implementation of the Council's directive of 1978 on toxic and dangerous waste. This examination brought to light certain weaknesses and shortcomings in the implementation of this directive.

The enquiry also demonstrated the economic importance of the waste treatment sector (about 7% of the GNP) and the extent of transfrontier shipment of waste, and in particular of toxic and dangerous substances. The European Parliament ratified the conclusions of its committee of enquiry in two resolutions, voted in March and April 1984 respectively. These resolutions, which address criticisms to both Commission and Council, request that the list of toxic and dangerous substances in the 1978 directive be completed and clarified as a matter of urgency, and underline the need to formulate a more ambitious European policy on waste, for both environmental and economic reasons. Finally, in its two resolutions Parliament asks the Council to speed up its examination of the proposal on transfrontier shipment of toxic waste, expressing the wish that the legal form of the proposal be not a "directive" but a "regulation" directly applicable by Member States.

(c)   The 1991 directive on hazardous waste

On 5 August 1988, the Commission sent the Council a proposal for a Council directive on hazardous waste intended to replace Directive 78/319/EEC. The Commission indicated that it had chosen the expression "hazardous" waste as being wider and more comprehensive than the former "toxic and dangerous" waste. The definition of "hazardous waste" is qualified by the reference to three annexes – a list of types or categories of hazardous waste, a list of substances or materials which render a waste hazardous and a list of hazard characteristics. The definition proposed is close to that of the OECD and, in the Commission's view, should make for very precise designations of waste covering all national situations. In addition, it lends itself to a detailed codification of hazardous waste, suitable for use in the notification procedure for transfrontier shipments of hazardous waste.

Table 5.5: Council Directive of 12 December 1991 on hazardous waste

ANNEX I

CATEGORIES OR GENERIC TYPES OF HAZARDOUS WASTE LISTED ACCORDING TO THEIR NATURE OR THE ACTIVITY WHICH GENERATED THEM (*) (WASTE MAY BE LIQUID, SLUDGE OR SOLID IN FORM)

ANNEX I.A

Wastes displaying any of the properties listed in Annex III and which consist of:

1. anatomical substances; hospital and other clinical wastes;
2. pharmaceuticals, medicines and veterinary compounds;
3. wood preservatives;
4. biocides and phyto-pharmaceutical substances;
5. residue from substances employed as solvents;
6. halogenated organic substances not employed as solvents excluding inert polymerized materials;
7. tempering salts containing cyanides;
8. mineral oils and oily substances (e.g. cutting sludges, etc.);
9. oil/water, hydrocarbon/water mixtures, emulsions;
10. substances containing PCBs and/or PCTs (e.g. dielectrics etc.);
11. tarry materials arising from refining, distillation and any pyrolytic treatment (e.g. still bottoms, etc.);
12. inks, dyes, pigments, paints, lacquers, varnishes;

(*) Certain duplications of entries found in Annex II are intentional.

Table 5.5 continued

13. resins, latex, plasticizers, glues/adhesives;

14. chemical substances arising from research and development or teaching activities which are not identified and/or are new and whose effects on man and/or the environment are not known (e.g. laboratory residues, etc.);

15. pyrotechnics and other explosive materials;

16. photographic chemicals and processing materials;

17. any material contaminated with any congener of polychlorinated dibenzo-furan;

18. any material contaminated with any congener of polychlorinated dibenzo-p-dioxin.

ANNEX I.B

Wastes which contain any of the constituents listed in Annex II and having any of the properties listed in Annex III and consisting of:

19. animal or vegetable soaps, fats, waxes;

20. non-halogenated organic substances not employed as solvents;

21. inorganic substances without metals or metal compounds;

22. ashes and/or cinders;

23. soil, sand, clay including dredging spoils;

24. non-cyanidic tempering salts;

25. metallic dust, powder;

26. spent catalyst materials;

27. liquids or sludges containing metals or metal compounds;

28. residue from pollution control operations (e.g. baghouse dusts, etc.) except (29), (30) and (33);

29. scrubber sludges;

30. sludges from water purification plants;

31. decarbonization residue;

32. ion-exchange column residue;

33. sewage sludges, untreated or unsuitable for use in agriculture;

34. residue from cleaning of tanks and/or equipment;

35. contaminated equipment;

36. contaminated containers (e.g. packaging, gas cylinders, etc.) whose contents included one or more of the constituents listed in Annex II;

37. batteries and other electrical cells;

38. vegetable oils;

39. materials resulting from selective waste collections from households and which exhibit any of the characteristics listed in Annex III;

40. any other wastes which contain any of the constituents listed in Annex II and any of the properties listed in Annex III.

The list of substances or material corresponds to the annex to the original Directive 78/319/EEC, supplemented by several groups of substances.

The list of hazard characteristics contains the list of characteristics laid down by Directive 79/831/EEC of 18 September 1979 (amending for the sixth time Directive 67/548/EEC relating to the classification, packaging and labelling of dangerous substances) (see p. 238). The only wastes which have been excluded are those excluded by the framework Directive 75/442/EEC, and the hazardous wastes subject to special Community rules.

Table 5.6: Council Directive of 12 December 1991 on hazardous waste

ANNEX II

CONSTITUENTS OF THE WASTES IN ANNEX I.B. WHICH RENDER THEM HAZARDOUS WHEN THEY HAVE THE PROPERTIES DESCRIBED IN ANNEX III (*)

Wastes having as constituents:

C1 beryllium; beryllium compounds;
C2 vanadium compounds;
C3 chromium (VI) compounds;
C4 cobalt compounds;
C5 nickel compounds;
C6 copper compounds;
C7 zinc compounds;
C8 arsenic; arsenic compounds;
C9 selenium; selenium compounds;
C10 silver compounds;
C11 cadmium; cadmium compounds;
C12 tin compounds;
C13 antimony; antimony compounds;
C14 tellurium; tellurium compounds;
C15 barium compounds; excluding barium sulfate;
C16 mercury; mercury compounds;
C17 thallium; thallium compounds;
C18 lead; lead compounds;
C19 inorganic sulphides;
C20 inorganic fluorine compounds, excluding calcium fluoride;
C21 inorganic cyanides;
C22 the following alkaline or alkaline earth metals: lithium, sodium, potassium, calcium, magnesium in uncombined form;
C23 acidic solutions or acids in solid form;
C24 basic solutions or bases in solid form;
C25 asbestos (dust and fibres);
C26 phosphorus: phosphorous compounds, excluding mineral phosphates;
C27 metal carbonyls;
C28 peroxides;
C29 chlorates;
C30 perchlorates;
C31 azides;

(*) Certain duplications of generic types of hazardous wastes listed in Annex I are intentional.

Table 5.6 continued

C32 PCBs and/or PCTs;
C33 pharmaceutical or veterinary compounds;
C34 biocides and phyto-pharmaceutical substances (e.g. pesticides, etc.);
C35 infectious substances;
C36 creosotes;
C37 isocyanates; thiocyanates;
C38 organic cyanides (e.g. nitriles, etc.);
C39 phenols; phenol compounds;
C40 halogenated solvents;
C41 organic solvents, excluding halogenated solvents;
C42 organohalogen compounds, excluding inert polymerized materials and other
     substances referred to in this Annex;
C43 aromatic compounds; polycyclic and heterocyclic organic compounds;
C44 aliphatic amines;
C45 aromatic amines;
C46 ethers;
C47 substances of an explosive character, excluding those listed elsewhere in this Annex;
C48 sulphur organic compounds;
C49 any congener of polychlorinated dibenzo-furan;
C50 any congener of polychlorinated dibenzo-p-dioxin;
C51 hydrocarbons and their oxygen; nitrogen and/or sulphur compounds not otherwise
     taken into account in this Annex.

ANNEX III

PROPERTIES OF WASTES WHICH RENDER THEM HAZARDOUS

H1   'Explosive': substances and preparations which may explode under the effect of
     flame or which are more sensitive to shocks or friction than dinitrobenzene.

H2   'Oxidizing': substances and preparations which exhibit highly exothermic reactions
     when in contact with other substances, particularly flammable substances.

H3-A 'Highly flammable':

     – liquid substances and preparations having a flash point below 21°C (including
       extremely flammable liquids), or

     – substances and preparations which may become hot and finally catch fire in
       contact with air at ambient temperature without any application of energy, or

     – solid substances and preparations which may readily catch fire after brief contact
       with a source of ignition and which continue to burn or to be consumed after
       removal of the source of ignition, or

     – gaseous substances and preparations which are flammable in air at normal
       pressure, or

     – substances and preparations which, in contact with water or damp air, evolve
       highly flammable gases in dangerous quantities.

H3-B 'Flammable': liquid substances and preparations having a flash point equal to or
     greater than 21°C and less than or equal to 55°C.

H4   'Irritant': non-corrosive substances and preparations which, through immediate,
     prolonged or repeated contact with the skin or mucous membrane, can cause
     inflammation.

H5   'Harmful': substances and preparations which, if they are inhaled or ingested or if
     they penetrate the skin, may involve limited health risks.

Table 5.6 continued

H6	'Toxic': substances and preparations (including very toxic substances and preparations) which, if they are inhaled or ingested or if they penetrate the skin, may involve serious, acute or chronic health risks and even death.
H7	'Carcinogenic': substances and preparations which, if they are inhaled or ingested or if they penetrate the skin, may induce cancer or increase its incidence.
H8	'Corrosive': substances and preparations which may destroy living tissue on contact.
H9	'Infectious': substances containing viable micro-organisms or their toxins which are known or reliably believed to cause disease in man or other living organisms.
H10	'Teratogenic': substances and preparations which, if they are inhaled or ingested or if they penetrate the skin, may induce non-hereditary congenital malformations or increase their incidence.
H11	'Mutagenic': substances and preparations which, if they are inhaled or ingested or if they penetrate the skin, may induce hereditary genetic defects or increase their incidence.
H12	Substances and preparations which release toxic or very toxic gases in contact with water, air or an acid.
H13	Substances and preparations capable by any means, after disposal, of yielding another substance, e.g. a leachate, which possesses any of the characteristics listed above.
H14	'Ecotoxic': substances and preparations which present or may present immediate or delayed risks for one or more sectors of the environment.

Notes

1. Attribution of the hazard properties 'toxic' (and 'very toxic'), 'harmful', 'corrosive' and 'irritant' is made on the basis of the criteria laid down by Annex VI, part I A and part II B, of Council Directive 67/548/EEC of 27 June 1967 of the approximation of laws, regulations and administrative provisions relating to the classification, packaging and labelling of dangerous substances ([1]), in the version as amended by Council Directive 79/831/EEC ([2]).

2. With regard to attribution of the properties 'carcinogenic', 'teratogenic' and 'mutagenic', and reflecting the most recent findings, additional criteria are contained in the Guide to the classification and labelling of dangerous substances and preparations of Annex VI (part II D) to Directive 67/548/EEC in the version as amended by Commission Directive 83/467/EEC ([3]).

Test methods

The test methods serve to give specific meaning to the definitions given in Annex III. The methods to be used are those described in Annex V to Directive 67/548/EEC, in the version as amended by Commission Directive 84/449/EEC ([4]), or by subsequent Commission Directives adapting Directive 67/548/EEC to technical progress. These methods are themselves based on the work and recommendations of the competent international bodies, in particular the OECD.

([1]) OJ No L 196, 16.8.1967, p. 1.
([2]) OJ No L 259, 15.10.1979, p. 10.
([3]) OJ No L 257, 16.9.1983, p. 1.
([4]) OJ No L 251, 19.9.1984, p. 1.

The other amendments concern the provisions of Directive 78/319/EEC which no longer satisfy the requirements of correct management of hazardous wastes. Many advances have been made in this sector since 1978, and the quantities of waste treated have grown considerably. The mixing of hazardous waste with other waste is prohibited, unless this practice is a necessary part of the treatment or recycling of the waste. Under the proposal, Member States may make collection and transport operations subject to authorization. In addition, the carriage of hazardous waste is subject to special conditions, which are deemed to be fulfilled if the Member State implements the provisions applicable to the carriage of hazardous products provided for in the international conventions, such as the ADR (European Agreement concerning the International Carriage of Dangerous Goods by Road (1957)), RID (International Regulations concerning the Carriage of Dangerous Goods by Rail (1924)), MARPOL (International Convention for the Prevention of Pollution from Ships (1973/1978)), etc. (The full list of relevant international transport conventions is set out in Annex 2 to Directive 84/631/EEC.)

The Council adopted the directive on 12 December 1991 as Directive 91/689/EEC.[5]

In October 1993, the Commission's proposal to amend the above directive was published. Article 1(4), which defines hazardous waste, is replaced and the Commission is obliged to draw up a Community list of hazardous waste in accordance with the procedure in Article 18 of Directive 75/442/EEC (the so-called "adapting to technical progress procedure"), taking into account the origin and the composition of the waste and, where necessary, limit values of concentration. Any subsequent decision by a Member State to consider categories of waste as hazardous shall be notified to the Commission with a view to adaptation of the Community list.[6]

On 21 February 1994 the Council adopted Common Position (EC) No 7/94 on the proposed amendment. The amendment was subsequently adopted as Council Directive 94/31/EC of 27 June 1994. The amendment gives Member States until 27 June 1995 (rather than 12 December 1993) to implement the principal directive. It also substitutes 27 June 1995 for 31 December 1993 as the date on which Directive 78/319/EEC on toxic and dangerous waste is to be repealed.[7]

(d)   The 1992 proposal for a directive on the incineration of hazardous waste

In May 1992 the Commission submitted to the Council a proposal for a directive on the incineration of hazardous waste.[8] The proposal set out emission limits and combustion conditions for air pollutants in order to prevent or keep to a minimum the impact on health and the environment. Measures to protect the soil and groundwater from discharges were also included. The proposed controls would apply to solid or liquid hazardous wastes as defined in Article 1 of Directive 91/689 and would cover both dedicated hazardous waste incineration plants, clinical waste and sewage sludge incinerators and plants which use such waste as a supplementary fuel. A full description and composition of the waste would be required for delivery and reception, as well as a sampling procedure and the availability of safe storage

---

[5] OJ No L 377 of 31/1/2/91.
[6] OJ No C 271/16 of 7/10/93.
[7] OJ No L 168/28, July 1994.
[8] OJ No C 130 of 1/5/92.

and pre-treatment facilities. Plants would need to be designed, equipped and operated according to specific combustion conditions and emission limits.

The proposal establishes average daily/half-hourly emission values for dust, organic substances, sulphur dioxide, hydrogen chloride/fluoride and carbon monoxide; and half-hourly to four-hourly limit values for thallium, mercury, lead, cadmium and other heavy metals.

Table 5.7: Proposal for a Council Directive on the incineration of hazardous waste

Article 8

Member States shall ensure that:
1. incineration plants have to be designed, equipped and operated in such a way that at least the following emission limit values are not exceeded in the exhaust gas:

(a) *daily average values*
1.	total dust	5 mg/m^3
2.	gaseous and vaporous organic substances, expressed as total organic carbon	5 mg/m^3
3.	hydrogen chloride (HCl)	5 mg/m^3
4.	hydrogen fluoride (HF)	1 mg/m^3
5.	sulphur dioxide (SO$_2$)	25 mg/m^3

(b) *half-hourly average values*
1.	total dust	10 mg/m^3
2.	gaseous and vaporous organic substances, expressed as total organic carbon	10 mg/m^3
3.	hydrogen chloride (HCl)	10 mg/m^3
4.	hydrogen fluoride (HF)	2 mg/m^3
5.	sulphur dioxide (SO$_2$)	50 mg/m^3

(c) *all average values over the sample period of a minimum of half and a maximum of four hours*
1.	Cadmium and its compounds, expressed as cadmium (Cd)	0.05 mg/m^3
2.	Thallium and its compounds, expressed as thallium (Tl)	0.05 mg/m^3
3.	Mercury and its compounds, expressed as mercury (Hg)	0.05 mg/m^3
4.	Antimony and its compounds, expressed as antimony (Sb)	0.05 mg/m^3
5.	Arsenic and its compounds, expressed as arsenic (As)	0.05 mg/m^3
6.	Lead and its compounds, expressed as lead (Pb)	0.05 mg/m^3
7.	Chromium and its compounds, expressed as chromium (Cr)	0.05 mg/m^3
8.	Cobalt and its compounds, expressed as cobalt (Co)	0.05 mg/m^3
9.	Copper and its compounds, expressed as copper (Cu)	0.5 mg/m^3
10.	Manganese and its compounds, expressed as manganese (Mn)	0.05 mg/m^3
11.	Nickel and its compounds, expressed as nickel (Ni)	0.05 mg/m^3
12.	Vanadium and its compounds, expressed as vanadium (V)	0.05 mg/m^3
13.	Tin and its compounds, expressed as tin (Sn)	0.05 mg/m^3

These average values cover also gaseous and the vapour forms of the relevant heavy metal emissions as well as their compounds;

2. the emission of dioxins and furans shall be minimised by the most progressive techniques. To this end every effort must be made to ensure that all average values measured over the sample period of a minimum of six hours and a maximum of 16 hours do not exceed a guide value of 0.1 mg/m^3.

This guide value is defined as the sum of the concentrations of the individual dioxins and furans evaluated in accordance with Annex I;

Table 5.7 continued

3. the results of the measurements made to verify compliance with the limit and guide values set out in Articles 7 and 8 shall be standardised under the conditions laid down in point 2 of Article 12;

4. where hazardous wastes are additionally incinerated in plants which are not solely destined for the incineration of such wastes, the provisions of point 6 of Article 7 and points 1, 2 and 3 of this Article shall only apply to that part of the volume of exhaust gas resulting from the incineration of the wastes.

Appropriate emission limit and guide values for the relevant pollutants emitted in the exhaust gas of such plants as set out in Annex II shall be laid down.

Because of the difficulty in measuring furans and dioxins, the proposal sets only a guideline value of 0.1 nanograms per cubic metre, expressed as toxic equivalents. The proposal prohibits the discharge of waste water from the purification of combustion gases in new plant.

Measures are proposed for encouraging the recycling of heat produced from waste incineration for use as energy on site or elsewhere. Requirements are set out for continuous measuring and monitoring of substances and emission limits and for periodic sampling obligations to make sure values are not exceeded. Within three years of the directive's adoption, existing plant would have to comply with the standards. Operating permits would be reviewed at five-year intervals. A technical committee would be set up to assess progress concerning the development of the abatement technology necessary to meet the stringent standards contained in the directive.

In June 1993 the Commission published an amended proposal which took account of 18 parliamentary amendments which were accepted by the Commission.[9] The directive was adopted by the Council on 16 December 1994 (OJ No L 365 of 31/12/94).

2.   The transfrontier shipment of hazardous waste

(a)   The 1984 directive on the supervision and control of the transfrontier shipment of hazardous waste

On 17 January 1983 the Commission sent the Council a proposal for a directive on the supervision and control of the transfrontier shipment of hazardous waste in the Community. This proposal aimed to establish a complete and uninterrupted chain of supervision and control, when hazardous waste is shipped across the national borders of Member States. The proposal comes into the framework of the general provisions of the 1978 directive on toxic and dangerous waste (see p. 191). It was drawn up as a result of the constant increase in the cross-border shipment of hazardous waste and the numerous accidents and incidents which had occurred. In fact it had become clear that the control of waste was being interrupted at the national borders of Member States, even in the countries where there was a particularly strict internal system of control. In addition, the countries to which the waste was shipped did not generally receive sufficient information to enable them to carry out an efficient control, since the wastes were often classified differently, or were inadequately described, labelled or packaged.

[9] OJ No C 190/5 of 14/7/1993.

The Council adopted this directive (84/631/EEC) on the supervision and control within the Community of the transfrontier shipment of hazardous waste on 6 December 1984.[10] It did not use the legal form of the "regulation" as the European Parliament had wished.

The directive concerns all transfrontier shipment of toxic and dangerous waste, the latter being defined by the specific directive of 20 March 1978. That directive considers "toxic or dangerous waste" to be any waste containing or contaminated by one or more of the substances or materials appearing on a specific list (see p. 192) in such quantities or concentrations as to constitute a risk to health or the environment. Within the framework of the transfrontier shipment directive poly-chlorinated biphenyls (PCB) have been added to this list.

The directive covers all cases of transfrontier shipment, be it across internal or external borders of the Community. The most common case involves the shipment of waste from one Member State to another, but it can also be the shipment in transit by one or more Member States, or else the shipment into a Member State from a third country. The central element of the directive concerns the setting up of a compulsory system of prior notification. The directive stipulates that any holder of waste intending to ship waste across a border must notify the competent author-ity of the Member State responsible for acknowledging receipt of the notification. A copy of the notification must be sent to the competent authorities of the other Member States, and, where applicable, to the third state (or states) of destination or transit. The notification must be made by means of a special uniform document called a "consignment note" (see Table 5.8).

The holder of the waste must give in this "consignment note" precise and detailed information, in particular on:

- the source and composition of the waste, including the producer's identity, and in the case of waste from various sources, a detailed inventory of the waste, and the identity of the original producers;
- the provisions made for routes and insurance against damage to third parties;
- the measures taken to ensure the safety of transport;
- the existence of any contractual agreement with the consignee of the waste, who should possess adequate technical capacity for the disposal of the waste in ques-tion under conditions presenting no danger to human health or the environment.

Where the waste is stored, treated or deposited within a Member State, the consignee must also possess a special permit.

The practical aspects of this system of control can prove rather complex in that objections to the proposed shipment can be made both by the Member State of despatch and by the Member States of transit and of destination. The basic principle retained by the directive only allows a shipment within the Community if the com-petent authority of the Member State of destination or, in the case of a shipment coming from a third state and in transit through the Community, of the last Member State through which the shipment is due to pass, has acknowledged receipt of the notification. The competent authorities of these states have a maximum of one month after receipt of the notification, either to acknowledge receipt or to raise an objection on the proposed shipment.

[10] OJ No L 326 of 13/12/84.

Table 5.8: Council Directive of 6 December 1984
Supervision and control within the European Community of the
transfrontier shipment of hazardous waste

CONTENT OF THE UNIFORM CONSIGNMENT NOTE

SECTION A

Information to be provided on notification

(See General Instructions – paragraph 1)

1. Holder of the waste (a)

2. General notification or notification of a single shipment

3. (a) Consignee of the waste (a)

   (b) Permit No (where applicable)

   (c) Information relating to the contractual agreement between the holder and the consignee

4. Producer(s) of the waste (a)

5. (a) Carrier(s) transporting the waste (a)

   (b) Licence No (where applicable) (b)

6 (a) Country of origin of the waste

   (b) Competent authority (c)

7. (a) Expected countries of transit

   (b) Competent authority (c)

8. (a) Country of destination of the shipment

   (b) Competent authority (c)

9. Planned date(s) of shipment(s) (d)

10. Means of transport envisaged (road, air, sea, etc.)

11. Information relating to insurance against damage to third parties (f)

12. Name and physical description of the waste and its composition (e)

(a) Full name and address, telephone and telex number and the name, address, telephone or telex number of the person to be contacted.

(b) Where there is no specific licence, the carrier should be able to demonstrate that he complies with the rules of the Member State concerned in respect of transport of such waste.

(c) Full name and address, telephone and telex number. This information is obligatory only where the countries concerned are Member States. In other cases it should be provided if known.

(d) In the case of a general notification covering several shipments, either the expected dates of each shipment or, if this is not known, the expected frequency of the shipments will be required.

(e) The nature and the concentration of the most characteristic components, in terms of the toxicity and other dangers presented by the waste will be required together with, if possible, an analysis referring to the method of disposal envisaged, particularly in the case of an initial shipment.

(f) Examples of information to be included where such insurance is required: insurer, policy number, last day of validity.

Table 5.8 continued

13. Method of packing envisaged
14. Quantit(y)(ies) (kg) (g)
15. UN classification
16. Process by which the waste was generated
17. Nature of the risk: Explosive / Reactive / Corrosive / Toxic / Flammable / Other
18. Outward appearance of the waste at ... °C : Powdery or Pulverulent / Solid / Viscous or Syrupy / Sludgy / Liquid / Gaseous / Other Colour
19. Place of generation of the waste
20. Place of disposal of the waste
21. Method of disposal of the waste
22. Other information
23. Declaration by the holder that the information is correct, place, date, signature of holder.

SECTION B

Acknowledgement

(See General Instructions – paragraph 2)

1. Date of receipt of notification
2. Date on which acknowledgement is sent
3. Period of validity of acknowledgement
4. Whether acknowledgement applies to a single shipment or to several shipments
5. Date, signature and stamp of competent authority.

SECTION C

Transport arrangements

(See General Instructions – paragraph 3)

1. Serial No of shipment
2. Identification of means of transport
3. No and type of containers, markings, numbers, etc.
4. Exact quantities (kg)
5. Customs posts of entry in the country(ies), whose territory is to be passed through
6. Special conditions (if any) set by Member States concerned regarding the transport across their territory
7. Declaration by the holder and the carrier that the information is correct; place, date, signature of holder and carrier.

SECTION D

Receipt by the consignee

(See General Instructions – paragraph 4)

Declaration by the consignee that he has received the waste for disposal and the quantity thereof; place, date, signature of the consignee.

(g) In the case of a general notification covering several shipments, both the total quantity and the quantities for each individual shipment will be required.

Table 5.8 continued

SECTION E

Customs endorsement

(See General Instructions – paragraph 5)

1. Address of customs post

2. Declaration that the waste has been exported from the customs territory of the Community

3. Date of exit

4. Date, stamp and signature of customs authority.

GENERAL INSTRUCTIONS

NB: Any competent authority may require further information or documentation to supplement the information provided on the consignment note.

1. Section A of the consignment note must be completed by the holder and sent to the competent authority of the Member State of destination of the waste or, in the case of waste exported to a destination outside the Community or of waste in transit through the Community, to the competent authority of the last Member State through which the shipment is due to pass, with copies to the third State of destination and to the competent authorities of the other Member States concerned with the shipment.

2. Section B must be completed by the competent authority of the Member State to whom the notification is addressed and returned to the holder of the waste within one month of receipt of the notification.

A transfrontier shipment of hazardous waste may not be carried out until after receipt of the acknowledgement of notification supplied by the competent authority referred to above. The acknowledgement must accompany the shipment.

Apart from the control mechanism based on the "notification" and on the "acknowledgment of receipt", the directive also states the conditions with which transfrontier shipment must comply with regard to packaging, labelling, and instructions to be followed in the event of danger or accident. It also specifies that Member States must designate border crossing-points for the shipment of hazardous waste. As far as responsibility and insurance are concerned, the directive foresaw that the Council would determine not later than 30 September 1988 the conditions for implementing the civil liability of the producer of the waste.

The directive came into force on 1 October 1985.

(b)   The Commission's 1985 implementing directive

In order to facilitate the implementation of the "shipment of dangerous waste" directive, the Commission adopted on 2 July 1985 an implementing directive allowing for the finalizing of the different forms needed for the implementation of this directive, accompanied by the practical instructions needed for filling out and sending these forms.[11]

---

[11] OJ No L 272 of 12/10/85.

(c)   The amending directive of 1986

On 7 October 1985, i.e. just a few days after the official date for the coming into force of the directive, the Commission sent the Council a proposal intended to amend certain provisions in the directive of 6 December 1984. Following the work carried out in this area within the United Nations Environment Programme (UNEP), and especially within the OECD (Basle Conference 27–28 September 1985) the Commission judged it necessary to improve the control and safety conditions in the case of the shipment of dangerous waste to third countries.

The Council adopted this amending directive (86/279/EEC) on 12 June 1986,[12] so as to take into account the risks of pollution likely to arise outside the Community (see also the proposal for a regulation on the export of certain dangerous chemicals (p. 255)). The basic principle retained in the amending directive is that in the case of a shipment of dangerous waste from a Member State to a third country, the holder of the waste shall obtain the agreement of the third country destination before embarking upon the usual notification procedure provided for in the directive of 6 December 1984.

(d)   Export of toxic waste

On 13 July 1988, the Commission sent a Communication to the Council entitled "Export of toxic waste" (COM (88) 365 final). The Commission noted that recent events had given sharp prominence to problems connected with the export of toxic waste from the Community to certain developing countries. It had become quite clear that a proportion, and possibly a very large proportion, of such exports took place in breach of elementary concern for human health and protection of the environment, as well as of Community legal requirements.

The Communication noted that exports of toxic waste from the Community are, in principle, governed by Council Directives 84/631/EEC and 86/279/EEC. Under these directives the holder of the waste must notify the competent authorities of the planned export and must provide the necessary information to justify authorization of shipment. This should include proof that the consignee possesses "adequate technical capacity" for the disposal of the waste in question under conditions presenting no danger to human health or the environment as well as evidence of the agreement of the country of destination. If properly applied, these two requirements gave some reassurance as to the safety of the operation; but evidence was mounting that some strengthening of the legislation might be necessary.

The Commission was in possession of information showing that the requirements of these directives had certainly not been met in connection with contracts for the importation of very large quantities of waste into a number of African countries which did not possess the necessary technical capacity to deal safely with the type of waste concerned. This was a matter of rapidly growing political concern. The Council of Environment Ministers on 16 June 1988 had instructed the Presidency to make known their wish to see urgent Community action on this problem. The European Parliament in its Resolution of 19 May condemned "massive exportation of hazardous waste to developing countries". The United States authorities had made clear their dismay at recent revelations about export of

[12] OJ No L 181 of 4/7/86.

hazardous waste. The recent Organization of African Unity Summit at Addis Ababa had underlined its opposition to this traffic. The OECD was currently finalizing an international Agreement on the Control of Transfrontier Movements of Hazardous Wastes and the United Nations Environment Programme was pursuing work on a global convention on the movements of waste.

Against this background, the Commission viewed it as a matter of urgency that concrete steps be taken to tackle the abuses in connection with the export from the Community of hazardous waste. The central aim should be to reduce this trade to the lowest possible level. The Commission would pursue the following steps with all feasible speed:

(a) to bring maximum stringency to the full and rapid incorporation into Member State law of Council Directives 84/631/EEC and 86/279/EEC, and the full implementation of these directives in practice;
(b) to come forward very shortly with a new directive on hazardous waste which, *inter alia*, will strengthen Directive 84/631/EEC by establishing a more precise and uniform definition of hazardous waste as well as more precise rules for the transport and elimination of waste and fuller information requirements (see p. 201);
(c) to examine whether, in the light of experience within the Community, further Community legislation is needed on the prior assessment of environmental hazards and on the continuing management of sites for the dumping of hazardous waste;
(d) to come forward with a draft mandate for Community participation in the negotiation of the UNEP Convention on the movement of waste;
(e) to examine rapidly the possibilities of drawing on Community and Member State resources and expertise to establish a system to provide developing countries, where they request it, with technical and other assistance to tackle the problems posed by hazardous waste.

At its meeting of 24 November 1988 the Environment Council adopted a Resolution concerning transfrontier movements of hazardous waste to third countries. The Resolution:

1. STRESSES the urgency of agreeing a system at the widest possible international level to ensure effective control of transfrontier movements and disposal of hazardous waste;
2. WELCOMES the negotiations under way in OECD and UNEP to this end in which the Community and the Member States are playing an active role;
3. NOTES that the provisional results of these negotiations reflect on a wider scale the principles laid down in the EEC Directives dealing with the same issue; in particular the principles of reduction of waste to a minimum level, prior informed consent, safe disposal, and the responsibility of the producer for the proper management of his waste;
4. RECALLS that under Council Directive 84/631/EEC, as amended by Council Directive 86/279/EEC, any export of hazardous waste to third countries is subject to specific controls;
5. RECOGNIZES the ban on imports of hazardous waste imposed by a number of third countries;
6. REQUESTS Member States, in cooperation with the Commission, to encourage the development of the effective management of hazardous waste at source and of the technology for the processing of hazardous waste, the exchange of technical

information and the development of trained manpower resources for the safe handling, processing and disposal of hazardous waste; and to elaborate necessary standards and technical guidelines for waste disposal installations.

7. REQUESTS the Commission and the Member States to give due priority to the
provisions to developing countries when they so request for information on the
risks pertaining to the incorrect disposal of hazardous waste and of technical and
other assistance to enable them to deal with the problems posed by hazardous
waste.

8. INVITES the Member States to further the development of an adequate and
environmentally compatible infrastructure in the Member States for the disposal of
all types of waste.

A Global Convention on the Transfrontier Movement of Hazardous Wastes was
negotiated in March 1989 in Basle, Switzerland under the auspices of the United
Nations Environment Programme. The Community signed the convention, being
authorized to do so at a special meeting of the Environment Council, convened in
Basle itself during the final negotiating session.

*(e)   The 1990 proposal for a regulation to replace Directive 84/361 on the
supervision and control of the transfrontier shipment of waste*

On 26 October 1990 the Commission sent the Council a proposal for a regulation to
replace the 1984 directive as the latter had been found to be defective in operation.[13] The regulation would also give effect to the Basle Convention on
Transfrontier Movements of Hazardous Wastes and their Disposal and to the provisions of the Fourth Lomé Convention banning the export of hazardous wastes from
the Community to the ACP states, as well as establish procedures to control the
movement of wastes between and within EC Member States. The proposal prohibits the export of hazardous waste to and the import from countries which are not
parties to the Basle Convention. It also bans the export of any waste to third countries unless the country of import gives its written consent, the Member State from
which the waste is despatched is satisfied that the waste will be dealt with in an
environmentally benign way, and either the waste is to be recycled or cannot be
disposed of in the EC. The proposal gives Member States discretion to refuse or
allow the import of any kind of waste from third countries, besides requiring the
return of shipments where disposal cannot be undertaken as planned. The proposal
requires the movement of any kind of waste between the competent authorities
between or within Member States to be subject to the approval of the competent
authorities. Non-hazardous waste that is for recycling is not included in the
proposal.

The directive was adopted as Directive 259/93 on the supervision and control of
shipments of waste within, into and out of the European Community.[14]

The Basle Convention entered into force on 5 May 1992. The Council Decision
approving the Basle Convention on behalf of the Community was published in the
Official Journal on 16 February 1993.[15]

---

[13] COM (90) 415 of 26/10/90.
[14] OJ No L 30 of 6/2/93.
[15] OJ No L 39/1 of 16/2/93.

IV. PARTICULAR CATEGORIES OF WASTE

1. Waste oils

(a) The 1975 directive on the disposal of waste oils

Studies undertaken by the Commission had shown the importance of oil and water pollution resulting from the treatment and combustion of waste oils. A more recent phenomenon of incidental air pollution resulting from the treatment and combustion of waste oils could also be added to this pollution. Apart from the aspect of environmental protection, studies had illustrated that not enough waste oils were recycled. In view of these studies the Commission presented a proposal to the Council on 25 March 1974 concerning the disposal of waste oils. The main aims of this proposal were environmental protection, and maximum re-use of waste oils.

The Council adopted the directive on the disposal of waste oils on 16 June 1975.[16] It was the first directive to be adopted by the Council in the sector of waste management.

It should be noted that this first directive in the area of waste contains original provisions from the financial point of view, more specifically in the form of the charges introduced in favour of undertakings dealing with the disposal of waste oils, and from the point of view of the exchange of technical information between the Commission and the Member States.

According to the directive, Member States are required to take the necessary measures to ensure the safe collection and disposal of waste oils and to ensure that as far as possible this disposal is carried out by recycling, i.e. by regeneration and/or combustion other than for destruction.

The directive prohibits any discharge of waste oils into the water or soil, and any processing of waste oils causing air pollution which exceeds national or Community standards.

In order to respect these objectives, Member States must designate the undertakings responsible for the collection and disposal of waste oils. Each undertaking of waste oils must obtain a permit granted by the competent authorities after examination of the installations. The undertakings must be inspected periodically by the authorities. As a reciprocal concession for the obligations imposed by the Member States on the undertakings dealing with the collection or disposal of waste oils, the directive provides for the possibility of indemnities being granted for the service rendered. These indemnities, which must respect certain conditions outlined in the directive, can be financed by a charge imposed directly on waste oils or on products which after use become transformed into waste oils.

The directive stipulates that any establishment producing, collecting or disposing of more than 500 litres of waste oil per year must keep a record of the quantity, quality, origin and location of the waste oils, including the dates of their receipt and despatch. The information contained in this record must be conveyed to the competent authorities on request.

---

[16] OJ No L 194 of 25/7/75.

Finally the directive contains a general provision stipulating that any person or undertaking holding waste oils must, if they are unable to comply with the precautionary measures provided for by the directive, put the waste oils at the disposal of an authorized elimination undertaking.

(b)   The 1986 amending directive on the disposal of waste oils

On 29 January 1985 the Commission presented the Council with a proposal amending the 1975 directive on the disposal of waste oils. The Commission proposed to amend the 1975 directive because of the major potential risks to the environment that waste oils represent. Apart from the fact that in some cases Member States had taken different national measures for applying the 1975 directive, which had led to significant distortions, serious gaps had come to light regarding the collection of waste oils and the control of their combustion or burning. The collection system had often proved inadequate and the practice of individuals carrying out motor oil changes had reached worrying proportions. Similarly it had become clear that the uncontrolled burning of waste oils in small plants raised important health and environmental risks, due to the diffusion of heavy metals, in particular lead, and other dangerous substances contained in the oils such as PCB/PCT.

The Council adopted this amending directive on the disposal of waste oils on 22 December 1986.[17] The directive limits the field of application solely to mineral-based waste oils, synthetic oils being excluded from now on since they are covered by other directives, for example the PCB/PCT directive (see point 2 below).

It lays down specific stricter provisions concerning the disposal of waste oils by regeneration and combustion, with the understanding that Member States must give priority to regeneration. The oils processed by regeneration must not contain concentrations of PCB/PCT higher than 50 ppm.

Where waste oils are disposed of by combustion, the directive, with a view to combating air pollution, establishes Community emission limit values for a certain number of pollutants, in particular heavy metals, when the oils are burned in plants having a thermic input of 3 MW or more (see Table 5.9). The directive also provides for programmes of promotion and public awareness aimed at ensuring suitable storage and collection of waste oils.

2.   The disposal of PCB and PCT

The Council adopted Directive 76/403 on the disposal of PCBs and PCTs on 6 April 1976.[18] The directive covers not only polychlorinated biphenyls and polychlorinated terphenyls, but also any mixture containing these substances. PCBs are chlorinated organic compounds which due to their stability and good dielectric characteristics have been widely used in hydraulic fluids, transformers and capacitors, lubricants and plasticizers. It was discovered, however, that they accumulate in the tissue of plants and animals and are probably carcinogenic. Fires with PCBs produce highly toxic polychlorinated dibenzo-dioxins and polychlorinated dibenzo-furans.

---

[17] OJ No L 42 of 12/2/87.
[18] OJ No L 108 of 26/4/76.

Table 5.9: Directive of 22 December 1986 amending Directive 75/439/EEC on the disposal of waste oils

Emission limit values (^{1}) for certain substances emitted as a result of the combustion of waste oils in plants with a thermal input of 3 MW (LHV) or more

Pollutant		Limit value mg/Nm^3		
Cd		0.5		
Ni		1		
	either (^{2})		or (^{2})	
Cr	⎫		Cr ⎫	
Cu	⎬ 1.5		Cu ⎬ 5	
V	⎭		V ⎭	
Pb	5		Pb	
Cl (^{3})		100		
F (^{4})		5		
SO$_2$ (^{5})		–		
Dust (total) (^{5})		–		

(^{1}) These limit values, which may not be exceeded when waste oils are burned, indicate the mass concentration of emissions of the aforementioned substances in waste gas, in terms of the volume of waste gas in the standard state (273 K; 1 013 hPa), after deduction of the water vapour moisture content, and of a 3 % oxygen content by volume in waste gas.
In the case of the second subparagraph of Article 8 (3), the oxygen content will be that which corresponds to normal operating conditions in the particular process concerned.
(^{2}) It shall be for the Member States to lay down which of these options shall apply in their country.
(^{3}) Inorganic gaseous compounds of chlorine expressed as hydrogen chloride.
(^{4}) Inorganic gaseous compounds of fluorine expressed as hydrogen fluoride.
(^{5}) It is not possible to determine limit values for these substances at this stage. The Member States will independently set emission standards for discharges of these substances taking into account the requirements of Directive 80/779/EEC (OJ No L 229, 30.8.1980, p. 30).

According to the directive, the Member States are required to take the necessary measures to:

• prohibit the uncontrolled discharge, dumping and tipping of PCB/PCT and of objects and equipment containing such substances, i.e. electrical or hydraulic equipment (transformers, condensers, etc.);
• make compulsory the disposal of waste PCB and PCT by ensuring the collection, destruction or regeneration of these substances, all of these operations to be carried out without endangering human health and without harming the environment.

To put these provisions into action, Member States must designate and, if necessary, set up installations and undertakings which must obtain the authorization of the competent control authorities. Anyone holding PCB/PCT must in accordance with the directive hold it available for disposal by the authorized installations or undertakings. In line with the "polluter pays" principle, the cost of disposal must be borne by the holder or producer of the PCB/PCT.

Further restrictions on PCB/PCTs were incorporated in the Council's framework Directive 76/769 EEC on the marketing and use of dangerous substances. Under that directive, PCBs and PCTs may only be used in closed system electrical equipment, large condensers and for certain other applications. Council Directive 85/467/EEC bans all new uses of PCBs and PCTs and terminated, as of 30 June 1986, the exemptions allowed under Directive 76/769/EEC. The secondhand sale of equipment containing PCBs or PCTs and fluids was also banned as of the same date.

In October 1988 the Commission submitted a proposal to the Council for a directive to cover the handling and disposal of those PCBs which entered into circulation before the 1985 ban. It would replace Directive 76/403 with a new set of provisions to reduce the risks which PCBs present to human health and to the environment by means of more effective management of used PCBs and by improving the conditions under which they are disposed of. *Inter alia*, the proposal would prohibit the incineration of PCBs at sea; require the licensing of incinerators which dispose of PCBs and the licensing of retrofilling operations; require the preparation of national plans to dispose of PCBs; and require the compilation of inventories of larger PCB-filled equipment and the labelling of such equipment. The proposal defines PCBs as any mixture which contains more than 0.005% (50 parts per million) of PCBs, PCTs or PCBTs.

In 1991 the Commission sent an amended proposal to the Council which also proposed to prohibit exports to third countries and imports from such countries with adequate disposal facilities of their own. Furthermore, it proposed provisions for disposal licensing, inspection of disposal facilities, the civil liability of disposal facilities, the maintenance of registers of PCB waste deliveries, and standards for the operation of disposal facilities.

3. Waste paper

On 14 May 1980 the Commission sent to the Council a proposal for a Recommendation concerning the re-use of waste paper and board. This Recommendation was in line with the 2nd Environmental Action Programme of 1977 which provided for priority in work on waste to be given among other things to the question of waste paper. The other motivations for Community action in this area were that waste paper represented a significant percentage of urban waste and that the Community had to make up its deficit of raw materials for the manufacture of pulp and paper by significant imports from third countries. Finally, from the environmental point of view, the use of waste paper instead of cellulose or wood pulp would enable savings of energy and fresh water to be made, and would produce fewer effluents and less atmospheric pollution, while contributing towards easier waste disposal.

The Council adopted the Recommendation on the re-use of waste paper and the use of recycled paper on 3 December 1981.[19] This text recommends Member States and Community institutions to implement policies and measures aimed at promoting the use of recycled paper and board. These measures will aim in particular to:

[19] OJ No L 355 of 10/12/81.

- encourage the use of recycled and recyclable paper and board, especially in public administrations and services;
- encourage the use of products such as inks or glues which do not preclude the subsequent recycling of paper and board;
- implement programmes of consumer and manufacturer education and awareness;
- develop uses for waste paper otherwise than as raw material for the manufacture of paper and board.

4. Containers of liquid for human consumption

On 23 April 1981 the Commission presented the Council with a proposal for a directive on containers of liquids for human consumption.

The purpose of this proposal was to implement a series of measures relating to the production, marketing, use and disposal of containers of liquids for human consumption, in order to reduce the impact on the environment of the disposal of these containers and to encourage a reduction in the consumption of energy and raw materials.

The proposal came within the framework of Community activities in the area of the rational management of solid wastes, containers representing a substantial and growing part of the waste collected by the municipal authorities (30–50% of the total weight of household wastes). The cost of disposing of household waste was continually rising and had to be covered by the local authority.

The Council adopted the directive on containers of liquids for human consumption on 27 June 1985.[20] To reach the objectives of environmental protection and reduced consumption of energy and raw materials, Member States must draw up programmes for reducing the tonnage and volume of containers of certain liquids for human consumption. The liquids covered by the directive appear in Table 5.10.

The national programmes must be drawn up for the first time for a period beginning 1 January 1987. They were to be revised and updated regularly, at least every four years, taking into account, in particular, technical progress and changing economic circumstances.

Within the framework of these programmes, the Member States must take measures designed in particular to:

- facilitate the refilling and recycling of containers of liquids for human consumption;
- maintain and, where possible, increase the proportion of refilled or recycled containers where the conditions of industrial activity and the market permit;
- develop consumer education in the advantages of using refillable containers and recyclable containers;
- encourage the technical development and placing on the market of new types of container, with the aim in particular of reducing the consumption of raw materials, facilitating recycling and the final disposal of container waste and achieving overall energy savings;
- as regards non-refillable containers and as far as it is economically feasible, promote the selective collection of containers, and develop effective processes for retrieving containers from household waste.

[20] OJ No L 176 of 6/7/85.

Table 5.10: Directive of 27 June
Containers of liquids for human consumption

LIQUIDS FOR HUMAN CONSUMPTION REFERRED TO IN ARTICLE 2

1. Milk and liquid milk products, whether or not flavoured, with the exception of yoghurt and kefir.

2. Edible oils ([1]).

3. Fruit or vegetable juices and fruit nectar.

4. Natural spa water, spring water, aerated water and table water.

5. Non-alcoholic refreshing drinks.

6. Beer, including non-alcoholic beer.

7. Wine made from fresh grapes; grape must with fermentation arrested by the addition of alcohol.

8. Vermouths, and other wines made from fresh grapes flavoured with aromatic plants or extracts.

9. Cider, perry, mead and other fermented beverages.

10. Ethyl alcohol, not denatured, with an alcoholic strength of less than 80% by volume; spirits, liqueurs and other spirituous beverages; compound alcoholic preparations for the manufacture of beverages.

11. Fermentation vinegar and diluted synthetic acetic acid ([1]).

([1]) Most containers used for oil and vinegar are unsuitable for refilling but may be suitable for recycling.

All of these measures can be taken either by legislative or administrative means, or by voluntary agreements at national or local level.

In implementing these provisions, Member States must ensure that they respect both the provisions of the EEC Treaty on the free movement of goods, and the hygiene and public health factors.

The directive also contains certain specific provisions concerning consumer information. New refillable containers must carry an appropriate indication drawing attention to the refillable nature of the container in question. The consumer must also be clearly informed of the amount of deposit payable in the case of a deposit system.

By September 1988, nine programmes had been officially communicated to the Commission. Four countries – namely France, the Netherlands, the United Kingdom and Germany – proposed a series of voluntary measures. Two countries – Denmark and Ireland – proposed obligatory measures. In the case of three countries – Greece, Spain and Portugal – it was not clear whether the measures were to be voluntary or obligatory.

5. Sewage sludge

On 13 September 1982 the Commission sent the Council a proposal for a directive on the use of sewage sludge in agriculture, which aimed to define and regulate the conditions under which sewage sludge can be used on agricultural land.

The Community's interest in the problems caused by sewage sludge goes back to the 1st Action Programme of 1973. Since then the Community has launched research programmes into the question of sewage sludge, both within the framework of scientific and technical cooperation with third countries (1971–1979 COST68 Action), and internally in the form of concerted research (1977) (see Chapter 11).

The Waste Management Committee set up within the Commission in 1976 (see p. 187) judged that the use of waste in agriculture constituted a priority area for action at Community level. The quantities of sewage sludge produced by waste water treatment stations would undoubtedly increase significantly, thus presenting a disposal problem. It was estimated that 45% of this sludge was dumped without control, 7% was incinerated, 19% was dumped at sea and 29% was used in agriculture. The proportion of sludge used in agriculture could therefore usefully be increased since it provides the soil with organic matter containing phosphorus and nitrogen. But in order to avoid any risk to health or the environment, its use in agriculture must be regulated from the point of view of quality and quantity. The residual sludge can in fact contain significant quantities of heavy metals (iron; lead; copper; zinc) or other chemical elements. The use of sewage sludge in agriculture should therefore be encouraged, while avoiding any contamination of the food chain, animals or plants.

The Council adopted this directive on the protection of the environment, and in particular of the soil, when sewage sludge is used in agriculture, on 12 June 1986.[21] The particular importance of this directive should not be overlooked. Apart from constituting a new legal text in the area of waste, it is also the first directive which involves the protection of the soil in general, and the first to deal directly with both agricultural and environmental aspects.

The general aim of the directive is to regulate the use of sewage sludge in agriculture in such a way as to prevent harmful effects on soil, vegetation, animals and man, while encouraging its correct use.

The sludge covered by the directive is mainly the residual sludge from sewage plants treating domestic or urban waste waters, sludge from industrial plants being excluded from the field of application and having to be covered by a specific national regulation.

According to the directive, Member States must, first, prohibit the use of sewage sludge in agriculture where the concentration of heavy metals in the soil which is to receive the sludge, exceeds certain limit values laid down by the directive (see Table 5.11 – Annex 1A). Secondly, the directive requires Member States to regulate the use of sludge in such a way that the accumulation of heavy metals in the soil does not lead to these limit values being exceeded. To achieve this, Member States may choose between two categories of limit values to be observed:

- either they must observe the limit values for concentrations of heavy metals in sludge which may be introduced into the soil per unit of area per year (see Table 5.11 – Annex 1B);
- or they must observe the limit values for the quantities of heavy metals which can be introduced into cultivated soil per unit per year (see Table 5.11 – Annex 1C). The directive also requires Member States to carry out an analysis of the sludge.

[21] OJ No L 181 of 4/7/86.

Table 5.11: Directive of 12 June 1986 Protection of the environment, and in particular of the soil, when sewage sludge is used in agriculture

ANNEX IA

LIMIT VALUES FOR CONCENTRATIONS OF HEAVY METALS IN SOIL

(mg/kg of dry matter in a representative sample, as defined in Annex II C, of soil with a pH of 6 to 7)

Parameters	Limit values ([1])
Cadmium	1 to 3
Copper ([2])	50 to 140
Nickel ([2])	30 to 75
Lead	50 to 300
Zinc ([2])	150 to 300
Mercury	1 to 1.5
Chromium ([3])	–

([1]) Member States may permit the limit values they fix to be exceeded in the case of the use of sludge on land which at the time of notification of this Directive is dedicated to the disposal to sludge but on which commercial food crops are being grown exclusively for animal consumption. Member States must inform the Commission of the number and type of sites concerned. They must also seek to ensure that there is no resulting hazard to human health or the environment.

([2]) Member States may permit the limit values they fix to be exceeded in respect of these parameters on soil with a pH consistently higher than 7. The maximum authorized concentrations of these heavy metals must in no case exceed those values by more than 50%. Member States must also seek to ensure that there is no resulting hazard to human health or the environment and in particular to ground water.

([3]) It is not possible at this stage to fix limit values for chromium. The Council will fix these limit values later on the basis of proposals to be submitted by the Commission, within one year following notification of this Directive.

ANNEX I B

LIMIT VALUES FOR HEAVY-METAL CONCENTRATIONS IN SLUDGE FOR USE IN AGRICULTURE

(mg/kg of dry matter)

Parameters	Limit values
Cadmium	20 to 40
Copper	1 000 to 1 750
Nickel	300 to 400
Lead	750 to 1 200
Zinc	2 500 to 4 000
Mercury	16 to 25
Chromium ([1])	–

([1]) It is not possible at this stage to fix limit values for chromium. The Council will fix these limit values later on the basis of proposals to be submitted by the Commission within one year following notification of this Directive.

Table 5.11 continued

ANNEX I C

**LIMIT VALUES FOR AMOUNTS OF HEAVY METALS WHICH MAY BE
ADDED ANNUALLY TO AGRICULTURAL LAND, BASED ON A 10-YEAR
AVERAGE**

(kg/ha/yr)

Parameters	Limit values ([1])
Cadmium	0.15
Copper	12
Nickel	3
Lead	15
Zinc	30
Mercury	0.1
Chromium ([2])	–

([1]) Member States may permit these limit values to be exceeded in the case of the use of sludge on land which at the time of notification of this Directive is dedicated to the disposal of sludge but on which commercial food crops are being grown exclusively for animal consumption. Member States must inform the Commission of the number and type of sites concerned. They must also ensure that there is no resulting hazard to human health or the environment.

([2]) It is not possible at this stage to fix limit values for chromium. The Council will fix these limit values later on the basis of proposals to be submitted by the Commission within one year following notification of this Directive.

The practical methods of the sludge analysis, which must be carried out at least every six months, and of the soil analysis, are the subject of two technical annexes to the directive. The directive also provides for reference methods for the sampling and analysis of sludge and soils. It stipulates that only sludge which has received appropriate treatment may be used in agriculture. The purpose of this treatment by means of biological, chemical or heat processes, or by long-term storage, is to reduce the fermentability of the sludge, and more generally, any health hazards. The Member States are nevertheless able to authorize under certain conditions the use of untreated sludge in agriculture if it is injected or worked into the soil. The directive also prohibits under certain conditions, particularly where time limits are not respected, the use and spreading of sludge on soil used for grassland, forage crops, and for fruit and vegetable crops.

As far as control is concerned, the directive requires Member States to keep records in which they must register in particular the quantities of sludge produced and supplied for use in agriculture; the composition and properties of the sludge; the type of treatment carried out; the names and addresses of the recipients.

6. Waste and the titanium dioxide industry

Since most of the waste coming from the titanium dioxide industry is discharged into the aquatic environment, mainly at sea, the rules adopted by the Community concerning this waste are examined in the chapter on water pollution (see pp. 98ff).

7.   Radioactive waste

This question is dealt with in Chapter 15 on nuclear security (see p. 470).

8.   Municipal waste

(a)   89/429/EEC: Council Directive of 8 June 1989 on the prevention of air pollution from existing municipal waste incineration plants

Council Directive 75/442/EEC on waste requires waste to be disposed of without endangering human health or the environment. Any establishment responsible for waste disposal must therefore obtain an authorization from the competent authority.

Directive 84/360/EEC on the fight against atmospheric pollution from industrial installations requires all new industrial installations, and in particular waste incinerators, to be subject to prior authorization to ensure that all the necessary measures have been taken to avoid atmospheric pollution.

Directive 85/337/EEC on environmental impact assessment requires installations for domestic waste to be subject to an assessment in those cases where the Member States consider their characteristics require it.

The Council directive of 8 June 1989 on the prevention of air pollution from existing municipal waste incineration plants [22] sets two stages for the adaptation of existing installations. By 30 June 1994 all installations authorized before 30 June 1989 must meet the minimum conditions laid down by the directive. By 30 June 1999, all these installations must respect the conditions imposed on "new" installations. This means that for the less efficient installations there is a period of five years after which they must either be re-equipped or taken out of service. The directive also lays down standards for dust emissions.

(b)   89/369/EEC: Council Directive of 8 June 1989 on the prevention of air pollution from new municipal waste incineration plants

Directive 84/360/EEC already requires all new installations to adopt the necessary measures to prevent atmospheric pollution. This implies that if the emission limits set by the directive are inadequate, in a specific situation, to prevent a significant level of pollution, then other supplementary measures must be taken.

The Council directive of 8 June 1989 sets the emission limits, expressed as concentrations (MG/M3), applicable to new incinerators.

As far as dust particles are concerned, the value varies according to the size of the installation so as to avoid any unnecessary investments in the smallest installations in terms of cost of separation per tonne of pollutant. In all cases, the use of an electro-filter is essential, although the required efficiency of this filter, and so the cost, is again linked to the size of installation.

The values set for heavy metals vary according to the degree of danger they represent to health and the environment. The emphasis throughout this directive is on the use of the best available technology not involving excessive cost. On environmental grounds, Member States have the right, while respecting the treaty, to impose stricter measures than are foreseen by the directive.

[22] OJ No L 203 of 15/7/89.

**Table 5.12: Council Directive of 8 June 1989 on the prevention of air
pollution from new municipal waste incineration plants**

EMISSION LIMIT VALUES IN MG/NM^3 AS A FUNCTION OF THE
NOMINAL CAPACITY OF THE INCINERATION PLANT

Pollutants	less than 1 tonne/h	1 tonne/h or more but less than 3 tonnes/h	3 tonnes/h or more
Total dust	200	100	30
Heavy metals			
– Pb + Cr + Cu + Mn	–	5	5
– Ni + As	–	1	1
– Cd and Hg	–	0.2	0.2
Hydrochloric acid (HCI)	250	100	50
Hydrofluoric acid (HF)	–	4	2
Sulphur dioxide (SO$_2$)	–	300	300

9.   The 1991 proposal for a directive on the landfill of waste

In May 1991 the Commission sent to Council a proposal for a directive on the
landfill of waste.[23] The proposal set out to harmonize technical and operational
standards with the aim of securing a higher level of environmental protection and
reducing distortion of industrial competition throughout the EC.

The draft set out to regulate landfill, where this is a reasonable waste management option. It does not list disposal priorities but does contain brief stipulations
concerning waste unsuitable for landfill. The draft proposed systems of site
classification and waste assessment with site permits to cover stipulated aspects of
control. Where necessary, waste would be tested according to specified test protocols and, where joint disposal of different classes of waste is proposed, in accordance with compatibility criteria. Operators would retain responsibility for
restoration, monitoring and, where required, clean-up during an adequate post-
closure period. To this end, an aftercare fund would be set up to provide finance in
cases where costs could not be recouped from operators.

An amended proposal was published by the Commission in June 1993, following
Parliament's opinion.[24] The amendments, *inter alia*, enhance the definitions of
"treatment" and "leachate"; expand Article 6 by adding time limits (application for
a permit); forbid the "dilution" of waste in order to meet waste acceptance criteria.
Parliament's amendment to ban joint disposal is accepted in Article 10, which also
includes a five-year transitional period for those countries where it is currently
legally practised and clarifies the type of waste that can be deposited in a
monolandfill. Other amendments require that at least 30 years after the closure of
the landfill or for as long as the site poses an active risk, leachate from the site and

---

[23] COM (91) 102, OJ No C 192 of 23/7/91.
[24] COM (93) 416, OJ No C 285 of 21/10/93.

the groundwater regime are monitored and analysed at least twice a year. Article 19 is lengthened considerably in relation to information to be included in annual reports from Member States and a new Article 20a is added on training and information.[25]

European Union environment ministers, meeting in June 1994, reached political agreement on European Parliament amendments, subject to reserve, on the directive on the landfill of waste.

10.   Council directive on packaging and packaging waste

In August 1992 the Commission's proposal for a Council directive on packaging and packaging waste was published.[26] *Inter alia*, the directive is intended to minimize current differences in national provisions concerning the management of packaging and packaging waste which tend to distort competition, affect the free movement of goods and give rise to differences in the level of protection of the environment. To attain these objectives the directive establishes targets and essential requirements which packaging must meet, and provides for measures for the prevention of the production of packaging waste and for the promotion of return, re-use and recovery operations relating to packaging and packaging waste in order to ensure public health and the protection of the environment.

The specific targets proposed in the draft directive under Article 4 were as follows:

- 90% by weight of the packaging waste output to be removed for the purpose of *recovery* from the waste stream within 10 years of the implementation date of the directive, recovery being defined in Annex II.B to Directive 75/442 EEC (see p. 186);
- within this general recovery target, 60% by weight of each material of the packaging waste output to be removed from the waste stream for the purpose of recycling, as defined in Annex II.A to Directive 75/442/EEC.

Member States were to specify intermediate targets in their waste management plans aiming at 60% recovery and 40% recycling rates with dates to be indicated.

Under Article 5, Member States were within five years of the directive's implementation date to:

- provide for the return of all used packaging and/or all packaging waste from the consumer;
- ensure that the used packaging and/or packaging waste is effectively re-used or recovered.

Annex I set out the markings to be used to indicate re-usable and recoverable packaging. Annex II set out the essential requirements to be met before packaging could be placed on the Community market. These included requirements specific to the manufacturing and composition of packaging, as well as requirements dealing with re-usability and recoverability (including the recovery of energy).

Article 11 stated that economic instruments could be adopted by Member States, in accordance with the provisions of the treaty, to promote the objectives of the directive.

[25] COM (93) 275 final SYN 335, 10 June 1993, OJ No C 212/33 of 5/8/93.
[26] OJ No C 209/46 of 15/8/1992.

On 9 September 1993, following the opinions of the European Parliament and the Economic and Social Committee the Commission published an amended proposal,[27] *inter alia*, setting a limit of five years for the attainment of intermediate targets (60% by weight of the packaging waste output to be removed from the waste stream for the purpose of recovery, with 40% by weight of each material being removed for the purpose of recycling) and elaborating the criteria for the use of economic instruments, with explicit mention of the avoidance of distortion of competition and obstacles to trade, as well as compatibility with other tax legislation. The instruments must take into account the "polluter pays" principle.

In Annex II, individual limits are established for lead, cadmium, chrome and mercury present in packaging or packaging components (as opposed to the sum of concentration levels) and a definition of 100% biodegradable packaging has been added.

On 4 March 1994, the Parliament and Council adopted Common Position (EC) No 13/94 on the draft directive[28] and in June 1994 the environment ministers reached political agreement.

11.   Council Directive of 18 March 1991 on batteries and accumulators containing certain dangerous substances (91/157/EEC)[29]

Under this directive, adopted under Article 100a of the EEC Treaty, Member States are to prohibit, as from 1 January 1993, the marketing of:

- alkaline manganese batteries for prolonged use in extreme conditions containing more than 0.05% of mercury by weight;
- all other alkaline manganese batteries containing more than 0.025% of mercury by weight.

Alkaline manganese button cells and batteries composed of button cells are exempted from this provision.

Table 5.13: Council Directive of 18 March 1991 on batteries and accumulators containing certain dangerous substances

ANNEX I

BATTERIES AND ACCUMULATORS COVERED BY THE DIRECTIVE

1. Batteries and accumulators put on the market as from the date laid down in Article 11 (1) and containing:
   - more than 25 mg mercury per cell, except alkaline manganese batteries,
   - more than 0.025% cadmium by weight,
   - more than 0.4% lead by weight.

2. Alkaline manganese batteries containing more than 0.025% mercury by weight placed on the market as from the date laid down in Article 11 (1).

[27] OJ No C 258 of 21/10/93.
[28] OJ No C 107/16 of 15/4/94.
[29] OJ No L 78 of 26/3/91.

Table 5.14: The fifth environment action programme: strategic chart for a Community management policy on hazardous and other wastes

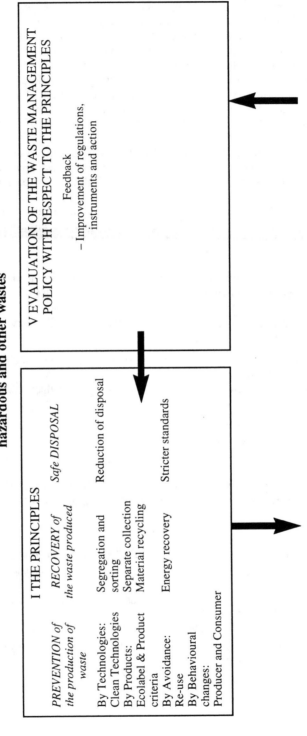

V EVALUATION OF THE WASTE MANAGEMENT POLICY WITH RESPECT TO THE PRINCIPLES

Feedback
– Improvement of regulations, instruments and action

I THE PRINCIPLES

PREVENTION of the production of waste	RECOVERY of the waste produced	Safe DISPOSAL
		Reduction of disposal
By Technologies: Clean Technologies	Segregation and sorting	
By Products: Ecolabel & Product criteria	Separate collection Material recycling	
By Avoidance: Re-use	Energy recovery	Stricter standards
By Behavioural changes: Producer and Consumer		

II THE REGULATORY FRAMEWORK	III THE OBJECTIVES	IV THE ACTIONS

GENERAL APPLICATION
Framework Directive on Waste
 	
Directive on Hazardous Waste
 	
Regulation on the Control on shipments of waste
 	
Proposal of Directive on Civil Liability for damages to the environment
 	
SPECIFIC APPLICATION
A. *On specific types of wastes:*
 	
Directives on:
  Waste oils
  – PCBs and PCTs
  – Sewage sludge
  – Packaging
  – Batteries
 	
Priority waste streams:
  – Used tyres
  – Halogenated Solvents
  – Used cars
  – Demolition waste
  – Hospital waste
  – Municipal waste
 	
B. On specific types of waste: management operations
 	
Directives and technical standards for:
Waste Incineration (Municipal and Industrial Waste)
Landfill disposal
	Strict implementation of Community legislation through:
	
	Reliable Data on:
	  – Waste production & characteristics
	  – Waste treatment facilities
	
	Waste management
	
	Minimization of movements of waste
	
	Establishment of recycling circuits and opening of market options for recycled materials
		Development of data basis on:
		  – Waste production & characteristics
		  – Waste treatment facilities
		
		Establishment of Integrated waste management systems: plans, network, facilities
		
		Development of ecological balances for evaluation of waste management alternatives
		
		Development & application of economic instruments specifically designed towards waste management
		
		Development and promotion of:
		  – Clean Technologies
		  – Ecoproducts
		  – Segregation & sorting systems
		  – Recycling circuits
		  – Safe disposal processes
		
		Implementation of self-sufficiency and proximity principles
		
		Development of product specifications to provide the use of recycled materials
		
		Development & application of community instruments for financial support:
		  – LIFE (ACE, NORSPA, MEDSPA)
		  – Regional funds
		  – Research & development funds

Member States are required to take appropriate steps (Article 4) to ensure that spent batteries and accumulators are collected separately with a view to their recovery or disposal and to draw up programmes (Article 6) to this end. Such programmes should achieve the following objectives:

- reduction of the heavy-metal content of batteries and accumulators;
- promotion of marketing of batteries and accumulators containing smaller quantities of dangerous substances and/or less polluting substances;
- gradual reduction, in household waste, of spent batteries and accumulators as set out in Table Table 5.13;
- promotion of research aimed at reducing the dangerous-substance content and favouring the use of less-polluting substances;
- separate disposal of spent batteries and accumulators as indicated in Table 5.13.

The first programmes were to cover a four-year period starting on 18 March 1993.

V. FUTURE ACTION

The Community's 5th Environmental Action Programme – Towards Sustainability[30] – presents the Community's future waste management policy and programme. It argues that the problems to which waste gives rise are both specific and relatively complex: waste is not only a potential source of pollution; it can also constitute secondary raw materials. The choice of priorities in this sector has direct economic and environmental consequences and is of direct relevance not only to environment policies but to technology, economic and consumer policies.

Management of waste generated within the Community will be a key task of the 1990s. Current upward trends in waste generation must be halted and reversed in terms of both volumes and environmental hazard and damage. A Community strategy for waste management to the year 2000 has already been published[31] and endorsed by the Council.[32] This strategy includes a hierarchy of waste management options in which primary emphasis is laid on waste prevention, followed by promotion of recycling and use, and then by optimization of final disposal methods for waste which is not re-used. Table 5.14 indicates the strategic flow-chart for waste management.

This strategy will be pursued and enforced under the 5th Action Programme. In particular more attention will be given to the prevention of waste and solving waste problems at source, the encouragement of re-use and recycling of waste by, *inter alia*, separation at source, prioritization of waste streams and the encouragement of a rational network of disposal facilities. Further, application of lifecycle analysis will be promoted so as to encourage the intervention of all people concerned in order to attain targets to be achieved within a limited period. Hazardous waste requires particular attention in relation to both preventing waste and encouraging maximum recycling and the development of an EC-wide infrastructure for safe disposal.

---

[30] COM (92) 23 final – Vol II, 27 March 1992, and OJ No C 138 of 17/5/93.
[31] Sec (89) 934 final, September 1989.
[32] Council Resolution of 7 May 1990, OJ No C 122.

Economic and fiscal instruments such as charges and levies will be applied, wherever appropriate. The 5th Programme indicates that "the legislative package of measures on waste management must also be rounded off by the adoption of specific directives on packaging, the incineration of industrial and toxic wastes, on the control and recuperation of landfill sites, and a more general directive on civil liability for damage."

Table 5.15 indicates overall objectives, targets for the year 2000 and the actions required in the short term.

Table 5.15: The fifth environment action programme: waste

Objectives	EC Targets up to 2000	Actions	Time-frame	Sectors/actors
* overall target: rational and sustainable use of resources				Industry Agriculture Transport Energy Tourism
Municipal waste				
* prevention of waste (closing of cycles)	* waste management plans in Member States	* landfill Directive operational	before 1995	EC+MS+LAs Industry
* maximal recycling and reuse of material	* stabilization of quantities of waste generated at EC average 300 kg/capita (1985 level[1]; on a country by country basis no exceedance of 300 kg/capita	* directive on packaging operational	1995	EC+MS+LAs Industry
* safe disposal of any waste which cannot be recycled or reused in following ranking order:	* recycling/reuse of paper, glass and plastics of at least 50% (EC average)	* cleaner technologies + product design	progressive	Ind+Public+ EC+MS+LAs
– combustion as fuel	* Community-wide, infrastructure, for safe collection, separation and disposal	* policy on priority waste streams, stop on landfill for specific wastes (legislation + voluntary agreements)	ongoing	EC+MS+LAs Ind+NGOs+ Public
– incineration	* no export outside EC for final disposal	* reliable EC-data on waste generated, collected and disposed	1995	EC+MS+LAs +EEA
– landfill	* recycling/reuse of consumer products	* system of liability in place	2000	EC+MS
	* market for recycled materials	* economic incentives and instruments (incl. deposit return systems + vol. agreements)	ongoing	MS+EC+ Ind.
	* considerable reduction of dioxin emissions (90% reduction on 1985 levels by 2005)	* standards for dioxin emissions from municipal waste incineration	before 1994	EC+MS+LAs

Table 5.15 continued

Objectives	EC Targets up to 2000	Actions	Time-frame	Sectors/ actors
Hazardous waste				
* prevention of waste (closing of cycles) * maximal reuse/ recycling of material * safe disposal of any waste which cannot be recycled or reused following ranking order: – combustion as fuel – incineration – landfill	* no export outside EC for final disposal * waste management plans set up in Member States * EC-wide infrastructure for safe collection, separation and disposal * market for recycled materials	* landfill Directive operational	before 1995	EC+MS+LAs Industry
		* Directive on incineration of hazardous waste operational	1995	EC+MS+LAs Industry
		* policy on priority waste streams, stop on landfill for specific waste	ongoing	EC+MS+Ind +LAs+NGOs+ Public
		* cleaner technologies	ongoing	Ind.+EC+MS
		* reliable EC-data on waste generated, collected and disposed	1995	EEA+MS+LAs EC+Ind
		* setting up of bourse de dechets	before 1995	EC+MS+Ind
		* system of liability in place	2000	EC+MS
		* inventory of risks	1995	EC+MS+Ind
		* economic incentives and instruments, incl. vol. agreements	ongoing	MS+EC+ Ind.

(¹) Based on EUROSTAT and OECD statistics

Chapter 6

The Control of Chemicals

I. INTRODUCTION

Community regulations regarding the control of chemicals have gone through several phases which are linked on the one hand to the basic principles of the Common Market, and on the other to the establishment of an environmental protection policy.

In a first phase around 1965, the Community adopted a certain number of measures concerning the classification, packaging and labelling of dangerous chemical substances to be applied when such substances entered the market of the Community. The accent at that time was placed largely on the need to avoid obstacles to commercial exchanges of these substances between Member States. The differences between national regulations in fact prevented the creation of a true common market for these products, the importance of which was growing rapidly, both in volume and value.

In a second phase, around 1975, the Community concentrated much more on consumer protection, while not forgetting the importance of the smooth operation of the Common Market. A group of measures was taken with a view to banning or limiting the commercialization of dangerous substances and preparations contained in certain specific products.

In a third phase, from 1979 onwards, the Community entered into a more systematic and preventive policy of management and control of chemical products which corresponded more to objectives of environmental protection.

Different measures were thus taken in order to avoid, as far as possible, risks to health and the environment. These measures concerned both dangerous substances and industrial chemical activities (production; storage; transport). As far as substances were concerned, the provisions were aimed primarily at new chemical substances, prior to their introduction to the market. In the case of existing chemical substances, the Commission first started to draw up a complete inventory of substances, which is an essential prerequisite for the establishment of a more systematic control policy.

In a fourth phase beginning at the end of the 1980s, the Commission signalled its intention to extend the field of application of the policy on the control of chemicals to cover the international aspects. Until that time Community regulations regarding chemical substances and preparations had mainly concerned the internal market of the Community. In 1986 however the Commission proposed the adoption of a specific Community regulation regarding the export of dangerous chemical products to developing countries. The Community's actions regarding the protection of the ozone layer – a major international concern – have been discussed in the previous chapter.

II.   THE CONTROL OF EXISTING CHEMICALS

1.   Community regulation on the classification of dangerous substances

(a)   1967 framework directive

On 27 June 1967[1] the Council adopted the first directive on the classification, packaging and labelling of dangerous substances. This important directive represents the basis for a group of regulations concerning the management of dangerous chemicals, which will continue to develop in the future. It defines dangerous substances and preparations as being those which are "explosive, oxidizing, flammable, toxic, harmful, corrosive, and irritant". It clearly classifies the dangerous substances according to the different categories mentioned above. It also sets out detailed rules which Member States must apply for the packaging and labelling of dangerous substances.

The 1967 directive was amended on five occasions up to 1979, in order to adapt it to the latest advances in science and technology, or to clarify a particular provision.[2]

A new amendment, the 6th amending directive, was made in 1979. It clarified and strengthened the provisions of the 1967 directive on dangerous substances, and also introduced compulsory prior notification for any new chemicals placed on the market. It required quantities of one tonne per annum or more to be notified to the European Commission via the competent authorities of the Member States along with a technical dossier containing the results of specified tests for physicochemical, toxicological and ecotoxicological properties, a declaration of adverse effects and proposals for the classification of the substance, its labelling and recommended precautions. Lower quantities did not have to be notified, although the notifier was obliged to submit a limited announcement to the competent authorities of the Member State in which the substance is supplied.

On 25 April 1984[3] the Commission also adapted to technical progress the 1967 "classification" directive regarding test methods for determining the toxicity and ecotoxicity of chemical substances and preparations.

A proposal for a 7th amending directive was made in 1990.[4] The proposal was aimed at the classification, packaging, labelling and notification of new substances which had come on to the Community market since 18 September 1981. The major change proposed by the 7th amendment concerned the notification of substances to

---

[1]   OJ No 196 of 16/8/67.

[2]   Amendments were made on 13 March 1969 (OJ No 68 of 19/3/69); 6 March 1970 (OJ No L 59 of 14/3/70); 22 March 1971 (OJ No L 74 of 29 /3/71); 21 May 1973 (OJ No L 167 of 25/6/73); and 24 June 1975 (OJ No L 183 of 14/7/75).

[3]   OJ No L 251 of 19/9/84.

[4]   COM (89) 575.

be placed on the European Community market in quantities of less than one tonne per annum. Instead of the limited announcements provided for under the 6th amendment, the 7th amendment proposed a reduced notification similar in format to full notifications for quantities of more than one tonne but with a more limited package of test results. It also proposed that for quantities of less than 100 kg per annum the required data package would be even more limited, with a complete exemption for amounts under 10 kg.

Several other important revisions were proposed. Although the classification, packaging and labelling of all dangerous substances would remain for the most part unchanged, the term "dangerous for the environment" was revised to recognize different environmental media and a labelling symbol was proposed for those substances falling into this category. Also, a new article in the proposed directive would facilitate the sharing of test data in order to reduce testing on vertebrates. The proposal also aimed to bring non-agricultural pesticides and fertilizers into the scope of the directive.

The proposed amendment was adopted by the Council in 1992 as Directive 92/32/EEC.[5]

In addition to amendments adopted by the Council, the annexes to the directive had by the end of 1994 been adapted over 20 times by the Commission through the adaptation procedure.

(b)   Sectoral directives by products

Parallel with the 1967 directive which aims to regulate the classification or packaging of all dangerous substances and preparations at a general or horizontal level, the Community also adopted regulations in the 1970s on some specific dangerous preparations, that is, mixtures of solutions of dangerous substances. The Council thus adopted the following directives:

- on 4 June 1973, a directive on the classification and packaging of solvents;[6]
- on 7 November 1977, a directive on the classification and packaging of paint, varnishes, printing inks and adhesives and similar products;[7]
- on 26 June 1978, a directive on the classification and packaging of pesticides.[8]

(c)   1988 directive on the classification and packaging of dangerous preparations

On 29 July 1985 the Commission sent the Council a proposal on the classification, packaging and labelling of dangerous preparations. This proposal is a counterpart to the 1967 directive on dangerous substances, and particularly to its 6th amendment adopted by the Council in 1979.

From the industrial and commercial points of view it is clear that preparations, i.e. mixtures and combinations of several substances, represent a growing proportion of the chemical sector.

The risks which such preparations cause to the health of consumers and to the environment can be made even more serious in that the different components of the preparation often have considerable additional or multiplying effects. In the

[5] OJ No L 154 of 5/6/92.
[6] OJ No L 189 of 11/7/73 and OJ No L 229 of 30/8/80.
[7] OJ No L 303 of 28/11/77 and OJ No L 157 of 6/683.
[8] OJ No L 206 of 29/7/78 and OJ No L 88 of 7/4/81.

Commission's view, Community legislation in the area of dangerous preparations would therefore be all the more useful in the extent to which it is able to contribute to the better working of the Common Market, by reducing obstacles to trade caused by different classification and labelling systems. On several occasions, when adopting directives on specific preparations or products (solvents/paints and varnishes/pesticides), the Council had moreover asked the Commission to produce a general proposal covering all dangerous preparations. The proposal submitted by the Commission responded to the Council's request and made it possible to bring together in one text all of the existing legal rules and to extend the regulation to cover all dangerous preparations, with the exception mainly of medicinal products, radioactive substances, munitions and explosives, and cosmetic products.

The main provisions of the proposal aimed to classify and label preparations according to the degrees of danger they can represent, regardless of the use of those preparations. To this end, the proposal established a conventional method of evaluating the dangers from the toxicity point of view, and for the classification of preparations again uses the same definitions as those in the 6th amendment to the "dangerous substances" directive, i.e. of preparations which are very toxic/harmful/corrosive/irritant, etc.

Finally, the proposal made detailed provision for the packaging (sturdiness/airtightness) and labelling of dangerous preparations.

The Council adopted this directive on 7 June 1988.[9]

2. The Community regulation on the marketing and use of dangerous substances

The 1973 1st Action Programme indicated that for some dangerous substances and preparations it is not enough only to regulate their classification, packaging or labelling, as the Community started to do in 1967; it is also necessary at times to prohibit or limit the marketing and use of some of these substances.

On 25 July 1974 the Commission therefore sent the Council a proposal for a directive limiting the marketing and use of certain dangerous substances and preparations. This proposal relied to a great extent on the work already carried out by the Organization for Economic Cooperation and Development (OECD). The Council adopted this directive on 27 July 1976,[10] but greatly reduced the field of application suggested by the Commission. The only substances covered initially were polychlorinated biphenyls (PCB and PCT) and monomer vinyl chloride (VCM), the use of which can, under certain conditions, cause risks to human health and the environment. Since this first directive of 1976, Community regulations on the marketing and use of dangerous chemicals have been constantly adapted and extended.

(a)   1976: first directive restricting the use of PCB, PCT and VCM

The directive adopted by the Council on 27 July 1976 (Directive 76/769) stipulates that the marketing of polychlorinated biphenyls (PCB) and polychlorinated

---

[9] OJ No L 262 of 27/9/76.
[10] OJ No L 262 of 27/9/76.

terphenyls (PCT) and preparations with a PCB or PCT content higher than 0.1% by weight, is prohibited, with the exception of the following categories:

- closed system electrical equipment; transformers; resistors; and inductors;
- large condensers (1 kg total weight);
- small condensers in certain conditions;
- heat-transmitting fluids in closed-circuit heat-transfer installations, except in installations for processing foodstuffs, feedingstuffs, pharmaceutical and veterinary products;
- hydraulic fluids used in underground mining equipment and in machinery servicing cells;
- primary and intermediate products for further processing into other products which are not prohibited under the directive.

For monomer vinyl chloride, the directive specifies that this substance may not be used as aerosol propellant for any use whatsoever. The Council of Social Affairs Ministers also adopted a directive on 29 June 1978 concerning the protection of workers exposed to monomer vinyl chloride.[11]

(b)   1979: banning of the use of dangerous chemicals in ornamental objects and textile articles (1st amendment of the directive of 27 July 1976)

On 24 July 1979 the Council adopted a directive which completes the list of chemical substances, the marketing or use of which are prohibited or regulated.[12] The amendment adopted aims to prohibit, due to the dangers they represent for health, the marketing of:

- toxic, harmful, corrosive, explosive or inflammable liquids in the sense of the "classification" directive of 27 June 1967, used in ornamental objects such as lamps and ashtrays;
- tris (2.1 dibromoprophyl) phosphate in textile articles such as pyjamas or undergarments.

(c)   1982: banning of the use of benzene in toys (2nd amendment of the directive of 27 July 1976)

On 22 November 1982 the Council added benzene as a dangerous substance, the use of which is prohibited in toys when the concentration of benzene is higher than 5 mg/kg in comparison with the weight of the toy.[13]

(d)   1982: relaxing of the conditions for the use of PCT (3rd amendment to the directive of 27 July 1976)

On 3 December 1982 the Council temporarily relaxed the rules established by the directive of 27 July 1976 for PCTs (polychlorinated terphenyls).[14] The amendment adopted stipulates that until 1984 the Member States may allow the use on their territories of thermoplastic materials containing no more than 50% PCT. This possibility has not been extended beyond 1984.

[11] OJ No L 197 of 22/7/85.
[12] OJ No L 197 of 3/8/79.
[13] OJ No L 339 of 1/12/82.
[14] OJ No L 350 of 10/12/82.

(e)   1983: banning of the use of dangerous chemicals in textile articles and in jokes and hoaxes (4th amendment to the directive of 27 July 1976)

On 16 May 1983 the Council adopted a new list of five chemical substances, the marketing of which is prohibited when used in certain objects.[15]

- The use of tris-aziridinyl-phosphinoxide and polybrominatedbiphenyls is therefore prohibited in textile articles.
- "Panama" powder, ammonium sulphide and volatile esters of bromo-acetic acids are prohibited in jokes and hoaxes or similar objects.

(f)   1983: first stage in regulation of the marketing and use of asbestos (5th amendment to the directive of 27 July 1976)

On 7 March 1980 the Commission presented a proposal aimed at the regulation of the marketing and use of asbestos, a substance which is widely used, especially in the building sector, but which also represents a serious danger to health.

The Council adopted this directive in two stages, the first on 19 September 1983,[16] the second on 20 December 1985 (see p. 234). At the first stage, the main provisions contained in the directive concern both the prohibiting of the placing on the market of the most dangerous asbestos, known as "blue asbestos" (crocidolite), and the compulsory use of a specific label for all other asbestos fibres. The ban on the marketing of blue asbestos was nevertheless tempered by the possibility given to each Member State to allow blue asbestos on its territory until 30 June 1988 and, for Member States which so wish, to authorize the use of asbestos in the following three products: asbestos-cement pipes; seals; and torque converters.

For asbestos fibres other than blue asbestos, the Council did not follow the Commission's more restrictive proposals at this first stage. Indeed, rather than making provision of a general regulation on marketing and use, the Council restricted itself at this point to a simple obligation to provide information, in the form of a label, drawing the users' attention to the health dangers of asbestos and specifying the safety measures to follow.

(g)   1985: strengthening of the 1976 regulation on the marketing and use of PCB and PCT (6th amendment to the directive of 27 July 1976)

On 3 October 1984 the Commission presented the Council with a proposal aimed at considerably strengthening the Community regulation in force since 1976 on the marketing and use of PCB/PCT in the Community. This proposal was produced as a result of research which confirmed the harmful effects of PCB/PCT on health and the environment, and as a result of the particular dangers which PCB/PCT represent in the event of fires, and of the progress made in the perfection of substitute products which can be used in electrical installations.

The Council adopted this directive on 1 October 1985.[17] In particular, it makes provision for the following measures, which concern new equipment as well as existing equipment containing PCB/PCT.

---

[15] OJ No L 147 of 6/6/83.
[16] OJ No L 263 of 24/9/83.
[17] OJ No L 269 of 11/10/85.

For new equipment, the directive practically withdraws the exemptions which had been authorized in the 1976 directive. From 1 July 1986 at the latest, the introduction into the market of electrical equipment (transformers/condensers) and fluids in heat-transfer installations and mines is therefore prohibited when this equipment and these fluids contain PCB/PCT.

The directive also prohibits the marketing of preparations and mixtures, including waste oils, with a PCB or PCT content higher than 0.01% by weight, or 100 ppm; the maximum content authorized by the 1976 directive was 10 times higher at 0.1% or 1000 ppm.

The use of old existing equipment is authorized until it has been disposed of or until the end of the service life, Member States nevertheless being able to prohibit the use of such equipment within their territories before the end of the service life. Finally, the directive stipulates that the placing on the secondhand market of equipment, plant and fluids containing PCB/PCT is prohibited from 1 July 1986 onwards.

(h)   1985: second stage of the regulation on the marketing and use of asbestos (7th amendment to the directive of 27 July 1976)

On the basis of a Commission proposal dated 7 March 1980, the Council adopted a directive on 20 December 1985[18] which, with the aim of protecting health and the environment, puts further restrictions on the marketing and use of products containing asbestos. While the purpose of the first-stage directive (see p. 233) was mainly to regulate the use of the most dangerous asbestos ("blue asbestos" or crocidolite), the directive of 20 December 1985 concerns the other asbestos fibres, and especially "white asbestos" (chrysotile). The directive therefore makes provision for six new bans on the marketing of current products containing asbestos fibres which belong to the following groups: chrysotile; amosite; anthophylillite; actinolite; tremolite. The six products which contain asbestos fibres and are covered by the ban are:

- toys;
- paints and varnishes;
- items for smoking (pipes, cigarette holders);
- finished products in powder form;
- catalytic filters used in heaters using liquefied gas;
- materials and preparations applied by spraying.

For this last category, the Member States may, however, allow the use within their own territories of bituminous compounds containing asbestos when these materials are intended for undersealing vehicles for anti-corrosion protection. Member States must conform with this directive by 31 December 1987 at the latest.

(i)   The 1989 proposal to amend Directive 76/769

The 9th amendment to Directive 76/769 prohibited the placing on the market of substances or preparations if they contain more than 0.1% or more of pentachlorophenol and its salts and esters, collectively referred to as PCP. PCP is used in preservative treatments for timber, masonry and textiles, and to a lesser extent as a biocide or preservative in a variety of industrial products and processes. PCP is

---

[18] OJ No L 375 of 31/12/85.

extremely effective for these purposes and, in particular, for the treatment of dry rot, for which there are very few suitable alternatives. The toxic nature of the substance requires it to be subject to strict control. The general ban on PCP contains four derogations. Continued use was allowed in industrial installations for the following purposes:

- the treatment of timber intended for structural use, which must not be used inside a building for decorative purposes, or for food containers;
- the treatment of heavy duty textiles, which must not be used for clothing or decorative purposes;
- as a synthesizing or processing agent in industry;
- the treatment of dry rot and cubic fungi in historical buildings and in emergency situations.

The uses of PCP were thus limited to those where it performs an important function for which there is currently no alternative substance and where usage is of such a limited nature as to minimize exposure of humans and the environment. The derogations were to be reviewed not more than three years after the entering into force of the directive in order to take into account the possible development of suitable substitutes.

The proposal was adopted as Council Directive 91/173/EEC on 21 March 1991.[19]

(j) The 11th amendment to Directive 76/769 (Council Directive adopted on 18 June 1991 as 91/339/EEC)[20]

The 11th amendment concerned three substances: monomethyl-tetrachlorodiphenyl methane, monomethyl-dichlorodiphenyl methane, and monomethyl-dibromo-diphenyl methane. The three were marketed under the trade names of Ugilec 141, Ugilec 121 and DBBT respectively. All had been developed as substitutes for PCBs the marketing and use of which were banned, apart from certain very limited exceptions, by the 6th amendment to the directive. The three substances are used as hydraulic fluids in deep lignite mines where machinery has to operate at very high temperatures for which water-based fluids cannot be used. All three have hazardous properties similar to those of PCBs which caused the latter to be banned: they are toxic, do not degrade naturally and tend to accumulate in living tissues. The amendment permitted the continued use of Ugilec 141 (the only one of the three actually in use within the Community) for three years after the directive's adoption. After that, it may still be used in plant or machinery already in service until this is disposed of or reaches the end of its service life. The other two substances would be prohibited outright one year after the directive's adoption.

(k) The 1991 proposal for a directive amending Directive 76/769 (12th amendment)

In 1991 the Commission sent the Council a proposal for a directive to amend the original 1976 directive. The proposal arose mainly as a result of concern in some Member States, particularly Germany, about the dangers posed to human

[19] OJ No L 85 of 5/4/91.
[20] OJ No L 186 of 12/7/91.

health and the environment by the combustion of a group of chemicals known as polybromobiphenyl ethers (PBBEs), certain of which have special properties which inhibit the spread of fire and consequently are used as flame retardants in textiles and plastics. When compounds and plastics containing them are burnt or exposed to heat, polybromodioxins (dioxins) and polybromofurans (furans) are released, these highly toxic substances then accumulating in animal tissues.

The Commission proposed the immediate prohibition of seven of these substances: mono, di, tri, tetra, hexa, hepta and nona bromobiphenyl ether. None of the seven is currently in widespread use. The remaining three of the group, deca, octa and penta, widely used as flame retardants, would be banned five years after the proposal was adopted. Furthermore, the proposal would limit the concentrations of the substances placed on the market in formulations and products to less than 0.1% by mass, effectively preventing any use as a flame retardant.

3. Cadmium

The 4th Environmental Action Programme indicated (para. 3.3.6) that "the Commission is carefully reviewing, on an 'across the board' basis, the environmental problems caused by cadmium". On 21 April 1987, the Commission sent to the Council a proposed action programme to deal with environmental pollution by cadmium, indicating that exposure to cadmium had steadily increased because of the large-scale use of cadmium in the last decade and that the WHO provisional tolerable weekly intake of 400/500 mg per person, which had been widely adopted, had already been reached in some areas.

At its meeting of 3 December 1987, the Environment Council approved a Resolution[21] concerning a Community Action Programme to combat environmental pollution by cadmium.

In this Resolution, the Council stressed that, in the light of the result of scientific and technical studies, the major elements of the strategy for cadmium control in the interests of the protection of human health and the environment should be the following:

- limitation of the uses of cadmium to cases where suitable alternatives do not exist;
- stimulation of research and development:
- of substitutes and technological derivatives, in particular, encouragement of the development of further alternatives to the use of cadmium in pigments, stabilizers and plating;
- related to the cadmium content of the raw materials used for the production of phosphate fertilizers;
- of varieties of tobacco and food plants with a lower cadmium content;
- collection and recycling of products containing cadmium, for example batteries;
- development of a strategy designed to reduce cadmium input in soil, for example by appropriate control measures for the cadmium content of phosphate fertilizers based on suitable technology not entailing excessive costs, taking into account environmental conditions in the different regions of the Community;
- combating significant sources of airborne and water pollution.

[21] OJ No C 30 of 4/2/88.

At the same time as it adopted the Resolution, the Council invited the Commission to submit proposals for Community rules concerning a source-oriented approach to pollution by other heavy metals, to be combined, if necessary, with action programmes on the lines of the cadmium programme.

4.   Council directive on the prevention of environmental pollution by asbestos

On 19 March 1987, the Council adopted a directive (87/217) on the prevention and reduction of environmental pollution by asbestos, based on the proposal of the Commission of 29 November 1985[22] (COM (85) 632 final).

The directive supplements provisions already in force (see p. 171) requiring Member States to take the measures necessary to ensure that asbestos emissions into the air, asbestos discharges into the aquatic environment, and solid asbestos waste are, as far as reasonably practicable, reduced at source and prevented. In the case of the use of asbestos, these measures should entail using the best available technology not entailing excessive cost, including, where appropriate, recycling or treatment.

As far as emissions of asbestos to air are concerned, Member States have to take the measures necessary to ensure that the concentration of asbestos emitted through the discharge ducts into the air during use of asbestos does not exceed a limit value of 0.1 mg/m^3 of asbestos per m^3 of air discharge.

As far as discharges into the aquatic environment are concerned, Member States have to take the measures necessary to ensure that all aqueous effluent arising in the manufacture of asbestos cement is recycled or, where this is not economically feasible, that the disposal of liquid waste containing asbestos does not result in pollution of the aquatic environment. To this end, the Council fixed a limit value of 30 grams of total suspended matter per m^3 of aqueous effluent discharged.

Member States are also required to take the measures necessary to ensure that:

- activities involving the working of products containing asbestos do not cause significant environmental pollution by asbestos fibres or dust;
- the demolition of buildings, structures and installations containing asbestos does not cause significant asbestos environmental pollution.

III.   THE CONTROL OF NEW CHEMICALS

For new chemicals the 1973 1st Action Programme indicated that the Commission would investigate the measures required to harmonize and strengthen control by the public authorities over certain substances or new synthetic products before they are marketed. This investigation would concentrate in particular on the improvement and harmonization of quantitative analysis techniques, long-term toxicity and standardization of toxicity tests, and especially on compulsory prior submission of samples. A study carried out by the Commission showed that the number of synthesized compounds could reach an annual figure of 250,000, only a few hundred of

---

[22] Proposed 29/11/85 – COM (85) 632, adopted OJ No L 85 of 28/3/87.

which find their way into the various commercial channels. The use of some of these compounds could have serious ecological consequences if they were placed on the market without prior assurance that they represent no foreseeable danger to man and the environment.

1. The Community framework regulation on the marketing of new chemical substances: Adoption in 1979 of the 6th amendment to the "classification" directive of 1967

On 20 September 1976, the Commission presented the Council with a proposal amending for the sixth time the directive of 27 June 1967 on the classification, packaging and labelling of dangerous substances (see p. 229).

In fact this proposal, far from being a simple amendment, constitutes the Community framework regulation on chemicals, particularly the control of new chemical substances.

Unlike the five preceding amendments which were mainly of a technical nature, the 6th amendment not only replaces the different provisions in force under the "classification of dangerous substances" directive of 27 June 1967, by codifying and strengthening them, but also introduces compulsory notification, on the basis of tests, prior to the marketing of any new chemical substance.

The Commission produced this proposal as a result of considerable scientific developments in the chemical industry, a sector in the forefront of research and development. This development led to a rapid increase in both the number and quantity of new synthetic chemical compounds, thus presenting serious problems for the control of these substances. In the Commission's view, the risks which uncontrolled new chemical substances impose on health and the environment in general, demand that a harmonized surveillance system be established in the Community before such substances are put on the market.

The Council adopted this important directive on 18 September 1979.[23] First, the directive completes, clarifies and strengthens the definition and criteria of the "classification" directive of 27 June 1967 on substances and preparations considered to be dangerous, namely "explosive, oxidizing, extremely flammable, highly flammable, flammable, very toxic, toxic, harmful, corrosive, irritant, dangerous for all environment, carcinogenic, teratogenic, and mutagenic". All existing chemical substances must be classified into the different categories referred to above, according to the provisions of the directive. The directive does not apply to medicinal products, narcotics and radioactive substances.

Secondly, the directive introduces into Community legislation important provisions for the control of new chemical substances. Any manufacturer or importer into the Community must supply, at least 45 days before the marketing of a new substance, a notification including the following four elements:

● a basic technical dossier supplying the information necessary for evaluating the foreseeable risks, whether immediate or delayed, which the substance may entail for man and the environment. This must at least contain specific and detailed information on the following areas: identity of the substance; physico-chemical properties; toxicological studies; and the possibility of rendering the substance harmless (see Table 6.2);

[23] OJ No L 259 of 15/10/79.

Table 6.1: Council Directive of 18 September 1979 amending for the sixth time Directive 67/548/EEC on the approximation of the laws, regulations and administrative provisions relating to the classification, packaging and labelling of dangerous substances

GENERAL CLASSIFICATION AND LABELLING REQUIREMENTS FOR DANGEROUS SUBSTANCES

PART I

A. Save where otherwise provided in the separate Directives on dangerous preparations, the substances and preparations shall be classified as very toxic, toxic or harmful according to the following criteria:

   (a) classification as very toxic, toxic or harmful shall be effected by determining the acute toxicity of the commercial substance or preparation in animals, expressed in LD_{50} or LC_{50} values with the following parameters being taken as reference values:

Category	LD_{50} absorbed orally in rat mg/kg	LD_{50} percutaneous absorption in rat or rabbit mg/kg	LC_{50} absorbed by inhalation in rat mg/litre/four hours
Very toxic	≤ 25	≤ 50	≤ 0.5
Toxic	25 to 200	50 to 400	0.5 to 2
Harmful	200 to 2 000	400 to 2 000	2 to 20

   (b) if facts show that for the purposes of classification it is inadvisable to use the LD_{50} or LC_{50} values as a principal basis because the substances or preparations produce other effects, the substances or preparations shall be classified according to the magnitude of these effects.

PART II

B. – Corrosion criteria: for the record
    – Irritation criteria: for the record

C. If the facts show the existence of effects other than the acute effects indicated by experiments with animals, e.g. carcinogenic, mutagenic, allergenic, sub-acute or chronic effects, the substances or preparations shall be classified according to the magnitude of these effects.

D. Guide for the labelling of dangerous substances and criteria for the choice of phrases allocated to dangerous substances indicating the special risks (R phrases) and the safety advice (S phrases): for the record.

● a declaration concerning the unfavourable effects of the substance in terms of the various uses envisaged;
● the proposed classification and labelling of the substance in accordance with the directive;
● proposals for any recommended precautions relating to the safe use of the substance.

Table 6.2: Directive of 18 September 1979 amending for the sixth time Directive 67/548/EEC on the approximation of the laws, regulations and administrative provisions relating to the classification, packaging and labelling of dangerous substances

INFORMATION REQUIRED FOR THE TECHNICAL DOSSIER ('BASE SET') REFERRED TO IN ARTICLE 6 (1)

When giving notification the manufacturer or any other person placing a substance on the market shall provide the information set out below.

If it is not technically possible or if it does not appear necessary to give information, the reasons shall be stated.

Tests must be conducted according to methods recognized and recommended by the competent international bodies where such recommendations exist.

The bodies carrying out the tests shall comply with the principles of good current laboratory practice.

When complete studies and the results obtained are submitted, it shall be stated that the tests were conducted using the substance to the marketed. The composition of the sample shall be indicated.

In addition, the description of the methods used or the reference to standardized or internationally recognized methods shall also be mentioned in the technical dossier, together with the name of the body or bodies responsible for carrying out the studies.

1. IDENTITY OF THE SUBSTANCE

1.1.   **Name**

1.1.1.   Names in the IUPAC nomenclature

1.1.2.   Other names (usual name, trade name, abbreviation)

1.1.3.   CAS number (if available)

1.2   **Empirical and structural formula**

1.3   **Composition of the substance**

1.3.1.   Degree of purity (%)

1.3.2.   Nature of impurities, including isomers and by-products

1.3.3   Percentage of (significant) main impurities

1.3.4.   If the substance contains a stabilizing agent or an inhibitor or other additives, specify: nature, order of magnitude: ... ppm; ... %

1.3.5.   Spectral data (UV, IR, NMR)

1.4.   **Methods of detection and determination**

A full description of the methods used or the appropriate bibliographical references

Table 6.2 continued

2. INFORMATION ON THE SUBSTANCE

2.1.   **Proposed uses**

2.1.1. Types of use

Describe: the function of the substance ....

the desired effects ....

2.1.2. Fields or application with approximate breakdown

(a) closed system

– industries ....

– farmers and skilled trades ....

– use by the public at large ....

(b) open system

– industries ....

– farmers and skilled trades ....

– use by the public at large ....

2.2.   **Estimated production and/or imports for each of the anticipated uses or fields of application**

2.2.1. Overall production and/or imports in order of tonnes per year 1; 10; 50; 100; 500; 1 000 and 5 000

– first 12 months .... tonnes/year

– thereafter .... tonnes/year

2.2.2   Production and/or imports, broken down in accordance with 2.1.1 and 2.1.2, expressed as a percentage

– first 12 months ....

– thereafter ....

2.3.   **Recommended methods and precautions concerning:**

2.3.1. handling ....

2.3.2. storage ....

2.3.3. transport ....

2.3.4. fire (nature of combustion gases or pyrolysis, where proposed uses justify this)

2.3.5. other dangers, particularly chemical reaction with water

2.4.   **Emergency measures in the case of accidental spillage**

2.5.   **Emergency measures in the case of injury to persons** (e.g. poisoning)

Table 6.2 continued

3. PHYSICO-CHEMICAL PROPERTIES OF THE SUBSTANCE

3.1.   **Melting point**

.... °C

3.2.   **Boiling point**

.... °C .... Pa

3.3.   **Relative density**

.... $(D_4{}^{20})$

3.4.   **Vapour pressure**

.... Pa at .... °C

.... Pa at .... °C

3.5.   **Surface tension**

.... M/m (........................... °C)

3.6.   **Water solubility**

.... mg/litre (...................... °C)

3.7.   **Fat solubility**

Solvent – oil (to be specified)

.... mg/100 g solvent (.......................... °C)

3.8.   **Partition coefficient**

n-octanol/water

3.9.   **Flash point**

.... °C ☐ open cup ☐ closed cup

3.10. **Flammability** (within the meaning of the definition given in Article 2 (2) (c), (d) and (e))

3.11. **Explosive properties** (within the meaning of the definition given in Article 2 (2) (a))

3.12. **Auto-flammability**

.... °C

3.13. **Oxidizing properties** (within the meaning of the definition given in Article 2 (2) (b))

4. TOXICOLOGICAL STUDIES

4.1.   **Acute toxicity**

4.1.1. Administered orally

LD_{50} .... mg/kg

Effects observed, including in the organs ....

Table 6.2 continued

4.1.2.   Administered by inhalation

LC$_{50}$ .... (ppm) Duration of exposure .... hours

Effects observed, including in the organs ....

4.1.3.   Administered cutaneously (percutaneous absorption)

LD$_{50}$ .... mg/kg

Effects observed, including in the organs ....

4.1.4.   Substances other than gases shall be administered via two routes at least, one of which should be the oral route. The other route will depend on the intended use and on the physical properties of the substance.

Gases and volatile liquids should be administered by inhalation (a minimum period of administration of four hours).

In all cases, observation of the animals should be carried out for at least 14 days.

Unless there are contra-indications, the rat is the preferred species for oral and inhalation experiments.

The experiments in 4.1.1, 4.1.2 and 4.1.3 shall be carried out on both male and female subjects.

4.1.5.   Skin irritation

The substance should be applied to the shaved skin of an animal, preferably an albino rabbit.

Duration of exposure .... hours

4.1.6.   Eye irritation

The rabbit is the preferred animal.

Duration of exposure .... hours

4.1.7.   Skin sensitization

To be determined by a recognized method using a guinea-pig.

4.2.   **Sub-acute toxicity**

4.2.1.   Sub-acute toxicity (28 days)

Effects observed on the animal and organs according to the concentrations used, including clinical and laboratory investigations ....

Dose for which no toxic effect is observed ....

4.2.2.   A period of daily administration (five to seven days per week) for at least four weeks should be chosen. The route of administration should be the most appropriate having regard to the intended use, the acute toxicity and the physical and chemical properties of the substance.

Unless there are contra-indications, the rat is the preferred species for oral and inhalation experiments.

Table 6.2 continued

4.3.	**Other effects**

4.3.1.   Mutagenicity (including carcinogenic pre-screening test)

4.3.2.   The substance should be examined during a series of two tests, one of which should be bacteriological, with and without metabolic activation, and one non-bacteriological.

5. ECOTOXICOLOGICAL STUDIES

5.1.   **Effects on organisms**

5.1.1.   Acute toxicity for fish

LC_{50} .... (ppm) Duration of exposure determined in accordance with Annex V (C)

Species selected (one or more) ....

5.1.2.   Acute toxicity for daphnia

LC_{50} .... (ppm) Duration of exposure determined in accordance with Annex V (C)

5.2.   **Degradation**

– biotic

– abiotic

The BOD and the BOD/COD ratio should be determined as a minimum

6. POSSIBILITY OF RENDERING THE SUBSTANCE HARMLESS

6.1.   **For industry/skilled trades**

6.1.1   Possibility of recovery ....

6.1.2.   Possibility of neutralization ....

6.1.3.   Possibility of destruction:

– controlled discharge ....

– incineration ....

– water purification station ....

– others ....

6.2.   **For the public at large**

6.2.1   Possibility of recovery ....

6.2.2.   Possibility of neutralization ....

6.2.3.   Possibility of destruction:

– controlled discharge ....

– incineration ....

– water purification station ....

– others ....

Apart from the basic technical dossier, the directive also requires that any person or firm giving notification of a substance must inform the competent authority of the results of studies and tests referred to in Table 6.2. In the light of the information received the competent authority can require the notifier to carry out additional tests in accordance with Table 6.3.

Table 6.3: Council Directive of 18 September 1979 amending for the sixth time Directive 67/548/EEC on the approximation of the laws, regulations and administrative provisions relating to the classification, packaging and labelling of dangerous substances

ADDITIONAL INFORMATION AND TESTS REQUIRED UNDER ARTICLE 6 (5)

Any person who has notified a substance to a competent authority in accordance with the requirements of Article 6 of this Directive shall provide at the request of the authority further information and carry out additional tests as provided for in this Annex.

If it is not technically possible or if it does not appear necessary to give information, the reasons shall be stated.

Tests shall be conducted according to methods recognized and recommended by the competent international bodies where such recommendations exist.

The bodies carrying out the tests shall comply with the principles of good current laboratory practice.

When complete studies and the results obtained are submitted, it shall be stated that the tests were conducted using the substance marketed. The composition of the sample shall be indicated.

In addition the description of the methods used or the reference to standardized or internationally recognized methods shall also be mentioned in the technical dossier, together with the name of the body or bodies responsible for carrying out the studies.

LEVEL 1

Taking into account:

– current knowledge of the substance,

– known and planned uses,

– the results of the tests carried out in the context of the base set,

the competent authority may require the following additional studies where the quantity of a substance placed on the market by a notifier reaches a level of 10 tonnes per year or a total of 50 tonnes and if the conditions specified after each of the tests are fulfilled in the case of that substance.

Table 6.3 continued

Toxicological studies

– Fertility study (one species, one generation, male and female, most appropriate route of administration)

If there are equivocal findings in the first generation, study of a second generation is required.

It is also possible in this study to obtain evidence on teratogenicity.

If there are indications of teratogenicity, full evaluation of teratogenic potential may require a study in a second species.

– Teratology study (one species, most appropriate route of administration)

This study is required if teratogenicity has not been examined or evaluated in the preceding fertility study.

– Sub-chronic and/or chronic toxicity study, including special studies (one species, male and female, most appropriate route of administration)

If the results of the sub-acute study in Annex VII or other relevant information demonstrate the need for further investigation, this may take the form of a more detailed examination of certain effects, or more prolonged exposure, e.g. 90 days or longer (even up to two years).

The effects which would indicate the need for such a study could include for example:

(a) serious or irreversible lesions;

(b) a very low or absence of a 'no effect' level;

(c) a clear relationship in chemical structure between the substance being studied and other substances which have been proved dangerous.

– Additional mutagenesis studies (including screening for carcinogenesis)

A. If results of the mutagenesis tests are negative, a test to verify mutagenesis and a test to verify carcinogenesis screening are obligatory.

If the results of the mutagenesis verification test are also negative, further mutagenesis tests are not necessary at this level; if the results are positive, further mutagenesis tests are to be carried out (see B).

If the results of the carcinogenesis screening verification test are also negative, further carcinogenesis screening verification tests are not necessary at this level; if the results are positive further carcinogenesis screening verification tests are to be carried out (see B).

B. If the results of the mutagenesis tests are positive (a single positive test means positive), at least two verification tests are necessary at this level. Both mutagenesis tests and carcinogenesis screening tests should be considered here. A positive result of a carcinogenesis screening test should lead to a carcinogenesis study at this level.

Table 6.3 continued

Ecotoxicology studies

– An algal test: one species, growth inhibition test.

– Prolonged toxicity study with Daphina magna (21 days, thus study should also include determination of the 'no-effect level' for reproduction and the 'no-effect level' for lethality).

   The conditions under which this test is carried out shall be determined in accordance with the procedure described in Article 21 in the light of the methods laid down in Annex V (C) for acute toxicity tests with Daphnia.

– Test on a higher plant.

– Test on an earthworm.

– Prolonged toxicity study with fish (e.g. Oryzias, Jordanella, etc.; at least a period of 14 days; thus study should also include determination of the 'threshold level').

   The conditions under which this test is carried out shall be determined in accordance with the procedure described in Article 21 in the light of the methods adopted under Annex V (C) for acute toxicity tests with fish.

– Tests for species accumulation; one species, preferably fish (e.g. Poecilla reticulata).

– Prolonged biodegradation study, if sufficient (bio)degradation has not been proved by the studies laid down in Annex VII, another test (dynamic) shall be chosen with lower concentrations and with a different inoculum (e.g. flow-through system).

   In any case, the notifier shall inform the competent authority if the quantity of a substance placed on the market reaches a level of 100 tonnes per year or a total of 500 tonnes.

   On receipt of such notification and if the requisite conditions are fulfilled, the competent authority, within a time limit it will determine, shall require the above tests to be carried out unless in any particular case an alternative scientific study would be preferable.

LEVEL 2

If the quantity of substance placed on the market by a notifier reaches 1 000 tonnes per year or a total of 5 000 tonnes, the notifier shall inform the competent authority. The latter shall then draw up a programme of tests to be carried out by the notifier in order to enable the competent authority to evaluate the risks of the substance for man and the environment.

The test programme shall cover the following aspects unless there are strong reasons to the contrary, supported by evidence, that it should not be followed:

– chronic toxicity study,

– carcinogenicity study,

– fertility study (e.g. three-generations study); only if an effect on fertility has been established at level 1,

Table 6.3 continued

– teratology study (non-rodent species) study to verify teratology study at level 1 and experiment additional to the level 1 study, if effects on embryos/foetuses have been established,

– acute and sub-acute toxicity study on second species: only if results of level 1 studies indicate a need for this. Also results of biotransformation studies and studies on pharmacokinetics may lead to such studies,

– additional toxicokinetic studies.

Ecotoxicology

– Additional tests for accumulation, degradation and mobility.

The purpose of this study should be to determine any accumulation in the food chain.

For further bioaccumulation studies special attention should be paid to the solubility of the substance in water and to its n-octanol/water partition coefficient.

The results of the level 1 accumulation study and the physicochemical properties may lead to a large-scale flow-through test.

– Prolonged toxicity study with fish (including reproduction).

– Additional toxicity study (acute and sub-acute) with birds (e.g. quails): if accumulation factor is greater than 100.

– Additional toxicity study with other organisms (if this proves necessary).

– Absorption – desorption study where the substance is not particularly degradable.

2. The Consultative Committee on the Toxicity and Ecotoxicity of Chemical Compounds

On 28 June 1987[24] the Commission appointed a scientific committee to examine the toxicity and ecotoxicity of chemical compounds. This committee is made up of experts from the Member States. It should assist the Commission to keep the impact of chemical compounds on health and the environment under constant review. Its role is purely consultative.

3. The different inventories of chemical substances

To assist it in the management and control of chemical substances, the Commission has at its disposal the following inventories:

(a) ECDIN system

More than an inventory, this system is actually a data bank containing information on the characteristics and behaviour of chemical pollutants. This data bank was

---

[24] OJ No L 198 of 22/7/78.

created in 1973, as a pilot project, under the different research programmes of the Community.

(b)   EINECS (European Inventory of Existing Chemical Substances)

The creation of this inventory is specifically provided for in the 6th amendment of 1979. It contains all the "existing" basic chemical substances, i.e. those placed on the market between 1971 and 18 September 1981. The inventory includes a total of approximately 95,000 substances and was published at the end of 1986. None of the substances included in the EINECS will need to be subject to prior notification in the sense of the 6th amendment.

(c)   ECOIN (European Core Inventory)

This inventory constitutes a sub-set of the general EINECS inventory. It consists of the best-known and most widely marketed substances as of 18 September 1981. It was published in 1981 and covers approximately 34,000 substances.

(d)   Commission Decision 85/71/EEC – List of Notified Substances[25]

The Decision establishes the procedure for publication of the European Community List of Notified Substances (ELINCS) in the Official Journal of the European Communities. The list is to be published annually by 31 December, covering the period 1 July to 30 June. The list contains the number of the notification and the identity of each substance. This identity consists of its trade name(s) and its chemical name in the IUPAC Nomenclature. However, chemicals which are not classified as hazardous may be recorded under their trade name(s) at the request of the competent authority of a Member State for up to three years.

4.   The 1986 directive on the application of the principles of "good laboratory practice" for tests on chemical substances

On 24 July 1985 the Commission presented the Council with a proposal on the application in the Community of so-called "good laboratory practice" (GLP) for tests on chemical substances. The Council adopted the directive on 18 December 1986.[26] This text requires the laboratories of the Member States which carry out tests on chemical products to respect the principles of good laboratory practice specified in a decision of the OECD on 12 May 1981. In submitting the results of the tests, the laboratories must certify that the OECD principles have been respected. The Member States must carry out inspections and study checks of the laboratories in accordance with the recommendations of the OECD in this area. The requirement to follow the principles of good laboratory practice makes it possible both to ensure a higher quality in the carrying out of the tests, and to guarantee a certain comparability of these tests, thus limiting the repetition of tests in the Member States. The directive is general in scope, in that it applies not only to the tests on new chemical substances provided for in the 6th amendment of 1976 but

[25]   OJ No L 30 of 2/2/85.
[26]   OJ No L 15 of 17/1/87.

also to the tests prescribed by other Community provisions (pharmaceutical prod-ucts, pesticides, etc.).

Council Directive 88/320/EEC of 9 June 1988 on the inspection and verification of Good Laboratory Practice[27] provides for a harmonized system for study audit and inspection of laboratories to ensure that they are working under GLP condi-tions. Under Council Decision 89/569/EEC of 28 July 1989 the EEC accepted the OECD decision/recommendation on compliance with principles of GLP which established a framework for the conclusion of arrangements between OECD member countries on mutual recognition of compliance with GLP.[28]

5. The 1990 proposal for a regulation on the evaluation and control of the environmental risks of existing substances

On 14 September 1990 the Commission submitted a proposal to the Council for a regulation for the collection of information on existing substances, their subse-quent evaluation and, where appropriate, their control. Existing substances are classified as those listed in the European Inventory of Existing Commercial Chemical Substances (EINECS). The information collected would be separated into three phases. Manufacturers or importers who had produced or imported an existing substance at least once in the three years preceding the adoption of the regulation would be required to submit specified information direct to the Commission. In the first phase, information on all the existing substances listed in Annex 1 to the proposal (i.e. substances produced or imported in quantities exceeding 1000 tonnes per annum) would be submitted within six months of the proposal's adoption. The information submitted would have to include quantity, potential uses and data on toxicological, ecotoxicological and physico-chemical properties.

In the second phase, a similar obligation would fall on manufacturers and importers dealing with substances in quantities exceeding 1000 tonnes per annum but not listed in the Annex. The information would have to be submitted within 18 months of the proposal's adoption. The third phase would require submission on a timescale of four and a half years for a reduced package of information for existing substances produced or imported in quantities of 10–1000 tonnes per annum. The information so gathered would be used to draw up priority lists of those substances which appear to warrant detailed risk evaluation. The lists would be compiled by a management committee made up of representatives of all Member States and chaired by the Commission which would allocate priority substances to national competent authorities. The competent authorities in each Member State would review the data already collected and notify the Commission if they considered additional data was necessary. The Commission would then submit a proposal to the management committee for a request for additional data.

The regulation was adopted in 1993 as 793/EC on the evaluation and control of the risks of existing chemical substances.[29]

[27] OJ No L 145 of 11/6/88.
[28] OJ No L 315 of 28/10/89.
[29] OJ No L 84 of 5/4/93.

IV.   THE CONTROL OF DANGEROUS INDUSTRIAL CHEMICAL ACTIVITIES

1.   The 1982 directive on the major accident hazards of certain industrial activities

Accidents such as the one at Flixborough in 1973 and the one in Seveso in 1976 have highlighted the safety problems represented by chemical factories. In order to prevent accident hazards at source through a better integration of safety considerations into the various stages of design, production and operation of dangerous industrial activities, the Commission produced a proposal aiming to control certain dangerous industrial chemical activities. Having consulted the chemical industry and the consultative committee on safety, hygiene and health protection in the workplace, the Commission submitted this proposal to the Council on 19 July 1979.

The Council adopted this directive on the major accident hazards of certain industrial activities on 24 June 1982.[30] Its adoption was delayed by general differences of opinion amongst the Member States on the provisions to be applied to transfrontier industrial installations. Before looking at the general provisions of the directive, its importance must be underlined, as must the repercussions it has had, not only because of its close link with the Seveso accident, but also because it is the first Community text in the area of civil protection or safety.

The directive's field of application covers both production or transformation operations carried out in the chemical or energy related industrial installations listed in Table 6.4 using dangerous substances, and also individual operations involving the storage of certain dangerous substances (see Table 6.5). The directive does not apply to nuclear, military, mining or toxic and dangerous waste disposal installations.

The general structure of the directive consists of two main sections: the first concerns the general obligations of manufacturers; the second, more detailed, sets out a specific "notification" system for particularly dangerous substances.

The first part of the directive obliges all manufacturers of very toxic, toxic, flammable or explosive substances to take the necessary measures to prevent major accidents (e.g. emissions of harmful substances; explosion; fire, etc.) and to limit their consequences for man and the environment. To this end the manufacturer must be able to prove to the control authorities that he has evaluated the risk of major accidents, taken appropriate safeguard measures and informed, trained and equipped persons who work on the industrial site concerned.

The second part of the directive lays down that, without regard to the general security obligations mentioned above, each manufacturer must address to the control authorities a detailed "notification" when the industrial activity in question involves, in quantities which are laid down in the directive, particularly dangerous substances. The dangerous substances listed in the directive number 180.

The notification which has to be sent to the control authorities and which must be periodically updated, must include three types of information:

● information on the dangerous substances (identity of the substance; potential hazard; quantity; chemical or physical behaviour);

---

[30]   OJ No 230 of 5/8/82.

Table 6.4: Council Directive of 24 June 1982
Major accident hazards of certain industrial activities

INDUSTRIAL INSTALLATIONS WITHIN THE MEANING OF ARTICLE 1

1. – Installations for the production or processing of organic or inorganic chemicals using for this purpose, in particular:

   – alkylation

   – amination by ammonolysis

   – carbonylation

   – condensation

   – dehydrogenation

   – esterification

   – halogenation and manufacture of halogens

   – hydrogenation

   – hydrolysis

   – oxidation

   – polymerization

   – sulphonation

   – desulphurization, manufacture and transformation of sulphur-containing compounds

   – nitration and manufacture of nitrogen-containing compounds

   – manufacture of phosphorous-containing compounds

   – formulation of pesticides and of pharmaceutical products.

   – Installations for the processing of organic and inorganic chemical substances, using for this purpose, in particular:

   – distillation

   – extraction

   – solvation

   – mixing

2. Installations for distillation, refining or other processing of petroleum or petroleum products.

3. Installations for the total or partial disposal of solid or liquid substances by incineration or chemical decomposition.

4. Installations for the production or processing of energy gases, for example, LPG, LNG, SNG.

5. Installations for the dry distillation of coal or lignite.

6. Installations for the production of metals or non-metals by the wet process or by means of electrical energy.

Table 6.5: Council Directive of 24 June 1982
Major accident hazards of certain industrial activities

STORAGE AT INSTALLATIONS OTHER THAN THOSE COVERED BY ANNEX I ('ISOLATED STORAGE')

The quantities set out below relate to each installation or group of installations belonging to the same manufacturer where the distance between the installations is not sufficient to avoid, in foreseeable circumstances, any aggravation of major-accident hazards. These quantities apply in any case to each group of installations belonging to the same manufacturer where the distance between the installations is less than approximately 500 m.

Substances or groups of substances	Quantities (tonnes) ≥	
	For application of Articles 3 and 4	For application of Article 5
1. Flammable gases as defined in Annex IV (c) (i)	50	300 ([1])
2. Highly flammable liquids as defined in Annex IV (c) (ii)	10 000	100 000
3. Acrylonitrile	350	5 000
4. Ammonia	60	600
5. Chlorine	10	200
6. Sulphur dioxide	20	500
7. Ammonium nitrate	500 ([2])	5 000 ([2])
8. Sodium chlorate	25	250 ([2])
9. Liquid oxygen	200	2 000 ([2])

([1]) Member States may provisionally apply Article 5 to quantities of at least 500 tonnes until the revision of Annex II mentioned in Article 19.

([2]) Where this substance is in a state which gives it properties capable of creating a major-accident hazard.

- information on the installations (geographical location; number of persons working on the site; safety measures taken, etc.);
- information on possible major-accident situations (emergency plans; persons responsible for safety).

Although the directive in a general way applies both to new industrial activities and to existing activities, it nonetheless allows for supplementary delays for those industrialists who have old plants. These delays, running respectively to 1985 and 1989, are intended to permit industrialists to conform gradually to the provisions of the directive, in particular with regard to the notification.

The directive also contains special provisions for situations when the industrial installations belonging to the same manufacturer are less than 500 metres apart. It also specifies that Member States must inform persons liable to be affected by a major accident of the safety measures and of the correct behaviour to adopt in the event of an accident. This information must also be made available to the other

Member States in cases of transfrontier industrial installations. With regard to this, a separate declaration was published in the Official Journal of the European Communities indicating that the Member States must consult each other, within the framework of their bilateral relations, about the measures to be taken to prevent major accidents and to limit their consequences to man and the environment.

Apart from the rules on safety which must be applied by industry and control authorities, the directive also includes several provisions on the reciprocal exchange of information between industrialists, Member States and the Commission. All manufacturers are thus required to inform the control authorities as soon as a major accident occurs. For their part, the Member States must inform the Commission of major accidents occurring within their territories.

On the basis of the information received, the Commission must set up and put at the disposal of the Member States a register containing a summary and analysis of the major accidents that have occurred.

2.   The amending directive of 1987

On 4 November 1985 the Commission sent the Council a proposal for an amending directive intended to revise the technical annexes of the 1982 framework directive. The Council adopted this amending directive on 19 March 1987.[31] This limited revision of the annexes is intended generally to strengthen the provisions of the 1982 directive, for example by clarifying certain definitions, adding new substances, and especially by reducing the quantitative thresholds for certain dangerous substances. The maximum quantities, intended to set in motion the notification procedure, for the substances which were behind the Bhopal catastrophe in India in 1984, namely, carbonyl chloride (Phosgene) and methyl isocyanate, are thus reduced from 20 tonnes to 750 kg and from 1 tonne to 150 kg respectively.

During the examination of this directive, the Commission indicated that it would follow with great attention the implementation of the 1982 directive, and that in the light of the experience gained, it would later present a more fundamental and systematic revision of the substances covered by the directive on major accident hazards.

At its meeting on 16–17 June 1988, the Environment Council adopted a common position, pending the final opinion of the European Parliament, on a proposal for a directive amending for the second time Directive 82/501/EEC on the major accident hazards of certain industrial activities.[32]

The aim of the directive was to extend the scope of Directive 82/501/EEC to include all storage of dangerous chemicals, packaged or loose, whatever the site.

The directive would also strengthen the information provisions by specifying a minimum number of items of information that must be supplied to the public; these include: the nature of the hazards to which the population and the environment are exposed, measures to be taken in the event of an accident, whether emergency plans exist, and details of how to obtain further information.

The Council adopted Directive 88/610/EEC on 24 November 1988.[33]

For the eco-audit regulation see Chapter 13, p. 439.

[31] OJ No L 85 of 28/3/87.
[32] OJ No L 336 of 7/12/88.
[33] OJ No L 336 of 12/7/91.

V. THE EXPORT AND IMPORT OF DANGEROUS CHEMICALS

1. The 1988 Regulation No. 1734/88

On 2 July 1986 the Commission sent the Council a proposal for a regulation on Community exports and imports of certain dangerous chemicals.[34] Although this proposal covered both exports and imports and concerns all third countries, it is clear that the main problem it wished to tackle was that of the export to developing countries of chemical products which are already prohibited or strictly regulated in the Community. Indeed, at Community level a large number of directives prohibited or strictly regulated the marketing and use of many industrial products, including pesticides. These substances continued to be produced for export to third countries, and in particular to developing countries.

In order to improve the protection of public health and the environment in developing countries, the proposal made provision for a centralized common notification and information procedure at Community level for the export of 23 chemicals which are already prohibited or strictly regulated in the Community (mercury; HCH; PCB; PCT; DDT, etc.).

As far as the practical aspects of the export notification system are concerned, the proposal made provision for two phases. During a first phase a simplified notification system would be set up. Any enterprise wishing to export a substance covered by the regulation to a third country would have to inform a central competent authority designated by each Member State. This national authority would send the notification form giving the characteristics of the substance concerned to the Commission. The Commission would then be responsible for sending the notification to the third country importing the substance. It would centralize and publish the notifications periodically, and would inform the competent national authorities of any reaction from the importing country. This system of simple notification conformed with the international codes existing in this area, drawn up by the OECD and UNEP.

In a second phase, which should in theory have commenced on 31 December 1988, the regulation proposal envisaged a more sophisticated system of notification and information based on the principle of the "informed choice". According to this system, the third country involved would have 60 days in which to react to the Commission's notification. If the third country did not react in the period prescribed, the substance would be exported to it.

As for the import into the Community of chemicals which are prohibited or strictly regulated in a third country, the draft regulation allowed in theory for the application of the same provision as for exports, but with the difference that the regulation did not refer to any specific list of regulated substances in the third countries. Whether it is for exports or imports, the Commission's role in centralizing the information for the whole of the Community should simplify the procedure in that there will only be one notification needed per product and per their country importer. Moreover, only the Member State exporting a substance to a third country for the first time is required to inform the Commission. The authorization or refusal of the export will then be made by the competent authority of the Member States without any new notification procedure.

[34] OJ No C 117 of 15/7/86.

Among the other provisions made by the regulation, substances intended for export must be subject to the same rules for packaging and labelling as apply in the Community, which has not been the case in the past.

Finally, the regulation makes provision for an annual exchange of information between the Commission and the Member States on the functioning of the notification system.

The Council had several discussions on this proposal for a regulation and finally reached agreement at its meeting of 3 December 1987.

The regulation, as adopted, provides for a notification procedure, rather than a system of prior informed consent or choice. The notification is provided on an Export Notification Form which also contains references to relevant Community legislation; labelling requirements; details of the risks associated with the chemical; advice on the safety precautions necessary to its use; and any additional information that may be useful or of interest.

No Export Notification Form is required for the second and subsequent export of the substance from the EC to the same third country, but the export papers must contain the reference number allocated at the time of the first export.

At the end of 1991 21 chemicals were subject to export notification.

At its meeting of 3 December 1987, the Council also agreed on the text of a Resolution inviting the Commission to examine in greater detail, and if appropriate, to make proposals concerning the system of "prior informed consent". Europe Environment in its 12 December 1987 edition,[35] commented on the results of the 3 December 1987 Council:

> The argument over whether or not the export of dangerous chemicals to third countries should only be authorized after the importing country has given its "prior informed consent" has been polarized from the outset with the Commission, The Netherlands and Denmark supporting the principle and others refusing to accept anything more than the principle that they should be fully informed of the dangers involved, if possible before the cargo arrives at their ports, i.e. "prior notification". It would then be up to individual countries to take whatever action they considered appropriate to protect their citizens. In order to bridge the gap, it was agreed on 3 December 1987 to introduce an obligation on exporting Member States to notify importing countries in advance of the dangers involved whenever a substance restricted within the EEC was being shipped there for the first time, along with a revision clause. Before 1990 and every two years afterwards, the Commission is to report to the Council on the regulation's implementation, so that it can "consider the possibility of introducing the principle of prior informed consent".

> The notification system adopted was very similar to the "London Guidelines" adopted on 17 June 1987 by the Governing Council of the United Nations Environmental Programme (UNEP) which were already operated under the aegis of UNEP's International Register of Potentially Toxic Chemicals (IRPTC). European Commissioner, Stanley Clinton-Davis, who had long been campaigning for stricter trade safeguards, disassociated himself from the Council's decision saying that it did not go far enough.

2. The 1986 proposal for a Decision authorizing the Commission to negotiate within the OECD and UNEP

At the same time as the proposal for a regulation, the Commission sent the Council on 2 July 1986 a proposal for a Decision[36] aimed at authorizing it to negotiate an

---

[35] Eu. Env., Vol 289, 12/12/87, pp. 14–15.
[36] OJ No C 177 of 15/7/86.

amendment of the notification procedures which had existed since 1984 within the framework of the OECD and UNEP regarding the exchange of dangerous chemicals (recommendations of the Council of the OECD of 4 April, and of the Governing Council of UNEP of 28 May 1984).

These negotiations were basically intended to develop and strengthen the procedures drawn up by these two international organizations, in order to make them conform to the provisions of the Community regulation, in particular by introducing the principle of the "informed choice" for third countries importing dangerous chemicals.

In the light of the outcome of the Environment Council's discussions of 3 December 1987 and in particular the adoption of the Council Resolution discussed above, the Council did not take a position on the Commission's proposal for a Decision.

3. Council Regulation EEC/428/89 – Export of certain chemical products

The regulation requires that eight chemical products (used for the development or production of chemical weapons) be subjected to a prior export authorization or equivalent measures by the Member States. Such authorization is not to be granted if there is a risk of the products being delivered to belligerent countries.

4. The 1992 Regulation 2455/92 on the export and import of dangerous chemicals

On 17 December 1990 the Commission sent the Council a proposal for a regulation on the export and import of dangerous chemicals. In the preamble of the 1988 regulation, the Council had stated that it would consider before July 1990 the possibility of introducing into the regulation the principle of "prior informed consent" – PIC. At the same time, the Council adopted Resolution 88/C170/91 inviting the Commission to examine the question of PIC in greater detail and to submit, if necessary, in the light of developments in international practices, suitable proposals for the possible adjustment of the 1988 regulation.

In the meantime, UNEP and FAO had made considerable progress in setting up an international notification and PIC procedure for the export of banned and severely restricted chemicals. An amendment to the "London Guidelines" incorporating PIC was agreed at a meeting of experts organized in New York 13–16 February 1989 and adopted by the UNEP Governing Council on 25 May 1989. The Commission had participated in discussions with UNEP, FAO and other organizations and thought it necessary to ensure a common participation of the EC in the international notification and PIC system. The 1990 proposal sought to attain this objective by introducing the principle of PIC into the 1988 regulation by means of a scheme complementary to the joint scheme operated by UNEP and FAO, and by adding to the list of chemicals in Annex I of the regulation that are subject to the export notification procedure.

The exporter of a chemical subject to notification as being banned or severely restricted to certain uses by Community legislation is required to give at least 30 days' notice to the designated authority in its own state, which authority shall ensure that the appropriate authorities of the country of destination receive notification of the intended export. The PIC procedure gives an importing country the opportunity to refuse or apply conditions to the import of a banned or severely restricted chemical.

The regulation was finally adopted on 23 July 1992.[37]

VI.   GENETICALLY MODIFIED ORGANISMS

1.   90/219/EEC: Council Directive of 23 April 1990 on the contained use of genetically modified micro-organisms[38]

In its Communication to the Council "A Community framework for the regulation of Biotechnologies" (COM 86/573 fin), the Commission announced its intention to come forward with proposals covering two distinct aspects of the use of genetic material: (a) the level of physical and biological confinement – control of accidents and management of waste resulting from industrial use; (b) authorization of the release of GMOs in the environment.

The Communication also pointed out that GMOs could lead to improvements in health and the environment through the perfection of more precise biological instruments for the protection of food and the more efficient treatment of waste.

The Commission's proposal of 4 May 1988 for a Council directive on the contained use of genetically modified micro-organisms dealt with the contained use of genetically modified micro-organisms including questions of waste and accident prevention. While some naturally occurring micro-organisms might also be of concern in that they may present dangers to plants, animals or the environment in general, the Commission considered that in the first instance priority should be given to a legal framework which would both provide adequate protection and at the same time allow society to benefit from this rapidly evolving technology.

The Commission was, however, working towards the development of coherent methods of risk assessment in this field and would on this basis examine if and how the accompanying proposal could be modified or extended to cover non-genetically modified micro-organisms.

Genetically modified micro-organisms can be released to the environment in the course of their contained use in two different ways:

● routine release in normal operating conditions, e.g. as wastes or in airborne emissions;
● accidental release in abnormal operating conditions, i.e. significant release in the environment following an event which causes the activity to get out of control.

In certain cases such releases will pose risks to human health and the environment; it is therefore necessary to:

1. Identify these cases.
2. Adopt working practices and containment measures corresponding to the hazard the micro-organism represents.

---

[37] OJ No L 251 of 29/8/92.
[38] COM 88/0160 and COM 89/0409. Council Directive 90/219 EEC published in OJ L 117 of 8/5/90, p. 1.

3. Prevent the accidental release of hazardous micro-organisms and limit the consequences of any such accident which may occur.

The proposal for a directive covered the steps from 1 to 3.

For the purpose of this directive, genetically modified micro-organisms are divided into two groups: micro-organisms presenting a minimal hazard (Group I) to which relatively simple rules of good hygiene and safety practice shall be applied, and other micro-organisms (Group II) where containment, waste control and in some cases emergency response procedures are essential.

In all cases, users have to declare the fact that they are carrying out operations involving genetically manipulated micro-organisms to the responsible authorities and carry out a hazard assessment. A system of notification to the competent authority is then established, to allow effective monitoring and control of the correctness of the classification and of the containment measures applied.

The time schedule and the content of the notification is dependent upon the classification of the micro-organisms and on the scale of the operation involved. In respect of the latter the Commission considered it more appropriate to adopt a flexible approach and distinguish the activities on the basis of their purpose. "Industrial scale operations" would include manufacturing processes and pilot plants, whereas "non-industrial scale operations" would include teaching, research and development activities.

In order to ensure that the probability of accidental release is reduced to a minimum, the proposal envisaged special provisions in such cases of higher risk or incertitude. These are represented by the industrial scale operations using micro-organisms belonging to Group II. The notification in this case will be more detailed and the user will prove that he has studied possible causes of accidents, anticipating the combination of events which might lead to an unintended release and adopted safety measures and emergency response plans where appropriate. The user must also forward to the competent authority the information necessary to set up an emergency plant for the area surrounding the installation, should an accident occur.

In addition, the proposal for a directive provides for the competent authorities to be notified of accidental releases occurring in their territory and for an effective preventive and monitoring system to be set up at Community level. General provisions are made for the adapting of the directives to technical progress.

Technical annexes laying down containment and waste measures are largely drawn from the 1986 OECD Recommendation on safety considerations for application of recombinant DNA.

The Council held a discussion on the proposal at its meetings on 24 November 1988 and on 2 March 1989. The European Parliament gave its opinion on 24 May 1989. The amendments accepted by the Commission aimed to differentiate still further between the procedures foreseen, according to the potential risk of the confined uses in question, and also to clarify further the provisions in case of accident. Other amendments also introduce provisions covering confidentiality which are aimed at protecting sensitive commercial information and allowing for the wide diffusion of non-confidential information as well as wider consultation.

The Council adopted the directive on 23 April 1990.

Table 6.6: Council Directive of 23 April 1990 on the contained use of genetically modified micro-organisms

ANNEX I A

PART 1

Techniques of genetic modification referred to in Article 2 (b) (i) are, *inter alia*:

(i)   recombinant DNA techniques using vector systems as previously covered by Recommendation 82/472/EEC ([1]);

(ii) techniques involving the direct introduction into a micro-organism of heritable material prepared outside the micro-organism including micro-injection, macro-injection and micro-encapsulation;

(iii) cell fusion or hybridization techniques where live cells with new combinations of heritable genetic material are formed through the fusion of two or more cells by means of methods that do not occur naturally.

PART 2

Techniques referred to in Article 2 (b) (ii) which are not considered to result in genetic modification, on condition that they do not involve the use of recombinant-DNA molecules or genetically modified organisms:

(1)   *in vitro* fertilization;

(2)   conjugation, transduction, transformation or any other natural process;

(3)   polyploidy induction.

ANNEX I B

Techniques of genetic modification to be excluded from the Directive, on condition that they do not involve the use of genetically modified micro-organisms as recipient or parental organisms:

(1)   mutagenesis;

(2)   the construction and use of somatic animal hybridoma cells (e.g. for the production of monoclonal antibodies);

(3)   cell fusion (including protoplast fusion) of cells from plants which can be produced by traditional breeding methods;

(4)   self-cloning of non-pathogenic naturally occurring micro-organisms which fulfil the criteria of Group I for recipient micro-organisms.

([1]) OJ No 213, 21. 7. 1982, p.15.

Table 6.7: Council Directive of 23 April 1990 on the contained use of genetically modified micro-organisms

ANNEX II

CRITERIA FOR CLASSIFYING GENETICALLY MODIFIED MICRO-ORGANISMS IN GROUP I

A. *Recipient or parental organism*

- non-pathogenic;

- no adventitious agents;

- proven and extended history of safe use of built-in biological barriers, which, without interfering with optimal growth in the reactor or fermentor, confer limited survivability and replicability, without adverse consequences in the environment.

B. *Vector/Insert*

- well characterized and free from known harmful sequences;

- limited in size as much as possible to the genetic sequences required to perform the intended function;

- should not increase the stability of the construct in the environment (unless that is a requirement of intended function);

- should be poorly mobilizable;

- should not transfer any resistance markers to micro-organisms not known to acquire them naturally (if such acquisition could compromise use of drug to control disease agents).

C. *Genetically modified micro-organisms*

- non-pathogenic;

- as safe in the reactor or fermentor as recipient or parental organism, but with limited survivability and/or replicability without adverse consequences in the environment.

D. *Other genetically modified micro-organisms that could be included in Group I if they meet the conditions in C above*

- those constructed entirely from a single prokaryotic recipient (including its indigenous plasmids and viruses) or from a single eukaryotic recipient (including its chloroplasts, mitochondria, plasmids, but excluding viruses);

- those that consist entirely of genetic sequences from different species that exchange these sequences by known physiological processes.

Table 6.8: Council Directive of 23 April 1990 on the contained use of genetically modified micro-organisms

ANNEX III

SAFETY ASSESSMENT PARAMETERS TO BE TAKEN INTO ACCOUNT, AS FAR AS THEY ARE RELEVANT, IN ACCORDANCE WITH ARTICLE 6 (3)

A. Characteristics of the donor, recipient or (where appropriate) parental organism(s)

B. Characteristics of the modified micro-organism

C. Health considerations

D. Environmental considerations

A. *Characteristics of the donor, recipient or (where appropriate) parental organism(s)*

- names and designation;
- degree of relatedness;
- sources of the organism(s);
- information on reproductive cycles (sexual/asexual) of the parental organism(s) or, where applicable, of the recipient micro-organism;
- history of prior genetic manipulations;
- stability of parental or of recipient organism in terms of relevant genetic traits;
- nature of pathogenicity and virulence, infectivity, toxicity and vectors of disease transmission;
- nature of indigenous vectors:

  sequence,

  frequency of mobilization,

  specificity,

  presence of genes which confer resistance;
- host range;
- other potentially significant physiological traits;
- stability of these traits;
- natural habitat and geographic distribution. Climatic characteristics of original habitats;
- significant involvement in environmental processes (such as nitrogen fixation or pH regulation);
- interaction with, and effects on, other organisms in the environment (including likely competitive or symbiotic properties);
- ability to form survival structures (such as spores or sclerotia).

B. *Characteristics of the modified micro-organism*

- the description of the modification including the method for introducing the vector-insert into the recipient organism or the method used for achieving the genetic modification involved;
- the function of the genetic manipulation and/or of the new nucleic acid;
- nature and source of the vector;

Table 6.8 continued

- structure and amount of any vector and/or donor nucleic acid remaining in the final construction of the modified micro-organism;
- stability of the micro-organism in terms of genetic traits;
- frequency of mobilization of inserted vector and/or genetic transfer capability;
- rate and level of expression of the new genetic material. Method and sensitivity of measurement;
- activity of the expressed protein.

C. *Health considerations*

- toxic or allergenic effects of non-viable organisms and/or their metabolic products;
- product hazards;
- comparison of the modified micro-organism to the donor, recipient or (where appropriate) parental organism regarding pathogenicity;
- capacity for colonization;
- if the micro-organism is pathogenic to humans who are immunocompetent:
  (a) diseases caused and mechanism of pathogenicity including invasiveness and virulence;
  (b) communicability;
  (c) infective dose;
  (d) host range, possibility of alteration;
  (e) possibility of survival outside of human host;
  (f) presence of vectors or means of dissemination;
  (g) biological stability;
  (h) antibiotic-resistance patterns;
  (i) allergenicity;
  (j) availability of appropriate therapies.

D. *Environmental considerations*

- factors affecting survival, multiplication and dissemination of the modified micro-organism in the environment;
- available techniques for detection, identification and monitoring of the modified micro-organism;
- available techniques for detecting transfer of the new genetic material to other organisms;
- known and predicted habitats of the modified micro-organism;
- description of ecosystems to which the micro-organism could be accidentally disseminated;
- anticipated mechanism and result of interaction between the modified micro-organism and the organisms or micro-organisms which might be exposed in case of release into the environment;
- known or predicted effects on plants and animals such as pathogenicity, infectivity, toxicity, virulence, vector of pathogen, allergenicity, colonization;
- known or predicted involvement in biogeochemical processes;
- availability of methods for decontamination of the area in case of release to the environment.

Table 6.9: Council Directive of 23 April 1990 on the contained use of genetically modified micro-organisms

ANNEX IV

CONTAINMENT MEASURES FOR MICRO-ORGANISMS IN GROUP II

The containment measures for micro-organisms from Group II shall be chosen by the user from the categories below as appropriate to the micro-organism and the operation in question in order to ensure the protection of the public health of the general population and the environment.

Type B operations shall be considered in terms of their unit operations. The characteristics of each operation will dictate the physical containment to be used at that stage. This will allow selection and design of process, plant and operating procedures best fitted to assure adequate and safe containment. Two important factors to be considered when selecting the equipment needed to implement the containment are the risk of, and the effects consequent on, equipment failure. Engineering practice may require increasingly stringent standards to reduce the risk of failure as the consequence of that failure becomes less tolerable.

Specific containment measures for Type A operations shall be established taking into account the containment categories below and bearing in mind the specific circumstances of such operations.

Specifications	Containment Categories		
	1	2	3
1. Viable micro-organisms should be contained in a system which physically separates the process from the environment (closed system)	Yes	Yes	Yes
2. Exhaust gases from the closed system should be treated so as to:	Minimize release	Prevent release	Prevent release
3. Sample collection, addition of materials to a closed system and transfer of viable micro-organisms to another closed system, should be performed so as to:	Minimize release	Prevent release	Prevent release
4. Bulk culture fluids should not be removed from the closed system unless the viable micro-organisms have been:	Inactivated by validated means	Inactivated by validated chemical or physical means	Inactivated by validated chemical or physical means
5. Seals should be designed so as to:	Minimize release	Prevent release	Prevent release
6. Closed systems should be located within a controlled area	Optional	Optional	Yes, and purpose-built
(a) Biohazard signs should be posted	Optional	Yes	Yes
(b) Access should be restricted to nominated personnel only	Optional	Yes	Yes, via airlock

Table 6.9 continued

Specifications	Containment Categories		
	1	*2*	*3*
(c) Personnel should wear protective clothing	Yes, work clothing	Yes	A complete change
(d) Decontamination and washing facilities should be provided for personnel	Yes	Yes	Yes
(e) Personnel should shower before leaving the controlled area	No	Optional	Yes
(f) Effluent from sinks and showers should be collected and inactivated before release	No	Optional	Yes
(g) The controlled area should be adequately ventilated to minimize air contamination	Optional	Optional	Yes
(h) The controlled areas should be maintained at an air pressure negative to atmosphere	No	Optional	Yes
(i) Input air and extract air to the controlled area should be HEPA filtered	No	Optional	Yes
(j) The controlled area should be designed to contain spillage of the entire contents of the closed system	Optional	Yes	Yes
(k) The controlled area should be sealable to permit fumigation	No	Optional	Yes
7. Effluent treatment before final discharge	Inactivated by validated means	Inactivated by validated chemical or physical means	Inactivated by validated chemical means

Table 6.10: Council Directive of 23 April 1990 on the contained use of genetically modified micro-organisms

ANNEX V

Part A

Information required for the notification referred to in Article 8:

– name of person(s) responsible for carrying out the contained use including those responsible for supervision, monitoring and safety and information on their training and qualifications;

– address of installation and grid reference; description of the sections of the installation;

– a description of the nature of the work which will be undertaken and in particular the classification of the micro-organism(s) to be used (Group I or Group II) and the likely scale of the operation;

– a summary of the risk assessment referred to in Article 6 (2).

Part B

Information required for the notification referred to in Article 9 (2):

– the date of submission of the notification referred to in Article 8;

– the parental micro-organism(s) used or, where applicable the host-vector system(s) used;

– the source(s) and the intended function(s) of the genetic material(s) involved in the manipulation(s);

– identity and characteristics of the genetically modified micro-organism;

– the purpose of the contained use including the expected results;

– the culture volumes to be used;

– a summary of the risk assessment referred to in Article 6 (2).

Part C

Information required for the notification referred to in Article 10 (1):

– the information required in Part B;

– description of the sections of the installation and the methods for handling the micro-organisms;

– description of the predominant the meteorological conditions and of the potential sources of danger arising from the location of the installation;

– description of the protective and supervisory measures to be applied throughout the duration of the contained use;

– the containment category allocated specifying waste treatment provisions and the safety precautions to be adopted.

Part D

Information required for the notification referred to in Article 10 (2):

If it is not technically possible, or if it does not appear necessary to give the information specified below, the reasons shall be stated. The level of detail required in response to each

Table 6.10 continued

subset of considerations is likely to vary according to the nature and the scale of the proposed contained use. In the case of information already submitted to the competent authority under the requirements of this Directive, reference can be made to this information by the user:

(a) the date of submission of the notification referred to in Article 8 and the name of the responsible person(s);

(b) information about the genetically modified micro-organism(s):

  – the identity and characteristics of the genetically modified micro-organism(s),

  – the purpose of the contained use or the nature of the product,

  – the host-vector system to be used (where applicable),

  – the culture volumes to be used,

  – behaviour and characteristics of the micro-organism(s) in the case of changes in the conditions of containment or of release to the environment,

  – overview of the potential hazards associated with the release of the micro-organism(s) to the environment,

  – substances which are or may be produced in the course of the use of the micro-organism(s) other than the intended product;

(c) information about personnel:

  – the maximum number of persons working in the installation and the number of persons who work directly with the micro-organism(s);

(d) information about the installation:

  – the activity in which the micro-organism(s) is to be used,

  – the technological processes used,

  – a description of the sections of the installation,

  – the predominant meteorological conditions, and specific hazards arising from the location of the installation;

(e) information about waste management:

  – types, quantities, and potential hazards of wastes arising from the use of the micro-organism(s),

  – waste management techniques used, including recovery of liquid or solid wastes and inactivation methods,

  – ultimate form and destination of inactivated wastes;

(f) information about accident prevention and emergency response plans:

  – the sources of hazards and conditions under which accidents might occur,

  – the preventive measures applied such as safety equipment, alarm systems, containment methods and procedures and available resources,

  – a description of information provided to workers,

  – the information necessary for the competent authority to enable them to draw up or establish the necessary emergency response plans for use outside the installation in accordance with Article 14;

(g) a comprehensive assessment (referred to in Article 6 (2)) of the risks to human health and the environment which might arise from the proposed contained use;

(h) all other information required under Parts B and C if it is not already specified above.

2.   90/220/EEC: Council Directive of 23 April 1990 on the deliberate release into the environment of genetically modified organisms[39]

On 4 May 1988 the Commission also submitted a proposal to the Council concerning the deliberate release of genetically modified organisms.

In the Commission's view, the possible hazards from the release to the environment of genetically modified organisms (GMOs) are of various types:

- pathogenicity to humans, animals or plants;
- disruptive effects on ecosystems: displacement of natural populations, alteration of ecological cycles and interactions;
- transfer of the novel genetic traits to other species with undesired effects;
- excessive dependence on species lacking genetic variation.

However, public concern about genetic engineering was growing, and it was easy to imagine the public's response in case of harm to people or the environment caused by a GMO deliberately introduced into the environment. Moreover, genetic engineering would sharply increase the number of organisms with new traits introduced into the environment. These reasons made it urgently necessary to provide protection to people and the environment from the possible risks related to these new techniques.

The present approach, which focuses on the new technique of genetic engineering, is the first and most urgent step in the regulatory process; however, this will not impede evolution towards a more organism-related approach. Thus, the Commission will, as experience and knowledge on the matter build up, undertake to regulate the release of certain categories of naturally occurring organisms, such as known human, plant or animal pathogens, and non-indigenous organisms. Moreover, different categories of organisms and/or techniques may be established, allowing different requirements for organisms of different levels of risk.

The proposed directive would establish a case-by-case notification and endorsement procedure for the deliberate release of GMOs. Before carrying out a release, the person responsible for it should submit a notification to the competent authority of his Member State, including a detailed risk assessment where the possible hazards associated with the release must be identified.

However, understanding that there is a clear quantitative difference in the level of risk between experimental releases (carried out under very controlled conditions, strictly limited in space and time, closely monitored) and commercial ones (with limitations only in areas and conditions of use), two different procedures would be established; one for experimental releases where each competent authority is fully responsible for the releases carried out in its Member State, and a second one for the placing on the market of genetically modified organisms for a given use, where consultation and agreement with the other Member States is needed before the product is endorsed for its placing on the market.

In the Commission's view, the endorsement procedure had the advantage over an authorization procedure, in that it leaves responsibility with the notifier. Moreover, in such a little-known field as this, the decisions as to the safety of a release and its conditions must be the result of a dialogue between notifier and competent authority.

In this largely unexplored area, the exchange of information is likely to play an essential role in gaining experience. Therefore, provision is made for information exchange among the Member States through the Commission. This information sharing will be without restriction for the Commission and the competent author-

---

[39] COM 88/160 and COM 89/408. Council Directive 90/220/EEC of 23 April 1990 published in OJ L 117 of 8/5/90 p. 15.

ities, provided that absolute confidentiality is guaranteed for these data. The experience from the chemicals sector, where notification units for new chemical substances have been working for years with excellent results, encouraged the Commission to pursue this goal.

Table 6.11: Council Directive of 23 April 1990 on the deliberate release into the environment of genetically modified micro-organisms (90/220/EEC)

ANNEX II

INFORMATION REQUIRED IN THE NOTIFICATION

The notifications for a deliberate release referred to in Article 5 and for placing on the market referred to in Article 11 must provide the information set out below.

Not all the points included will apply to every case. It is to be expected, therefore, that individual notifications will address only the particular subset of considerations that are appropriate to individual situations. In each case where it is not technically possible or it does not appear necessary to give the information, the reasons shall be stated.

The level of detail required in response to each subset of considerations is also likely to vary according to the nature and the scale of the proposed release.

The description of the methods used or the reference to standardized or internationally recognized methods shall also be mentioned in the dossier, together with the name of the body or bodies responsible for carrying out the studies.

I. GENERAL INFORMATION

A. *Name and address of the notifier*

B. *Information on personnel and training*

    (1) Name of person(s) responsible for planning and carrying out the release including those responsible for supervision, monitoring and safety, in particular, name and qualifications of the responsible scientist;

    (2) Information on training and qualifications of personnel involved in carrying out the release.

II. INFORMATION RELATING TO THE GMO

A. *Characteristics of (a) the donor, (b) the recipient or (c) (where appropriate) parental organism(s):*

    1. scientific name;

    2. taxonomy;

    3. other names (usual name, strain name, culgivar name, etc.);

    4. phenotypic and genetic markers;

    5. degree of relatedness between donor and recipient or between parental organisms;

    6. description of identification and detection techniques;

    7. sensitivity, reliability (in quantitative terms) and specificity of detection and identification techniques;

    8. description of the geographic distribution and of the natural habitat of the organism including information on natural predators, preys, parasites and competitors, symbionts and hosts;

    9. potential for genetic transfer and exchange with other organisms;

    10. verification of the genetic stability of the organisms and factors affecting it;

Table 6.11 continued

11. pathological, ecological and physiological traits:

   (a) classification of hazard according to existing Community rules concerning the protection of human health and/or the environment;

   (b) generation time in natural ecosystems, sexual and asexual reproductive cycle;

   (c) information on survival, including seasonability and the ability to form survival structures e.g.: seeds, spores or sclerotia;

   (d) pathogenicity: infectivity, toxigenicity, virulence, allergenicity, carrier (vector) of pathogen, possible vectors, host range including non-target organism. Possible activation of latent viruses (proviruses). Ability to colonize other organisms;

   (e) antibiotic resistance, and potential use of these antibiotics in humans and domestic organisms for prophylaxis and therapy;

   (f) involvement in environmental processes: primary production, nutrient turnover, decomposition of organic matter, respiration, etc.

12. Nature of indigenous vectors:

   (a) sequence;

   (b) frequency of mobilization;

   (c) specificity;

   (d) presence of genes which confer resistance.

13. History of previous genetic modifications.

B. *Characteristics of the vector:*

   1. nature and source of the vector;

   2. sequence of transposons, vectors and other non-coding genetic segments used to construct the GMO and to make the introduced vector and insert function in the GMO;

   3. frequency of mobilization of inserted vector and/or genetic transfer capabilities and methods of determination;

   4. information on the degree to which the vector is limited to the DNA required to perform the intended function.

C. *Characteristics of the modified organism:*

   1. Information relating to the genetic modification:

      (a) methods used for the modification;

      (b) methods used to construct and introduce the insert(s) into the recipient or to delete a sequence;

      (c) description of the insert and/or vector construction;

      (d) purity of the insert from any unknown sequence and information on the degree to which the inserted sequence is limited to the DNA required to perform the intended function;

      (e) sequence, functional identity and location of the altered/inserted/deleted nucleic acid segment(s) in question with particular reference to any known harmful sequence.

Table 6.11 continued

2. Information on the final GMO:

(a) description of genetic trait(s) or phenotypic characteristics and in particular any new traits and characteristics which may be expressed or no longer expressed;

(b) structure and amount of any vector and/or donor nucleic acid remaining in the final construction of the modified organism;

(c) stability of the organism in terms of genetic traits;

(d) rate and level of expression of the new genetic material. Method and sensitivity of measurement;

(e) activity of the expressed protein(s);

(f) description of identification and detection techniques including techniques for the identification and detection of the inserted sequence and vector;

(g) sensitivity, reliability (in quantitative terms) and specificity of detection and identification techniques;

(h) history of previous releases or uses of the GMO;

(i) health considerations:

   (i) toxic or allergenic effects of the non-viable GMOs and/or their metabolic products;

   (ii) product hazards;

   (iii) comparison of the modified organism to the donor, recipient or (where appropriate) parental organism regarding pathogenicity;

   (iv) capacity for colonization;

   (v) if the organism is pathogenic to humans who are immunocompetent

     – diseases caused and mechanism of pathogenicity including invasiveness and virulence,

     – communicability,

     – infective dose,

     – host range, possibility of alteration,

     – possibility of survival outside of human host,

     – presence of vectors or means of dissemination,

     – biological stability,

     – antibiotic-resistance patterns,

     – allergenicity,

     – availability of appropriate therapies.

III. INFORMATION RELATING TO THE CONDITIONS OF RELEASE AND THE RECEIVING ENVIRONMENT

A. *Information on the release:*

1. description of the proposed deliberate release, including the purpose(s) and foreseen products;

Table 6.11 continued

    2. foreseen dates of the release and time planning of the experiment including frequency and duration of releases;

    3. preparation of the site previous to the release;

    4. size of the site;

    5. method(s) to be used for the release;

    6. quantities of GMOs to be released;

    7. disturbance on the site (type and method of cultivation, mining, irrigation, or other activities);

    8. worker protection measures taken during the release;

    9. post-release treatment of the site;

    10. techniques foreseen for elimination or inactivation of the GMOs at the end of the experiment;

    11. information on, and results of, previous releases of the GMOs, especially at different scales and in different ecosystems.

B. *Information on the environment (both on the site and in the wider environment):*

    1. geographical location and grid reference of the site(s) (in case of notifications under Part C the site(s) of release will be the foreseen areas of use of the product);

    2. physical or biological proximity to humans and other significant biota;

    3. proximity to significant biotopes or protected areas;

    4. size of local population;

    5. economic activities of local populations which are based on the natural resources of the area;

    6. distance to closest areas protected for drinking water and/or environmental purpose;

    7. climatic characteristics of the region(s) likely to be affected;

    8. geographical, geological and pedological characteristics;

    9. flora and fauna, including crops, livestock and migratory species;

    10. description of target and non-target ecosystems likely to be affected;

    11. a comparison of the natural habitat of the recipient organism with the proposed site(s) of release;

    12. any known planned developments or changes in land use in the region which could influence the environmental impact of the release.

IV. INFORMATION RELATING TO THE INTERACTIONS BETWEEN THE GMOs, THE GMOs AND THE ENVIRONMENT

A. *Characteristics affecting survival, multiplication and dissemination:*

    1. biological features which affect survival, multiplication and dispersal;

    2. known or predicted environmental conditions which may affect survival, multiplication and dissemination (wind, water, soil, temperature, pH, etc.);

    3. sensitivity to specific agents.

Table 6.11 continued

B. *Interactions with the environment:*

1. predicted habitat of the GMOs;

2. studies of the behaviour and characteristics of the GMOs and their ecological impact carried out in simulated natural environments, such as microcosms, growth rooms, greenhouses;

3. genetic transfer capability:

    (a) post-release transfer of genetic material from GMOs into organisms in affected ecosystems;

    (b) post-release transfer of genetic material from indigenous organisms to the GMOs;

4. likelihood of post-release selection leading to the expression of unexpected and/or undesirable traits in the modified organism;

5. measures employed to ensure and to verify genetic stability. Description of genetic traits which may prevent or minimize dispersal of genetic material. Methods to verify genetic stability;

6. routes of biological dispersal, known or potential modes of interaction with the disseminating agent, including inhalation, ingestion, surface contact, burrowing, etc.;

7. description of ecosystems to which the GMOs could be disseminated.

C. *Potential environmental impact:*

1. potential for excessive population increase in the environment;

2. competitive advantage of the GMOs in relation to the unmodified recipient or parental organism(s);

3. identification and description of the target organisms;

4. anticipated mechanism and result of interaction between the released GMOs and the target organism;

5. identification and description of non-target organisms which may be affected unwittingly;

6. likelihood of post-release shifts in biological interactions or in host range;

7. known or predicted effects on non-target organisms in the environment, impact on population levels of competitors: preys, hosts, symbionts, predators, parasites and pathogens;

8. known or predicted involvement in biogeochemical processes;

9. other potentially significant interactions with the environment.

V. INFORMATION ON MONITORING, CONTROL, WASTE TREATMENT AND EMERGENCY RESPONSE PLANS

A. *Monitoring techniques:*

1. methods for tracing the GMOs, and for monitoring their effects;

2. specificity (to identify the GMOs, and to distinguish them from the donor, recipient or, where appropriate, the parental organisms), sensitivity and reliability of the monitoring techniques;

3. techniques for detecting transfer of the donated genetic material to other organisms;

4. duration and frequency of the monitoring.

Table 6.11 continued

B. *Control of the release:*

1. methods and procedures to avoid and/or minimize the spread of the GMOs beyond the site of release or the designated area for use;

2. methods and procedures to protect the site from intrusion by unauthorized individuals;

3. methods and procedures to prevent other organisms from entering the site.

C. *Waste treatment:*

1. type of waste generated;

2. expected amount of waste;

3. possible risks;

4. description of treatment envisaged.

D. *Emergency response plans:*

1. methods and procedures for controlling the GMOs in case of unexpected spread;

2. methods for decontamination of the areas affected, e.g. eradication of the GMOs;

3. methods for disposal or sanitation of plants, animals, soils, etc. that were exposed during or after the spread;

4. methods for the isolation of the area affected by the spread;

5. plans for protecting human health and the environment in case of the occurrence of an undesirable effect.

ANNEX III

ADDITIONAL INFORMATION REQUIRED IN THE CASE OF NOTIFICATION FOR PLACING ON THE MARKET

A. *The following information shall be provided in the notification for placing on the market of products, in addition to that of Annex II:*

1. name of the product and names of GMOs contained therein;

2. name of the manufacturer or distributor and his address in the Community;

3. specificity of the product, exact conditions of use including, when appropriate, the type of environment and/or the geographical area(s) of the Community for which the product is suited;

4. type of expected use: industry, agriculture and skilled trades, consumer use by public at large.

B. *The following information shall be provided, when relevant, in addition to that of point A, in accordance with Article 11 of this Directive:*

1. measures to take in case of unintended release or misuse;

2. specific instructions or recommendations for storage and handling;

3. estimated production in and/or imports to the Community;

4. proposed packaging. This must be appropriate so as to avoid unintended release of the GMOs during storage, or at a later stage;

5. proposed labelling. This must include, at least in summarized form, the information referred to in points A. 1, A. 2, A. 3, B. 1 and B. 2.

Table 6.12: The fifth environment action programme: flow diagram showing the selection process for dealing with existing chemicals

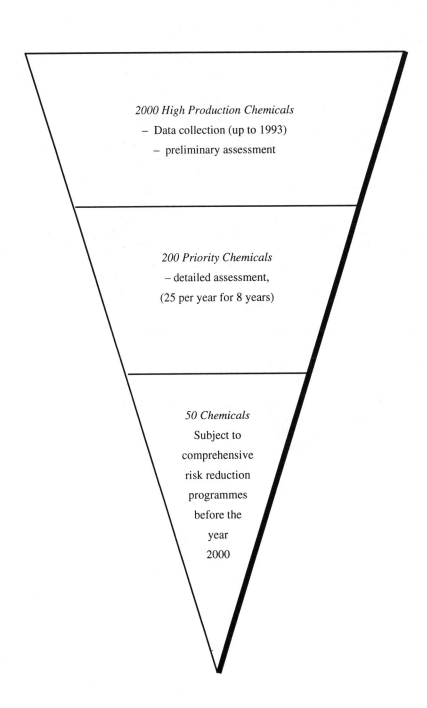

2000 High Production Chemicals
– Data collection (up to 1993)
– preliminary assessment

200 Priority Chemicals
– detailed assessment,
(25 per year for 8 years)

50 Chemicals
Subject to
comprehensive
risk reduction
programmes
before the
year
2000

On the other hand, given the public concern about genetic engineering, it was considered essential that the information necessary for evaluating the risk and adopting safety measures be made available to the public.

The European Parliament gave its first reading to the proposal on 25 May 1989, adopting a number of amendments, some of which were accepted by the Commission.

The Council adopted the directive on 23 April 1990. The directive introduces a notification system covering all genetically modified micro-organisms, plants and animals through all stages of release to the environment. Techniques of genetic modification the products of which are included or excluded from the scope of the directive are defined in Annex I.

The directive provides for a step-by-step and case-by-case review of each individual release by government before a permit can be issued. At the stage of experimental releases, the notifier must prepare a risk assessment according to the criteria set out Annex II to the directive and submit it to their national competent authority which has 90 days to consider the notification and authorize the release.

In the case of products, the manufacturer or importer must submit a detailed notification to the competent authority in the Member State where the product will first be placed on the market. The competent authority has 90 days to consider the file and to decide whether to reject the notification or to put it forward for the Community permit procedure. If the notification is sent forward, the Commission and the Member States have a further 60 days to consider the dossier and consult about it. They can propose modifications to the permit. Once a product has received the written consent of the competent authority in a Member State, other Member States are not allowed to impose new restrictions on it.

VII.   FUTURE ACTION

The 5th Environment Action Programme provides a flow diagram showing the process for dealing with existing chemicals (Table 6.12).

Priority actions to be taken over the remains of this decade in respect of industrial risks, chemicals and biotechnology are set out in Table 6.13 below.

Table 6.13: The fifth environment action programme: risk management

Objectives	Targets up to 2000	Measures	Time-frame	Actors
(a) Industrial Activity				
– Management of Industrial Risks	Improved safety standards	Comprehensive appraisal of experience within the framework of D.82/501	1993/4	*EC*
	Development of safety management standards	Report to Council and Parliament, including any necessary programme of action	1995	*EC*
	Improvement in, and harmonisation of, implementation measures	Development of standards for risk assessment and management	ongoing	*Standards Institutes*
	100% coverage of dangerous establishments	Comprehensive review of implementation	1994, 1998	*EC*
– General Environment Controls	Improved management and procedural standards	Development of standard for environmental management systems	ongoing	*Standards Institutes*
		Eco-audit (progressive)	1994 ⇒	*Enterprise*
(b) Chemicals Control				
– Data Collection	Effective notification procedure for all chemicals	Notification of all new chemicals	ongoing	*EC, MS, Industry*
		Data collection of all existing chemicals. Council regulation on existing chemicals	1992 ⇒	*EC, MS, Industry*
– Hazard Identification	Maintenance/improvement of existing classification criteria	Continual update in the light of scientific and technical progress	ongoing	*EC, MS*
		Extension of list of classified substances	ongoing	*Manufacturers + importers*

Table 6.13 continued

Objectives	Targets up to 2000	Measures	Time-frame	Actors
– Risk Assessment	Common principles for assessments	Amendment of Directive 67/548/EEC	1992/3	EC
	Assessment of 2000 high production volume chemicals	Council regulation on existing chemicals	1993 ⇒	EC, MS, Industry
	Assessment of 500 active substances in non-agricultural pesticides	Council Directive on non-agricultural pesticides	1994 ⇒	EC, MS, Industry
– Risk Management	Strengthen links between classification and control measures	Establish the Advisory Committee on chemicals risk reduction	1992	EC + Industry
– Risk Reduction	Risk reduction programmes for 50 priority chemicals	Legislation + voluntary agreements	1994 ⇒	EC, MS, Industry
(c) Biotechnology				
– Risk management for Contained	100% coverage of all installations and activities	Comprehensive review of implementation	ongoing	EC
Use of GMOs	Effective safety measures for use of GMOs in research & industry	Development of more detailed criteria	1992 ⇒	EC + MS
– Risk management for release of GMOs to the environment	Effective approval procedure for all releases in the Community, both for research and industry	Comprehensive review of implementation and technical adaptation	ongoing	id
	Oversight of export of GMOs to third countries	Proposal for regulatory instrument	1992	EC

Table 6.13 continued

Objectives	Targets up to 2000	Measures	Time-frame	Actors
– Risk assessment	Common approaches and principles for environmental risk assessment	Development of risk assessment methodologies	1993 ⇒	EC + MS + Standards Institutes (e.g. CEN)
	Common testing methods, identification methods, etc.	Assessment and common acceptance of methods	1993 ⇒	
	Safe transport of GMOs	EC legislation	1992	EC + MS
(d) Protection of animals used for experimental purposes				
Reduction in animal experimentation	50% reduction in the number of vertebrate animals used for experimental purposes	Directive 86/609/EEC (see also Maastricht Declaration on the protection of animals)	ongoing	EC, MS, Industry

Chapter 7

Noise

I. INTRODUCTION

The actions carried out by the Community against noise nuisance have certain characteristics which make them differ noticeably from those in other sectors of Community Environment Policy, such as water, air or waste. Two major elements characterize Community action against noise. The first concerns its very close link with industrial and commercial aspects; the second concerns the relationship which is often established between Community noise legislation and standards already existing at international level.

The close links with industrial aspects come about because measures should essentially be taken at the very source of the noise, that is, directly at the level of industrial products which are particularly noisy and generally of a high added value, such as modes of transport (cars, motorcycles, planes, trains) or constructional plant and equipment. Furthermore, the 1973 1st Environmental Action Programme did not contain a specific chapter on noise. It was only in the 2nd and 3rd Programmes of 1977 and 1983 that this aspect of Community policy was added and that various specific measures against noise were envisaged. In fact, historically speaking, Community actions against noise nuisances were first conceived within the framework of the general programme for the "general elimination of technical barriers to trade" of 29 May 1969. A supplement to this programme, adopted on 21 May 1973, then added the sector of constructional plant and machinery to the products which should come under Community regulations. Originally then, it was essentially in order to suppress the economic distortions likely to be created through disparities existing between the specifications of certain noisy products and equipment, that the Commission came to put forward a number of proposals for directives to the Council.

The only legal basis of these directives is Article 100 of the EEC Treaty (bringing together legislation with a view to facilitating the workings of the Common Market), while "environment" directives generally referred originally both to Article 100 and to Article 215, the latter forming the legal basis of all new policies not expressly provided for by the (unamended) treaty, such as Community Environment Policy. What is more, as is the case with a certain number of "technical barrier" directives, such as those dealing with motor vehicles, a large number of anti-noise directives include an "optional harmonization" aspect (see chapter on the introduction of the "clean car", pp. 141 ff). The mixed nature of a large number of "noise" directive proposals, which include both a part which regulates Community approval of the products concerned in order to ensure that they circulate freely within the Community, and also a part intended to define maximum sound limits, nevertheless resulted in a delay in the adoption of these directives by the Council. This is why several proposals concerning construction plant and equipment presented to the Council by the Commission from 1974–1975 onwards, were only adopted by the former 10 years later in 1984. So the reason for this delay is due, not to the clauses dealing with the limiting of noise emissions, but to the problems of the free circulation of these products, and more exactly, to the attitude to be taken regarding goods imported from third countries.

Such problems of free circulation are particularly relevant in those Member States, such as France or Italy, which have a major industry producing "noisy" products (constructional plant and equipment, lawnmowers, motorcycles, etc.). On the other hand, the Member States which are basically importers or consumers of these products (e.g. Denmark or the Netherlands), tend to demand very strict anti-noise standards, while at the same time wanting to see wider circulation of these products, be they from the Community or from third countries.

The second characteristic of Community actions against noise nuisances concerns the important role played by the standards established by other international organizations such as the ISO (International Standards Organization) or the ICAO (International Civil Aviation Organization). The reason why Community regulations take into account standards established at a wider international level is explained both by the technical complexity of anti-noise actions, particularly where measuring methods are concerned, and by the importance of commercial exchange currents of which these products are the object at international level (planes, cars, etc.).

In this respect, one should look at the potential consequences which the new movement towards technical harmonization and standardization defined by the Council on 7 May 1985,[1] might have on the legislative approach followed until now, regarding noise.

This new direction in fact means that the definition of the technical characteristics of products depends on standards, most of which are European.

This new policy of "referring to standards" is intended to keep to a minimum the number of individual directives which are excessively technical, and which concern specific products. Directives of this type should in theory be limited in the future to the essential safety requirements of the products. In the light of these considerations it seems that in some respects noise directives were already anticipating the new approach of harmonization and standardization, in that directives were already largely referring to pre-established standards at international level. At the same time it would equally appear that these directives correspond to a large extent to the criticisms levelled by the "new approach", i.e. the setting up of a large number of fragmented directives concerning specific products and being of an excessively technical nature. It is still too early at this stage to be able to foresee the consequences that the new approach, defined by the Council in 1985 in the area of harmonization and standardization, is likely to have in the years to come on Community noise legislation. At the beginning of this new approach, the Commission should no doubt reflect deeply on the characteristics and nature of its legislative work in the area of noise nuisances.

---

[1] OJ No C 136 of 4/6/86.

II.   NOISE CRITERIA

For noise, as for the other sectors of environment policy, the Commission first consulted acoustic experts and carried out studies with a view to analysing the adverse
or undesirable effects of man's exposure to noise. On the basis of this work, and
taking into account the studies carried out on a worldwide level by the International
Labour Organization, the Commission sent a Communication to the Council on 3
December 1976 concerning the determining of criteria for establishing the links
between the different exposures to noise and the observable effects. According to
the definition of the environmental action programme, the term "criteria" signifies
"the relationship between the exposure of a target to pollution or nuisance and the
risk or magnitude of the adverse or undesirable effect resulting from the exposure
in given circumstances". The Council acted on this Communication on noise criteria in 1977. The Communication divides the adverse effects of noise into five categories: sleep interference; speech interference; annoyance; performance of tasks;
hearing damage. In determining the criteria the population as a whole was considered. The effects of noise can, however, vary considerably depending on the individuals and the categories of the population concerned. The elderly, the ill or very
young children are categories of the population who are highly sensitive to noise.
The study carried out by the Commission does not cover certain specific noises
such as vibrations, supersonic waves or music. The curve of exposure/effect varies
according to each type of noise. The basic elements of the Commission's
Communication are given in Table 7.1.

Table 7.1: Commission communication of 3 December 1976
Determination of noise criteria

(a)   *Sleep interference*

–   35dB(A) is the non-fluctuating (less than 5dB) continuous indoor level up to which
        reports concerning sleep disturbance or awakenings are constant from about 10% of
        the subjects tested irrespective of the cause.

–   The continuous equivalent indoor level above which the pattern of sleep (e.g. EEG)
        is changed in more than 10% of the subjects and above which the percentage of
        reports is significantly increased is between 40dB(A) (about 20% reports) and
        50dB(A) (about 50% reports).

–   Changed activation of the central nervous system, which may lead to awakening, is
        observed if an increase of 10dB or more occurring in 0.5 sec. or less is superimposed
        on a continuous background level.

–   Reduced sleeping ability of the particularly sensitive population (e.g. old, sick,
        convalescent) has been demonstrated at values approximately 10dB below those
        mentioned above.

(b)   *Speech interference*

–   A continuous equivalent level of 65dB(A) makes normal conversation just possible at
        1 metre.

–   A continuous equivalent level of 45dB(A) or less introduces no problems in normal
        conversation at a distance of 1 metre. At greater distances lower levels correspond to
        these effects on speech intelligibility.

Table 7.1 continued

–   In special situations where the contents of the message have to be completely understood, for example teaching in classrooms medical consultations, the levels of background noise corresponding to the levels in paragraphs 2.1 and 2.2 should preferably be about 10dB lower.

–   For television viewing, listening to the radio, or telephone conversations, in cases where the background noise levels show large variations with time, equivalent noise levels corresponding to the levels in paragraphs 2.1 and 2.2 are about 5dB lower.

(c)   *Annoyance*

–   Under average town living conditions, outside noise which emanates from transportation and industrial sources of 45dB(A) equivalent daytime noise levels will generally cause about 15% of the population to be highly annoyed. 65dB(A) will generally cause about 40% of the population to be highly annoyed.

–   In noisier living conditions, city centres and near industrial sites, somewhat higher noise levels will correspond to the above described effects. On the other hand in quieter situations such as rural areas the described effects will occur at correspondingly lower levels. Tones and impulsive noises present in the environment increase the level of annoyance at each value of the equivalent noise level.

–   During periods where the sensitivity to noise is greater, such as periods of rest or relaxation, the corresponding noise levels are lower.

(d)   *Performance of tasks*

The findings of laboratory work show in general:

–   A steady noise, without special significance, would not appear to interfere with most human activities that do not require acoustic information in order to be carried out. This is so even where the steady level is relatively high, possibly as high as 90dB(A) at some times.

–   Intermittent or impulsive noise has a more marked disturbing effect than steady noise.

–   High frequency noise components (above about 200 Hz) usually cause worse interference with performance than do low frequency components.

–   Noise does not have a notable effect on overall performance – but high levels of noise can cause variations in the performance of sequential tasks. There can here be a complete breakdown of performance or a total absence of reaction to stimuli, sometimes followed by a compensating improvement.

–   Noise affects the quality of work more than the quantity.

–   Complicated tasks, demanding considerable concentrations, are more easily influenced by noise than simple tasks.

(e)   *Hearing damage*

High level noise can cause permanent impairment to hearing, different to age and illness, and which can lead to a handicap. Such a handicap can be avoided for the great majority of the population if the noise level to which they are exposed over their whole lifetime is less than a 24 hour daily value of equivalent continuous sound level, Leq., of 80dB(A); higher levels of continuous noise may only be endured, with no damage occurring, for shorter periods of time. The damage risk is greater if impulsive noise is added to continuous noise – the human ear cannot tolerate without damage, noise having an instantaneous value greater than 150dB(A).

Table 7.1 continued

In the determination of these criteria, it was considered that specific noise sources such as aircraft, traffic, musical noise etc. were likely to produce different levels of acceptability. The exposure/effect curves for each type of noise are not identical.

It was also considered that because of interindividual differences between members of the general population, the effects of noise can vary considerably.

In the determination of these criteria the population as a whole was considered. Additional considerations should be given to hypersensitive sections of the population, for example, old people, the sick and the very young.

This proposal concerning the determination of criteria for noise does not cover vibrations, and subsonic and supersonic waves, which will be the subjects of further studies.

III.   MOTOR VEHICLE NOISE

1.   The noise of cars, buses and lorries

(a)   The framework directives of 1970

Motor vehicle noise, that is essentially cars, buses and lorries, constitutes the major nuisance, especially in urban areas. OECD studies carried out in large towns such as Chicago, London, Paris and Nice have shown that traffic noise comes top of the list of noise nuisances experienced by the population (36%), followed by aircraft noise (9%) and railway trains (5%).

In the 1950s most countries in Europe introduced measures to limit motor vehicle noise. These not having been standardized, the International Standardization Organization (ISO) was asked to draw up a precise and reproducible method of measuring noise. This standardized method was published in 1964 and the Commission took it into account when preparing its first directive proposal on motor vehicle noise.

On 6 February 1970 the Council adopted the directive on the approximation of the laws of the Member States relating to the permissible sound level and the exhaust system of motor vehicles.[2] This directive applies to all motor vehicles intended for use on the road, and having at least four wheels, with the exception of tractors, agricultural machinery and civil engineering equipment. It established noise emission limits to be respected by private cars, buses and lorries.

(b)   The directives amending the 1970 framework directive

(i) Council directives.   Although the 1970 framework directive has already led to a significant reduction in noise nuisance in urban centres, this reduction has been rendered insufficient due to the continued increase in the number of vehicles and growing demands to protect the urban population against noise nuisance. In 1976 the Commission therefore sent the Council a proposal amending the 1970 directive and making the authorized noise limits more stringent. Because of the complexity of the subject, the proposal included short and long-term action programmes.

[2] OJ No L 42 of 23/2/70.

The short-term programme aimed to achieve a reduction in the noise limits without changing fundamentally the test method. A significant reduction of about 50% was envisaged for buses in particular. The long-term programme made provision for the drawing up of a new noise measurement method, better reflecting the real conditions in which vehicles are used in urban traffic.

Table 7.2: Council Directive of 3 September 1984 amending Directive 70/157/EEC on the approximation of the laws of the Member States relating to the permissible sound level and the exhaust system of motor vehicles

5.2.2.1. LIMIT VALUES

The sound level measured in accordance with items 5.2.2.2 to 5.2.2.5 of this Annex shall not exceed the following limits:

	Vehicle categories	*Values expressed in dB(A)*
5.2.2.1.1.	Vehicles intended for the carriage of passengers and equipped with not more than nine seats, including the driver's seat	77
5.2.2.1.2.	Vehicles intended for the carriage of passengers and equipped with more than nine seats, including the driver's seat, and having a maximum permissible mass of more than 3.5 tonnes and:	
5.2.2.1.2.1.	– with an engine power of less than 150 kW	80
5.2.2.1.2.2.	– with an engine power of not less than 150 kW	83
5.2.2.1.3.	Vehicles intended for the carriage of passengers and equipped with more than nine seats, including the driver's seat; vehicles intended for the carriage of goods:	
5.2.2.1.3.1	– with a maximum permissible mass not exceeding 2 tonnes	78
5.2.2.1.3.2.	– with a maximum permissible mass exceeding 2 tonnes but not exceeding 3.5 tonnes	79
5.2.2.1.4.	Vehicles intended for the carriage of goods and having a maximum permissible mass exceeding 3.5 tonnes	
5.2.2.1.4.1.	– with an engine power of less than 75 kW	81
5.2.2.1.4.2.	– with an engine power of not less than 75 kW but less than 150 kW	83
5.2.2.1.4.3.	– with an engine power of not less than 150 kW	84

However,
– for vehicles of categories 5.2.2.1.1 and 5.2.2.1.3, the limit values shall be increased by 1 dB(A) if they are equipped with a direct injection diesel engine,
– for vehicles with a maximum permissible mass of over two tonnes designed for off-road use, the limit values are increased by 1 dB(A) if their engine power is less than 150 kW and 2 dB(A) if their engine power is equal to or greater than 150 kW.'

The Council adopted this amending directive on 8 March 1977.[3] In so doing it made the following declaration: "Efforts should be made to achieve a noise level of around 80 decibels (A) for all categories of motor vehicles by 1985. The levels decided on will have to take into account what is technically and economically feasible at the time. Moreover, they will have to be established sufficiently early to give manufacturers an adequate transition period in which to improve their products."

In line with this declaration, the Council adopted a new directive on 3 September 1984 reducing the permitted noise levels of motor vehicles.[4] The noise levels to be respected by 1 October 1988 at the latest are shown in Table 7.2.

On 28 June 1991 the Commission sent the Council a proposal for a directive to amend the 1970 directive. The proposal's main effect would be to introduce stricter noise standards for all new motor vehicles with four or more wheels. The Commission also proposed to consolidate the various previous amendments to the original directive and to introduce some refinements to test procedures. Introduction dates for the new limits would be 1 October 1994 for new type approvals and 1 October 1995 for all new registrations. A new article would establish clear rules for the use by Member States of fiscal incentives to encourage the earlier introduction of vehicles that comply with the new limits. Given that at higher vehicle speeds, noise from tyre/road surface contact is now the main source of noise, engine noise having been greatly reduced, the proposal also contains a commitment for the Council to agree before 1 October 1995 on measures to limit noise from this source.

As adopted by the Council on 10 November 1992, the amended directive (92/97/EEC) states that as from October 1 1995 Member States may not grant EEC type-approval certification for vehicles not meeting the new requirements and as from 1 October 1996 shall prohibit the entry into service of motor vehicles which do not so comply.

The new limits as agreed by the Council are shown in Tables 7.3 and 7.4.

Table 7.3: Reduced noise values for vehicles in dB(A)

	92/97	84/424	77/212	70/157
Cars	74	77	80	82
Buses over 3.5 tonnes				
less than 200 HP	78	80	82	89
over 200 HP	80	83	85	91
Buses and goods vehicles				
less than 2 tonne	76	78	81	84
over 2 and under 3.5 tonne	77	79		
Goods vehicles over 3.5 tonnes				
less than 100 HP	77	81		
over 100 and under 200 HP	78	83	86	89
over 200 HP	80	84	88	91

Note: for cars and goods vehicles of less than 3.5 tonnes with diesel engines the limit values are 1 dB(A) higher.

[3] OJ No L 66 of 12/3/77.
[4] OJ No L 238 of 6/9/84.

Table 7.4: Reduction in noise limits in dB(A)

	1970	1983	1988/9
Cars	84	80	77
Heaviest buses	89	85	83
Heaviest lorries	89	88	84

It should, however, be stressed that the first directives on the noise levels of vehicles, as with the directives concerning motor vehicles, were "optional", i.e. the Member States are not legally required to make their manufacturers respect them. They cannot however refuse to grant "approval" to vehicles from the Community if those vehicles respect the limit values of the directive. With the 1992 amendments the noise limits became mandatory.

(ii) Technical implementation directives of the Commission. The Commission has adopted, on the basis of its own areas of responsibility, two directives aimed at adapting the 1970 framework directive to scientific and technical advances:

● on 7 November 1973 it adopted a directive on the adaptation of the test conditions for the provisions on vehicle exhaust;[5]
● on 13 April 1981 it adopted a directive introducing a new method of noise measurement from October 1984 onwards; this new method, though it does not change the permitted noise levels, nevertheless leads to a reduction in the permitted noise level for certain vehicle categories of 3 decibels;[6]
● on 3 July 1984 it adopted a directive (84/372/EEC) to improve the measurement of sound levels in urban traffic conditions as approved by the United Nations Economic Commission for Europe in Regulation 51;[7]
● on 17 July 1989, the Commission adopted a directive (89/491/EEC) adapting the Annex to take into account technical changes to vehicles using unleaded petrol.[8]

2. Motorcycle noise

On 31 December 1984 the Commission sent the Council a proposal for a directive on the approximation of the laws of the Member States on the approval of motorcycles, including in particular provisions on permissible sound levels and exhaust systems. Motorcycles do represent a significant source of noise, especially in built-up areas. They are also frequently used at full throttle, and a 20% increase in speed often leads to a doubling of the sound intensity emitted.

The Council adopted the directive (78/1015/EEC) on the permissible sound level and exhaust system of motorcycles on 23 November 1978.[9] The directive's field of application is limited to two-wheeled motorcycles with a maximum speed of over 50 km/hr intended for use on roads, thus excluding "off-road" vehicles. This direct-

[5] OJ No L 321 of 22/11/73.
[6] OJ No L 131 of 18/5/81.
[7] OJ No L 196 of 26/7/84.
[8] OJ No L 238 of 15/8/89.
[9] OJ No L 349 of 13/12/78.

Table 7.5: Council Directive of 18 December 1986 amending Directive 78/1015/EEC on the approximation of the laws of the Member States relating to the permissible sound level and exhaust system of motorcycles

Motorcycle category by cubic capacity (in cm^3)	Sound level limits in dB (A) and dates of entry into force for national type approval of motorcycle			
	First stage limits in dB (A)	Dates of entry into force for national approval	Second stage limits in dB (A)	Dates of entry into force for national approval
1. ≤ 80	77	1 October 1988	75	1 October 1993
2. > 80 ≤ 175	79	1 October 1989	77	31 December 1994
3. > 175	82	1 October 1988	80	1 October 1993

ive, which is also an optional one, fixes the permissible sound levels according to the cylinder capacity of the motorcycle. The sound levels and the exhaust system are an integral part of the EEC approval procedure. The technical annexes of the directive define the requirements to be respected concerning measuring instruments, conditions and methods. When adopting the directive in 1978, the Council undertook to decide on a further reduction in the maximum noise level of motorcycles by 31 December 1984.

On 14 September 1984 the Commission therefore presented the Council with a proposal amending the 1978 framework directive. The Council adopted this directive (87/56/EEC) on 18 December 1986.[10] It specifies the methods to use for measuring sound emissions, making it more representative of the actual use of motorcycles in urban traffic. It reduces the number of categories of motorcycles dealt with by the 1979 directive, and greatly strengthens the limit values for the permissible noise level to come into force in two stages in 1988 and 1993 respectively (see Table 7.4).

Council Directive 89/235/EEC was adopted as part of the package of measures to establish the Single Market by 1993. It extended the scope of the principal directive to cover replacement exhaust systems and their components and defined a new test procedure in a new Annex II.[11]

3.   Tractor noise

A directive (74/151/EEC) establishing the characteristics of agricultural or forestry tractors was adopted by the Council on 4 March 1974.[12] Among the different technical specifications that tractors must respect in order to circulate freely in the Community are the maximum noise limit levels. The levels are 89 dB(A) for tractors weighing more than 1.5 tonnes unladen and 85 dB for those over 1.5 tonnes.

[10] OJ No L 24 of 27/1/87.
[11] OJ No L 98 of 11/4/89.
[12] OJ No L 84 of 28/3/74.

A second Council directive (77/311/EEC) of 29 March 1977 fixed permissible limit levels with the specific aim of protecting the hearing of tractor drivers.[13] This directive is more directly linked to work legislation.

IV. CONSTRUCTIONAL PLANT AND EQUIPMENT NOISE

1. Framework directives of 1978 and 1984

On 31 December 1974 the Commission sent two proposals for directives to the Council, concerning both the technical and administrative procedures concerning construction plant and equipment (EEC approval; free movement, etc.) and also a general method of measuring the level of sound emissions from such construction plant and equipment. These two proposals, like all the "motor vehicle" directives, provided for a legal system based on partial or "optional" harmonization. The directives' field of application covers all material, equipment, installations and plant used to carry out work on building sites.

(a)   1978 framework directive on the method of measuring the noise emission of construction plant and equipment

In drawing up this proposal the Commission took into account the noise standards envisaged by the International Standardization Organization. This is of particular importance in the case of construction plant, since trade in such material goes well beyond the borders of the Community.

The Council adopted the directive (79/113/EEC) on the determination of the noise emission of construction plant and equipment on 19 December 1978.[14] This directive, which is basically a technical one, defines and harmonizes the conditions and methods of measuring noise emissions from construction plant used outdoors (type of noise; how to express the results; measuring site, etc.). The Council amended this directive on 7 December 1981[15] in order to include a new technical annex making it possible to determine the noise of construction plant, not only outdoors, but also specifically with regard to the operator's position (Council Directive 81/1051).

The 1978 directive also makes provision for a simplified procedure for adapting to technical progress, and this procedure was used by the Commission on 11 July 1985 when it adopted a directive (85/405/EEC) amending certain technical provisions.[16]

(b)   1984 framework directive on the common administrative procedures for the approval of construction plant

More than 10 years of extensive discussions and negotiations were needed before the Council finally adopted on 17 September 1984[17] the framework directive on

[13] OJ No L 105 of 28/4/77.
[14] OJ No L 33 of 8/2/79.
[15] OJ No L 376 of 30/12/81.
[16] OJ No L 233 of 30/8/85.
[17] OJ No L 300 of 19/11/84, original Commission proposal COM (74) 2195 of 14/4/75.

the approximation of the legislations of the Member States concerning common provisions for construction plant and equipment. The delay in the adoption of this directive was mainly due to the problems presented by the sanctioning and approval of construction plant imported into the Community. Member States having large industries producing civil engineering equipment were worried that the Community procedures might over-facilitate the importation of such equipment into the Community. The 1984 directive sets the conditions and requirements which the plant must fulfil in order to be approved within the Community.

2.   Directives for the application of the framework directive

From 1974–1975 onwards, in line with the two 1974 proposals for the framework directives, the Commission sent the Council a number of proposals specifically regulating the permissible noise level corresponding to each type or category of construction plant: concrete breakers, picks, motor-compressors, cranes, current generators, earth-moving machines. All of these specific proposals being linked from the legal point of view to the framework directives as far as EEC approval and examination procedures are concerned, the Council could only unfreeze and approve them at the same time as it approved the framework directive. The individual directives which were therefore adopted by the Council on 17 September 1984 are the following:

- directive (84/533/EEC) on the permissible sound power level of compressors;[18]
- directive (84/534/EEC) on the permissible sound power level of tower cranes;[19]
- directive (84/535/EEC) on the permissible sound power level of welding generators;[20]
- directive (84/536/84) on the permissible sound power level of power generators;
- directive (84/537/EEC) on the permissible sound power level of concrete breakers and picks.[21]

A sixth directive (86/662/EEC) on noise emission limits for earth-moving machines, i.e. hydraulic excavators, rope-operated excavators, dozers, loaders and excavator-loaders, was adopted by the Council on 22 December 1986.[22]

It should be noted that all of the "construction plant" directives contain a provision allowing Member States to regulate the use of this equipment in certain particularly sensitive zones, in order to reduce the nuisance caused by the noise emitted. Most of these directives indicate that the Council will decide, on the basis of a Commission proposal, and no later than five years after their adoption, on new reductions in the noise levels for each type of equipment in question. They also make provision for a simplified procedure for adapting the various technical annexes to technical progress. The Commission made use of this procedure on 11 July 1985 to amend certain technical methods contained in the annexes in all the directives.[23]

---

[18] OJ No L 300 of 19/11/84.
[19] *Ibid.*
[20] *Ibid.*
[21] *Ibid.*
[22] OJ No L 284 of 31/12/86.
[23] OJ No L 233 of 30/8/85.

Finally, as far as the noise measurement method is concerned, it should be noted that these directives refer to what is known as a "static" method, i.e. the measurement of plant motor noise when it is not active. However, the last directive on earth-moving equipment adopted by the Council in 1986 marks an interesting development in this respect. This directive not only fixes the permissible sound power levels for noise emitted into the environment, and to the operator's position, it also makes provision for the establishment in the future (six years) of noise levels measured by an actual "dynamic" method, i.e. when the plant is in up and running movement and in operation. The Commission is called upon to draw up a proposal to establish the permissible noise levels.

V. AIRCRAFT NOISE

1. The work of the International Civil Aviation Organization

Another sector in which the Community has undertaken action against noise at source concerns aircraft noise. In undertaking this action the Commission has relied largely on the work already carried out by the International Civil Aviation Organization (ICAO). In Montreal in 1971 this international organization adopted an initial group of standards and recommendations on aircraft noise, known as "Annex 16 to the International Convention on Civil Aviation". A first amendment to "Annex 16" was adopted in 1973. Among other things, it concerns subsonic jet aircraft with a maximum take-off weight greater than 5700 kg, powered by engines with a bypass ratio greater than 2, which received their first individual certificate of airworthiness after 1 March 1972.

These sound levels also applied to subsonic jet aircraft with a maximum take-off weight exceeding 28,500 kg and powered by engines with a bypass ratio less than 2 if the first certificate of airworthiness was issued before 1 January 1976. A second amendment to Annex 16 was adopted in 1975. It extends the field of application of the noise standards of Annex 16 to cover all recent jet aircraft, irrespective of weight, and introduced recommended practices for the noise certification of light propeller aircraft.

2. The 1979 directive on aircraft noise

On 2 April 1976 the Commission sent a proposal to the Council for a directive on the limitation of noise emissions from subsonic aircraft. This proposal was intended to incorporate most of the noise standards of the ICAO's Annex 16 into a text on Community law. In view of the extensive work already carried out by the ICAO in this area, the Commission felt that the most effective and rapid way of limiting aircraft noise was by imposing the uniform application in all Member States of the European Community, of the ICAO's standards in Annex 16. These standards were no more than recommendations for the member countries of the Chicago Convention on International Civil Aviation, and only became compulsory when integrated into the national legislation of the Member States. The majority of Community Member States were already basing themselves on the principles of Annex 16, but there were important differences between national legislation at a practical level from both the technical and legal points of view. Some Member States, for example, were basing themselves on the first Annex 16 amendment of 1973; others, however, had also incorporated the second amendment of 1975 into their legislation. In other Member States again, none of the legislation on aircraft noise took into account the ICAO's recommendations. These differences not only limited the effectiveness of the attempts to combat aircraft noise, but also created distortions in competition between airlines for the purchase of aircraft.

The Council adopted the directive (80/51/EEC) on the limitation of noise emissions from subsonic aircraft on 20 December 1979.[24] This directive makes it compulsory for all Member States to adhere to the most recent noise standards adopted by the ICAO. It also makes mandatory the recommendations taken within the European Civil Aviation Conference (ECAC) concerning the restricted use of non-certificated aircraft. The directive establishes an "EEC noise limitation certificate", i.e. a document by which the Member State which has registered an aircraft recognizes that such aircraft meet the requirements of the directive. This EEC certificate must be mutually recognized between all the Member States. The directive also makes provision for checks on compliance by aircraft with the noise standards, and for exchange of information between the different control authorities regarding these checks. The directive covers not only aircraft registered in the Member States of the Community, but also all third country civil aircraft landing or taking off in a Member State.

Directive 80/51 prevented any further non-noise certificated aircraft (so-called Chapter 1 aircraft) being put on the register of Member States and required the removal of such aircraft from registers by 31 December 1986.

3.   The amending directive of 1983

On 28 September 1981 the Commission presented the Council with a proposal amending the 1979 directive on aircraft noise. The Council adopted this directive (83/206/EEC) on 21 April 1983.[25] This is firstly intended to incorporate into Community legislation the technical amendments made in 1981 by the ICAO to Annex 16. Secondly, it prohibits subsonic civil aircraft registered in third countries and not complying with the standards of Annex 16 (Chapter 1 aircraft) from using Community territory after 31 December 1987. The Member States are however able to grant a temporary derogation for this category of aircraft until 31 December 1989.

4.   The amending directive of 1989

In 1989 the Council approved a directive (89/629/EEC) further limiting noise emissions from civil subsonic jet aeroplanes.[26] Under the directive Member States would have to ensure that, as from 1 November 1990, civil subsonic jet aeroplanes registered or leased for use in their territory, or in the territory of another Member State, may not be operated in their territory unless granted a noise certificate to the standards at least equal to those specified in Part II, Chapter 3, Volume 1 of Annex

---

[24] OJ No L 18 of 24/1/80.
[25] OJ No L 117 of 4/5/83.
[26] OJ No L 363 of 13/12/89.

16 to the Convention on International Civil Aviation, 1st edition (November 1981). The above provision would not apply to aeroplanes on the national registers of Member States on 1 November 1990 and no deadline was given in the directive for the operation of aircraft meeting Chapter 2 standards. Exemptions are allowed in certain specified cases, such as for aircraft of historic interest. Member States may make further limited exemptions for economic reasons until 31 December 1995. These must be reported to the Commission.

5. The amending directive (92/14/EEC) of 2 March 1992[27]

This directive on the limitation of the operation of aeroplanes covered by Part II, Chapter 2, Volume 1 of Annex 16 to the Convention on International Civil Aviation, 2nd edition (1988) is aimed at the gradual elimination over a period of years of Chapter 2 aircraft, taking into account the ecological factors, the technical feasibility and the economic implications. Directive 92/14 bans the operation of aircraft not meeting Chapter 3 standards after 1 April 1995. However, Chapter 2 aircraft which are less than 25 years old may continue to operate until 1 April 2002. Particular attention is given to developing countries and temporary exemptions specified for the airlines of some developing countries which otherwise might have had to cease aircraft operations regarded as vital to their economies.

6. Helicopter noise

On 13 October 1981 the Commission sent the Council a proposal for a directive on the limitation of noise emitted from helicopters.[28] An amendment to the ICAO's Annex 16 adopted in 1981 did introduce noise standards and an international certification procedure for helicopter noise. The Commission's proposal was intended to make these standards uniformly mandatory throughout the Community, following the same legal and technical structure as for aircraft. The Council has not yet adopted this directive. It seems that the standards proposed by the Commission, although not particularly stringent, are technically complicated to implement, and are likely to be rapidly overtaken by scientific and technical progress.

VI. ACTIONS IN OTHER AREAS

1. Lawnmower noise

On 18 December 1978 the Commission submitted a proposal to the Council for a directive on the permissible sound power level of lawnmowers, which are particularly noisy pieces of machinery, causing considerable nuisance.

The Council adopted this directive on 17 September 1984, at the same time as the series of directives concerning construction plant.[29] The directive fixes the limit

[27] OJ No L 76 of 23/3/92.
[28] OJ No C 275 of 27/10/81.
[29] OJ No L 300 of 19/11/81.

values for the sound power level according to the cutting width of the lawnmower and determines the method of measuring the noise levels.

In order to inform the consumer, the directive requires that the noise level be indicated on each lawnmower, along with the marks identifying the manufacturer and the type of lawnmower. It also describes the administrative procedures to be followed by the manufacturer or importer to ensure that the lawnmowers conform with the requirements of the directive; the certificates of conformity must be mutually recognized by the Member States in order to guarantee the free movement of the products within the Community. Finally, the directive stipulates that Member States can regulate the use of lawnmowers in particularly sensitive zones.

On 22 March 1988, the Council adopted a directive (88/180/EEC) amending Directive 84/538/EEC on the permissible sound power level of lawnmowers.[30] Under the amended directive, Member States shall take all appropriate measures to ensure that lawnmowers may not be placed on the market unless:

● their sound power levels do not exceed the permissible level for the cutting width of the mower as shown in the following table:

Table 7.6: Council Directive of 17 October 1974
Permissible sound power levels of lawnmowers

Cutting width of lawnmower (L)	Permissible sound power level in dB(A)/pW
L ≤ 50 cm	96
50cm <L ≤ 120 cm	100
L > 120 cm	105

For lawnmowers with a cutting width exceeding 120 cm, the sound-pressure level of airborne noise in (dB(A)), measured at the operator's position should not exceed the level of 90 dB(A).

Annex I was adapted to technical progress by Commission Directive 87/252/EEC of 7 April 1987.[31] Requirements for limiting the sound power level at the operator's position were introduced by Council Directive 88/181/EEC.[32]

2. Domestic appliance noise

On 19 June 1982 the Commission presented the Council with a proposal for a framework directive on noise emitted by household equipment.

The Council adopted this directive (86/594/EEC) on 1 December 1986.[33] It covers all household equipment intended for private use in dwellings (refrigerators, dishwashers, washing machines, etc.). The text agreed on by the Council is less ambitious than that proposed by the Commission in that it only makes provision for the rules concerning the information and publication of noise levels of different equipment, in cases where Member States decide to inform the public and the consumer.

---

[30] OJ No L 81 of 26/3/88.
[31] OJ No L 117 of 5/5/87.
[32] OJ No L 81 of 26/3/88.
[33] OJ No L 344 of 1/12/86.

The directive does not therefore impose any general obligation regarding information on the noise emitted by household equipment, and does not establish any maximum permissible noise level, unlike the "construction plant" directives, for example. The directive considers, in line with the new standardization approach of 1985, that it is up to the private standardization organization (European Standardization Committee (CEN) and European Electrotechnical Standardization Committee (CENELEC)) to determine the harmonized standards in this area.

The directive establishes the general principles on the publication of information on noise emitted by household equipment when a Member State makes such information compulsory in its territory (labelling requirements, for example). It also defines the technical requirements needed to carry out checks on the noise levels declared by the manufacturers and importers.

3.   Train noise

On 7 December 1983 the Commission presented the Council with a proposal for a directive concerning the noise emissions of rail-mounted vehicles,[34] namely traction engines (locomotives), carriages and electric trains.

This proposal appeared to cause considerable difficulties due to the significant cross-border movement of railway equipment coming from third countries, and particularly from countries in Eastern Europe, which do not comply with internationally recognized standards.

The proposal was withdrawn by the Commission in August 1993.[35]

4.   Acoustic standards in housing

Under the 4th Environment Action Programme (1987–1992), the Commission worked on different projects with a view to drawing up a directive proposal fixing acoustic standards for housing, which would take into consideration the international standards already existing within the framework of the ISO (International Standardization Organization). No proposal has so far been made to the Council.

VII.   THE PROTECTION OF WORKERS FROM NOISE

On 15 October 1982 the Commission presented the Council with a first proposal for a directive on the protection of workers against noise in the framework of the Community social action programme.

The Council approved this first directive (88/188/EEC) concerning the protection of workers from risks due to exposure to noise at work on 12 May 1986.[36] This directive is intended to reduce to the lowest reasonably practical level, the risks resulting from the exposure of workers to noise. It provides for the drawing up of a programme of measures aimed at reducing noise when exposure exceeds 90 dB(A) and if this is impossible, the use of individual protectors for workers. These protectors must be made available to workers for levels exceeding 85 dB(A).

[34] OJ No C 354 of 29/12/83.
[35] OJ No C 228/4 of 24/8/93.
[36] OJ No L 137 of 24/5/86.

The directive also sets up a regular check on the hearing of workers in order to diagnose any loss of hearing due to noise exposure. For new installations it makes provision for the application of the principle of reducing risks to the lowest possible level at the design and construction stages. Finally, it makes provision for consultation with workers' representatives regarding the establishment of programmes and measures intended to reduce noise in the workplace.

VIII. FUTURE ACTION

With the exception of the directive on noise in the workplace, all the measures on noise that have been adopted to date by the Community have been concerned with noise from products. They mainly involve modes of transport (motor vehicles, motorcycles, aircraft), construction plant or some specific products such as lawnmowers.

The 1977 2nd Environmental Action Programme set out the general framework for a body of measures such as the definition of quality objectives, specific regulations for sensitive areas, or noise-related charges. In practice, however, the Commission was not to progress beyond the product-oriented approach.

In subsequent action programmes, noise is recognized as an environmental problem which, according to surveys of public opinion, remains of considerable importance.

The Commission considered that the product-oriented approach was still valid, and that it should continue to be pursued in the future, while extending its scope.

First and foremost the Commission wanted to look more closely at a method of measuring noise which would not be exclusively "static", as is currently the case for the construction plant directives for example, but a "dynamic" method, i.e. combining all the noises produced when the machine is actually in movement.

Secondly, the Commission felt that by liaising with transport policy a form of inspection of motor vehicle noise could be established within the framework of the "technical control" carried out in Member States. A Community approach to noise-related landing charges for aircraft which would be consistent with the "polluter pays" principle might also be suggested with a view to contributing to a solution to the problem of aircraft noise.

Overall the Commission would try to combine the establishment of noise emission limits for specific products with the fixing of ambient noise levels. The Member States would thus be able to move towards policies which penalize or discourage the sale of noisy products in favour of more silent ones, so creating pressure on manufacturers to develop less "polluting" articles.

In practice, many of these ambitions remained unfulfilled during the period of the 3rd and 4th Environmental Action Programmes. Moreover, the new emphasis on "subsidiarity" which surrounded the Maastricht Treaty seemed likely to limit major Community initiatives in the noise field unless they were product related.

However, the 5th Environment Programme, under the section on The Urban Environment (5.5.) indicates that noise is one of the most pressing problems in urban areas. More than 16% of the population suffers at night time from noise levels, mainly resulting from road and air traffic, over leq 65 dB(A). This causes serious health risks. The primary objective, according to the 5th Environment Programme, is "to remedy this situation, before tackling other levels".

Table 7.7 indicates EC targets for noise up to the year 2000 and related actions.

Table 7.7: The fifth environment action programme: noise

Objective	EC Targets up to 2000	Actions	Time-frame	Sectors/actors
* no person should be exposed to noise levels which endanger health and quality of life	Night-time exposure levels in Leq dB(A):			Transport + Industry
	* exposure of the population to noise levels in excess of 65 should be phased out; at no point in time a level of 85 should be exceeded	* inventory of exposure levels in the EC	before 1994	EEA + MS + LAs
		* noise abatement programme to be set up	before 1995	MS + LAs
	* proportion of population at present exposed to levels between 55–65 should not suffer any increase	* further reductions of noise emissions (cars, trucks, aircraft, cranes, mowers, etc.) Directives to be presented progressively, aiming at implementation not later than 2000	before 1995	EC + MS + Industry
	* proportion of population at present exposed to levels less than 55 should not suffer any increase above that level	* standardization of noise measurement and ratings	continuous	EEA + EC + MS
		* measures to influence behaviour, such as driving cars, flight procedures, industrial processes operating at night-time	id	MS + LAs + EC
		* measures related to infrastructure and physical planning, such as better zoning around airports, industrial areas, main roads and railways	id	MS + LAs

(1) OJ N°L 163, 89/369/EEC and OJ N°L 203, 89/429/EEC
(2) OJ N°L 135, 30.5.1991, 91/271/EEC
(3) COM (90) 218 of 27 June 1990
(4) Source: ECMT report on Transport policy and the environment, OECD, Paris, 1990

Chapter 8

Flora and Fauna

I. INTRODUCTION

The protection of flora and fauna constitutes one of the most recent areas of Community actions in the environmental field, and one which in any case followed on from actions against pollution and nuisances. The implementation of this new policy met with numerous difficulties at Council level, since certain Member States questioned the political and legal basis of Community action in this area, in that it was moving away somewhat from the truly economic activities on which the treaty is based. So it is that the Council's first decisions in this sector were only taken in the years 1979–1980. Furthermore, the 1973 1st Action Programme hardly mentioned this sector, which nevertheless represents an important element of a true environmental protection policy. Not until the 1977 2nd Action Programme was there some description of certain actions in the area of the protection of flora and fauna. In this respect, it should be stressed that the support given to the Commission by the European Parliament was a determining factor in the implementation of this new dimension of Community Environment Policy.

As far as the actual content of the policy is concerned, there is a certain preponderance of actions of an international or external nature, which the Community carries out either by means of international conventions, or at the level of trade policy, particularly in the area of Community import regulations. However, the adoption by the Council on 21 May 1992 of a directive on the conservation of natural habitats and of wild fauna and flora is likely to do much to redress the balance.

II. THE PROTECTION OF CERTAIN SPECIES

1. The protection of birds

(a) The Council directive of 1979

On 20 October 1976 the Commission presented the Council with a proposal for a directive on the conservation of birds in the Community.

Scientific studies carried out by the Commission had brought to light a reduction in the number of bird species, and, for some species, a reduction in population levels. These phenomena could represent a serious threat to the conservation of the natural environment, due to the danger of weakening of the biological balance and of the regulating biological mechanisms. This threat is made even greater by the growing use of chemicals to combat pests, such as insects or rodents. The reasons for this situation stem mainly from the pressure being put on the habitats and also from the pressures caused by hunting. As far as habitats are concerned, pollution, and, more generally, certain activities carried out by man (rural and coastal development, intensification of farming, increased civil engineering work) have a determining influence on the levels of population of bird species, especially in certain sensitive areas such as wetlands and woodlands. With regard to hunting, the use of methods of mass or non-selective destruction also has a harmful effect on population levels. Scientific observations have also shown that the bird species living wild in the European territories of the Member States are largely migratory species, which implies that effective protection of such species can only be achieved at transfrontier level.

On 2 April 1979 the Council adopted the directive on the conservation of wild birds.[1] It covers the protection, management and control of more than 400 species of wild birds. It applies not only to the birds themselves, but also to their eggs, nests and habitats. The Member States must take measures to maintain the population of all species of birds living in the wild state at a level which corresponds to ecological requirements, or to adapt the population to that level, in particular by maintaining or re-establishing a sufficient diversity and area of habitats.

The directive sets up different legal measures depending on the situation of the bird species concerned:

- A first category of species (Annex I of the directive) is the subject of special conservation measures concerning their habitat (creation of special protection areas), the specific prohibiting of hunting (the prohibiting of the deliberate killing or capture of birds, destruction of their nests or eggs), and restrictive trade measures. Special exemptions are nevertheless provided for in the cases of certain species (Annex III of the directive – parts 1, 2 and 3), the conditions of application of these exemptions being controlled by the Commission. The seven species listed in Annex III/1 may be sold if they have been killed, captured or otherwise legally acquired. The 10 species listed in Annex III/2 may be exempted from the prohibition by a Member State after consultation with the Commission. A further nine species listed in Annex III/3 are to be the subject of further study by the Commission with a view to inclusion in Annex III/2.
- A second category (Annex II) includes 74 species which may be hunted under certain strictly defined conditions, for example, depending on the population level of the species in question, its geographical distribution, and its reproduction rate; 24 of these species may be hunted throughout the Community (Annex II, part 1), 48 others only in certain Member States (Annex II, part 2).

Moreover, as far as the means of hunting are concerned, the directive prohibits the use of methods of large-scale or non-selective capture which might cause the local disappearance of a species. In this respect the directive mentions the following methods: explosives, nets, mirrors, aeroplanes, motor vehicles, electrocuting apparatus, etc.

[1] OJ No L 103 of 2/4/79.

Commission Directive 85/411/EEC amending the 1979 directive

The original list of 74 "particularly vulnerable" species was increased to 144 species by Commission Directive 85/411/EEC in 1985.[2]

The 1991 Commission Directive 91/244 amending the 1979 directive[3]

On 6 March 1991 the Commission approved a directive adding to the list of particularly vulnerable species in Annex I, bringing the total number of species listed to 175. The number of species listed in Annex III/2 was also increased to 21.

Council Directive 94/24/EC of 8 June 1994 amending the 1979 directive

The directive introduces a revised Annex II/2 to Directive 79/409/EEC. The revised annex includes certain species which could not previously legally be hunted, but which have now been added to the list because of their geographical distribution and population levels.

(b)   The Council Resolution of 1979

Parallel with the 1979 directive, the Council also adopted a Resolution on 2 April 1979 concerning the methods of implementing the directive, both from the point of view of the Member States and of the Commission.[4] The Resolution concerns in particular the choice by Member States of the special protection areas to be created on their territories, and the wetlands of international importance to be used for the protection of birds.

2.   The protection of whales

(a)   The 1981 Council Regulation (348/81/EEC) prohibiting the import for commercial purposes of whale products into the Community

On 29 April 1980 the Commission presented the Council with a proposal for a regulation instituting common rules for cetacean whale and sperm whale products. The Commission proposed to prohibit the commercial exploitation of whale products, since this trade might lead to the extinction of certain cetacean species and to a change in the marine ecology.

Since substitute products for all cetacean products, and in particular for oils, were already available, the Commission did not envisage any major difficulties for industry in abandoning the use of cetacean products. The Council adopted this regulation on 20 January 1981.[5]

As of 1 January 1982 the regulation makes provision for the introduction into the Community of cetacean products being made subject to an import licence, which would under no circumstances be issued for products to be used for commercial purposes. The products covered by the regulation appear in Table 8.1. It should however be stressed that the significance of the 1981 "cetaceans" regulation was

---

[2] OJ No L 233 of 30/8/85.
[3] OJ No L 115 of 8/5/91.
[4] OJ No C 14 of 18/1/83.
[5] OJ No L 39 of 12/2/81.

Table 8.1: Council Regulation (EEC) No 348/81 of 20 January 1981
Common rules for imports of whales or other cetacean products

CCT heading No	Description
ex 02.04 C	Meat and edible meat offals of cetaceans, fresh, chilled or frozen
ex 02.06 C	Meat and edible meat offals of cetaceans, salted, in brine, dried or smoked
ex 05.09	Whalebone and the like, unworked or simply prepared but not cut to shape, and hair and waste of these products
ex 05.15 B	Meat and meat offals of cetaceans, unfit for human consumption
ex 15.04	Fats and oils of cetaceans, whether or not refined
ex 15.08	Oils of cetaceans, boiled, oxidized, dehydrated, suphurized, blown, or polymerized by heat in vacuum or in inert gas, or otherwise modified
ex 15.12	Oils and fats of cetaceans, wholly or partly hydrogenated or solidified or hardened by any other process, whether or not refined, but not further prepared
15.15 A	Spermaceti, crude, pressed or refined, whether or not coloured
ex 16.03	Extracts and juices of the meat of cetaceans
ex 23.01 A	Flours and meals of the meat and offals of cetaceans, unfit for human consumption
ex Chapter 41	Leather treated with oil, whether or not modified, of whales or of other cetaceans

All the products listed below which have been treated with oil, whether or not modified, of whales or of other cetaceans or which have been made from leather treated with such oil:

ex Chapter 42	Articles of leather; saddlery and harness; travel goods, handbags and similar containers
ex Chapter 43	Fur skins and manufactures thereof
ex Chapter 64	Footwear, gaiters and the like; parts of such articles.

somewhat lessened by the adoption by the Council on 3 December 1982 of the Regulation on the application in the Community of the Convention on International Trade in Endangered Species of Wild Fauna and Flora (Washington Convention), in that this also includes cetacean species and has a wider field of application than that of the actual "cetacean" regulation of the Community.

Commission Regulation No 3786/81 prescribed the form of the import licence.[6]

(b)   1979 Commission proposal regarding the Community's participation in the International Whaling Convention

On 4 September 1979 the Commission presented the Council with a proposal for a Decision on the Community's participation in the 1946 International Whaling Convention. The Council has not pursued this proposal due to Denmark's opposition to such a move.

---

[6] OJ No L 377 of 31/12/81.

3.   The protection of seal pups

(a)   The First Directive of 1983 banning the import of seal pup skins into the Community until 1985

On 20 October 1982 the Commission sent the Council a proposal for a regulation aimed at banning the Community importation of the skins of certain seal pups, and of other products derived from these animals.

The Commission produced this proposal in response to the moral outcry expressed by a large part of the public both in the Community and in the rest of the world, regarding the hunting methods used, and following several resolutions adopted by the European Parliament. Before drawing up the proposal the Commission consulted with Canada and Norway with a view to achieving a ban on the hunting of seal pups, but these consultations did not lead to any positive results. Finally, since some Member States had already taken or were planning to take national measures to prohibit trade in seal pup skins, the Commission felt that distortions in competition within the Community might arise if such a proposal were not produced.

The Council decided that for political and legal reasons there should be a two-stage approach.

(i) On 5 January 1983 the Council and the governments of the Member States meeting within the Council, first adopted a Resolution on seal pups.[7] This Resolution called upon the Commission, in collaboration with the countries concerned (Canada and Norway), to examine further the methods and circumstances of the killing of harp and hooded seal pups. It also called upon the Commission to report back before March 1983 so that the Council could take the appropriate measures before the beginning of the 1983 hunting period. In the meantime the Member States undertook to take appropriate measures at national level with a view to preventing the importation into their territories of the furskins of harp and hooded seal pups.

(ii) Shortly afterwards, on 28 March 1983, the Council finally adopted a directive (83/129/EEC) concerning the banning of the importation into the Member States of the skins and derivative products of harp and hooded seal pups.[8] This directive is a direct extension of the Resolution of 5 January 1983. Coming into force on 1 October 1983, the directive banned the commercial importation into the territories of the Member States, of the skin and derivative products of harp and hooded seal pups. The banning measure remained in force until 1 October 1985. This import ban is not applicable to products resulting from the traditional hunting practised by the Inuit people (Eskimos).

The products covered by the ban are:

● raw furskins and furskins, tanned or dressed, of harp seal pups ("white-coat") and hooded seal pups ("blue-blacks") of less than three months;
● articles produced from these furskins.

(b)   The Second Directive of 1985 extending the ban on the importation of seal pup skins to 1989; indefinite extension, 1989

On 14 June 1985 the Commission presented the Council with a proposal amending the directive of 28 March 1983 which was to expire on 1 October 1985. The

[7] OJ No C 14 of 18/1/83.
[8] OJ No L 91 of 9/4/83.

amendment would extend for an unspecified period the banning of the importation into the Community of seal pup skins. The Commission felt that an indefinite extension of the directive was justified by the fact that contacts with Norway and Canada had not brought any new elements to the situation, although these countries had decided to set up an independent Royal Commission of Enquiry to look into all of the problems presented by seal hunting. The European Commission considered, moreover, that the negative reactions which would probably arise in public opinion if the directive were not extended, would be likely to have additional detrimental effects both on the fur industry and on the means of survival of the Inuits of Canada and Greenland. Finally, the Commission noted that in most of the Member States the legislation adopted did not have any time-limits, as was already the case in the United States and that this legislation would therefore probably be maintained after 1 October 1985, which might create distortions in the workings of the Common Market.

The Council did not follow the proposal of the Commission in its entirety. On 27 September 1985 it did adopt a directive (85/444/EC)[9] extending the importation ban, but only for a period of four years, namely up to 1 October 1989. It also asked the Commission to report back to it before 1 October 1987 on developments in the area of the conservation of the seal species concerned, and in the commercial situation of the market in seal skins derived from the Inuits' traditional hunting. The products covered by the new four-year importation ban are the same as those in the directive of 28 March 1983. At the Council meeting of 8 June 1989, the import ban was prolonged indefinitely under Directive 89/370/EEC.[10]

4.   African elephant ivory: Regulation 2496/89 (OJ 240, 17/08/89)

As a result of ivory poaching, the African elephant population fell from 1.3 million in the 1970s to just 760,000 by 1987. At such a rate of decline, it was forecast that several elephant populations would become extinct within a few years, including those from some of the most famous national parks of East Africa. The killing of elephants was taking place against the policy of the African governments, serving only the interests of a small group of speculators. By the late 1980s, the ivory trade was estimated at having reached a value of some $120 million a year – almost twice the amount spent on conservation. The fall in the average weight of tusks reaching markets to only 5 kg indicated that many elephants were being killed before reaching sexual maturity.

The African elephant was already listed in Appendix II of CITES. In 1986, within the framework of CITES, a quota system was introduced for the international ivory trade whereby each country organized its ivory trade while also providing an international control system. Yet 80% of world ivory trade was taking place outside the system. Accordingly, the WWF, the IUCN, the CITES Secretariat and the Commission drew up an action plan and a strategy for the conservation of the African elephant involving $15 million. A contribution of Ecu 500,000 in 1988 made it possible to implement the plan immediately.

Adopting measures similar to those taken by the US, the EC imposed a restriction on ivory imports as of 17 August 1989 with certain exemptions, such as for antiques, and hunting trophies where the catch had contributed to the conservation of the population in question.

[9] OJ No L 259 of 1/10/85.
[10] OJ No L 163 of 4/6/89.

5. Leghold traps: Regulation 3254/91

On 26 June 1989 the Commission sent the Council a proposal for a regulation banning the use of leghold traps and limiting the import of pelts and products derived from their use. The aim of the proposal was to promote the conservation of certain species of wild animal hunted for their fur. Leghold traps are widely regarded as being unnecessarily cruel as they inflict much pain on the animals caught, often condemning them to a slow and traumatic death.

Adopted by the Council on 4 November 1991, Council Regulation (EEC) No 3524/91 bans the use of leghold traps in the Community as of 1 January 1995.[11] The import of pelts and products from species listed in the annex is also banned, i.e. badger, beaver, bobcat, coyote, ermine, fisher, lynx, marten, musk rat, otter, raccoon, sable, and wolf. The Commission can exempt countries from the import ban where it believes the use of leghold traps is effectively prohibited or that the above species are taken in accordance with internationally agreed humane trapping standards. Pelts originating in such countries need a certificate for re-export.

Table 8.2: Council Regulation (EEC) No 3254/91 of 4 November 1991 prohibiting the use of leghold traps in the Community and the introduction into the Community of pelts and manufactured goods of certain wild animals species orginating in countries which catch them by means of leghold traps or trapping methods which do not meet international humane trapping standards

ANNEX I

List of species referred to in article 3 (1)

Beaver:	*Castor canadensis*
Otter:	*Lutra canadensis*
Coyote:	*Canis latrans*
Wolf:	*Canis lupus*
Lynx:	*Lynx canadensis*
Bobcat:	*Felis rufus*
Sable:	*Martes zibellina*
Raccoon:	*Procyon lotor*
Musk rat:	*Ondatra zibethicus*
Fisher:	*Martes pennanti*
Badger:	*Taxidea taxus*
Marten:	*Martes americana*
Ermine:	*Mustela erminea*

[11] OJ No L 308 of 9/11/91.

Table 8.3: Council Regulation (EEC) No 3254/91 of 4 November 1991 prohibiting the use of legholds traps in the Community and the introduction into the Community of pelts and manufacturered goods of certain wild animal species originating in countries which catch them by means of leghold traps or trapping methods which do not meet international humane trapping standards

Other goods referred to in article 3 (1)

CN code	Description
ex 4103	Other raw hides and skins (fresh, or salted, dried, limed, pickled or otherwise preserved, but not tanned, parchment-dressed or further prepared), whether or not dehaired or split, other than those excluded by note 1 (b) or 1 (c) to chapter 41
ex 4103 90 00	Other
ex 4301	Raw furskins (including heads, tails, paws and other pieces or cuttings, suitable for furriers' use), other than raw hides and skins of Code 4101, 4102, or 4103
ex 4301 40 00	Of beaver, whole, with or without head, tail or paws
ex 4301 80	Other furskins, whole, with or without head, tail or paws
ex 4301 80 50	Of wild felines
ex 4301 80 90	Other
ex 4301 90 00	Heads, tails, paws and other pieces or cuttings, suitable for furriers' use
ex 4302	Tanned or dressed furskins (including heads, tails, paws and other pieces or cuttings), unassembled, or assembled (without the addition of other materials), other than those of Code 4303: – whole skins, with or without head, tail or paws, not assembled
ex 4302 19	Other
ex 4302 19 10	Of beaver
ex 4302 19 70	Of wild felines
ex 4302 19 90	Other
ex 4302 20 00	Heads, tails, paws and other pieces or cuttings, not assembled
ex 4302 30	Whole skins and pieces or cuttings thereof, assembled
ex 4302 30 10	'Dropped' furskins Other
ex 4302 30 35	Of beaver
ex 4302 30 71	Of wild felines
ex 4302 30 75	Other
ex 4303	Articles of apparel, clothing accessories and other articles, of furskin
ex 4303 10	Articles of apparel and clothing accessories
ex 4303 10 90	Other
ex 4303 90 00	Other

III.   INTERNATIONAL TRADE IN ENDANGERED SPECIES OF WILD FAUNA AND FLORA

1.   The Community framework regulation of 1982

On 29 July 1980 the Commission presented the Council with a proposal for a regulation intended to set up within the Community a common system of implementation of the provisions of the 1973 Washington Convention on International Trade in Endangered Species of Wild Fauna and Flora. In order to protect these species the convention institutes rigorous measures for the restriction and control of international trade in animals and plants belonging to endangered species and in products obtained from these species. The exportation or importation of endangered species of fauna and flora is thus subject to a compulsory licence or certificate issued by the *ad hoc* management bodies designated by the states which are party to the convention. The endangered species are listed and classified in different categories depending on the extent to which they are endangered:

● trade in the species appearing in Annex I of the convention is subject to a particularly strict regulation which amounts in practice to an almost total ban on their trade;
● Annex II includes all the species which might be endangered in the future, if trade in these species is not subject to strict regulation intended to prevent any exploitation which would be incompatible with their survival. It also includes certain species which must be the subject of regulation if the control of their trade at international level is to be effective;
● Annex III includes species endangered by illegal exploitation within the contracting states themselves, requiring the cooperation of the other parties to the convention in order to control their trade.

For the species in Annexes II and III of the convention, provision is made to ensure that trade can only be carried out after an export permit has been issued by the states concerned and in the light of certain criteria for the protection of the species and of the judicious use of live natural resources.

The Council adopted this regulation (EEC/3626/82) on the implementation in the Community of the Convention on International Trade in Endangered Species of Wild Fauna and Flora on 3 December 1982.[12]

The regulation has two main characteristics. First, it aims to ensure a uniform implementation within the Community of the provisions of the convention. This harmonization approach mainly concerns commercial policy instruments, especially from the point of view of customs controls and administrative formalities. The regulation makes provision for the mutual recognition of decisions taken by the competent authorities in the different Member States, and stipulates that the licences and certificates issued in one Member State are valid throughout the Community.

The second characteristic of the regulation is that it institutes a more stringent protection system than that in the Washington Convention for more than 250 species of fauna and flora which are particularly at risk, including some sensitive species such as whales, seals and turtles. This more stringent Community system is to be seen in two

---

[12] OJ No L 384 of 31/12/82.

areas. First, the Community applies to some of the species listed in Annex II of the convention the more stringent system of Annex I, namely a ban in imports for commercial reasons (Annex C, part 1, of the Community regulation). Secondly, for certain other species also listed in Annexes II and III of the convention, the Community requires not only an export permit as provided for by the convention, but also an import permit. This import permit can only be issued if certain criteria regarding the conservation of the species are respected: no harmful effect on the conservation of the species; proof of adequate facilities for accommodating the species in the case of a living animal, etc. (Annex C, part 2, of the Community regulation).

Finally, it is important to note that, apart from the measures for international trade, the regulation also makes provision for a general ban on the sale of certain species within the Community itself.

2.   Implementation regulations amending the framework regulation of 1982

Since 1982 the Community framework regulation has been amended on several occasions by the Council and by the Commission, mainly to incorporate the amendments adopted by the management body of the Washington Convention which every two years brings together the states which are contracting parties to the convention. These amendments concern either points of procedure, or more generally the endangered species mentioned in the different annexes of the convention.

Amendments adopted by the Council:

- 3645/83 – the procedure for applying Article 4 (regulation of trade in Annex II species)[13]
- 1831/85 – amendments of Appendix II of Annex A and parts I and II of Annex C to allow stricter controls on wild populations of cyclamen while respecting the practice of artificial propagation of cyclamens within the Community[14]
- 1422/87 – allowing ranches propagating birdwing butterflies to export their products. The most endangered species of birdwing butterfly was retained in part I of Annex C while the other species were transferred to part 2.[15]

Amendments adopted by the Commission:

- 577/84 – moves Giant Panda from Appendix II to Appendix I[16]
- 1451/84 – adds seven species of snake to Appendix III[17]
- 1452/84 – takes into account the adoption of a new taxonomic system for birds[18]
- 1422/85 – introduces amendments following Fifth Meeting of the parties to CITES[19]
- 2295/86 – takes into account revisions to the control system for plants in Appendices II and III and animals in Appendix III adopted by the Fourth[20] Meeting of the parties to CITES

---

[13] OJ No L 367 of 28/12/83.
[14] OJ No L 173 of 3/7/85.
[15] OJ No L 136 of 26/6/87.
[16] OJ No L 64 of 6/3/84.
[17] OJ No L 64 of 6/3/84.
[18] OJ No L 140 of 26/5/84.
[19] OJ No L 136 of 26/5/87.
[20] OJ No L 201 of 24/7/86.

- 1540/87 – introduces taxonomic and other amendments as agreed by the parties[21]
- 3143/87 – introduces amendments following Sixth Meeting of the parties[22]
- 869/88 – brings nomenclature into harmony with the International Convention on the Harmonized Commodity Description and Coding System agreed in 1983 by the Customs Cooperation Council[23]
- 3188/88 – covers increase in export quotas for Nile or African crocodiles[24] from Madagascar and Malawi
- 197/90 – introduces amendments agreed at Seventh Meeting of the parties (Lausanne 1989), including a ban on the import of raw and worked ivory from the African elephant (see below)[25]
- 3675/91[26] – US Brown Bear
- 1970/92 – introduces amendments agreed at Eighth Meeting of the parties (March 1992)[27]
- 1534/93 – amends Annex A to the original regulation and replaces list of Orchideae species in Appendix I[28]

3. Proposal of November 1991 for a regulation laying down provisions with regard to possession of and trade in specimens of species of wild fauna and flora

On 6 December 1991 the Commission sent the Council a proposal for a regulation which would revise Regulation 3626/82 which implements CITES in full throughout the Community.[29] In the years following the entering into force of Regulation 3626/82 significant changes had occurred: more information on the conservation status of species and on patterns of trade in those species had been obtained; changes to CITES itself had occurred as a result of conference resolutions; other Community legislation had been enacted; and the Single Market had been introduced. On this basis, the Commission concluded that a complete revision of the 1982 regulation was necessary. The proposal drafted by the Commission would have a considerable impact upon patterns of trade in those species currently covered by the 1982 regulation, with controls extending to include specimens bred in captivity or artificially propagated on a large scale within the Community.

The Commission's proposal, along with other subsidiary regulations, would replace the existing 1982 regulation. It would strengthen controls and extend the list of species in which trade would be controlled or monitored. It contains measures which take into account the establishment of the Single Market, besides incorporating controls already contained in the Habitats Directive, the Wild Birds Directive and the Leg-Hold Trap Regulation.

The proposed regulation is considerably wider in scope than existing Community legislation. It contains five annexes, of which A to C correspond broadly to CITES

---

[21] OJ No L 147 of 6/6/87.
[22] OJ No L 299 of 2/10/87.
[23] OJ No L 87 of 31/3/88.
[24] OJ No L 285 of 19/10/88.
[25] OJ No L 29 of 31/1/90.
[26] OJ No L 349 of 18/12/91.
[27] OJ No L 201 of 20/7/92.
[28] OJ No L 151 of 23/6/93.
[29] COM (91) 448 (OJ No C 26 of 3/2/92).

Appendices I, II and III, but which list many more species on the more restrictive annexes. Annex D lists non-CITES species for which there is a need to monitor, while Annex E lists species indigenous to individual Member States which are controlled by them and listed at their request. The species listed in Annexes C and D would be allowed to enter the Community provided the importer completed and presented to the customs authorities an import declaration. Given that with the Single Market most existing customs checks at the internal borders of the European Union have ceased, as far as CITES is concerned the Commission proposes to replace these checks with a system of tight internal controls on possession and movement of Annex A specimens. The proposal could require Member States to establish a register of the authorized locations for live specimens, perhaps with certificates of legality for which a fee would be charged, and to monitor their movements, for which authorization would be required. Sale and purchase of Annex A species and products would be banned completely unless special exemption had been acquired, the 1982 regulation controlling only the sale. The Commission would be able to set down extra restrictions on possession for critically endangered species. The proposal also calls for further restrictions for other species, such as those unlikely to survive transportation or long periods in captivity. Species listed in Annexes B and D would not be allowed to be used for various commercial purposes unless the specimens in question could be shown to have been acquired in accordance with conservation legislation.

On 21 January 1994, following the opinion of the European Parliament based on the report of Mr Hemmo Muntingh, a Dutch MEP,[30] the Commission presented an amended proposal to Council and Parliament. Public pressure on the Commission, including a visit paid by former Environment Commissioner Carlo Ripa di Meana to his successor in Brussels, Mr Yannis Palaeokrassas, ensured that the Commission dropped its reported plans to repeal the separate Seals Directive (see above p. 302) and to include the species of seal concerned in the new CITES regulation.[31]

IV.   THE PROTECTION OF HABITATS

Habitats Directive: 92/43/EEC (OJ L 206, 22/07/92)

The Community's 4th Environment Action Programme indicates that in the area of the protection of fauna and flora, and that of nature conservation in general, the Commission will over the coming years ensure the effective implementation of the measures already adopted. New measures will also be proposed with a view to protecting not only birds and their habitats, but also all wild species of fauna and flora. These measures will aim to preserve genetic diversity and to guarantee the rational utilization of species and ecosystems. With this aim in mind, a general list will be drawn up covering the sites in the Community which are protected under the various categories of protected areas. In addition the Commission will try to

[30] PE 204.175/fin of 15/6/93.

[31] See *The Sunday Telegraph*, London – article by Boris Johnson and Grey Neale entitled "EC to lift ban on seal skin exports" dated 21/11/93 and further article by Christopher Lockwood in the *Daily Telegraph* of 2/12/93 "Europe retains ban on sealskin imports".

encourage the improved implementation of the Berne Convention on the conservation of threatened plant and animal species in Europe.

On 21 September 1988, the Commission sent to the Council a proposal[32] for a Council directive on the protection of natural and semi-natural habitats and of wild fauna and flora. In its Explanatory Memorandum the Commission indicated that the fundamental aim of the proposal is to establish, at the latest by the year 2000, a comprehensive network of protected areas aimed at ensuring the maintenance of threatened species and threatened types of habitat in all the regions of the Community where they occur, thus achieving more effective implementation within the Community of the Berne Convention on the conservation of European wildlife and natural habitats as well as other complementary measures appropriate to the Community framework.

The Council held a first discussion of the Commission's proposal at its meeting of 24 November 1988. It was finally adopted on 21 May 1992 (92/43/EEC). As adopted, the directive identifies species and habitat types defined as being of special Community interest and endows them with "favourable conservation status", the concept around which the directive revolves. Divided into two main parts covering the protection of species and the conservation of habitats, the directive extends the protection mechanisms set up in the 1979 Wild Birds Directive to the areas and species identified above. The directive also imposes obligations on the Member States similar to those contained in the Berne Convention on the Conservation of European Wildlife.

The notion of favourable conservation status is based on a range of criteria, including population dynamics, the amount left of a given habitat, and the natural range of species. The directive seeks to maintain or restore favourable conservation status while taking into account socio-economic and cultural needs and what are described as "regional and local characteristics".

Annex I lists 168 habitat types. Habitats are defined as being of Community interest where they are threatened within their natural range, have a limited natural range, or where they constitute an outstanding example of one or more biogeographical regions: Alpine, Atlantic, Continental, Macaronesian or Mediterranean. The habitats listed are classified in the same way as those in the CORINE biotypes programme. Some are specific to a given region, others defined according to strict criteria, while others have a broader description, such as estuaries. The list includes 42 habitat types for which it is deemed the Community has a special responsibility because a significant part of their natural range occurs within Community territory.

Annex II lists plant and animal species deemed to be of special Community interest and whose habitats need special designation for their effective conservation. These species are categorized as endangered, vulnerable, rare, or endemic and needing special attention.

Annex IV (a) and (b) lists animal and plant species respectively of Community interest which are subject to strict protection: all deliberate capture and killing of wild animal specimens is prohibited, as is deliberate disturbance, taking of eggs, disturbance of breeding sites and nesting places. Many of the species are the same as those listed in Annex II. As regards plants, deliberate picking, collecting, uprooting or destruction of wild specimens is forbidden. The transport, sale and exchange of both listed flora and fauna are also forbidden.

---

[32] OJ No C 247 of 21/9/88.

Table 8.4: Council Directive 92/43/EEC of 21 May 1992 on the conservation of natural habitats and of wild fauna and flora

ANNEX I

NATURAL HABITAT TYPES OF COMMUNITY INTEREST WHOSE CONSERVATION REQUIRES THE DESIGNATION OF SPECIAL AREAS OF CONSERVATION

Interpretation

Code: The hierarchical classification of habitats produced through the Corine programme ([1]) (Corine biotopes project) is the reference work for this Annex. Most types of natural habitat quoted are accompanied by the corresponding Corine code listed in the Technical Handbook, Volume 1, pp. 73–109, Corine/Biotope/89/2.2, 19 May 1988, partially updated 14 February 1989.

The sign 'x' combining codes indicates associated habitat types, e.g. 35.2 × 64.1 – Open glassland with *Corynephorus* and *Agrostis* (35.2), in combination with continental dunes (64.1).

The sign '*' indicates priority habitat types.

COSTAL AND HALOPHYTIC HABITATS

Open sea and tidal areas

11.25	Sandbanks which are slightly covered by sea water all the time
11.35	*Pasidonia beds
13.2	Estuaries
14	Mudflats and sandflats not covered by sea water at low tide
21	*Lagoons
–	Large shallow inlets and bays
–	Reefs
–	Marine 'columns' in shallow water made by leaking gases

Sea cliffs and shingle or stony beaches

17.2	Annual vegetation of drift lines
17.3	Perennial vegetation of stony banks
18.21	Vegetated sea cliffs of the Atlantic and Baltic coasts
18.22	Vegetated sea cliffs of the Mediterranean coasts (with endemic *Limonium spp.*)
18.23	Vegetated sea cliffs of the Macaronesian coasts (flora endemic to these coasts)

Altantic and continental salt marshes and salt meadows

15.11	*Salicornia* and other annuals colonizing mud and sand
15.12	Spartina swards (*Spartinion*)
15.13	Altantic salt meadows (*Glauco-Puccinellietalia*)
15.14	*Continental salt meadows (*Puccinellietalia distantis*)

Mediterranean and thermo-Atlantic salt marshes and salt meadows

15.15	Mediterranean salt meadows (*Juncetalia maritimi*)
15.16	Mediterranean and thermo-Atlantic halophilous scrubs (*Arthrocnemetalia fructicosae*)
15.17	Iberia halo-nitrophilous scrubs (*Pegano-Salsoletea*)

([1]) Corine: Council Decision 85/338/EEC of 27 June 1985 (OJ No L 176, 6, 7, 1985, p. 14).

Table 8.4 continued

Salt and gypsum continental steppes

15.18	*Salt steppes (*Limonietalia*)
15.19	*Gypsum steppes (*Gypsophiletalia*)

COASTAL SAND DUNES AND CONTINENTAL DUNES

Sea dunes of the Atlantic, North Sea and Baltic coasts

16.211	Embryonic shifting dunes
16.212	Shifting dunes along the shoreline with *Ammophila arenaria* (white dunes)
16.221 to 16.227	*Fixed dunes with herbaceous vegetation (grey dunes):
	16.221 *Galio-Koelerion albescentis*
	16.222 *Euphorbio-Helichrysion*
	16.223 *Crucianellion maritimae*
	16.224 *Euphorbia terracina*
	16.225 *Mesobromion*
	16.226 *Trifolio-Gerantietea sanguinei, Galio maritimi-Geranion sanguinei*
	16.227 *Thero-Airion, Botrychio-Polygaletum, Tuberarion guttatae*
16.23	*Decalcified fixed dunes with *Empetrum nigrum*
16.24	Eu-atlantic decalcified fixed dunes (*Calluno-Ulicetea*)
16.25	Dunes with *Hyppophae rhamnoides*
16.26	Dunes with *Salix arenaria*
16.29	Wooded dunes of the Atlantic coast
16.31 to 16.35	Humid dune slacks
1.A	Machairs (*in machairs in Ireland)

Sea dunes of the Mediterranean coast

16.223	*Crucianellion maritimae* fixed beach dunes
16.224	Dunes with *Euphorbia terracina*
16.228	*Malcolmietalia* dune grasslands
16.229	*Brachypodietalia* dune grasslands with annuals
16.27	*Dune juniper thickets (*Juniperus spp.*)
16.28	Dune scleorophyllous scrubs (*Cisto-Lavenduletalia*)
16.29×42.8	*Wooded dunes with *Pinus pinea* and/or *Pinus pinaster*

Continental dunes, old and decalcified

64.1×31.223	Dry sandy heaths with *Calluna* and *Genista*
64.1×31.227	Dry sandy heaths with *Calluna* and *Empetrum nigrum*
64.1×35.2	Open grassland with *Corynephorus* and *Agrostis* of continental dunes

FRESHWATER HABITATS

Standing water

22.11×22.31	Oligotrophic waters containing very few minerals of Atlantic sandy plains with amphibious vegetation: *Lobelia, Littorelia* and *Isoetes*
22.11×22.34	Oligotrophic waters containing very few minerals of West Mediterranean sandy plains with *Isoetes*
$22.12 \times (22.31$ and 22.32)	Oligotrophic waters in medio-European and perialpine area with amphibious vegetation: *Littorella* or *Isoetes* or annual vegetation on exposed banks (*Nanocyperetalia*)

Table 8.4 continued

22.12 × 22.44	Hard oligo-mesotrophic waters with benthic vegetation of chara formations
22.13	Natural eutrophic lakes with *Magnopotamion* or *Hydrocharition-type* vegetation
22.14	Dystrophic lakes
22.34	*Mediterranean temporary ponds
–	*Turloughs (Ireland)

Running water

Sections of water-courses with natural or semi-natural dynamics (minor, average and major beds) where the water quality shows no significant deterioration

24.221 and 24.222	Alpine rivers and the herbaceous vegetation along their banks
24.223	Alpine rivers and their ligneous vegetation with *Myricaria germanica*
24.224	Alpine rivers and their ligneous vegetation with *Salix elaegnos*
24.225	Constantly flowing Mediterranean rivers with *Glaucium flavum*
24.4	Floating vegetation of ranunculus of plane, submountainous rivers
24.52	*Chenopodietum rubri* of submountainous rivers
24.53	Constantly flowing Mediterranean rivers: *Paspalo-Agrostidion* and hanging curtains of Salix and *Populus alba*
–	Intermittently flowing Mediterranean rivers

TEMPERATE HEATH AND SCRUB

31.11	Northern Atlantic wet heaths with *Erica tetralix*
31.12	*Southern Atlantic wet heaths with *Erica ciliaris* and *Erica tetralix*
31.2	*Dry heaths (all subtypes)
31.234	*Dry coastal heaths with *Erica vagans* and *Ulex maritimus*
31.3	*Endemic macaronesian dry heaths
31.4	Alpine and subalpine heaths
31.5	*Scrub with *Pinus mugo* and *Rhododendron hirsutum* (*Mugo-Rhododenretum hirsuti*)
31.622	Sub-Arctic willow scrub
31.7	Endemic oro-Mediterranean heaths with gorse

SCLEROPHYLLOUS SCRUB (MATORRAL)

Sub-Mediterranean and temperate

31.82	Stable *Buxus sempervirens* formations on calcareous rock slopes (*Berberidion p.*)
31.842	Mountain *Genista purgans* formations
31.88	*Juniperus communis* formations on calcareous heaths or grasslands
31.89	*Cistus palhinhae* formations on maritime wet heaths (*Junipero-Cistetum palhinhae*)

Mediterranean arborescent matorral

32.131 to 32.135	Juniper formations
32.17	*Matorral with *Zyziphus*
32.18	*Matorral with *Laurus nobilis*

Thermo-Mediterranean and pre-steppe brush

32.216	Laurel thickets
32.217	Low formations of euphorbia close to cliffs
32.22 bis 32.26	All types

Table 8.4 continued

Phrygana

33.1	*Astragalo-Plantaginetum subulatae phrygana*
33.3	*Sarcopoterium spinosum phrygana*
33.4	Cretan formations (*Euphorbieto-Verbascion*)

NATURAL AND SEMI-NATURAL GRASSLAND FORMATIONS

Natural grasslands

34.11	*Karstic calcareous grasslands *(Alysso-Sedion albi)*
34.12	*Xeric sand calcareous grasslands *(Koelerion glaucae)*
34.2	Calaminarian grasslands
36.314	Siliceous Pyrenean grasslands with *Festuca eskia*
36.32	Siliceous alpine and boreal grass
36.36	Siliceous *Festuca indigesta* Iberian grasslands
36.41 bis 36.45	Alpine calcareous grasslands
36.5	Macaronesian mountain grasslands

Semi-natural dry grasslands and scrubland facies

34.31 to 34.34	On calcareous substrates (*Festuco Brometalia*)
	(*important orchid sites)
34.5	*Pseudo-steppe with grasses and annuals (*Thero-Brachypodietea*)
35.1	*Species-rich *Nardus* grasslands, on siliceous substrates in mountain
	areas (and submountain areas, in continental Europe)

Sclerophyllous grazed forests (dehesas)

32.11	With *Quercus suber* and/or *Quercus ilex*

Semi-natural tall-herb humid meadows

37.31	Molinia meadows on chalk and clay (*Eu-Molinion*)
37.4	Mediterranean tall-herb and rush meadows (*Molinio-Holoschoenion*)
37.7 and 37.8	Eutrophic tall herbs
–	*Cnidion venosae* meadows liable to flooding

Mesophile grasslands

38.2	Lowland hay meadows (*Alopecurus pratensis, Sanguisorba officinalis*)
38.3	Mountain hay meadows (British types of *Geranium sylvaticum*)

RAISED BOGS AND MIRES AND FENS

Sphagnum acid bogs

51.1	*Active raised bogs
51.2	Degraded raised bogs
	(still capable of natural regeneration)
52.1 and 52.2	Blanket bog (*active only)
54.5	Transition mires and quaking bogs
54.6	Depressions on peat substrates (*Rhynchosporion*)

Calcareous fens

53.3	*Calcareous fens with *Cladium mariscus* and *Carex davalliana*
54.12	*Petrifying springs with tufa formation (*Cratoneurion*)
54.2	Alkaline fens
54.3	*Alpine pioneer formations of *Caricion bicoloris-atrofuscae*

Table 8.4 continued

ROCKY HABITATS AND CAVES

Scree

61.1	Siliceous
61.2	Eutric
61.3	Western Mediterranean and alpine thermophilous
61.4	Balkan
61.5	Medio-European siliceous
61.6	*Medio-European calcareous

Chasmophytic vegetation on rocky slopes

62.1 and 62.1A	Calcareous sub-types
62.2	Silicicolous sub-types
62.3	Pioneer vegetation of rock surfaces
62.4	*Limestone pavements

Other rocky habitats

65	Caves not open to the public
–	Fields of lava and natural excavations
–	Submerged or partly submerged sea caves
–	Permanent glaciers

FORESTS

(Sub)natural woodland vegetation comprising native species forming forests of tall trees, with typical undergrowth, and meeting the following criteria: rare or residual, and/or hosting species of Community interest

Forests of temperature Europe

41.11	*Luzulo-Fagetum* beech forests
41.12	Beech forests with *Ilex* and *Taxus*, rich in epiphytes (*Ilici-Fagion*)
41.13	*Asperulo-Fagetum* beech forests
41.15	Subalpine beech woods with *Acer* and *Rumex arifolius*
41.16	Calcareous beech forest (*Cephalanthero-Fagion*)
41.24	*Stellario-Carpinetum* oak-hornbeam forests
41.26	*Galio-Carpinetum* oak-hornbeam forests
41.4	*Tilio-Acerion* ravine forests
41.51	Old acidophilous oak woods with *Quercus robur* on sandy plains
41.53	Old oak woods with *Ilex* and *Blechnum* in the British Isles
41.86	*Fraximus angustifolia* woods
42.51	*Caledonian forest
44.A1 to 44.A4	*Bog woodland
44.3	*Residual alluvial forests (*Alnion glutinoso-incanae*)
44.4	Mixed oak-elm-ash forests of great rivers

Mediterranean deciduous forests

41.181	*Apennine beech forests with *Taxus* and *Ilex*
41.184	*Apennine beech forests with *Abies alba* and beech forests with *Abies nebrodensis*
41.6	Galicio-Portuguese oak woods with *Quercus robur* and *Quercus pyrenaica*

Table 8.4 continued

41.77	*Quercus faginea* woods (Iberian Peninsula)
41.85	*Quercus trojana* woods (Italy and Greece)
41.9	Chesnut woods
41.1A × 42.17	Hellenic beech forests with *Abies borissi-regis*
41.1B	*Quercus frainetto* woods
42.A1	Cypress forests *(Acero-Cupression)*
44.17	*Salix alba* and *Populus alba* galleries
44.52	Riparian formations on intermittent Mediterranean water-courses with *Rhododendron ponticum, Salix* and others
44.7	Oriental plane woods *(Plantation orientalis)*
44.8	Thermo-Mediterranean riparian galleries *(Nerio-Tamariceteae)* and south-west Iberian Peninsula riparian galleries *(Securinegion tinctoriae)*

Mediterranean sclerophyllous forests

41.7C	Cretan *Quercus brachyphylla* forests
45.1	*Olea* and *Ceratonia* forests
45.2	*Quercus suber* forests
45.3	*Quercus ilex* forests
45.5	*Quercus macrolepis* forests
45.61 to 45.63	*Macaronesian laurel forests *(Laurus, Ocotea)*
45.7	*Palm groves of *Pheonix*
45.8	Forests of *Ilex acquifolium*

Alpine and subalpine coniferous forests

42.21 to 42.23	Acidophilous forests *(Vaccinio-Piceetea)*
42.31 and 42.32	Alpine forests with larch and *Pinus cembra*
42.4	*Pinus uncinata* forests (*on gypsum or limestone)

Mediterranean mountainous coniferous forests

42.14	*Appenine *Abies alba* and *Picea excelsa* forests
42.19	*Abies pinsapo* forests
42.61 to 42.66	*Mediterranean pine forests with endemic black pines
42.8	Mediterranean pine forests with endemic Mesogean pines, including *Pinus mugo* and *Pinus leucodermis*
42.9	Macaronesian pine forests (endemic)
42.A2 to 42.A5 and 42.A8	*Endemic Mediterranean forests with *Juniperus spp.*
42.A6	*Tetraclinis articulata* forests (Andalusia)
42.A71 to 42.A73	*Taxus baccata* woods

The shorter Annex V lists species of flora and fauna which, although of Community interest, may be taken and exploited "subject to management measures", such as surveillance, operation of closed seasons, the regulation of trade, and licensing systems. In certain cases, such as to prevent serious crop damage or in the interest of public health and safety, a derogation may be granted. It must be established, though, that there exists no satisfactory alternative and that the conservation status of the species is not threatened.

Table 8.5: Council Directive 92/43/EEC of 21 May 1992 on the conservation of natural habitats and of wild fauna and flora

ANNEX II

ANIMAL AND PLANT SPECIES OF COMMUNITY INTEREST WHOSE CONSERVATION REQUIRES THE DESIGNATION OF SPECIAL AREAS OF CONSERVATION

Interpretation

(a) Annex II follows on from Annex I for the establishment of a consistent network of special areas of conservation.

(b) The species listed in this Annex are indicated:

  – by the name of the species or subspecies, or

  – by the body of species belonging to a higher taxon or to a designated part of that taxon.

  The abbreviation 'spp.' after the name of a family or genus designates all the species belonging to that family or genus.

(c) *Symbols*
  An asterisk (*) before the name of a species indicates that the species is a priority species.

  Most species listed in this Annex are also listed in Annex IV.

  Where a species appears in this Annex but does not appear in either Annex IV or Annex V, the species name is followed by the symbol (o); where a species which appears in this Annex also appears in Annex V but does not appear in Annex IV, its name is followed by the symbol (V).

(A) *ANIMALS*

VERTEBRATES

MAMMALS

INSECTIVORA

Talpidae

  Galemys pyrenaicus

CHIROPTERA

Rhinolophidae

  Rhinolophus blasii
  Rhinolophus euryale
  Rhinolophus ferrumequinum
  Rhinolophus hipposideros
  Rhinolophus mehelyi

Vespertilionidae

  Barbastella barbastellus
  Miniopterus schreibersi
  Myotis bechsteini
  Myotis blythi

  Myotis capaccinii
  Myotis dasycneme
  Myotis emarginatus
  Myotis myotis

RODENTIA

Sciuridae

  Spermophilus citellus

Castoridae

  Castor fiber

Microtidae

  Microtus cabrerae
  *Microtus oeconomus arenicola

CARNIVORA

Canidae

Table 8.5 continued

*Canis lupus (Spanish populations: only those south of the Duero; Greek populations: only those south of the 39th parallel)

Ursidae

*Ursus arctos

Mustelidae

Lutra lutra
Mustela lutreola

Felidae

Lynx lynx
*Lynx pardina

Phocidae

Halichoerus grypus (V)

*Monachus monachus
Phoca vitulina (V)

ARTIODACTYLA

Cervidae

*Cervus elaphus corsicanus

Bovidae

Capra aegagrus (natural populations)
*Capra pyrenaica pyrenaica
Ovis ammon musimon (natural populations – Corsica and Sardinia)
Rupicapra rupicapra balcanica
*Rupicapra ornata

CETACEA

Tursiops truncatus
Phocoena phocoena

REPTILES

TESTUDINATA

Testudinidae

Testudo hermanni
Testudo graeca
Testudo marginata

Cheloniidae

*Caretta caretta

Emydidae

Emys orbicularis
Mauremys caspica
Mauremys leprosa

SAURIA

Lacertidae

Lacerta monticola
Lacerta schreiberi

Gallotia galloti insulanagae
*Gallotia simonyi
Podarcis lilfordi
Podarcis pityusensis

Scincidae

Chalcides occidentalis

Gekkonidae

Phyllodactylus europaeus

OPHIDIA

Colubridae

Elaphe quatuorlineata
Elaphe situla

Viperidae

*Vipera schweizeri
Vipera ursinii

Table 8.5 continued

AMPHIBIANS

CAUDATA

Salamandridae

Chioglossa lusitanica
Mertensiella luschani
*Salamandra salamandra aurorae
Salamandrina terdigitata
Triturus cristatus

Proteidae

Proteus anguinus

Plethodontidae

Speleomantes ambrosii
Speleomantes flavus
Speleomantes genei
Speleomantes imperialis

Speleomantes supramontes

ANURA

Discoglossidae

Bombina bombina
Bombina variegata
Discoglossus jeanneae
Discoglossus montalentii
Discoglossus sardus
*Alytes muletensis

Ranidae

Rana latastei

Pelobatidae

*Pelobates fuscus insubricus

FISH

PETROMYZONIFORMES

Petromyzonidae

Eudontomyzon spp. (o)
Lampetra fluviatilis (V)
Lampetra planeri (o)
Lethenteron zanandrai (V)
Petromyzon marinus (o)

ACIPENSERIFORMES

Acipenseridae

*Acipenser naccarii
*Acipenser sturio

ATHERINIFORMES

Cyprinodontidae

Aphanius iberus (o)
Aphanius fasciatus (o)
*Valencia hispanica

SALMONIFORMES

Salmonidae

Hucho hucho (natural populations) (V)
Salmo salar (only in fresh water) (V)
Salmo marmoradus (o)
Salmo macrostigma (o)

Coregonidae

*Coregonus oxyrhynchus (anadromous
    populations in certain sectors of the
    North Sea)

CYPRINIFORMES

Cyprinidae

Alburnus vulturius (o)
Alburnus albidus (o)
Anaecypris hispanica
Aspius aspius (o)
Barbus plebejus (V)
Barbus meridionalis (V)
Barbus capito (V)
Barbus comiza (V)
Chalcalburnus chalcoides (o)
Chondrostoma soetta (o)
Chondrostoma polylepis (o)
Chondrostoma genei (o)
Chondrostoma lusitanicum (o)
Chondrostoma toxostoma (o)
Gobio albipinnatus (o)
Gobia uranoscopus (o)
Iberocypris palaciosi (o)
*Ladigesocypris ghigii (o)
Leuciscus lucomonis (o)
Leuciscus souffia (o)
Phoxinellus spp. (o)
Rutilus pigus (o)
Rutilus rubilio (o)
Rutilus arcasii (o)
Rutilus macrolepidotus (o)
Rutilus lemmingii (o)
Rutilus friesii meidingeri (o)
Rutilus alburnoides (o)
Rhodeus sericeus amarus (o)
Scardinius graecus (o)

Table 8.5 continued

Cobitidae

Cobitis conspersa (o)
Cobitis larvata (o)
Cobitis trichonica (o)
Cobitis taenia (o)
Misgurnis fossilis (o)
Sabanejewia aurata (o)

PERCIFORMES

Percidae

Gymnocephalus schraetzer (V)
Zingel spp. [(o) except Zingel asper
and Zingel zingel (V)]

Gobiidae

Pomatoschistus canestrini (o)

Padogobius panizzai (o)
Padogobius nigricans (o)

CLUPEIFORMES

Clupeidae

Alosa spp. (V)

SCORPAENIFORMES

Cottidae

Cottus ferruginosus (o)
Cottus petiti (o)
Cottus gobio (o)

SILURIFORMES

Siluridae

Silurus aristotelis (V)

INVERTEBRATES

ARTHROPODS

CRUSTACEA

Decapoda

Austropotamobius pallipes (V)

INSECTA

Coleoptera

Buprestis splendens
*Carabus olympiae
Cerambyx cerdo
Cucujus cinnaberinus
Dytiscus latissimus
Graphoderus bilineatus
Limoniscus violaceus (o)
Lucanus cervus (o)
Morimus funereus (o)
*Osmoderma eremita
*Rosalia alpina

Lepidoptera

*Callimorpha quadripunctata (o)
Ceononympha oedippus
Erebia calcaria
Erebia christi
Eriogaster catax

Euphydryas aurinia (o)
Graellsia isabellae (V)
Hypodryas maturna
Lycaena dispar
Maculinea nausithous
Maculinea teleius
Melanagria arge
Papilio hospiton
Plebicula golgus

Mantodea

Apteromantis aptera

Odonata

Coenagrion hylas (o)
Coenagrion mercuriale (o)
Cordulegaster trinacriae
Gomphus graslinii
Leucorrhina pectoralis
Lindenia tetraphylla
Macromia splendens
Ophiogomphus cecilia
Oxygastra curtisii

Orthoptera

Baetica ustulata

Table 8.5 continued

MOLLUSCS

GASTROPODA

Caseolus calculus
Caseolus commixta
Caseolus sphaerula
Discula leacockiana
Discula tabellata
Discus defloratus
Discus guerinianus
Elona quimperiana
Geomalacus maculosus
Geomitra moniziana
Helix subplicata
Leiostyla abbreviata

Leiostyla cassida
Leiostyla corneocostata
Leiostyla gibba
Leiostyla lamellosa
Vertigo angustior (o)
Vertigo genesii (o)
Vertigo geyeri (o)
Vertigo moulinsiana (o)

BIVALVIA

Unionoida

Margaritifera margaritifera (V)
Unio crassus

(b) PLANTS

PTERIDOPHYTA

ASPLENIACEAE

Asplenium jahandiezii (Litard.) Rouy

BLECHNACEAE

Woodwardia radicans (L.) Sm.

DICKSONIACEAE

Culcita macrocarpa C. Presl.

DRYOPTERIDACEAE

*Dryopteris corleyi Fraser-Jenk.

HYMENOPHYLLACEAE

Trichomanes speciosum Willd.

ISOETACEAE

Isoetes boryana Durieu
Isoetes malinverniana Ces. & De Not.

MARSILEACEAE

Marsilea batardae Launert
Marsilea quadrifolia L.
Marsilea strigosa Willd.

OPHIOGLOSSACEAE

Botrychium simplex Hitchc.
Ophioglossum polyphyllum A. Braun

GYMNOSPERMAE

PINACEAE

*Abies nebrodensis (Lojac.) Mattei

ANGIOSPERMAE

ALISMATACEAE

Caldesia parnassifolia (L.) Parl.
Luronium natans (L.) Raf.

AMARYLLIDACEAE

Leucojum nicaeense Ard.
Narcissus asturiensis (Jordan(Pugsley
Narcissus calcicola Mendonça
Narcissus cyclamineus DC.
Narcissus fernandesii G. Pedro
Narcissus humilis (Cav.) Traub
*Narcissus nevadensis Pugsley
Narcissus pseudonarcissus L.
   subsp. nobilis (Haw.) A. Fernandes
Narcissus scaberulus Henriq.

Narcissus triandrus (Salisb.) D. A. Webb
   subsp. capax (Salisb.) D. A. Webb.
Narcissus viridiflorus Schousboe

BORAGINACEAE

*Anchusa crispa Viv.
*Lithodora nitida (H. Ern) R. Fernandes
Myosotis lusitanica Schuster
Myosotis rehsteineri Wartm.
Myosotis retusifolia R. Afonso
Omphalodes kuzinskyana Willk.
*Omphalodes littoralis Lehm.
Solenanthus albanicus (Degen & al.)
   Degen & Baldacci
*Symphytum cycladense Pawl.

Table 8.5 continued

CAMPANULACEAE

Asyneuma giganteum (Boiss.) Bornm.
*Campanula sabatia De Not.
*Jasiorea crispa (Pourret) Samp.
    subsp. serpentinica Pinto da Silva
Jasione lusitanica A. DC.

CARYOPHYLLACEAE

*Arenaria nevadensis Boiss. & Reuter
Arenaria provincialis Chater & Halliday
Dianthus cintranus Boiss. & Reuter
    subsp. cintranus Boiss. & Reuter
Dianthus marizii (Samp.) Samp.
Dianthus rupicola Biv.
*Gypsophila papillosa P. Porta
Herniaria algarvica Chaudri
Herniaria berlengiana (Chaudhri) Franco
*Herniaria latifolia Lapeyr.
    subsp. litardierei gamis
Herniaria maritima Link
Moehringia tommasinii Marches.
Petrocoptis grandiflora Rothm.
Petrocoptis montsiccina O. Bolos &
    Rivas Mart.
Petrocoptis pseudoviscosa Fernandez
    Casas
Silene cintrana Rothm.
*Silene hicesiae Brullo & Signorello
Silene hifacensis Rouy ex Willk.
*Silene holzmanii Heldr. ex Boiss.
Silene longicilia (Brot.) Otth.
Silene mariana Pau
*Silene orphanidis Boiss.
*Silene rothmaleri Pinto da Silva
*Silene velutina Pourret ex Loisel.

CHENOPODIACEAE

*Bassia saxicola (Guss.) A. J. Scott
*Kochia saxicola Guss.
*Salicornia veneta Pignatti & Lausi

CISTACEAE

Cistus palhinhae Ingram
Halimium verticillatum (Brot.) Sennen
Helianthemum alypoides Losa & Rivas
    Goday
Helianthemum caput-felis Boiss.
*Tuberaria major (Willk.) Pinto da Silva &
    Roseira

COMPOSITAE

*Anthemis glaberrima (Rech. f.) Greuter
*Arthemisia granatensis Boiss.
*Aster pyrenaeus Desf. ex DC.
*Aster sorrentinii (Tod) Lojac.

*Carduus myriacanthus Salzm. ex DC.
*Centaurea alba L.
    subsp. heldreichii (Halacsy) Dostal
*Centaurea alba L.
    subsp. princeps (Boiss. & Heldr.)
    Gugler
*Centaurea attica Nyman
    subsp. megarensis (Halacsy & Hayek)
    Dostal
*Centaurea balearica J. D. Rodriguez
*Centaurea borjae Valdes-Berm. & Rivas
    Goday
*Centaurea citricolor Font Quer
Centaurea corymbosa Pourret
Centaurea gadorensis G. Bianca
*Centaurea horrida Badaro
*Centaurea kalambakensis Freyn & Sint.
Centaurea kartschiana Scop.
*Centaurea lactiflora Halacsy
Centaurea micrantha Hoffmanns. & Link
    subsp. herminii (Rouy) Dostál
*Centaurea niederi Heldr.
*Centaurea peucedanifolia Boiss. & Orph.
*Centaurea pinnata Pau
Centaurea pulvinata (G. Bianca) G.
    Bianca
Centaurea rothmalerana (Arènes) Dostál
Centaurea vicentina Mariz
*Crepis crocifolia Boiss. & Heldr.
Crepis granatensis (Willk.) B. Bianca &
    M. Cueto
Erigeron frigidus Boiss. ex DC.
Hymenostemma pseudanthemis (Kunze)
    Willd.
*Jurinea cyanoides (l.) Reichenb.
*Jurinea fontqueri Cuatrec.
*Lamyropsis microcephala (Moris)
    Dittrich & Greuter
Leontodon microcephalus (Boiss. ex
    DC.) Boiss.
Leontodon boryi Boiss.
*Leontodon siculus (Guss.) Finch & Sell
Leuzea longifolia Hoffmanns. & Link
Ligularia sibirica (L.) Cass.
Santolina impressa Hoffmanns. & Link
Santolina semidentata Hoffmanns. &
    Link
*Senecio elodes Boiss. ex DC.
Senecio nevadensis Boiss. & Reuter

CONVOLVULACEAE

*Convolvulus argyrothamnus Greuter
*Convolvulus Fernandes Pinto da Silva &
    Teles

Table 8.5 continued

CRUCIFERAE

Alyssum pyrenaicum Lapeyr.
Arabis sadina (Samp.) P. Cout.
*Biscutella neustriaca Bonnet
Biscutella vincentina (Samp.) Rothm.
Boleum asperum (Pers.) Desvaux
Brassica glabrescents Poldini
Brassica insularis Moris
*Brassica macrocarpa Guss.
Coincya cintrana (P. Cout.) Pinto da Silva
*Cioncya rupestris Rouy
*Coronopus navasii Pau
Diplotaxis ibicensis (Pau) Gomez-Campo
*Diplotaxis siettiana Maire
Diplotaxis vicentina (P. Cout.) Rothm.
Erucastrum palustre (Pirona) Vis.
*Iberis arbuscula Runemark
Iberis procumbens Lange
   subsp. microcarpa Franco & Pinto da
   Silva
*Ionopsidium acaule (Desf.) Reichenb.
Ionopsidium savianum (Caruel) Ball ex
   Arcang.
Sisymbrium cavanillesianum Valdes &
   Castroviejo
Sisymbrium supinum L.

CYPERACEAE

*Carex panormitana Guss.
Eleocharis carniolica Koch

DIOSCOREACEAE

*Borderea chouardii (Gaussen) Heslot

DROSERACEAE

Aldrovanda vesiculosa L.

EUPHORBIACEAE

*Euphorbia margalidiana Kuhbier &
Lewejohann
Euphorbia transtagana Boiss.

GENTIANACEAE

*Centaurium rigualii Esteve Chueca
*Centaurium somedanum Lainz
Gentiana ligustica R. de Vilm. & Chopinet
Gentianella angelica (Pugsley) E. F.
   Warburg

GERANIACEAE

*Erodium astragaloides Boiss. & Reuter
Erodium paularense Fernandez-Gonzalez
   & Izco
*Erodium rupicola Boiss.

GRAMINEAE

Avenula hackelii (Henriq.) Holub
Bromus grossus Desf. ex DC.
Coleanthus subtilis (Tratt.) Seidl
Festuca brigantina (Markgr.-Dannenb.)
Markgr.-Dannenb.
Festuca duriotagana Franco & R. Afonso
Festuca elegans Boiss
Festuca henriguesii Hack.
Festuca sumilusitanica Franco &
   R. Afonso
Gaudinia hispanica Stace & Tutin
Holcus setiglumis Boiss. & Reuter
   subsp. duriensis Pinto da Silva
Micropyropsis tuberosa Romero – Zarco
   & Cabezudo
Pseudarrhenatherum pallens (Link)
   J. Holub
Puccinellia pungens (Pau) Paunero
*Stpa austroitalica Martinovsky
*Stipa bavarica Martinovsky & H. Scholz
*Stipa veneta Moraldo

GROSSULARIACEAE

*Ribes sardum Martelli

HYPERICACEAE

*Hypericum aciferum (Greuter)
N. K. B. Robson

JUNCACEAE

Juncus valvatus Link

LABIATAE

Dracocephalum austriacum L.
*Micromeria taygetea P. H. Davis
Nepeta dirphya (Boiss.) Heldr. ex Halacsy
*Nepeta sphaciotica P. H. Davis
Origanum dictamnus L.
Sideritis incana
   subsp. glauca (Cav.) Malagarriga
Sideritis javalambrensis Pau
Sideritis serrata Cav. ex Lag.
Teucrium lepicephalum Pau
Teucrium turredanum Losa & Rivas
   Goday
*Thymus camphoratus Hoffmanns. & Link
Thymus carnosus Boiss.
*Thymus cephalotos L.

LEGUMINOSAE

Anthyllis hystrix Cardona, Contandr. &
   E. Sierra
*Astragalus algarbiensis Coss. ex Bunge

Table 8.5 continued

*Astragalus aquilanus Anzalone
Astragalus centralpinus Braun-Blanquet
*Astragalus maritimus Moris
Astragalus tremolsianus Pau
*Astragalus verrucosus Moris
*Cytisus aeolicus Guss. ex Lindl.
Genista dorycnifolia Font Quer
Genista holopetala (Fleischm. ex Koch)
Baldacci
Melilotus segetalis (Brot.) Ser.
subsp. fallax Franco
*Ononis hackelii Lange
Trifolium saxatile All.
*Vicia bifoliolata J. D. Rodriguez

LENTIBULARIACEAE

Pinguicula nevadensis (Landb.) Casper

LILIACEAE

Allium grosii Font Quer
*Androcymbium rechingeri Greuter
*Asphodelus bento-rainhae P. Silva
Hyacinthoides vicentina (Hoffmanns. &
Link) Rothm.
*Muscari gussonei (Parl.) Tod

LINACEAE

*Linum muelleri Moris

LYTHRACEAE

*Lythrum flexuosum Lag.

MALVACEAE

Kosteletzkya pentacarpos (L.) Ledeb.

NAJADACEAE

Najas flexilis (Willd.) Rostk. &
W. L. Schmidt

ORCHIDACEAE

*Cephalanthera cucullata Boiss. & Heldr.
Cypripedium calceolus L.
Liparis loeselii (L.) Rich.
*Ophrys lunulata Parl.

PAEONIACEAE

Paeonia cambessedesii (Willk.) Willk.
Paeonia parnassica Tzanoudakis
Paeonia clusii F. C. Stern
subsp. rhodia (Stearn) Tzanoudakis

PALMAE

Phoenix theophrasti Greuter

PLANTAGINACEAE

Plantago algarbiensis Samp.
Plantago almogravensis Franco

PLUMBAGINACEAE

Armeria berlengensis Daveau
*Armeria helodes Martini & Pold
Armeria negleta Girard
Armeria pseudarmeria (Murray)
Mansfeld
*Armeria rouyana Daveau
Armeria soleirolii (Duby) Godron
Armeria velutina Welv. ex boiss. &
Reuter
Limonium dodartii (Girard) O. Kuntze
subsp. lusitanicum (Daveau) Franco
*Limonium insulare (Beg. & Landi)
Arrig. & Diana
Limonium lanceolatum (Hoffmanns. &
Link) Franco
Limonium multiflorum Erben
*Limonium pseudolaetum Arrig. & Diana
*Limonium strictissimum (Salzmann)
Arrig.

POLYGONACEAE

Polygonum praelongum Coode & Cullen
Rumex rupestris Le Gall

PRIMULACEAE

Androsace mathildae Levier
Androsace pyrenaica Lam.
*Primula apennina Widmer
Primula palinuri Petagna
Soldanella villosa Darracq.

RANUNCULACEAE

*Aconitum corsicum Gayer
Adonis distorta Ten.
Aquilegia bertolonii Schott
Aquilegia kitaibelii Schott
*Aquilegia pyrenaica D. C.
subsp. cazorlensis (Heywood) Galiano
*Consolida samia P. H. Davis
Pulsatilla patens (L.) Miller
*Ranumculus weyleri Mares

RESEDACEAE

*Reseda decursiva Forssk.

ROSACEAE

Potentilla delphinensis Gren. & Godron

Table 8.5 continued

RUBIACEAE

  *Galium litorale Guss.
  *Galium viridiflorum boiss. & Reuter

SALICACEAE

  Salix salvifolia Brot.
    subsp. australis Franco

SANTALACEAE

Thesium ebracteatum Hayne

SAXIFRAGACEAE

  Saxifraga berica (Beguinot) D. A. Webb
  Saxifraga florulenta Moretti
  Saxifraga hirculus L.
  Saxifraga tombeanensis Boiss. ex Engl.

SCROPHULARIACEAE

  Antirrhinum charidemi Lange
  Chaenorrhinum serpyllifolium (Lange)
    Lange subsp. lusitanicum R. Fernandes
  *Eupharasia genargentea (Feoli) Diana
  Euphrasia marchesettii Wettst. ex
    Marches.
  Linaria algaviana Chav
  Linaria continhou Valdés
  *Linaria ficalhoana Rouy
  Linaria flava (Poiret) Desf.
  *Linaria hellenica Turrill
  *Linaria ricardoi Cout.
  *Linaria tursica B. Valdes & Cabezudo
  Linaria tonzigii Lona
  Odontites granatensis Boiss.
  Verbascum litigiosum Samp.
  Veronica micrantha Hoffmanns. & Link
  *Veronica oetaea L.-A. Gustavson

SELAGINACEAE

  *Globularia stygia Orph. ex Boiss.

SOLANACEAE

  *Atropa baetica Willk.

THYMELAEACEAE

  Daphne petraea Leybold
  *Dayphe rodriguezii Texidor

ULMACEAE

  Zelkova abelicea (Lam.) Boiss.

UMBELLIFERAE

  *Angelica heterocarpa Lloyd
  Angelica palustris (Besser) Hoffm.
  *Apium bermejoi Llorens
  Apium repens (Jacq.) Lag.
  Athamanta cortiana Ferrarini
  *Bupleurum capillare Boiss. & Heldr.
  *Bupleurum kakiskalae Greuter
  Eryngium alpinum L.
  *Eryngium viviparum Gay
  *Laserpitium longiradium Boiss.
  *Naufraga balearica Constans & Cannon
  *Oenanthe conioides Lange
  Petagnia saniculifolia Guss.
  Rouya polygama (Desf.) Coincy
  *Seseli intricatum Boiss.
  Thorella verticillatinundata (Thore) Brig.

VALERIANACEAE

  Centranthus trinervis (Viv.) Beguinot

VIOLACEAE

  *Viola hispida Lam.
  Viola jaubertiana Mares & Vigineix

Lower plants
BRYOPHYTA

Bruchia vogesiaca Schwaegr. (o)
*Bryoerythrophyllum machadoanum
  (Sergio) M. Hill (o)
Buxbaumia viridis (Moug. ex Lam. &
  DC.) Brid. ex Moug. & Nestl. (o)
Dichelyma capillaceum (With.) Myr. (o)
Dicranum viride (Sull. & Lesq.) Londb.
  (o)
Distichophyllum carinatum Dix. &
  Nich. (o)
Drepanocladus vernicosus (Mitt.)
  Warnst. (o)
Jungermannia handelii (Schiffn.)
  Amak. (o)

Mannia triandra (Scop.) Grolle (o)
*Marsupella profunda Lindb. (o)
Meesia longiseta Hedw. (o)
Nothothylas orbicularis (Schwein.) Sull.
  (o)
Orthotrichum rogeri Brid. (o)
Petalophyllum ralfsii Nees & Goot. ex
  Lehm. (o)
Riccia briedleri Jur. ex Steph. (o)
Riella helicophylla (Mont.) Hook. (o)
Scapania massolongi (K. Muell.) K.
  Muell. (o)
Sphagnum pylaisii Brid. (o)
Tayloria rudolphiana (Gasrov)
  B. & G. (o)

Table 8.5 continued

SPECIES FOR MACARONESIA
PTERIDOPHYTA

HYMENOPHYLLACEAE

Hymenophyllum maderensis Gibby & Lovis

DRYOPTERIDACEAE

*Polystichum drepanum (Sw.) C. Presl.

ISOETACEAE

Isoetes azorica Durieu & Paiva

MARSILIACEAE

*Marsilea azorica Launert & Paiva

ANGIOSPERMAE

ASCLEPIADACEAE

Caralluma burchardii N. E. Brown
*Ceropegia chrysantha Svent.

BORAGINACEAE

Echium candicans L. fil.
*Echium gentianoides Webb & Coincy
Myosotis azorica H. C. Watson
Myosotis maritima Hochst. in Seub.

CAMPANULACEAE

*Azorina vidalii (H. C. Watson) Feer
Musschia aurea (L. f.) DC.
*Musschia wollastonii Lowe

CAPRIFOLIACEAE

*Sambucus palmensis Link

CARYOPHYLLACEAE

Spergularia azorica (Kindb.) Lebel

CELASTRACEAE

Maytenus umbellata (R. Br.) Mabb.

CHENOPODIACEAE

Beta patula Ait.

CISTACEAE

Cistus chinamadensis Banares & Romero
*Helianthemum bystropogophyllum Svent.

COMPOSITAE

Andryala crithmifolia Ait.
*Argyranthemum lidii Humphries
Argyranthemum thalassophylum (Svent.) Hump.
Argyranthemum winterii (Svent.) Humphries
*Atractylis arbuscula Svent. & Michaelis
Atractylis preauxiana Schultz.
Calendula maderensis DC.
Cheirolophus duranii (Burchard) Holub
Cheirolophus ghomerytus (Svent.) Holub

Cheirolophus junonianus (Svent.) Holub
Cheirolophus massonianus (Lowe) Hansen
Cirsium latifolium Lowe
Helichrysum gossypinum Webb
Helichrysum oligocephala (Svent. & Bzamw.)
*Lactuca watsoniana Trel.
*Onopordum nogalesii Svent.
*Onopordum carduelinum Bolle
*Pericallis hadrosoma Svent.
Phagnalon benettii Lowe
Stemmacantha cynaroides (Chr. Son. in Buch) Ditt
Sventenia bupleuroides Font Quer
*Tanacetum ptarmiciflorum Webb & Berth

CONVOLVULACEAE

*Convolvulus caput-medusae Lowe
*Convolvulus lopez-socasii Svent.
*Convolvulus massonii A. Dietr.

CRASSULACEAE

Aeonium gomeraense Praeger
Aeonium saundersii Bolle
Aichryson dumosum (Lowe) Praeg.
Monanthes wildpretii Banares & Scholz
Sedum brissemoretii Raymond-Hamet

CRUCIFERAE

*Crambe arborea Webb ex Christ
Crambe laevigata DC. ex Christ
*Crambe sventenii R. Petters ex Bramwell & Sund.
*Parolinia schizogynoides Svent.
Sinapidendron rupestre (Ait.) Lowe

CYPERACEAE

Carex malato-belizii Raymond

DIPSACACEAE

Scabiosa nitens Roemer & J. A. Schultes

Table 8.5 continued

ERICACEAE

Erica scoparia L.
subsp. azorica (Hochst.) D. A. Webb

EUPHORBIACEAE

*Euphorbia handiensis Burchard
Euphorbia lambii Svent.
Euphorbia stygiana H. C. Watson

GERANIACEAE

*Geranium maderense P. F. Yeo

GRAMINEAE

Deschampsia maderensis (Haeck. & Born.)
Phalaris maderensis (Menezes) Menezes

LABIATAE

*Sideritis cystosiphon Svent.
*Sideritis discolor (Webb ex de Noe) Bolle
Sideritis infernalis Bolle
Sideritis marmorea Bolle
Teucrium abutiloides L'Hér
Teucrium betonicum L'Hér

LEGUMINOSAE

*Anagyris latifolia Brouss. ex Willd.
Anthyllis lemanniana Lowe
*Dorycnium spectabile Webb & Berthel
*Lotus azoricus P. W. Ball
Lotus callis-viridis D. Bramwell & D. H.
Davis
*Lotus kunkelii (E. Cheuca)
D. Bramwell & al.
*Teline rosmarinifolia Webb & Berthel.
*Teline salsoloides Arco & Acebes.
Vicia dennesiana H. C. Watson

LILIACEAE

*Androcymbium psammophilum Svent.
Scilla maderensis Menezes
Semele maderensis Costa

LORANTHACEAE

Arceuthobium azoricum Wiens & Hawksw

MYRICACEAE

*Myrica rivas-martinezii Santos.

OLEACEAE

Jasminum azoricum L.
Picconia azorica (Tutin) Knobl.

ORCHIDACEAE

Goodyera macrophylla Lowe

PITTOSPORACEAE

*Pittosporum coriaceum Dryand. ex Ait.

PLANTAGINACEAE

Plantago malato-belizii Lawalree

PLUMBAGINACEAE

*Limonium arborescens (Brouss.) Kuntze
Limonium dendroides Svent.
(Limonium spectabile (Svent.) Kunkel &
Sunding
*Limonium sventenii Santos &
Fernandez Galvan

POLYGONACEAE

Rumex azoricus Rech. fil.

RHAMNACEAE

Frangula azorica Tutin

ROSACEAE

*Bencomia brachystachya Svent.
Bencomia sphaerocarpa Svent.
*Chamaemeles coriacea Lindl.
Dendriopterium pulidoi Svent.
Marcetella maderensis (Born.) Svent.
Prunus lusitanica L.
subsp. azorica (Mouillef.) Franco
Sorbus maderensis (Lowe) Docle

SANTALACEAE

Kunkeliella subsecculenta Kammer

SCROPHULARIACEAE

*Euphrasia azorica Wats
Euphrasia grandiflora Hochst. ex Seub.
*Isoplexis chalcantha Svent. &
O'Shanahan
Isoplexis isabelliana (Webb & Berthel.)
Masferrer
Odontites holliana (Lowe) Benth.
Sibthorpia peregrina L.

SELAGINACEAE

*Globularia ascanii D. Bramwell & Kunkel
*Globularia sarcophylla Svent.

SOLANACEAE

*Solanum lidii Sunding

Table 8.5 continued

UMBELLIFERAE

Ammi trifoliatum (H. C. Watson)
    Trelease
Bupleurum handiense (Bolle) Kunkel
Chaerophyllum azoricum Trelease
Ferula latipinna Santos

Melanoselinum decipiens (Schrader &
    Wendl) Hoffm.
Monizia edulis Lowe
Oenanthe divaricata (R. Br.) Mabb.
Sanicula azorica Guthnick ex Seub.

VIOLACEAE

Viola paradoxa Lowe

Lower plants

BRYOPHYTA

*Echinodium spinosum (Mitt.) Jur. (o)   *Thamnobryum fernandesii Sergio (o)

The directive also provides for the setting up of a coherent European ecological network of sites of Community significance: Natura 2000. The network will cover three types of site: sites listed in Annexes I and II, and the "Special Protection Areas" set aside for birds in accordance with the Wild Birds Directive. The aim is to maintain or restore to a favourable conservation status in the areas covered. Financial contributions to the network from Member States are calculated according to the extent to which the habitats listed in Annexes I and II are found on their territory.

The setting up of the network will involve a number of stages. In the first stage, by June 1995 the Member States must send the Commission a list of sites which are potentially of Community importance. Such sites can either be natural habitat types listed in Annex I or be the habitats of species listed in Annex II. The sites are chosen in accordance with criteria aimed at facilitating the identification of their relative conservation importance. In particular, Member States must indicate which sites contain priority habitats and species. If the Commission believes that a Member State has omitted to list a site containing a priority habitat type or species, it can initiate a consultation procedure with the Member State in question. If after six months the issue remains unresolved, the Commission can propose to the Council that the site be defined as being of Community importance, in which case the Council must approve the Commission's proposal by unanimity. Throughout the consultation procedure, the site remains protected.

In the second stage, the Commission, based on the 12 national lists and in conjunction with the Member States, produces a list of sites of Community importance. Criteria used in drawing up the list, contained in Stage 2 of Annex III of the directive, include the number of habitat types present, size of the site, and its national importance. Those Member States where more than 5% of national territory is defined as containing priority habitat types or species can request that the Annex III criteria be applied more flexibly in determining which sites are of Community importance. The final list must be adopted by the Commission by June 1998 after having been approved by qualified majority by a committee of Member State representatives.

The third stage involves the designation by the Member States concerned of the above sites as special areas of conservation or SACs. This must be done within six years with priority being accorded to those sites most threatened by destruction or degradation. Member States are obliged to set up the necessary conservation measures for SACs, including management plans and, where needed, undertake administrative, contractual or statutory steps.

Member States are obliged to protect all sites designated as being of Community importance, whether or not they have been classified as SACs. In particular, they must: take appropriate steps to avoid the deterioration of the habitats or disturbance of the species concerned; and subject to an impact assessment all plans or projects which are likely to have a significant effect on the sites but which are not directly connected to the management of the site. Approval for such projects must only be granted where it has been proven that they will not adversely affect the site. In addition, where it has been shown that such a project would indeed cause damage to the site but that for "reasons of overriding public interest" it must nevertheless be implemented, the Member State is obliged to take all measures necessary to ensure the overall coherence of Natura 2000. Where priority sites are concerned, approval may only be granted to damaging projects on the grounds of environmental improvements of primary importance or of human health or public safety. Otherwise, the Commission must first give its opinion on the project. The above obligations also apply to the Special Protection Areas (SPAs) contained in the 1979 Birds Directive.

In general terms, the Member States must monitor sites, giving special attention to priority sites, and ensure that planning and development policies promote sound management of landscape features which are of importance to wildlife. The directive also makes provision for the Commission to undertake periodic reviews of the extent to which Natura 2000 effectively contributes to the conservation of habitats and species.

Given the limited application of the "polluter pays" principle to nature conservation and that the financial burden of implementing the directive will be distributed unevenly between the Member States, reflecting the distribution of habitats and species themselves, the directive provides for Community co-financing to assist Member States with the costs involved. Such financial assistance is restricted, however, to maintaining or re-establishing favourable conservation status at priority sites.

Finally, the Member States and the Commission are to promote scientific research and the exchange of information. Member States must provide the Commission with reports on implementation at six-year intervals. In turn, the Commission is obliged to produce and publish a composite report within two years. Amendments to Annex IV require unanimity in Council, those to the other annexes qualified majority.

V. THE PROTECTION OF ANIMALS

1. The protection of animals used for experimental purposes

(a) The 1986 directive

On 20 December 1985 the Commission sent the Council a proposal for a directive on the protection of animals used for experimental or other scientific purposes. The proposal owed its origin principally to pressures originating in the European

Parliament and to the commitments given by the Commission in the context of parliamentary discussion of environmental and animal welfare issues. The proposal aimed to integrate into the framework of the Community rules, the principles and objectives of the Council of Europe Convention on the Protection of Vertebrate Animals, in order to ensure an integral and coherent application of the provisions of this convention in all the Member States. It also included some new elements which went beyond the provisions of the convention and which would provide additional guarantees for the protection of the animals.

The Commission based itself mainly on the following principles:

- to define and limit clearly the purposes of scientific research experiments;
- to reduce to a minimum the number of animals used;
- to reduce the degree of suffering inflicted on the animals;
- to prohibit the use of endangered animals and species;
- to avoid the unnecessary duplication of experiments, and to encourage the mutual recognition of procedures;
- to involve only persons considered to be competent to perform the experiments.

The Council adopted this directive (86/278/EEC) as well as the comprehensive technical annexes on 24 November 1986.[33] It has, however, somewhat limited the effect of some of the provisions proposed by the Commission, for example the principle of prior authorization of experiments, and the list of the different objectives for which experiments can be carried out on vertebrate animals (with regard to the latter, see the Resolution which follows).

The directive, first, prohibits in principle experiments carried out on animals belonging to the endangered species in the Washington Convention and in the Community regulation of 1982 (see p. 306). With regard to the care and accommodation of the animals, Member States must ensure that laboratory animals are provided with appropriate housing, food, water and care, and are checked daily. Each Member State must designate a competent authority to verify that the provisions of the directive are properly carried out.

The directive sets out a number of conditions and requirements to be respected in the carrying out of the experiments, for example, with regard to the choice of species which should in principle be bred animals; the need to use general or local anaesthetic; the re-use of the animals; whether or not the animal should be kept alive at the end of the experiment, etc. It also makes a number of provisions concerning the breeding establishments supplying the animals. These must be approved by the control authority and a record must be kept of the number and the species of the animals sold or supplied. The animals must be provided with an identification mark, mainly to avoid stray animals (especially dogs and cats) being used in experiments.

Finally, the directive attaches great importance to the use of trained and qualified staff, both for the carrying out of the experiments, and for the checking and management of the supplying breeding establishment. Equally it urges the Member States to recognize the validity of experiments carried out in other Member States, in order to avoid any unnecessary duplication of experiments. Every three years, Member States must inform the Commission of measures taken to implement the directive. On the basis of this information, the Commission will prepare a report for the Council and the European Parliament.

33 OJ No L 358 of 18/12/86.

(b)   The 1986 Resolution of the Member States on the purpose of experiments using animals[34]

On 24 November 1986 the Member States meeting within the Council also adopted a Resolution in which they undertake not to authorize the use of animals for experiments, except for the following purposes: the prevention of disease; the protection of the environment; scientific research; education; forensic enquiries. Moreover, since these experiments would not be covered by the directive of 24 November 1986, the Member States undertake to apply rules which will be no less stringent than those fixed by the directive.

Questions of competence lay behind the adoption of the above resolution. The directive was based on Article 100. Though there were clear commercial implications in animal testing and possible distortions of competition, some Member States were reluctant to admit that the Community had a general competence in this field.

2.   The 1991 proposal for a zoo directive

The 1989 Work Programme for the Commission stated that: "the Commission will propose in the course of the year, standards for the protection of animals in zoos". In making its proposal for a Council directive laying down minimum standards for the keeping of animals in zoos,[35] the Commission estimated that there were over a thousand zoos in the European Community, exhibiting to the public a wide variety of exotic animals. Collections varied considerably, not only between Member States, but also from one zoo to another: some were public, some private. Some are professionally run with adequate resources, others lack staff and experience.

The last 20 years, the Commission argued, had seen a steady accumulation of information and experience on the basic requirements of wild animals kept in captivity. As a consequence there was now sufficient knowledge available for all European zoos to be able to provide at least a minimum degree of necessary care and accommodation in order to ensure that their animals have the correct nutrition, veterinary attention and social conditions in which to express their most fundamental behavioural and physiological needs.

Legislation on the keeping of animals in zoos varied significantly from one Member State to the next. Countries with specific legislation on zoos, such as Denmark, France, the United Kingdom and Belgium, required that they be registered with a competent authority in order to operate and zoos were therefore subject to a series of conditions spanning the whole of zoo management, including animal welfare and public safety aspects. Many Member States also imposed further restrictions on the granting of state subsidies to zoos in view of their essentially commercial nature.

The variation in national laws regarding zoos had many potentially negative consequences. Not only are wild animals kept in captivity subject to different conditions but international efforts for conserving threatened species might also be jeopardized as a result.

The Commission's proposal of 30 August 1991 defines what is meant by the term zoo and establishes measures which Member States must take to ensure that animals kept in zoos are adequately housed and pose no danger to the public. As a result of

[34]   OJ No C 331 of 23/12/86.
[35]   COM (91) 177 final of 30/8/91, OJ C 249/14 of 24/9/91.

widely differing standards in the various Member States, the proposal sets down standards of safety, record keeping, staffing and inspection by independent authorities. It requires all zoos to be licensed by a competent authority. In addition, the proposal calls upon Member States to encourage zoos to promote conservation and public education. Under the proposal, Member States would be required to submit regular reports to the Commission regarding the implementation of the directive.

The zoos directive proved to be a casualty of the debate over "subsidiarity" which took place in the context of the Maastricht Treaty preparations. With the specific inclusion of the subsidiarity principle in Maastricht (see p. 496), the Commission was under pressure to trawl for proposals which could be withdrawn. The zoos directive seemed a plausible candidate particularly in view of the fact that the Commissioner, Carlo Ripa di Meana, who had fought so long and hard for it inside the Commission, had now returned to Italy. In the event, pressure from the European Parliament ensured that the Commission's proposal, rather than being completely withdrawn, was converted into a recommendation. Even in this attenuated form, the proposal still awaits adoption by the Council.

VI.   FUTURE ACTION

The 5th Action Programme observes that, in spite of measures taken by international agencies, the Community and individual Member States, the major threats to nature conservation and maintenance of biodiversity persist and in some areas are increasing. Habitats are converted to human uses and the species that occupy them are made homeless. Much of the development which has occurred and is continuing to take place is in contradiction to mankind's fundamental desire to live in harmony with nature and to enjoy and derive pleasure from it.

The 5th Programme argues that the case for preserving nature goes beyond this: in the first place, it is a necessary element in the overall maintenance of the ecological balance; furthermore, nature provides an invaluable genetic bank which is essential to medical, biological, agricultural and other scientific progress.

For most species of flora and fauna the splitting up and isolation of habitats, mainly because of infrastructural works (including high-tension electricity cables), pose the greatest threat. If habitats become too small and if connecting zones between them are blocked or lost, essential migration may be precluded, with consequential extinction in the case of some species.

The Community strategy will be aimed at the maintenance of European biodiversity primarily through sustainable land management in and around habitats of Community and wider importance. An interrelated network of habitats, based on the concept of Natura 2000 as indicated in the Habitats Directive (see p. 309), should be created through the restoration and maintenance of habitats themselves and of corridors between them. The creation and maintenance of this network will be very much dependent on how carefully transport, agricultural and tourist policies are shaped and pursued in the future.

The programme sets three targets for the period up to 2000: the maintenance or restoration of natural habitats and species of wild fauna and flora at a favourable conservation status; the creation of a coherent European network of protected sites; and the strict control of abuse and trade in wild species. To achieve these

Table 8.6: The fifth environment action programme: diagram on nature conservation

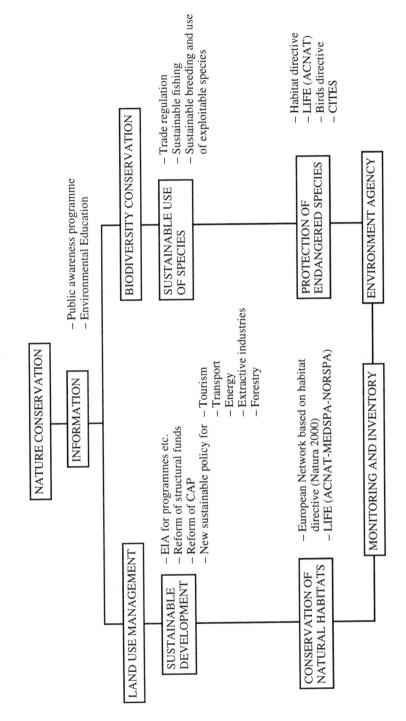

objectives, the programme lists a number of existing instruments and measures, such as reform of the CAP; the updating of the 1979 Birds Directive; CITES; the Habitats Directive; and the environmental assessment of plans and programmes.

Table 8.6 outlines the strategic approach to the protection of nature and biodiversity.

Table 8.7 sets out the targets for 2000 and the instruments necessary in the short run to have the Network and the surveillance of European biodiversity partly operational in the year 2000.

Table 8.7: The fifth environment action programme: nature and biodiversity

Targets up to 2000	Instruments	Time-frame	Sectors/actors
Maintenance of biodiversity through sustainable development and management in and around natural habitats of European and global value: and through control of use and trade of wild species			Agriculture Forestry, Fisheries Transport Tourism Energy Industry
1. Maintenance or restoration of natural habitats and species of wild fauna and flora at a favourable conservation status	* Habitat directive	1992 ⇒	EC, MS, LAs, NGOs, Farmers
	* Updating of Directive 79/409/EED on wild birds	ongoing	EC + MS + LAs
2. Creation of a coherent European network of protected sites	* setting of criteria for identification of habitats, buffer zones and migratory corridors	1992–1993	Id + NGOs + Farmers
– Natura 2000: flagship programmes of carefully selected and managed natural areas with the EC.	* action programmes for the efficient conservation and monitoring of the sites designed for Natura 2000	1991–1993	Id
3. Strict control of abuse and trade of wild species.	* Iventory, monitoring systems, and recovery plans for endangered and overexploited species	1991–1992	Id

Table 8.7 continued

Targets up to 2000	Instruments	Time-frame	Sectors/actors
	* regulations concerning Internal and International trade of endangered species	1992 ⇒	Id + UNEP (CITES)
	* International Conventions (Biodiversity, Alpes, Regional agreements under Bonn Convention)	1992 ⇒	*MS* + EC + UNEP (CITES + BONN CONVENTION)
	* Reform of CAP (notably zonal programmes for support of environmentally friendly agricultural practices)	ongoing	*EC, MS*, LAs
	* Environmental assessment of plans and programmes	1995 ⇒	*MS, LAs*, EC
	* Programmes for promotion of public awareness	1992 ⇒	Id + *NGOs*
	* Measures to maintain and protect forests	progressive	EC, *MS* + forest-owners

Part Two

Specific Aspects of Community Environment Policy

Chapter 9

Preventive Action

Part One: Financial Instruments

I. THE 1984 REGULATION CREATING A "MINI-FUND" FOR THE ENVIRONMENT

On 13 January 1983 the Commission sent the Council a proposal for a regulation intended to initiate financial Community actions in the area of the environment, i.e. to lay the foundations for a European Fund for the environment, following the example of other funds already existing in the Community.

In presenting this proposal the Commission was working on the basis that standardizing the legislative action cannot in itself constitute the only face of a truly dynamic environmental protection policy. Such a policy should in fact be of an increasingly preventive nature and should consequently have recourse to methods and actions other than the approximation of laws and regulations.

The Commission received decisive support from the European Parliament in achieving this. In 1982 the Parliament took an important budgetary initiative by introducing four new Community budget lines intended to support financially certain actions in favour of environmental protection. Strengthened by the Parliament's political support and by the experience gained since 1982 in the use of these budget lines, the Commission suggested in its proposal for a regulation that the Council go beyond individual actions and institute a financial instrument involving two specific budget lines, namely, clean technologies and the protection of certain sensitive zones of Community interest. On 28 June 1984 the Council adopted this regulation on actions by the Community in favour of the environment, or "ACE Regulation", for a period of just three years.[1]

The conditions retained by the Council were considerably more restrictive than those proposed by the Commission. The fields of application selected by the Council as being eligible for financial support from the Community are shown in the following table:

[1] OJ No L 176 of 3/7/84.

Table 9.1

(a) demonstration projects aimed at developing new "clean" technologies, i.e. technologies which cause little or no pollution and which may also be more economical in the use of natural resources, in the following industrial sectors:

Surface treatments

- Reduction of the amount of surface scouring solvents (in particular chlorinated solvents) in effluent;
- lacquering processes producing little residue and recovery of solvents used in industrial lacquering processes;
- galvanizing and cadmium-plating processes producing little residue, designed to avoid mixed metal hydroxide sludge (special waste);
- replacement of cadmium in surface treatment processes.

Leather industry

- Reduction of the amount of chromium salts and organic residues (mainly fats) in effluent by altering tanning processes;
- processing of solid waste.

Textile industry

- Reduction of the amount of not-easily degradable chemicals used in textile finishing processes (de-sizing, bleaching, dyeing, preparation for printing and dressing) which are contained in effluent; use of non-polluting additives.

Cellulose and paper industries

- Reduction of effluent by developing zero-discharge layouts for these industries;
- pulp-bleaching processes causing less pollution;
- cellulose disintegration processes causing little pollution;
- development of de-inking processes.

Mining and quarrying

- Recovery and processing of wastes.

Chemical industry

- Alteration or replacement of processes, in order to reduce pollution caused by production residues containing chlorinated hydrocarbons produced during processes using organo-chlorine compounds;
- development of sulphurizing processes producing little residue in the organic chemistry sector, the waste products and effluent of which are highly dangerous;
- recovery and processing of solvents.

Agri-food industry

- Reduction of effluent pollution by perfecting processes using zero-discharge layouts, for example, in sugar refineries and oil mills and in the manufacture of margarine;
- knackers' yards;
- reduction of the amount of ammonium and ammonia in effluent processing and recovery of by-products and waste products of the agri-food industries.

(b) demonstration projects aimed at developing new techniques and methods for measuring and monitoring the quality of the natural environment;

(c) projects providing an incentive and aimed at contributing towards the maintenance or re-establishment of seriously threatened biotopes which are the habitat of endangered species and are of particular importance to the Community, under the 1979 directive on the conservation of wild birds (see p. 237).

The financial provisions made by the regulation were the following:

- the global funds came to a total of 13 million Ecu for the three years 1984/1985/1986, 6.5 million Ecu being intended for the "clean technologies" and "measuring techniques" sectors, and 6.5 million Ecu for the "bird biotopes" sector;
- the financial support from the Community could comprise a maximum of 30% of the cost of the project for the first two sectors, and 50% for the third sector.

For the selection and management of projects the Commission was obliged to refer to an advisory committee of representatives of the Member States.

Moreover, the regulation stipulated that the Commission's decision on whether to grant or refuse Community financial support applied upon expiry of a period of 20 working days, if no Member States had referred the matter to the Council within that period. Where the matter was referred to the Council, the latter had to take a decision on the Commission's decision by a qualified majority within 40 working days.

Since the 1984 regulation was due to run out in 1987, on 30 December 1986 the Commission sent the Council and the Parliament a new proposal[2] intended to extend for an unlimited period these Community financial actions in the area of the environment, while widening the field of application and introducing more flexibility.

The Council agreed to the proposal at the meeting of environment ministers on 21–22 May 1987. The main features of the agreement were as follows:

1. The regulation would run for four years.
2. The regulation would specify that the sum considered necessary for that period is 24 million Ecu. That amount could be reviewed after one year on the basis of a Commission proposal and on the basis of a report on the experience gained. The appropriations would be entered in the general budget of the European Communities.
3. In the third year, the Council, acting unanimously on a Commission proposal, would decide whether to extend and adapt the regulation.
4. The scope of the regulation would cover:
   (a) demonstration projects aimed at developing new clean technologies, i.e. technologies which cause little or no pollution and which may also be more economical in the use of natural resources;
   (b) demonstration projects aimed at developing techniques for recycling and re-using waste, including waste water;
   (c) demonstration projects aimed at developing techniques for locating and restoring sites contaminated by hazardous wastes or hazardous substances;
   (d) demonstration projects aimed at developing new techniques and methods for measuring and monitoring the quality of the natural environment;
   (e) projects providing an incentive and aimed at contributing towards the maintenance or re-establishment of seriously threatened biotopes which are the habitat of endangered species and are of particular importance to the Community, under Directive 79/409/EEC;
   (f) projects providing an incentive and aimed at contributing towards the protection or re-establishment of land threatened or damaged by fire, erosion and desertification.

---

[2] OJ No C 18 of 24/1/87.

5. The rate of the Community's contribution to the measures financed under this regulation would not exceed:
   - 30% for projects covered by Article 1(1)(a), (b) and (c) (clean technologies, waste recycling/re-use techniques, locating and restoring contaminated sites);
   - 50% for other projects;
   - 75%, exceptionally, in the case of projects covered by Article 1(1)(e) provided they are related to species in danger of extinction in the Community.
6. The management arrangements would be in accordance with those provided for in the existing regulation.

The proposal was finally adopted by the Council on 23 July 1987 as Council Regulation 2242/87/EEC of 23 July 1987, on action by the Community relating to the environment.[3] The ACE programme ran until 30 July 1991.

II. REGULATION ON ACTION BY THE COMMUNITY RELATING TO NATURE CONSERVATION (ACNAT)

ACNAT was proposed partly as a replacement for ACE, partly because during discussions on the Habitats Directive it became clear that agreement would not be reached unless financial arrangements to assist implementation were resolved at the same time. The regulation (EEC No 3907/91) was adopted by the Council on 19 December 1991 with funding established at a level of 50 million Ecu over two years.[4]

The purpose of ACNAT was to make Community funding available at a rate of 50% and, in certain circumstances, at a rate of 75% in order to help maintain or re-establish seriously threatened habitats of Community importance, or for measures to re-establish or conserve endangered species under the Birds Directive (79/409/EEC) or the Habitats Directive (92/43/EEC). The regulation was to apply initially for two years during which period the Commission would be obliged to submit an annual report on implementation to the European Parliament, the Council and the Economic and Social Committee. Funding decisions would be made by the Commission upon the advice of an Advisory Committee made up of representatives of the Member States. In contrast to the ACE Regulation, the Commission would not be required to communicate its decisions to the European Parliament, Council or Member States before they entered into effect.

This regulation came about when it did as a result of the Member States' position on the proposal presented by the Commission on 16 August 1988 for a directive on the protection of natural and semi-natural habitats and wild fauna and flora. Despite a generally positive position on the part of the Member States, most of them argued that the successful implementation of such a directive would depend on the availability of adequate financial resources at Community level. Until then, the Commission had planned to present a financial proposal for the implementation measures after adoption of the Habitats Directive. Instead, it found itself obliged to come forward with measures covering the biotopes area of the ACE Regulation and the Species area. In order to meet the concerns expressed by the Member States

---

[3] OJ No L 207 of 29/7/87.
[4] OJ No L 370 of 31/12/91.

it was felt necessary to create a specific instrument concerning Community actions for nature protection. The finance available under such an instrument should allow for Community support to be given to the most urgent projects.

There was general agreement that the actions carried out under Regulations 1872/84 and 2242/87 had made an important contribution to the maintenance of a number of biotopes of major importance for the conservation of birds in the Community. However, the financial means available had been inadequate compared to the levels of demands. For example, 1987–1988 requests covered five times the amount available for the total period covered by the regulation.

Extending the field of application to cover different types of species and habitat in the new directive made it essential to provide for increased funds. At the same time, the speed of economic growth, notably in the richest regions as far as genetic diversity is concerned, made the need for action in the area of conservation still more urgent in order to avoid the depletion of European natural heritage.

In the case of agricultural or forest areas, efforts would be made to harmonize the interventions made with the possibilities offered by Regulations 797/85 (Article 19: environmentally sensitive areas) and 3529/86 (protection of forests against fires).

Given the two totally different types of action financed under the previous ACE Regulation (A: demonstration projects for which support could be given to any group or individual on the basis of calls for tender; B: incitation projects for which support could be given to Member States at their request at any time) – involving different evaluation procedures and models – it was felt wise to abandon this approach when extending the regulation to cover biotopes and species of wild fauna and flora and to replace it by an independent regulation allowing for Community action (and financial support) for the conservation of nature.

III. ACTIONS FOR THE PROTECTION OF THE ENVIRONMENT IN THE MEDITERRANEAN BASIN (MEDSPA)

1. Commission Communication of 23 April 1984

On 23 April 1984 the Commission sent the Council a Communication on the protection of the environment in the Mediterranean basin.[5] In it, the Commission announced its intention to carry out, over a period of five years, a series of specific actions with a view to contributing to the setting up of a programme for the protection of the environment in the Mediterranean basin.

The field of application of these actions was to cover the whole of the Mediterranean basin, including regions both within and outside the Community.

Apart from the particular importance which the Community attaches to the Mediterranean region from the economic, political, historic and cultural points of view, it should be noted that the Council, when adopting the 3rd Environmental Action Programme (1982–1986) had considered environmental protection in this region to be a priority area. Ecologically speaking, the Mediterranean is indeed subject to a variety of demands and pressures, due in particular to the demographic density of its shores, the growing industrialization of its coasts, the development of tourism, and the considerable amount of maritime traffic. These activities often

---

[5] OJ No C 133 of 24/5/84.

result in microbiological pollution due to the discharge of waste waters coming from built-up areas, in industrial pollution, and in pollution by hydrocarbons. Often soil erosion and the progressive destruction of wildlife are added to this pollution.

In order to remedy this situation, the Commission made provision for the undertaking of a series of Community actions intended to assist in the solving of the priority problems of the region. These actions were grouped together under the "action plan for the protection of the environment in the Mediterranean" (MEDSPA). This programme was a complement to the so-called "IMP" programmes (Integrated Mediterranean Programmes)[6] which aimed mainly at the economic development of the Mediterranean regions of the Community, particularly with regard to the adaptation of these regions to the entry into the Community, of Spain, Greece and Portugal, and also to the different actions carried out in the framework of the Convention of Barcelona on the protection of the Mediterranean Sea against pollution (see pp. 405ff).

As far as the methods and procedures of the MEDSPA action plan were concerned, the Commission envisaged a financial allowance, under the general budget of the Community, of the order of 5 million Ecu spread over a period of five years. The annual total was determined by the joint budgetary authority of the Council and Parliament. In order to assist the Commission in implementing the action plan, it set up an advisory committee, consisting of experts on the Mediterranean environment. Among the priority tasks of this committee was the establishment of a data bank including a list of all the existing projects, intended to avoid any unnecessary overlap with other actions.

The areas of action covered by the MEDSPA plan mainly concerned the problems of water resources and sea pollution, and to a lesser extent the problems of urban and industrial waste and the rational management of space. Among these areas the Commission set out to determine, in consultation with the committee of experts, a certain number of specific projects, which would be of an essentially pilot nature and which would have a public impact. The projects were carried out in close collaboration with the Member States concerned and were only financed by the Commission up to a certain percentage (generally 50% of the cost). The first projects were selected in 1986 and started from 1987 onwards.

It should be noted that the Parliament indicated its support for the MEDSPA plan proposed by the Commission, while the Council did not take a position on it, feeling that the plan falls more into the Commission's general competences in the area of management and execution.

2.   Council Regulation (EEC) No 563/91 of 4 March 1991 on action by the Community for the protection of the environment in the Mediterranean region (MEDSPA)

The MEDSPA regulation adopted by the Council (EEC No 563/91) on 4 March 1991 follows on from the 1987 Commission strategy and action plan for the protection of the environment in the Mediterranean region.[7]

---

[6] IMP = Integrated Mediterranean Programmes. These programmes were adopted by the Council on 23 July 1985 and had their own budget of 1.6 billion Ecu over a period of seven years (OJ No L 197 of 27/7/85).

[7] OJ No L 63 of 9/3/91.

It covers the whole of the Mediterranean region, both within and outside the Community, as well as the Spanish and Portuguese territories of the Iberian Peninsula south of the river Tagus and not on the Mediterranean coast. The initial phase of the MEDSPA programme was to run for five years starting from 9 March 1991. In 1994, the Commission was to submit an assessment report to the Council, accompanied by proposals for priority measures for a second five-year phase.

The objectives of MEDSPA were to increase efforts to protect and improve the quality of the environment and strengthen the effectiveness of Community Environment Policy in the region concerned; to encourage the integration of the environmental dimension into other areas of Community policy; to increase cooperation and coordination of environmental protection in the region concerned by integrating Community action and the operations carried out at regional, national and international level; and to encourage appropriate technology transfer to protect the Mediterranean environment.

The initial amount allocated for the execution of the MEDSPA programme during the first two years was 25 million Ecu. Priority measures for the first five years of the programme appear in Annex I of the regulation. These include, for the Community:

Table 9.2: Council Regulation (EEC) No 563/91 of 4 March 1991 on action by the Community for the protection of the environment in the Mediterranean region (medspa)

ANNEX

MEDSPA ACTION

1. Priority measures eligible under this Regulation

   A. Action in the Community
      - for coastal towns with fewer than 100 000 inhabitants and small islands: collection, treatment, storage and disposal of waste water and solid waste,
      - collection, treatment, storage, recycling and disposal of sewage sludge and toxic and dangerous waste,
      - treatment of water from ships' tanks containing residues of oil and other chemicals,
      - integrated management of biotopes of Community interest in coastal regions,
      - protection of soil threatened or degraded by fire or desertification; protection of land against coastal erosion.

   B. Action in non-Community Mediterranean countries
      - help with the establishment of the requisite environmental administrative structures,
      - technical assistance required for the establishment of environmental policies and action programmes.

2. Operations to deal with a problem likely, within a short time, to give rise to a lasting change in the ecological conditions in the area concerned may also be regarded as priority measures.

- action for small coastal towns and islands in the area of the collection, treatment, storage and disposal of waste water and solid waste;
- collection, treatment, storage and disposal of sewage sludge and toxic and dangerous waste;
- treatment of water from ships' tanks;
- integrated management of coastal biotopes of Community interest;
- protection of soil at risk from fire, desertification or coastal erosion.

Priority action in non-Community countries includes help with setting up appropriate administrative structures, as well as technical assistance with the establishment of environment policies and programmes. In addition, provision is made for actions needed to deal with particularly urgent ecological problems.

According to the regulation, the Community can contribute up to 50% of the total cost of public investment projects and pilot or demonstration schemes; a maximum of 30% in the case of private investment projects for non-commercial purposes, and 100% in the case of information and public awareness raising campaigns and for measures implemented on the initiative of the Commission itself. The Commission is assisted in the execution of the programme by a management committee composed of representatives of the Member States.

IV.   NORSPA – SPECIFIC ACTION TO PROTECT THE ENVIRONMENT IN THE COASTAL AREAS AND COASTAL WATERS OF THE IRISH SEA, NORTH SEA, BALTIC SEA AND NORTH-EAST ATLANTIC

The general improvement of the aquatic environment, and in particular of the North Sea and Mediterranean, was one of the priority areas of the 4th Environmental Action Programme.

In January 1991 the Commission sent the Council a proposal for a regulation on the protection of the Community's northern seas.

The NORSPA proposal was seen as completing the action started with MEDSPA – thus permitting the protection of all the marine and coastal areas of the Community, and intervention in favour of particularly sensitive and threatened areas such as the North and Baltic Seas.

It proposed using Community funds in two five-year phases to promote certain measures in targeted sectors and was designed to reinforce and supplement existing Community financial instruments, especially the programmes of regional actions to protect the environment (ENVIREG), the PHARE programme for measures in East European countries and the Structural Funds. Projects receiving funds from NORSPA, however, would not be obtaining funding from these other programmes as well.

Aware of the particular environmental problems of certain seas, the European Parliament allocated 2 million Ecu in 1989 and 1990 respectively to allow for the launch of a number of demonstration and stimulation projects in the zones concerned. The Council had also underlined on several occasions the need to take urgent action to prevent pollution of the marine environment and to make global improvements in water quality in the Community.

The Rhodes Council Declaration of December 1988 stressed the need for particular attention to be given to the serious environmental problems facing the marine and coastal areas of the Community. In 1984, 1987 and 1990 the Ministers responsible for the environmental protection of the North Sea and the watercourses running into it, met to define a common action to strengthen the environmental protection of that sea. The third International North Sea Conference which took place in The Hague on 7–8 March 1990 resulted in the adoption by the participants of a number of concrete measures – NORSPA was part of the Community response to this effort.

NORSPA's aim was to put into place a mechanism which allows for full account to be taken of pollution problems and the need for increased protection of coastal areas and waters in the regions targeted. Its specific objectives were to intensify the efforts already being made in environmental protection and improvement in the areas concerned; to strengthen the effectiveness of Community actions covering the environment in those areas under other policy sectors; to increase cooperation between countries bordering the areas concerned by integrating Community actions with operations run at local, national and international levels; and to promote the development and use of new technologies.

NORSPA measures are divided between action within the EC and that under-taken in littoral third countries in the sea areas covered. Within the Community, a range of measures would be eligible for support: action to reduce nutrient input to coastal areas, to reduce inputs of dangerous substances via rivers, estuaries and the atmosphere, as well as from dumping and pollution from ships and offshore instal-lations, and measures to accelerate the application of emission standards from industrial point sources.

Suitable habitat management measures and action to reduce or limit coastal erosion were also eligible for support. In third countries eligible measures were limited to cooperation and exchange of experience, including transfer of clean or low-emission technologies between seaboard states, and technical assistance to set up environmental action programmes and policies.

Funding could be used for capital grants towards investment, financial contribu-tions towards demonstration or pilot projects, or measures to raise awareness and provide incentives. NORSPA could cover up to 50% of costs in the case of public investments and 30% in the case of private investments. The Commission is assisted by the same Consultative Committee as manages the MEDSPA programme.

NORSPA was adopted by the Council on 19 December 1991 (EEC Regulation No 3908/91).[8] During its first phase (to 31 December 1992) NORSPA funding was set at 16.5 million. In adopting NORSPA, the Council recognized that the regula-tion would need subsequently to be incorporated into LIFE (see following section) when the Council had concluded its deliberation on that particular proposal.

V. REGULATION ESTABLISHING A FINANCIAL INSTRUMENT FOR THE ENVIRONMENT ("LIFE")

In 31 January 1991 the Commission published proposals for a single all-embracing financial instrument for the environment ("LIFE"). The instrument would subsume the other specific funds (ACNAT, MEDSPA, NORSPA), and would also allow the

---

[8] OJ No L 377 of 31/12/91.

Table 9.3: Council Regulation (EEC) No 3908/91 of 19 December 1991 on Community action to protect the environment in the coastal areas and coastal waters of the Irish Sea, North Sea, English Channel, Baltic Sea and North-East Atlantic Ocean (Norspa)

ANNEX

NORSPA ACTION

1. Priority measures eligible under this Regulation (*)

     A. *Action in the Community*

        – reduction of nutrient inputs, including those due to agricultural activities,

        – reduction of inputs of persistent, toxic and potentially bioaccumulative substances,

        – reduction of dumping of sewage sludge and of contaminated dredged materials,

        – treatment of water from ships' tanks containing residues of oil and other chemicals,

        – speeding up of the application of emission standards by industries responsible for significant pollution from specific sources,

        – promotion of the conservation of marine life,

        – integrated management of biotopes of Community interest,

        – protection of soil threatened or degraded by forest fires, coastal erosion or the disappearance of the dune belt.

     B. *Action in certain non-Community countries with Baltic coasts (**)*

        – help with the establishment of the requisite environmental administrative structures,

        – technical assistance required for the establishment of environmental policies and action programmes.

2. Operations to deal with a problem likely, within a short time, to give rise to a lasting change in the ecological conditions in the area concerned may also be regarded as priority measures.

(*)   These measures are based on, *inter alia*, discussions held in various relevant international fora.

(**) This action does not apply to the member countries of EFTA.

Commission to grant financial assistance in an extremely wide range of new areas. The objectives of LIFE would strengthen the effectiveness of the administrative structures necessary to implement environmental legislation; to help control and reduce pollution; to help protect sensitive areas and endangered species; and to provide technical and financial support to third countries in order to implement international conventions or tackle common problems. Within these broad aims, the Commission proposed to draw up programmes and priorities annually, after consultation with an advisory committee comprising representatives of the Member States.

Table 9.4: The fifth environment action programme: coastal zones

Objective	EC Targets up to 2000	Instruments	Time-frame	Sectors/actors
* sustainable development of coastal zones and their resources in accordance with the carrying capacity of coastal environments	* higher priority to the environmental needs of coastal zones, through inter alia, better coordination between relevant EC policies and between policies at the EC, national and regional levels	* framework of integrated management plans on appropriate levels	before 1998	MS + LAs+ EC
	* operational framework for integrated planning and management	* better know-how and exchange of experience	continuous	MS + LAs+ EC
		* creation and improvement of data bases and relevent indicators	before 1995	MS + LAs + EC
	* development of criteria for a better balance of land use and conservation and use of national resources	* pilot projects on integrated management of coastal zones	1993–1994	MS + LAs + EC
	* awareness raising of the public, competent authorities and economic sectors	– information compaigns – education – professional training – financial support for demonstration projects and innovative approaches (LIFE)	1992 ⇒	MS + LAs + EC *Tourist sector* Transport Enterprises Agriculture General public
		* Improvement of criteria to ensure sustainability of projects and programmes (incl. EIA)	1993	MS + EC

Council Regulation 1973/92/EEC establishing a unified financial instrument for the environment was published in the Official Journal in July 1992.[9] As adopted by the Council, the objective of LIFE is to contribute to the development and implementation of Community environmental policy and legislation by financing.

The instrument and the funding it supplies are divided into five parts.

1. Promotion of sustainable development and the quality of the environment

Actions in this area account for 40% of funding and seek to:

- establish and develop new clean technologies, i.e. those which create little or no pollution and make fewer demands on resources, with emphasis placed on innovative methods capable of reducing or eliminating pollution at source. Six priority areas were identified for 1994: surface treatments, tanneries, the graphic industry, the plastics industry, metal processing, and the agri-food industry;
- develop techniques for the collection, storage, recycling and disposal of waste, especially toxic and dangerous wastes and waste water;
- establish and develop models to integrate environmental factors into land-use planning and management, and socio-economic activities, including tourism;
- improve the quality of the environment in the urban area both in central and peripheral zones, including the development of environmentally friendly transport systems and initiatives for the management of commercial traffic.

2. Protection of nature and habitats

Covering 45% of funding, actions to protect nature and habitats relate to the Wild Birds Directive 79/409/EEC and the Habitats Directive 92/43. With regard to wild birds, LIFE aims to maintain or restore biotopes which are the habitat of endangered species or seriously threatened habitats which are of particular importance to the Community, or to implement measures to conserve or re-establish endangered species. In particular, wetlands of international importance are included. Concerning the Habitats Directive, LIFE seeks to maintain or re-establish types of natural habitats of Community interest and species of flora and fauna of Community interest as defined by Annexes I and II of the Habitats Directive. Funding is also provided for emergency actions with immediate impact to halt the decline of priority habitats or species, as well as for the protection and conservation of fresh groundwater and fresh surface water.

3. Administrative structures and environment services

In this sector, which accounts for 5% of available funding, LIFE is intended to support actions which aim to foster cooperation between the authorities of the Member States, especially concerning the control of transboundary and global environmental problems. Assistance can also be provided to equip, modernize or develop monitoring networks in the context of a strengthening environmental legislation.

[9] OJ No L 206 of 22/7/92.

4.   Education, training and information

Funding for the dissemination of knowledge regarding sound environmental management is also 5% of the total available.

5.   Actions outside Community territory

A further 5% is available for technical assistance for the setting up of environmental policies and action programmes, and assistance in the event of an ecological emergency. Funding in this area is limited to the southern and eastern shores of the Baltic and to the Mediterranean. In 1994, priorities included support for the Baltic Sea environmental action programme established with regard to the Helsinki Conference.

The finance required for the first operational phase of LIFE up to the end of 1994 is an estimated 400 million Ecu. The Commission's LIFE programme for 1994 included support for:

- the introduction of clean technologies into six sectors: surface treatments, tanneries, graphic and plastic industries, metal processing, and agri-food industry;
- development and implementation of models to integrate the environment in the land-use planning and management of the rural environment;
- sustainable tourism;
- the conservation of special protection areas (SPAs) and the recovery of priority species, wild birds and wetlands of international importance;
- demonstration actions relating to the integrated management of water catchment areas;
- coordination, modernizing and development of monitoring networks.[10]

Generally the rate of Community assistance shall be subject to the following ceilings:

- 30% of the cost in the case of actions involving the financing of income-generating investments;
- 100% of the cost of measures designed to provide the information necessary for the execution of an action and of technical assistance measures implemented on the Commission's initiative;
- 50% of the cost of other actions.

VI.   FORESTS

(See also Chapter 13.II.)

1.   The 1986 regulations on the protection of forests against fires and acid rain

On 27 June 1983 the Commission sent the Council a proposal for a regulation setting up a Community action programme intended to increase the protection of forest against fires and acid rain.

[10] OJ No C 270/7 of 6/10/93.

The Council adopted this proposal on 17 November 1986[11] in the form of two separate regulations, but in so doing it considerably reduced the scope of the Commission's proposal with regard to the field of application and the total finance granted.

The regulation on the "protection of forests against atmospheric pollution" is essentially intended to launch scientific actions making it possible to assist Member States to establish a periodic inventory of the damage caused to forests by air pollution. To draw up this inventory, a network of observation posts will be created. Pilot projects intended to finalize the methods of maintaining and restoring damaged forests will also be eligible for finance. The financial contribution of the Community will be limited to 30% of the cost of each project.

The regulation, which is valid for five years, makes provision for a total budget of 10 million Ecu. The second regulation on "forest fires" makes provision for a group of preventive measures but not for any direct intervention in the combating of forest fires. The preventive measures envisaged concern in particular:

● forestry operations designed to reduce the risks (purchase of brush-clearance equipment; provision of forest roads, firebelts and water supplies);
● the installation of fixed or mobile look-out structures;
● the organization of information campaigns.

These preventive measures could be supplemented by the training of highly specialized personnel and by encouragement of the harmonization of techniques and equipment. The financial participation of the Community in these actions cannot exceed 30% of the cost of each project. The funds available come to a total of 20 million Ecu for a period of five years.

The Council has undertaken to re-examine the financial aspects of these two regulations in 1989 in the light of experience gained during the first two years of their implementation.

2.   Protection of forests against fire: Regulation 2158/92 (OJ 217 of 31/07/92)

On 23 July 1992, the Council agreed a regulation setting up a scheme aimed at reducing the number of forest fire outbreaks and the extent of the areas burnt when fires did occur. Running for a five-year period from 1 January 1992, the scheme seeks to identify the causes of forest fires and the ways in which they can be combated, including information and education campaigns and studies. Support is provided for setting up or improving systems of prevention, especially infrastructures such as forest paths, water supply points, firebreaks, cleared and felled areas. The scheme also sets out to improve forest monitoring systems including both fixed and mobile systems.

The regulation requires Member States to classify their territory according to the degree of forest fire risk. High risk areas are those where the permanent or cyclical risk of forest fire presents a serious threat to the ecological balance and safety of persons and goods, or where it speeds up the process of desertification. Only areas situated in Portugal, Spain, Greece, and certain parts of France and Italy can be classified as high risk. Medium risk are those areas where, although not permanent

[11]   OJ No L 326 of 21/11/86, Regulations EEC No 3528/86 and 3529/86 of 17 November 1989.

or cyclical, the risk of forest fire still presents a significant threat to forest ecosystems. Remaining areas are classified as low risk.

Member States are required to provide the Commission with forest fire protection plans for the areas classified as high or medium risk. Within three months of the plans being forwarded, the Commission, after consulting the Standing Forestry Committee, will deliver its opinion on the plans. As of 1 January 1993, Community financing of measures in high- and medium-risk areas became subject to the adoption of such plans and the implementation of the measures they contain. Funding was set at Ecu 70 million, including Ecu 12 million for 1992.

VII.   THE STRUCTURAL POLICIES

The Community's Structural Funds – that is to say the European Regional Development Fund (ERDF), the European Social Fund (ESF) and the guidance element of the European Agricultural Guidance and Guarantee Fund (EAGGF) – are applied in the Community to strengthen economic and social cohesion and benefit the poorer regions of the Community. A major reform of their operation was agreed in 1988; the financial resources available for assisting the weaker regions were increased and concentrated on specific objectives. The budget was doubled in real terms between 1987 and 1993; in 1992 it represented about 27% of the overall Community budget.

Of these funds, the ERDF makes the most important contribution towards economic development through its direct intervention in the financing of productive investments and infrastructures. Many of its interventions have consequences for the environment. Within the ERDF, funds devoted to "environmental projects" have risen considerably from around 100 million Ecu per year in 1985–1987 to some 700 million Ecu per year in the early nineties, partly as a result of ENVIREG and other Community initiatives. The ESF, in its support of training and job creation, and the EAGGF in its interventions on rural development and eco-farming also contribute to the protection and improvement of the environment.

The 5th Environmental Action Programme indicates that, in the case of the ERDF, future Fund-assisted development will take account of the environmental implications. Member States will be encouraged to take an integrated approach, taking full account of the environmental impact at an early stage in the formulation of plans and programmes and avoiding environmental degradation that could be irreversible or would require costly corrective action in future.

The opportunities and incentives to promote responsible management of land, forest and ecosystems through both the EAGGF and ESF will increase as the Common Agricultural Policy is reoriented towards a better balanced and more dynamic management of the rural areas of the Community.

VIII.   THE EUROPEAN INVESTMENT BANK

Environmental protection has constituted an important criterion for EIB project selection and appraisal for most of the last 20 years. In 1983, a formal declaration of intent on environmental policy was made by the EIB and in 1984 the Board of

Governors laid down the foundations of Bank policy enabling it to intervene in favour of environmentally related projects throughout the entire Community. Since 1988 the Bank has maintained cooperation with the World Bank within the framework of the Environmental Programme for the Mediterranean (EPM). One result of this cooperation is the Mediterranean Technical Assistance Programme (METAP), whose objective is to function as a catalyst for environmental investment in the region. Further opportunities for increased cooperation are envisaged – for instance, co-financing investment within ENVIREG.

For its operating purposes the Bank has adopted a definition of the environmental which covers water-related projects, solid waste disposal, air pollution control, heritage conservation and certain urban pollution-reducing projects. There has been a sharp increase in Bank environmental lending in member countries in recent years (rising to 15% of total lending in 1989) and a widening of types of environmental investment covered.

Part Two: Other Preventive Instruments

I. ENVIRONMENTAL IMPACT ASSESSMENT

1. The 1985 "environmental impact assessment" directive

On 16 June 1980 the Commission presented the Council with a proposal for a directive concerning the evaluation of the environmental effects of certain public and private projects. This proposal aimed to introduce into national administrative procedures for the authorization of projects, common rules and principles allowing for a prior evaluation of the effects of the project on the environment.

Such prior assessment, in the Commission's view, is essential to a proper understanding of the environmental consequences of the construction of major public or private projects. Economic activities are constantly putting increasing pressure on the natural environment, in congestion of certain areas, particularly in urban centres, in unhealthy living conditions, often dangerously so, or even in accidents or catastrophes due, for example, to bad soil management.

Moreover, with several Member States already having, or being in the process of putting together, legislation concerning impact studies, too great a disparity between those laws could only lead to differences in investments in the Community, and so to distortions in competition, with negative effects on the workings of the Common Market.

Financially speaking, the costs involved in impact assessments generally constitute a very small percentage of the total cost of a project, of the order of 0.25% to 0.75%. It has also been proved that the costs of these preventive measures are often lower than those which might be incurred at a later stage.

The Council adopted the directive on the assessment of the effects of certain public and private projects on the environment on 27 June 1985 after nearly five years of extensive discussions.[12]

This directive marks a fundamental step in Community Environment Policy in that it signifies the implementation of a truly preventive approach to environmental problems, even if the provisions agreed on by the Council are significantly

---

[12] OJ No L 175 of 5/7/85.

restrained compared with the initial proposals of the Commission, and often include various derogations or exceptions.

The basic principle of the directive is that any developer, public or private, of a project which might have significant effect on the environment, is obliged to provide information to the competent public authorities in the area of the environment. This information must be taken into consideration by the public authorities responsible for granting the authorization for the project in question. The directive defines a "project" as any execution of construction works or of other installations or schemes, as well as any other interventions in the natural surroundings and landscape.

The directive's provisions concerning the type of projects which should be subject to impact assessment and the content of that assessment are the following.

(a) Type of projects to be subject to impact assessment

The directive applies to projects having a significant effect on the environment, particularly due to their nature, size or location. The directive divides such projects into two categories:

- first, projects which must in all circumstances be subject to impact assessment (Annex I of the directive) (see Table 9.1);
- secondly, projects of which there is a far greater number, which do not always have significant effects on the environment and which should only be subject to an impact assessment when the Member States consider that the nature of the project requires it (Annex II of the directive) (see Table 9.2).

For this last category of projects, the Member States thus have considerable freedom of choice. They must nevertheless carry out an examination of each project in order to determine which should be subject to an impact assessment. To do this they may establish specific criteria or thresholds.

(b) Content of the assessment procedure

The evaluation procedure or impact assessment is intended to identify, describe and evaluate the direct and indirect effects of a project on:

- human beings, fauna and flora;
- soil, water, air, climate and the landscape;
- the interaction between these factors;
- material assets and the cultural heritage.

The first stage of the assessment procedure consists in gathering information. This is the responsibility of the developer, who is defined as being either the applicant for authorization for a private project or the public authority which initiates a project. The information to be provided mainly concerns:

- the technical description of the project;
- the parts of the environment likely to be affected;
- alternative solutions studied by the developer;
- the significant effects on the environment;
- the measures envisaged to avoid or reduce pollution or nuisance or any other negative effect on the environment.

Table 9.5: Council Directive of 27 June 1985 Assessment of the effects of certain public and private projects on the environment

PROJECTS SUBJECT TO ARTICLE 4 (1)

1. Crude-oil refineries (excluding undertakings manufacturing only lubricants from crude oil) and installations for the gasification and liquefaction of 500 tonnes or more of coal or bituminous shale per day.

2. Thermal power stations and other combustion installations with a heat output of 300 megawatts or more and nuclear power stations and other nuclear reactors (except research installations for the production and conversion of fissionable and fertile materials, whose maximum power does not exceed 1 kilowatt continuous thermal load).

3. Installations solely designed for the permanent storage or final disposal of radioactive waste.

4. Integrated works for the initial melting of cast-iron and steel.

5. Installations for the extraction of asbestos and for the processing and transformation of asbestos and products containing asbestos: for asbestos-cement products, with an annual production of more than 20 000 tonnes of finished products, for friction material, with an annual production of more than 50 tonnes of finished products, and for other uses of asbestos, utilization of more than 200 tonnes per year.

6. Integrated chemical installations.

7. Construction of motorways, express roads ([1]) and lines for long-distance railway traffic and of airports ([2]) with a basic runway length of 2 100 m or more.

8. Trading ports and also inland waterways and ports for inland-waterway traffic which permit the passage of vessels of over 1 350 tonnes.

9. Waste-disposal installations for the incineration, chemical treatment or landfill of toxic and dangerous wastes.

PROJECTS SUBJECT TO ARTICLE 4 (2)

1. Agriculture

    (a) Projects for the restructuring of rural land holdings.

    (b) Projects for the use of uncultivated land or semi-natural areas for intensive agricultural purposes.

    (c) Water-management projects for agriculture.

([1]) For the purposes of the Directive, "express road" means a road which complies with the definition in the European Agreement on main international traffic arteries of 15 November 1975.

([2]) For the purposes of this Directive, "airport" means airports which comply with the definition in the 1944 Chicago Convention setting up the International Civil Aviation Organization (Annex 14).

Table 9.5 continued

(d) Initial afforestation where this may lead to adverse ecological changes and land reclamation for the purposes of conversion to another type of land use.

(e) Poultry-rearing installations.

(f) Pig-rearing installations.

(g) Salmon breeding.

(h) Reclamation of land from the sea.

2. *Extractive industry*

(a) Extraction of peat.

(b) Deep drillings with the exception of drillings for investigating the stability of the soil and in particular:
   - geothermal drilling,
   - drilling for the storage of nuclear waste material,
   - drilling for water supplies.

(c) Extraction of minerals other than metalliferous and energy-producing minerals, such as marble, sand, gravel, shale, salt, phosphates and potash.

(d) Extraction of coal and lignite by underground mining.

(e) Extraction of coal and lignite by open-cast mining.

(f) Extraction of petroleum.

(g) Extraction of natural gas.

(h) Extraction of ores.

(i) Extraction of bituminous shale.

(j) Extraction of minerals other than metalliferous and energy-producing minerals by open-cast mining.

(k) Surface industrial installations for the extraction of coal, petroleum, natural gas and ores, as well as bituminous shale.

(l) Coke ovens (dry coal distillation).

(m) Installations for the manufacture of cement.

3. *Energy industry*

(a) Industrial installations for the production of electricity, steam and hot water (unless included in Annex I).

(b) Industrial installations for carrying gas, steam and hot water; transmission of electrical energy by overhead cables.

(c) Surface storage of natural gases.

(d) Underground storage of combustible gases.

(e) Surface storage of fossil fuels.

(f) Industrial briquetting of coal and lignite.

(g) Installations for the production or enrichment of nuclear fuels.

(h) Installations for the reprocessing of irradiated nuclear fuels.

Table 9.5 continued

    (i) Installations for the collection and processing of radioactive waste (unless included in Annex I).

    (j) Installations for hydroelectric energy production.

4. *Processing of metals*

    (a) Iron and steelworks, including foundries, forges, drawing plants and rolling mills (unless included in Annex I).

    (b) Installations for the production, including smelting, refining, drawing and rolling, of non-ferrous metals, excluding precious metals.

    (c) Pressing, drawing and stamping of large castings.

    (d) Surface treatment and coating of metals.

    (e) Boilermaking, manufacture of reservoirs, tanks and other sheet-metal containers.

    (f) Manufacture and assembly of motor vehicles and manufacture of motor-vehicle engines.

    (g) Shipyards.

    (h) Installations for the construction and repair of aircraft.

    (i) Manufacture of railway equipment.

    (j) Swaging by explosives.

    (k) Installations for the roasting and sintering of metallic ores.

5. *Manufacture of glass*

6. *Chemical industry*

    (a) Treatment of intermediate products and production of chemicals (unless included in Annex I).

    (b) Production of pesticides and pharmaceutical products, paint and varnishes, elastomers and peroxides.

    (c) Storage facilities for petroleum, petrochemical and chemical products.

7. *Food industry*

    (a) Manufacture of vegetable and animal oils and fats.

    (b) Packing and canning of animal and vegetable products.

    (c) Manufacture of dairy products.

    (d) Brewing and malting.

    (e) Confectionery and syrup manufacture.

    (f) Installations for the slaughter of animals.

    (g) Industrial starch manufacturing installations.

    (h) Fish-meal and fish-oil factories.

    (i) Sugar factories.

Table 9.5 continued

8. *Textile, leather, wood and paper industries*

    (a) Wool scouring, degreasing and bleaching factories.

    (b) Manufacture of fibre board, particle board and plywood.

    (c) Manufacture of pulp, paper and board.

    (d) Fibre-dyeing factories.

    (e) Cellulose-processing and production installations.

    (f) Tannery and leather-dressing factories.

 9. *Rubber industry*

    Manufacture and treatment of elastomer-based products.

10. *Infrastructure projects*

    (a) Industrial-estate development projects.

    (b) Urban-development projects.

    (c) Ski-lifts and cable-cars.

    (d) Construction of roads, harbours, including fishing harbours, and airfields (projects not listed in Annex I).

    (e) Canalization and flood-relief works.

    (f) Dams and other installations designed to hold water or store it on a long-term basis.

    (g) Tramways, elevated and underground railways, suspended lines or similar lines of a particular type, used exclusively or mainly for passenger transport.

    (h) Oil and gas pipeline installations.

    (i) Installation of long-distance aqueducts.

    (j) Yacht marinas.

11. *Other projects*

    (a) Holiday villages, hotel complexes.

    (b) Permanent racing and test tracks for cars and motor cycles.

    (c) Installations for the disposal of industrial and domestic waste (unless included in Annex I).

    (d) Waste water treatment plants.

    (e) Sludge-deposition sites.

    (f) Storage of scrap iron.

    (g) Test benches for engines, turbines or reactors.

    (h) Manufacture of artificial mineral fibres.

    (i) Manufacture, packing, loading or placing in cartridges of gunpowder and explosives.

    (j) Knackers' yards.

12. *Modifications to development projects included in Annex I and projects in Annex I undertaken exclusively or mainly for the development and testing of new methods or products and not used for more than one year.*

Although most of this information must be provided in all cases, the directive does allow for a certain degree of flexibility; some information is only required in so far as it corresponds to the state of progress in the authorization procedure and in so far as the developer can realistically be expected to gather it, bearing in mind the extent of knowledge and the technique of assessment methods. Since public authorities often possess useful or even essential information for the developer, the directive also authorizes these authorities to make information available to the developer.

The second stage of the procedure is consultation with the authorities, and with the public concerned by the project. The information given by the developer must be made available to the responsible authorities in the area of the environment and to the public, in order to give them the opportunity to express their opinion before the project is started.

In this respect it should be noted that the directive contains an important provision concerning the communication of information to other Member States, when it is a case of transfrontier projects likely to have a significant effect on the environment of several Member States.

Finally, the third stage of the assessment procedure concerns the taking into consideration of the information by the competent authority when deciding whether to authorize the project.

The result of the assessment study will be just one of the factors allowing the competent authority to grant or refuse authorization. Even if other aspects necessarily intervene when the decision on authorization is taken, it is clear that it will no longer be possible to ignore the "environment" factor, as has often been the case in the past. Once the decision has been taken the competent authority will have to inform the public concerned of the nature of the decision and of all the conditions attached to it.

Generally, it can be seen that this directive, which restricts itself to fixing certain common principles for the assessment of effects on the environment, will certainly not ensure an optimal and harmonized application of an impact assessment procedure in the Member States. The directive seems to recognize this, since it asks the Commission to draw up a report after five years on its use and effectiveness, and to present, if necessary, other proposals to ensure a better harmonization of legislations and practices of the Member States.

To date, no such report has been forthcoming, apparently due to the failure of certain Member States to provide reports to the Commission. This Community regulation nevertheless represents a fundamental step towards a better preventive approach on the plan of environment policy, in that this policy is recognized from now on as being an integral component of good land and natural resources management.

2. The Commission's proposal of 16 March 1994 to amend Council Directive 85/337/EEC

On 16 March 1993 the Commission sent to the Council a proposal for a Council directive amending Directive 85/337/EEC. The proposal was based chiefly on the findings of the report on the implementation of the directive which the Commission sent to Parliament and Council in April 1993.[13] (see Table 9.6.)

---

[13] COM (93) 28 of 2/4/1993.

Under Directive 85/337 EEC, projects falling within the scope of Annex I of the directive must always be subject to an environmental impact assessment (EIA); an EIA is required for a project falling into Annex II only if the Member State considers it necessary on the basis of the characteristics of the project. The implementation of the directive in respect of Annex II projects has been inconsistent from Member State to Member State and the Commission now proposes to amend the directive to clarify:

(i)   the circumstances in which Annex II projects will be required to undergo an environmental assessment, i.e. where they are liable to have a significant effect on special protection areas designated by Member States and communicated to the Commission in accordance with directives on environmental protection;

(ii) the selection procedure to be applied in the case of Annex II projects.

In its amendment, the Commission proposed no specific measures to introduce ex-post monitoring of environmental impact, even though the report on implementation mentioned above had highlighted the technical shortcomings of the assessment procedure provided for by the directive, which makes no provision for monitoring the effects on the environment which result from the implementation of the project.

II.   1985 DECISION ON AN INFORMATION SYSTEM ON THE STATE OF THE ENVIRONMENT AND NATURAL RESOURCES OF THE COMMUNITY (CORINE[14])

On 14 October 1983 the Commission presented the Council with a proposal for a Decision aimed at the adoption of a work programme for the first phase of the implementation of an information system on the state of the environment and natural resources of the Community. This first phase, lasting four years, was meant to cover the years 1984–1987.

From the point of view of strengthening the preventive nature of Community Environment Policy, the Commission considered that it was essential to be aware of the state of the environment and the natural resources of the Community, and to be able to follow developments in these areas on a regular basis. The lack of sufficiently comparable information at Community level on the different aspects of the environment was in fact making it difficult for the Commission to implement the priority actions retained by the Council within the 3rd Action Programme.

The information system should be set up progressively and should be limited at first to the following three priority areas:

● biotopes of major importance for nature conservation;
● acid deposition;
● protection of the environment in the Mediterranean region.

It also made provision for measures to improve the comparability and availability of information.

On 27 June 1985 the Council adopted a decision on a work programme for the Commission concerning an experimental project for the gathering, coordination and

---

[14] CORINE = CoOrdination INformation Environment.

Table 9.6: Proposal for a Council Directive amending Directive 85/337/EEC on the assessment of the effects of certain public and private projects on the environment

ANNEX IIA

SELECTION CRITERIA REFERRED TO IN ARTICLE 4(3)

1. *Characteristics of the project*

The characteristics of the project must be considered having regard, in particular, to:

- the size of the project (^{1});
- the use of natural resources;
- the production of waste;
- pollution and nuisances;
- the risk of accidents;
- the impact on the natural and historical heritage having regard to the existing functions of the areas likely to be affected (such as tourism, urban settlement, agriculture).

2. *Location of the project*

The environmental sensitivity of geographical areas likely to be affected by the project must be considered, having regard, in particular, to:

- the relative abundance, quality and regenerative capacity of natural resources in the area;
- the absorption capacity of the natural environment, paying particular attention to the following areas:

  (a) wetlands;
  (b) coastal zones;
  (c) mountain and forest areas;
  (d) nature reserves and parks;
  (e) areas already classified or protected under Member States' legislation;
  (f) areas in which the environmental quality standards laid down in Community legislation have already been exceeded;
  (g) densely populated areas;
  (h) landscapes of historical, cultural or archaeological significance.

(^{1}) The size of the project must be considered in relation to the duration, frequency and reversibility of its likely impacts.

consistency of information on the state of the environment and natural resources in the Community.[15]

While accepting the three priority areas suggested by the Commission, for the implementation of the information system, i.e. biotypes of major importance for nature conservation, acid deposition, and the protection of the environment in the Mediterranean region, the Council somewhat reduced the dimension of the programme and judged it necessary to start off with an experimental phase.

This programme, which was limited to a period of four years, should enable a judgment to be made regarding the possibility of establishing definitively a truly

---

[15] OJ No L 176 of 6/7/85.

Community-wide information system on the state of the environment and natural resources.

The funds set aside for this programme amounted to a total of 4 million Ecu, instead of the 5.8 million Ecu requested by the Commission. To ensure the carrying out of the programme the Commission would be assisted by a committee made up of representatives of the Member States.

III. THE EUROPEAN ENVIRONMENT AGENCY

The idea of a European Environment Agency was first proposed by the Commission's President Jacques Delors when he outlined the Commission's 1989 Programme to the European Parliament in January of that year. He spoke of the "introduction of a European system of environmental measurement and verification which could be the precursor of a European environmental agency".

Environment Commissioner Carlo Ripa di Meana supported the call for such a body in a speech delivered in February 1989, stressing the importance of enforcing European Community legislation and of integrating environmental concerns into other policies.

The services of the Commission worked rapidly to produce the text of a draft regulation in discussion with experts from the Member States and advice from an informal Council of Environment Ministers held in Caceres, Spain in May 1989. The Commission's draft was published on 12 July 1989.[16] It emphasized the networking concept under which Member States would link their own environmental monitoring and observation networks to European "thematic centres". The European Environment Agency's role would principally be to ensure coherence, consistency and comparability of data and to ensure publication of the results.

The Commission's proposal was noted by the European Council held in the summer of 1989 which requested the Environment Council to consider it at the earliest possible opportunity.

The Environment Committee of the European Parliament considered the proposal at its meetings between September 1989 and February 1990. The Environment Committee was of the opinion, in particular, that the Agency should be more of an environmental inspectorate. When the Council adopted Regulation EEC/1210/90 of 7 May 1990, it made a gesture in the Parliament's direction by agreeing to decide within two years after the entry into force of the regulation on further tasks including (Article 20):

associating in the monitoring of the implementation of Community environmental legislation, in cooperation with the Commission and existing competent bodies in the Member States.

The regulation formally establishing the European Environment Agency and the European Environment Information and Observation Network was adopted by the Council on 7 May 1990. However, the regulation was unable to enter into force until the Council decided on a seat for the new Agency. The European Parliament,

---

[16] COM (89) 303.

increasingly frustrated at the Council's failure to take a decision on this matter, threatened legal action to make it possible for the work of the Agency to begin, pending a formal decision concerning its location. A decision was finally reached at the Brussels summit of October 1993 as part of a package agreement concerning various institutions with Copenhagen being chosen as the seat for the Environmental Agency.

As adopted by the Council, the regulation (EEC 1210/90 of 7 May 1990)[17] on the establishment of the European Environment Agency and the European Environment Information and Observation Network is intended to provide the Community and the Member States with objective reliable and comparable information at European level enabling them to take the requisite measures to protect the environment, to assess the results of these measures and to inform the public about the state of the environment. It will provide technical and scientific support to these ends.

Priority (Article 3) will be given to the following areas of work:

- air quality and atmospheric emissions;
- water quality, pollutants and water resources;
- the state of the soil, of the fauna and flora, and of biotopes;
- land use and natural resources;
- waste management;
- noise emissions;
- chemical substances which are hazardous for the environment;
- coastal protection.

Article 3 specifies that, in particular, transnational, plurinational and global phenomena shall be covered and that the socio-economic dimension shall also be taken into account.

The network will be made up of three groups: the main elements of the existing national environmental information networks; national focal points to be nominated by the Member States for the coordination and transmission of the information to be supplied to the Agency and other institutions in the network; and topic centres to be designated by the Management Board of the Agency and to be responsible for cooperating with the Agency on specific subjects of special interest. The Management Board will consist of one representative of each Member State, two representatives of the Commission and two scientific personalities to be designated by the European Parliament and will be headed by an Executive Director. The work of the Agency will be based on a multi-annual work programme to be adopted by the Management Board after consultation with a special Scientific Committee and the Commission. The Agency will be open to countries outside the Community, and provision is made for the future extension of its work to cover additional tasks relating in particular to the criteria for the eco-label scheme; promotion of the use and transfer of clean technologies within and beyond the Community; and the establishment of environmental impact assessment criteria with a view to the possible revision of the EIA Directive.

The first multi-annual work programme (MAWP) (1994–1999) was adopted by the Management Board at its fifth meeting on 25–26 July 1994.

[17] OJ No L 158 of 23/6/90.

IV. PROPOSAL FOR A DECISION ADOPTING A FOUR-YEAR PROGRAMME 1993–1996 TO DEVELOP REGULAR OFFICIAL STATISTICS ON THE ENVIRONMENT

In December 1992 the Commission sent a proposal to Council for a four-year programme to develop environmental statistics on the environment.[18] The 5th Environmental Action Programme agreed by the Environment Council on 16 December 1992 underlines the priority areas for EC environmental policy and stresses the importance of reliable statistical information. The Statistical Programme of the European Communities set out in the Council Resolution of 19 June 1989 (OJ No C 161, 28/6/89) also calls for the development of environmental statistics.

The proposal calls for the adoption of a four-year programme the aim of which will be to produce a key set of environmental statistics by 1995, which would then be integrated with the statistics provided by the Member States. The objective was to coordinate the development of official environmental statistics between EUROSTAT (the statistical office of the European Communities), the statistical services of other Community organizations and international organizations and those of the Member States.

The Commission proposed four priority areas:

- economic statistics of current expenditure and investment for environmental protection;
- statistics of the management of waste and dangerous products, quality and management of water;
- linkage of transport and energy statistics to environmental statistics;
- integration of environmental statistics in industrial, agricultural and forestry surveys.

V. PROPOSAL FOR A DIRECTIVE ON INTEGRATED POLLUTION PREVENTION AND CONTROL

On 14 September 1993 the Commission sent to the Council a proposal for a framework directive on integrated pollution prevention and control (IPC).[19] The concept of IPC has been growing in importance within the Commission and the Community in recent years. Indeed, the 5th Environmental Action Programme lists IPC as a priority field of action. The growing importance of IPC reflects the increasing realization that no one part of the environment is separate from another and that it functions as an integrated whole.

The main environmental aim of IPC is thus to prevent or solve pollution problems rather than merely transferring them from one part of the environment to another. In fact, stepping up controls on one medium can create an incentive to release and/or transfer pollution to another. The proposal emphasizes the use of BAT – Best Available Techniques – as a means of preventing inputs of substances harmful to the environment or reducing them to a minimum.

[18] COM (92) 483 final; OJ No C 328/8 of 12/12/92.
[19] OJ No C 311/6 of 17/11/93 – (COM (93) 423 final).

The Commission proposes that no existing installation (of those engaged in processes listed in Annex I) should be operated later than 30 June 2005 without a permit. The permit must set emission limit values based on what is actually achievable through the use of best available techniques. The Commission's proposed definition of "best available techniques" is as follows:

> "best available techniques" (BAT) signifies the latest stage in the development of activities, processes and their methods of operation which indicate the practical suitability of particular techniques as the basis of emission limit values for preventing, or where that is not practicable, minimizing emissions to the environment as a whole, without predetermining any specific technology or other techniques.
>
> "techniques" include both the technology used and the way in which the installation is designed, built, maintained, operated and decommissioned. The techniques must be industrially feasible, in the relevant sector, from a technical and economic point of view.
>
> "available" techniques means those developed on a scale which allows implementation in the relevant industrial context, under economically viable conditions, whether or not the techniques are used or produced inside the Member State in question, as long as they are reasonably accessible to the operator.
>
> "best" means most effective in achieving a high level of protection for the environment as a whole, taking into account the potential benefits and costs which may result from action or lack of action.

The permit shall also contain suitable monitoring requirements, specifying the measurement methodology, frequency and evaluation procedure and an obligation to supply the competent authority with data required for checking compliance with the permit.

The emission limit values must also be set (Article 9) with the aim of ensuring that environmental quality standards are not breached.

The directive specifies (Article 15) that Member States are to be informed by 1 July 1998 of the emission limit values and the best available techniques from which these values are derived for the various categories of installation.

This would have three main aims. Firstly, the Commission and the Member States would be able to compare standards established at Member State level. In turn, this would allow greater priority to be given to future proposals regarding those industrial sectors where environmental standards are the most diverse. Secondly, the exchange of information concerning environmental quality standards and BAT would help the Commission and the Member States in setting future European level standards. Thirdly, the exchange of information could help resolve problems of imbalance in technological potential within the EC.

VI.   COUNCIL DIRECTIVE 90/313/EEC – ACCESS TO INFORMATION

The directive on the freedom of access to information on the environment came into force on 31 December 1992. Though it was signalled in the 4th Action Programme, its emergence as a draft from the Commission in November 1988 and its eventual adoption by the Council on 23 June 1990 owed much to the dedication of Dr Hans Scheuer, a German official in DG XI who championed the directive at a time when the Commission's own environmental hierarchy seemed less than enthusiastic.

The directive requires public authorities or bodies in the Member States with public responsibilities for the environment which hold information on the environment to make such information available to the public both by the publication of periodic reports containing general information and by the provision of specific information requested by any legal or natural person.

The directive provides a structure and a procedure for disseminating environmental information, which must be made available to any person, whether or not they are a citizen or resident of the Member State in question. No justification need be given for requesting the information and refusal or failure to provide it can be followed up by an appeals procedure. A reasonable charge may be made for the information.

The directive permits certain exemptions, such as for national defence, public security, commercial secrets, and cases before the courts. Also exempt is the disclosure of environmental information whose dissemination could actually threaten the environment, for example the location of nesting sites of rare species.

Based on reports submitted to it by the Member States, the Commission must report to the Council and the European Parliament on the implementation of the directive, as well as propose revisions, by 31 December 1996.

VII.   PROPOSAL FOR A COUNCIL DIRECTIVE ON CIVIL LIABILITY FOR DAMAGE CAUSED BY WASTE (COM (91) 219)

The amended proposal of 1991 is at the present time on hold pending discussion of the Communication on environmental liability (see below).

VIII.   EC GREEN PAPER ON REMEDYING DAMAGE TO THE ENVIRONMENT (COM (93) 47)

With the failure of the Council to adopt the draft directive on civil liability for damage caused by waste, the Commission sought to generalize the discussion by presenting a Green Paper on Remedying Damage to the Environment. The paper explores the merits and demerits of fault-based and strict liability regimes. Recalling the Community's own defective product legislation (Directive 85/374/EEC) as well as the proposed directive on civil liability for damage caused by waste, the paper argues:

> A strict liability regime can increase incentives for better risk management and provide legal certainty for those economic enterprises subject to such a regime. It can also help implement the "polluter pays" principle for certain types of economic activities. It means that this system guarantees that the cost of damage caused by an economic activity is borne by the operator.

However, the Green Paper also recognizes the problems linked to strict liability, notably the potential burden on industry and those situations where multiple parties are involved. The Green Paper suggests, somewhat controversially,[20] that the public authorities should be responsible for compensation in cases where damage is created by activities which fully complied with standards set in the relevant permit.

The Green Paper envisages the creation of a joint compensation scheme which would "enable responsibility for costs to be shared fairly within the economic sector most closely connected to the presumed source of the damage". On a practical level this integrated "environmental" liability regime could take the form of the following alternatives:

- in the event of damage attributable to the action of a single liable party, compensation would be sought via civil liability;
- if the damage could not be attributed to the activities of a liable party (i.e. the liable party could not be identified), joint compensation mechanisms, as decentralized as possible, could be used.

---

[20] See article by David Wilkinson, EELR June 1993, p. 159.

Table 9.7: The fifth environment action programme: horizontal measures

Objectives	Targets up to 2000	Actions	Time-frame	Actors
1. IMPROVEMENT OF DATA	– Improvement of Base-line data	* Community programme for environmental statistics	1992 ⇒	EEA + EC
		* National statistics on environment	1995	MS
		* Regional and Community statistics	1995	EC
	– Development of Environmental Indicators	* Indicators of general progress and trends	1995 / 1997	EC / EC
	– Regular assessment of quality and progress	* National and Community reports on the state of the environment	1995 / 2000	MS / EC
	– Inventory of polluting emissions and discharges, and waste	* Published inventories (progressive)	1994 ⇒	EC, Enterprise
2. SCIENTIFIC RESEARCH AND TECHNOLOGICAL DEVELOPMENT	– Considerable reinforcement of investments in general environment + energy R + D	* New R & D programme	1992/96	Enterprise +MS+EC
	– Specific programmes as low carbon technology, biomass, and other renewable energies		1993	id
	– Extended programmes on biotechnology, including its use in integrated pest control in agriculture		1995	id
	– Expanded programme on clean technologies, recycling technologies, recyclable and reusable materials		1993	id
3. SECTORAL AND SPATIAL PLANNING	Integrated socio-economic development plans	* Integrated Regional Development Plans	1992 ⇒	MS, LAs, EC
		* Integrated Transport Management Plans up to 2000	1994	MS, LAs, EC
		* Integrated Coastal Management Plans	1998	MS, LAs, EC
		* Integrated Transport Plans for 2010	1997	MS, LAs, EC
		* Environmental Impact Assessment at planning and at project level	1995 ⇒ ongoing	MS, LAs, EC
		* EIA applied to ERDF – aimed programmes + projects	1993 ⇒	MS, LAs, EC

Table 9.7 continued

Objectives	Targets up to 2000	Actions	Time-frame	Actors
4. GETTING THE PRICES RIGHT				
a) Evaluation and accounting	Evaluation of environmental resource stock	* Preliminary guidelines linked to "Improvement of Data"	1993 1995	EC EEA, EC, MS
	Development of renewable resource indicators	* "Shadow" GNP tables showing natural resource values	1995 ⟹	MS + EC
	Modification of key economic indicators	* Formal GNP tables	1999 ⟹	id
	Cost/benefit analysis	* Development + implementation of a coherent programme internalizing external costs	1992 ⟹	MS + Ind.
	Institutions of environmental accounting mechanism	* Consultations with professional organizations	1992	EC
		* Community guidelines	1993	
		* Parallel accounts in companies	2000 ⟹	{ Accountants + Profess. Bodies + EC
	Disclosure of environmental issues in the accounts of enterprises	* Consultation with MS, Industry and professional organizations	1992/3	EC, MS, Industry & Prof. Bodies
	Instruments	* EC Directive	1994	EC + MS
b) Fiscal incentives	Integration of environment protection requirements into fiscal policies	* Promotion of fiscal incentives for environment	1993	MS + EC
c) Charges	Improved transparency of charging systems	* Review of national and local levies and charges	1993	MS + LAs
		– collation of data		EC
d) State aids	Application of polluter pays principle	* Comprehensive review of State Aids in environment field	1992/3	EC + MS

Table 9.7 continued

Objectives	Targets up to 2000	Actions	Time-frame	Actors
e) Other economic and market-related instruments	– Environmental Audit of all major public and private enterprises	* Directive on Eco-audits	1992	EC + MS +
		Ecoaudits	1994	Accountants
		* Consultations with MS, Industry and insurance institutions	1992/3	EC + MS, LAs + Enterprise
		* Initiation of scheme of performance Bonds in respect of covenants and licence conditions	1995	MS + LAs + Insurance companies
	– Integrated liability and joint responsibility	* Directive on civil liability for damage caused by waste	1993 ⇒	EC + MS
		* Discussion document on civil liability and joint responsibility systems	1992	EC
		* Adoption of EC regulation	1995	EC + MS
	– Deposit/Refund systems	* Progressive implementation	ongoing	MS, Enterpr
		Reports on progress and effectiveness	1995/8	EC + MS
5. PUBLIC INFORMATION AND EDUCATION	– Improved level of general information	* Public access to environm. info	1993	LAs, MS, EC
		* Regular state-of-environment reports	1995 ⇒	LAs, MS
	– Specific information campaigns on selected themes	* Waste, energy consumption, transport etc. (to be decided by Environment Policy Review Group)	1992 ⇒	EC, MS, public utilities
	– Improved Consumer information	* Ecological labelling	1993	EC, MS
		* Integrated Environmental/Consumer Safety label	1998	EC, MS, Standards Institutes
	– Integrated environment into all primary and secondary school curricula	* Report on current situation and proposal on developments	1992	EC
		* Programme of pedagogic research	1992/3	MS, Ed. Ins EC
		* Adoption of general guidelines	1993	MS

Table 9.7 continued

Objectives	Targets up to 2000	Actions	Time-frame	Actors
		* Preparation of books/teaching aids	ongoing	Enterprise Educ. Insts.
		* Training of teachers	1993 ⇒ 2000	MS
		* Integration into school curricula		MS, Educ. Insts.
		* Programme of seminars, summer schools, colloquies	1993 ⇒	EC
		* Annual update of progress		
6. PROFESSIONAL EDUCATION AND TRAINING	– Integration of environmental studies in a representative proportion of third-level institutions	* Report on current situation for all sectors * Incorporation of environment studies	1992 1993	EC National Educ. Insts.
		* Idem of environment faculties	id	id
	– Vocational training programmes for technicians, machine operators, agronomists, foresters and other appropriate workers and trainers	* Pedagogic research, preparation of books and teaching aids	1992 ⇒	Educ. Insts. Enterprise
	– Professional training courses, seminars and workshop for planners, accountants, auditors	* Co-ordination among professional institutes, development of guidelines and procedures	1992 ⇒	EC + Prof. Bodies
	– Ongoing programme of courses and seminars for policy planners, transport managers, agricultural advisers, tourism operators	* Idem	id	id

Table 9.7 continued

Objectives	Targets up to 2000	Actions	Time-frame	Actors
7. FINANCIAL SUPPORT MECHANISMS	Full integration of environmental dimension in disbursement of structural funds (with effect from the ratification of the new Treaty)	* Take account of environmental impact	1993 ⇒	MS, LAs, EC
	FEOGA aid to be orientated to favour sustainable, integrated farming and rural development	* Progressive re-orientation price to income supports	1992 ⇒	EC
		* Land management contracts	1992 ⇒	MS + EC
		* Rural Development Programme	Progressive	id
		* Forest Development Programme	id	Forest Enterprises, MS + EC
	LIFE to be developed as a "booster mechanism" for effective implementation of environment policy	* initiation of LIFE	1992	EC + MS
		* Comprehensive review and extension as appropriate	1995	id
	New Cohesion Fund	* Special boost for air, waste water, waste treatment etc.	1993–1998	EC + MS + LAs
	New financial support mechanisms to assist SMEs	* Comprehensive survey of difficulties and needs	1992/93	EC, MS. Industry Organizations
		* Comprehensive review of State Aids in environment field	1993	EC

Chapter 10

The Economic Aspects of Pollution Control

I. THE POLLUTER PAYS PRINCIPLE (P.P.P.): THE COUNCIL RECOMMENDATION OF 1975

One of the general principles approved by the Council in 1973 when adopting the 1st Environmental Action Programme was that of the "polluter pays" (see p. 14). The Council recognized that the costs incurred in preventing and suppressing nuisances fall as a matter of principle to the polluter. There can, however, be exceptions and special arrangements, particularly during periods of transition, provided that no major distortions result with regard to international trade and investments. The Council felt that, without prejudice to the implementation of the provisions of the treaties, there was a need to specify exactly how the "polluter pays" principle should be applied at Community level. In addition, when exceptions are made to this principle, it was felt that the importance of progressively eliminating regional imbalances within the Community should also be taken into consideration.

In order to define the means of applying the polluter pays principle, on 5 March 1974 the Commission sent the Council a draft Recommendation regarding "cost allocation and action by public authorities on environmental matters".

The Council adopted this Recommendation on 3 March 1975.[1] It invites the Member States to conform, in respect of allocation of costs and of action by public authorities in the field of environmental protection, to the principles and rules governing their application contained in the Commission's Communication of 1974 – which is included in its entirety in the Council's Recommendation.

The principles retained by the Council with regard to "polluter pays", and the rules governing their application, are the following:

(a) In order to avoid distortions of competition affecting trade and the location of investments which would be incompatible with the proper functioning of the Common Market, the costs connected with the protection of the environment against pollution should be allocated according to the same principles throughout the Community.

(b) The European Communities and the Member States in their national legislation on environmental protection, must apply the polluter pays principle, under which natural or legal persons governed by public or private law who are responsible for pollution must pay the costs of such measures as are necessary

---

[1] OJ No L 176 of 3/7/84.

to eliminate that pollution or to reduce it. Consequently, environmental protection should not in principle depend on policies which rely on grants of aid and place the burden of combating pollution on the community.

(c) A polluter is someone who directly or indirectly damages the environment or who creates conditions leading to such damage.

(d) Under the polluter pays principle, standards and charges, or a possible combination of the two, are the major instruments of action available to public authorities for the avoidance of pollution.

(e) The purpose of charges shall be to encourage the polluter to take the necessary measures to reduce the pollution he is causing as cheaply as possible (incentive function) and/or make him pay his share of the costs of collective measures, for example, purification costs (redistribution function). Charges should however be fixed so that primarily they fulfil their incentive function.

(f) Income from charges may be used either to finance measures taken by public authorities or to help finance installations set up by an individual polluter, provided that the latter, at the specific request of the public authorities, is seen to render a particular service to the community, by reducing his pollution level to below that set by the competent authorities. In the latter instance, the financial aid granted must be limited to compensating for the services thus rendered by the polluter to the community.

In line with Articles 92 *et seq.* of the EEC Treaty, income from charges may also be used to finance the installations of individual polluters for protecting the environment.

(g) Polluters will be obliged to pay the charges and expenditure on pollution control measures (investment in anti-pollution installations and equipment, introduction of new processes, cost of running anti-pollution installations, etc.), even when these go beyond the standards laid down by the public authorities.

The costs to be borne by the polluter under the polluter pays principle should include all the expenditure necessary to achieve an environmental quality objective, including the administrative costs directly linked to the implementation of anti-pollution measures.

The cost to the public authorities of construction, buying and operating pollution monitoring and supervision installations may, however, be borne by those authorities.

(h) Exceptions to the polluter pays principle may be justified in limited cases:
- Where the immediate application of very stringent standards or the imposition of substantial charges is likely to lead to serious economic disturbances by giving rise to greater social loss. It may then prove necessary to allow some polluters time to adapt their products to the new standards and to grant aid for a limited period of time. Such measures may, in any case, apply only to existing production plants and existing products.
- Where, in the context of other policies (e.g. regional, industrial, social and agricultural policies, or scientific research and development policy), investment is affecting environmental protection benefit from aid intended to solve certain industrial, agricultural or regional structural problems.

(i) The following three categories of financing shall not be considered contrary to the polluter pays principle:
- financial contributions which might be granted to local authorities for the construction and operation of public installations for the protection of the

environment, the cost of which could not be wholly covered in the short term from the charges paid by polluters using them;

● financing designed to compensate for the particularly heavy costs which some polluters would be obliged to meet in order to achieve an exceptional degree of environmental cleanliness;

● contributions granted to foster activities concerning research and development with a view to implementing techniques, manufacturing processes and products causing less pollution.

It is to be noted that the Community's commitment to the polluter pays principle was reaffirmed by Article 130R of the Single European Act (see p. 489) and the Maastricht Treaty.

II.　STATE AIDS IN ENVIRONMENTAL MATTERS

1.　The first Commission Memorandum of 1974 on state aids in environmental matters

In a Memorandum addressed to the Member States on 6 November 1974 concerning the Community approach to state aids in environmental matters, the Commission considered that during a transitional period state aids designed to assist firms in adapting to laws imposing major new burdens relating to environmental protection, should be able to qualify for exemption under Article 92, paragraph 3 of the EEC Treaty. This provision stipulated that "State aids designed to promote the execution of an important project of common European interest" can be considered to be compatible with the Common Market. In its Memorandum the Commission expresses the view that the protection of the environment constitutes such a "project of common interest", so justifying exemption from the general rule of the Common Market. This general rule, which is laid down in the Treaty of Rome of 1957, prohibits state aids which distort competition between firms in so far as such aids have an effect on trade between Member States.

(a)　Conditions for the application of exemption under Article 92, paragraph 3(b) of the EEC Treaty

In granting this exemption, the Commission did not wish to encourage Member States to make financial investments in the form of state aids in favour of firms. But, considering that the polluter pays principle could not yet be applied in a general and uniform way in the Community, the Commission wished merely to inform the Member States of the general criteria which it intends to follow with regard to state aids in the area of the environment, in view of the general provisions of the treaty on state aids. To this end, the Commission established a certain number of conditions that the Member States must respect if they wish to make use of the exemption under Article 92, paragraph 3(b). These are the following:

(i) The optimal exemption would only be open to the Member States for a period of six years from 1 January 1975 to 31 December 1980.

(ii) In order to qualify for exemption, national aids would have to satisfy the following two criteria:

- they would have to be necessitated by new major obligations and regulations imposed by the state or by the Community on the recipient firms in relation to environmental protection;
- they would have to be granted to finance investments necessary to the adaptations which these firms would have to make to their plants in operation at 1 January 1975 in order to satisfy the stated obligations.

Such additional investment might be involved either in acquiring new equipment to reduce or eliminate pollution or nuisances or in adopting new production processes having the same effect; in the latter case aid should not be granted in respect of that part of the new investment whose effect is to increase productive capacity. The cost of replacing and operating the investments should be borne fully by the relevant firms.

(iii) When expressed as a net after-tax subsidy calculated by reference to the common method set out in the Commission Memorandum to the Council in Regional Aid Schemes,[2] state aids were not to exceed:
- 45% of the value of the beneficiary investment for investments in 1975 and 1976;
- 30% for investments in 1977 and 1978;
- 15% for investments in 1979 and 1980.

The Commission felt that this degressive scale was justified because the Member States had to be aware of the need to make polluters pay the price of their pollution as quickly as possible, and because firms had to be made to treat the investments required to eliminate pollution as a matter of urgency.

The maximum aid, although it was high, took account of the degree of effort required of businesses which had thought out their activities in an economic context where environmental costs were insufficiently taken into account. These maximum limits had to be respected, even where the relevant investments might benefit from several specifically environmental aid schemes.

(iv) Each year the Member States had to give a statistical report for the past year on the aids granted and the investments involved in each industry. As required by the general provisions of the treaty with regard to state aids (Article 93 of the EEC Treaty) the Commission was thus in a position to monitor the application of these aid schemes and to act where necessary in order to tighten disciplines should it be found that schemes were liable to create problems in certain industries as regards competition and trade within the Community.

If all of the above conditions were met, the Member States would be able to implement both aid schemes in favour of given industries or regions, and general schemes applicable to any particular industry or region. Any scheme which did not meet the above conditions had to be modified, otherwise the Commission had to declare it incompatible with the functioning of the Common Market, unless the aids satisfied the general application rules defined in Article 92, paragraph 3(a) or 3(c) of the EEC Treaty.

(b) Application of the general rules of the EEC Treaty if state aids do not respect the conditions of exemption under Article 92, paragraph 3(b)

[2] OJ No C 111 of 4/11/71 and OJ No C 31 of 3/2/79.

If the conditions and limits fixed by the Commission regarding exemption under Article 92, paragraph 3(b) were not respected, the Commission applied the following criteria to state aids on environmental matters:

(i) State aids in the area of the environment cannot be considered to be compatible with the Common Market unless they respect the general conditions concerning the exemptions provided for under Article 92, paragraphs 3(b) and 3(c) of the EEC Treaty. These exemptions concern aids intended to encourage the development of "certain activities" (para. 3(a)) or "certain regions" (para. 3(c)). Consequently, these provisions exclude the application by Member States of general aid schemes, which depend on the discretionary power of national administrations alone and which can apply to any firm regardless of its geographic location or industrial sector.

(ii) In order to be authorized by the Commission, state aids must also be granted with the aim of adapting the firms to the new obligations and restrictions imposed on them by the demands of environmental protection. This aim must be reflected in the nature of the aid and in the definition of the beneficiaries. As far as the nature of the aid is concerned, it must aim to facilitate the research/development activities of firms with a view to achieving less polluting products or techniques, or to allow firms to establish new installations for the elimination of pollution or nuisance.

For firms receiving state aids corresponding to the criteria outlined above, the aid can only be granted to existing firms in cases of a sudden and considerable modification to the environmental obligations and restrictions. Under this group of criteria only state aids in the area of the environment which, for example, assist the functioning of firms, or which are granted to new firms, can in principle be considered by the Commission to be compatible with the Common Market.

2.   The second Commission Memorandum of 1980 on state aids on environmental matters

In a second Memorandum addressed to the Member States in 1980, the Commission took the view that the transitional period of six years established in 1974 for the provision of specific aid for the environment was too short to achieve the objective set, namely the general and uniform implementation of the polluter pays principle in the Community. It therefore decided on 2 July 1980 to grant Member States a new transitional period of six years, thereby extending to 31 December 1986 the period during which state aids for the environment could, with the introduction of a few minor amendments, continue to be granted to firms.

Three reasons led the Commission to grant a new exemption period authorizing the Member States to give national aids in the area of the environment:

● the economic recession which set in at the beginning of the transitional period meant that the funds Member States were able to set aside for environmental protection had to be restricted and attempts to regulate the question were hampered;

● the complexity of environmental problems made the preparation of laws and regulations at both national and Community levels a long and difficult task;

- delays caused by this situation attracted particular attention from public opinion, resulting in increased demands for actions and improvements to the environment extending far beyond what had been achieved by governments to date.

The granting of national aids in the area of the environment is subject, during the period from 1 January 1981 to 31 December 1986, to the following conditions:

- only undertakings having installations in operation for at least two years prior to the entry into force of the environmental standards in question will be eligible for financial assistance;
- the rate of aid will be uniformly maintained at 15% of the value of the investment aided, throughout the whole of the transitional period; the rate applying for the last two years (1979–1980) of the first transitional period is thus extended for six years;
- the Member States must send the Commission an annual report on the application of their aid programmes. This report must show the total aid granted (expressed as a net subsidy) and the total investments which have received aid. These totals must be divided according to the industrial sector, region and category of anti-pollution action in question: water, air, noise, solid and effluent wastes.

As far as the system to be applied from 1 January 1987 onwards is concerned, the Commission decided to extend the current legal situation for the period of the 4th Action Programme (1987–1992). However, the Commission specified that this extension would be subject to revision in the light of the findings of the examination under way into the application by Member States of the polluter pays principle (P.P.P.).

III. THE 1978 COUNCIL RECOMMENDATION TO THE MEMBER STATES REGARDING THE METHODS FOR ASSESSING POLLUTION CONTROL COSTS IN INDUSTRY

On 8 December 1977 the Commission presented the Council with a draft Recommendation to the Member States concerning methods for assessing pollution control costs in industry. The Commission noted that the methods used and the data obtained in this area varied among the Member States and that it was therefore difficult to compare them at Community level.

It therefore proposed that the Member States adopt a body of common principles for future studies into the cost of pollution control in industry. This common framework was based on models produced in certain industrial sectors, and taking into consideration the work of the OECD.

The Council adopted this Recommendation on assessing pollution control costs in industry on 19 December 1978.[3] The Recommendation, which is addressed to the Member States, completes and makes more specific that of 3 March 1975 on the charging of costs in the area of the environment, better known as the polluter pays principle (P.P.P.). The assessment of costs is intended, first, to determine the extent of the charge which should be assumed by the economy as a whole or by the different industrial sectors, when the authorities take environmental protection measures. Secondly, such an assessment should provide indications as to the means of reducing the pollution to the lowest possible costs. To assess these costs the Member States must wherever possible apply the following principles:

---

[3] OJ No L 5 of 9/1/79.

(a) Cost data concerning the cost of pollution control measures should be collected in such a way that an evaluation of each of the following cost categories is available separately for each pollution control technique identified in the technical survey:
  • Investment costs (new or replacement): expenditure on the construction or acquisition of plant and equipment; expenditure on the construction or acquisition of buildings; expenditure on the acquisition of land and/or the market value of land already owned; expenditure on improvements; expenditure on loss of output during transition.
  • Running costs: expenditure on labour; expenditure on energy; expenditure on materials other than energy; expenditure on services; expenditure on rents; expenditure on repairs.
(b) The above mentioned data should not include value added tax and should be calculated as gross costs, without making deduction for any subsidies.
(c) The cost data should be accompanied by the following information:
  • the market value of any materials recovered or saved as a result of the operation of the pollution control plant in question;
  • the exact levels of the values of emissions by the relevant production plant;
  • the annual production capacity and the annual production volume of the production process.
(d) As regards measures taken only partly for environmental reasons, an absolute amount attributable to pollution control should be determined as precisely as possible and the criteria used for its derivation stated. The amount should be expressed as a proportion of the total cost of the measures concerned.

IV. FUTURE ACTION

The 5th Environment Action Programme states that, in order to get the prices right and to create market based incentives for environmentally friendly economic behaviour, the use of economic and fiscal instruments will have to constitute an increasingly important part of the overall approach. The fundamental aim of these instruments will be to internalize all external environmental costs incurred during the whole life-cycle of products from source through production, distribution, use and final disposal, so that environmentally friendly products will not be at a competitive disadvantage in the market place *vis-à-vis* products which cause pollution and waste. The 5th Action Programme commits the Commission to exploring the use of charges and levies as well as fiscal incentives and notes that, with the differential taxes already being applied in the case of leaded and unleaded petrol and with the proposal for the "Carbon tax" (see p. 174), there is already movement in this direction. The Programme states:

> This evolution will be encouraged over the period covered by this Programme with a view to overall modernization and rationalization of fiscal systems to render them more responsive to the need to protect the natural resource base and the environment. In this regard, it is now widely accepted as economically more efficient to tax those activities which damage the economic resource structure, including the environment, and to reduce the burden of those taxes which can have a negative effect of employment and investment. Every care should be taken however, to avoid increases in the overall burden of taxation.

Chapter 11

Research

1. Since 1961, under the Euratom Treaty, the Community has been carrying out research into the effects of ionizing radiation and its implications for the environment. However, this specific research comes more into the area of the development of atomic energy than that of environmental protection. The first attempts to coordinate environmental research at Community level date from 1967 when the PREST (Working Party on Scientific and Technological Research Policy of the Medium-Term Economic Policy Committee), considering that environmental protection was a most appropriate subject for scientific cooperation, established an expert group on nuisances and asked it to prepare research projects to be undertaken jointly. However, this initial joint research rapidly went beyond the limits of the Community of the six Member States, and it was decided to associate third countries in the research. Thus, from the outset of Community environmental research, the Community has turned to the exterior, and particularly to other non-Community European countries, offering its cooperation on research matters. Environmental protection was particularly suitable for this kind of scientific and technical cooperation, in that pollution is no respecter of borders. Since 1971 the Community has signed three "scientific and technical cooperation" agreements (COST), concerning oxides of sulphur, micropollutants in water, and sewage sludge processing respectively.

2. It was not until 1972–1973 however, that a real Community environmental research policy was launched, which benefited both from well-established structures and from substantial funds from the Community budget. The preparation of this research policy took place in close association with the discussions held within the Council of Ministers within the framework of the adoption of the 1st Environmental Action Programme of 1973 (see Table 11.1). Indeed the drawing up of the research action programme had to rely on a body of scientific and technical knowledge regarding the natural environment, ecology, toxicology, chemistry, technology, etc. The knowledge available frequently being insufficient, it consequently had to be complemented by research and development actions.

These research actions are carried out either directly by the Community in its Joint Research Centre (JRC), or indirectly via coordinated national research actions in the Member States. This coordination is carried out by the Commission either in the form of shared cost actions carried out between the Community and the Member States or in the form of "concerted" actions which make it easier to follow different research projects carried out in the Member States. It was in this context

Table 11.1: European Communities' Environmental Programme/Community Research Programme (1973)

Programme	A. Research already undertaken or approved[1]	B. Other research possibly to be undertaken
Part Two		
Title 1: Measures to reduce pollution and nuisances		
Chapter 1: Objective evaluation of the risks to human health and to the environment from pollution	1. Data bank on chemical pollutants 2. Noxiousness of lead 3. Epidemiological surveys	1. Thermal rejects 2. Acoustic irritants 3. Problem of unpleasant smells
Chapter 2: Setting of standards	4. Effects of micropollutants on humans, including biochemical toxicology and the biotelemetry of toxic effects 5. Ecological effects of pollutants, including bioindicators of water pollution 6. Remote sensing of atmospheric pollution 7. Mathematical models of the diffusion of atmospheric pollution 8. Analysis of organic micro-pollutants in water (COST 64b) 9. Multidetection unit (contribution to COST 64b) 10. Physico-chemistry of SO_2 (COST 61a) 11. Uptake of SO_2 by soil and vegetation (contribution to (COST 61a)	4. Marine pollution from the continent 5. Physical model for studies on the diffusion of atmospheric pollutants

Table 11.1 continued

Programme	A. Research already undertaken or approved[1]	B. Other research possibly to be undertaken
Chapter 3: Specific action on environment pollution		
Section 1: Exchange of information between the surveillance and monitoring networks	1. Data bank on chemical pollutants 6. Remote sensing of atmospheric pollution	6. Improvement of methods of analysis and measurement of pollutants
Chapter 9: Action to be taken on the economic aspects of anti-pollution measures	1. Data bank on chemical pollutants	
Chapter 10: Research projects (p.m.)		
Chapter 11: Dissemination of knowledge relating to environment protection	1. Data bank on chemical pollutants	
Title II: Action to improve the environment		
Chapter 1: Protection of the natural environment		13. Structure and function of ecological systems 14. Ecological effects of modern production techniques employed in farming 15. Integrated campaign against harmful insects 16. Improvement of the quality of agricultural products 17. Utilization of waste water for irrigation purposes 18. Water supply and administration of water resources

Table 11.1 continued

Programme	A. Research already undertaken or approved[1]	B. Other research possibly to be undertaken
Chapter 2: Depletion of certain natural resources		
Chapter 3: Urban development and improvement of amenities (p.m.)		
Chapter 4: Improvement of the working environment (p.m.)		
Chapter 5: European Foundation for the Improvement of Working and Living Conditions		19. Long-term perspective of living and working conditions
Chapter 6: Promotion of awareness of environmental problems and education		20. Organization of instruction on the environment at various educational levels

[1]As part of the multiannual Research and Training Programme and COST projects.

that in 1973 the first pluriannual environmental research programme was launched. Research and development requirements having grown, this first programme has been followed by several others, the last of which was adopted in 1991.

It should be noted that the idea of an "environmental research programme" in fact covers two different categories of programmes. The first involves "direct" research, the second "indirect" research. While the Commission ensures a close link between these two categories from the point of view of staff and research themes, legally speaking these programmes are entirely separate.

This explains how the Council has been able to adopt programmes at different dates and why the periods for the carrying out of the programmes often do not coincide, while it is also possible for their periods of duration to differ (three, four or five years, depending on the case in question). This difference was particularly clear in the fourth "environmental research programme". The "direct" research section of this programme covered the years 1984–1990. The research programmes are also often revised before they expire, in order to adapt them to new developments. In order to facilitate the coordination of the different research actions, the Commission is assisted by an Advisory Committee on Programme Management for Environmental Research working in the sector of environment and natural resources and made up of experts from the Member States.

3. Generally speaking, the Community's environmental research policy can be seen to represent an important aspect both of environmental policy and of the global scientific research policy of the Community. During the last decade the "environment" research programmes have been significantly expanded both with regard to the themes of research covered and to the funds and personnel made available from this research. The widening of the field covered is largely explained by the development of disturbing environmental phenomena such as acid rain or accidents which involve dangerous chemicals, and by the desire to alter the direction of Community research which was originally centred on questions linked with atomic energy.

From the structural point of view Community environmental research calls on all the mechanisms and channels which are open to Community research, namely the "direct" actions carried out by the Community's Joint Research Centre (JRC) which is mainly based in Ispra in Italy, the "indirect" actions which rely on the coordination by the Commission of research actions undertaken in the Member States, or the "COST" actions which cover research carried out jointly by the Community, its Member States and third countries, mainly Austria, Switzerland and Sweden. Finally, it should be noted that parallel to these "environmental" research actions, which are directly supportive of the different Community Environmental Action Programmes, the Community is also pursuing very important research programmes in the area of nuclear energy, which also deserve mention in that they undoubtedly contribute to environmental protection in the broad sense of the term. These programmes concern, for example, nuclear safety (safety of fuel reactors), health protection against radioactive material (radio-protection), or the management and storing of radioactive waste.

I. THE FIRST "ENVIRONMENTAL" RESEARCH PROGRAMME (1973–1976)

The first environmental research programme was decided by the Council in 1973, a few months before the adoption of the 1st Environmental Action Programme. This first research programme, which is part of the Community's pluriannual research programme, included both "direct" and "indirect" research actions. It was specifically established in order to provide scientific and technical support to the "reduction of pollution and nuisance" section of the 1st Action Programme. In particular it was meant to provide the scientific and technical knowledge needed to evaluate objectively the risks to man and the environment resulting from pollution and nuisance, to improve the pollution measurement methods, and to manage information in the area of the environment.

1. Direct research (JRC)

Direct research actions were agreed by the Council on 14 May 1973.[1] Undertaken at the Common Research Centre (CRC) in Ispra, they were to be carried out over a period of four years, from 1 January 1973 to 31 December 1976. They involved a

---

[1] OJ No L 153 of 9/6/73.

staff of 142 people and a budgetary allowance of 13 million Ecu. The research covered the following four areas:

- analysis and monitoring of pollution (including development of a multi-detection unit, remote sensing of air pollutants, and a pilot data bank of environmental chemicals);
- fate and effects of pollutants;
- models and system analysis applied to the eutrophication of a lake and to air pollution;
- thermal pollution and catalytic oxidation of water pollutants.

2.   Indirect research (contract actions)

Indirect research actions were the subject of a Council Decision of 18 June 1973.[2] They received Community finance of 6.3 million Ecu and were to take place over three years, from 1 January 1973 to 31 December 1975. These actions mainly had to be carried out in the form of research contracts made by the Commission with different laboratories or national research institutes. The funding of these contracts is shared between the Community budget and those of the Member States. The research was to cover the following areas:

- establishment of a data bank on environmental chemicals;
- harmful effects of lead;
- epidemiological surveys of the effects of air and water pollution;
- effects of micropollutants on man;
- ecological effects of water pollution;
- remote sensing of air pollution.

The research actions carried out via contracts are managed by the Commission which must submit an annual report to the Council on the execution of the programme. To assist the Commission in implementing these research actions, the Council also decided in 1973 to appoint an Advisory Committee on the Management of Environmental Research Programmes made up of experts put forward by the Member States. In particular this committee must examine the requests for participation received from the different laboratories of the Member States.

In 1978 the Commission published a final report on research actions launched under this first programme of indirect research. A total of 127 shared-cost contracts were signed and completed, the maximum contribution by the Community usually amounting to 50% of the total cost of each project. Of these 127 projects, 10 concerned area no. 1 (data bank), 27 area no. 2 (harmful effects of lead), 16 area no. 5 (water pollutants) and 10 area no. 6 (remote sensing of air pollution). The following can be mentioned by way of illustration of these research actions:

- an epidemiological survey aimed at establishing correlations between air pollution and respiratory diseases in children;
- a study of pollution in streams of the Luxembourg–Saarland–Lorraine region in relation to the establishment of quality objectives for these watercourses;
- a pilot project for the development of a data bank on environmental chemicals (ECDIN project);

[2] OJ No L 189 of 11/7/73.

- a project for the development of mutagenicity testing methods for environmental pollutants, in order to improve the techniques for assessing long-term effects of pollution on human health;
- research on chronic toxicity of lead at low level which has served as a scientific basis for the preparation of a directive on the monitoring of the degree of contamination of the population by lead (see p. 132);
- a project designed to facilitate the development of better techniques for the treatment and utilization of sewage sludge;
- the drawing up of a list of over 1000 organic micropollutants identified in surface water in order to establish, with a view to evaluating, the potential toxicity of these waters and to guide the development of treatments for drinking water.

II.   THE SECOND ENVIRONMENTAL RESEARCH PROGRAMME (1976–1980)

1.   Direct research (JRC)

On 18 July 1977[3] the Council agreed on a general research programme to be executed by the Joint Research Centre for a period of four years from 1977 to 1980. This programme, which mainly covered nuclear safety and future energies, also included a section on environmental protection and natural resources. Of a total of 345 million Ecu, 35 million were devoted to environmental research covering the following four areas: air; water; chemicals; renewable resources.

2.   Indirect research (contract actions)

On 15 March 1976 the Council adopted a second pluriannual environmental research and development programme[4] for a period of five years from 1976 to 1980. This programme had a staff of 10 and a budget of 16 million Ecu. It was to be undertaken via contracts made by the Commission with the research institutes or laboratories of the Member States, the funding generally being split 50/50 between the Community budget and that of the Member States. The four main areas of research were the following:

- the establishment of criteria (exposure-effect relationships) for environmental pollutants;
- environmental information management, especially with regard to problems of new chemicals likely to endanger health or the environment;
- improvement of the environment; the planned research concerned the structure and function of ecosystems, biogeochemical cycles, reclamation of spoiled or waste land, remote sensing of environmental disturbances and the ecological implications of land development and modern methods of farming.

[3] OJ No L 200 of 8/8/77.
[4] OJ No L 74 of 20/3/76.

The Council's Decision of 15 March 1976 also made provision for an assessment and revision of the research programme during its third year of execution. The Commission therefore, having carried out an overall re-examination of the environmental research programmes under way, and having asked for the opinion of the Advisory Committee on Programme Management, proposed to the Council in 1978 that it amend and expand this second Community environmental research programme. The revision was mainly intended to integrate the latest and most accurate environmental problems with regard to health and the protection of the natural environment.

The Council adopted the Decision regarding the revision of the second environmental research programme on 9 October 1979.[5] This revision increased the budget from 16 million to 20.8 million Ecu, and extended the four areas of research defined in 1976 as follows:

- the first area of research, aimed at the establishment of health criteria for pollutants and environmental chemicals, concerned in particular, heavy metals, organic micropollutants and new chemicals, asbestos, air quality, water quality, thermal discharges, sea pollution and noise nuisance;
- the second area of research mainly concerned the collection and handling of data on chemicals in the framework of the ECDIN (Environmental Chemicals Data and Information Network);
- the third area of research concerned water pollution, and especially the development of advanced water treatment methods, the environmental effects of waste, and the development of clean technologies;
- the fourth area of research was centred on the following three topics: ecosystems and biogeochemical cycles (the establishment of an ecological cartography, reduction of the ozone layer, and accumulation of CO_2 in the atmosphere); reclamation of waste land; bird protection (protection of habitats).

III. THE THIRD ENVIRONMENTAL RESEARCH PROGRAMME (1980–1985)

1. Direct research (JRC)

On 13 March 1980 the Council agreed on the research programme to be undertaken by the Joint Research Centre for a new period of four years, from 1 January 1980 to 31 December 1983.[6] Out of a staff of over 2000 people and a total budget of over 500 million Ecu, nearly half of the staff and budget were devoted to nuclear safety and the fuel cycle (reactor safety; plutonium fuel and research into actinides; safety of nuclear materials and management of fissionable matter). The section concerning the study of the protection of the natural environment represented a staff of approximately 300 people, and a budget of the order of 50 million Ecu. This section was subdivided into two areas:

- the first area, concerning environmental protection in the full sense of the term, for the most part merely followed on from the actions undertaken since 1973 by

[5] OJ No L 258 of 13/10/79.
[6] OJ No L 72 of 18/3/80.

the JRC in the area of the environment, namely chemicals, water and air quality and heavy metals. A new action was nevertheless added concerning the impact on the environment of major non-nuclear fuel installations (power plants);
- the second area, of a more innovative nature, concerned spatial remote sensing and consisted of two projects on agriculture and sea protection.

2. Indirect research (contract and concerted actions)

In December 1979 the Council decided to carry out a greater rationalization of all the Community's environmental research programmes. Before pronouncing on the Commission's proposal for a third environmental research programme therefore, the Council first asked the Commission to draw up an inventory of all the environmental research actions under way. This inventory made it possible for the Council to group together four categories of research actions being carried out in 1980, namely:

- the direct action programme being carried out by the Joint Research Centre;
- the second indirect action programme of 1976–1980, revised on 9 October 1979;
- a first research programme in the area of climatology (1980–1984) decided by the Council on 18 December 1979;[7]
- a number of specific concerted actions decided by the Council in 1977 and 1978 in the areas of sewage sludge,[8] analysis of organic micropollutants in water,[9] and of the physico-chemical behaviour of atmospheric pollutants. The concerted action involved strict coordination at Community level, carried out by the Commission, of research activities going on within the research programmes of the Member States, and where relevant of the Joint Research Centre;
- a group of COST cooperation actions (scientific and technical cooperation) agreed with third countries in 1979 and involving the same areas of research as the concerted actions referred to above (COST 68 b – COST 64 b – COST 61 a bis plus COST 47, an action on marine benthic ecosystems).

In the light of this inventory the Council adopted on 3 March 1981 the third environmental research programme[10] and decided to bring together into a single programme the indirect and concerted actions adopted in 1977–1978.

The new programme agreed by the Council ran for a period of five years from 1 January 1981 to 31 December 1985. It received a budget of 43 million Ecu and a staff of 16 people. The scientific and technical content of the programme was subdivided into two sections, one being devoted to environmental protection, the other to climatology.

The five areas of research making up the "environmental protection" section are mentioned in Table 11.2.

The section on climatology covers two areas of research, the first entitled "Understanding Climate" (reconstruction of past climates, climate modelling and predictions), the second concerning man/climate interactions (effect on agriculture and water resources; chemical pollution through accumulation of carbon gases, etc.).

---

[7] OJ No L 12 of 17/1/80.
[8] OJ No L 267 of 19/10/77.
[9] OJ No L 311 of 4/11/78.
[10] OJ No L 101 of 11/4/81.

**Table 11.2: Research areas of the 3rd environmental research
programme 1981–1985**

	Indirect action (contracts and coordination)	*Concerted action*
Research area 1: Sources, pathways and effects of pollutants		
1.1. Heavy metals	×	–
1.2. Organic micro-pollutants and new chemical products	×	(1) Analysis of organic micro-pollutants in water (COST 64b *bis*) until 31 December 1983) Research topics and distribution of work among Member States are shown in Table 1, point C
1.3. Asbestos and other fibres	×	–
1.4 Air quality	×	(2) Physico-chemical behaviour of atmospheric pollutants (COST 61a *bis*) (until 31 December 1983) Research topics and distribution of work among Member States are shown in Table 2, point C
1.5 Surface and underground freshwater quality	×	–
1.6. Thermal pollution	×	–
1.7. Marine environment quality	×	(3) Benthic coastal ecology (COST 47): 1. Sedimentary bottoms 2. Rocky bottoms – intertidal 3. Rocky bottoms – subtidal
1.8. Noise pollution	×	–
Research area 2: Reduction and prevention of pollution and nuisances		
2.1. Sewage sludge	–	(4) Treatment and use of sewage sludge (COST 68 *bis*) (until 31 December 1983) Research topics and distribution of work among Member States are shown in Table 3, point C

Table 11.2 continued

	Indirect action (contracts and coordination)	Concerted action
2.2. Pollution abatement technologies	×	−
2.3. Clean technologies	×	−
2.4. Ecological effects of solid waste disposal	×	−
2.5. Oil pollution cleaning techniques	×	×
2.6. Impact of new technologies	×	×
Research area 3: Protection, conservation and management of natural environments		
3.1. Ecosystems studies	×	−
3.2. Biogeochemical cycles	×	−
3.3. Ecosystems conservation	×	−
3.4. Bird protection	×	×
3.5. Reclamation of damaged ecosystems	×	−
Research area 4: Environment information management		
4.1. Data bank on environment chemicals	×	−
4.2. Evaluation, storage and exploration of data	×	−
4.3. Ecological cartography	×	−
Research area 5: Complex interactive systems: man-environment interactions	×	×

IV.   THE FOURTH ENVIRONMENTAL RESEARCH PROGRAMME (1986–1990)

1.   Direct research (JRC)

By a decision of 22 December 1983, the Council extended the general research programme of the Community which was being carried out by the Joint Research

Centre.[11] This programme, lasting four years, was to be carried out between 1 January 1984 and 31 December 1987. It has an overall budget of 700 million Ecu, of which 100 million are devoted to the "environmental" sub-programme. This sub-programme covers the following three areas:

- protection of the environment (chemicals; environmental quality; energy and environment);
- aero-spatial remote sensing techniques (agriculture; sea protection; natural disasters);
- industrial risks (prevention of accidents; control of accidents).

As with the preceding JRC programmes, the major part of the research is devoted to problems of nuclear fission, and in particular to problems of the safety of reactors, the management of radioactive waste and nuclear fuels. Studies will be carried out in particular into the storing of radioactive waste in continental geological formations and in deep ocean sediment. Other studies will concentrate, for example, on the modelling of accidents in reactors and on the release of fissionable products in the case of damage.

2.   Indirect research (contract and concerted actions)

On 10 June 1986 the Council adopted the decision on the fourth environmental research programme.[12] This has a budget of 75 million Ecu for a period of five years and will be carried out from 1 January 1986 to 31 December 1990. This total includes the expense incurred by the staff of 19 people implementing the programme through shared-cost contract actions, concerted actions and coordination and training activities. The scientific content of the programme includes the continuation and broadening of the research actions carried out since 1973 in the area of environment, and since 1981 in the area of climatology. Moreover, as the Commission had proposed, the Council has added to these two areas of research, a third component concerning major technological hazards.

As far as the "environmental protection" sub-programme is concerned the studies cover 11 research subjects (see Table 11.3) and have a budget of 55 million Ecu, of which 5 million are reserved for concerted actions.

Within the framework of this sub-programme a particular effort will be made in the area of acid depositions, toxic waste and soil protection. Two new actions will also be undertaken in the area of air quality inside buildings and the protection of species (loss of genetic diversity due to the effects of urbanization and agricultural practices).

The "climatology" sub-programme which has a budget of 17 million Ecu, has two distinct sections. The first returns in greater depth to the research actions already under way since 1981 within the framework of the third programme concerning:

- the physical basis of climate (climatic changes, seasonal forecasting (three–six months, etc.);
- climate sensitivity (for example, the consequences of enhanced CO_2);

[11] OJ No L 3 of 5/1/84.
[12] OJ No L 159 of 14/6/86.

Table 11.3: Research areas of the 4th environmental research programme 1986–1990

PROTECTION OF THE ENVIRONMENT

Funding: total	55 000 000 ECU
– contract research	50 450 000 ECU
– concerted actions	4 550 000 ECU

Scientific content of the programme

Reference to the subthemes contained under the following 11 research topics is of an indicative nature:

1. Health effects of pollutants

- Chronic and late effects at low exposure levels and early indicators of health effects,
- Epidemiology and exposure trends.

2. Ecological effects of pollutants

- Effects on sensitive key species,
- Effects on ecosystems.

3. Assessment of chemicals

- Development and assessment of testing procedures,
- Replacement of vertebrates used for toxicity testing,
- Structure/activity relationships (SAR),
- Evaluation of chemicals.

4. Air quality

- Analysis, sources, transport, transformation and deposition of pollutants,
- Effects of air pollution on the natural environment,
- Effects of air pollution on materials,
- Stratospheric chemistry,
- Remote-sensing techniques,
- Indoor-air quality.

5. Water quality

- Analytical methods,
- Biotic and abiotic degradation of pollutants,
- Eutrophication,
- Remote-sensing techniques.

6. Soil quality

- Analytical methods,
- Behaviour of pollutants in soil,
- Effects of pollutants in soil,
- Effects of agricultural and forestry practice on soil quality.

Table 11.3 continued

7. *Noise research*

   - Effects of noise on the cardiovascular system,
   - Comparison between effects of impulse noises and those of continuous noises,
   - Synergism between noise and vibrations.

8. *Ecosystem research*

   - Basic research on the functioning of ecosystems,
   - Effects of agricultural practice and urbanization on ecosystems, loss of genetic diversity,
   - Environmental oceanography,
   - Bio-geochemical cycles,
   - Conservation of flora and fauna.

9. *Waste research*

   - Waste management,
   - Organic wastes,
   - Toxic and dangerous waste,
   - Abandoned disposal sites.

10. *Reduction of pollution*

   - Advanced abatement technologies,
   - Clean technologies.

11. *Scientific basis of environmental legislation and management including the development of scientific criteria for environmental impact assessment.*

Concerted actions

Concerted actions may be implemented in the following areas within the scientific programme :

1. Air-pollution effects on terrestrial and aquatic ecosystems;

2. Physico-chemical behaviour of atmospheric pollutants;

3. Organic micropollutants in the aquatic environment;

4. Treatment and use of organic sludge and liquid agricultural waste;

5. Coastal benthic ecology;

6. Indoor-air quality and its impact on man;

7. Protection of species;

8. New technologies and environmental protection
   - environmental impact of new technological processes,
   - environmental impact of new technological products,
   - use of new technologies for environmental protection;

9. Compatibility of fibres with the environment and health.

- climatic effects (on water, agricultural land, forest resources, on sea resources and fisheries, on soil, particularly with regard to desertification).

Particular emphasis will be put on the concentration of CO_2 due to the combustion of fossil fuels, and on the climatic consequences of this phenomenon on natural resources and especially on forests.

The second section of the "climatology" programme which was added by the Council and which constitutes a new action, concerns natural hazards, and especially seismic risks. Studies will aim in particular at the creation of a data bank on seismological and earthquake damage. Education and training actions will be undertaken.

The third sub-programme on "major technological hazards" has been greatly reduced in comparison with the initial more ambitious proposals of the Commission following the accidents occurring in the chemical and petrochemical industries or in the area of transport (Bhopal, Bantry Bay, etc.). The actions to be carried out in this area will in fact only be of a pilot nature and will only have a budget of 3 million Ecu. The studies to be undertaken will cover:

- physical and chemical phenomena and mitigation of consequences of accidents (risk analysis and replacement of dangerous techniques);
- assessment and management of risks (probability of occurrence of accidents according to the geographic and human context).

It should be noted from the point of view of Community institutional procedure, that the Council's decision on this fourth environmental research programme led to a number of criticisms from the European Parliament. In particular it reproached the Council for having severely reduced the funding of this programme (75 million Ecu instead of the 105 million originally requested by the Commission), and this precisely at a time of numerous environmental problems (chemical accidents; acid rain; nuclear accidents, etc.). This is why the Parliament, which shares the budgetary authority with the Council, asked for a concertation procedure to be undertaken with the Council before the final adoption of the Decision on the fourth environmental research programme.

V. SCIENTIFIC AND TECHNICAL COOPERATION BETWEEN THE COMMUNITY AND THIRD COUNTRIES IN THE AREA OF THE ENVIRONMENT

1. Scientific and technical cooperation (COST)

Since the beginning of the implementation of a Community environmental research programme, the Community decided to associate with other European countries with a view to broadening the field of scientific cooperation and carrying out joint research actions. Three scientific and technical cooperation agreements (COST) were therefore signed on 23 November 1971, concerning the following areas:

- the physico-chemical behaviour of oxides of sulphur in the atmosphere (COST 61a/1972–1976);

Table 11.4: Cost Agreement of 19 March 1979 on research into treatment and use of sludge

Research topics	Division of research among contracting parties					
	EEC	Switzerland	Austria	Sweden	Norway	Finland
1. Sludge stabilization and odour problems:						
– Definition and determination of 'degree of stability' and relation to odour nuisance	×			×	×	
– Comparative evaluation of stabilization procedures	×	×	×	×	×	×
2. Problems related to sludge dewatering:						
– Research on water binding forces	×	×		×	×	
– Development and standardization of methods for the assessment of dewatering properties						
– Problems related to the use of flocculants	×	×		×		×
– Comparative evaluation of thickening and dewatering equipment	×	×		×	×	×
3. Analytical problems related to sludge treatment and use:						
– Characterization of pathogens and evaluation of disinfection procedures	×	×			×	×
– Characterization and determination of pollutants (heavy metals, persistent organic compounds) in sludge and development of standardized analytical method	×	×	×	×		
4. Environmental problems related to sludge use:						
– Special processing of sludge for agricultural use (e.g. composting) including the improvement of disinfection procedure and pollutant removal	×	×	×		×	×
– Transfer of pollutants to plants and harmful effect on vegetation	×	×		×	×	×
– Effects of long range sludge application on soil quality and ground water	×		×	×	×	×
– Optimum land use of sludge, including sludge from dephosphatation plants	×	×	×	×	×	×

- the analysis of organic micropollutants in water (COST 64b/1972–1974);
- treatment of sewage sludge (COST 68/1973–1974).

It should be noted that these three agreements on areas of environmental protection were the first to be the subject of this kind of scientific cooperation with third countries, and can therefore be considered to be precursors which opened the way for the "COST" agreements in areas other than that of the environment, particularly those of food research and medical research. Among the most recent COST agreements, there is for example COST 48, concluded by the Council on 14 July 1986, which concerns research into biotechnology in the area of aquatic biomass. On the same day the Council also concluded COST 87 concerning the area of plant cultures.

The three COST agreements signed in 1971 having given encouraging results and having provided mutual advantages, the Council decided in 1979 to renew the agreements with Austria, Portugal, Finland, Norway, Sweden and Switzerland, while broadening the field of research. These agreements were thus extended and are still in force.

Concertation between the contracting parties to the agreements takes place within a "Community-COST" concertation committee, the secretariat of which is provided by the Commission.

Although all the parties remain entirely responsible for the research undertaken by the national research institutes, a project director is appointed by the Commission with the agreement of the participating countries. As an illustration of a COST agreement, Table 11.4 shows the division of the research work to be undertaken by the contracting parties of COST 68 bis on the treatment and utilization of sewage sludge. This agreement was concluded by the Council on 19 March 1979.[13]

2. COST agreement: "Concerted" community research actions

The first COST operation agreements signed with third countries originally involved closer concertation in the area of research between the Member States of the Community themselves on one hand, and the Commission on the other. The successful working of these agreements assumed increased harmonization beforehand of the research work undertaken by the Member States and by the Commission in the Joint Research Centre. So-called "concerted" actions were therefore needed which allowed the Commission to act as a "catalyst" and to play a larger coordinating role than is the case in "contract" actions.

The three areas of research covered by the 1971 COST agreements were later the subject of three "concerted" Community actions which were decided on by the Council in 1977–1978.[14] These three actions (sewage sludge – micropollutants in water – atmospheric pollutants) were integrated from 1981 onwards into the third indirect environmental research programme. An example of "concerted" Community action appears in Table 11.5. This table, which shows the division of research to be undertaken between the Member States and the Joint Research Centre, concerns the analysis of organic micropollutants in water.

[13] OJ No L 72 of 23/3/79.
[14] OJ No L 311 of 4/11/78.

Table 11.5: "Concerted" Community Research Action of 9 October 1978 containing the analysis of organic micropollutants in water

Research topics	Division of research work								
	B	D	DK	F	I	IRL	NL	UK	JRC
1. Sampling and sample treatment									
– General development and evaluation of methods		×	×		×		×	×	×
– methods for sampling sediments and indicator organisms									
2. Gas chromatographic analysis	×	×	×	×	×	×	×	×	×
3. Coupling gas chromatographs and mass spectrometers	×		×	×		×			×
4. Other separation techniques									
– development of methods for liquid chromatography			×				×	×	×
– improvement of equipment									
– other separation techniques									
5. Data collection and processing									
– hard copy spectrum collection	×	×	×	×	×	×	×	×	×
– establishment of a spectrum library									
6. Establishment of inventories									
– inventory of pollutants	×	×	×	×	×	×	×	×	×
– collection of data on conversion									

VI.   STEP AND EPOCH

On 20 November 1989, on the basis of a Commission proposal submitted the previous year, the Council adopted a Decision establishing the STEP and EPOCH environmental R & D programmes for the period 1989–1992.[15] These programmes provide scientific and technical back-up for Community Environment Policy, with the accent on the development of preventive and anticipatory policies. They also aim to improve and streamline the level of global research activities in the Community, partly through coordination of national environmental R & D programmes.

The STEP programme deals with various aspects of environmental protection (health; chemical risks; air and water quality; soil and groundwater protection; ecosystems and clean technologies), cultural heritage, major technological risks and fire safety, while EPOCH concentrates on various aspects of climatology and natural hazards.

1.   STEP

On 20 November 1989 the Council adopted a Decision concerning a specific-multiannual environment related R & D programme – Science and Technology for Environmental Protection (STEP) – for the years 1989 to 1992.

Article 8 of the Decision authorizes the Commission to negotiate agreements with European third countries with which the Community has concluded framework agreements for scientific and technical cooperation in order to associate such countries wholly or partly within the STEP programme. The Community having already concluded framework agreements with Austria, Finland and Norway on 9 February 1987 (9840/86), the Commission submitted a proposal for the association of the three countries with the STEP programme. Their association would enable researchers and research bodies from the three countries to participate in STEP and, in particular, allow them to submit relevant research proposals to the Commission and, where these were approved, to receive financial support. Austria, Finland and Norway would also make financial contributions to the programme calculated proportionally according to GDP.

2.   EPOCH

The European Programme on Climatology and Natural Hazards, EPOCH, was agreed by the Council on 20 November 1989.

Framework agreements for scientific and technical cooperation were agreed between the Community and Iceland and Sweden on 29 September 1989 and 9 February 1987. In 1991 the Commission submitted to Council a proposal for the two countries to be associated with both the EPOCH and STEP programmes on the same basis as Austria, Finland and Norway were with STEP.

---

[15] 89/625/EEC: Council Decision of 20 November 1989 on two specific research and development programmes in the field of the environment – STEP and Epoch (1989–1992).

VII.   THIRD FRAMEWORK PROGRAMME 1990–1994

On 23 April 1990, the Council adopted the Third Framework Programme for research and development in the area of environment. The programme will run for five years with a budget of 5.7 billion Ecu, as well as a supplementary budget of 900 million Ecu. Within the framework programme, 15 specific programmes for research and technical development (RTD) are provided for:

- information technologies;
- communication technologies;
- development of telematics systems in areas of general interest;
- industrial and materials technologies;
- measurement and testing;
- environment;
- marine science and technology;
- biotechnology;
- agricultural and agro-industrial research;
- biomedical and health research;
- life sciences and technologies for developing countries;
- non-nuclear energies;
- nuclear fission safety;
- controlled thermonuclear fusion;
- human capital and mobility.

Most of these programmes are to be implemented via shared-cost research projects or concerted research actions. In shared-cost projects, Community participation is in principle 50% of total project costs, whereas as regards concerted research actions, the Community only reimburses coordination costs rather than the costs of research itself.

VIII.   THE FIFTH ENVIRONMENTAL RESEARCH PROGRAMME (1991–1994)

The programme constitutes the follow-up to the STEP, EPOCH and REWARD research programmes which ran from 1989–1992. It seeks to expand and reinforce ongoing research projects by adopting a more integrated, multidisciplinary and transnational approach by taking into account the global aspects of environmental issues, as well as the growing importance of Community environmental policy. To this end, the programme contains six general objectives:

- to provide the scientific data and technical know-how to enable the Community effectively to carry out environmental actions in accordance with title VII of the treaty;
- to increase the productivity of the Community's research activities by better coordination of national R & D programmes and the minimization of overlaps;
- to reinforce the Community's role in international conventions concerning the protection of the atmosphere by improving fundamental knowledge on the greenhouse effect;

- to provide a basis for a European contribution to international programmes concerning global environmental problems, whilst concentrating on areas of particular interest to Europe;
- to provide a sound technical basis for environmental quality norms, safety and technical norms and methodologies for environmental impact assessment, and to support the European Environmental Agency;
- to help strengthen the social and economic cohesion of the Community through the promotion of scientific and technical quality and the incorporation into environmental research of socio-economic aspects.

In addition, the programme contains four specific objectives. First, to contribute to the understanding of the processes governing environmental change and to assess the impact of human activity. Secondly, to improve environmental quality standards by the encouragement of technological innovation at the pre-competitive stage and to protect and rehabilitate the environment. Thirdly, to expand and deepen the understanding of the economic, legal, ethical and health aspects of environmental policy and management, and fourthly, to assist in the resolution of problems of national interest by means of a systems approach and interdisciplinary research.

The programme is subdivided into four main areas: participation in global change programmes; technologies and engineering for the environment; research on economic and social aspects of environmental issues; and technological and natural risks.

The programme is open to all persons and organizations (industrial firms, universities, higher education institutes, research organizations, etc.) established in the European Community. Organizations from European third countries can participate fully in the programme under the same conditions as organizations from the Member States where their country of origin has signed an agreement with the Community for full association. At the time of writing, no such agreements were in force. Otherwise, they can participate in the programme on a project by project basis, in which case they are not eligible for funding from the Community.

In order to participate, persons or organizations must submit a proposal which falls within the scope and objectives of the programme and which conforms to specific criteria, such as being innovative, of a pre-competitive character, having a European dimension, and being transnational, i.e. involving at least two independent participants from different Member States.

IX. SPECIFIC RESEARCH PROGRAMMES

1. Special research programme on the recycling of paper and board

On 17 April 1978 the Council adopted a research programme on the recycling of paper and board[16] (indirect research action). This research action was to take place over a period of four years from 1 January 1978 and was to be carried out by contracts. Bearing in mind the Community's great dependence on third countries for paper, the programme aimed to improve technologies for the recovery and

---

[16] OJ No L 107 of 21/4/78.

recycling of paper and board, especially with regard to the quality of recycled paper. Among the specific research themes there appears in particular the problems of de-inking and the health problems caused by using recycled fibres.

2.   Special research programme on the recycling of urban and industrial waste

On 12 November 1979 the Council agreed on a specific research programme on the recycling of urban and industrial waste[17] (indirect research action). This programme, which aimed to reduce the Community's dependence on third countries for raw materials, was to be carried out over a period of four years with a budget of 9 million Ecu. The areas of research concentrated on the sorting of household waste, the thermal treatment of waste, the fermentation, hydrolysis and recovery of rubber waste. The Commission was to ensure the carrying out of the contract actions and was responsible for the coordination of the different research activities which were divided between the Member States. It was assisted by an advisory committee made up of experts from the Member States. This research programme was extended on 17 May 1982 and integrated into the programme on secondary raw materials (recycling of metal – urban and industrial waste, etc.).[18]

3.   REWARD

The REWARD programme (REcycling WAste and R & D) ran from 1989 to 1992 following on from the Community's first waste recycling programme (1986–1989). It covered three broad areas of research: sampling, analysis and classification of wastes; recycling technologies; and fuel and energy production from waste. The programme had five objectives. First, to raise the percentage of recycling and re-utilization of waste by the development of economically viable technologies. Secondly, to improve the management of raw materials and of energy resources. Thirdly, to help alleviate problems of waste disposal and of environmental pollution. Fourthly, to boost industrial competitiveness by the development of innovative technologies, the use of recycled materials and the promotion of recyclable materials. Fifthly, it sought to further the coordination of relevant research and development projects in Europe.

A total of 6 million Ecu were provided for REWARD to cover, *inter alia*, shared-cost contracts research, coordination activities, workshops and symposia. Pilot or demonstration projects were not eligible for funding as they were covered by other sources of funding.

[17] OJ No L 193 of 20/11/79.
[18] OJ No L 174 of 21/6/82.

Chapter 12

International Conventions

Since the Community's first environmental action programme, the international dimension of the Community's environmental policy has remained a priority. The adoption of internal rules in particular areas has often been followed by measures to ensure the Community's adherence or accession to international treaties or conventions in those areas as well as its participation in the mechanisms, e.g. committees, commissions or conferences of the parties, which have been established under such treaties or conventions. The 5th Environmental Action Programme recalls that over the past 20 years, the Community has been playing an important part in international action in the field of the environment. The Community is a contracting party to some 30 conventions and international agreements, and is actively supporting the work of different international and regional institutions, such as UNEP, UN-ECE, OECD and the Council of Europe. In pursuance of its obligations under the treaty, as amended by the Single European Act, and under Article 130.r of the new Treaty on European Union, the Community's involvement in international environmental action will be stepped up over the period covered by the programme.

I. CONVENTIONS IN THE AREA OF WATER POLLUTION

1. The Paris Convention for the Prevention of Marine Pollution from Land-Based Sources (1974)

The first session of the conference on marine pollution from land-based sources was held in Paris in 1973 at France's initiative. This conference, in which most of the Western European countries bordering the North Atlantic participated, was intended to put together regulations for an important sector of marine pollution which was not yet covered by any international conventions, namely, pollution brought into the sea by rivers, estuaries, and pipelines, as well as by direct discharges into the sea from the shore. Since the drawing up of the Oslo and London Conventions in 1972, significant progress had been made in the control of sea pollution due to discharges or dumping from ships. Other conventions drawn up within the framework of the International Maritime Organization (IMO) were aimed at controlling the accidental or deliberate discharging of oil at sea.

The diplomatic conference in Paris ended on 4 June 1974 with the adoption of the text of a Convention for the Prevention of Maritime Pollution from Land-Based Sources. This draft convention was open for signature up until 31 May 1975. The Paris Convention covers the maritime zone of the North-East Atlantic. According to the convention, the contracting parties undertake:

● to eliminate, if necessary by stages, pollution from land-based sources by substances listed in the convention;
● to limit strictly pollution from land-based sources by other substances also listed in the convention.

In order to respect these undertakings, the Member States must implement, individually or jointly, programmes and measures, including, if appropriate, the establishment of specific regulations or standards together with time limits. The convention defines "pollution from land-based sources" as being the pollution of the maritime area through watercourses and from the coast, including introduction through pipelines and from manmade structures such as floating platforms or artificial islands.

On 3 March 1975, following a proposal by the Commission, the Council adopted two texts concerning the Paris Convention:

● In a "Decision" the Council agreed to conclude the Paris Convention on behalf of the Community, and thus become a contracting party;[1] in so doing it decided that the Community should be represented by the Commission on the executive body responsible for the management of the convention. As one of the Member States of the Community, namely Italy, was not a party to the convention, the Council also defined the internal rules and procedures to be followed by the Community within the framework of the convention.
● In a "Resolution" adopted at the same time as the Decision, the Council invited the Member States concerned to sign the convention before 31 May 1975.[2] In this Resolution the Council also asked the Commission to ensure that the provisions of the convention were implemented in a coherent and coordinated way in relation to Community legislation on the control of industrial discharges of dangerous substances (see p. 74).

(a)   The implementing programme on the discharge of mercury and cadmium

On 20 December 1985 the Council approved on behalf of the Community an initial series of specific implementing programmes and measures, negotiated within the framework of the Paris Convention.[3] These programmes, which concern the discharge of mercury and cadmium, were considered to be compatible with the Community directives already existing in that area (see p. 85).

(b)   The protocol on atmospheric pollution at sea

On 22 December 1986[4] the Council decided to ratify, on behalf of the Community, the protocol amending the Paris Convention with a view to including provisions on the prevention of atmospheric pollution at sea.

[1] OJ No L 194 of 25/7/75.
[2] OJ No C 168 of 25/7/75.
[3] OJ No L 375 of 31/12/85.
[4] OJ No L 24 of 27/1/87.

The Oslo and Paris Conventions (see pp. 403 and 409) were later superseded by a new convention which combined their terms into a single text known as the Convention on the Protection of the Environment of the North-East Atlantic (Paris Convention). The Community signed the convention on 27 September 1992 and is currently in the process of ratifying it.

2. The Barcelona Convention for the Protection of the Mediterranean Sea against Pollution (1976)

(a)   The framework convention and the first protocol for dumping operations

At the initiative of the United Nations Environment Programme (UNEP), the countries bordering the Mediterranean were invited to Barcelona in 1975 to attend a first inter-governmental meeting on the protection of the Mediterranean Sea. During this meeting an "action plan" was adopted to protect the Mediterranean against pollution. This action plan included:

● integrated planning of the development and management of the resources of the Mediterranean basin;
● a coordinated programme of research, monitoring and exchange of information, and an assessment of the state of pollution;
● the drawing up of a framework convention for the protection of the marine environment of the Mediterranean, including various protocols corresponding to each of the principal sources of pollution.

On 8 December 1975 the Council authorized the Commission to participate in the negotiations for the drawing up of the convention which were held in Barcelona in 1976. These negotiations resulted in a text for a framework convention and two additional protocols, one for cooperation in the combating of pollution by hydrocarbons, the other for pollution due to dumping operations carried out by ships and aircraft.

Subject to conclusion at a later date, the Community signed the convention on 13 September 1976, together with the protocol for dumping operations. The conclusion of these two international legal acts was decided by the Council on 25 July 1977.[5]

This convention is particularly important, not only from the point of view of environmental protection, but also politically speaking, in that it brings together the majority of countries bordering the Mediterranean, including Israel, Libya, Morocco, Tunisia, Greece and Turkey. It also enables the Community to be present in its own right in this sensitive region of the world, and to offer its cooperation and assistance (see p. 405). As far as the content of the convention is concerned, it includes not only general provisions concerning different sources of pollution (pollution due to dumping operations; pollution resulting from the exploitation of the sea's continental shelf; pollution from land-based sources; pollution resulting from accidents), but also provisions on the continuous monitoring of pollution, on scientific and technological cooperation, on liability and compensation for damage, and on the settlement of disputes and arbitration. The protocol for dumping operations carried out by ships and aircraft prohibits the dumping of certain specific

[5] OJ No L 240 of 19/9/77.

dangerous substances, and subjects the dumping of other substances or waste to the issuing of a special permit.

(b) The second protocol for cooperation in combating pollution caused by hydrocarbons in emergency situations

Following the serious accidents of 1978 (*Amoco-Cadiz* and *Tamio*) which resulted in oil slicks (see p. 117), the Council also decided on 19 May 1981[6] to conclude the "hydrocarbons" protocol drawn up in 1976, thus allowing the Community to become a contracting party to the second protocol of the Barcelona Convention. This protocol makes provision for cooperation between the contracting parties on monitoring of the sea and on the implementation of emergency plans and methods of combating pollution caused by hydrocarbons and other harmful substances.

(c)   The third protocol for pollution from land-based sources

On 28 February 1983 the Council decided to approve on behalf of the Community a new protocol to the Barcelona Convention concerning pollution from land-based sources.[7] This protocol, which was drawn up in 1978 by the contracting parties to the framework convention, makes provision for the implementation of programmes and measures including common emission standards and standards for use with a view to reducing or eliminating, depending on the type of substance in question, pollution from land-based sources in the Mediterranean.

(d)   The fourth protocol for protected areas of the Mediterranean

On 1 March 1984, the Council agreed that the Community should also become a contracting party to the fourth protocol of the Barcelona Convention concerning specially protected areas of the Mediterranean.[8] This protocol is intended to protect and improve the state of resources and natural sites in the Mediterranean Sea, as well as the state of the natural heritage of the region, particularly by creating specially protected marine areas. These areas will be created with the aim of safeguarding sites which are of biological and ecological value, together with sites of particular importance because of their scientific, aesthetic, historic, archaeological, cultural or educational interest. They will also help to preserve the genetic diversity of species and representative types of ecosystems.

(e)   Measures concerning bathing waters and shellfish waters

On 28 August 1985 the Council authorized the Commission to participate in negotiations with the other contracting parties to the Barcelona Convention, with a view to fixing standards for bathing waters and shellfish waters. It is the first time that such specific measures have been envisaged within the framework of the Barcelona Convention. These measures must be compatible with existing Community legislation in these two areas (see pp. 32 and 41). The parties to the Barcelona Convention adopted a recommendation regarding the quality of bathing waters on 13 September 1985.

[6] OJ No L 162 of 19/6/81.

[7] OJ No L 67 of 12/3/83.

[8] OJ No L 68 of 10/3/84.

3. Protection of the waters of the Rhine against pollution

(a) Convention for the Protection of the Rhine against Chemical Pollution

In 1963 the states concerned by the pollution of the Rhine, namely Switzerland, France, Germany, Luxembourg and the Netherlands, decided in Berne to create an International Commission for the Protection of the Rhine against Pollution (Berne Agreement of 29 April 1963). The 1st Environmental Action Programme of 1973 also specifically stressed the problems being caused by the growing pollution of the Rhine and its tributaries. The International Commission for the Protection of the Rhine against Pollution, meeting at ministerial level in 1972, 1973 and 1975 decided to regulate the pollution of the Rhine and therefore drew up a draft convention. In order to ensure coherence with actions carried out at Community level, the Council authorized the Commission on 20 January 1976 to participate in the negotiations on this convention, so that the Community could be a contracting party to it, along with the Member States concerned.

On 25 July 1977[9] the Council decided to ratify, on behalf of the Community, the Convention for the Protection of the Rhine against Chemical Pollution. On the same day it also ratified an "additional agreement" to the Berne Agreement of 1963. This amendment was made necessary by the Community's participation in the convention on chemical pollution. Taking into consideration the various uses of the waters of the Rhine (water for human consumption; leisure; fishing, etc.), the convention makes provision for a body of measures designated to eliminate or reduce pollution caused by certain chemical substances listed in an annex to the convention. Several implementing measures were taken by the Council in 1982 and 1985 in order to implement the provisions of the convention. These measures, which are based to a very large extent on Community legislation, concern questions such as discharges of mercury[10] or cadmium[11] into the Rhine.

Subsequent Council decisions dealt with carbon tetrachloride and mercury.[12]

(b) Convention for the Protection of the Rhine against Salt Pollution

The member countries of the International Commission for the Protection of the Rhine also signed in 1976 a second convention concerning salt pollution of the Rhine. However, due to opposition raised by Alsace to this convention which makes provision for the injection of salt into the Alsatian subsoil, the French government was unable to ratify the convention. Amendments made at a later date enabled an agreement to be reached with France in 1981.

The first stage of the programme, lowering salt disposal into the Rhine by 20 kg per second, was implemented by January 1987. However, Environment Ministers of the five Rhine riparian countries, meeting in Bonn in October 1988, were unable to agree on the financial burden-sharing necessary to permit the second-stage reductions – a further 40 kg on the present total of around 300 kg – to be implemented beginning January 1989. The Community is not a contracting party to this convention.

---

[9] OJ No L 240 of 19/9/77.
[10] OJ No L 210 of 19/7/82.
[11] OJ No L 175 of 5/7/85.
[12] OJ No L 183 of 14/7/88.

(c)   Draft convention for the protection of the Rhine against thermal pollution

On 12 June 1986 the Council authorized the Commission to participate in negotiations on the drawing up of this draft convention.

4.   The Magdeburg Convention on the International Commission for the Protection of the Elbe (1990) (OJ L 321, 23/11/91)

Originally with three signatories (the Community, Germany, and the then Czech and Slovak Republic), the convention was signed in October 1990. It set up a Commission to prepare surveys of point sources, to propose quality objectives and discharge limit values. The convention became possible as a result of German unification and the changing political situation in Central and Eastern Europe. The Council authorized the Community's participation on 18 November 1991.[13]

5.   The Regensburg Cooperation Agreement on the Management of the Waters of the Danube (1980)

On 8 August 1980 the Council authorized the Commission to participate in negotiations for a cooperation agreement between Germany and Austria on the management of the waters of the Danube. The negotiations carried out by the Commission were intended to allow the Community to become a party to this agreement, which affects Community competences in the area of water pollution, and in particular the base directive of 4 May 1976. On 22 December 1986 the Council decided to sign this convention on behalf of the Community, which was then concluded in December of the following year. The convention only applies to part of the Danube Basin, where it sets out to protect the watercourse and groundwater sources from pollution, to regulate the flow of the Danube, and to coordinate emergency systems. It also established a Standing Commission on Management of Water Resources.

On 22 March 1990, the Community and the Federal Republic of Germany, on the one hand, and Austria, on the other, agreed to cooperate in the management of the water resources of the Danube Basin.[14]

6.   Convention on the Protection of the Marine Environment of the Baltic Sea (1974)

In 1974 the countries bordering the Baltic Sea (Denmark, Finland, the Federal Republic of Germany, the German Democratic Republic, Poland, Sweden and the USSR) adopted a Convention on the Protection of the Marine Environment of the Baltic Sea Area. This convention covers the principal sources of marine pollution, including pollution from land-based sources and discharges of dangerous substances at sea. On 21 July 1977 the Council authorized the Commission to open negotiations with a view to permitting the Community, through its competences in the areas covered, to become a contracting party to the convention, alongside the two Member States concerned (Denmark and the Federal Republic of Germany). These negotia-

---

[13] OJ No L 321 of 23/11/91.
[14] OJ No L 90 of 5/4/90.

tions have not yet been concluded due to the particular political circumstances of the convention; the Community did not accede to the convention until it was renegotiated in 1992. The renegotiation of the convention also saw the accession of Estonia, Lithuania, Latvia, the Czech and Slovak Republics and the Ukraine. The German Democratic Republic ceased to be a signatory upon German reunification in 1990, while Russia took over the international obligations of the former Soviet Union.

7.   The Convention for the Protection of the Marine Environment and the Coastal Areas of East Africa (1985)

On 19 June 1986 the Council decided to sign on behalf of the Community, and subject to its conclusion at a later date, the Convention for the Protection of the Marine Environment and the Coastal Areas of East Africa. The Community's participation in this convention was made necessary for legal reasons, since the provisions of the convention can affect the Community laws applicable to the French overseas territory of the Ile de la Reunion. This regional convention was drawn up in 1985 under the United Nations Environment Programme (UNEP) and brings together the following countries: the Seychelles, Madagascar, France, Somalia, Mozambique and Kenya.

8.   The Convention of Cartagena (Colombia) for the Protection and Improvement of the Marine Environment and the Coastal Areas of the Caribbean Region (1983)

In 1982 the Community participated in negotiations for the drawing up of a convention designed to protect the marine environment of the Caribbean. These negotiations having allowed the Community to become a contracting party to the convention, alongside the Member States concerned (France, the Netherlands, the United Kingdom), the Community signed the convention on 24 March 1983, subject to its conclusion at a later date. The reasons for the Community's participation in this convention are both legal and political. Legally speaking, the geographic field of application and the very content of the convention affect Community legislation on sea pollution. Moreover, from the political point of view, the European Council, meeting in Copenhagen in 1978, felt that the Community should make the prevention and combating of sea pollution a major objective, particularly with regard to its activities within the relevant international bodies. In addition, a number of the Caribbean countries participating in this convention maintain special links with the Community through the Lomé Convention and the system of association between overseas countries and territories.

9.   Protection of the North Sea

(a)   1972 Oslo Convention for the Prevention of Sea Pollution by Dumping Operations Carried out by Ships and Aircraft in the North Sea and in the North-East Atlantic

On 19 December 1978 the Commission sent the Council a proposal for a Decision designed to open negotiations with a view to the Community becoming a party to the Oslo Convention of 1972 which regulates waste dumping operations in the North Sea. The Council was unable to reach an agreement on this proposal, due to objections raised by Denmark. The Commission, nevertheless, has observer status within the body dealing with the management of the Oslo Convention.

(b)   1983 Bonn Agreement for cooperation in dealing with pollution of the North Sea by hydrocarbons and other harmful substances

On 28 June 1984 the Council approved the Community's participation in the Bonn Agreement of 1983[15] in which Germany, Belgium, France, Norway, the United Kingdom, Sweden, the Netherlands and Ireland also participate. It should be noted that the 1983 Agreement follows an initial agreement dating back to 1969 which only concerned pollution caused by hydrocarbons. Due to the considerable increase in the maritime transport of dangerous chemicals, the contracting parties to the agreement decided in 1983 to extend its field of application to cover a specific list of dangerous chemicals. The Bonn Agreement applies when the presence or threat of hydrocarbons or other pollutant or potentially pollutant substances, constitutes a serious or imminent threat to the coastlines of the countries concerned. The agreement makes provision for a system of information exchange between the parties and for mutual aid measures in cases of accidents.

10.   The Law of the Sea Convention (1982)

In 1970 the United Nations General Assembly decided to convene a third conference on the law of the sea, with a view to adopting a convention dealing with all matters relating to the law of the sea. The first conference was held in 1958 and resulted in the adoption of four distinct international conventions of the territorial seas, the high seas, fishing and the continental shelf. The second conference took place in 1960 in an attempt to resolve certain specific problems relating to the breadth of the territorial seas and fishing limits. The work undertaken by this conference was not completed until 1970 when the General Assembly adopted a "declaration on the principles regulating the ocean floor". This declaration contained in particular the well-known principle according to which the international zone of the ocean floor and its resources constitute the "common heritage of humanity". The third conference on the law of the sea began work in 1973. It decided to create three commissions, one of which had specific responsibility for studying the questions of the preservation of the marine environment and of scientific marine research. From the outset the Community followed the work of the conference in an observer capacity. In this respect the Council decided that the Member States should try to adopt common approaches to all the subjects entering into Community competences. The work of the third conference on the law of the sea, started in 1973, finally resulted nearly 10 years later in the adoption on 30 April 1982 of an international convention consisting of more than 300 articles and nine annexes. This considerable piece of legal codification provides a body of regulations covering all maritime questions, and also includes a section devoted to the

[15] OJ No L 188 of 16/7/84.

protection and conservation of the marine environment. This section consists of more than 40 articles concerning:

- measures designed to prevent, reduce or control the different types of pollution: pollution from land-based sources; pollution caused by activities connected with the ocean floor; pollution by dumping; pollution by shipping, etc.;
- worldwide and regional cooperation (in cases of damage; emergency anti-pollution plans);
- continuous monitoring and ecological assessment.

The convention determines the respective powers of the contracting parties with regard to the implementation of the different rules established by the convention in the area of the protection of the marine environment.

The Convention on the Law of the Sea was signed on 7 December 1984 by all of the Member States of the Community with the exception of the United Kingdom and Germany. These countries, together with the United States, do not accept the specific provisions of the convention concerning the regions governing the ocean floor. The Community itself signed the convention in accordance with Annex 9 which covers the participation of international organizations. This annex stipulates that international organizations may also participate in the convention when a majority of its Member States have already signed it. It should be noted that the Convention on the Law of the Sea entered into force in 1994, the required total of 60 ratifications having been reached. The Community has not yet been in a position to ratify.

11. Maritime conventions on the safety of shipping

In a Communication on 27 April 1978 on the control of sea pollution (see Chapter 3) the Commission requested the Council to accelerate ratification of the following conventions:

(a) The MARPOL Convention

This convention, which was drawn up in London in 1973 in the framework of the International Maritime Organization (IMO), lays down more stringent construction standards for tankers, and designates special zones, such as the Baltic or the Mediterranean, in which discharges of tank washings are banned. A protocol adopted in 1978 considerably strengthened the preventive measures to be respected by tankers, in particular by requiring the use of on-board tank-washing systems for tankers exceeding a certain tonnage.

(b) The SOLAS Convention

This 1974 Convention was also drawn up within the framework of the International Maritime Organization (IMO), and was also tightened up in 1978. It establishes precise rules on construction, stability, radio communications, life-saving equipment, etc. The additional protocol of 1978 covers the inspection of instruments and gear and the operation of shipping in general, and in particular of tankers (mandatory duplication of elements in the steering system, for example).

(c)   Convention No. 147 of the International Labour Office

Drawn up in 1976 within the framework of the United Nations' International Labour Office, Convention No. 147 is a convention according to which the parties undertake to adopt minimum social provisions for the crews of ships and minimum standards of safety and accident prevention on board ships.

(d)   The 1982 Paris Memorandum on "Port State Control"

In 1980 the French government invited the ministers responsible for maritime affairs in 13 European countries to Paris to discuss concrete measures designed to improve the safety of shipping, as well as pollution prevention measures. Following these discussions a "Memorandum of Understanding on Port State Control" was signed in Paris in 1982 by all the then Member States of the Community (with the exception of Luxembourg which does not have any maritime areas) together with Spain, Portugal, Norway and Finland. The Commission took part in these negotiations and was to be represented in the body set up to monitor the operation of the scheme. The measures covered by the Memorandum mainly concern a harmonized and concerted approach with regard to the inspection of foreign registered shipping entering European ports, with a view to detecting vessels which fail to meet the standards laid down in international conventions. These measures, which came into force on 1 July 1982, should lead to an improvement in safety standards in shipping by encouraging shipowners to carry out the necessary modifications, and by discouraging the entry into European ports of shipping which does not fulfil the safety standards.

12.   Draft European Convention for the Protection of International Watercourses against Pollution (Strasbourg Convention)

In July 1975 the Council authorized the Commission to negotiate the Community's participation in the above Convention but work on the draft, begun by the Council of Europe in 1969, was never completed. In practice, the adoption by the Community of the 1st Environmental Action Programme in 1973 and the first Community measures in the area of water pollution rendered the Strasbourg Convention superfluous, as far as the Member States of the Community were concerned. An effort was made to bring the Strasbourg text into line with Community directives but the draft has not yet been completed.

II.   CONVENTIONS IN THE AREA OF AIR POLLUTION

1.   The 1979 Geneva Convention on Long-range Transboundary Air Pollution

(a)   The 1979 Geneva Convention

The Final Act of the Conference on Security and Cooperation in Europe (CSCE) signed in Helsinki in 1975 included in its economic section a chapter on cooperation in the area of environmental protection. This conference brought together all of the countries of Western and Eastern Europe, as well as the United States and Canada. Since for general political reasons the Soviets wished to increase East–West economic cooperation, President Brezhnev in 1976–1977 launched the idea of "pan-European conferences on economic cooperation" in the three areas of energy, transport and the environment. Although reluctant with regard to these initiatives, the Western countries, which preferred to emphasize political and human rights aspects, finally agreed in 1979 to a so-called "high level meeting" on environmental protection. Two themes were selected for this meeting: first, the theme of air pollution suggested by the Western countries under pressure from the northern countries, and secondly, the theme of recycling, the re-use of waste and clean technologies proposed by the Eastern countries which wanted above all to obtain technology transfers.

As far as air pollution is concerned, the northern countries, affected for many years by acid deposition inflicting damage on the lakes and forests of Scandinavia, had since the 1960s been vainly requesting the other Western countries to draw up a convention under the OECD. In 1979, taking advantage of the political support of the USSR and of all the Eastern bloc countries, the northern countries were finally able to achieve the acceptance of the idea of an international legal instrument to combat air pollution. The result was the Geneva Convention on Long-Range Transboundary Air Pollution – a convention which has both political and environmental significance. From the political point of view, it was the first time that the European Economic Community as such had become a contracting party to a convention of a purely East–West context, thus benefiting from the explicit recognition of the Soviet Union. The Community signed the Geneva Convention in November 1979, and the Council decided officially to conclude and ratify it on 11 June 1981.[16] From the environmental point of view, the Community played an important role in the drawing up of this convention, bringing with it an approach which was both dynamic and realistic, despite the often divergent positions of its Member States. In return this convention provided an incentive and a stimulus for the internal policy of the Community on air pollution, which until then had made no real breakthrough, no major directive having been adopted by the Council at that stage (see p. 127).

The Geneva Convention basically represents a general framework convention. It stipulates that the contracting parties will develop policies and strategies designed to eliminate and reduce as far as possible air pollution, in particular emission of sulphur compounds. To this end the parties must take measures for the management and monitoring of air pollution, in particular by using the best available technology which is economically feasible. The convention also contains certain obligations concerning the exchange of information, consultations, research and monitoring.

(b)   The 1984 protocol on the financing of the programme for monitoring air pollution in Europe (EMEP)

On 12 June 1986[17] the Council decided to ratify on behalf of the Community, the protocol to the Geneva Convention produced in 1984 which ensures the long-term financing of the programme for monitoring long-range transmission of air pollution in Europe, or the EMEP programme. In ratifying this protocol the Community and its Member States undertook to provide 50% of the finance for this monitoring

[16]   OJ No L 171 of 27/6/81.
[17]   OJ No L 181 of 4/7/86.

programme, the Community itself contributing more than 3% of the total cost of the programme.

(c)   The Helsinki protocol on the reduction of sulphur emissions

On 10 January 1985 the Commission presented the Council with a proposal for a Decision authorizing it to participate in negotiations concerning a protocol to the Geneva Convention, with a view to establishing a reduction in sulphur emissions. This protocol makes provision for a reduction in national sulphur emissions or their cross-boundary flux, of 30% compared with 1980, to be achieved by 1993 at the latest. It was signed in Helsinki on 9 July 1985 by 21 signatories to the Geneva Convention, including the USSR, Hungary and several Member States of the Community (Germany, Italy, France, Belgium, the Netherlands, Luxembourg and Denmark). Due to the differences existing between Member States regarding a compulsory reduction of sulphur emissions (see p. 153) the Council did not give its agreement to the Commission's proposal. The Community as such has not therefore been able to sign the Helsinki protocol on the reduction of sulphur emissions.

(d)   The Sofia protocol on NOx

On 23 July 1991 the Commission sent the Council a proposal for a Decision on EC accession to the Protocol to the 1979 Geneva Convention on long-range transboundary air pollution concerning the control of emissions of nitrogen oxides or their transboundary fluxes, the so-called NOx or Sofia protocol. This protocol required contracting parties to take effective measures to reduce their total national emissions of NOx or their transboundary fluxes to their 1987 levels by 1994. It also required parties to apply fixed emission standards for new mobile and fixed sources as well as to take anti-pollution measures for large fixed sources. Provision was made for the parties to exchange information and technology with the executive of the convention, to develop monitoring and research and to work towards a follow-up agreement to take effect in January 1996.

Council Decision 93/361/EEC approved the accession of the European Community to the above protocol.[18]

2.   The 1985 Vienna Convention on the Protection of the Ozone Layer

Following the preparatory work carried out in 1981 under the United Nations Environment Programme (UNEP), a convention designed to protect the ozone layer of the stratosphere was adopted in Vienna in 1985. In view of the Community's own competences in the areas covered by the convention, in particular in the areas of research and the regulation of chlorofluorocarbon emissions (see p. 166), the Council decided on 20 March 1985 to sign this convention on behalf of the Community, alongside the Member States, subject to conclusion at a later date. The general objective of the protection of the ozone layer only being attainable at a wider international level, the convention is of global dimension. It was signed in Vienna on 22 March 1985 by the Community and by more than 22 countries, including the USSR, the United States, and several developing countries (Chile, Peru, Egypt, Burkina Faso, Morocco, etc.).

---

[18] OJ No L 149/14 of 21/6/93.

The Community's participation in this convention has led to a number of legal and political difficulties. It will participate in the agreement as an "organization of regional economic integration". The nature of its participation has been based largely on that of its participation in the 1979 Geneva Convention on transboundary air pollution.

The Vienna Convention can be considered to be a framework convention, since its provisions are of a very general nature. The principal clause of the convention requires the contracting parties to take the appropriate measures to protect human health and the environment against the harmful effects resulting or likely to result from the human activities which alter or are likely to alter the ozone layer. Nevertheless, recognizing that the simple precautionary measures of the convention regarding emissions of chlorofluorocarbons would not be sufficient for the protection of the ozone layer, the countries participating in the Vienna Conference in 1985, together with the Community, also adopted a specific resolution which made provision for the drawing up in 1987 of an additional protocol to the convention, designed to control the use of chlorofluorocarbons on a worldwide level.

See also Chapter 4 – Air – The control of fluorocarbons in the environment.

3. The United Nations Framework Convention on Climate Change

The opening for signature in Rio de Janeiro on 4 June 1992 of the United Nations Framework Convention on Climate Change was seen by many as one of the most important events of the Earth Summit. The Intergovernmental Negotiating Committee for a Framework Convention on Climate Change (INC/FCCC) had been established by the United Nations General Assembly in December 1990 (Resolution 45/212) and had met six times under the chairmanship of Mr Jean Ripert of France, a former high official of the United Nations. The scientific basis of the INC/FCCC's discussions derived mainly from the technical assessments and methodological work of the Intergovernmental Panel on Climate Change (IPCC) and on the whole this aspect of the INC's work was not a major source of contention. It was recognized on all sides that the IPCC, established jointly in 1988 by the United Nations Environment Programme (UNEP) and the World Meteorological Organization (WMO) under the chairmanship of Mr Bert Bolin of Sweden, represented one of the most massive scientific exercises ever undertaken by the United Nations system and that, though IPCC's findings would certainly be refined or modified over time in the light of new evidence, the Panel's reports provided as sound a scientific basis for an understanding of, and response to, global warming and other important climatic issues as could be expected in the circumstances.

Perhaps even more significant for the negotiation of a Framework Convention on Climate Change were the political considerations. The approach of the Rio Conference, like the prospect of hanging for a condemned man, tended to concentrate the mind wonderfully. The challenge to "have something ready for Rio" was considerable. The INC needed the stimulus of UNCED as much as UNCED needed the glamour and visibility that would be associated with the signature in Rio of a climate convention. The difficulties were nevertheless very real and it was not until the evening of Saturday 9 May 1992 after several all-night negotiating sessions that Mr Ripert, INC/FCCC'S Chairman, was able to propose that the text of the draft convention be adopted and recommended for signature at UNCED in Rio de Janeiro.

Throughout the negotiations, the major stumbling blocks were the fundamental issues of the commitments to be made by states, the financial mechanisms to be used, and the reporting required.

The industrialized countries, most notably the European Community and the United States, took different views of the specific commitments they would be ready to make to limit their emissions of carbon dioxide and other greenhouse gases. The Council of the European Communities, at its meeting on 29 October 1990, had indicated its willingness to take actions aimed at reaching stabilization of total CO_2 emissions at 1990 levels in the Community as a whole. Though the specific measures to achieve those objectives were not necessarily all in place in the Community (a "carbon tax", for example, had been mooted by the Commission but not yet approved by the Council – see p. 176), the European Community on the whole stuck to its line throughout the negotiations and sought to have a clear commitment about targets and timetables in respect of CO_2 emission reductions included in the text of the convention.

The United States, on the other hand, was reluctant to see such targets and timetables (certainly not those embraced by the EC) and argued anyway in favour of an "all sources, all sinks" approach under which countries might receive credit for actions already taken to reduce the emission of greenhouse gases other than CO_2, for example CFCs, or to increase carbon sinks or reservoirs, for example through reforestation or afforestation. The United States linked President Bush's willingness to participate in the Rio Summit with progress made in the INC towards satisfying its concerns. This tactic, judged by many to be crude if effective, did nothing to improve the United States' image in the run-up to Rio. As negotiations within the INC continued, many asked: would a convention with no clear targets and commitments be worth having?

The developing countries were, for the most part, eager to secure commitments from the developed countries so as to begin to bring global warming under control. As they saw it, it was the industrialized world which had created the problem, using up a scarce global resource, namely the atmosphere's absorptive capacity. Unless the OECD countries were ready to reduce their own emissions, the net effect, so the developing countries feared, would be not only to limit their own prospects for development but to subject them (particularly the countries with arid or low-lying lands or with heavily populated river deltas) to the adverse effects of an environmental problem that had not been of their making.

Not all developing countries, of course, were agreed as to the precise commitments which should be sought. The oil-producing nations, for example, led by Saudi Arabia were not anxious to see explicit references to the need to impose carbon or energy taxes as one means of achieving reductions in CO_2 emissions. This reluctance would be reflected not only in the text of the Climate Change Convention as finally adopted but also in UNCED's difficult debate on the "atmosphere" chapter of Agenda 21.

As far as the financial mechanisms are concerned, the industrialized countries were united in preferring the Global Environmental Facility (GEF) as the mechanism through which financial and technological resources would flow from North to South. They received some satisfaction under Article 21 of the convention which entrusts the operation of the convention's "financial mechanism" to the GEF on an interim basis. G77 countries insisted, however, that the GEF "should be appropriately restructured and its membership made universal".

As far as reporting requirements under the Climate Change Convention are concerned, developed countries commit themselves to providing specific and detailed information on the progress they are making towards the goal of returning their "anthropogenic emissions of carbon dioxide and other greenhouse gases not controlled by the Montreal Protocol" to their 1990 levels. (Note: the text of the convention does not commit the developed countries to achieving the stabilization goal – as the European Community wanted – but only to reporting progress made towards achieving the goal, a subtle but important distinction.) The reporting requirements that apply to developing countries are more general, on a different timescale and are related to the availability of finance and the transfers of technology.

President Collor of Brazil was the first to sign the United Nations Framework Convention on Climate Change at a ceremony which took place in the Conference Centre at Rio Centro on 4 June 1992. During the course of the next 10 days the Convention was signed by over 150 countries and by the European Community. In order for the Convention to enter into force, it must be ratified, accepted, approved or acceded to by national legislatures in at least 50 countries, a process which it was estimated might take two years. Arrangements were made for a Convention secretariat to function on an interim basis in the meantime.

The Council decided on the conclusion of the convention by the Community on 21 December 1993. The convention entered into force in 1994.

III.   CONVENTIONS IN THE AREA OF THE PROTECTION OF FLORA AND FAUNA

1.   The 1973 Washington Convention on International Trade in Endangered Species of Flora and Fauna

On 31 December 1976 the Commission sent the Council a Recommendation aimed at authorizing it to enter into negotiations regarding the Community's participation in the Washington Convention drawn up in 1973 to control the international trade in endangered species of flora and fauna (see also p. 306).

The Council authorized the Commission to open these negotiations on 15 March 1977. In 1983 the "conference of the parties", which constitutes the executive body of the convention, voted on an amendment to the text of the convention, making it possible to include the European Economic Community. However, since the necessary number of ratifications of this amendment has not been achieved, the Community's participation has not yet come into effect.

2.   The 1979 Berne Convention on the Conservation of the Wildlife of Europe's Natural Environment

This convention, drawn up in 1979 in the framework of the Council of Europe, is designed to ensure the conservation of wild flora and fauna and of their natural habitats, by promoting cooperation between the different States of the Council of Europe. The convention gives particular attention to vulnerable endangered species.

On 3 December 1981 the Council decided to conclude this convention on behalf of the Community.[19] Eighteen other European states are contracting parties to it.

The convention makes provisions for strict measures for the protection of habitats and the conservation of species, for example by prohibiting certain types and methods of hunting, and by controlling trade in animals. These measures vary according to the extent to which the different species are threatened. The convention contains a list of species of flora (Annex 1) and fauna (Annex II) which should be particularly strictly protected. It also contains specific provisions for migratory species (see also p. 309).

3. The 1979 Bonn Convention on the Conservation of Migratory Species of Wild Animals

This convention, drawn up in 1979 under the United Nations Environment Programme (UNEP) aims to conserve threatened migratory species of wild animals.

On 24 June 1982 the Council decided to conclude this convention on behalf of the Community.[20] About 20 other states are contracting parties to this convention, including several developing countries (Cameroon, Egypt, India, Nigeria) and one Eastern European country.

The convention establishes the principle according to which states on whose territory are found populations of threatened migratory species must take the conservation and management measures appropriate for the species in question, covering the whole of the geographic area in which the threatened species is found. These measures vary depending on whether the species concerned requires immediate and strict protection actions due to its "unfavourable conservation status" (species listed in Appendix I) or whether it is to be the subject of later international agreements on conservation and management (Appendix II species).

The convention also covers measures for controlling the taking of animals belonging to the species in question, conservation and management plans, the maintenance of networks of suitable habitats, and the control of discharges of substances which are harmful to migratory species.

The first meeting of the management body of the convention, which brings together the contracting parties and the countries having observer status, took place in 1985 and the second took place in 1988. Subsequent meetings took place in every other year, with the latest being held in Fort Lauderdale, Florida in November 1994.

4. The 1985 Convention of the Council of Europe on the Protection of Vertebrate Animals used for Experimental Purposes

In 1982, and again in February 1985, the Commission brought to the attention of the Council the question of the participation of the Community in the Council of

---

[19] OJ No L 38 of 10/2/82.
[20] OJ No L 210 of 19/7/82.

Europe's draft convention on the protection of vertebrate animals used for experimental purposes. However, the legal problems connected with the Community's competences in the areas covered by the draft convention prevented the Council from arriving at any concrete decision.

The convention having been definitely adopted by the Council of Europe on 31 May 1985, the Commission presented the Council with a new Communication on 20 December 1985, requesting the signing of the convention by the Community and its Member States in order to allow this international agreement to come into force as soon as possible. The convention has been open to signature by the Member States of the Council of Europe and of the European Community since December 1985. It has two major objectives, namely a reduction in the number of animals used for experimental purposes, and the prevention of any unnecessary suffering by the animals during the experiments.

On 24 November 1986 the Council decided to sign the convention on behalf of the Community, subject to conclusion at a later date.[21] On the same day it adopted a Resolution requesting those Member States which had not already done so to sign the convention as soon as possible (see also p. 329).

5.   Convention on Biological Diversity

Signed by the European Community and the Member States at the 1992 UN Conference on Environment and Development in Rio de Janeiro, the convention seeks to conserve biological diversity and ensure the sustainable use of biological resources. The convention also aims for an equitable distribution of the benefits accruing from the use of genetic resources. By enabling developing countries to reap the benefits from maintaining and preserving their biological resources, the convention seeks to ensure that a true economic value is attributed to such resources. The convention covers appropriate transfer of technology, funding, and access to genetic resources. Each signatory is required to set up a system of protected areas. The Community is given competence for some areas of the convention under the Habitats Directive.

On 25 October 1993 the Council approved the conclusion of the convention by the Community.[22]

IV.   OTHER CONVENTIONS

1.   Proposal for a Decision concerning the conclusion of the Convention on Environmental Impact Assessment in a Transboundary Context

The Convention on Environmental Impact Assessment in a Transboundary Context was negotiated under the auspices of the UN Economic Commission for Europe. It was adopted at Espoo, Finland on 25 February 1991 and signed by several UNECE member countries including EC Member States and by the Community the day after.

[21] Mr Stanley Johnson, co-author of the present work, signed on behalf of the European Community.
[22] OJ No L 309/1 of 13/12/93; COM (92) 509.

Consistent with the Community's own Directive 85/337/EEC on environmental impact assessment of certain public projects, the convention sets up arrangements for cooperation and consultation between the signatories where a significant adverse transboundary impact is probable due to certain types of proposed activities. Appendix I to the convention lists 17 types of major development to which its conditions apply and for which the actual impact assessment itself would be carried out by the government and public of the country concerned.

The proposed Decision[23] would provide for the EC to approve the convention and facilitate simultaneous ratification by the Community and the Member States.

2.   Basle Convention on Transboundary Movements of Hazardous Waste

The EC and 35 other countries signed the Basle Convention on the Control of the Transboundary Movements of Hazardous Waste and their disposal in 1989. The Council agreed on 7 February 1994 that the European Union should conclude the convention and become a party to the convention from 8 May 1994. The waste shipments Regulation (259/93/EEC) implements the Basle Convention in the Union (see p. 208) and applies from 6 May 1994.

[23] Transmitted to the Council of 26 June 1994.

Table 12.1: The fifth environment action programme: international environmental issues

Objectives	Targets up to 2000	Measures required	Principle actors
1. Preservation of Global Biodiversity	* no further deterioration of ecosystems and habitats necessary to maintain diversity of species and within species	* Global Convention on Biodiversity	International Community
		* National and Regional Strategies on Biodiversity – preventive approach, EIA – inventories – protection of forests, wetlands and other species – rich ecosystems	All Countries (EC + MS)
		* Increased technical and financial Assistance to Developing Countries * Valuation of biological resources * Global Climate Change Convention	Industrialized Countries (including EC) id
2. Control of Global Warming	* Stabilisation of CO_2 emissions at 1990 levels * Limitation or reduction of CH_4 emissions	– Protocol on CO_2 emission reductions – Protocol on limitation of CH_4 emissions – Increased technical and financial Assistance to Developing and CEE Countries	International Community
	* Increased energy effiency	* National and Regional Strategies including	Individual States, Regions, including EC + MS
	* Protection/enhancement of Greenhouse gases reservoirs/sinks	– Inventories of Greenhouse gases + sinks – Increased energy efficiency – Promotion of renewable sources of energy – Economic/fiscal incentives	
3. Protection of Ozone Layer	* Phase-out of production and use of CFCs, Halons, Carbontetrachloride and I.I.I. trichlorethane	* Full implementation of Montreal Protocol (incl. technical and financial assistance) * Review of scientific data and response * EC Regulations	International Community id EC + MS
4. Protection of Forests	* Maintenance/reinstatement of forests at least at 1990 levels	* Global agreement on protection, development and management of forests	International Community + ITTO
	* Substantial reafforestation programmes for tropical, temperate and boreal forest areas	* Implementation of forest provisions in global conventions on biodiversity and climate change * ITTO "Target 2000" on timber trade	id
	* Integrated protection/sustainable management of forest areas	* Reduced timber consumption, including promotion of recycling of paper and board * Restructuring of relevant international organisations e.g. ITTO, TFAP, UNEP	Producing + importing countries, ITTO, EC, GATT id International Community

Table 12.1 continued

Objectives	Targets up to 2000	Measures required	Principle actors
		* National strategies for promotion, enhancement and protection of forests	All countries
		* Finalization of pilot programme on Brazilian rain-forest; extension to other forest areas	Brazil, EC, World Bank, G-7, other countries
		* Increased technical and financial assistances to developing countries	International Community
		* Monitoring of global forest coverage, including remote sensing	EC / id
5. Promotion of sustainable development	* Relief of pressure on the environment in developing countries resulting from population growth and poverty	* Adoption and implementation of "Agenda 21"	UNCED participants
		* Effective implementation of provisions on sustainable development in Lomé IV	EC + ACP
	* Integration of environmental objectives and criteria into macro-economic reform programmes	* Effective implementation of environmental guidelines for co-operation between EC and ALA countries	EC + ALA
	* Solution of critical problems for the development process in developing countries and in Central and Eastern Europe	* Effective implementation of Nicosia Charter	Mediterranean Countries
		* PHARE national and regional programmes	EC, EIB, MAP, World Bank / International Community
		* Increased technical and financial assistance to all developing countries for the formulation and implementation of national and regional programmes for sustainable development	EC, World Bank, G-24, EIB, Multinational companies, financial institutions, Research and Technological Bodies

	– energy demand supply
	  – land degradation + desertification
	  – water resources
		– institutional strengthening
		  – financial resources
		  – scientific and technical transfer, co-operation and assistance	

		* Increased public health and environmental awareness
		  – government, local and regional authority and corporate decision-makers
		  – general public
			International Community / Individual countries / NGOs

		* Codes of conduct for enterprises	International Community / EC, MS, Enterprises Community, BC, PHARE, World
		* Investment in environmental clean-up in former centrally planned countries	3rd, EB, BERD, Financial institutions

Chapter 13

The Integration of Environmental Protection in the Other Community Policies

The 1983 3rd Action Programme gave itself as a general objective the integration of the environmental dimension in the other policies of the Community. One of the foremost instruments for this integration was the implementation of a procedure for the evaluation of the effect on the environment in cases of public or private development projects (see p. 354).

The 4th Action Programme for 1987–1992 emphasized even more clearly the need to integrate the protection of the environment in the other policies, since "it has now become clear that there can be no lasting economic and social progress if environmental problems are not taken into consideration as an essential element in economic and social development".

Given the pre-eminence of the agricultural policy within the Community, as well as the specific problems faced by that policy (overproduction, soil quality, etc.), the relationship between environment and agriculture constitutes a fundamental element in arriving at this integration. A second area in which integration must be improved over the coming years concerns the economic and social policy in general in all its sectors: industry, employment, energy, transport, consumer protection, etc. The specific relationship between environment and development aid is dealt with in the next chapter.

I. AGRICULTURE AND ENVIRONMENT

1. The first actions carried out within the framework of the three environment programmes of 1973, 1977 and 1983

The actions carried out within the framework of these programmes have usually been limited to specific measures in the area of agricultural structures or to studies instigated by the Commission. In order to bring about increased consideration of environmental protection in the policy of agricultural structures, the Community has adopted normative or financial measures. These were aimed at supporting agriculture in disadvantaged areas, particularly in mountain areas,[1] and encouraging

[1] OJ No L 128 of 19/5/75.

reafforestation or the suspension of certain agricultural activities to improve the structures and the environment.

In order to evaluate the ecological consequences of modern farming techniques the Commission has also initiated studies aimed at increasing knowledge of the effects on the natural environment of certain practices such as monoculture, intensive use of fertilizers, abuse of pesticides, intensive breeding, land developments causing draining or destruction of wetlands.

In the case of pesticides, studies have concentrated mainly on the development of substitute methods, and on the control of residues in foodstuffs. As far as intensive breeding is concerned, studies have centred on nuisances caused by animal excrement, smells and noise. In the case of mineral fertilizers, research is being carried out into the long-term consequences of eutrophication of water and the increase of nitrates in underground waters.

2. The global reflection on agriculture and environment: the "green" book of 1985

In 1985 the Commission set about a global reflection on the agricultural policy of the Community which resulted in the presentation to the Council of two Communications on "the perspectives of the Common Agricultural Policy" (green book) and "the future of European Agriculture". This reflection pays particular attention to the environmental problems caused by modern farming techniques.

(a) The "green book" states that the role of agriculture in a modern industrialized economy includes not only economic and social functions, but also the conservation of the rural environment. At a time when the Community is self-sufficient in many agricultural products, and therefore obliged to manage its productive capacity in a prudent way, environmental considerations gain in relative importance.

In fact, agriculture has a direct and profound impact on the environment of the European Community: two-thirds of the surface of the Community is devoted to agricultural production. In the last decades, agriculture has undergone a technological revolution which has profoundly changed farming practices. There is growing concern about the effects of such changes on the environment – a concern which is expressed not only among the urban population but also to a lesser extent among those engaged in agriculture, whose basic resources are soil, water and the genetic diversity of plant and animal species. The problems are most evident in the northern regions of the Community, where the introduction of modern agricultural techniques is more advanced, but they are manifesting themselves also in the Mediterranean regions, and sometimes in specific ways (forest fires in arid zones).

Regulation and control of practices harmful to the environment

The development of modern agricultural techniques has played an important role in the increase in agricultural activity. But these techniques are the cause of the extinction of species of flora and fauna and of the destruction of valuable ecosystems such as wetlands, and in some cases have increased risks of ground and surface water pollution, e.g. excessive nitrate levels.

In this context, agriculture has to be considered as a sector of economic activity which, like the other sectors with potentially harmful activities, should be subject to reasonable public prescriptions and controls designed to avoid deterioration of the environment. In general, the principle of "polluter pays" should apply, and it would not be normal for farmers to be compensated by the public authorities for the introduction of such rules.

The expanding use of pesticides and chemical fertilizers involves a number of environmental risks, especially with regard to their long-term effects. The excessive use of fertilizers, whether of natural origin (animal wastes, etc.) or not, risks damaging water supplies through pollution by nitrates. In the case of pesticides, definition of product standards with respect to environmental risks, approval of products before use, restriction of product distribution to persons with approved qualifications and facilities for storing and application of the products, warnings against excessive usage, are measures which could be envisaged in a first stage to limit these risks. In addition, it would be necessary that the agricultural advisory and extension services, even more than in the past, provide competent advice to farmers, and that research efforts to develop new and less harmful products or methods are supported.

Common action is also needed to control the problems arising from intensive livestock production – common action, not only in the interest of protecting the environment, but also with a view to ensuring fair conditions of competition. Such action could take the form of the issue of permits for the construction of buildings for intensive livestock production and for the exercise of such activities. The conditions of such permits would have to include provisions for prior evaluation of the environmental impact, hygiene standards, sufficient capacity for storing and, if necessary, for recycling the animal wastes as well as appropriate plans for their spreading on the land or for other non-polluting uses.

Appropriate planning procedures, including a full environmental impact assessment, should also be introduced for major projects affecting the use of land (reparcelling, changes in the water regime, roads, etc.), especially in the case of public funding of such projects. A particular problem in this context is the drainage of agricultural land. It is encouraged in all Member States by aids from public authorities, and is assisted in some cases by Community funds. There is growing evidence, however, that the intensification and extension of drainage particularly in the wetlands has led to the degradation or loss of important habitats for wildlife. The destruction of such valuable ecosystems is generally irreversible, and the question is therefore posed whether public aids for this activity can still be justified.

Promotion of practices friendly to the environment

At least as important as the "passive" protection of the environment is a policy designed to promote farming practices which conserve the rural environment and protect specific sites. Generally speaking such practices would be less intensive (and thereby less productive) and could have an effect to a limited extent on the growth of agricultural production.

Two types of action could be envisaged in this context not only in less-favoured areas or marginal zones, but in many other regions of the Community:

● First of all measures in order to introduce or maintain agricultural practices compatible with the need for the protection of nature. Elements of such measures could be, for example, observance of low limits on use of fertilizers and pesticides; acceptance of rules for the use of pasture; abandonment of drainage and irrigation works; change of land use to other agricultural production, or planting of trees, maintenance of stone walls, hedges or ponds.

The areas for such management measures might be: areas where agriculture should be maintained in certain traditional forms (e.g. buffer zones adjoining nature reserves, zones for the protection of groundwater); ecological corridors in areas of highly developed agriculture, for example, a strip of 5–10 m along watercourses, ponds and coasts would protect not only habitats but water as a resource itself.

In some areas where the environmental balance is particularly threatened, practices friendly to the environment should be made compulsory by law. In other cases, they could be introduced on a voluntary basis in the form of management contracts between public authorities and the farmers concerned.

Society should recognize the resulting external benefits of such measures by providing the financial resources to permit farmers to fulfil these tasks. Corresponding payments would at the same time support and diversify farmers' incomes and contribute to the control of production.

- Next, buying out or renting out of land by public authorities for environmental purposes (protection of nature and wildlife; creation of ecological refuges or corridors; provision of recreational amenities). In many cases farmers could even be asked to stay on the land and to manage it according to its new functions.

According to some estimates, up to 10% of the Community's agricultural surface could be reasonably used for such purposes. The medium and long-term environmental objective would be to create a coherent network of larger protected zones, interlinked by ecological refuges and corridors which should facilitate exchange of species, thus contributing to their preservation and development. At the same time, the measures suggested might – to a limited extent – supplement and diversify the income of the farmers concerned and could in some cases even have a stimulating effect on rural tourism.

(b) In the document entitled "A Future for European Agriculture", the accent is on measures to support agricultural activity in areas where it is essential for land improvement, the maintaining of social balance, and the protection of the environment and the landscape. The Commission also underlines the need to promote better awareness among farmers of environmental problems. To establish a fair balance between the sometimes opposed needs of agricultural development and conservation of the natural environment, a number of actions must be taken concerning the use of agro-chemical products, treatment of agricultural wastes and the conservation of species, habitats and landscapes.

3. Commission Communication of June 1988 on environment and agriculture

The Commission's 4th Environmental Action Programme, 1987–1992, strongly emphasized the need for agricultural and environmental policy to be integrated. As a first step towards this aim, the Commission released, in June 1988, a paper reviewing environmental problems in agriculture, and setting out proposed action before the end of 1988 (COM (88) 338 final).

The paper states that before the end of 1988 the Commission will take action in four specific areas:

1. Present a proposal, based on one presented in 1976, for a directive concerning the marketing of plant protection products (this represents the first stage towards harmonization of controls on the sale, supply and use of pesticides in the Community).
2. Present a proposal concerning the production and marketing of agricultural products and foodstuffs obtained without the use of synthetic chemicals (this represents a first step in encouraging organic farming).
3. Present a proposal for a directive concerning the protection of fresh surface and ground waters and coastal waters against pollution from livestock manure and from overuse of nitrogenous compounds (this would tackle the pollution problems associated with intensive livestock units and with excessive use of artificial fertilizers).
4. Present a proposal for the revision of Directive 85/337/EEC concerning the assessment of the effects of certain private and public projects on the environment (this would make clear that such assessments will normally be required for major agricultural projects, including the restructuring of farms and changes in water regimes).

This paper also commits the Commission to a study of the use of economic instruments to reduce consumption of artificial fertilizers and pesticides, and to a review of large-scale arterial drainage projects. The Commission also proposes to examine financial participation in existing measures, the coordination of measures taken by Member States, promoting awareness of farmers for new options, and the need to promote alternative economic activities in rural areas, while respecting environmental needs.

4. The Council Directive of 12 December 1991 concerning the protection of waters against pollution caused by nitrates from agricultural sources (91/676/EEC)

In line with the undertaking mentioned in paragraph 3 above, the Commission transmitted the above proposal to the Council on 21 December 1988. The aim of the proposal was to prevent the concentration of nitrate reaching a level at which it could interfere with the legitimate uses of the water or could lead to eutrophication. Community waters have many and various uses. They are not only a source of drinking waters but are also a valuable touristic resource, a medium of transportation, a source of recreational activity, they support fisheries and even have a worth for their own intrinsic beauty. The proposal is designed to control the various diffuse sources of nitrate pollution so that they do not impair these and other legitimate uses of Community waters.

Problems with nitrate pollution are not expected to occur in all Community waters, fresh waters, groundwaters, estuarial, coastal and marine waters. Certain areas are at far greater risk than others. The proposal therefore concentrates on introducing measures for these vulnerable areas. Under it, Member States are asked to designate waters affected or likely to be affected by pollution from nitrogen compounds based on criteria laid out in Table 3.15.

These criteria relate to:

(a) the concentration of nitrate in waters used as sources for drinking water supplies, and

(b) the potential for waters to become eutrophic.[2]

Where waters cross national boundaries, provision is made for Member States to cooperate in designating the appropriate vulnerable areas.

Within the vulnerable zones Member States will need to take a number of measures. The disposal of animal manure poses a great problem for a number of Member States, particularly because manure is often regarded by the farmer as a waste product rather than a nutrient source. This proposal lays down the maximum quantity of different animals' manure that can be applied to the land. It also requires Member States to establish rules covering the method of application of manures and the capacity of storage facilities.

Furthermore, Member States are required to establish land application rates for chemical fertilizer, taking into account the rates at which different crops take up nitrogen from the soil and the amount of nitrogen in the soil including that which has been applied by the application of other types of fertilizers such as sewage sludge, animal manures, etc.

For those vulnerable zones which have been designated due to the problems of eutrophication, Member States will have to ensure that sewage treatment works discharging to waters flowing to or in these zones will treat their effluent such that the concentration of nitrate is less than 10 mg/l.

In addition, Article 4.3 lists a series of measures which Member States should also consider.

In order to decide which areas should be vulnerable zones and to track the progress that is being achieved, Member States will have to carry out regular monitoring. The details of the monitoring and the related analysis methods are outlined in Annex 4. Results of the monitoring will be sent to the Commission which will prepare a report at three-yearly intervals.

Table 13.1: Commission Proposal of 21 December 1988 Pollution of water by nitrates

Criteria for the designation of vulnerable zones

Vulnerable zones are those areas of land which drain directly or indirectly into one or more of the following waters:

(i)   surface fresh waters intended for the abstraction of drinking water which could contain more than 50 mg/l nitrate if protective action is not taken.

(ii) groundwaters intended for the abstraction of drinking water which contain more than 50 mg/l nitrate or could contain more than 50 mg/l nitrate if protective action is not taken.

(iii) natural freshwater lakes, other natural freshwater bodies, estuaries, coastal waters and seas which are found to be eutrophic or which in a short time may become eutrophic if protective action is not taken.

---

[2] The term "eutrophication" has been defined in Article 2 such that it only relates to waters which are nitrogen limited. Waters which are eutrophic and phosphorus limited are not covered by this proposal.

Table 13.2: Commission Proposal of 21 December 1988
Pollution of water by nitrates

Maximum number of manure-producing animals per hectare of land available for manure spreading

Animals	Maximum number of animals per hectare (1)
Dairy cows	2
Young stock or beef cattle	4
Fattening pigs	16
Sows with piglets	5
Turkeys, ducks	100
Laying hens	133
Young hens, 0–16 weeks	285

(1) Numbers are not cumulative.

Table 13.3: Commission Proposal of 21 December 1988
Pollution of water by nitrates

Measures to be considered in the elaboration of action programmes referred to in article 4.3

1. The restriction or banning of the ploughing in of vegetables.
2. Prevention of downward water movement beyond the crop root systems in irrigation systems.
3. The use of crop rotation systems and catch crops.
4. Covering of the soil by a crop or other vegetation for as long as possible.
5. The setting aside, or re-forestation, of agricultural land.
6. The diversification of agriculture.
7. The continuous training and education of farmers and producers.
8. Scientific and agronomic research on the behaviour of nitrogen in the soil and on crops.

The Council adopted the directive on 12 December 1991 in a more flexible form than originally proposed by the Commission.[3] The detailed requirements as regards stocking rates (as set out in Table 13.1) were not retained by the Council. The limit of 50 mg/l nitrate above which catchments were to be designated as vulnerable is presented as an average rather than an absolute.

5. Future action

The 5th Environmental Action Programme stresses that it is not only environmentally desirable, but it also makes sound agricultural and economic sense to seek to strike a more sustainable balance between agricultural activity and the natural

[3] OJ No L 375 of 31/12/91.

Table 13.4: The fifth environment action programme: agriculture and forestry

Objectives	Targets up to 2000	Actions	Time-frame	Actors
Maintenance of the basic natural processes indispensable for a sustainable agricultural sector notably by conservation of water, soil, and genetic resources	Standstill or reduction of nitrate levels in groundwaters.	Strict application of the nitrates directive	1994 ⇒	MS + AGR
	Reduced incidence of surface waters with a nitrate content exceeding 50 mg/l. or giving rise to eutrophication of lakes and seas.	Setting of regional emission standards for new litestock units (NH_3) and silos (silage)	Ongoing	MS + LAs
		Reduction programme for phosphate use.	1995	EC + MS
	Stabilisation or increase of organic material levels in the soil	Allocation of premiums and other compensating payments to be subject to full compliance with environmental legislation	1995 ⇒	EC MS + LAs + AGR
Decrease in the input of chemicals to the point that none of these processes be affected.	Significant reduction of pesticide use per unit of land under production and conversion of farmers to methods of integrated pest control, at least in all areas of importance for nature conservation	– Registration of sales and use of pesticides – Control on sale and use of pesticides – Promotion of "Integrated Control" (in particular training activities) and promotion of bio-agriculture	Ongoing 1995 1992 ⇒	EC + MS + AGR EC + MS + AGR EC + MS + AGR
Equilibrium between input of nutrients and the absorption capacity of soils and plants.				
Rural environment management permitting the maintenance of biodiversity and natural habitats and minimising natural risks (e.g. erosion, avalanches) and fires	15% of agricultural area under management contracts	Programmes for agriculture/environment zones with premiums co-financed by FEOGA	1992	MS + EC
		Protection of all endangered domestic animal races	Ongoing	MS

Table 13.4 continued

Objectives	Targets up to 2000	Actions	Time-frame	Actors
	Management plans for all rural areas in danger	Re-evaluation of licence conditions for irrigation and of state aids for drainage schemes	1995	MS + EC
		Training of farmers, promotion of exchange visits between regions with comparable environment management situations	1992 ⇒	EC + MS + LAs
Optimisation of forest area as to fulfil all their functions	Increase of forest plantation, including on agricultural land;	New afforestation and regeneration of existing forest, favouring the most adequate means for the environment (slow growing trees, mixed afforestation);	Ongoing	EC + MS + LAs + forest-owners
	Improved protection (health and forest-fires)	Further action against forest-fires	id	id

resources of the environment. The objectives and targets in the field of agriculture and forestry are set out in Table 13.4.

II.   FORESTRY AND THE ENVIRONMENT

Forests cover almost 54 million hectares of the European Community (64 million hectares if one includes areas of maquis and scrub woodland), which represents 24% of the land area of the Community and 42% of its agricultural land area. In composition, 58% of Community forests are deciduous and 42% coniferous. Privately owned forestry comprises 58% of the total and publicly owned forestry 42%.

The Community as a whole is the second largest consumer of timber in the world, but the Community is only 50% self-sufficient in timber and timber products at present. Forestry and related industries in the Community employ 2 million people, producing over 100 million m^3 of wood and related products. However, the Community is not self-sufficient in wood products and runs a trade deficit of Ecu 15–20 million per year in wood products.

Around 20% of trees in the Community's forests are clearly damaged, mainly as a result of atmospheric pollution (i.e. leaf or needle loss higher than 25% compared to normal foliage), while studies have indicated that EC harvest-loss attributable to air pollution is of the order of 30 million m^3, with an estimated value of Ecu 10 billion. Fire is also a major problem, with about 1% of the total forest area being destroyed by forest fires each year, the vast majority in the Mediterranean region.

1.   Development of the Community's policy

In 1981, the Commission submitted a proposal to the Council for a Resolution concerning the objectives and principles of a Community forestry policy.[4] At the time, this was supported by the European Parliament[5] and by the Economic and Social Committee.[6] However, the proposal was not endorsed by the Council of Ministers. In 1983, the Commission proposed a further Council Resolution concerning objectives and kinds of action for Community policy regarding forestry and forestry-based industries.[7]

In 1986 the Council adopted regulations which were aimed specifically at the protection of the Community's forests from fire and atmospheric pollution.[8]

Finally, in 1988 the Commission published its Communication "A Community Strategy and Action Programme for the Forestry Sector", with the Action Programme planned to run from 1989 to 1992.[9] The Council of Ministers did not formally adopt the strategy and action plan which the Commission published, but approved all of the proposed regulations set out within the Commission Communication.[10]

[3] OJ No L 375 of 31/12/91.
[4] COM (78) 621 final of 1/12/78.
[5] OJ No C 140 of 5/6/79.
[6] ESC opinion of 22/5/79.
[7] COM 83 (222).
[8] OJ No L 386 of 21/11/86.
[9] COM 88 (255).
[10] OJ No L 165 of 15/6/89.

Community forestry strategy

Within the Community Strategy document produced by the Commission, guidelines and principles were laid down for Community forestry policy. The key points of these guidelines are illustrated in the following sections.

Principles.   The following principles were established in the Forestry Strategy to guide Commission and Community action:

(a) it should supplement the work of Member States, regions, local authorities and private individuals, i.e. it should be complementary to national actions;
(b) the schemes launched must implement a long-term and integrated strategy; and
(c) the strategy must be selective in approach and concentrate on essential areas to be an effective policy.

Aims.   The Commission envisaged eight major aims for Community forestry strategy namely:

● to participate fully in land use planning and encourage the development of rural life in the Community by a more systematic and wider contribution on the part of the forestry sector to regional development, particularly in rural areas;
● to ensure the security of supply of renewable raw materials;
● *to contribute to environmental improvement* (emphasis added);
● to give the forestry sector its own dynamism;
● to protect the Community's forests against damage;
● to extend the role forests have as a natural setting for relaxation, recreation and culture;
● to participate in development in the most disadvantaged areas of the world; and
● to give forests and the forestry sector their full place in the formulation and implementation of Community policies.

Scope.   The areas in which the forestry strategy could be applied are identified in the Community Forestry Strategy document as the following:

Within the Community:

● forestry infrastructure, such as access roads;
● forestry management structures, whereby the rationalization of land ownership will lead to greater efficiency;
● development of silvicultural techniques and processing;
● harmonization of rules and regulations on product standards and quality;
● location and development of processing industries;
● development of forest owner associations; and
● development of certain sectors of production (i.e. cork and resins);

The Commission notes that most of the action that the Community could initiate in the above fields would not be of guaranteed effectiveness unless preceded or accompanied by action in the following areas:

(1) forestry inventories and forecasts;
(2) forestry research and technological development;
(3) education and public awareness; and
(4) training and forestry management consultancy.

Outside the Community:

(a) programmes and projects in developing countries, such as technical and financial support from the Community for forestry projects integrated into development programmes; and

(b) international organizations: the Community must take part in the forestry work of international organizations to protect and promote the world's forests by efficient integrated exploitation together with replanting programmes.

Means. The strategy document identifies three means of applying Community forestry strategy namely:

- promoting measures or procedures by granting financial incentives;
- launching Community supported forestry schemes; and
- coordinating national forestry policies.

Instruments. The strategy document identifies two mechanisms for the implementation of the Community's forestry strategy:

- On the administrative side, the Commission set up a Standing Forestry Committee to give opinions on the implementation of the strategy and to help coordinate forestry policy, besides establishing a forestry information system and a Community research network; and
- On the financial side, the Structural Funds are used within the Community, and the European Development Fund (EDF) and other instruments, e.g. the assistance programme for Asian and Latin American countries (ALA), are used for aiding developing countries. The European Investment Bank (EIB) is able to finance actions both inside and outside the Community.

Implementation. The forestry strategy advocates both medium- and long-term measures and is implemented in phases, each lasting four years. The first phase was planned to cover the period 1989–1992 and was seen as being of crucial importance in the development of an effective Community forest policy.

2.   Forestry Action Programme (1989–1992)

The first Forestry Action Programme (FAP), which was planned to run from 1989–1992, has focused on the following five priority areas:

- afforestation of agricultural land;
- development and optimal utilization of woodland in rural areas;
- cork production;
- forest protection; and
- back-up measures.

3.   Forest protection

The forest protection schemes adopted by the Council on 17 November 1986 were a significant first step on the way to establishing common European responsibility for safeguarding Community forests.[11]

---

[11] Council Regulations 3528 and 3529, OJ No L 386 of 21/11/86.

The provisions adopted were seen as needing to be reinforced and enhanced to give the Community a set of effective tools for protecting its forests against the main threats, which were identified as:

- atmospheric pollution;
- fire;
- disease; and
- weakening of the genetic potential.

(a) Protection of forests against atmospheric pollution

Acid rain and the other effects of atmospheric pollution from sulphur dioxide represent a serious threat to the environment and appear to be the principal cause of the decline of European forests. Most at risk are the forests of continental Europe as well as a number of forests in southern Europe. Research in this area has not produced any definitive conclusion concerning the interactions of the different factors involved in the decline of forests. As a result, there exists a great need for research to determine precisely the effects of atmospheric pollution.

Council Regulation 3528/86/EEC of 17 November 1986 (OJ L 326, 21/11/1986, p. 2) established a Community programme aimed a protecting forests against atmospheric pollution. The principle measures comprised:

- the establishment, at Community level, of a periodic review of forest damage, based on a common system of observation;
- the establishment, by the Member States, of periodic assessments of the health status of forests, to be given to the Commission;
- the completion of pilot and demonstration projects aimed at understanding the effects of atmospheric pollution, at improving observation and measurement techniques for forest damage, and at methods for restoring damaged forests; and
- the coordination and production, by the Commission, of the above policies.

The regulation took effect from 1 January 1987, and received a budget of Ecu 10 million for a five-year period. The financial commitment of the Community in approved projects was fixed at 30%.

According to a report by the Commission (CEC (89) 2153, 18 December 1989) on the inventory of forest damage, the Member States had presented during 1987 and 1988 a total of 22 projects of which 21 were approved, receiving total funding of Ecu 3,222,257. Regarding pilot projects, the Commission approved 37 out of 66 projects proposed in 1987 and 1988, granting them a total of Ecu 2,886,609 of financial assistance.

Council Regulation 1613/89/EEC of 29 May 1989 amended Regulation 3528/86/EEC with the following measures:

- the Community financial commitment to approved projects was to be raised from 30% to 50%;
- the budget was to be increased from 10 million Ecu to 17 million Ecu for the five-year period;
- pilot projects under way were to be enhanced by measures by the Community; and
- a programme was to be established to explore methods for the gathering of information concerning atmospheric pollution and its effects on forest.

Regulation 3528/86/EEC, as modified by Regulation 1613/89/EEC expired on 31 December 1992. However on 23 July 1992 the Council of Ministers extended and tightened the existing legislation. Regulation 3528/86/EEC was extended for another five years and provided with funding of Ecu 29.4 million.[12]

The regulation has already resulted in the creation of a Community network for monitoring the condition of Community forests which examines the issue of forest die-back. Work is now being conducted on establishing an intensive monitoring system for forests through the International Concerted Programme (PIC-forests) for the Evaluation and Surveillance of the effects of Atmospheric Pollution on Forests, which has been set up within the framework of the Convention on Long-Range Transboundary Air Pollution.

This new regulation is more far-reaching than the one it replaces in so far as it combines the European "tree observation plots" network with a more intensive system of forestry surveillance. As a result of this new measure, it should be possible to learn more about the complex interactions between forestry ecosystems and pollutants. The regulation also envisages pilot schemes for upgrading forests and improving forest observation methods.

(b) Protection of forests against fires

The number of forest fires in the Community is considerable, especially in the Mediterranean region. For the five southern Member States (France, Spain, Greece, Italy and Portugal), it has been estimated that there are 26,000 fires annually, with an average of 18 burning at any one time. About 1% of the forest area of the Community (500,000 ha) is destroyed by fire each year in the five southern Member States (France 0.9%, Spain 1.9%, Greece 0.8%, Italy 0.4%, Portugal 2.6%). During the 1980s, about 4.5 million hectares were burnt, which corresponds to the entire wooded area of France's Mediterranean region. During 1990 and 1991, the situation deteriorated. In the first nine months of 1991, more than 200,000 ha of forest in Spain was burnt and more than 130,000 ha was burnt in Portugal.

Several Council Regulations have been adopted to protect Community forests against fire damage. The first was Council Regulation 3529/86/EEC of 17 November 1986 (OJ L 326 21/11/1986, p. 5). This related to the protection of Community forests from fire by establishing a Community policy to encourage Member States to reinforce forestry fire protection with the following preventative measures:

- encouragement of silvicultural operations designed to reduce the risks of forest fires;
- encouragement to stock forest clearing equipment;
- construction of fire breaks and water hydrants;
- installation of fixed or mobile observation posts;
- organization of information campaigns; and
- assistance in establishing interdisciplinary centres to carry out and disseminate analytical studies on the topic.

These measures are complementary in encouraging the development of highly specialized forestry personnel, in encouraging the harmonization of techniques and materials for fire fighting, and in the coordination of research.

[12] 2157/92/EEC.

The regulation took effect from 1 January 1987, and was provided with a budget of Ecu 20 million for a period of five years. Under the regulation, the Commission provides up to 30% of the funding for fire prevention projects.

According to the last Commission report (CEC (89) 2153 final, 18 December 1989) for the first two years of the programme, 132 projects have been submitted to the Commission. Of these, 88 were awarded a total of Ecu 9,171,284. After two years of the regulation being in force, it was apparent that the majority of the projects proposed concentrated on preventive action, such as information and surveillance projects.

Council Regulation 1614/89/EEC of 29 May 1989 modified Regulation 3529/86/EEC reinforcing Community action aimed at the protection of forests against fires. Under this regulation, the Community would fund 30–50% of approved projects and a budget of Ecu 20–31.5 million was approved for a five-year period. In addition the Community was to support pilot projects and experimentation with new technology aimed at improving forestry fire protection measures.

Regulation 3529/86/EEC, as amended by Regulation 1614/89/EEC, expired on 31 December 1992. The regulation was renewed on 23 July 1992 for a further five years, amended so as to:

- focus Community action on areas where there is a high risk of fires breaking out;
- induce the Member States to develop coherent strategies for protecting forests against fires; and
- develop an information system (database) on forests in order to provide an opportunity to upgrade the protection systems and in particular the methods for assessing the causes of forest fires.

It is proposed that the level of Community funding should be as high as 80% of the total needed in high-risk regions, 30% for medium-risk regions and 15% for others. Ecu 70 million has been provided to assist in combating forest fires.

4.   Forests as carbon dioxide sinks

The Community is committed to stabilizing its CO_2 emissions at 1990 levels by the year 2000. In the context of measures to be developed to assist in reaching the target, the Commission has recognized that measures aimed at increasing the scale and effectiveness of CO_2 sinks within the Community have an important part to play in the overall emissions stabilization strategy.

Of the recognized forms of CO_2 sink that could be amenable to policy measures, forests are those where a contribution might be readily achieved and where policy actions might be developed. In the United States, for example, the Conservation Reserve Programme has already been developed for some time and well over a million hectares of trees have been planted under that programme.

The IPCC[13] workshop "Carbon Balance of the World's Forested Ecosystems – Towards a Global Assessment" held in May 1992 also recognized the importance of the potential contribution of forests to CO_2 stabilization and reduction policies.

---

[13] Intergovernmental Panel on Climate Change.

The Commission has initiated a research effort in this area. This may become an important imperative for the continuation and development of Community forestry policy, as such policies will pass the subsidiarity criteria as being best performed at Community level.

5. 5th Environmental Action Programme

Under the 5th Environmental Action Programme, "Towards Sustainability", agriculture has been highlighted as one of the target sectors of the programme and forestry has been addressed within this. The objective for forestry is the "optimization of forest area so as to fulfil all their functions". In order to do this, twin policies of increasing afforestation and improved forest protection against fires have been established for some time.

Within the Action Programme, the Commission sees that this is best undertaken by a mix of Community and Member State action, with the Community providing the context within which Member States may operate. Such an approach indicates the likelihood that future forest policy will be neither wholly Community based nor wholly Member State based, but a mixture of the two.

6. Other environmental issues

A European Commission report produced in collaboration with the International Cooperative Programme on Assessment and Monitoring of Air Pollution Effects on Forests, has concluded that the condition of European forests has continued to deteriorate and that nearly 20% of trees show clear sign of damage.[14]

The primary cause of forest damage was identified as transboundary atmospheric pollution leading to increased acidification of forest soils. In many areas atmospheric deposition loads exceeded critical levels. This may act as an impetus to further strengthening measures to protect Community forests from atmospheric pollution.

The contribution of woods and forests to the maintenance of biodiversity, the protection of habitat and the quality of landscape is also of crucial importance. Forests which are to be safeguarded for ecological reasons may be of a different character, and may need to be managed differently, from those which are exploited primarily for other purposes.

In 1992 the United Nations Economic Commission for Europe (UNECE) and the Food and Agriculture Organization (FAO) published a forest resource assessment.[15] The survey concluded that forest resources in temperate areas are continuing to increase. The report points out that environmental and other non-wood values of forests in temperate zone regions are increasingly important to society, both in absolute terms and in relation to wood production. Most countries are reported to expect to see more policy and planning directed at specific non-wood functions, especially forestry protection, water regulation and water quality, nature conservation and recreation. However, the importance of wood production will be maintained. Forestry policies are reported to be beginning to respond to the

---

[14] Forest Conditions in Europe: 1992 EEC and UN/ECE.
[15] UN/ECE Forests Resource Assessment 1990 (EC/TIM/60).

conflicts between the different functions of forests using conflict resolution methods. As a result, it is likely that as the perceived value of forests increases, so their quality will improve and extent will increase.

III. INDUSTRY AND THE ENVIRONMENT

1. Industry and the internal market

The integration of environmental problems in industrial policy should be viewed in a wider context than that of the prevention or control of pollution and procedures for evaluating environmental impact.

The site and design of industrial installations, the choice of products and processes, the management of industrial wastes, should all also take ecological aspects into account. Another important objective from the point of view of industry involves passing environmental legislation far enough in advance to allow industry sufficient time to adapt to the new standards for production, industrial strategy and long-term investments. Since all of these problems could not be resolved by legislation, the Commission also intends to encourage a better relationship between the environment and industry by collaborating with the different sectors, drawing up, in collaboration with the different industrial sectors, guiding principles and codes of conduct.

It is, however, likely that the imposition of increasingly severe environmental standards will pose serious problems for old industries whose installations are often obsolete, as well as in some cases for small and medium-sized enterprises. Nevertheless, it is clear that generally speaking, competitiveness of Community industry on world markets in the 1990s and beyond will partly depend on the conformity of its products to environmental standards which are at least as strict as those of its competitors. In the opposite situation, Community producers will lose their share of the market, not only on international markets, but also on the internal market.

It is recognized that pollution leads to a waste of resources which is often linked to obsolete technologies. Within the context of the completion of the Community internal market by 1992, it was important to arrive at a harmonization of national environmental standards which still differ greatly from one Member State to another. The Single Act therefore indicated that the increasing standardization of environmental protection legislations would be based on a high level of protection.

The 5th Environmental Action Programme singles out public and private enterprise, and in particular manufacturing industry, as being among the key targets of, and participants in, environmental policy.

2. The 1993 Regulation allowing voluntary participation by companies in the industrial sector in a Community eco-management and audit scheme

On 6 March 1992 the Commission sent a proposal to the Council for a Council regulation allowing voluntary participation by companies in the industrial sector in a Community Eco-audit scheme.

In its Explanatory Memorandum[16] the Commission pointed out that successive Community Environmental Action Programmes, in particular the 4th (1987–1992) had stressed the need to develop more integrated policies promoting multi-media approaches to the environment and the cutting of pollution at source. Under the pressure of the growing number of regulations, particularly in the form of the Community's environmental legislation, companies engaged in manufacturing activities, and particularly industrial activities, were assuming responsibilities for performing more and more complex tasks which played a decisive part in the environmental protection field. The proposal set out to establish a voluntary scheme which would recognize industrial sites where firms had set up, within the framework of a company policy, environmental management systems, including regular audits and public reports on environmental performance. The public, suppliers and consumers would be provided with information about the commitment of the company to improving environmental performance and to reducing the impact on the environment resulting from operations at the site. The recognition brought by registration with Eco-audit, including the right to use a "logo", would encourage industry to develop more environmentally friendly policies.

The European Parliament gave its opinion in January 1993[17] and the ECOSOC in December 1992.[18] The Commission's amended proposal was sent to the Council in March 1993.[19] Under the amended proposal, the title of the scheme was changed to "eco-management and audit", various recitals were amended and new ones added and some of the articles were more specifically defined. The Eco-Management and Audit Scheme (EMAS) was adopted by the Environment Ministers at their meeting on 23 March 1993 and published in the Official Journal on 10 July 1993,[20] the date for implementation being set for the spring of 1995 to give time for the establishment of an effective accreditation scheme for verifiers.

The key features of the EMAS Scheme as adopted by the Council are as follows:[21]

● Commitments by companies participating on a voluntary basis, including the adoption of a company environmental policy and conducting an environmental review of the registered site.
● The validation of the environmental statement to be carried out by an officially appointed, independent and accredited environmental verifier.

EMAS is essentially a management tool which should allow companies throughout the European Union to apply high standards of environmental management and to evaluate the environmental impact of their activities.[22]

---

[16] COM (91) 459 final of 5/3/92; OJ No C 76/2 of 27/3/92.
[17] Valverde Lopez Report, 3–005/93, 11 January 1993.
[18] OJ No C 332/44 of 16/12/92.
[19] COM (93) final, 16/3/93; OJ No C 120/3 of 30/4/93.
[20] OJ No L 168/1 of 10/7/93.
[21] See Juan Xiberta, "The Eco-Management and Audit Scheme", *European Environmental Law Review*, March 1994.
[22] *Ibid.*

Table 13.5: Council Regulation (EEC) No 1836/93 of 29 June 1993 allowing voluntary participation by companies in the industrial sector in a Community eco-management and audit scheme

ANNEX I

REQUIREMENTS CONCERNING ENVIRONMENTAL POLICIES, PROGRAMMES AND MANAGEMENT SYSTEMS

A. *Environmental policies, objectives and programmes*

1. The company environmental policy, and the programme for the site, shall be established in writing. Associated documents will explain how the environmental programme and the management system at the site relate to the policy and systems of the company as a whole.

2. The company environmental policy shall be adopted and periodically reviewed, in particular in the light of environmental audits, and revised as appropriate, at the highest management level. It shall be communicated to the company's personnel and be publicly available.

3. The company's environmental policy shall be based on the principles of action in section D.

   The policy will aim, in addition to providing for compliance with all relevant regulatory requirements regarding the environment, at the continual improvement of environmental performance.

   The environmental policy and the programme for the site shall address, in particular, the issues in section C.

4. *Environmental objectives*

   The company shall specify its environmental objectives at all relevant levels within the company.

   The objectives shall be consistent with the environmental policy and shall quantify wherever practicable the commitment to continual improvement in environmental performance over defined time-scales.

5. *Environmental programme for the site*

   The company shall establish and maintain a programme for achieving the objectives at the site. It shall include:

   (a) designation of responsibility for objectives at each function and level of the company;

   (b) the means by which they are to be achieved.

   Separate programmes shall be established in respect of the environmental management of projects relating to new developments, or to new or modified products, services or processes, to define:

1. the environmental objectives to be attained;

2. the mechanisms for their achievement;

3. the procedures for dealing with changes and modifications as projects proceed;

4. the corrective mechanisms which shall be employed should the need arise, how they shall be activated and how their adequacy shall be measured in any particular situation in which they are applied.

Table 13.5 continued

B. *Environmental management systems*

The environmental management systems shall be designed, implemented and maintained in such a way as to ensure the fulfilment of the requirements defined below.

1. *Environmental policy, objectives and programmes*

The establishment and periodical review, and revision as appropriate, of the company's environmental policy, objectives and programmes for the site, at the highest appropriate management level.

2. *Organization and personnel*

Responsibility and authority

Definition and documentation of responsibility, authority and interrelations of key personnel who manage, perform and monitor work affecting the environment.

Management representative

Appointment of a management representative having authority and responsibility for ensuring that the management system is implemented and maintained.

Personnel, communication and training

Ensuring among personnel, at all levels, awareness of:

(a) the importance of compliance with the environmental policy and objectives, and with the requirements applicable under the management system established;

(b) the potential environmental effects of their work activities and the environmental benefits of improved performance;

(c) their roles and responsibilities in achieving compliance with the environmental policy and objectives, and with the requirements of the management system;

(d) the potential consequences of departure from the agreed operating procedures.

Identifying training needs, and providing appropriate training for all personnel whose work may have a significant effect upon the environment.

The company shall establish and maintain procedures for receiving, documenting and responding to communications (internal and external) from relevant interested parties concerning its environmental effects and management.

3. *Environmental effects*

Environmental effects evaluation and registration

Examining and assessing the environmental effects of company's activities at the site, and compiling a register of those identified as significant. This shall include, where appropriate, consideration of:

(a) controlled and uncontrolled emissions to atmosphere;

(b) controlled and uncontrolled discharges to water or sewers;

(c) solid and other wastes, particularly hazardous wastes;

(d) contamination of land;

(e) use of land, water, fuels and energy, and other natural resources;

(f) discharge of thermal energy, noise, odour, dust, vibration and visual impact;

(g) effects on specific parts of the environment and ecosystems.

Table 13.5 continued

This shall include effects arising, or likely to arise, as consequences of:

1. normal operating conditions;

2. abnormal operating conditions;

3. incidents, accidents and potential emergency situations;

4. past activities, current activities and planned activities.

Register of legislative, regulatory and other policy requirements

The company shall establish and maintain procedures to record all legislative, regulatory and other policy requirements pertaining to the environmental aspects of its activities, products and services.

4. *Operational control*

Establishment of operating procedures

Identification of functions, activities and processes which affect, or have the potential to affect, the environment, and are relevant to the company's policy and objectives.

Planning and control of such functions, activities and processes, and with particular attention to:

(a) documented work instructions defining the manner of conducting the activity, whether by the company's own employees or by others acting on its behalf. Such instructions shall be prepared for situations in which the absence of such instructions could result in infringement of the environmental policy;

(b) procedures dealing with procurement and contracted activities, to ensure that suppliers and those acting on the company's behalf comply with the company's environmental policy as it relates to them;

(c) monitoring and control of relevant process characteristics (e.g. effluent streams and waste disposal);

(d) approval of planned processes and equipment;

(e) criteria for performance, which shall be stipulated in written standards.

Monitoring

Monitoring by the company of meeting the requirements established by the company's environmental policy, programme and management system for the site; and for establishing and maintaining records of the results.

For each relevant activity or area, this implies:

(a) identifying and documenting the monitoring information to be obtained;

(b) specifying and documenting the monitoring procedures to be used;

(c) establishing and documenting acceptance criteria and the action to be taken when results are unsatisfactory;

(d) assessing and documenting the validity of previous monitoring information when monitoring systems are found to be malfunctioning.

Non-compliance and corrective action

Investigation and corrective action, in case of non-compliance with company's environmental policy, objectives or standards, in order to:

(a) determine the cause;

Table 13.5 continued

(b) draw up a plan of action;

(c) initiate preventive actions, to a level corresponding to the risks encountered;

(d) apply controls to ensure that any preventive actions taken are effective;

(e) record any changes in procedures resulting from corrective action.

5. *Environmental management documentation records*

Establishing documentation with a view to:

(a) present in a comprehensive way the environmental policy, objectives, and programme;

(b) document the key roles and responsibilities;

(c) describe the interactions of system elements.

Establishing records in order to demonstrate compliance with the requirements of the environmental management system, and to record the extent to which planned environmental objectives have been met.

6. *Environmental audits*

Management, implementation and review of a systematic and periodical programme concerning:

(a) whether or not environmental management activities conform to the environmental programme, and are implemented effectively;

(b) the effectiveness of the environmental management system in fulfilling the company's environmental policy.

C. *Issues to be covered*

The following issues shall be addressed, within the framework of the environmental policy and programmes and of environmental audits.

1. Assessment, control, and reduction of the impact of the activity concerned on the various sectors of the environment.

2. Energy management, savings and choice.

3. Raw materials management, savings, choice and transportation; water management and savings.

4. Waste avoidance, recyling, reuse, transportation and disposal.

5. Evaluation, control and reduction of noise within and outside the site.

6. Selection of new production processes and changes to production processes.

7. Product planning (design, packaging, transportation, use and disposal).

8. Environmental performance and practices of contractors, subcontractors and suppliers.

9. Prevention and limitation of environmental accidents.

10. Contingency procedures in cases of environmental accidents.

11. Staff information and training on environmental issues.

12. External information on environmental issues.

Table 13.5 continued

D. Good management practices

The company's environmental policy shall be based on the principles of action set out below; the activities of the company shall be checked regularly to see if they are consistent with these principles and that of continual improvement in environmental performance.

1. A sense of responsibility for the environment amongst employees at all levels, shall be fostered.

2. The environmental impact of all new activities, products and processes shall be assessed in advance.

3. The impact of current activities on the local environment shall be assessed and monitored, and any significant impact of these activities on the environment in general, shall be examined.

4. Measures necessary to prevent or eliminate pollution, and where this is not feasible, to reduce pollutant emissions and waste generation to the minimum and to conserve resources shall be taken, taking account of possible clean technologies.

5. Measures necessary to prevent accidental emissions of materials or energy shall be taken.

6. Monitoring procedures shall be established and applied, to check compliance with the environmental policy and, where these procedures require measurement and testing, to establish and update records of the results.

7. Procedures and action to be pursued in the event of detection of non-compliance with its environmental policy, objectives or targets, shall be established and updated.

8. Cooperation with the public authorities shall be ensured to establish and update contingency procedures to minimize the impact of any accidental discharges to the environment that nevertheless occur.

9. Information necessary to understand the environmental impact of the company's activities shall be provided to the public, and an open dialogue with the public should be pursued.

10. Appropriate advice shall be provided to customers on the relevant environmental aspects of the handling, use and disposal of the products made by the company.

11. Provisions shall be taken to ensure that contractors working at the site on the company's behalf apply environmental standards equivalent to the company's own.

3.   Council Regulation 92/880(EEC) of 23 March 1992 on a Community eco-label award scheme

In February 1991, the Commission sent the Council a proposal based on Article 130S for a regulation on a Community eco-label award scheme.[23] This proposal was drawn up in the light of the Council's request in its Resolution of 7 May 1990 that such a system be established at Community level, taking into account the environmental impact of the products in question throughout their life-cycle. Prior to

---

[23] COM (91) 37 of 11/2/91; OJ No L 99 of 11/4/92.

Table 13.6: Council Regulation (EEC) No 1836/93 of 29 June 1993 allowing voluntary participation by companies in the industrial sector in a Community eco-management and audit scheme

ANNEX II

REQUIREMENTS CONCERNING ENVIRONMENTAL AUDITING

The audit will be planned and executed in the light of the relevant guidelines in the ISO 10011 international standard (1990, Part 1, in particular paragraphs 4.2, 5.1, 5.2, 5.3, 5.4.1, 5.4.2) and other relevant international standards, and within the framework of the specific principles and requirements of this Regulation (*).

In particular:

A. *Objectives*

The site's environmental auditing programmes will define in writing the objectives of each audit or audit cycle including the audit frequency for each activity.

The objectives must include, in particular, assessing the management systems in place, and determining conformity with company policies and the site programme, which must include compliance with relevant environmental regulatory requirements.

B. *Scope*

The overall scope of the individual audits, or of each stage of an audit cycle where appropriate, must be clearly defined and must explicitly specify the:

1. subject areas covered;

2. activities to be audited;

3. environmental standards to be considered;

4. period covered by the audit.

Environmental audit includes assessment of the factual data necessary to evaluate performance.

C. *Organization and resources*

Environmental audits must be performed by persons or groups of persons with appropriate knowledge of the sectors and fields audited, including knowledge and experience on the relevant environmental management, technical, environmental and regulatory issues, and sufficient training and proficiency in the specific skills of auditing to achieve the stated objectives. The resources and time allocated to the audit must be commensurate with the scope and objectives of the audit.

(*) For the specific purpose of this Regulation, the terms of the abovementioned standard will be interpreted as follows:
- "quality system" shall read "environmental management system",
- "quality standard" shall read "environmental standard",
- "quality manual" shall read "environmental management manual",
- "quality audit" shall read "environmental audit",
- "client" shall read "the company's top management",
- "auditee" shall read "the site".

Table 13.6 continued

The top company management shall support the auditing.

The auditors shall be sufficiently independent of the activities they audit to make an objective and impartial judgment.

D. *Planning and preparation for a site audit*

Each audit will be planned and prepared with the objectives, in particular, of:

– ensuring the appropriate resources are allocated,

– ensuring that each individual involved in the audit process (including auditors, site management, and staff) understands his or her role and responsibilities.

Preparation will include familiarization with activities on the site and with the environmental management system established there and review of the findings and conclusions of previous audits.

E. *Audit activities*

1. On-site audit activities will include discussions with site personnel, inspection of operating conditions and equipment and reviewing of records, written procedures and other relevant documentation, with the objective of evaluating environmental performance at the site by determining whether the site meets the applicable standards and whether the system in place to manage environmental responsibilities is effective and appropriate.

2. The following steps, in particular, will be included in the audit process:

    (a) understanding of the management systems;

    (b) assessing strengths and weaknesses of the management systems;

    (c) gathering relevant evidence;

    (d) evaluating audit findings;

    (e) preparing audit conclusions;

    (f) reporting audit findings and conclusions.

F. *Reporting audit findings and conclusions*

1. A written audit report of the appropriate form and content will be prepared by the auditors to ensure full, formal submission of the findings and conclusions of the audit, at the end of each audit and audit cycle.

    The findings and conclusions of the audit must be formally communicated to the top company management.

2. The fundamental objectives of a written audit report are:

    (a) to document the scope of the audit;

    (b) to provide management with information on the state of compliance with the company's environmental policy and the environmental progress at the site;

    (c) to provide management with information on the effectiveness and reliability of the arrangements for monitoring environmental impacts at the site;

    (d) to demonstrate the need for corrective action, where appropriate.

Table 13.6 continued

G. Audit follow-up

The audit process will culminate in the preparation and implementation of a plan of appropriate corrective action.

Appropriate mechanisms must be in place and in operation to ensure that the audit results are followed up.

H. Audit frequency

The audit will be executed, or the audit cycle will be completed, as appropriate, at intervals no longer than three years. The frequency for each activity at a site will be established by the top company management, taking account of the potential overall environmental impact of the activities at the site, and of the site's environmental programme depending, in particular, on the following elements:

(a) nature, scale and complexity of the activities;

(b) nature and scale of emissions, waste, raw material and energy consumption and, in general, of interaction with the environment;

(c) importance and urgency of the problems detected, following the initial environmental review or the previous audit;

(d) history of environmental problems.

this proposal, the 4th Action Programme had underlined the need to put into place a policy in favour of clean products. The prospect of several different systems operating within the Community, based on different criteria, made some kind of Community system all the more necessary, particularly since at the time the proposal was published one Member State (Germany) had already introduced a national eco-label system for clean products and other countries were thinking of doing the same. However, the regulation does allow for existing and future independent systems to continue for a period of five years – after which the Commission will look again at how best to proceed in the light of the experience gained.

The regulation aims gradually to introduce in all the EC Member States a voluntary scheme for the award of a Community eco-label to products with a reduced environmental impact. Criteria will be worked out for the award of the eco-label to individual product groups, such as washing machines, paper products and detergents, with the exception of food, drink and pharmaceutical products. It is hoped that such a scheme will encourage manufacturers to design and produce products which have a reduced environmental impact, and will help to provide consumers with better information on the environmental performance of certain products compared with others in the same category.

The main elements of the scheme, adopted as Council Regulation 880/92,[24] are as follows:

● product groups have to be defined and ecological criteria have to be adopted for each such group by the Commission, after Community-wide consideration of proposals. The principal interest groups are consulted on all proposals. The cri-

[24] OJ No L 99 of 11/4/92.

teria have to be based on a "cradle-to-grave" assessment of a product's environmental impact;

● each Member State has to designate a competent body which is responsible for receiving applications from manufacturers or importers for the award of the eco-label to their products. The competent body decides on applications on the basis of the product group definitions and ecological criteria which have been previously adopted;

● each decision to award an eco-label to an individual product must first be cleared with the competent bodies in all Member States (during a 30-day period). This clearance ensures that the successful applicant can enjoy Community-wide recognition of his eco-label award;

● a successful applicant is required to sign a contract with the competent body for the issue of the eco-label during a specified period. The competent body charges fees, both for the application and for the annual use of the eco-label;

● the EC Commission must publish in the Offical Journal details of product group definitions and ecological criteria that have been adopted; of products awarded the eco-label and their manufacturers or importers; and of the names and addresses of the competent bodies.

Thanks to an amendment to the Commission's original proposal introduced by the European Parliament in its opinion of 10 December 1991, the Commission is required to consult a Consultation Forum (made up of representatives of industry, commerce, consumer and environmental organizations) on all proposals for the definition of product groups and ecological criteria, before it submits its proposals to the Regulatory Committee (consisting of representatives of Member States). The proposals themselves are drawn up on the basis of preparatory work done by a national competent body in consultation with interest groups.

The "cradle-to-grave" assessment means that the complete life-cycle of a product group is analysed, starting with the extraction of the raw materials, progressing through the production, distribution and use phases, and ending with disposal after use. An assessment matrix appears in the regulation (see brochure). The eco-label itself will be in the form of a flower as shown below.

Since the adoption of the regulation, problems have arisen with the national competent authorities.

IV.   SOCIAL POLICY AND THE ENVIRONMENT

There are a number of links between the environment policy and social policy, notably in the areas of the protection of workers, professional training and working conditions in general. What is more, in the crucial area of employment the strengthening of environment policy will undoubtedly generally have positive effects on job creation, thanks to investments made in the area of environment, and the manufacture of new products linked to the quality of the environment. Even if in certain cases at the micro-economic level environmental regulations may have increased industrial costs and had a short-term negative impact on employment, it is now recognized, in particular following work carried out on this matter by the OECD, that numerous environmental measures contribute directly or indirectly to the creation of jobs: for example, measures taken to avoid decline in town centres, to rehabilitate disused land, or to remedy the deterioration of natural sites.

The Community's 1st Environmental Action Programme, adopted 22 November 1973, indicated that the Commission would propose the creation of a European Foundation for the Improvement of Living and Working Conditions. On 26 May 1975, the Council adopted the regulation establishing the Foundation in Dublin and it has since then undertaken numerous research projects relating to the working environment, the urban environment, etc.

On an experimental basis the Commission has already provided financial support in 1985 and 1986 for a limited number of pilot actions in the areas of professional training and job creation. In 1987 it planned to extend these actions considerably. To this end it proposed a five-year programme (1988–1992) of "demonstration projects" in the area of environment and employment. This programme, which should have a budget of approximately 60 million Ecu, is intended to show in each Member State how measures taken in the area of environment can contribute to job creation.

It will thus be possible to gather together experiences and information from which the different sectors of activity and administration will be able to benefit in the future. The demonstration projects will involve both the control of industrial pollution, including developing clean technologies, and also the development of infrastructures. They will concern small and medium-sized enterprises in particular. The proposal has been discussed on several occasions by the Council but it has not yet proved possible to reach agreement.

V. THE OTHER POLICIES: REGIONAL, ENERGY, TRANSPORT, CONSUMER PROTECTION

1. Regional policy

As regards regional policy, the integration of environmental aspects in the planning and execution of regional development programmes is of growing importance. This integration must basically be achieved through preventive actions, but in less economically developed regions it is the case that environmental measures are sometimes delayed because of their financial impact on existing enterprises, or else cause numerous difficulties at the application level due to a lack of basic environmental infrastructures. To overcome these problems, the Commission intended to submit to the Council in 1987, within the framework of the Regional Funds of the Community (FEDER), a Community "regional environment-development" programme specifically designed to assist disadvantaged regions to apply the Community directives in the area of the environment.

The submission of this proposal was, however, delayed, priority being given to the major reform of the Structural Funds agreed by the Council in late 1988 and to the elaboration of new rules for the various component sectors.

The regulation governing the Structural Funds, as adopted in 1988,[25] distinguishes five objectives:

1. The development and structural adaptation of the poor regions of the EC (less than 75% of the average per capita GDP).
2. The conversion of the regions affected by industrial decline and high unemployment rates in manufacturing industries.
3. The decrease of long-term unemployment.
4. The facilitating of the entry of young people to the labour market.
5. The reform of the agricultural policy by (a) adaptation of agricultural structures and (b) rural development.

Article 7 of the basic regulation (2052/88 EEC) states that all actions of the Structural Funds, including the European Investment Bank and other financial instruments, must be carried out in conformity with the treaty and with all decisions based upon the treaty and the different fields of policy for the Community, including EC competition policy and the rules for contracting-out of public works and environmental protection.

In the implementing regulation for the ERDF (No 4252/88 EEC), the types of investment that are eligible for co-financing are described. Mention is made of "productive investments and infrastructure to protect the environment, if related to economic activities".

It is specified that all actions undertaken in the context of the Community Support Frameworks (CSFs) must respect EC environmental legislation. The operational programmes (OPs) contain similar conditions. Once a programme has been decided by the European Commission, a Monitoring Committee is established in which the Commission and the national and regional authorities, as well as other institutions that are concerned with the execution of the programme, are represented.

The European Court of Auditors has pointed out that the obligation for environmental aspects to be controlled by the Monitoring Committee is rarely fulfilled.[26]

ENVIREG[27] as adopted is a programme within the Structural Funds aimed at supporting urban waste water treatment plants, solid waste discharge systems, the management of toxic industrial waste as well as maritime water protection and biotope protection in coastal areas. An amount of 500 million Ecu was to be available for the coastal areas of Objective 1 regions and Mediterranean zones for Objective 2 regions.

2. Energy policy

(See also under Chapter 4, Air.)

As far as energy is concerned, a satisfactory balance must be achieved between energy and environmental objectives. Energy production depends very largely on the use of fossil fuels and inevitably causes atmospheric pollution problems.

---

[25] Regulation 2052/88 EEC, OJ No L 185 of 15/7/88; Regulation 4235–4256/88 EEC, OJ No L 374 of 31/12/88.
[26] Special Report No 3/92 "Environment". See also article by Dr Hendrik Fehr and Ir. Diana D van der Stelt-Scheele entitled "The EC Environmental Policy in Relation to the EC Structural Funds: A Critical Analysis of its Application", published in *European Environmental Law Review*, October 1992.
[27] Communication of the Commission No C 115/3 of 9/5/90.

Table 13.7: The fifth environment action programme: energy

Measures up to 2000	Instruments	Time-frame	Actors
awareness building and incentives aimed at sustainable energy use and behavioural changes	* information to, education and training of end-users	1993 onwards	MS + EC + public + Energy sector
	* agreements with industry on efficiency	ongoing	MS + Ind + EC
	* codes of conduct to be adopted by the actors concerned	ongoing	Energy sector + MS + Ind + EC
	* economic and fiscal instruments	ongoing	EC + MS
	* removal of restrictive rules	1993 onwards	MS + EC
energy efficiency programmes	Implementation of PACE, SAVE and national efficiency Programmes, including:	ongoing	EC + MS + Ind + Energy sector
	* least cost planning		Ind + Energy sector
	* energy efficiency standards for appliances, products and vehicles		EC + MS + Ind + Transport sector
	* efficiency standards for energy technology		EC + Ind
	* buildings insulation standards		MS + Ind + EC
	* minimization of methane leakages from natural gas distribution systems		MS + Energy sector
technology programmes	Implementation of THERMIE and JOULE Programmes, including:	ongoing	EC + MS + Ind + Energy sector
	* R&D of new energy technologies and promotion and use thereof		id
	* R&D on renewables (i.e. biomass)		id
promotional programme	ALTENER: promotion of renewable energy	1993 onwards	id
	* Pilot projects and standardisation		
nuclear safety programmes	Study on safety and waste aspects of nuclear energy	ongoing	EC + MS + Energy sector

Environmental demands also affect energy cost and the competitive position of different energy sources. Conservation measures and the rational use of energy and non-fossil alternative energy sources contribute to the improvement of the quality of the air. In fossil fuel power stations technologies should be used which allow for considerable reduction at a reasonable cost of polluting emissions which can have serious consequences on ecosystems and the climate.

Some specific programmes, e.g. SAVE and ALTENER, have been described in Chapter 4, Air. Table 13.7 sets out the measures necessary up to the year 2000, the instruments needed and the actors involved in order to make the first important steps to the achievement of a sustainable energy policy.

3. Transport

With transport there is an important interaction with environmental problems, be they problems of noise, air pollution or impact on landscapes. In this respect, particular attention should be given to the acceptability of motor vehicles from the environmental point of view in order to diminish polluting emissions and noise levels. With regard to the infrastructure of transport, harmful environmental effects should be kept to a minimum, and new means of communication should be the object of prior evaluation of their effect on the environment.

The 5th Environmental Action Programme notes that the polluting emissions of transport represent a very high share of overall emissions in the Community – about 90% of all lead emissions, about 50% of all NOx emissions and about 30% of all VOC emissions. In urban areas, traffic causes almost 100% of the CO emissions, 60% of HC and NOx emissions, and about 10% of SO_2 emissions. Transport accounts for 22% of all CO_2 emissions. Of this, 80% of emissions arise from road transport and more than 55% from the private car alone. Furthermore, the transport sector – in particular, road and air traffic – is reckoned to be the biggest contributor to the problem of noise.

On 20 February 1992, the Commission published a Green Paper on the Impact of Transport on the Environment: A Community Strategy for Sustainable Mobility[28] which, *inter alia*, proposes a strategy for "sustainable mobility" involving a combination of:

- improved land-use/economic development planning at local, regional, national and transnational levels, to reduce the need for mobility and allow for the development of alternatives to road transport;
- improved coordination in the planning of and investment in transport infrastructure networks and facilities;
- incorporation of the real costs of both infrastructure and environment in investment policies and decisions and in user costs and charges;
- improvement of the competitive position of environment-friendly modes, such as railways, inland and sea-navigation and combined transport;
- development of urban transport, which gives priority to collective transport and to adequate link-up between different stages of journeys;
- continued technical improvement of vehicles and fuels;

[28] COM (92) 46 final of 20/2/92.

Table 13.8: The fifth environment action programme: transport

Measures up to 2000	Instruments	Time-frame	Actors
(a) Infrastructures			
– Land-use planning	EIA	2000	*MS/LAs*
– Infrastructure investments, urban transport, trans-shipment facilities, rail enhancement, goods handling, inland waterways/sea traffic	Structural Funds	1995	*MS/LAs* + EC
– Infrastructure charging			EC
	Road taxes and different forms of Road pricing	1993	MS + EC
		id	id
(b) Fuels & vehicles			
Progressive technical improvement of vehicles:	– R & D	before '95	*Industry* + EC
– exhaust and noise emissions, fuel consumption, performance, final disposal	– regulation	2000	EC + MS
	– vehicle testing (contr. techn)	before '98	MS + EC
	– Recycling of parts	2000	*Industry*
	– Fiscal incentives	2000	MS + EC
Composition & consumption of fuels:	– R & D	before '95	*Industry* + EC
– alternative fuels, cleaner fuels	– Fiscal incentives	2000	MS + EC
– complete move to unleaded petrol by 2000	– regulation	1995	EC + MS
(c) User Behaviour			
– driver information & education on a more rational use of the car	– campaigns in media, speed limits and other physical constraints	ongoing	*LAs/MS* + EC + NGOs
– improved public/collective transport	– investments, land-use plans	2000	*LAs/MS* + EC Transp. authorities
– discouragement of road traffic in cities	– charges, high parking fees, car pooling e.g. positive discrimination (lower tolls) of car poolers	before '95	*LAs* + MS Public
– development of economic and fiscal incentives		id	*Toll operating Companies,* Public
– development of inter-active communication infrastructures	– logging and tracking systems, electronic home, video conferences	ongoing	EC + MS + *Industry*

- promotion of environmentally rational use of the private car, and changes in driving rules and habits, including speed limits.

Table 13.8 gives an indication of measures and instruments needed, the actors involved on different levels but acting in parrtnership, and the time-frame envisaged.

4.   Consumer protection

In the area of consumer protection certain interests have a lot in common with the objectives of environmental protection. Such is the case, for example, with regard to water or drink quality, and more generally with the design and durability of products. Moreover, programmes for consumer education and information should give a larger place to the environmental aspects of products and services.

In organizational terms the links between environment and consumer protection have been strong, since the consumer policy unit until 1986 was allied to the environment unit within the Commission's services (first as part of the Environment and Consumer Protection Service, subsequently, as part of DG XI when it was the Directorate-General for Environment, Consumer Protection and Nuclear Safety). Within the European Parliament, environment and consumer matters have for many years now been handled by the same Committee.

5.   The 1990 Green Paper on the Urban Environment

In June 1990 the Commission published its Green Paper on the Urban Environment. It was prepared in response to the Commission's commitment within the framework of the 4th Environmental Action Programme to carry out a detailed examination of urban environmental problems. The Paper looks at the main causes of inner-city environmental degradation and lays out possible guidelines for Community action. It identifies the full range of issues facing the Community's major urban areas and sets out 27 suggested lines of action. The Paper's objectives include the creation, or re-creation of towns and cities which provide an attractive environment for the people who live in them and the reduction of the cities' contribution to global solution. Member States would need to cooperate with the Commission to draw up guidelines for sound environmental action.

Council Resolution of 28 January 1991[29] welcomed the Green Paper in general. It stressed that, in accordance with the principle of subsidiarity, the primary responsibility for urban policy and management lay with local authorities, regions and national governments. There was, however, a Community dimension to the development of future policy within this area. This dimension covered:

The Council recognized the importance of a reliable source of data as a guide to the development of the urban environment and indicated that the European Environment Agency should play an important role in this respect. Finally, it invited the Commission to set up a working group of national representatives and independent experts.

---

[29] OJ No C 33 of 8/2/91.

Table 13.9: Council Resolution of 28 January 1991 on the Green Paper on the urban environment

3. recognizes that, while in accordance with the principle of subsidiarity the primary responsibility for the definition of policy for, and the management of, the urban environment lies with local authorities, regions and national governments, there is a Community dimension to the development of future policy in this area.

This dimension covers:

(a) the impact on urban environment of Community policies in many areas, particularly those related to the preparation for, and establishment of, the single market, regional development, energy and transportation;

(b) the very close interrelationship between those factors which are recognized as the cause of problems at the city level and those which give rise to contribution to global problems such as acid rain and the greenhouse effect; and the need therefore to ensure that solutions at the local level contribute to the solution of regional and global problems. Urban policies need therefore to be part of wider environmental policies;

(c) the common nature of the problems facing cities, which underlines the value of cooperation and exchange of information between cities, in which the Community can assist in the search for effective solutions;

(d) the importance of improving urban environments that are degraded or threatened by degradation, *inter alia* as a factor of social and economic cohesion within the Community;

(e) recognition of the importance to the Community as a whole of the historic and cultural heritage that our cities represent.

The 5th Environmental Action Programme recalled the Green Paper on the Urban Environment. It pointed out that in the Community, about 80% of the population lives in cities and towns. Urban areas are thus the places where the problems of the environment touch most the quality of life of citizens.

The 5th Environmental Action Programme argues that one of the most pressing problems in urban areas is that of noise. More than 16% of the population suffers at night from noise levels, mainly resulting from road and air traffic, over leq 65 dB(A). (See also Chapter 7 on Noise.)

VI. ENVIRONMENTAL EDUCATION

On 24 May 1988, the Council of Ministers of Education adopted a Resolution on environmental education.[30]

The Resolution lays down that:

The objective of environmental education is to increase the public awareness of the problems in this field, as well as possible solutions, and to lay the foundations for a fully informed and active participation of the individual in the protection of the envir-

---

[30] OJ No C 177 of 6/7/88.

onment and the prudent and rational use of natural resources. For the achievement of this objective environmental education should take into account particularly the following guiding principles:

- the environment as the common heritage of mankind,
- the common duty of maintaining, protecting and improving the quality of the environment, as a contribution to the protection of human health and the safeguarding of the ecological balance,
- the need for a prudent and rational utilization of natural resources,

- the way in which each individual can, by his own behaviour, particularly as a consumer, contribute to the protection of the environment.

The achievement of this objective and implementation of the guiding principles should be promoted both at the level of the Member States and at European Community level.

A. Action to be taken at Member State level

Within the limits of their own specific education policies and structures, the Member States will make every effort to implement the following measures:

(a) each Member State, taking account of regional situations, and in cooperation with parents, local bodies and other relevant bodies, should promote the introduction of environmental education in all sectors of education, including vocational training and adult education. It would appear appropriate that its current policy on environmental education should be set out in a document and made available to schools and other educational institutions.

The document should take account of the fact that environmental education is an interdisciplinary subject of relevance to many fields of teaching;

(b) for the carrying out of these tasks, it would appear important for the relevant authorities of the Member States:
- to give consideration to the basic aims of environmental education when drawing up curricula and organizing interdisciplinary courses,
- to encourage extracurricular school activities by means of which theoretical knowledge of the environment acquired in school can be put into practice,
- to take appropriate measures to develop teachers' knowledge of environmental matters in the context of their initial and in-service training,
- to undertake specific action to provide teachers and pupils with appropriate teaching materials.

It would appear appropriate to prepare, implement and improve these priority activities with the help of pilot and research projects;

(c) specialists who.. are particularly concerned with environmental problems should, through appropriate vocational training facilities, have the opportunity to acquire new knowledge or bring their knowledge in this field up to date. Relevant environmental content should also be introduced into initial vocational training and university training with a view to influencing those with future professional responsibilities in a direction which is most favourable to the conservation of the environment and natural resources.

B. Action to be taken at Community level

In order to reinforce the action of the Member States and achieve effective collaboration in this field, the Commission, assisted by a working party of representatives of Member States, appointed by the Commission on the proposal of the Member States concerned, is invited to take the following initiatives:

(a)   Exchange of information

- production of an inventory of initiatives taken in the Member States and at Community level with a view to facilitating their transposition and systematic comparison,
- organization of meetings, seminars and symposia about aims and methods of environmental education, as well as for examining the specifically European aspects;

(b)   Improvement of the documentation for teachers and pupils

- measures to place basic documentation on various Community issues in the environment sphere, as well as results of Community research programmes, at the disposal of teachers and pupils,
- organization of summer courses at European institutes of higher education for teaching specialists so as to enable them to exchange experience and identify new methods of teaching in the environment sphere,
- production of a European guide to institutes of higher education offering courses in disciplines concerned with environment problems;

(c)   Incorporation of environmental education into current activities

- encouragement for initiatives by young people for young people or partnerships in the environment sphere based on the existing Community ad hoc arrangements,
- promotion of meetings between young Europeans on topics of environmental protection through the "Youth for Europe Scheme" (YES) and the "Young Workers' Exchange Scheme",
- insertion of the topic "Environmental education" into the "Study visits for education specialists" (Orion) programme so as to enable a certain number of national, regional or local specialists in environment education to visit another Member State in order to exchange information and improve their work through incorporation of a European dimension,
- encouragement for cooperation between institutes of higher education operating in the environment sphere by using the opportunities offered by the Erasmus programme to promote the mobility of students and European teaching staff and the development of common teaching materials,
- encouragement, in the environment sphere, for cooperation between institutes of higher education and industry as regards training in new technologies by using the Comett programme.

Chapter 14

Environment and Development Aid

Since the beginning of the 1960s a special relationship of cooperation has existed between the developing countries and the Community, the latter having had an environmental protection policy since the early 1970s.

It is, however, only relatively recently, since the beginning of the 1980s, that the importance of the relationship between "environment" and "development" has been recognized. This is equally true on a worldwide level, both from the point of view of the other industrialized countries which provide most of the bilateral and multilateral aid (the United States, Canada, the Nordic countries) and also from that of the recipient countries, despite the awareness-raising efforts carried out in this area for over 10 years by the United Nations Environment Programme.

This failure to take environmental protection into account in development aid policy is illustrated, for example, by the Lomé I (1975) or Lomé II (1979) Conventions which make hardly any reference to the environment. However, following the dramatic consequences of drought and desertification experienced in Africa for several years, a major change in attitude has taken place at Community and worldwide levels alike. As far as the Community is concerned, the real turning point came in 1983–1984. In 1983 the 3rd Environmental Action Programme established for the first time a certain number of objectives in the area of environmental protection in developing countries. The programme refers, for example, to the conservation of tropical forests, water management, and the formulation of national conservation strategies. In 1984 the Council, both in the form of the environment ministers, and of the ministers responsible for developing cooperation, adopted several Resolutions indicating the willingness of the Community and of its Member States to integrate the environmental dimension into development aid policies.

I. THE INTERNAL COMMITMENTS OF THE COMMUNITY: RESOLUTIONS OF THE COUNCIL AND THE MEMBER STATES IN THE AREAS OF ENVIRONMENT AND DEVELOPMENT

1. The general Resolution of 1984 on the relationship between environment and development

On France's initiative, the Council and the governments of the Member States adopted a general Resolution on 3 October 1984 concerning the relationship between environment and development.

This Resolution underlines the need for the Community to consider environmental protection as an integral part of its development cooperation policy. It invites the Commission to increase the integration of the environmental dimension into the Community development aid policy. In particular, the Council and the Member States announce their commitment to the principles of the Declaration signed in 1980 by the United Nations Environment Programme (UNEP) and by 10 multilateral development aid institutions, concerning environment policies and procedures regarding economic development. According to this declaration, special attention must be given to the conservation of tropical forests, to the combating of desertification, to water management, and to the setting up of environmentally compatible systems of agriculture and energy usage.

2.   The 1984 Resolution on new forms of cooperation in the area of the environment (Solidarité Eau)

On 3 October 1984, also on France's initiative, the Council and the governments of the Member States adopted a Resolution specifically devoted to new forms of cooperation between the Community and developing countries in the area of water.[1] This Resolution emphasizes the need to encourage voluntary local or regional initiatives, either in public or private, which aim to carry out concrete and timely actions in favour of the management, use and protection of water in developing countries. The Resolution led to a new form of cooperation and aid to African countries regarding the different uses of water, in particular in agriculture, drinking water and the endangered natural environment. This programme, better known as "solidarité eau", allows for an original and effective form of collaboration between European local or regional authorities and those of developing countries.

3.   The 1984 Resolution on the inclusion of environmental considerations in Community Development Policy

In November 1984 the Commission sent the Council a Communication on the inclusion of environmental considerations in the development policy of the Community, together with a draft Council Resolution. The Communication contains a worrying analysis of the environmental situation in developing countries. Despite a lack of reliable information it would appear that the extent of deforestation, soil degradation, lack of water resources and desertification, has reached alarming proportions, particularly in certain regions of Africa. To the regional problems, must also be added the pollution of the air, the seas, and the continental waters, the use of dangerous substances and the extinction of animal and plant species. Parallel to this general deterioration of the environment, a population explosion is being experienced which is due to the decline of major diseases but which also contributes to environmental deterioration.

The worrying environmental situation in developing countries is confirmed in particular by the disappearance of forest areas due to a general shortage of firewood, by the overcrowding of livestock in grazing areas, especially around water sources, and by increased land cultivation which is detrimental to fallow areas and which

[1] OJ No C 272 of 12/10/84.

brings with it the use of chemicals. All of these factors highlight the inadequacy of the environmental training of the decision-makers, as well as, more generally speaking, the lack of any inclusion of environmental considerations in the development policies of the developing countries, with or without external aid.

In its Communication, the Commission also reviews the recent efforts of the Community and puts forward a number of suggestions for the improvement of the environmental situation in developing countries. Since 1982 a significant financial effort has been made by the Community in favour of projects carried out for larger environmental ends (hydraulic projects in villages, or anti-desertification projects for example). Apart from concrete projects carried out *in situ* a new budget line entitled "ecology in developing countries" has made it possible since 1982 to carry out training activities to increase awareness among the African and European development sectors. Parallel to these actions the Commission has undertaken appraisals and awareness-raising activities designed to establish a long-term policy and to lead to real environmental management in developing countries. To this end certain thematic actions are considered a priority. The three themes selected concern:

- the fight against desertification;
- development of domestic and wild livestock;
- management of water resources.

For the future, the Commission also wants to improve the coordination of the development policies of Member States and of other providers of finance, such as the European Investment Bank (EIB), and to point those policies in the direction of environmental protection.

On 6 November 1984 the Council and the governments of the Member States adopted a Resolution on the inclusion of environmental considerations in Community development policy. In this Resolution the Council and the Member States confirm the principles and objectives aimed at integrating the environmental dimension into the development policy of the Community and also acknowledge the Commission's Communication.

4.   The 1986 Resolution on the protection of natural resources and the fight against desertification in Africa

On 27 January 1986 the Commission presented the Council with a Communication on the protection of natural resources and the fight against desertification in Africa, which also included a draft Council Resolution. This Communication responds to the European Council's request made in Milan in June 1985 for all European aid, both Community and bilateral, to give priority to environmental protection, and in particular to the fight against desertification. In the Communication the Commission proposes a coherent policy including:

- adapted research policies;
- actions to increase awareness among the populations concerned;
- coordination between the Commission and the Member States with other donors;
- a concentration of the financial means available (Lomé Convention, food aid, Southern Mediterranean countries, Non-Governmental Organizations).

On 17 April 1986 the Council decided, on the basis of the Commission's Communication, to implement a European Community long-term plan of action with a view to combating desertification, and so adopted a Resolution which defines the major directions to follow for the implementation of such a plan. The Resolution emphasizes the need to give priority to actions to combat the degradation of natural resources in developing countries, relying largely on the active participation of the populations. This will include both direct actions (reforestation; anti-erosion projects) and indirect actions (training; research; rational use of energy resources including firewood, etc.). In order to be really effective, these actions require both a concentration of means and a certain continuity. In particular every effort should be made to obtain the assistance of local authorities, which implies a greater administrative decentralization and the participation of local and international Non-Governmental Organizations. Finally, the importance of what is at stake, and the dimension of the desertification problem, demands coordination between the beneficiary countries, the donors and the governmental organizations. This coordination requires greater coherence of the aid plans of the Community and its Member States, in order to encourage aid to the rural sector, and in particular measures for the protection of natural resources.

5.   Council Regulation on conservation of tropical forests

Following its Communication on Tropical Forests (COM (89) 410; OJ No C 264 of 16/10/89), the Commission on 19 March 1993 published a proposal for a Council Regulation on operations to promote the conservation and sustainable management of tropical forests, defined as being the forests, savannahs and trees and their respective ecosystems, that are found within the tropics and subtropics in both dry and humid climates, including their human populations, whether or not indigenous and other populations of forest regions who utilize the forest or whose actions affect the forest.[2] Conservation is defined as including all actions to preserve, rehabilitate and rationally manage tropical forests and sustainable forest management is defined as the planned utilization of forests in a manner compatible with the conservation of forest ecosystems for future generations. The Community will provide financial support or technical expertise.

The Commission published an amended proposal on 10 June 1994.[3]

II.   EXTERNAL COMMITMENTS OF THE COMMUNITY: THE LOMÉ CONVENTION AND OTHER AGREEMENTS

1.   Lomé III Convention (1984)

The first two Lomé Conventions associating the Community and the countries of Africa, the Caribbean and the Pacific (ACP) paid little attention to environmental protection and Lomé I (1975) made no reference to it whatsoever. Lomé II (1979) only referred to the questions of energy saving and firewood. Consequently, from

[2] OJ No C 78 of 19/3/93.
[3] OJ No C 201 of 23/7/94.

the point of view of the application of the conventions, only 1.5% of the subsidies under Lomé I and 3% under Lomé II were made for reforestation or soil conservation projects.

Shortly before the signing of Lomé III on 8 December 1984, the Community redirected its aid policy in the area of the environment, as is illustrated by the three Resolutions adopted by the Council at the end of 1984. This redirection was given an important place in the new Lomé III Convention which associated the Community for a period of five years, i.e. until 1990, with 66 African, Caribbean and Pacific countries. For the first time the convention devoted a considerable amount of space to the aspects of environmental protection and natural resources. Among the general objectives of cooperation, Article 11 of the convention stipulated that in the area of efforts for environmental protection and the restoration of natural resources, cooperation contributed in particular to actions against drought and desertification and implemented thematic actions to this end.

"Thematic actions" are long-term interventions of more than five years, this being the minimum period required for the restoration of ecological balances.

Chapter 2 of Title I of the convention was thus entirely devoted to action against drought and desertification. Among the priority aspects the convention refers to better control of water (inventory of underground water-layers), the setting up of a system for the prevention and combating of bush fires and deforestation, together with the education of the populations. In Lomé III, environment was integrated into the three following areas of cooperation: agricultural and rural development; the development of fishing; and the development of energy potential. The convention also referred several times to the regional dimension of environmental problems. Environmental protection was of course mentioned explicitly among the projects likely to benefit from the financial and technical aid of the Community. Generally these projects had to be the subject of prior assessment, not only from the technical, economic and social points of view, but also from the environmental point of view. Finally, the convention made provision for two main agents in environmental protection, namely local authorities and Non-Governmental Organizations (NGOs), especially with a view to giving maximum encouragement to micro-projects and concrete operations in the field (the installation of solar pumps for waterboring, etc.).

2. Lomé IV Convention (1989)

Lomé IV, signed on 15 December 1989 and which came into force on 1 September 1991, runs until 2000 and provides for funding of Ecu 12 billion during the first five years.[4]

The principle of sustainable development is set out in the General Principles. Title I (Articles 33 to 41) deals with environment while in Title II, covering agricultural cooperation, food security and rural development, special attention is also given to sustainable development. Article 4 states that "development shall be based on a sustainable balance between its economic objectives, the rational management of the environment, and the enhancement of natural and human resources". Article 6 asserts that "priority must be given to environmental protection and conservation of natural resources, which are essential conditions for sustainable and balanced development from both the economic and human viewpoints".

---

[4] Consisting of grants, soft loans and interest rate rebates.

Environmental protection and restoration are recurring themes throughout the convention. Indeed, protection and improvement of natural resources and the environment, as well as the restoration of the ecological balance, are two of the convention's main aims. Continued emphasis is given to desertification, as well as to the preservation of tropical forests and biological diversity, to the rational use of and protection of water resources, and to the balance between urban and rural areas. Such issues are contained in national programmes negotiated by the Community with individual ACP states. Environment was given such a high priority in order to try to achieve an immediate improvement in living conditions in ACP states and as a safeguard for future generations.

Article 35 of the convention gives priority to three activities: the preventive principle; the systematic assurance of the ecological soundness of all programmes and operations at all their stages; and trans-sectoral approaches which take into consideration indirect as well as direct environmental impact. Among the specific sectors identified, in the area of energy development (Title VII), the convention notes that one of the main aims is to conserve "biomass resources, particularly fuel wood, by encouraging alternative solutions, improving consumption techniques and habits, and using energy and energy resources in a rational and sustainable manner".

A specific problem taken up in Article 39 of the convention is the question of toxic waste, the export to ACP countries of which it bans. Furthermore, the convention undertakes wide-ranging commitments to monitor and control the ban, besides providing for consultation between the signatories on major environmental hazards caused either by global problems or industrial technology.

3.   The 1992 United Nations Conference on Environment and Development (UNCED)

The UNCED or Earth Summit took place in Rio de Janeiro at Head of State and Government level. The decision to convene the conference was taken at the United Nations General Assembly resolution 44/228 of December 1989, which was based upon the report of the World Commission on Environment and Development, this commenting on progress since the 1972 Conference on the Human Environment in Stockholm. Given that the Stockholm Conference was the main stimulus for the birth of the Community's environmental policy, the 1992 Rio Summit 20 years on provided an opportune moment to assess the progress made by the Community during two decades of environmental policy.

The Commission produced a report to the conference and a Communication to the Council entitled "A Common Platform: Guidelines for the Community" which served as a basis for the conclusions of the Environment Council of 12 December 1991. In those conclusions the Council indicated that:

> Ministers meeting in the Environment Council believe that the United Nations Conference on Environment and Development to be held in Rio de Janeiro in June 1992 provides a unique opportunity for enhanced cooperation between all nations with a view to achieving sustainable development worldwide.
>
> The European Community and its Member States acknowledge their responsibilities in this process, have played a leading role in the preparatory work so far and pledge their full commitment to contribute to a successful outcome of the Conference. They will work towards adopting at Rio an Earth Charter and a relevant and effective Agenda

21; signing the biodiversity and climate conventions; and adopting a declaration on forests to be reinforced thereafter by an international legally binding convention.

At Rio in June 1992, over 150 countries as well as the European Community signed the Framework Convention on Climate Change (see p. 415), and the Convention on Biological Diversity (see p. 419). UNCED also adopted:

- an Authoritative Statement of Principles for a Global Consensus on the Management, Conservation and Sustainable Development of All Types of Forests;
- a Declaration on Environment and Development; and
- a 600-page document known as Agenda 21 as a guide for future national and international action in the field of environment and development.

4.   Convention on Climate Change

The UNCED also saw the signing of a framework convention on climate change aimed at stabilizing atmospheric concentrations of greenhouse gases (GHGs) at a safe level. The final text, signed by more than 150 countries and also by the European Community itself, was the result of 18 months' difficult negotiations. To enter into effect, the convention must be ratified by at least 50 of the signatories.

The stabilization of emissions at 1990 levels by 2000 is held up as a desired objective, although the convention contains no obligations to do so. Contracting parties to the convention will be required however to publish national or regional action programmes concerning carbon sinks and emissions, as well as national inventories of emissions.

As part of the Community's effort to reduce carbon emissions, on 27 May 1992, just before the UNCED, the Commission proposed the introduction of a tax on energy/carbon. The tax would begin with a tax of US$3 per barrel of oil equivalent, rising by US$1 each year to a rate of US$10. But the Community's effort in this area and the effectiveness of the convention itself were limited by the unwillingness of the United States, and to a certain extent Japan, to commit themselves to a legally binding date for the reduction of CO_2 emissions. At the time of writing, the Commission was still awaiting the opinion of the European Parliament.

5.   Convention on the Protection of Biodiversity

The convention was signed at the UNCED by the European Community in its own rights and by more than 150 countries but not at that time by the United States, which declared it could not accept the clauses referring to intellectual property rights or the financial conditions which it saw as being too far removed from the Global Environment Facility. The United Kingdom, France and Japan also expressed similar concerns and after signature the EC issued a statement on three points: regret at the insufficient environmental objectives contained in the convention; scrupulous respect for the financial conditions set out; and the need to respect existing rules relating to intellectual property rights.

The result of more than two years of negotiations under the auspices of UNEP, the convention seeks to conserve the world's biological and genetic diversity, as well as to ensure the sustainable use of genetic resources and the equitable distribution, namely between the developed and developing countries, of benefits accruing from their exploitation. The convention covers transfer of technology, funding and access to genetic resources. Signatories are obliged to set up a system of specially protected areas and to draw up national plans to conserve biodiversity which must be integrated into other policies. It draws a distinction between natural or *in-situ* conservation and *ex-situ* conservation, such as botanical gardens and gene banks.

The terms of the convention are, however, considerably weakened by a qualifying clause which states that action need only be taken to the extent that it is possible and so far as it is necessary. Nevertheless, the convention can be seen as representing an important basic tool and a reference point for the progressive implementation of conservation strategies.

6.   Rio Declaration on Forests

In its long and awkward title, the declaration states that it is not legally binding but serves as a global consensus on the management, conservation and ecologically viable exploitation of all types of forest. The declaration is based on 15 principles covering use of forest resources, management criteria, financial resources and research. It notes that states possess a sovereign and inalienable right to exploit their forests, but reiterates the need for sustainable management practices and underlines the intrinsic and ecological value of forests for both indigenous populations and the world as a whole. On the global scale, the declaration also refers to the role of forests in preserving biodiversity and ensuring climatic stability.

7.   Agenda 21

Over 800 pages long, Agenda 21 addresses almost 40 different topics, divided into four main areas: economic and social; conservation and management of natural resources; strengthening the role of major economic and social actors in society; and implementation measures. Agenda 21 sets out to check pollution and to halt the divide between North and South through greater international cooperation and consultation. The section concerning natural resources covers, *inter alia*, atmosphere, land management, forests, deserts, mountains, water, chemicals and waste. Agenda 21 is not a legally binding text but rather a political undertaking at the highest level. As such, there is a certain ambiguity surrounding the time scale it addresses, the costs involved, and implementation and control mechanisms. Nevertheless, the UN has estimated the cost of its implementation from 1993–2000 at some US$600 billion per annum, of which $125 billion is hoped to come from international aid.

At their Summit meeting in Lisbon on 26 and 27 June 1992, the European Community's Heads of State and Government adopted the following conclusions with regard to the Rio Conference:

The European Council welcomes the results of the United Nations Conference on Environment and Development (UNCED) held at Rio de Janeiro from 3 to 14 June 1992 and in particular the acceptance by the international community at the highest level of the aim of sustainable development worldwide. It also noted with satisfaction the role played by the Community and its Member States in the Conference.

The European Council invites all participating states to proceed rapidly to the implementation of the measures agreed at Rio.

The Community and its Member States, for their part, are prepared to commit themselves to the following eight-point plan:

- to ratify the climate change convention and publish national plans for implementing it;
- to publish national plans for action on biodiversity, and to establish the basis for ratification of the convention;
- to publish national plans for implementation of the forest principles;
- to give financial support to developing countries for the implementation of Agenda 21 through Official Development Assistance (ODA) and for the replenishment of the Global Environmental Facility (GEF);
- to put their weight behind establishing an international review process for the forest and desertification principles;
- to take the lead in the restructuring of the GEF so that it can in time be established as the permanent financial mechanism for the climate change and biodiversity conventions.[5]

8.   Other agreements

(a)   Cooperation agreements with Mediterranean countries

Under the cooperation agreements concluded in 1978 between the Community and the Maghreb countries on the one hand (Algeria, Morocco, Tunisia) and the Mashrak countries on the other (Jordan, Lebanon, Syria, Egypt), the parties agree to encourage cooperation in the area of environmental protection.

(b)   International conventions

The Community is a contracting party to various international conventions specifically concerning environmental protection, and in which many developing countries also participate. These conventions are either of a worldwide or a regional nature. There is the Washington Agreement, for example, on the international trade of endangered species of wild flora and fauna (CITES); the Bonn Convention on the conservation of migratory birds; the Barcelona and Cartagena (Colombia) Conventions concerning the protection of the waters of the Mediterranean and of the Caribbean respectively, the Vienna Convention on the protection of the ozone layer, etc. (see Chapter 12).

(c)   The Committee of International Development Institutions on the Environment (CIDIE)

On 1 February 1980 in New York the Commission and the European Investment Bank (EIB) along with nine other international organizations involved in financial development aid (the World Bank, Arabian Bank for Economic Development, ASEAN Bank, International American Development Bank, United Nations Environment Programme, etc.), signed a "Declaration concerning environmental policy and the procedures for economic development". This declaration makes provision for the integration of appropriate ecological measures in the organization

---

[5] Europe Environment No 390 of 30/6/92.

and execution of economic development activities. To this end, a Committee of International Development Institutions on the Environment (CIDIE) was set up, in which the Commission and the European Investment Bank (EIB) both participate, and where an exchange of information and experiences in the area of the environment takes place. This exchange of information is designed to respond to the objectives defined in the "World Conservation Strategy" drawn up by the United Nations in March 1980 to which the Commission, the European Parliament and the Member States of the Community all subscribe.[6]

(d)   The OECD Recommendations on environment and development

The Organization for Economic Cooperation and Development (OECD), which includes the United States and Japan, as well as the countries of Western Europe, adopted a Recommendation on 20 June 1985 concerning the environmental assessment of development aid projects and programmes. This Recommendation was completed on 23 October 1986 by a second Recommendation, designed to specify the measures and methods intended to facilitate the environmental assessment of aid projects. The Community decided to associate itself with these two recommendations which were drawn up jointly by the Committee on Development Aid (DAC) and the Environment Committee of the OECD.

9.   Central and Eastern Europe (CEE); the former Soviet Union

The 5th Environmental Action Programme observes that the momentous political changes in Central and Eastern Europe have had a major impact on the international political agenda, with environmental issues featuring very high on the list of priorities for discussion. The improvement of environmental standards and the protection of human health and quality of life have been highlighted by the new democratic governments as priorities to be addressed in parallel with the process of economic reform and liberalization.

Environmental degradation in many CEE regions is severe; in some areas the damage already incurred may be irreversible. Although the extent and type of degradation varies from country to country, and from region to region, common problems prevail. These problems include extensive acid rain damage to forests (up to 75% of Polish forests are said to be affected), and the poisoning of complete river systems (the water of the Vistula is unfit even for industrial use). There is a permanent high risk of serious industrial accidents particularly in the nuclear and chemical fields.

Since the beginning, environmental protection has been an integral part of the Community's PHARE programme of assistance for economic reform in Central and Eastern Europe.

Total PHARE assistance for 1990 amounted to 500 million Ecu; it rose to 785 milliom Ecu in 1991 and for the period 1992 to 1994 averaged around 1000 million Ecu a year (countries – Albania, Bulgaria, Czech Republic, Estonia, Hungary, Latvia, Lithuania, Poland, Romania, Slovakia, Slovenia). Environment and nuclear safety over the period 1990 to 1993 accounted for 9.6% of PHARE allocations. This proportion may diminish in the future as PHARE focuses on

[6] OJ No C 147 of 16/6/80.

longer-term objectives but is still likely to be significant. Moreover, environmental spending is likely to be increasingly linked with other PHARE objectives, notably privatization and structural reform of the economy where Coopers is probably a market leader.

TACIS started off at 400 million Ecu for 1991 under Council Regulation 2157/91 of 15 July 1991 and the cumulative total of funds now available under TACIS amounts to around 1870 million Ecu. The 1994 budget is 540 mEcu (countries originally – Armenia, Azerbaijan, Belarus, Georgia, Kazakhstan, Kyrgystan, Moldova, Russia, Tajikistan, Turkmenistan, Ukraine, Uzbekistan; now also including Mongolia).

Though Council Regulation (EEC, EURATOM) No 2157/91 did not specify the environment as one of the priorities for the Community's technical assistance under the TACIS programme, many TACIS projects and programmes, for example those in the energy sector, were of considerable relevance for the environment.

In a 1993 revision of the regulation, the reference to energy was expanded to include nuclear safety, and telecommunications was also added.

The TACIS Nuclear Safety Programme was based on the policy recommendations of the G7 issued after the Munich Summit held in July 1991 and was endorsed by the European Community's Lisbon Summit held in June 1992. The programme covers nuclear safety activities in the Russian Federation and Ukraine. The overall objectives of the programme are to improve the safety of operating nuclear plants and other civilian nuclear fuel and waste treatment facilities, and to promote regional cooperation on nuclear safety among countries operating Soviet-designed power facilities.

At the end of 1994, it seemed likely the TACIS Regulation would be revised to permit, amongst other things, specific reference to environmental objectives. A draft amendment to the regulation is now circulating in the Commission which would allow TACIS programmes specifically to include the environment. If adopted by the Council, which seems likely, the amended regulation would probably come into effect on 1 January 1996.

Chapter 15

The Community and Nuclear Safety

In 1974, the Council adopted several important Resolutions concerning the Community's energy policy. These Resolutions were influenced to a great extent by the serious oil crisis which was raging at the time and which was forcing the Community to modify its energy strategy as a matter of urgency. The first Resolution, adopted on 17 September 1974,[1] concerns a new strategy for energy policy. First, with regard to the demand for energy, it provides for a reduction in the rate of growth of internal consumption through measures for rational and economic use of energy. As far as the availability of energy is concerned, and particularly with the aim of improving the safety of supplies, the Resolution foresees the development of electricity from nuclear sources, as well as the development of the hydrocarbon and fuel resources of the Community.

A second Council Resolution, adopted on 17 December 1984, specified the objectives to be reached in 1985, with a view to reducing the Community's dependence on imported energy. To this end the proportion of nuclear energy in relation to the total needs for primary energy was supposed to increase from 1% in 1973 to around 13% by 1985. In another Resolution concentrating specifically on energy and the environment and adopted on 3 March 1975[2], the Council noted that nuclear energy was to become one of the main sources of energy supply, and that it would therefore be necessary, given the nature of this energy source, to study the specific problems liked to the development of nuclear energy, such as the risks of radiation, safety of reactors, release of heat, radioactive waste and the recycling of nuclear fuel. These problems first started to be researched in depth from 1985 onwards within the European Community of Atomic Energy (EURATOM). Indeed, according to Article 1 of the Euratom Treaty, the Community's mission is to "contribute to the raising of the standard of living in the Member States and to the development of relations with the other countries by creating the conditions necessary for the speedy establishment and growth of nuclear industries". In the preamble to the Euratom Treaty the six founder Member States describe themselves as being "resolved to create the conditions necessary for the development of a powerful nuclear industry which will provide extensive energy resources, and lead to the modernization of technical processes ...".

---

[1] OJ No C 153 of 9/7/75.
[2] OJ No C 168 of 25/7/75.

I. NUCLEAR SAFETY BEFORE CHERNOBYL

1. Health protection

(a) Community research programme on radiation protection

Since 1960 the Commission has instigated a considerable amount of research into radiation protection (see p. 381) which has led to the fixing of "permissible" levels of radiation for workers and the public in general. In the area of radiotoxicology, particular attention has been paid to long-life radionuclides like plutonium. A lot of research has also been carried out into the transfer of radioactive elements and other pollutants in the different areas making up the environment.

In 1976 the Council adopted a first programme of research and training on radiation protection lasting five years (1976–1980) in order to increase knowledge of the dangers of ionizing radiations for individuals, animals and plants. This programme was extended by a second programme for the period 1980–1984. On 12 March 1985[3] the Council agreed on a third programme for the period 1980–1989. Research, carried out both through contracts and at the Joint Research Centre, concentrates in particular on radioactive carcinogens, the genetic effects and the non-stochastic effects of ionizing radiations.

(b) Fixing of Community standards of health protection from ionizing radiations: the framework directive of 1959

Since 1959 the Council has established basic standards concerning health protection for the general public and workers against ionizing radiations,[4] regardless of origin: nuclear industry energy; scientific research; natural or medical radiation. The basic standards were modified in 1962, 1966, 1976, 1980 and 1984 in the light of developments in scientific knowledge in the area of radiation protection.

The Council fixed these standards in accordance with Article 30 of the Euratom Treaty which provides for the regulation of activities which are dangerous due to ionizing radiations, in order to protect the health of workers and the general public. The directive establishes two series of base standards depending on whether it is a matter of the individual safety of workers exposed to ionizing radiations or of the protection of the public in general. As far as the protection of workers is concerned, the directive calls for the implementation of a system of radiation prevention and evaluation, as well as thorough medical surveillance. With regard to the protection of the public, the directive essentially imposed a surveillance and inspection procedure in normal circumstances, and a mechanism for intervention in an emergency. The surveillance is to be carried out both over critical groups of the population, in areas where such groups exist, and over the area as a whole for the population in general. The field of application of this important directive is extremely large, since it covers the production, transport, handling, possession, storing, treatment and elimination of natural and artificial radioactive substances. Each of these activities must be subject to prior declaration and authorization in each Member State. The directive fixes the maximum permitted doses measured in becquerels for exposed

---

[3] OJ No L 83 of 23/3/85.
[4] OJ No L 11 of 20/2/59.

workers and for the public. To this end there are technical annexes which determine for the different nuclides the maximum annual levels of incorporation by inhalation or ingestion, as well as levels of concentration in the air.

On 3 September 1984 the Council also adopted a directive (84/466) fixing measures of radiological protection for people undergoing medical radiation following medical examinations and treatments.[5]

(c) Prior information to the Commission on all discharges of radioactive waste

According to Article 37 of the Euratom Treaty, all plans for installations involving the disposal of radioactive waste must be communicated to the Commission by the Member States. The Commission has a period of six months in which to examine whether or not there is a risk of radioactive contamination of water, soil or air.

2.   Protection of the environment

(a) Thermal discharges

Any electric power station, be it traditional or nuclear, discharges heat into the water or the air. The heating of water used for cooling power stations causes many environmental problems. These are studied under the Community research programme, particularly with regard to the characteristics of cooling towers. The towers make it possible to eliminate a large proportion of the overheating of the receiving waters, but also cause difficulties and nuisances: spoiling of the landscape; consumption of large quantities of water through evaporation; creation of a micro-climate characterized by fog and reduced sunlight in the surrounding area, etc.

(b) Radioactive wastes

Some nuclear waste has a high level of radioactivity which can last for thousands of years. In order to study the different methods of isolating or destroying these wastes, the Community has set up several research programmes which are carried out in different laboratories in the Member States, as well as in the common research centre at Ispra. The first research programme on the storing of radioactive wastes was adopted by the Council on 26 June 1975.[6] This programme was extended on 18 March 1980[7] and 12 March 1985[8] respectively. This last programme, carried out essentially through indirect research, covers a period of five years and has a budget of 62 million Ecu. The Commission ensures the carrying out of this programme with the help of a consultative committee on nuclear energy and waste storage, created in 1984. The programme aims to perfect and demonstrate a system of managing radioactive wastes which ensures the maximum possible protection of the public and the environment. For example, it involves studies of methods which allow for a reduction of the volume of wastes, for the solidifying of liquid wastes in order to avoid danger of leakage, or for separating long-term radioactive wastes from other types. The research also covers the improvement of

[5] OJ No L 265 of 5/10/84.
[6] OJ No L 178 of 9/7/75.
[7] OJ No L 78 of 23/3/80.
[8] OJ No L 83 of 23/3/85.

draining installations; storing in artificial shelters or geological formations; burying near the surface; safety of protection structures. The construction and use of underground installations on a pilot basis are also planned in Germany, Belgium, and France. In order to look at the long-term perspectives and to give more coherence to the research on radioactive wastes, the Council adopted a Resolution on 18 February 1980 which established the main points of a Community action plan on radioactive wastes.[9] This action plan covers the period 1980–1992 and in addition to technical measures allows for continued research into long-term highly radioactive wastes as well as periodic information to the public on this.

(c)   The close-down of nuclear power stations

As with any installation, a nuclear power station will one day cease to function. For this reason the Community has set up various studies concerning in particular the large light-water power stations. Different methods of dismantling have been considered: maintaining the structure while allowing safe access to the station; demolishing the superstructure while leaving the foundations and other underground structures in concrete; total demolition of the installation.

A first research programme devoted specifically to the dismantling of nuclear installations was agreed upon in 1979. On 31 January 1984[10] the Council decided to continue the programme for five years (1984–1988). The research involved in particular dismantling and decontamination techniques, as well as the treatment of specific wastes (steel; concrete; graphite).

3.   The safety of nuclear equipment

The installation of nuclear power stations requires equipment of a very high level of safety. Very strict standards must be respected in order to take into account any unforeseeable accident or abnormal malfunction: earthquake; explosion; plane crash; war; sabotage, etc. Each Member State has its own national legislation on standards. Nevertheless, in the light of the Council Resolution of 22 July 1965 on the technological problems of nuclear safety,[11] the Commission has initiated two types of action in the area of safety standards. First, it has carried out a progressive harmonization of national safety criteria and standardization of equipment. This harmonization effort was completed by mutual information on approval legislation and on the administrative procedures existing in the different Member States. Next the Commission used them in technological installations of its research centre to carry out a systematic analysis of the possibilities of accidents and the perfection of preventive detection methods of possible failure of reactors.

4.   The transport of radioactive material

The volume of transport of irradiated fuels having considerably increased, there is a need to research into conditions of maximum security for the circulation of radioactive material. The main problems concern the radiation effects when it is

---

[9]   OJ No C 51 of 29/2/80.
[10]   OJ No L 36 of 8/2/84.
[11]   OJ No C 185 of 14/8/85.

being transported, the prevention of serious accidents involving fissionable or radioactive materials, and protection from theft or acts of sabotage. Strict measures concerning packaging have been laid down by the International Atomic Energy Agency in Vienna, in which the Member States of the Community are involved. The Community has also carried out certain actions aiming to harmonize the approval procedures and formalities with regard to transport, and to ensure adequate training of workers handling radioactive packages.

5.   The control of the use of fissionable materials

The Euratom Treaty made the Community responsible for controlling the use of radioactive materials in order to ensure that these materials are not diverted for uses other than the stated uses, and are not used for ends other than those for which the company intended them. Commission inspectors are therefore responsible for checking the information which all enterprises dealing with nuclear materials or civil installations are obliged to give them. Any enterprise handling radioactive material must provide the Commission with the plans and capacity of its installations, the nature of the materials used and produced, and the technical processes used. When they visit an installation the inspectors carry out both an accounting check and a technical control.

II.   PLANS FOR INCREASED NUCLEAR SAFETY FOLLOWING CHERNOBYL

In a Resolution of 13 January 1976, the European Parliament drew the attention of the Commission and the Council to a certain number of conditions relating to the development of nuclear energy in the Community. In particular, the Parliament felt it was necessary to have a Community policy regarding the siting of nuclear power stations, bearing in mind the foreseeable effects on the population. It also pronounced itself in favour of a harmonization of the requirements relating to the authorization for power stations, and of stricter conditions for the transport of radioactive material. The serious accident which occurred on 26 April 1986 at the Soviet power station at Chernobyl led the Commission to present an outline Communication to the Council on 16 June 1986 on the consequences of the Chernobyl accident. This outline Communication follows on from the immediate emergency measures taken by the Community to control agricultural products originating from Eastern European countries.

1.   Emergency measures relating to the control of agricultural products

On 13 May 1986 the Council adopted an initial provisional regulation[12] banning the import of certain agricultural products from the Soviet Union and other Eastern

---

[12] OJ No L 127 of 13/5/86.

European countries until 31 May 1986. A second regulation adopted by the Council on 30 May 1986[13] lifted the import ban, but submitted the import into the Community of agricultural products coming from these countries to strict controls until 30 September 1986. These were carried out in the form of tests based on objective criteria. A Commission regulation of 5 June 1986[14] specified the method to be used when carrying out these tests.

The Council Regulation of 13 May 1986[15] was successively extended until 30 December 1989. In parallel, the Commission continued its work in order to arrive at a permanent system concerning maximum permitted radioactivity levels for foodstuffs in the event of nuclear accident.[16] The Council dedicated several sessions to the consideration of a Commission proposal submitted on 16 June 1987 and finally approved a Regulation 3954/87 on 22 December 1987.[17]

Regulation 737/90 clarifies and renews the temporary measures on the import of agricultural products.[18]

2.   The outline Communication of the Commission of 16 June 1986

In this Communication to the Council, the Commission felt that the first information on the Chernobyl accident justified the urgent adoption by the Community of an initial set of internal measures and initiatives within the framework of its international relations. Such action, the Commission stated, is all the more necessary in view of the fact that nuclear power is now an essential component of the Community's energy balance. It accounts for one-third of electricity production and makes it possible to save the equivalent of 100 million tonnes of oil each year. The Commission's proposals concerned the following five areas of action: health protection; plant safety; emergency procedures; international action; and research. The body of measures suggested by the Commission aims to ensure a certain consistency between Member States with regard to public information, both on a preventive basis and in the event of a crisis.

(a)   Health protection

(i) The Commission must first make a thorough assessment of the whole of Chapter III of the Euratom Treaty relating to health protection (Articles 33–35 and 36–37). In particular it will examine the question of whether or not it is necessary to revise the 1984 directive fixing the basic standards for protection against the dangers of radiation (see p. 471).

(ii) With regard to the contamination of foodstuffs the Commission will draw up a proposal aimed at setting maximum tolerance limits for the radioactive contamination of agricultural products, be they produced in the Community or imported from third countries.

---

[13] OJ No L 146 of 31/5/86.

[14] OJ No L 152 of 6/6/86.

[15] Council Regulations 3020/86/EEC, OJ No L 280/79 of 1/10/86; 624/87/EEC, OJ No L 58/101 of 28/2/87; 3955/87/EEC, OJ No L 371/14 of 30/12/87.

[16] OJ No C 174 of 2/7/87.

[17] OJ No L 371 of 30/12/87.

[18] OJ No L 83 of 30/3/90.

(b)   Intrinsic and operational safety of installations

In the area of nuclear installations there is at present no compulsory Community standard limiting radioactive emissions into the air and water. The Commission will examine the possibility of applying such emission standards to nuclear installations, based on the concept of the best technology available, and in the knowledge that in any case the basic standards will remain in force.

Safety standards for nuclear equipment (withstanding the effects of earthquakes, for example) exist in each Member State, but the criteria can vary from one Member State to another. The Commission will examine the effect of the application of the Council Resolution of 1975 on the technological problems of nuclear safety as well as the problems of harmonization of safety standards.

There are no existing Community provisions concerning prior information to the public. The Commission will therefore examine the possibility of enforcing provisions for prior information to the public on what to do in case of an accident.[19]

The Commission also feels that the international exchange of information and joint analysis of incidents occurring in nuclear installations should be made more effective. With this in mind it will draw up a proposal aiming to set up a compulsory system of Community reporting on incidents in nuclear power stations.

As regards transport of radioactive substances, the Commission will present a proposal designed to make the application in Member States of the provisions of the international agreements on the transport of dangerous substances obligatory. As regards the disposal of radioactive substances, the Commission will present a proposal designed to make the application in Member States of the provisions of the international agreements on the disposal of dangerous substances obligatory.

As regards the disposal of radioactive waste at sea which, as is the case with all types of waste, is subject to the provisions of the London Dumping Convention, the Commission will draw up a proposal aimed at making the Community party to this convention.

(c)   Emergency procedures

The Commission will draw up a proposal for the setting up of an interim Community information system in case of nuclear accident.[20] This proposal will constitute the Community contribution to an international convention to be negotiated within the framework of the International Atomic Energy Agency. This convention will oblige the contracting parties to provide and exchange information in case of an alert or radioactive accident. The Chernobyl accident having proved the usefulness of a system of mutual assistance, the Commission also intends to present the Council with a proposal on the implementation of a Community system for mutual assistance in emergencies.

(d)   International action

According to the Commission, the Community should become a party to two international conventions, the negotiation of which was decided within the International

---

[19] The Commission put forward on 8 June 1988 a draft Council resolution relating to the information of the public on health protection measures to be applied in the event of a radiological emergency.

[20] Adopted as Council Decision 87/600/Euratom of 14 December 1987 on Community arrangements for the early exchange of information in the event of a radiological emergency (OJ No L 371 of 30/12/87).

Atomic Energy Agency: convention on rapid information,[21] and convention on mutual assistance in emergencies.[22] The Commission also proposes to participate actively with its experts in the evaluation of the Chernobyl accident.

(e) Research

Certain specific problems highlighted by the Chernobyl accident necessitate the modification of Community research programmes currently in hand. The Commission will propose to make these changes.

It should be noted that it is up to the Council to examine and formally to adopt, over the coming months, each of the proposals which the Commission committed itself to presenting within the framework of its Communication of 16 June 1986.

3.   The Communication of the Commission of 20 August 1986 on health protection

On 20 August 1986 the Commission sent a Communication to the Council on the development of measures taken by the Community in applying Chapter III of the Euratom Treaty on health protection. This Communication is intended to prepare the measures for improvement of the protection of the health of the citizens and the environment, which the Commission will propose formally to the Council over the coming months. The priority among these measures is the establishment of an inter-Community system for the rapid exchange of information in cases of unusually high levels of radioactivity or of a nuclear accident.

4.   Council Directive 92/3/Euratom of 3 February 1992 on the supervision and control of shipments of radioactive waste between Member States and into and out of the Community[23]

Article 2b of the Euratom Treaty defines one of the main tasks of the Community as being to establish uniform safety standards for the health protection of the population and workers and to oversee their implementation. In virtue of Chapter 3 of the Euratom Treaty the Council has since 1959 adopted a series of directives establishing basic safety standards for the health protection of the public and workers against the dangers resulting from ionizing radiation. The Council Directive of 15 July 1980 (80/838/EURATOM), modified by Directive 84/467/EURATOM, sets out the basic standards and explicitly includes the transport of radioactive substances in its field of implementation. However, it does not contain any specific provisions covering this area, limiting itself to general requirements which apply to any activity carrying with it a risk from ionizing radiation.

---

[21] The IAEA General Conference in September 1986 adopted a convention on early notification of a nuclear accident. This convention was immediately signed by all EC Member States and came into force in October of the same year but to date has been ratified only by Denmark. Thus, the subsequent Council Decision of December 1987 that the Community adhere to the convention cannot be officially implemented, since Article 102 of the Euratom Treaty requires that in such cases the Commission be first notified by all Member States that they have effectively ratified the instrument in question.

[22] The Commission proposed the adhesion of the Community to the convention on mutual assistance in the event of nuclear accident (also adopted by the IAEA General Conference in September 1986) in January 1987. The Council has not yet approved the proposal.

[23] OJ No L 35 of 12/2/92.

In January 1988, a number of cases arose involving radioactive waste, notably that between Belgium and the Federal Republic of Germany, which led to a decision by the Member States concerned to order enquiries to examine the matter in depth.

The European Parliament set up a Committee of Enquiry, the main conclusions of which are contained in the European Parliament Resolution of 6 July 1988 on the handling and transport of nuclear material. This Resolution called in particular on the Commission to "present a global Community Regulation controlling trans-frontier transport of nuclear waste in so far as these are necessary". It also approves "the different proposals of the Enquiry Committee aimed at ensuring through a system of strict control and authorization, the registration of transfrontier transports from the place of origin to the stockage site".

A further Parliament Resolution was adopted on 27 October 1988, regarding the follow-up to be given to the Conclusions of its Committee of Enquiry and underlining the urgency of the required measures.

A European Commission group of experts looked into a number of aspects of the question, trying in particular to evaluate whether the international and Community provisions currently governing the transport of radioactive waste constituted a satisfactory guarantee of the safety of workers and the public. The Commission noted that the provisions of the agreements covering the transport of waste of weak and medium activity were in conformity with the requirements of the IAEA and guaranteed at all times an adequate level of safety. No sign was found indicating that the health of workers or other people had been put in danger because of transport operations.

However, the Commission arrived at the same disturbing conclusion as had the Committee of Enquiry – although there had been no infraction of the relevant legislation, some Member States had been shown to be incapable of maintaining their control of the radioactive waste throughout its life and of supervising its movement satisfactorily. The Commission therefore produced a proposal for a directive which adds the transport of radioactive waste to the activities which should come under a system of prior authorization according to Article 5 of Directive 80/836/ EURATOM and which provides for a common notification and transport system in order to avoid the risks associated with the loss of control of radioactive wastes by national authorities. The proposed system covers all transfers of radioactive waste in the Community, including transfers effected within one Member State, as well as the import and export of radioactive waste.

The system also includes a number of elements taken from the Basle Convention of 22 March 1989 on the Control of Transfrontier Movements and Disposal of Dangerous Waste. The main aim of the directive is to ensure that all movements of radioactive material are subject to a system of prior authorization and to assist the competent national authorities in keeping track of the movements.

5.   The 4th Lomé Convention

The 4th Lomé Convention signed on 15 December 1989 prohibits the export of dangerous and radioactive waste from the Community to an ACP country which is party to the convention. This does not however prevent a Member State, to which an ACP country has chosen to export waste for treatment, from returning the treated waste to the ACP country of origin.

The main elements of the system are that each transfer of radioactive waste must be notified to the competent authorities of the receiving Member State. If they are to be exported to a third country, the sending Member State must be informed and the agreement of the receiving country must be indicated.

The transport cannot take place before the competent authorities have acknowledged receipt of the notification authorizing the transfer.

Table 15.1: The fifth environment action programme: nuclear safety

Objectives	Targets up to 2000	Measures	Time-frame	Actors
(a) Upgrading of safety measures	Update existing Community Basic Safety Standards according to the 1990 ICRP recommendations	Amendment of Directive 80/836/EURATOM	1992 ⇛	EC, MS
	Keep BSS up to date with scientific developments and latest ICRP recommendations	As above	ongoing	EC, MS
	Harmonise Community nuclear safety requirements	Develop and implement Council decision of 25.07.1975	ongoing	EC, MS
	Extend Community safety culture to the countries of the former Soviet Union and Central and Eastern Europe	– Technical Assistance Programmes – Extend G-24 coordination to include the countries of the former Soviet Union	1991 ⇛ 1991 ⇛	EC, MS, Ind. EC, G-24
	International Framework Convention	Active support to the IAEA in the preparatory work	1992 ⇛	EC, IAEA
(b) Verification of monitoring installations article 35-EURATOM	Reactivation of a Treaty provision	– Define verification objectives and goals – Implementation	1991 ⇛ ongoing	EC EC + MS

Table 15.1 continued

Objectives	Targets up to 2000	Measures	Time-frame	Actors
(c) Strategy on waste management	Complete BSS to include transfers of radioactive waste	Supplement Amendment of Directive 80/836/EURATOM	1992 ⇒	EC, MS
	Strategic management plan for all radioactive waste	Establish, adopt and implement strategic plan	1992 ⇒	EC, MS, Industry
(d) Enhancement of public information and education	Radiation protection education in primary and secondary school	– Handbook for teachers	1992	EC, MS
		– Brochures, videos	ongoing	id
	Improve quality of public information	Standing conference on health and safety in the nuclear age	ongoing	EC
		Preparation and publication of a journalist's guide to nuclear power	1992	EC
		Recommendation for a harmonised approach to public information on indoor radon exposure 1	1993	EC
(e) Adequate training in radiation protection	Improve quality of ionising of different professional groups	Courses in different fields of radiation protection and nuclear safety	1992 ⇒	EC

Chapter 16

Monitoring of the Implementation of "Environment" Directives

I. THE ROLE OF THE COMMISSION AND THE COURT OF JUSTICE

According to the Treaty of Rome, the Commission is responsible for ensuring that Community law is properly implemented and for referring cases of infraction to the Court of Justice of the European Communities in Luxembourg. In the area of the environment most of the measures have been taken in the form of "directives" which mean that the Commission has to pay particular attention to the correct integration of the directives into national law. A directive binds all Member States with respect to the result to be achieved, but responsibility with regard to the form and means to be used to achieve the stated objectives is left up to the national authorities. However, the Community does not have any material means to impose respect of Community law, be it in the form of directives, regulations, or the general provisions of the treaty itself. In the sector of the environment, the question of checking the implementation of the texts has become increasingly important over recent years due to the growing number of directives passed by the Council. It would be a little unrealistic, not to say dangerously misleading, for Community Environment Policy to continue to adopt a large number of legal acts, if these were not actually going to be implemented by the Member States. Studies carried out by the Commission have shown that a serious problem exists in this respect, since the number of infractions in the environment sector has been constantly increasing since 1978.

In 1986, complaints and cases detected by the Commission's own enquiries, came to 192 as compared to 25 in 1978. In 1987, the level was roughly the same – at 188, but by 1992 had risen to 587 (see Table 16.1). The 1992 figures put the sector of the environment in first position, ahead of industrial affairs and agriculture, areas for which the law is far more extensive than that of environment. Aware of the importance of the situation, the European Parliament asked the Commission to make the monitoring of the respect of Community environment law a matter of priority in the future. In its resolution adopting the 4th Environmental Action Programme (1987–1992) the Council underlined the importance of Community law on the environment and called upon the Commission to send it and the Parliament regular reports on its application in order that environmental policy could be assessed. The importance of abiding by the obligations of environmental directives

Table 16.1: Complaints (C) and infringements detected by the Commission's own inquiries (I) since 1982 in the environment sector

		B		D		DK		E		F		GB		GR		IRL		IT		L		NL		P		Total	
		C	I	C	I	C	I	C	I	C	I	C	I	C	I	C	I	C	I	C	I	C	I	C	I	C	I
Environment, consumer protection and nuclear safety	1982	1	–	1	–	–	–	4	–	–	–	1	–	–	–	1	–	2	–	–	–	–	–	–	–	10	–
	1983	1	–	1	–	–	1	1	–	–	–	1	–	1	–	–	–	1	–	–	–	1	–	–	–	8	–
	1984	–	–	1	2	–	–	–	–	–	–	2	–	2	–	–	–	4	–	–	–	–	–	–	–	9	2
	1985	–	1	3	1	1	1	3	–	2	–	11	3	14	–	1	–	2	–	–	–	3	1	–	–	37	10
	1986	7	3	6	6	2	1	44	5	5	–	32	–	53	3	5	–	13	3	2	–	2	3	2	–	165	32
	1987	4	3	14	6	3	4	16	29	1	–	30	3	17	3	9	1	16	6	5	–	4	1	7	2	150	38

was a point also made in the 1992 Court of Auditors Special Report on the environment and by institutions in the Member States, including the House of Lords in the United Kingdom. The Commission will have to use all the means at its disposal, both its legal and political means, and also the provision of information to the public, to put a stop to certain deficiencies in the implementation of directives.

II.   THE SYSTEM FOR CHECKING THE IMPLEMENTATION OF "ENVIRONMENT" DIRECTIVES

To ensure that the Member States are correctly implementing the directives and other measures adopted under Community Environment Policy, which amounts to a total of several hundred texts, the Commission carries out two types of checks:

- the formal check on the integration of Community directives into national law; first, it is necessary to verify that the Member States have actually informed the Commission of the translation of Community provisions into national law; secondly it is also necessary to check that the national measures comply, both from the formal and the practical points of view, with requirements of Community law;
- the check on the practical implementation and the effective respect of the directives; this type of check is of course the most difficult for the Commission to carry out, in that theoretically any national or regional administrative act which would be contrary to Community law should, in principle, be subject to infringement proceedings. To perform the check, the Community can make use of the general powers of investigation provided for under Article 155 of the EEC Treaty, and of the specific national reports on the implementation of the directives which the Member States are required to send to the Commission periodically.

Moreover, the complaints made by individuals to the Commission, or where appropriate to the Court of Justice (Article 173, paragraph 2 of the EEC Treaty) can also help to bring to the attention of the Commission instances where Community law is not being respected. Generally speaking, numerous weaknesses and gaps in the implementation of environmental directives by Member States have been noted by the Commission:

- often inclusion of these directives in national law is delayed;
- they are often only partially incorporated;
- in practice the directives have sometimes been considered as recommendations, rather than provisions having a restrictive legal power;
- in some cases even the decisions of the Court of Justice recognizing an infringement on the part of a Member State, have not been followed.

The Commission has therefore had to enter into a large number of infringement proceedings against Member States, in accordance with Article 169 of the EEC Treaty. This article stipulates that if the Commission feels that a Member State has failed in one of the obligations imposed on it by the treaty or by Community law in general, it must draw up a "reasoned opinion" after first having allowed the State the opportunity to comment by sending it a letter of formal notice. Such letters are issued routinely when a Member State has not notified the Commission of national measures implementing directives which are due for implementation. If the State in question does not conform to the "reasoned opinion" in the period laid down by the Commission, it can be taken before the Court of Justice. Under Article 171 of the treaty, if the Court recognizes that a Member State has failed in its obligations, that State must take the necessary measures to respect the decision of the Court. The Treaty on European Union amended Article 171 so that if the Commission consider that a Member State has not complied with a judgment of the Court, it may refer the matter back to the Court with a recommendation that the Member State be fined a "penalty payment". The decision on whether to impose such a fine, and how much, will be up to the Court. In order to improve the situation regarding the implementation of directives, the Commission gave particular priority, during the course of the 4th Environmental Action Programme, to the monitoring of environmental legislation, as the European Parliament has requested. To this end, the Commission has not only continued to pursue and intensify legal actions under Article 169 of the treaty, it has also increased dialogue with national and regional administrations and in 1990 initiated "package" meetings with the central, regional or local authorities of the Member States to discuss the factual or legal aspects of alleged complaints, infringements or implementation of environmental directives. It has also endeavoured to increase public awareness, and to provide more information to local authorities and environmental protection associations. With this in mind, it intends to allow the public access to a computerized Community data bank on the implementation of Community law, to organize training seminars, and to encourage private individuals and associations to bring to its attention cases of failures to respect Community legislation.

Chapter 9 of the 5th Environmental Action Programme deals exclusively with the question of implementation and enforcement. It calls for better preparation of measures, including improved consultation, better integration accompanied by complementary measures, improved practical follow-up to legislative measures, both administrative and operative, and stricter checking and enforcement of compliance. To implement these reforms, the 5th Action Programme plans to establish three *ad hoc* dialogue groups:

- a consultative forum to provide for consultation and the exchange of information between the industry, business, regional and local authorities, professional associations, trade unions, environmental and consumer organizations and the relevant Directorates-General of the Commission;
- an implementation network made up of representatives of national authorities and the Commission which will aim at fostering common approaches on a practical level;
- an environment policy review group comprising representatives of the Commission and Member States at Director-General level to boost mutual understanding and facilitate an exchange of views on environmental policies and measures.

1. 91/692/EEC: Council Directive of 23 December 1991 standardizing and rationalizing reports on the implementation of certain directives relating to the environment

On 23 December 1991, the Council adopted a directive aimed at harmonizing the obligations of the Member States with regard to reporting requirements on the implementation of EC environment legislation.[1] This is seen as essential in order to facilitate the publication by the Commission itself of comprehensive reports on the implementation of legislation and to avoid unnecessary infraction procedures against Member States for failure to respect legislation. The directive provides for basic questionnaires to be drawn up by the Commission for each of the main sectors (water, air, waste, etc.) which the Member States must complete and return. On the basis of the information provided the Commission will draw up a report on the implementation of the directives operating in each sector.

2.   Eleventh annual report to the European Parliament on monitoring the application of Community law – 1993 – the environment[2]

The above report provides a useful insight into the application of Community environmental legislation. Action taken on cases of failure to notify in 1993 breaks down as follows:

- 90 Article 169 letters (95 in 1992);
- 26 reasoned opinions (18 in 1992);
- 7 cases referred to the Court of Justice (4 in 1992)
- 53 cases terminated (63 in 1992).

Table 16.2 shows progress made by 1993 in implementing environmental directives.

Incorrect application of environmental law in various parts of the Community is most commonly detected through complaints from Community citizens and through questions put by Members of the European Parliament. The directives that cause the greatest difficulty are those relating to waste, discharges into the aquatic environment, the protection of wild birds and environmental impact assessment.

[1] OJ No L 377 of 31/12/92.
[2] OJ No C 154 of 6/6/94.

Table 16.2: Eleventh annual report to the European Parliament on monitoring the application of Community law – 1993

3. Progress in implementing directives applicable to the environment

The results obtained by the Member States in 1993 are satisfactory, though Greece, Ireland and Italy 'could do better'

Member States	*Directives applicable on 31.12.1993*	*Directives for which measures have been notified*	*%*
Belgium	117	107	91
Denmark	117	115	98
Germany	119	108	91
Greece	119	100	84
Spain	117	106	90
France	117	111	95
Ireland	117	103	88
Italy	117	95	81
Luxembourg	117	108	92
Netherlands	117	108	92
Portugal	117	106	90
United Kingdom	117	106	90

Note: this table concerns the following Directives:

General matters: 85/337, 90/313, 90/656, 90/660.

Waste: 75/439, 75/442, 76/403, 78/319, 84/631, 85/339, 85/469, 86/121, 86/278, 86/279, 87/101, 87/112, 91/156, 91/157, 92/122, 93/86.

Water: 75/440, 76/160, 76/464, 78/176, 78/659, 79/869, 79/923, 80/68, 80/778, 81/855, 81/858, 82/176, 82/883, 83/29, 83/513, 84/156, 84/491, 86/280, 88/347, 90/415.

Air: 75/716, 80/779, 81/857, 82/884, 84/360, 85/203, 85/210, 85/580, 85/581, 87/219, 87/416, 88/609, 89/369, 89/427, 89/429.

Noise: 79/113, 80/51, 81/1051, 83/206, 84/533, 84/534, 84/535, 84/536, 84/537, 84/538, 85/405, 85/406, 85/407, 85/408, 85/409, 86/594, 86/662, 87/252, 88/180, 88/181, 89/514, 89/629, 92/14.

Nature: 79/409, 81/854, 83/129, 85/411, 85/444, 86/122, 89/370, 91/244, 91/271.

Chemicals: 79/831, 80/1189, 81/957, 82/232, 82/501, 83/467, 84/449, 86/431, 86/609, 87/18, 87/216, 87/217, 87/432, 88/302, 88/490, 88/610, 90/219, 90/220, 90/517, 91/325, 91/326, 91/410, 91/632, 92/32, 92/37, 92/69, 93/67, 93/90, 93/105.

Radiation protection: 80/836, 84/466, 84/467, 89/618, 90/641.

Chapter 17

The Place of the Environment in the Single European Act and the Maastricht Treaty

The drawing up of a new European treaty took place in 1985. It resulted in the production of a text called the "Single European Act" which was signed in Luxembourg by the Foreign Ministers of the Member States on 17 February 1986. It is called the "Single Act" because it brings together in one text both the provisions modifying the treaties establishing the European Communities and those on European political cooperation regarding foreign policy.

This revision of the EEC, ECSC and Euratom Treaties, for the first time devotes a special place to the environment ("Title VII"), which consists of three articles. The "internal market" chapter also contains some particular provisions concerning the protection of the environment. This inclusion of the environment in the Single European Act represents first and foremost an official recognition by the governments of the Member States of the Community's responsibility in the area of the environment, thus regularizing a situation which has actually been in existence for a number of years. This official recognition has made it possible explicitly to incorporate in the new treaty certain fundamental principles which are basic to any environmental protection policy. In this respect the new treaty first returns to a number of traditional principles such as that of the polluter pays, or of the priority to be given to preventive action. But it also sets out some relatively new principles, such as that of the protection of natural resources, the priority to be given to the rectification "at source" of environmental damage, or the principle under which environmental protection should also be incorporated into other Community policies. These new and promising principles are nevertheless accompanied by a certain number of concepts which are in danger of being used in a restrictive way by some governments. For example, there is the provision requiring the analysis of potential costs prior to any Community action, or for the justification of the most appropriate level of action, Community or national. Finally, contrary to the Commission's proposal which had argued in favour of the qualified majority vote, the negotiators of the new treaty have retained the rule of unanimity for the decision procedure within the Council on environmental matters except for those relating to the internal market (see under II).

I. THE NEW TITLE OF THE "SINGLE ACT" ON THE ENVIRONMENT

(a) The first article of this title (Article 130R) establishes the objectives, principles and conditions of implementation of the Community's action on the environment. In all, three objectives have been retained:

- to preserve, protect and improve the quality of the environment;
- to contribute towards protecting human health;
- to ensure a prudent and rational utilization of national resources.

As far as this last point on natural resources is concerned, the Member States stated in a declaration annexed to the Single Act that the Community's activities in the area of the environment should not interfere with national policies regarding the exploitation of energy resources.

The principles which form the basis of Community action on the environment should be those of preventive action, of polluter pays, of the rectification at source of environmental damage and of the integration of the environmental dimension in the other Community policies. During the preparation and implementation of the various activities in the field of the environment, the Community should neverthe-less take account of the following:

- the environmental conditions and the economic development of the regions;
- the potential benefits and costs of action or lack of action.

As far as finance is concerned, the new treaty stipulates that as a general rule it is up to Member States to ensure the carrying out of measures which are not of a Community nature.

At international level it specifies that the Community and Member States must cooperate with third countries and with the relevant international organizations, this provision in no way prejudicing the respective competences of the Member States and the Community in negotiating and concluding international agreements. Member States also consider in an annexed declaration that this provision does not affect the principles resulting from the judgment handed down by the Court of Justice in the *AETR* case.

(b) The second article of the "environment" chapter (Article 130S) deals with the decision procedure within the Council. It states that, "the Council, acting unanimously on a proposal from the Commission and after consulting the European Parliament and the Economic and Social Committee, shall decide what action is to be taken by the Community". The Council can nevertheless define those matters on which decisions are to be taken by a qualified majority. However, this last provision does not really introduce any new element, in that this possibility already existed within the Council. In fact a number of directives already provide for the creation of "committees on the adaptation to scientific and technical research" whose decisions are taken on the basis of the qualified majority. The areas of responsibility and the powers of these committees are nev-ertheless defined beforehand and on the basis of unanimity by the Member States within the Council.

(c) The third and final article of the "environment" chapter of the Single Act (Article 130T) specifies that the measures taken by the Community do not prevent any Member State from maintaining or introducing more stringent protective measures, provided that these are compatible with the treaty.

II.   THE ENVIRONMENT PROVISIONS IN THE NEW "INTERNAL MARKET" CHAPTER

(a) The new provisions on the realization of the internal market, i.e. an area without internal frontiers in which the free movement of goods, persons, services and capital is ensured, allow for the introduction of the qualified majority vote, even though the old Article 100 on the functioning of the Common Market which requires unanimity is retained. In the area of the internal market the exceptions foreseen requiring unanimity for decision-taking mainly concern fiscal questions, professions and the freedom of movement of capital. According to the new Article 100A, all the other measures contributing to the establishment and functioning of the internal market will however be taken by the Council on the basis of the qualified majority. Many of the environmental protection measures also have objectives and consequences which are directly linked to the functioning of the internal market. Apart from all the directives establishing product standards (vehicle exhaust; lead in petrol; sulphur in gas, oil, etc.), there are also other more general directives whose current legal basis is both Article 100 and Article 235 of the EEC Treaty. Although Article 100 of the EEC Treaty dealing with the harmonization of legislation with a view to achieving the effective functioning of the Common Market remains in force, it is likely that a number of directives will in future have their legal basis in the new Article 100A. Considerable recourse to this article would be all the more justifiable in the area of the environment, given that the provisions contained within it require the Commission to base the drawing up of its environment proposals on high levels of protection.

(b) The new Article 100A gives the Member States the right, after the adoption of a harmonization measure by the Council acting by a qualified majority, to apply more severe national provisions, on grounds relating to the protection of the environment or working environment. The possibility of departing from the harmonization measures adopted on the basis of a qualified majority as described in Article 100A, must be notified to and assessed by the Commission, and may be submitted to the Court of Justice in cases of improper use. This derogation clause represents an important qualification in the harmonization provision regarding the establishment of the internal market. It was imposed by the Danish government which also made a unilateral declaration on this subject, specifying that national measures taken by way of derogation must not constitute a disguised form of protectionism, but should be based solely on higher requirements in the areas of the working environment and environmental protection.

(c) Finally, within the framework of Article 100A, the Single Act provides for a new procedure for the intervention of and cooperation with the European Parliament. This procedure, the implementation of which appears somewhat complicated, while maintaining the driving force of the Commission, allows Parliament to influence more directly the Council's decision, with the understanding that the final decision rests with the Council.

The new treaty came into force in July 1987. The various provisions of this treaty clearly involved a number of uncertainties. The most important of these undoubtedly concerned the respective division of competencies between the Community and its Member States on the one hand, and the extent of recourse to the qualified majority on the other.

As far as the competencies and the choice of the level of action are concerned, the final text was sufficiently broad and vague to allow for numerous interpretations. It specified in the environment chapter (interestingly it is here, and nowhere else in the SEA, that the principle of subsidiarity is spelled out for the first time – in Article 130r(4)) which states that "the Community shall take action relating to the environment to the extent to which the objectives can be attained better at Community level than at the level of the individual Member States". As for the use in certain circumstances of the new Article 100A, allowing a decision to be taken on the basis of the qualified majority, instead of the general rule of unanimity provided for by Article 130R, it seemed likely that some Member States would endeavour to keep recourse to this type of majority decision down to a minimum, so as to retain intact their total power of decision.

The Commission took the view that environmental measures which were also Single Market measures, i.e. designed to remove barriers to trade or distortions in the conditions of competition, could legitimately be proposed on the basis of Article 100a and therefore be subject to qualified majority voting in the Council.

The Commission's view of this matter was specifically upheld by the European Court of Justice in the so-called titanium dioxide case where, the Council having struck down Article 100a as the legal basis for a directive in favour of Article 130(s), the European Court reinstated it.

There are some fields where the possibility of majority voting provided by the Single European Act effectively revolutionized Community environmental policy. A case in point were the so-called "clean car" directives where new stringent standards were introduced for exhaust emissions through procedures which involved using qualified majority voting in the Council, and the "cooperation procedure" whereby the European Parliament had the right to propose amendments at a second reading which, if they were adopted by the Commission, could only be amended or rejected by the Council by unanimity.

The Act further required that "environmental protection requirements shall be a component of the community's other policies" (Article 130R). This language survives, though in modified form, in the Maastricht Treaty.

With the adoption of the Single European Act in 1986 environmental policy became a formal competence of the Community. Was that of any practical significance? The answer to that question must be both positive and negative.

Positive, in so far as voting procedures could be speeded up and measures therefore adopted more rapidly by the Council (though there must be real doubt as to the long-term acceptability of some measures in cases where Member States find themselves outvoted. They may have to live with the text but simply fail to apply it.). Positive, in so far as accusations that the Commission or the Community is acting *ultra vires* in the environmental field will be harder to make and to sustain with the Community's environmental competence now clearly defined.

But negative too in the sense that these new and promising developments are nevertheless accompanied by a certain number of concepts which are in danger of being used in a restrictive way by some governments. For example, there is the provision requiring the analysis of potential costs prior to any Community action, or for the justification of the most appropriate level of action – the so-called subsidiarity principle. It was not hard to envisage circumstances where such references could be used not to advance but to retard Community environmental policy.

On balance, it is hard to argue that the inclusion of the environmental articles in the treaty as amended by the Single European Act was in and of itself sufficient to produce a massive impact on the Community's environmental policy. It was helpful but not crucial. More important, probably, was the fact that at the end of the 1980s the political framework was supportive on the whole. Worth noting in particular was the growing tendency of the European Council, which is the highest political authority of the Community, to pay particular attention to the environmental situation within the Community. This first became evident in 1978 when the European Council decided on a specific Community action on sea pollution, but also more recently in 1983 and 1985. In 1983 the Stuttgart European Council underlined the urgent need to speed up and reinforce the action carried out at all levels in the fight against environmental pollution. It put particular emphasis on the serious danger threatening European forest areas, and decided that environmental protection policy should be treated as a priority within the Community. In March 1985 at its Brussels session the European Council judged that environmental protection policy should become a fundamental part of economic, industrial, agricultural, and social policies set up by the Community and its Member States. It asked that the years to come be marked by significant progress in Community action for environmental protection in Europe and the rest of the world. The European Councils which took place in Hanover in June 1988, in Rhodes in December 1988 and in Dublin in June 1990 all returned to the environmental theme (see p. 22).

The year 1987 was declared by the Council as European Year of the Environment and saw the adoption of the Community's 4th Environmental Action Programme. It was also the year in which the report of the World Commission on Environment and Development, the so-called Brundtland Commission, was published, setting the stage for the United Nations Conference on Environment and Development (UNCED) to be held in June 1992.

The Brundtland Commission's report and the whole emphasis on sustainable development finds its reflection in the Maastricht Treaty with the reformulated Article 2 though, as it has been pointed out by various scholars,[1] there is a degree of confusion between the notions of sustainable progress, sustainable growth and sustainable development. Article 2 finally opts for the following language:

> The Community shall have as its task, by establishing a common market and an economic and monetary union and by implementing the common policies or activities referred to in articles 3 and 3a, to promote throughout the Community a harmonious and balanced development of economic activities, sustainable and non-inflationary growth respecting the environment, a high level of employment and of social protection, the raising of the standards of living and the quality of life, and economic and social cohesion and solidarity among Member States.

---

[1] See for example *Maastricht and the Environment* published by the Institute for Environmental Policy: Verhoeve, Bennett, Wilkinson, August 1992.

III. THE MAASTRICHT TREATY AND THE ENVIRONMENT

The Treaty on European Union entered into force on 1 November 1993. The standard legislative procedure for environmental legislation became the cooperation procedure whereby the Parliament has two readings and two opportunities to amend legislation, although the Council retains the final say. The co-decision procedure, newly introduced by the Maastricht Treaty, on the other hand, enables the Parliament in theory to veto proposals, even if the Council is unanimously in favour of them. Yet the Treaty on European Union, far from simplifying the legislative process for environmental policy, further complicated it by doubling the number of possible procedures from two to four.

Proposals for legislation can still be made on the basis of either Article 100a or 130s, the choice of legal basis determining the method of voting in Council, qualified majority voting or unanimity. The treaty did, however, considerably extend the scope of qualified majority voting so that it can now be regarded as the norm.

The treaty also increased the power of the European Parliament: first, by the extension in qualified voting which entitles the Parliament to participation in the cooperation, secondly by the introduction in Article 189b of a new procedure, that of "co-decision". Co-decision could result in the Parliament enjoying a say equal to that of the Council depending on the extent to which the Parliament is determined to find ways to exercise these powers to the full. It also provides for a conciliation procedure to resolve differences between the two institutions. Qualified majority voting, by removing the ability of one Member State on its own – or even two large Member States acting together – to veto a proposal, speeds up Council decisions, but the complicated co-decision procedure – with up to 11 separate stages – could end up slowing down the decision-making process.

The four possible procedures arising from the above changes are thus as follows:

Under Article 130s:

- qualified majority voting in Council and cooperation procedure with Parliament – effectively the norm now;
- qualified majority voting in Council and co-decision with Parliament – as regards general action programmes;
- unanimity in Council and consultation with Parliament – for a number of exceptional cases mentioned in Article 130s;

Under Article 100a:

- qualified majority voting and co-decision – for instances concerning the establishment of the Single Market.

Given that the text of the new Article 130s as amended by the Treaty on European Union is not clear, it is likely that there will be much argument between the various EC institutions as to which of the above procedures should apply and when. Article 130s specifies some areas where unanimity in Council will continue to be required: fiscal measures; town and country planning, land use (but not waste management and measures of "a general nature") and the management of water resources; measures significantly affecting a Member State's choice between different energy sources and the general structure of its energy supply. The vagueness of these rather broad categories is likely to add to the uncertainties concerning the choice of the three legislative procedures available under Article 130s.

Under Article 100a, the requirement for unanimity in the above exceptional areas no longer applies. Following the 1991 titanium dioxide case in which the Court of Justice ruled that in the case before it the goals of environmental protection and removal of market distortions were indivisible, and in which the Court pointed out that Article 100a made specific reference to the Commission's obligation when proposing measures for approximating the laws of the Member States to take as a basis a high level of environmental protection, the Commission might be expected to interpret broadly the applicability of Article 100a under which the Parliament now has power of co-decision with the Council. In its ruling on the waste directive, however, the Court judged that recourse to Article 100a is only possible when the measure has a direct bearing on the distortion of competition between undertakings, which was not the case in the regulation of waste in general terms.

As noted above, the co-decision procedure gives the Parliament a right of veto over proposed legislation and as such represents a significant increase in Parliament's powers. Besides applying to proposals based on Article 100a, it also applies to those based on Article 130s which concern "general action programmes setting out priority objectives to be attained". The 5th Environmental Action Programme, for example, includes specific, quantitative pollution reduction targets for the period up to 2000. Previous Environmental Action Programmes have also contained similar statements of intent to legislate which have not always been realized. Depending upon the interpretation of the amended Article 130s, the obligation to pass the necessary implementing legislation for an action programme could be deemed a legal obligation. In a Declaration attached to the Treaty on European Union, the Member States undertook to review in 1996 the "classification of Community acts with a view to establishing a hierarchy between the different categories of act".

The extension of qualified majority voting increased the likelihood that individual Member States will be required to implement policies to which they are opposed. This, in turn, could worsen the already serious problem of non-implementation of environmental legislation. In a Declaration (which is merely a political statement and is not legally binding) attached to the Treaty on European Union, the Heads of State and Government stressed that "each Member State should fully and accurately transpose into national law the Community directives addressed to it within the deadlines laid down therein". The Declaration went on to state that "measures taken by the different Member States should result in Community law being applied with the same effectiveness and rigour as in the application of their national laws". The treaty did introduce an important change in the field of implementation though, in its amendment to Article 171 whereby if the Commission believes a Member State has not complied with a judgment of the Court, it may refer the case back to the Court recommending that the Member State pay a fine or "penalty payment". The final decision rests with the Court. Failure to pay the fine could, in theory, result in the freezing of payments from Structural Funds or other sources.

The Maastricht Treaty also went beyond the Single European Act as far as environment was concerned by introducing into Article 130R(2) the so-called "precautionary principle". The treaty itself did not define the precautionary principle but it is defined in other texts, for example the Conclusions of the Bergen Ministerial Meeting on the Environment. Whereas *prevention* requires that chosen hazards be eliminated, the precautionary principle dictates that action to eliminate possible damaging impacts on the environment should be taken before even a causal link has been established by absolutely clear scientific evidence. Some commentators believe that the adoption of the precautionary principle as a principle of EC environmental law may well result in a considerable tightening of existing environmental regulatory standards.[2]

Whereas the Single European Act indicated that "environmental protection shall be a component of other policies of the Community", Maastricht states that "Environmental protection requirements must be integrated into the definition and implementation of other Community policies". This was to include the Community's external policies. As noted above, the Treaty on European Union also included a new Title XVII on development cooperation. Article 130u(1) requires Community policy to foster "the sustainable economic and social development of the developing countries". Why the treaty should apply the concept of sustainable *development* to the developing countries but sustainable *growth* to the Community is not clear.

The treaty also introduced several new areas of Community activity which to a certain extent are relevant to environmental protection. In most cases, the Community had already begun to take action in these "new" areas but their formal inclusion in the treaties will no doubt increase the number of proposals for legislation in these fields. The new areas include:

- a contribution to the attainment of a high level of health protection – Article 129(1) notes that the Community's role is a "contributory" one, implying that the main responsibility will remain with the Member States. As Article 130r(1) declares "protecting human health" as one of the objectives of Community environmental policy, problems of demarcation may arise between the two articles. Furthermore, Article 129(4) provides for co-decision, whereas Article 130 provides for the cooperation procedure;
- a contribution to the strengthening of consumer protection – as with health protection, problems of demarcation could occur between Article 129a which provides for a Community contribution to a high level of consumer protection and Article 130s. Again, Article 129 requires co-decision, Article 130s cooperation and sometimes unanimity;
- measures in the sphere of energy, civil protection and tourism – although the Treaty on European Union contains no specific titles relating to these areas, a declaration attached to the treaty suggests these issues will be reviewed on the basis of Commission proposals to be submitted to the Council by 1996;
- encouragement for the establishment of trans-European networks – Article 129b defines these as including transport, energy and telecommunications infrastructures;
- a contribution to the flowering of the cultures of the Member States – Article 128 provides the legal basis for encouraging cultural cooperation between the Member States, including in the area of the conservation and safeguarding of the cultural heritage of European significance. An amendment to Article 92 dealing with state aids means that financial support might be allowed for traditional forms of agriculture in order to preserve particular landscape features or specific breeds of farm animals.

[2] See David Freestone, "The 1992 Maastricht Treaty – Implications for European Environmental Law", *European Environmental Law Review*, June 1992.

IV. SUBSIDIARITY

The principle of subsidiarity had long been one of the recognized principles of Community Environment Policy. The first Council Resolutions approving or adopting the Community's Environmental Action Programmes were themselves explicitly given a double "*chapeau*". They were not only resolutions of the Council as such; there were also resolutions of the Representatives of the Member States meeting in the Council. The environment was always an area where competence was to be shared between the Community and the Member States. Not everything that featured in the environmental programmes would be performed at Community level. Some actions might fall wholly to Member States. Indeed, some actions might best be undertaken at purely local level.

Although the Single European Act did not itself use the term "subsidiarity", it is interesting to note (as recorded above) that the idea of subsidiarity is expressly stated in the new environment chapter (indeed this is the only such explicit reference in the SEA). Article 130R(4) provides "that action shall be taken only to the extent that the objective can be attained better at Community level".

In the Maastricht Treaty, the "subsidiarity principle" has been removed from the environment chapter and given greater prominence as one of the opening articles. The new Article 3B of the Maastricht Treaty states:

> In areas which do not fall within its exclusive competence, the Community shall take action, in accordance with the principle of subsidiarity, only if and in so far as the objectives of the proposed action cannot be sufficiently achieved by the Member States and can therefore, by reason of the scale or effects of the proposed action, be better achieved by the Community. Any action by the Community shall not go beyond what is necessary to achieve the objectives of this Treaty.

The Community's 5th Environmental Action Programme, entitled "Towards Sustainability", which was adopted by the Council in December 1992 goes out of its way to stress that environmental actions will take place at different levels – Community, Member State, local authority, non-governmental organizations, industry, agriculture, tourism, etc.

What weight will in the end be given to the principle of subsidiarity as far as environmental policy is concerned? Could we imagine a situation where the Commission was taken before the European Court for having failed to respect the subsidiarity principle? Could we imagine a clear ruling by the Court on this issue?

Laurens Jan Brinkhorst, a former Director-General of DG XI, the Commission's Environment Directorate, in a speech entitled "Maastricht – A Panacea or Pandora's Box"[3] has suggested that, whereas action in the field of polluting products or polluting industries can be justified at Community level, and even some measures of nature protection, action to improve the protection of animals could not. Mr Brinkhorst cited the question of bull-fighting. A Spanish audience might be ready to agree that measures to ban bull-fighting should not be proposed or adopted at EEC level. Indeed a Spanish audience might be of the view that such measures should not even be treated at a national level but should be left to the conscience and the customs of individual localities and communities.

But even here the issue is not entirely straightforward. The European Parliament has persistently called for animal protection measures to be adopted at Community level, even including an article to that effect in its own Draft Treaty on European

---

[3] *European Environmental Law Review*, January 1993.

Union, the precursor in a sense of the Maastricht Treaty. And it is worth noting that the same meeting of the European Council which adopted the Maastricht Treaty also adopted a declaration which stated that the Community should "pay full regard to the welfare requirements of animals" when drafting and implementing Community legislation on the common agricultural policy, transport, the internal market and research.

At the present time there is some pressure in some Member States to "repatriate" certain elements of Community environmental policy on the grounds that the principle of subsidiarity is not being respected. In the United Kingdom, those early directives on drinking water, bathing water, etc. are frequently under attack. Though these directives were originally adopted on the basis of unanimity there seems nonetheless to be a feeling that they run counter to the subsidiarity principle and should be rewritten.

One cannot help feeling, nevertheless, that the argument here is not so much a legal argument as one of practicality. The reality is that the implementation of these directives has proved costly. The reality is that had the full economic and financial implications been known they might not have been adopted in the form they were adopted.

We may in the future therefore confront a situation where ironically the very inclusion of the reference to subsidiarity in the treaty is used an excuse, or an alibi, to block or water down new proposals, or revise existing proposals. The law thereby would serve as a cloak for what are essentially political objections or motivations. The same could be said for those other provisions of the SEA's environment chapter which have been carried forward into Maastricht, particularly the articles which require full prior assessment of the scientific basis of proposals and their economic and financial implications.

Maastricht in short may be a powerful sword, but it may be a two-edged sword as far as the environment is concerned. Only time – and the force of public opinion (positive or negative) – will determine how the sword is used. Ultimately the progress of the Community's environmental policy, as for most other Community policies, will be determined by the political realities in the individual Member States and, though probably to a lesser extent in spite of the real increase in its powers, by the European Parliament. The outcome of the debate over the destiny of Europe – federal versus national, centralizing versus decentralizing, regulatory versus non-interventionist – will have a major impact on the Community's environmental policy. Indeed, the environment may provide the ground for some of the major battles in that debate.

Table 17.1: The fifth environment action programme: examples of shared responsibility

	EC	(*)Member State and Regional Governments	Local + Regional Authorities	Enterprises	General Public / Consumer
Planning					
– Economic and social development	Regional Devt: Cohesion	Economic Devt. plans: Growth management EIA	Regional Devt. Strategies EIA	Demand – infra-structure	NGO
– Physical planning	Directive 85/337/ EEC (EIA)	national, regional & local development plans; integration of services			EIA – public participation
– Networks	Euro network of roads, rail, air, communication- regional co-operation		Euro network of roads	Demand-distribution	
R & D					
– Media	R & D programmes, EEA	Focal points Tax concessions	Emission controls treatment	Env. R & D Biotechnology	
– Processes		Integrated pollution controls		Innovation, technology	
– Products		Fiscal incentives National waste mgt plans	Waste prevention policies	Design: equipment	Consumer demand ECO-labels
Communicative					
– Information	Dissemination Co-ordination EEA Eurostat statistical programme	State of Environment: Admin. structures; National statistical services	Performance of licenses, collation: assessment, dissemination	Ind. demand – predictability Insurance/ investment	NGOs concerned citizens, consumers
– Education	Platform for exchange of information and experience	Primary, secondary + university curricula: education aids, teachers		Demand for graduates with environmental training	
– Training	Support measures	Professional, vocational	Professional. vocational	On-the-job; insurance; service industry	Trades Unions

Table 17.1 continued

	EC	(*Member State and Regional Governments)	Local + Regional Authorities	Enterprises	General Public / Consumer
Market-based					
– Codes of conduct (vol. agreements)	Covenants, EC-codes	Sectoral agreements & covenants		Sectoral agreements	
– Resource Mgt (env. audit)	BC Directive Pilot Projects	Sectoral agreements: Own Service Audit	Own activity audit; operating licences	Management Tool, Investment Banks, Insurance premiums	Investors, public, consumer information
– Ecological labels	EC directive EEA	National Promotion coordination + Procedures		Product design	Consumer pressure
– Financial supports- (incl. state aids)	Overview of state aids and of EC financial instruments	Tax concessions grants.			
Normative					
– Env. protection	Habitats directive, ACNAT, NATURA 2000, Rural Developt.	Designation of sensitive habitats: nature parks	Spatial plans Local amenities		NGOs/public demand for facilities & quality of life
– Internal Mkt	Product standards Emission limits			Demand for avoidance of trade barriers	Demand for consumer choice
– Implementation of Internat. agrs	Regulations monitoring	National implementation		Sectoral implementation	

■ – Lead Rôle,   (grey) – Complementary Rôle,   □ – Position of influence

(*) It is appreciated that, because of differences in the constitutional and institutional arrangements in the Member States, competences are not shared in a common manner. Accordingly, as the title indicates, this table is intended to provide theoretical examples of shared responsibility which are not intended to interfere with existing divisions of competences. The reference to Regional Governments is used to cover sub-national governments such as the Länder in Germany and the regional administrations in Belgium, Italy and Spain which have certain exclusive competences in the fields of policy dealt with in this Programme.

Annex 1

RESOLUTION

OF THE COUNCIL OF THE EUROPEAN COMMUNITIES AND OF THE REPRESENTATIVES
OF THE GOVERNMENTS OF THE MEMBER STATES, MEETING WITHIN THE COUNCIL

Of 19 October 1987 On the continuation and implementation of a European Community policy and action programme on the environment (1987–1992)

(OJ No C 138 of 17/5/93)

(This text replaces the one which appears in OJ No C 289, 29. 10. 1987, p. 3)

THE COUNCIL OF THE EUROPEAN COMMUNITIES AND THE REPRE-SENTATIVES OF THE GOVERNMENTS OF THE MEMBER STATES, MEETING WITHIN THE COUNCIL,

Note that the projects to which the appended programme will give rise should in some cases be carried out at Community level and in others be carried out by the Member States;

With regard to the projects to be carried out by the Member States, the latter will supervise their proper execution, it being understood that for these projects the Council will exercise the coordinating powers laid down in the Treaties;

With regard to the projects in the programme to be carried out by the institutions of the European Communities:

THE COUNCIL OF THE EUROPEAN COMMUNITIES,

Having regard to the Treaty establishing the European Coal and Steel Community,

Having regard to the Treaty establishing the European Economic Community,

Having regard to the Treaty establishing the European Atomic Community,

Having regard to the draft from the Commission,

Having regard to the opinion of the European Parliament ([1]),

([1]) Opinion delivered on 14 May 1987.

Having regard to the opinion of the Economic and Social Committee (^{2}),

Whereas the Treaty establishing the European Economic Community, as amended by the Single European Act, provides for the development and implementation of a Community policy on the environment, and lays down the objectives and principles which should govern such policy;

Whereas the Declaration of the Council of the European Communities and of the Representatives of the Governments of the Member States, meeting within the Council, of 22 November 1973 (^{3}) calls for the implementation of a European Communities programme of action on the environment; whereas the action programme was extended and supplemented for the period 1977 to 1986 by the resolutions of the Council and the Representatives of the Governments of the Member States, meeting within the Council, of 17 May 1977 (^{4}) and of 7 February 1983 (^{5}); whereas the programme of action is still valid and whereas it should be updated, further implemented and supplemented for the period 1987 to 1992 by new tasks which prove to be necessary;

Whereas it is necessary, in accordance with the Treaty as amended by the Single European Act, to avoid the adoption by the Member States of divergent measures likely to bring about economic and competition distortions in the common market;

Whereas the European Year of the Environment, which begins on 21 March 1987, offers a welcome opportunity of initiating the changes of attitude and promoting the action necessary to give practical effect to these perceptions;

RECALLS that the Single European Act, which constitutes a new legal basis for Community policy on the environment, lays down that action by the Community relating to the environment shall have the following objectives:

– to preserve, protect and improve the quality of the environment,

– to contribute towards protecting human health,

– to ensure a prudent and rational utilization of natural resources;

RECALLS that the Single European Act lays down that:

– action by the Community relating to the environment shall be based on the principles that preventive action should be taken, that environmental damage should as a priority be rectified at source, and that the polluter should pay,

– environmental protection requirements shall be a component of the Community's other policies,

---

(^{2}) Opinion delivered on 14 May 1987 (not yet published in the Official Journal).
(^{3}) OJ No C 112, 20. 12. 1973, p. 1.
(^{4}) OJ No C 139, 13. 6. 1977, p. 1.
(^{5}) OJ No C 46, 17. 2. 1983, p. 1.

– within their respective spheres of competence, the Community and the Member States shall cooperate with third countries and with the relevant international organizations;

RECALLS, in conclusion, that the Single European Act also provides that in preparing its action relating to the environment, the Community will take account of:

– available scientific and technical data,

– environmental conditions in the various regions of the Community,

– the potential benefits and costs of action or of lack of action,

– the economic and social development of the Community as a whole and the balanced development of its regions;

RECALLS, moreover, that the Single European Act provides that the Community shall take action relating to the environment to the extent to which the above objectives can be attained better at Community level than at the level of the individual Member States; that, without prejudice to certain Community measures, Member States shall be responsible for financing and implementing other measures;

RECALLS, finally, that the Commission, in its proposals on health and environmental protection, takes as a basis a high level of protection as laid down in the relevant provisions of the Single European Act;

RECOGNIZES that the protection of the environment can help to improve economic growth and facilitate job creation;

WELCOMES the Commission's intention of working closely with industry, trade unions and interested non-governmental organizations in the drawing-up and implementations of environmental policy and programmes;

UNDERLINES the particular importance it attaches to the implementation of the Community legislation and INVITES the Commission to review systematically the application and the practical effects of existing Community policy and to provide regular reports on this to the Council and the European Parliament so that an assessment of the effectiveness of such a policy can be made and, *inter alia*, useful guidelines for future proposals determined;

DECLARES that, in view of the foregoing, and on the basis of past achievements, it is important for Community action to concentrate on the following priority areas while observing the respective powers of the Community and the Member States:

Pollution prevention

(a) reduction at source of pollution and nuisance in various areas:

– combating air pollution, *inter alia* by effective implementation of existing Council Directives on air quality and air pollution from industrial plants, and by adopting and implementing measures concerning emissions from large combustion plants and motor vehicles,

– combating fresh-water and marine pollution from specific or diffused sources, *inter alia*, by the implementation of Council Directive 76/464/EEC of 4 May 1976 on pollution caused by certain dangerous substances discharged into the aquatic environment of the Community (^{1}), and by the general improvement of the Community's aquatic environment in particular the North Sea and the Mediterranean,

– combating soil pollution, among others caused by agro-chemical products and toxic wastes,

– harmonized implementation of the existing Directives on toxic and dangerous wastes, in particular the transfrontier transport thereof.

In this context, Community action shall take particular account of the need to:

– prevent the transfer of pollution from one part of the environment to another,

– combat transfrontier pollution;

(b) control of chemical substances and preparations:

– evaluation, in particular through greater use of multi-environment studies, of risks to the environment and human health caused by chemical substances and preparations,

– identification and implementation of the most efficient and economical control measures for these substances which are a potential hazard for the environment and consumers' health;

(c) prevention of industrial accidents:

Measures for the general prevention of industrial accidents and an effective response and restriction of the consequences of accidents which might nevertheless occur, by:

– more effective implementation of Council Directive 82/501/EEC of 24 June 1982 on the major-accident hazards of certain industrial activities (^{2}),

– review of this Directive, if necessary, to include, *inter alia*, a possible widening of its scope,

– greater exchange of information on the matter between Member States;

(^{1}) OJ No L 129, 18. 5. 1976, p. 23.
(^{2}) OJ No L 230, 5. 8. 1982, p. 1.

(d) combating noise pollution at source;

(e) measures concerning the evaluation and best use of biotechnology with regard to the environment;

(f) effective action to protect the health of the population and the environment from harm through nuclear radiation both as a result of normal operations and in the circumstances of an accident;

Improvement in management of resources

(g) measures to protect and enhance Europe's natural heritage, in particular:

   – implementation of Council acts in force such as Regulation (EEC) No 3626/82 of 3 December 1982 on the implementation in the Community of the Convention on international trade in endangered species of wild fauna and flora ([2]) and Directive 79/409/EEC of 2 April 1979 on the conservation of wild birds ([3]),

   – the protection, as laid down in the Treaty, of areas of importance in the Community, *inter alia*, in the framework of Directive 79/409/EEC, or of areas which are particularly sensitive environmentally, and encouragement of the revival of areas which are environmentally impaired,

   – protection of forests against atmospheric pollution and forest fires, including the implementation of the measures laid down in Council Regulation (EEC) No 3528/86 of 17 November 1989 on the protection of the Community's forests against atmospheric pollution ([4]) and (EEC) No 3529/86 of 17 November 1986 on the protection of the Community's forests against fire ([5]);

(h) measures relating to natural or man-made hazards or disasters affecting public health and the environment, including both evaluation of risk and adequate response;

(i) encouragement of agricultural practices which are environmentally beneficial;

(j) protection of the soil, in particular by combating erosion, by conserving plant cover, by the prevention of damage caused by certain industrial and agricultural activities and by combating such damage while bearing in mind the various geomorphological characteristics of the different areas;

(k) improving water resources and the management of water, in particular by reducing water pollution, protecting catchment areas and encouraging the re-use of waste water;

([2]) OJ No L 384, 31. 12. 1982, p. 1.
([3]) OJ No L 103, 25. 4. 1979, p. 1.
([4]) OJ No L 326, 21. 11. 1986, p. 2.
([5]) OJ No L 326, 21. 11. 1986, p. 5.

(l) the development of improved waste management in relation to reduction of quantities, treatment, recycling and re-use;

(m) overall and integrated environmental protection of the Mediterranean region, taking particular account of all the specific aspects of that region when giving practical application to the action programme;

International activities

(n) support and, where appropriate, active participation by the Community and the Member States in the activities of international organizations concerned with environmental protection within the framework of their respective powers;

(o) cooperation with developing countries on environmental matters and on protection of natural resources, having particular regard to questions of desertification and water supply, tropical forests and the production and use of dangerous substances or products and technological cooperation;

Development of appropriate instruments

(p) improving the scientific bases of environment policy, *inter alia*, through appropriate research programmes;

(q) effective implementation of Council Directive 85/337/EEC of 27 June 1985 on the assessment of the effects of certain public and private projects on the environment (^{1}) and the integration of the environmental dimension in other Community policies;

(r) implementation of appropriate standards in order to ensure a high level of public health and environmental protection;

(s) development of efficient economic instruments such as taxes, levies, State aid, authorization of negotiable rebates with a view to implementing the principle that the polluter pays, in accordance with the Council Recommendation 75/436/Euratom, ECSC, EEC of 3 March 1975 regarding cost allocation and action by public authorities on environmental matters (^{2}) (the 'polluter pays' principle);

(t) encouraging the development, dissemination and distribution of clean technology, notably in the case of heavily polluting industries;

(u) improved access to information on the environment;

(v) increased effort to promote environmental education and training at appropriate levels, and greater public awareness;

(^{1}) OJ No L 175, 5. 7. 1985, p. 40.
(^{2}) OJ No L 194, 25. 7. 1975, p. 1.

NOTES the action programme set out in the Annex to this resolution and approves in general the guidelines;

UNDERTAKES to act on the Commission proposals wherever possible within nine months of the date on which they are submitted or, as the case may be, of the date on which the opinions of the European Parliament and of the Economic and Social Committee are submitted;

STATES that the decision to make available the financial resources necessary for implementing this resolution and the action programme attached thereto will be taken in accordance with the usual procedures, in compliance with Article 130 R of the Single European Act, and in particular paragraph 4 thereof.

Annex 2

RESOLUTION OF THE COUNCIL AND THE REPRESENTATIVES OF THE GOVERNMENTS OF THE MEMBER STATES, MEETING WITHIN THE COUNCIL

of 1 February 1993

on a Community programme of policy and action in relation to the environment and sustainable development

(OJ No C 138 of 17/5/93)

THE COUNCIL OF THE EUROPEAN COMMUNITIES AND THE REPRESENTATIVES OF THE GOVERNMENTS OF THE MEMBER STATES OF THE EUROPEAN COMMUNITIES, MEETING WITHIN THE COUNCIL,

Having regard to the Treaty establishing the European Coal and Steel Community,

Having regard to the Treaty establishing the European Economic Community,

Having regard to the Treaty establishing the European Atomic Energy Community,

Having regard to the draft from the Commission,

Having regard to the opinion of the European Parliament ([1]),

Having regard to the opinion of the Economic and Social Committee ([2]),

Whereas the Treaty establishing the European Economic Community, as amended by the Single European Act, explicitly provides for the development and implementation of a Community policy on the environment; whereas the Treaty on European Union signed at Maastricht on 7 February 1992 has as a principal object-ive the promotion of sustainable growth respecting the environment, and specifies the objectives and guiding principles of that policy and the factors which must be taken into account in its preparations;

Whereas the Declaration of the Heads of State and Government, meeting in Council on 26 June 1990, calls *inter alia* for a further action programme for the environment to be elaborated on the basis of the principles of sustainable develop-ment, preventive and precautionary action and shared responsibility;

([1]) Opinion delivered on 17 November 1992.
([2]) OJ No C 287, 4. 11. 1992, p. 27.

Whereas the Community and its Member States have acquired considerable experience in the development and implementation of environmental policy and legislation and have thereby enhanced protection of the environment;

Whereas the United Nations Conference on Environment and Development (UNCED) meeting in Rio de Janeiro, 3 to 14 June 1992, adopted the Rio Declaration and Agenda 21 which are aimed at achieving sustainable patterns of development worldwide as well as a declaration of forest principles; whereas important Conventions and climate change and biodiversity were opened for signature and were signed by the Community and its Member States; whereas the Community and its Member States also subscribed to Agenda 21 and the said Declarations;

Whereas at the European Council meeting in Lisbon on 27 June 1992 the Community and its Member States committed themselves to the rapid implementation of the principal measures agreed at UNCED;

Whereas the European Council meetings in Lisbon on 27 June 1992 and in Birmingham on 16 October 1992 invited the Commission and the Council to undertake work relating to the implementation of the principle of subsidiarity and the European Council meeting in Edinburgh on 11 and 12 December 1992 approved principles, guidelines and procedures for its practical application; whereas in accordance with the principle of subsidiarity, some aspects of the policy and specific actions embodied in the programme 'Towards sustainability' ([3]), hereafter referred to as the 'programme' fall to be carried out at levels other than those involving the competencies of the European Communities;

Whereas the strategy advanced in the programme relies on the satisfactory integration of environment and other relevant policies,

ACKNOWLEDGE that the programme presented by the Commission has been designed to reflect the objectives and principles of sustainable development, preventive and precautionary action and shared responsibility set out in the declaration of the Heads of State and the Government of the Community meeting in Council on 26 June 1990 and in the Treaty on European Union signed at Maastricht on 7 February 1992;

CONSIDER that in so far as it provides a comprehensive framework as well as a strategic approach to sustainable development the programme constitutes an appropriate point of departure for the implementation of Agenda 21 by the Community and the Member States;

NOTE that many current forms of activity and development are not environmentally sustainable and ENDORSE, accordingly, the general objective of progressively orientating human activity and development towards sustainable forms;

AGREE that the achievement of sustainable development calls for significant changes in current patterns of development, production, consumption and behaviour;

([3]) See page 5 of this Official Journal.

DECLARE that such changes imply a sharing of responsibility at global, Community, regional, national, local and even personal levels;

ACKNOWLEDGE that the programme when implemented will take into account the diversity of the various regions of the Community, and will be consistent with the objectives of strengthening economic and social cohesion, and will aim at a high level of protection of the environment;

NOTE that the conclusions of the European Councils at Birmingham on 16 October 1992 and Edinburgh on 11 and 12 December 1992 will guide the Community's work in relation to the principle of subsidiarity;

CALL on the Commission to ensure that all proposals it makes relating to the environment fully reflect that principle, and UNDERTAKE to consider those proposals on a case-by-case basis to ensure consistency with the principle;

ACKNOWLEDGE that, pursuant to the principle of subsidiarity and the concept of shared responsibility, some aspect of the policy and specific actions indicated in the programme fall to be implemented at levels other than that of the Community;

NOTE that the application of the principle of subsidiarity will not lead to a step backwards in Community policy or hinder its effective development in the future;

NOTE however that the policy will be made more effective if actions are taken at the appropriate level;

In so far as environment and development within the European Communities are concerned:

NOTE the report on the state of the environment which the Commission has published in conjunction with the programme; NOTE the generally positive impact that previous action programmes have made on certain environmental problems; NOTE that the end of the time-frame of the current action programme on the environment coincides with the completion of the Internal Market; NOTE that, during the fifth programme, the environmental dimension of the Internal Market should be reinforced;

CONSIDER, however, that the current measures do not appear to be sufficient to meet the increased pressures on the environment likely to arise in consequence of current and anticipated trends in economic and social activity within the Community and developments in neighbouring regions, especially central and eastern Europe and at a wider international level;

AGREE that more progressive, coherent and better coordinated policies and strategies for the environment and development involving all levels of society are called for;

ADVOCATE in order, *inter alia*, to reduce wasteful consumption of natural resources and to prevent pollution, the elaboration of the concept of life-cycle management of products and processes, particularly in relation to waste management, the use of clean or cleaner technology and the substitution of certain hazardous processes and substances with less hazardous processes and substances in the most cost-effective way;

ENDORSE the strategy of giving increased and appropriate attention to certain key sectors in a coordinated and comprehensive manner including through a strengthening of dialogue with the main actors in the sectors identified in the programme;

ACKNOWLEDGE the need for consideration of a comprehensive Community strategy and action plan for nature conservation and protection, especially in relation to biodiversity and forests;

REAFFIRM the crucial importance of ensuring that environmental concerns are taken fully into account from the outset in the development of other policies and in the implementation of those policies, and the need for appropriate mechanisms within the Member States, the Council and the Commission to help achieve this integration, upon which the strategy advanced in the programme relies;

INVITE the Commission to consider developing initiatives to this end, including examination of the possibilities for the following areas, and to report on its conclusions in due course:

– new mechanisms within the Commission to increase cooperation between policy areas in the development of proposed legislation including organizational aspects,

– the incorporation, in regular progress reports on the implementation of the programme and of Agenda 21, of specific assessments, sector by sector, of the contribution of other policy areas to the achievement of environmental objectives,

– the inclusion in new legislative proposals of a section dealing with the likely implications for the environment,

– the environmental dimension in the granting of community funds;

UNDERTAKE to consider at the national level, and at the level of the Council in its various formations, the introduction of comparable measures to achieve the same aims;

RECOGNIZE that the involvement of all levels of society in a spirit of shared responsibility requires a deepening and broadening of the range of instruments to complement normative legislation including, where appropriate,

– market-based and other economic instruments,

– research and development, information, education and training,

– financial support mechanisms,

– voluntary schemes;

NOTE the objectives, targets, actions and time-frames indicated in the programme, and consider that these constitute a useful start in moving towards sustainable development;

ACKNOWLEDGE the programme's contribution to efforts to fulfil the objective specified in the Treaty establishing the European Economic Community that the Community's environmental policy should take account of the potential benefits and costs of action or lack of action; INVITE the Commission to develop appropriate proposals in the light of such further study as may be necessary;

NOTE that sustainability of activity and development will not be attained within the life-span of this programme and, consequently, that further, still more progressive, measures will probably be necessary beyond the year 2000 in order to hand on the environment to the next generation in a fit state to maintain public health and social and economic welfare at a high level;

NOTE, also, that while many of the measures and actions are set within a time-frame which extends to 2000, and even beyond, it is intended to undertake a review of the programme before the end of 1995; in the meantime INVITE the Environmental Policy Review Group proposed in the programme, once it be established, to keep the implementation of the programme under review on the basis of regular reports from the Commission summarizing progress under the programme; as part of the review process consideration should be given to the relationship between trade and the environment;

CALL on the Commission in its reviews of the programme to give special attention to any necessary revision of objectives and priorities, after adequate consultation, especially with the Member States;

CONSIDER that in order to ensure that community measures on the environment are more effectively implemented, cooperation procedures between the Commission and the Member States should be further improved;

EMPHASIZE the importance of effective implementation and enforcement of Community legislation in all Member States; STRESS that due regard should be given both at the stage when legislation is proposed and when it is adopted to the quality of the drafting of the legislation, in particular in terms of the practicability of implementing and enforcing it; UNDERTAKE to discuss in Council the Commission's annual report on the state of implementation and enforcement of Community legislation in the Member States;

NOTE that, while Member States are responsible for the implementation and enforcement of measures agreed by the Council, the Commission will continue to be the appropriate body for the monitoring of that implementation and enforcement; CALL on the Commission to consider bringing forward proposals for helping to improve the functioning of enforcement agencies within the Member States and encouraging the spread of best practice;

STRESS the urgency of the European Environment Agency beginning work as soon as possible;

NOTE the proposal in the programme for the establishment of a consultative forum and an Environmental Policy Review Group and a network of enforcement agencies from the Member States; WELCOME the principle of wider and more systematic consultation with interested bodies;

In so far as environment and development at the wider international level are concerned,

ASSERT that the Community and the Member States will contribute positively to the implementation of effective strategies to deal with such problems as climate change, deforestation, desertification, depletion of the ozone layer and loss of bio-diversity and to fulfil as early as possible the commitments to which they have agreed upon ratification of relevant international Conventions;

UNDERTAKE to play a positive role in the formulation of programmes of sustain-able development including in the developing countries and in the countries of central and eastern Europe within the framework of the Community's cooperation and association agreements;

NOTE that many of the internal Community measures in the programme are designed to reduce wasteful consumption of resource and, thereby, will contribute to greater efficiency in resource management at the wider international level;

REAFFIRM their commitment to implement the eight point plan for follow-up to UNCED agreed at the Lisbon European Council. Tasks for the Community and its Member States which need to be addressed include:

– to establish the basis for ratification of the climate change and biodiversity Conventions with the aim of ratification by the end of 1993, and to prepare the relevant national strategies by the same time,

– to integrate the Rio Declaration, Agenda 21 and Statement of Forest Principles into appropriate policies of the Community and its Member States as soon as possible,

– to work to review, under the aegis of the Commission on Sustainable Development (CSD), the implementation of the forest principles, and to work towards the preparation of a possible forest convention,

– to participate positively in negotiations on a future desertification convention,

– to fulfil the commitments to strengthen assistance to developing countries in the field of sustainable development and to increase funding for Agenda 21 by iden-tifying financial support to be given to developing countries including significant new and additional resources;

in this regard, to put into concrete form the ECU 3 billion commitment which the European Community and its Member States made in Rio as an initial contribution to the prompt and effective implementation of Agenda 21 with priority being given to technology transfer, institutional capacity building, and poverty reduction;

– to work for the restructuring and replenishment of the global environment facility so that it can become the permanent financial mechanism for relevant new global environmental Conventions, in particular the climate change and biodiversity Conventions,

– to continue to give consideration to an earth increment to the International Development Association (IDA) for environment purposes;

NOTE that the implementation of the programme will make a major contribution to the follow-up to Agenda 21 by the European Community and its Member States;

STRESS the need to promote the participation of non-governmental organizations (NGOs) and other major groups in the follow-up to UNCED at the national and CSD levels;

STRESS the importance of establishing the CSD and the need for full participation of the Community in the work of the CSD in line with the conclusions agreed by the Council on 23 November 1992 and NOTE that the Community and the Member States will submit regular progress reports on the implementation of Agenda 21 to the CSD;

and, in the light of the foregoing,

SUBSCRIBE to the necessity for a programme of policy and action in relation to the environment designed to achieve a sustainable development path;

APPROVE the general approach and strategy of the programme 'Towards sustainability' presented by the Commission;

INVITE the Commission to come forward with appropriate proposals to give effect to the programme in so far as it pertains to action at Community level;

UNDERTAKE to decide on proposals submitted by the Commission as expeditiously as possible taking account of the relevant indicative objectives, targets and time-frames set out in the programme which will be discussed in the context of those proposals;

CALL on all Community institutions, Member States, enterprises and citizens to accept their relative responsibilities to protect the environment for this and future generations and to play their full part in implementing this programme.

Index

The index covers Chapters 1 to 17 but not the Annexes. Index entries are to page numbers, those in italic referring to the location of tables.

515